Patronal Politics

This book proposes a new way of understanding events throughout the world that are usually interpreted as democratization, rising authoritarianism, or revolution. Where the rule of law is weak and corruption pervasive, what may appear to be democratic or authoritarian breakthroughs are often just regular, predictable phases in longer-term cyclic dynamics – typical patronal politics. This is shown through in-depth narratives of the post-1991 political history of all post-Soviet polities that are not in the European Union. This book also includes chapters on tsarist and Soviet history and on global patterns.

Henry E. Hale is Associate Professor of Political Science and International Affairs at George Washington University, having earned his PhD at Harvard University, been a Fulbright Scholar, and held a Title VIII post-doctoral fellowship at the Kennan Institute of the Woodrow Wilson International Center for Scholars. His previous work has won two awards from the American Political Science Association, the Leon D. Epstein Outstanding Book Award for *Why Not Parties in Russia* (Cambridge, 2006) and the Alexander L. George Article Award for "Divided We Stand" (*World Politics*, 2005). His other publications include *Foundations of Ethnic Politics* (Cambridge, 2008), two edited volumes, and numerous articles. His research has been funded by the National Science Foundation, the Carnegie Corporation of New York, and (through a Title VIII program) the National Council for East European and Eurasian Research. In 2009–12, he served as director of the Institute for European, Russian, and Eurasian Studies (IERES) at George Washington University's Elliott School of International Affairs. He is currently editorial board chair of *Demokratizatsiya: The Journal of Post-Soviet Democratization.*

PROBLEMS OF INTERNATIONAL POLITICS

Series Editors
Keith Darden, *American University*
Ian Shapiro, *Yale University*

The series seeks manuscripts central to the understanding of international politics that will be empirically rich and conceptually innovative. It is interested in works that illuminate the evolving character of nation-states within the international system. It sets out three broad areas for investigation: (1) identity, security, and conflict; (2) democracy; and (3) justice and distribution.

Patronal Politics

Eurasian Regime Dynamics in Comparative Perspective

HENRY E. HALE

The George Washington University

CAMBRIDGE
UNIVERSITY PRESS

CAMBRIDGE
UNIVERSITY PRESS

32 Avenue of the Americas, New York NY 10013-2473, USA

Cambridge University Press is part of the University of Cambridge.

It furthers the University's mission by disseminating knowledge in the pursuit of education, learning and research at the highest international levels of excellence.

www.cambridge.org
Information on this title: www.cambridge.org/9781107423138

First published 2015

A catalogue record for this publication is available from the British Library

Library of Congress Cataloguing in Publication data
Hale, Henry E., 1966–
Patronal politics : Eurasian regime dynamics in comparative perspective / Henry E. Hale, George Washington University.
    pages   cm. – (Problems of international politics)
Includes bibliographical references and index.
ISBN 978-1-107-07351-7 (hardback) – ISBN 978-1-107-42313-8 (paperback)
1. Patronage, Political – Former Soviet Republics.   2. Political culture – Former Soviet republics. 3. Former Soviet republics – Politics and government.   I. Title.
JN6581.H35   2015
324.2'04–dc23   2014016288

ISBN 978-1-107-07351-7 Hardback
ISBN 978-1-107-42313-8 Paperback

Contents

Figures

Tables

Acknowledgments

While readers will ultimately be the judge of its quality, this book is far better than it otherwise would have been thanks to a large number of others who devoted great amounts of time and effort to helping me along over the years. Most of all, I thank my wife, Isabelle Kaplan, without whose support, insights, and editorial excellence I would not have been able to write this book.

I am also very grateful to those who provided research assistance at various points in time, including Wilder Bullard, Cristian Ciobanu, Marketa Janesova, Sergiu Manic, Justin Schoville, Jeremy Streatfield, Huan-Kai Tseng, and Paul Zachary. This research assistance was made possible by support from the Woodrow Wilson International Center for Scholars' Kennan Institute and George Washington University's (GW's) Institute for European, Russian, and Eurasian Studies (IERES) at the Elliott School of International Affairs, in particular IERES's Maria H. Davis European Studies Endowment. I am also deeply grateful to the dozens of individuals – far too many to name – who helped facilitate my field research in post-Soviet countries, sharing their own insights, recommending materials, and assisting me in finding the people with whom I wanted to meet.

GW's Political Science Department and IERES, where I am especially grateful to Directors Hope Harrison and Peter Rollberg, provided outstanding intellectual environments in which to develop these ideas, as did the Kennan Institute, where thanks to Director Blair Ruble and his outstanding associates I spent eight months during 2009 on a Title VIII Research Scholarship. I also benefited from time spent in residence at the Harvard Ukrainian Research Institute on a Fellowship in Ukrainian Studies (2004) and at the Carnegie Moscow Center (2007–8 and again 2012). Funding for other aspects of my research, including the extensive fieldwork across the region that the project involved, came from the Fulbright Scholar program (which supported research based in Moscow during 2007–8) and the Elliott School's Strategic Opportunities for Academic Reach (SOAR) initiative launched by Dean Michael Brown.

I owe a special debt to all who took whole days out of their busy schedules to read all or parts of the book as it was in progress and to provide me with invaluable feedback, including through two amazingly helpful workshops organized for the manuscript. The first was a Johan Skytte Manuscript Workshop held by the Johan Skytte Foundation at Uppsala University in Uppsala, Sweden, during May 27–8, 2011. This event featured extensive comments from Li Bennich-Bjorkman, Georgi Derluguian, Joakim Ekman, Johan Engvall, Oleksandr Fisun, Sverker Gustavsson, Gretchen Helmke, Kimitaka Matsuzato, Sven Oskarsson, William Reno, Graeme Robertson, Mattias Sigfridsson, Inge Snip, Alexei Trochev, and Sten Widmalm. The second was a "book incubator" workshop organized at IERES through the Program on New Approaches to Research and Security in Eurasia (PONARS Eurasia), funded by Carnegie Corporation of New York. Participants generously giving of their time included Nathan Brown, Wilder Bullard, Paul D'Anieri, Jeffrey Goldstein, Lisel Hintz, Cynthia McClintock, Eric McGlinchey, Kimberly Morgan, Nancy Myers, Robert Orttung, Margaret Paxson, Albert Schmidt, Alexander Sokolowski, Brian Taylor, Joshua Tucker, and Cory Welt (who organized the session). Timothy Colton and Alexandra Vacroux gave the manuscript a spin in their graduate class on post-Soviet politics at Harvard University, for which I thank them and their students. Rebecca Chamberlain-Creanga and Andrei Rogachevskii also provided very helpful detailed comments on earlier drafts. I am also grateful to Eric Lawrence and students in his Visualizing and Modeling Politics class at GW for their assistance in designing Figure 3.1.

Far more people than I can mention commented on pieces of this project that were presented at dozens of conferences and university lecture series over the years, including several PONARS Eurasia workshops and invited appearances at the Brookings Institution, Columbia University, George Mason University, Georgetown University, the European University at St. Petersburg (Russia), Indiana University, the Kennan Institute, the I. F. Kuras Institute of Political and Ethnic Studies of the National Academy of Sciences of Ukraine, the Kuras National University of Kharkiv (Ukraine), Lviv Polytechnic National University (Ukraine), Lviv State Agrarian University (Ukraine), Miami University, the Noravank Foundation (Armenia), Queen's University (Canada), the Royal Netherlands Academy of Arts and Sciences, the University of Tokyo, Stanford University, Uppsala University, the University of Chicago, the University of Michigan, the University of Pittsburgh, and the University of Washington.

I am also very grateful to Lewis Bateman and his colleagues at Cambridge University Press for their consistent support and guidance in developing this book. Finally, I wish to thank the publishers of the following articles for permission to include some of the material that originally came out there in the book:

Henry E. Hale, "Did the Internet Break the Political Machine? Moldova's 2009 'Twitter Revolution That Wasn't,'" *Demokratizatsiya: The Journal of Post-Soviet Democratization*, v. 21, no. 3, Fall 2013, pp. 481–505

Henry E. Hale, "Eurasian Polities as Hybrid Regimes: The Case of Putin's Russia," *Journal of Eurasian Studies*, v. 1, no. 1, 2010, pp. 33–41

Henry E. Hale, "Formal Constitutions in Informal Politics: Institutions and Democratization in Eurasia," *World Politics*, v. 63, no. 4, October 2011, pp. 581–617

Henry E. Hale, "Prezidentskii rezhim, revoliutsiia, i demokratiia: Sravnitel'nyi analiz Gruzii, Kyrgyzii, Rossii, i Ukrainy," *Pro et Contra*, no. 1, January–February 2008, pp. 6–21

Henry E. Hale, "The Putin Machine Sputters: First Impressions of Russia's 2011 Duma Election," *Russian Analytical Digest*, no. 106, December 21, 2011, pp. 2–5

Henry E. Hale, "Regime Cycles: Democracy, Autocracy, and Revolution in Post-Soviet Eurasia," *World Politics*, v. 58, no. 1, October 2005, pp. 133–65

Henry E. Hale, "Two Decades of Post-Soviet Regime Dynamics," *Demokratizatsiya: The Journal of Post-Soviet Democratization*, v. 20, no. 2, Spring 2012, pp. 71–7

Henry E. Hale, "The Uses of Divided Power," *Journal of Democracy*, v. 21, no. 3, July 2010, pp. 84–98

Note on Transliteration

Cyrillic (in this volume, Russian, Ukrainian, and Uzbek languages) source material is transliterated here using the Library of Congress system with the following exceptions:

General exceptions:
- Y is used at the beginning of soft vowels (ya, ye, yu) that are the first letters in words
- Soft signs are omitted at the end of proper names
- Common spellings are employed for words or names that widely appear in English-language media (e.g., Klitschko not Klychko)

Exceptions made for people's names:
- Soft signs are omitted from people's names (e.g., Yeltsin not Yel'tsin)
- The letter y is used at the end of names that would otherwise end in ii, yi, yy, or iy
- The letters ie are substituted for 'e (e.g., Glaziev not Glaz'ev or Glazev)
- The spellings people themselves use as authors of English-language publications are generally used here regardless of the above (e.g., Vladimir Gel'man, Serhiy Kudelia)

For Azerbaijani language sources that use the Latin alphabet, letters that do not appear in English are transliterated phonetically or by the English letter that best approximates the sound. Specifically, the following conversions are used:

ü	u
ö	o
ğ	gh
ı	i
ə	a
ç	ch
ş	sh

I

Introduction

Elections are civil war fought by nonviolent means. If some countries resolve their domestic disputes on the battlefield, others wage their wars on the stump and through the ballot box. The latter wars are no less real. Campaigns are launched, battle lines drawn, foot soldiers mobilized, flags flown, allies sought, passions inflamed, and victories won. Elections in many countries often have a special whiff of war, sitting precariously near the wrong end of the continuum between violence and nonviolence. There, tanks may not roll and guns may not fire, but other means of coercion replace them as keys to victory, frequently finding their way into the arsenals of at least one side.

This is not the face of "democracy" as typically depicted in American textbooks, but the United States' own history illustrates the point quite well. Early American elections – especially with the advent of industrialization – were as much the preserve of the political machine as issue politics, of the company town as the town assembly. Large segments of the population were denied the vote one way or another straight through to the Civil Rights Act of 1965 in some places, while in others even the dead lingered long on voter lists, posthumously casting ballots for those who controlled the rolls. In Frank Capra's famous 1939 film, the upright Mr. Smith who went to Washington was the exception to the Taylor machine's sorry rule. Taylor was fictional, but characters ranging from William ("Boss") Tweed to Huey Long to the senior Richard Daley were decidedly not. In fact, it might be fair to say that the most common world historical experience with elections has been of this more coercive sort, not the idealized version taught in schools and fought for by student activists.

As the twenty-first century approached, however, Western citizens, analysts, and leaders had largely come to see the "messiness" of elections as a political disease that is unusual and alien to the body politic, something unnatural to be exorcised. On one hand, this is a good thing, testimony to how far we have come as societies. And surely we should strive to eliminate coercion from democratic practice. On the other hand, the focus on the ideal has often come at the expense of understanding and anticipating the real, especially when it comes to countries newly emerging from autocratic rule. Nowhere is this more clear than with the demise of the USSR's totalitarian system, an event that arguably freed more states from dictatorship than any other of the twentieth century. At least, initially.

The region increasingly referred to as Eurasia[1] has taken Western observers on a roller-coaster ride of expectations ever since Mikhail Gorbachev launched his political reforms in the late 1980s. As the Berlin Wall fell, as the USSR's own constituent republics held free and competitive elections, and as newly elected leaders throughout the region declared and won independence from the Soviet Union, Western thinkers widely proclaimed the triumph of democracy and even the "end of history."[2] Political scientists classified these new countries as cases of "transition to democracy," the culmination of what Samuel Huntington labeled history's great "third wave" of democratization that had begun with Southern Europe in the 1970s before spreading to Latin America, Africa, and Asia.[3]

Disillusionment grew as the 1990s progressed, however. Authoritarian tendencies reappeared in almost all post-Soviet states except the Baltics, consternating Western policy makers and helping spawn at least three new directions in scholarship. One school deemphasized democratization and stressed instead democratic "consolidation," a task that increasingly appeared Sisyphean.[4] A

[1] The rest of this book, unless otherwise specified, will use this term to refer to the territory that was once part of the USSR.

[2] Francis Fukuyama, "The End of History and the Last Man," *National Interest*, Summer 1989, pp. 3–18.

[3] Valerie Bunce, "Should Transitologists Be Grounded?" *Slavic Review*, v. 54, no. 1, Spring 1995, pp. 111–27; Timothy J. Colton, "Politics," in Colton and Robert Legvold, eds., *After the Soviet Union: From Empire to Nations* (New York: W. W. Norton, 1992), pp. 17–48; M. Steven Fish, *Democracy from Scratch* (Princeton, NJ: Princeton University Press, 1995); Samuel P. Huntington, *The Third Wave* (Norman: University of Oklahoma Press, 1991); Terry Lynn Karl and Philippe C. Schmitter, "Modes of Transition in Latin America, Southern and Eastern Europe," *International Social Science Journal*, v. 43, June 1991, pp. 269–84; Michael McFaul, *Russia's Unfinished Revolution* (Ithaca, NY: Cornell University Press, 2001); Guillermo O'Donnell, "On the State, Democratization, and Some Conceptual Problems: A Latin American View with Some Glances at Postcommunist Countries," *World Development*, v. 21, no. 8, August 1993, pp. 1355–69. More recently, see Andrei Shleifer and Daniel Treisman, "A Normal Country," *Foreign Affairs*, v. 83, no. 2, March–April 2004, pp. 20–38.

[4] Valerie Bunce, "Rethinking Recent Democratization: Lessons from the Postcommunist Experience," *World Politics*, v. 55, no. 2, January 2003, pp. 167–92; Stephen E. Hanson, "Defining Democratic Consolidation," in Richard D. Anderson Jr., M. Steven Fish, Stephen E. Hanson, and Philip G. Roeder, *Postcommunism and the Theory of Democracy* (Princeton, NJ: Princeton University Press, 2001); Juan J. Linz and Alfred Stepan, *Problems of Democratic Transition and Consolidation: Southern Europe, South America, and Post-Communist Europe* (Baltimore: Johns Hopkins University Press, 1996); and Gerardo L. Munck, "The Regime Question: Theory Building in Democracy Studies," *World Politics*, v. 54, no. 1, October 2001, pp. 119–44.

second group argued for a shift in focus: What should be explained was not transition *from* authoritarian rule but transition back *toward* it, a process they saw as the new norm.[5] A third cohort proposed a more radical response: Eschewing the "transition paradigm" altogether, it posited that these countries could long remain in a "twilight zone" between democracy and dictatorship, governed by "hybrid regimes" that that might not be adequately characterized as "unconsolidated democracies" yet are not transitioning to anything else.[6]

But just when democratic pessimism seemed to have won the day, Westerners witnessed a "Bulldozer Revolution" topple Serbian nationalist strongman Slobodan Milosevic in 2000, a "Rose Revolution" unseat Georgia's weary Eduard Shevardnadze in 2003, an "Orange Revolution" upend former "red director" Leonid Kuchma's attempt to hand power to an anointed successor in Ukraine in 2004, and a "Tulip Revolution" overthrow the jaded Askar Akaev in Kyrgyzstan in 2005 – all in the name of democracy and with the backing of Western democracy advocates.[7] The Kyrgyz revolution was particularly stunning, a crack in the Central Asian bastion of postcommunist authoritarianism. Democracy, the cry went out, was again on the march! A slew of quick studies emerged to explain these "democratic breakthroughs," as they were almost universally received by Western scholars and policy makers, and to speculate on just how far the wave would go and how best to coax it along.[8]

As of 2014, however, most observers consider these post-Soviet "color revolutions" disappointments.[9] Georgia's revolutionary leader, the Columbia-

---

[5] M. Steven Fish, "The Dynamics of Democratic Erosion," in Richard D. Anderson Jr., M. Steven Fish, Stephen E. Hanson, and Philip G. Roeder, *Postcommunism and the Theory of Democracy* (Princeton, NJ: Princeton University Press, 2001); Philip G. Roeder, "Varieties of Post-Soviet Authoritarian Regimes," *Post-Soviet Affairs*, v. 10, no. 1, January 1994, pp. 61–101.

[6] Something like a manifesto for this school is Thomas Carothers, "The End of the Transition Paradigm," *Journal of Democracy*, v. 13, no. 1, January 2002, pp. 5–21. Other prominent work in this vein includes Larry Diamond, *Developing Democracy* (Baltimore: Johns Hopkins University Press, 1999); Larry Diamond, "Thinking about Hybrid Regimes," *Journal of Democracy*, v. 13, no. 2, April 2002, pp. 21–35; Jeffrey Herbst, "Political Liberalization in Africa after Ten Years," *Comparative Politics*, v. 33, no. 3, April 2001, pp. 357–75; Terry Lynn Karl, "The Hybrid Regimes of Central America," *Journal of Democracy*, v. 6, no. 3, July 1995, pp. 72–86; and Steven Levitsky and Lucan Way, "The Rise of Competitive Authoritarianism," *Journal of Democracy*, v. 13, no. 2, April 2002, pp. 51–65.

[7] Some trace this wave of ousted autocrats back even further, to Romania, Bulgaria, and Slovakia in the mid- to late 1990s. See Valerie J. Bunce and Sharon L. Wolchik, "Favorable Conditions and Electoral Revolutions," *Journal of Democracy*, v. 17, no. 4, October 2006, pp. 5–18.

[8] E.g., Adrian Karatnycky, "Ukraine's Orange Revolution," *Foreign Affairs*, v. 84, no. 2, March–April 2005, pp. 32–52; Michael McFaul, "Transitions from Communism," *Journal of Democracy*, v. 16, no. 4, July 2005, pp. 212–44; and Vitali Silitski, "Beware the People," *Transitions Online*, March 21, 2005.

[9] For example, Katya Kalandadze and Mitchell A. Orenstein, "Electoral Protests and Democratization: Beyond the Color Revolutions," *Comparative Political Studies*, v. 42, no. 11, November 2009, pp. 1403–25; Taras Kuzio, "Ambiguous Anniversary," *Business Ukraine*, November 24–30, 2008, pp. 12–16; Lincoln Mitchell, *The Color Revolutions* (Philadelphia:

educated Mikheil Saakashvili, found himself cracking down violently on peaceful demonstrators in November 2007, came under fire from democracy advocates for political strong-arm tactics and the constriction of independent mass media, and ultimately lost power in the wake of a major scandal involving prison torture. Kyrgyzstan's democratic hope, President Kurmanbek Bakiev, also restored the practices of his predecessor. Accused of corruption and media suppression, his overwhelming ballot box victories (including his 2009 reelection with 80 percent of the vote) failed to impress monitors as democratic and he himself was overthrown in the name of democracy in 2010. In fact, according to Freedom House's *Nations in Transit* study, both Kyrgyzstan and Georgia were less democratic in 2007 than they had been during the year prior to their "color revolutions."[10] Ukraine initially fared better in democracy ratings under "Orange" President Viktor Yushchenko, but after he lost in 2010 to the man he defeated in 2004, Viktor Yanukovych, observers once again began consigning Ukraine to the dedemocratizing camp.[11] Then in 2014, Yanukovych was again overthrown, perhaps the first man in history unseated *twice* by revolution. His successors once again promise a new, democratic, "European" beginning.

Stepping back for a moment, two observations seem appropriate. One is that both social scientists and policy makers appear to be chasing events in the post-communist world as much as explaining or anticipating them. There would thus seem to be strong grounds for us to reconsider the basic assumptions and models that we use, consciously or unconsciously, to interpret and anticipate political events in Eurasia.

A second observation is that there is indeed a great deal to be understood, that in fact a great puzzle of post-Soviet regimes now begs scholars for an explanation. If we step back a moment from our gyrating hopes and expectations, we are likely to be struck immediately by the extremely wide range in how the fragments of the former USSR look at any given moment after emerging from a single Soviet system two decades ago. On one extreme lies Turkmenistan, a land where the dictator abolished elections, renamed the month of January in his own honor, and erected a golden statue of himself that rotated so as always to face the sun.[12] The death of the self-proclaimed Turkmenbashi ("head of the Turkmen") in 2007 has so far produced little

University of Pennsylvania Press, 2012); Scott Radnitz, *Weapons of the Wealthy: Predatory Regimes and Elite-Led Protests in Central Asia* (Ithaca, NY: Cornell University Press, 2010).

[10] Jeannette Goehring, ed., *Nations in Transit 2008: Democratization from Central Europe to Eurasia* (New York: Freedom House, 2008), p. 44.

[11] Alexander J. Motyl, "The New Political Regime in Ukraine – toward Sultanism Yanukovych-Style?" Cicero Foundation Great Debate Paper, no. 10/06, July 2010; Christopher Walker and Robert Orttung, "From Revolution to Democracy," *Wall Street Journal*, March 7, 2011, online version, wsj.com.

[12] A colorful portrait can be found in Paul Theroux, "The Golden Man: Saparmurat Niyazov's Reign of Insanity," *New Yorker*, May 28, 2007, pp. 56–65.

change other than a new personality cult surrounding his successor, a former dentist who has rechristened himself Arkadag ("the protector").[13] Uzbekistan is similar, but with a slightly less vainglorious autocrat. At the other extreme sits Lithuania, a stable democracy comfortably nestled in the European Union. Latvia and Estonia also remain democratic and in the EU but face more questions than Lithuania due to reluctance to endow their larger local Russian populations with civic power.

Far more interesting, however, are the polities in between, the countries and unrecognized statelets that allow some real freedom for opposition politics – even in elections – but whose authorities also employ coercive methods to stack the deck in their own favor for any contest that matters. This indeed, is the vast bulk of the post-Soviet space: For much of the 1990s and 2000s, this has been a reasonably accurate description of Russia, Ukraine, Belarus, Moldova, all of the Caucasian states (Armenia, Azerbaijan, Georgia), most of Central Asia (Kazakhstan, Kyrgyzstan, Tajikistan), and all four of the separatist territories that have de facto broken away from their host countries (Abkhazia, Nagorno-Karabakh, South Ossetia, and Transnistria). In some sense, then, initial observers were right in expecting American democracy to take root after the demise of the USSR. They just got the American democracy of Boss Tweed rather than that of the New England town meeting.

Most striking of all, however, is the *dynamism* of post-Soviet regimes. And virtually all of this dynamism has come precisely from the hybrid polities. Since 1992, Turkmenistan and Uzbekistan have been quite stably autocratic while the Baltic countries have steadily sustained democratic regimes. It is the hybrid regimes that have so inspired and so frustrated Western onlookers, alternately moving toward or away from democracy and autocracy while never quite seeming to make a decisive leap to one or the other. It is the hybrid regimes that gave rise to the color revolutions as well as to the most potent attempts to replicate them, though here again, the result has not generally been an actual transition to democracy.

The lone exception for a time was Ukraine. For the period 2005–10, it became the *only* post-Soviet country to experience a real breakthrough to democracy, being rated fully "free" by Freedom House, since the Baltic countries first did it in the early 1990s.[14] But even Ukraine's democracy during this period was extraordinarily messy, a highly corrupt form of political competition that spawned seemingly permanent government instability and policy deadlock even in the face of economic calamity, the global financial crisis that wracked the region starting in 2008. Rather than the genteel public debates that Westerners have often seemed to expect, Ukraine's politics sometimes had the feel of the pitched, no-holds-barred battles that Martin Scorsese depicts

---

[13] *RFE/RL*, March 8, 2012.
[14] Christopher Walker, ed., *Nations in Transit 2011: The Authoritarian Dead End in the Former Soviet Union* (New York: Freedom House, 2011).

between rival political machines in his 2002 epic *The Gangs of New York*. This is not your grandfather's democracy. Or then again, maybe it is.

What we have in the former USSR, then, is what social scientists frequently call a grand natural laboratory, a large set of polities (fifteen countries and four unrecognized statelets) that emerged from a single starting point (Soviet rule) but were exposed to different "treatments" over the course of twenty years and wound up looking different at some points in time and similar at others. The fifteen East and Central European countries freed from communist regimes during 1989–91 and Mongolia might also be considered part of this same "experiment," giving us a total of thirty-five "cases" to work with. This situation affords us a chance to see precisely which treatments – and which preexisting conditions – are associated with which patterns. And now that nearly a quarter of a century has passed since each of these countries first held competitive nationwide elections, the time would seem ripe for drawing larger conclusions from all of the laboratory work that the field's leading scholars have been doing.

Making sense of these patterns requires shedding two comfortable Western assumptions about how politics works. First, it means replacing a theory of the ideal with a theory of the real. Virtually all of the most prominent textbooks in comparative politics and post-Soviet (mostly Russian) politics reflect the focus on the ideal, by which I mean Westerners' sense of how a democracy should work and what its central elements therefore are. Chapters on these political systems typically sport titles like "political participation," "political beliefs and culture," "parties and electoral politics," "associational groups," "the judiciary," "constitutional design," "public policy making," and sometimes "state building."[15] Surely this underlying conception of how politics is supposed to work, and what is likely to get in the way, also has something to do with Western comparative political science's overwhelming focus on these same topics, especially elections, political economy, ethnic politics, and state

---

[15] For example, leading comparative textbooks in recent years include Gabriel A. Almond, G. Bingham J. Powell Jr., Russell J. Dalton, and Kaare Strom, *Comparative Politics Today: A World View* (New York: Pearson, 2008); Michael Sodaro, *Comparative Politics: A Global Introduction* (Columbus: McGraw-Hill, 2007); Lowell Barrington, *Comparative Politics: Structures and Choices*, 2nd ed. (Boston: Cengage, 2012). Textbooks on the former Soviet countries include Vicki L. Hesli, *Governments and Politics in Russia and the Post-Soviet Region* (Boston: Houghton Mifflin, 2007); Thomas F. Remington, *Politics in Russia*, 6th ed. (Boston: Longman, 2010); Richard Sakwa, *Russian Politics and Society*, 4th ed. (London: Routledge, 2008); Eric Shiraev, *Russian Government and Politics* (New York: Palgrave Macmillan, 2010); Stephen White, *Understanding Russian Politics* (Cambridge: Cambridge University Press, 2011). The organization around formal institutions is only somewhat and inconsistently reduced in edited volumes intended for the classroom, such as Stephen K. Wegren, ed., *Return to Putin's Russia: Past Imperfect, Future Uncertain* (Lanham, MD: Rowman & Littlefield, 2012); and Stephen White, Richard Sakwa, and Henry E. Hale, eds., *Developments in Russian Politics*, 8th ed. (London: Palgrave Macmillan, 2014).

building, as indicated by the content of the field's major journals regardless of geographic area.

All this is fine and well when analyzing the United States or France. It may also be appropriate if one is primarily interested in why Russia, Georgia, or Kazakhstan is not becoming the United States or France. Indeed, virtually all of these publications do a fine job of documenting how each of these countries deviates from Western norms of policy making, participation, or what have you, and they ably communicate a great deal of information about each country. This approach can also be very useful for comparative scholarship that is primarily interested in local variations on a cross-national theme regardless of whether the theme is locally important. For this reason, such works are still very useful; I assign them in my own classes and have even written or edited some of them.

But the real stuff of politics in countries like Russia, Georgia, or Kazakhstan is not truly captured by topics like "participation," "parties and elections," "the judiciary," or "constitutional design" – at least, not in the straightforward way often assumed. Local politicians, the ones who actually exercise power, would surely emphasize other things if asked in private. That is, standard textbook chapters and many "normal science" publications on these themes in post-Soviet politics do not today give us a good sense of the distinct political *system* that functions in these polities, and of the logic that makes this system a system. Moreover, by breaking off different elements of this system and forcing each into its own Procrustean bed in our books, articles, and policy papers – a bed designed by research agendas originating in the West – we not only overlook but actively distract readers from this locally powerful logic. Without a well-articulated alternative framework for organizing all of these elements, Western observers are unlikely to come up with it on their own. We thus remain likely to continue chasing events in the post-Soviet world rather than truly explaining – not to mention anticipating – them. And this is a problem not only for policy makers and area specialists, but for comparativists seeking to develop the most potent and parsimonious theories.

Making sense of post-Soviet regime change also requires parting with a second assumption that is widespread in policy making and academic circles: that regime types are best identified in snapshots rather than dynamic patterns. Analysts typically consider where a country lies on the continuum between democracy and dictatorship at a given moment, defining that positioning as its current regime type, and then try to explain how it got there. This approach is typified by high-profile organizations (including Freedom House) that give each country a discrete "democracy rating" every year.[16] When this

---

[16] Many other such year-by-year ratings exist and are widely used by scholars. See especially Michael Coppedge and John Gerring, with David Altman, Michael Bernhard, Steven Fish, Allen Hicken, Matthew Kroenig, Staffan Lindberg, Kelly McMann, Pamela Paxton, Holli A. Semetko, Svend-Erik Skaaning, Jeffrey Staton, and Jan Teorell, "Conceptualizing and Measuring

same country changes position, moving toward democracy or autocracy, it is typically considered either to be on a "trajectory" toward democracy/ autocracy or to be displaying instability. Meeting a certain standard makes it a "democracy" for that year.

But much of what we have seen in the post-Soviet world over the past two decades, as described earlier, is movement *back and forth*. It may be that all this is simple instability, in which case there is no need for reconceptualization or further explanation of this movement. But it may also be that regime equilibria can be dynamic, that what we might be witnessing is regular, *cyclic* behavior characteristic of a certain underlying type of regime. What is most interesting and important about Georgia, for instance, might not be that it meets a standard for authoritarianism or is moving toward it in a given year, but precisely that it has displayed a pattern of moving back and forth between more democratic and more autocratic conditions. If this turns out to be a regular process underpinned by a systemic logic, we gain the power to anticipate a new round of "democratization" in the future, though also the perspective not to become too excited by it when it arrives. We need to augment the study of regime *change* with a science of *regime dynamics*.[17]

This book argues that such a regular process is in fact often at work, that much of what has been described as the "change" of a regime into something else actually reflects predictable dynamism within a single regime type. It can be discerned by systematizing insights from a large volume of important inductive studies – those seeking to characterize politics as it is understood locally – and infusing the result with a powerful logic of collective action to form a theory with broad practical and comparative application. Making this possible is an exciting, growing body of social science research that has pioneered our understanding of large patterns in how politics really works outside the West (and sometimes within it). These studies – usually grounded in strong and detailed knowledge of particular countries or regions – have tended to point to the importance of *informal politics*, the ways in which politics is often not what it

---

Democracy: A New Approach," *Perspectives on Politics*, v. 9, no. 2, June 2011, pp. 247–67; Monty G. Marshall, *Polity IV Project: Political Regime Characteristics and Transitions 1800– 2010* (2011), www.systemicpeace.org; Gerardo L. Munck, *Measuring Democracy: A Bridge between Scholarship and Politics* (Baltimore: Johns Hopkins University Press, 2009); Adam Przeworski, Michael E. Alvarez, Jose Antonio Cheibub, and Fernando Limongi, *Democracy and Development: Political Institutions and Well-Being in the World, 1950–1990* (New York: Cambridge University Press, 2000). On broader issues concerning the measurement of democracy and regime types more generally, see David Collier and Robert Adcock, "Democracy and Dichotomies: A Pragmatic Approach to Choices about Concepts," *Annual Review of Political Science*, v. 2, 1999, pp. 537–65.

[17] Prominent among existing studies of "regime dynamics," though in a sense somewhat different from the one in mind here, is Ruth Berins Collier and David Collier, *Shaping the Political Arena: Critical Junctures, the Labor Movement and Regime Dynamics in Latin America* (Princeton, NJ: Princeton University Press, 1991).

seems to outsiders.[18] There are formal laws on the books, but they are selectively or differentially enforced according to more fundamental unwritten (informal) rules of the game.[19] Market reforms are formally adopted under international pressure, but often remain on paper, masking new (informal) forms of state involvement in the economy.[20] Political parties formally appear on the ballot, but really (informally) serve a variety of purposes for the authorities, including acting as decoys, backups, or attack dogs.[21] This is the politics of the Potemkin village, the locally erected facade that threatens to fool the itinerant social scientist who does not stop to look deeper.[22]

What is hidden, or "the way things really work," is usually what will be called here the *patronalistic* dimension of politics. *Patronal politics* refers to politics in societies where individuals organize their political and economic pursuits primarily around the personalized exchange of concrete rewards and

[18] This theoretical tradition has roots in foundational insights of 1970s social science, many key contributions to which are collected in Steffen W. Schmidt, James C. Scott, Carl Lande, and Laura Guasti, *Friends, Followers, and Factions* (Berkeley: University of California Press, 1977). Some breakthrough conceptual works in the more recent wave of scholarship include Michael Bratton and Nicholas Van de Walle, "Neopatrimonial Regimes and Political Transitions in Africa," *World Politics*, v. 46, July 1994; Georgi Derluguian, *Bourdieu's Secret Admirer in the Caucasus: A World Systems Biography* (Chicago: University of Chicago Press, 2005); Gerald M. Easter, *Restructuring the State: Personal Networks and Elite Identity* (New York: Cambridge University Press, 2000); Venelin I. Ganev, *Preying on the State: The Transformation of Bulgaria after 1989* (Ithaca, NY: Cornell University Press, 2007); Anna Grzymala-Busse, "The Best Laid Plans: The Impact of Informal Rules on Formal Institutions in Transitional Regimes," *Studies in Comparative International Development*, v. 45, no. 3, September 2010, pp. 311–33; Herbert Kitschelt and Steven I. Wilkinson, eds., *Patrons, Clients, and Policies: Patterns of Democratic Accountability and Political Competition* (Cambridge: Cambridge University Press, 2007); Steven Levitsky and Gretchen Helmke, *Informal Institutions and Democracy: Lessons from Latin America* (Baltimore: Johns Hopkins University Press, 2006); Ellen Lust-Okar, *Structuring Conflict in the Arab World: Incumbents, Opponents, and Institutions* (Cambridge: Cambridge University Press, 2005); William Reno, *Warlord Politics and African States* (Boulder, CO: Lynn Rienner, 1998); Lucan A. Way, "Authoritarian State-Building and the Sources of Regime Competitiveness in the Fourth Wave: The Cases of Belarus, Moldova, Russia, and Ukraine," *World Politics*, v. 57, January 2005, pp. 231–61.

[19] Paul D'Anieri, *Understanding Ukrainian Politics: Power, Politics, and Institutional Design* (Armonk, NY: M. E. Sharpe, 2007); Vladimir Gel'man, "The Unrule of Law in the Making: The Politics of Informal Institution Building in Russia," *Europe-Asia Studies*, v. 56, no. 7, November 2004, pp. 1021–40; Stephen Holmes, "Introduction," *East European Constitutional Review*, v. 11, nos. 1–2, Winter/Spring 2002, pp. 90–1; Alena V. Ledeneva, *How Russia Really Works* (Ithaca, NY: Cornell University Press, 2006).

[20] Jerry F. Hough, *The Logic of Economic Reform in Russia* (Washington, DC: Brookings, 2001); David Woodruff, *Money Unmade* (Ithaca, NY: Cornell University Press, 1999).

[21] Henry E. Hale, "The Origins of United Russia and the Putin Presidency: The Role of Contingency in Party-System Development," *Demokratizatsiya: The Journal of Post-Soviet Democratization*, v. 12, no. 2, Spring 2004, pp. 169–94; Andrew Wilson, *Virtual Politics: Faking Democracy in the Post-Soviet World* (New Haven, CT: Yale University Press, 2005).

[22] Jessica Allina-Pisano, *The Post-Soviet Potemkin Village: Politics and Property Rights in the Black Earth* (New York: Cambridge University Press, 2008).

punishments through chains of actual acquaintance, and not primarily around abstract, impersonal principles such as ideological belief or categorizations like economic class that include many people one has not actually met in person. In this politics of individual reward and punishment, power goes to those who can mete these out, those who can position themselves as *patrons* with a large and dependent base of *clients*.

The sinews of power in post-Soviet countries, therefore, tend to be roughly hierarchical *networks* through which resources are distributed and coercion applied. These can exist outside formal institutions, such as parliament or the presidency, and they do not usually overlap with professional societies, issue advocacy groups, business associations, or even political parties. Instead, in post-Soviet Eurasia, networks rooted in three broad sets of collective actors typically constitute the most important building blocks of the political system, the moving parts in its regime dynamics:[23] (1) local political machines that emerged from reforms of the early 1990s, (2) giant politicized corporate conglomerates, (3) various branches of the state that are rich either in cash or in coercive capacity. Whoever controls these bosses, "oligarchs," and officials controls the country. And the most important function of a constitution in post-Soviet societies is arguably not to undergird the rule of law, which does not much exist, but to signal who (if anyone) is most likely to be patron-in-chief and to provide other focal points that help structure the way all these networks arrange and rearrange themselves – often in violation of the formal norms the constitution itself contains.

The most important distinction among patronalistic polities is whether these patronal networks are arranged in a single pyramid or multiple, usually competing pyramids.[24] Constitutions that declare a single dominant chief executive (sometimes a president, but sometimes also the head of a parliamentarist system) tend to tip systems toward the former. This is because such constitutions, even when their legal stipulations are not actually followed, shape expectations as to who wields ultimate power in a country. And ultimate power in patronalistic societies can be used not only to push for policies one supports, but also to direct favors to allies and to target opponents for punishment. Understanding

---

[23] Their formal bases are not necessarily essential to the existence of the network, however.

[24] The use of the terms "single-pyramid" and "competing-pyramid" to refer to the author's conceptualization is from Graeme Robertson and Matthew Green, personal communication. This echoes James C. Scott, who discusses different "pyramid" arrangements, though he also writes of "patron monopolies"; see James C. Scott, "Patron-Client Politics and Political Change in Southeast Asia," *American Political Science Review*, v. 66, no. 1, March 1972, pp. 91–113. Others have used terms like "centralized caciquismo," "bureaucratic neopatrimonialism," and "centralized cronyism"; respectively, see Kimitaka Matsuzato, "All Kuchma's Men: The Reshuffling of Ukrainian Governors and the Presidential Election of 1999," *Post-Soviet Geography and Economics*, v. 42, no. 6, September 2001, pp. 416–39; Aleksandr A. Fisun, *Demokratiia, neopatrimonializm i global'nye transformatsii* (Kharkiv: Konstanta, 2007), p. 176; and Gulnaz Sharafutdinova, *Political Consequences of Crony Capitalism inside Russia* (South Bend, IN: Notre Dame University Press, 2010).

that this is the way politics works, the country's machine bosses, oligarchs, and officials (whom we might collectively call *elites*)[25] have a strong incentive to fall into line or, even better, to get on the chief executive's good side by proactively working in his or her interest. The latter thus easily gains allies while would-be challengers start to face serious hurdles in rallying supporters, especially once opposition seems to be a lost cause. And the chief executive, understanding this, does everything in his or her power to divide and conquer the elites, playing them off each other and sowing discord among them. Power, then, is an odd self-fulfilling prophecy illuminated by a logic of collective action: So long as elites *expect* the formal chief executive to continue to be in charge in the future, few will dare even initiate an organized attempt to oust him or her because the risk of getting caught is too high and the perceived likelihood of success too low. This is the great power of expectations.

The recent political history of almost every post-Soviet country, therefore, has included the creation of a single pyramid of authority, a giant political machine based on selectively applied coercion and reward, on individualized favor and punishment. Local political actors even use the same imagery when describing this process in Russian, talking about President Vladimir Putin's, Kurmanbek Bakiev's, Leonid Kuchma's, and Mikheil Saakashvili's construction of a *piramida* of power, a *vertikal'* of authority. The 1990s in these places thus reflected parallel histories of self-interested political reform, crony privatization, and the sheer will to retain genuinely contested elections while making sure the "right" people always won them. In most cases, such processes played out in dynamic causal interaction with a formal presidentialist constitution that had its origins in the late Soviet period, producing a system that quite resembled authoritarianism despite the presence of some opposition figures on the ballot. The chief patron need not be a "president" for such political closure to occur, however. Where the constitution puts parliament on top, anyone who can control the parliament can also become patron-in-chief in virtually the same way a president can, though such a system can somewhat complicate the consolidation of a single-pyramid system. Thus we have seen single-pyramid systems emerge almost everywhere in the former Soviet Union, even in parliamentarist Moldova, though we also see how the latter's constitution nevertheless complicated the system's emergence and endurance. This is the logic at the heart of Eurasia's post-Soviet drift in the direction of (apparently) authoritarianism. Importantly, this logic distinguishes the highly patronalistic post-Soviet countries with formally concentrated executive

---

[25] Defined more precisely as persons who, slightly modifying the definition of John Higley and Michael G. Burton, "are able, by virtue of their authoritative positions in powerful organizations," networks, and "movements of whatever kind, to affect ... political outcomes" at the local or national level regularly and substantially." See Higley and Burton, "The Elite Variable in Democratic Transitions and Breakdowns," *American Sociological Review*, v. 54, no. 1, February 1989, pp. 17–32, p. 18.

power (the focus of this volume) from the less patronalistic postcommunist countries of Central and Eastern Europe with less formally concentrated executive power, where single-pyramid systems either have not tended to emerge or have been more readily demolished.

But the same logic that drives the creation of post-Soviet single-pyramid systems also dictates that they are highly vulnerable to crises brought about by anticipated leadership change when the leadership does not wield much genuine political support. When expected to leave the system and when too unpopular to win allies on the basis of something other than the methods of the political machine, incumbent chief patrons risk becoming lame-ducks. The people around them start to struggle openly over the succession, hoping to prevent their rivals from gaining supreme patronal power while aspiring to capture it for themselves. Seeking a major weapon in battle, elites suddenly become "democrats," mobilizing as many people as they can muster in the streets to fight for their cause. Thus we find that each of the events typically coded as post-Soviet "color revolutions" (those in Georgia, Kyrgyzstan, and Ukraine) had at least three characteristics in common: First, the country was already facing a succession struggle; second, the main challengers and ultimate victors had previously been part of the old "dictator's" administration; and third, the strongmen who were overthrown just also happened to be among the least popular leaders in the post-Soviet world.

Moreover, all three of these observations are also true of virtually all other instances in which incumbent single-pyramid presidents of post-Soviet countries were overthrown after the mid-1990s, when the initial institutional chaos of the independence period had passed. It will be shown that this includes not only "revolutions" with mass public participation, but also Armenian President Levon Ter-Petrossian's ouster at the hands of his own prime minister (Robert Kocharian) in 1998. The logic also proves surprisingly powerful in explaining patterns of politics in the four unrecognized statelets in the former Soviet space, with one of the most dramatic events possibly being Abkhazian President Vladislav Ardzinba's failed 2004 effort to hand over office to his chosen political heir, Raul Khajimba. The latter instance was particularly shocking because candidate Khajimba had enjoyed the open backing of Russian authorities, believed by many to be calling the political shots in this breakaway territory of Georgia. Indeed, here was a case of a true electoral revolution – complete with mass protests in the capital city – without any significant prodemocracy movement, Western democracy support, or revolutionary emissaries from countries like Serbia and Georgia seeking to spread their success in toppling dictators in their own countries. Similar events have rocked other unrecognized states in similar circumstances, ousting incumbent regimes in Transnistria in 2011 and South Ossetia in 2011–12. In fact, since the mid-1990s, this regularity has dominated what this book argues has been a related pattern of irregular regime cycles, the lone clear recent example of which during this period appears to have been Ukraine's 2014 "Euromaidan" revolution.

The same logic explains why Ukraine has been the lone post-Soviet country (or statelet) to experience a true sustained democratic interlude, and why this occurred precisely during 2005–10: Ukraine's revolution was the first to produce not only a new president, but also a constitutional reform that transferred significant formal power from the president to the parliament.[26] This helped catalyze a *balance* of formal and informal power between president and prime minister, two competing pyramids that could not defeat each other. Each side surely tried, even Viktor Yushchenko, the initially shining star of Ukrainian democratic hopes. But what stopped each attempt at usurpation was not the country's historic East-West divide, not European Union pressure, not democratic values, not leadership weakness, not civil society, and not economic development. Instead, each aggressive move to aggregate power in the hands of the prime minister or the president was stymied by an equal and opposite application of raw machine force by the other. And this opened up space for "third pyramids" to thrive without formal bases in one of the state's top two executive posts. This logic also explains why Ukraine's democratic episode was so unsatisfying to Ukrainians themselves: Its political machine was not eliminated, only *fragmented*, the patronalistic character of its society remaining largely unchanged. And there were serious flaws with the way its balance of power was established. Ukraine's political system thus remained quite open and competitive for five years, but governance suffered. In the end, Yanukovych's victory in a head-to-head competition with the most powerful rival political machine (that of Prime Minister Yulia Tymoshenko) disrupted the expectation of balanced patronalistic force, creating a fleeting opportunity that Yanukovych seized with gusto to restore a presidentialist constitution and start rebuilding a single-pyramid system.

When presidents were ousted in Kyrgyzstan (2005), Georgia (2003), Abkhazia (2004–5), Armenia (1998), South Ossetia (2012), and Transnistria (2011), mostly what changed was the patron at the top. Presidentialism remained embedded in their constitutions and was actually strengthened in Georgia and Kyrgyzstan until 2010. Moreover, these presidential ousters certainly did not wipe away the patronalistic relations so pervasive in each society, despite signs that Georgia may have made some progress on that front. And where presidentialist constitutions and patronalism have both remained in place, the rule has been that even the most inspiring revolutions in the name of democracy tend to be disappointing, followed by regression back toward single-pyramid politics--at least, until the next president becomes an unpopular lame-duck, setting in motion new revolutionary dynamics.[27]

---

[26] Kyrgyzstan and Georgia have both adopted similar constitutions reforms since 2010, and Ukraine has returned to this constitution after its 2014 revolution.

[27] One way readers can judge the claim of some predictability is to compare the expectations in the following publication with subsequent events: Henry E. Hale, "Regime Cycles: Democracy, Autocracy, and Revolution in Post-Soviet Eurasia," *World Politics*, v. 58, no. 1, October 2005,

All this should reshape our notions of democratization, autocratization, regime change, and hybrid regimes worldwide. At the most general level, it shifts our focus from the organization and instruments of authoritarian or hybrid regime rule to the crucial role of expectations in driving regime coherence and breakdown.[28] Power, to a significant degree, is a self-fulfilling prophecy. Dictators and hybrid regime presidents become vulnerable when the elites they rely upon to carry out their orders start expecting them to fall and therefore begin preparing for a future without these presidents, which in turn makes possible the breakdown of the coercive apparatus, no matter how well funded or well organized. This, one might argue, is precisely what the 2011 Arab uprisings were about, with protesters and regime leaders struggling to shape mass and elite expectations as to whether incumbent regime leaders were doomed, which in turn determined whether leaders' key allies (including militaries) defected "to the people" and prompted regime collapse or stuck together to impose a bloody crackdown and regime survival. "Opposition" in party or civil society form can disappear almost completely when a leader seems firmly in charge but then suddenly surge "out of nowhere" along with defections from the ruling camp when nothing but expectations changes. This calls into serious question the standard approach to regime transition, which has been to think in terms of "authorities" (often divided into hard-liners and soft-liners) and "opposition" as discrete "actors" whose relative strength can be taken as an independent factor driving processes of democratization and other forms of system change.[29] It also challenges the notion that politics is primarily organized around divides between rich and poor, and that this is what ultimately lies behind patterns of revolution and democratization.[30]

pp. 133–65. This article came out in 2006 (the journal was behind on its production schedule at the time) but is based on drafts produced in late 2004 and early 2005. This includes a first draft submitted on November 20, 2004 (before the crucial first presidential election runoff in Ukraine), for presentation at the symposium "Reconstruction and Interaction of Slavic Eurasia and Its Neighboring Worlds," Slavic Research Center, Hokkaido University, Sapporo, Japan, December 9, 2004, and an April 2005 draft circulated as PONARS Working Paper no. 24.

[28] Also implying this need and developing some useful propositions, but doing so in a somewhat different way and not addressing the question of expectations explicitly, is Bruce Bueno de Mesquita, Alastair Smith, Randolph M. Siverson, and James D. Morrow, *The Logic of Political Survival* (Cambridge, MA: MIT Press, 2003).

[29] This is one of many important points in Graeme B. Robertson, *The Politics of Protest in Hybrid Regimes: Managing Dissent in Post-Communist Russia* (New York: Cambridge University Press, 2011), pp. 12–13. Influential works in the prevailing tradition include Guillermo O'Donnell and Philippe C. Schmitter, *Transitions from Authoritarian Rule: Tentative Conclusions about Uncertain Democracies* (Baltimore: Johns Hopkins University Press, 1986); Huntington, *The Third Wave*; Steven Levitsky and Lucan A. Way, *Competitive Authoritarianism: Hybrid Regimes after the Cold War* (New York: Cambridge University Press, 2010); Michael McFaul, "The Fourth Wave of Democracy and Dictatorship: Noncooperative Transitions in the Postcommunist World," *World Politics*, v. 54, no. 2, January 2002, pp. 212–44; Milan W. Svolik, *The Politics of Authoritarian Rule* (New York: Cambridge University Press, 2012).

[30] Daron Acemoglu and James A. Robinson, *Economic Origins of Dictatorship and Democracy* (New York: Cambridge University Press, 2006); Carles Boix, *Democracy and Redistribution*

We need, then, to develop a social science of expectations, a systematic study of the kind of factors that influence mass and elite expectations as to whether and when specific regime leaderships and entire political systems are likely to end.[31] This will also facilitate a helpful reorientation of scholarship from a logic of regime change to a logic of regime dynamics, a logic that not only can anticipate the transition of a system from one type to another but can capture how the moving parts of highly patronalistic polities (such as oligarchic networks and regional political machines) arrange and rearrange themselves in regular, even predictable ways that might on the surface look like a regime "change" but that in reality reflect a stable core set of informal institutions and operating principles.[32]

Accordingly, this analysis holds lessons for policy making and democracy promotion. For one thing, a new, sharp focus on the politics of expectations will help us better understand when, where, and how different regime dynamics are likely to take place, as well as the possibility of true democratization. It also shows, however, that the ability of the international community to shape such expectations depends heavily on whether the West already exercises extensive and deep linkage and leverage with respect to the countries at hand.[33] Thus while the European Union has proven able to impact regime dynamics in Eastern Europe significantly, other international and U.S. efforts to influence the post-Soviet space – including transnational democracy promotion – have proven much weaker than often thought.

(New York: Cambridge University Press, 2003); Dan Slater, *Ordering Power: Contentious Politics and Authoritarian Leviathans in Southeast Asia* (New York: Cambridge University Press, 2010).

[31] The sources of expectations are already a subject of substantial research in the fields of both economics and political science when it comes to the economy, which is also clearly influenced by expectations, as in the central role of business and consumer confidence in driving patterns of investment and spending that are crucial for economic growth. See, for example, James E. Alt and K. Alec Chrystal, *Political Economics* (Berkeley: University of California Press, 1983); Christopher D. Carroll, "Macroeconomic Expectations of Households and Professional Forecasters," *Quarterly Journal of Economics*, v. 118, no. 1, February 2003, pp. 269–98; Raymond M. Duch and Randolph T. Stevenson, "Context and Economic Expectations: When Do Voters Get It Right?" *British Journal of Political Science*, v. 41, no. 1, January 2011, pp. 1–31; Thomas J. Sargent and Neil Wallace, "Rational Expectations and the Theory of Economic Policy," *Journal of Monetary Economics*, v. 2, no. 2, April 1976, pp. 169–83.

[32] This book defines "political regime" by paraphrasing Gerardo Munck's definition, which he distills from dominant accounts. A *political regime* is a set of rules that are at least strategically accepted and not normatively opposed by major actors and that govern which individuals have access to the most important state positions, how such access is obtained, and how binding state decisions are made. Importantly, these rules can be informal as well as formal. See Gerardo L. Munck, "Disaggregating Political Regime: Conceptual Issues in the Study of Democratization," Working Paper no. 228, Helen Kellogg Institute for International Studies, University of Notre Dame, Indiana, August 1996, pp. 6–8.

[33] The terms "linkage" and "leverage" are used in the sense described in Levitsky and Way, *Competitive Authoritarianism*.

The politics of expectations also has implications for the advice that countries should get during or after a true dictatorship collapses or when regime cycles serve up moments of flux when new ideas can be introduced.[34] Understanding that constitutions in highly patronalistic societies work more by shaping informal expectations than by being followed as legal documents, we gain insight into what kinds of constitutions generate the patterns of expectations that are most conducive to open politics. In fact, as imperfect as its outcome has been, Ukraine's experience between 2005 and 2010 – underpinned by a formal constitution that encouraged informal power networks to arrange themselves in multiple competing pyramids instead of one unified one – may yet yield a key to how true democratization can be achieved in highly patronalistic polities beyond Eurasia. Mongolia, a highly patronalistic country with a nonpresidentialist constitution that has had much democratic success in a highly nondemocratic neighborhood, seems to support such an interpretation, as do Bulgaria and Macedonia. Importantly, this advice would caution against uncritically recommending parliamentarism as the most promising arrangement for democratization, since parliamentarism can underpin single-pyramid systems and regime cycles in much the way presidentialist constitutions can.

Indeed, as alien as it may initially seem, Ukraine's 2005–10 outcome should ring rather familiar to readers in the United States in particular. It was there that the constitutional founders long ago discerned that autocracy was best thwarted not by the empowerment of any single person deemed to be a democrat but by a careful system of checks and balances combined with strong state governments that was designed to thwart the self-aggrandizing impulses of central executive power. Thus before we pronounce states in the post-Soviet region to be entirely outside Western political experience, we would do well to recall the histories of the United States and many countries now considered developed democracies that passed through similar periods when "democracy" was quite often the fierce battleground of political machines, rival company towns, packed courts, and merciless corrupt politicians. That said, as the chapters to follow will show, the kind of balances found capable of sustaining competitive politics in post-Soviet Eurasia may be different from those that developed over two centuries in the United States. All this is best illustrated not by taking the democratic ideal or even the dictatorial dystopia as our starting point for analysis, but by developing a compelling theory of the real.

The book unfolds as follows. After Chapter 2 elaborates the core logic of patronal politics and sets it in world historical context, Chapter 3 illustrates the logic by demonstrating how it can shed new light on a thousand years

---

[34] The logic of patronal politics is thus capable of supplying explanations as to when "critical junctures" are likely to arise, when contingent decisions can be made that produce long-lasting change (see Collier and Collier, *Shaping the Political Arena*). This will be discussed further in subsequent chapters.

of Eurasian history leading up to 1991, the momentous year of the USSR's demise. Chapter 4 shows how the logic can be used to develop a more specific theory of regime dynamics, predicting cyclic patterns in what on the surface appear to be "democratization," "autocratization," and "revolution."

The book then turns to testing these propositions empirically through in-depth, process-tracing analysis of regime dynamics in all twelve non-EU post-Soviet countries and all four unrecognized breakaway quasi-states (Abkhazia, Nagorno-Karabakh, South Ossetia, and Transnistria), analysis drawing on material in multiple local languages.[35] This material is collected from the author's own field observations of at least some sort everywhere except Nagorno-Karabakh and South Ossetia; extensive interviews with politicians, insiders, and experts; a detailed tracking of events in these polities over virtually the entire post-Soviet period as reported by local and foreign media (including some sources accessible only in local library archives); survey data where available; government documents; and a wide range of extraordinarily valuable secondary accounts produced by other academic researchers who specialize on each country or territory. Where different plausible interpretations exist of a given episode or where exactly what happened is unclear, this is generally noted, and where important the available narratives are weighed against each other by considering how well they fit the larger pattern of events. As readers will see from the use of all these sources, the logic of patronal politics resonates very well with how people who live and operate in these societies understand their own politics. On the basis of such research, Chapter 5 documents the emergence of the most important patronal networks and formal constitutional structure in each polity. Chapter 6 then describes and explains the successes and failures of the first post-Soviet patrons in arranging these patronal "building blocks" to create the single-pyramid systems that eventually emerged in nearly all of these places by the end of the 1990s. In so doing, this chapter demonstrates that, as expected, regularity in regime dynamics started to overcome irregularity after the initial turmoil of the transition from communist rule subsided.

With Chapter 7, the book shows how the patronal politics framework can account for both the occurrence and timing of virtually all ousters of patronal presidents that have occurred since the initial post-Soviet single-pyramid systems were built. It reveals how regularity in these ousters has been the norm and irregularity the exception. Chapter 8 then demonstrates that the theory also accurately explains why presidents in other post-Soviet countries have managed to keep their own networks in power, successfully managing any succession crises that have emerged. In Chapter 9, the volume explores what has happened after post-Soviet patronal presidents have been ousted. It reveals that

---

[35] This includes extensive use by the author of Russian (still widely used in all of these polities), Ukrainian, and Azerbaijani. Occasional use of other languages was made, sometimes with the aid of a dictionary or interpretation.

the result has tended to be a cyclic return of political closure rather than democratization regardless of how "democratic" the revolutionaries appeared to be, except where the revolution was accompanied by a constitutional shift away from presidentialism. Chapter 10 discusses the lone republic in the non-EU post-Soviet space featuring a truly parliamentarist constitution, Moldova, and dispels the myth that stronger parliaments generally tend to produce democratization, instead supplying some propositions as to what conditions make this more or less likely.

Chapter 11 takes a step back and draws some larger conclusions, showing how many factors that we often think of as influencing democratization are much less important than widely believed, including transnational democracy promotion, civil society organizations, privatization of the economy, opposition unity, regime resources and institutions, ethnolinguistic divides, and social media such as Twitter or Facebook. While these factors can matter, they are best treated as secondary in importance, at least in the post-Soviet space, most effective when the logic of patronal politics dictates they will be. The chapter also argues that the power of public opinion tends to be underestimated in highly patronalistic polities, including nondemocratic ones, and deserves more attention.[36] Chapter 12 concludes the volume by showing how the book's findings can shed new light on regime dynamics throughout the globe, dynamics ranging from the true democratization of many East European countries after 1989 to the 2011 Arab uprisings. In light of this world experience, it also considers the extent to which Eurasia is unique and weighs possible long-term scenarios for escaping the cycles of political opening and closure that have been a feature of the region's political landscape for the last quarter-century.

---

[36] This is a significant point of divergence from selectorate theory, which posits that nondemocratic regimes need not pay much attention to public opinion for "daily, routine politics." See Bueno de Mesquita et al., *The Logic of Political Survival*, p. 70.

2

Patronal Politics and the Great Power of Expectations

For many countries, pervasive "corruption" and low regard for the law are not simply a tumor on the body politic, something that can be isolated and excised.[1] Instead, they are more like the body's lifeblood. Not only do they course throughout the whole of society – connecting state, individual, and economy – but they deliver vital nourishment that keeps society functioning and growing. Paying a bribe, using one's position to help relatives, or circumventing legal "red tape" can be an indispensable means of getting almost anything done.[2] What is even more often missed by outsiders, however, is that these practices can also be a form of mass empowerment and even reflect a certain morality given the real choices they face. When officials are lazy or callous, offering a "gift" (bribe) can be one way citizens can get them to respond to their needs or simply do their job well. Badly underpaid officials can understand taking such gifts as a lesser of evils, necessary under the circumstances if they are to practice their professions while also feeding their families. The bureaucrat who fails to use his position to "look out for his own" can become not only ineffectual – lacking "favor bank" assets that can help him be a competent public servant – but seen as callous and even selfish, neglectful of his duties to family, friends, or community. The developer who fails to pay off the right people might find her plans to provide the community with sorely needed housing stymied.

People in such societies are caught in a vicious cycle. Not expecting others to behave according to formal rules, few risk working together when cheating is possible and the stakes are high without a side payment, a tight personal bond, or some kind of guarantee backed by force, the kind of force that can be supplied by a patron in high office or a criminal organization (if the two are

---

[1] World Bank President James D. Wolfensohn famously called for a campaign against the "cancer of corruption" in his October 1, 1996, Annual Meetings Address (one can find the text through http://web.worldbank.org).

[2] See Alena V. Ledeneva, *How Russia Really Works* (Ithaca, NY: Cornell University Press, 2006).

distinct).[3] Not expecting the government to implement policy impartially, citizens pressure their own patrons to milk that government for all they can while in office lest others suck the resources dry first. Social science might call this a social *equilibrium*: Given that everyone expects everyone else to behave this way, it makes no sense for an individual to behave differently since she would only wind up hurting herself and possibly those who depend on her, possibly severely.[4] Such people may all hate corruption and prefer a system where rules are impartially enforced. But so long as they do not expect everyone else to change his behavior at the same time, they are caught in a dilemma that is captured nicely by the title of Rasma Karklins's book, *The System Made Me Do It*.[5] And by "doing it," they can make a case that they are in fact morally right under the circumstances.[6] And so their predicament endures.

This is a picture of what this volume will call a highly *patronalistic* society. *Patronalism* refers to a social equilibrium in which individuals organize their political and economic pursuits primarily around the personalized exchange of concrete rewards and punishments, and not primarily around abstract, impersonal principles such as ideological belief or categorizations that include many people one has not actually met in person. Patronalism, then, involves collective action based far more on extended networks of actual acquaintance than on what Benedict Anderson cleverly calls "imagined communities," such as nations, ethnic groups, "socialists," "Republicans," "teachers," "the rich and the poor," or "supporters of gun control."[7] This does not mean that highly patronalistic societies cannot ever experience moments when people rally around some impersonalistic cause, as might happen when an outside force invades and catalyzes a broad, cooperative response by all local networks on the basis of territory or ethnicity rather than direct interpersonal connections.[8]

---

[3] Vadim Volkov, *Violent Entrepreneurs: The Use of Force in the Making of Russian Capitalism* (Ithaca, NY: Cornell University Press, 2002).

[4] More specifically, this sentence describes a Nash equilibrium. On the more specific concept of "corruption" as an equilibrium, see Pranab Bardhan, "Corruption and Development: A Review of Issues," *Journal of Economic Literature*, v. 35, no. 3, September 1997, pp. 1320–46. Similarly, see Anna Persson, Bo Rothstein, and Jan Teorell, "Why Anticorruption Reforms Fail – Systemic Corruption as a Collective Action Problem," *Governance*, v. 26, no. 3, July 2013, pp. 449–71.

[5] Rasma Karklins, *The System Made Me Do It: Corruption in Post-Communist Societies* (Armonk, NY: M. E. Sharpe, 2005). See also Daniel J. Beers, "Building Democratic Courts from the Inside Out: Judicial Culture and the Rule of Law in Postcommunist Eastern Europe," dissertation in Political Science, Indiana University, 2011.

[6] Lisa Cameron, Ananish Chaudhuri, Nisvan Erkal, and Lata Gangadharan, "Do Attitudes towards Corruption Differ across Cultures? Experimental Evidence from Australia, India, Indonesia and Singapore," University of Melbourne Department of Economics Research Paper no. 943, October 2006.

[7] Benedict Anderson, *Imagined Communities*, rev. ed. (New York: Verso, 1991). To reiterate one of his central points, by "imagined," Anderson does not mean that such communities do not exist, but that they consist of people who do not actually know each other, who actually "commune" only in the imagination.

[8] Rogers Brubaker thus famously defines "nation" as "contingent event" rather than a thing, "entity," or "real group." See Rogers Brubaker, *Nationalism Reframed: Nationhood and the National Question in the New Europe* (New York: Cambridge University Press, 1996), pp. 7, 16.

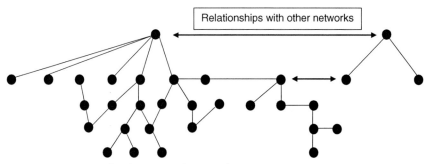

FIGURE 2.1. Example of a patronal network.

Note on interpretation: Dots represent individuals and lines indicate different mixes of coercive and mutually beneficial relationships, with vertical positioning indicating relative power in the relationships. As this diagram illustrates, patronal networks can be very complex combinations of relationships among patrons, clients, and equals, often including some lower-level actors who have ties to multiple actors in the same network. It can also happen that individuals at both higher and lower levels have ties to other networks with distinct leadership. When this volume follows locally common usage by discussing networks as hierarchical and invoking metaphors like "pyramid" and "vertical," therefore, this is naturally intended as a heuristically useful simplification of a complex reality. Works discussing different kinds of network arrangement variations within this general theme include Scott Radnitz, *Weapons of the Wealthy: Predatory Regimes and Elite-Led Protests in Central Asia* (Ithaca, NY: Cornell University Press, 2010), and James C. Scott, "Patron-Client Politics and Political Change in Southeast Asia," *American Political Science Review*, v. 66, no. 1, March 1972, pp. 91–113.

But this is the exception rather than the rule in highly patronalistic polities, where everyday politics and power struggles revolve around extended networks connecting people through actual personal acquaintance.[9]

Where economic or political inequality arises, as it does in all but the smallest and poorest human communities, patronal networks tend to take on a hierarchical character, though they also typically include many connections among equals (see Figure 2.1). Following a long research tradition, the most powerful people in these relationships can be called *patrons*, and more subordinate ones *clients*. Politics in patronalistic societies therefore revolves chiefly around personalized relationships joining extended networks of patrons and clients, and political struggle tends to take the form of competition among different patron-client networks. The term *patronal politics* refers to these relationships and this competition. One might reasonably substitute venerable academic terms like "patrimonialism," "neopatrimonialism," or "clientelism," but the conceptual

---

[9] This helps explain why moments of non-patronalistic mobilization, when they occur – for example, revolutionary collective action for democracy or against corruption – often involve great euphoria and hope for the transformation of society but also why disillusionment is so often eventually the result.

baggage they carry is more likely to distract than clarify for reasons that will be discussed later. In some cases, it will be helpful to refer to highly patronalistic societies as those often marked by "high levels of corruption" and "weak rule of law" because these are concepts more readily understood and measured, but establishing the concept of patronalism ensures we do not actually conflate these more specific (and normatively charged) terms with the underlying social equilibrium that helps *generate* these phenomena.

To understand how politics works in patronalistic societies, one must understand the logic of collective action that governs relations between the patrons and the clients and underpins interactions among the different patron-client networks. This logic treats power not only as a function of resources and organization, but crucially as a kind of self-fulfilling prophecy in which what people expect is often precisely what they get – *because* they expect it. The key, therefore, is to identify what shapes these expectations. By understanding the sources of patrons' and clients' expectations, we gain predictive power and uncover dynamics and patterns of what may appear to be "autocratization," "democratization," and "revolution" that are not fully understood through more conventional approaches, including theories of democratization, autocratization, and revolution as such.[10]

The pages that follow elaborate the core of this logic, which is then illustrated in Chapter 3 by showing its power to reinterpret a millennium of Eurasian history through 1991 and help clear up some long-standing debates among historians. Chapter 4 then elaborates further the logic of patronal politics, this time developing implications as to the likely consequences of certain formal institutions that have become common features of modern polities, including those in the former USSR: elections and constitutions. The result is a theory that goes a long way to explaining important regime dynamics over the first two decades of postcommunism, a claim that is supported in the subsequent chapters.

Why "Patronalism" and Not a Preexisting Concept?

The risk of introducing new terminology is to clutter further what is already an elaborately uncoordinated conceptual landscape, and it is not taken lightly. To defend the decision and to help readers understand how the new terminology of patronalism relates to existing concepts, the present section briefly discusses available alternatives that have been used productively for other purposes by other scholars and shows why patronalism is preferred for the purposes of this book. The main point is that patronalism is a more general notion than these

---

[10] It is important to keep in mind that this is an "ideal-type" depiction of reality in the sense discussed by Max Weber. Real-life systems are always more complicated than any simple logic would admit. But the ideal type highlights an important pattern that lends insight into how phenomena actually work. See Max Weber, "The Ideal Type," in Max Weber, *The Methodology of the Social Sciences*, translated and edited by Edward A. Shils and Henry A. Finch (Glencoe, IL: Free Press, 1949), especially pp. 89–94.

others, tending to subsume rather than deny them. Thus rather than "stretch" existing concepts, further clouding their own more specific meanings, the decision was made to move up a step in the "ladder of generality" by introducing a new, more general term.[11]

Clientelism

The present author originally worked with a long-standing line of scholarship on "clientelism" and attempted to refine and expand this older concept to fit the logic presented here instead of introducing new terms.[12] After several years of developing the ideas in this book and discussing them with colleagues, however, it became clear that "clientelism" simply has too many different (much more specific) prominent usages that tend to confuse audiences and distract them from this book's core logic when used to refer to it.[13] In at least some well-known social science work, for example, the concept of clientelism implies a focus on "clientele" that connotes a power shift from patrons to clients, something certainly not part of the present theory (though equally certainly not excluded from it);[14] is regarded as being in contrast with coercion or predation rather than including these practices as patronalism does[15]; or is defined as an explicitly electoral phenomenon whereas patronalism is not limited to such a context.[16] To use a term widely associated with such specific meanings is to introduce confusion in readers' understanding of my own argument, which is in fact about more than "clientelism" as so defined. And since these more specific usages are central to the research agenda on clientelism, I concluded that stretching the concept to capture everything meant by patronalism is also to put at risk the coordinated scholarly usage that has made this older research agenda productive.

[11] The classic work on the dangers of concept stretching (recommending instead climbing a "ladder of generality") is Giovanni Sartori, "Concept Misformation in Comparative Politics," *American Political Science Review*, v. 64, no. 4, 1970, pp. 1033–53.

[12] The most recent examples include Henry E. Hale, "Formal Constitutions in Informal Politics: Institutions and Democratization in Eurasia," *World Politics*, v. 63, no. 4, October 2011, pp. 581–617; and Henry E. Hale, "Two Decades of Post-Soviet Regime Dynamics," *Demokratizatsiya: The Journal of Post-Soviet Democratization*, v. 20, no. 2, Spring 2012, pp. 71–7.

[13] This is likely to be clear to anyone who compares the present chapter with the following review of the clientelism literature: Allen Hicken, "Clientelism," *Annual Review of Political Science*, v. 14, 2011, pp. 289–310.

[14] Simona Piattoni, "Clientelism in Historical and Comparative Perspective," in Simona Piattoni, ed., *Clientelism, Interests, and Democratic Representation: The European Experience in Historical and Comparative Perspective* (New York: Cambridge University Press, 2001), pp. 1–30, p. 7.

[15] Anna Grzymala-Busse, "Beyond Clientelism: Incumbent State Capture and State Formation," *Comparative Political Studies*, v. 41, nos. 4/5, April/May 2008, pp. 638–73, pp. 638–43.

[16] Herbert Kitschelt, "Clientelistic Linkage Strategies: A Descriptive Exploration," paper prepared for the Workshop on Democratic Accountability Strategies, Duke University, Durham, NC, May 18–19, 2011; Herbert Kitschelt and Steven I. Wilkinson, eds., *Patrons, Clients, and Policies: Patterns of Democratic Accountability and Political Competition* (Cambridge: Cambridge University Press, 2007), pp. 1–49, Piattoni, "Clientelism." See also Herbert Kitschelt, "Linkages between Citizens and Politicians in Democratic Polities," *Comparative Political Studies*, v. 33, nos. 6–7, 2000.

Patrimonialism

Weber intended this concept to capture rule based on "kin ties, patron-client relations, personal allegiances, and combinations thereof, with few formal rules and regulations."[17] As employed by many scholars, however, this concept is regarded as being in opposition to bureaucracy and "rational-legal" patterns of authority and was accordingly seen by Weber as a form of "traditional" authority; implies the personal *ownership* of the state (as "patrimony") by the leader; is often understood today as normatively implying backwardness; and is meant to capture one of several "legitimate" forms of domination. Scholarship in the patrimonialism tradition thus tends to revolve around these issues and is frequently distracted by arguments as to what Weber originally meant.[18]

Patronalism is not so limited as a concept. Patronalism is certainly not intended to imply either backwardness or legitimacy (though these are not ruled out), has no essential connotation of "tradition," and does not necessarily imply that the state (or prestate) is seen as the ruler's patrimony. More fundamentally, patronalism is not primarily a concept about rule or domination, much less legitimacy. Instead, patronalism connotes a broad *social equilibrium* that encompasses relations both inside and outside the realm of politics and the state. To be sure, one (but not the only) central question for the patronal politics research program is what kinds of rule are likely in highly patronalistic societies. And, certainly, with such a social equilibrium, patrimonial forms of legitimate domination are likely to be common. But so are breakdowns in both legitimacy and domination without society itself becoming any more or less patronalistic. Thus while patrimonial politics tends to be patronal politics, not all patronalism is patrimonial. Essentially the same is true for the concept of *sultanism*, which was invented by Weber as "an extreme case of patrimonialism" and as such is a much narrower concept.[19]

Neopatrimonialism

This concept was developed to redress some of the aforementioned problems with the notion of patrimonialism for studying contemporary societies. In

---

[17] Mounira M. Charrad and Julia Adams, "Introduction: Patrimonialism, Past and Present," *Annals of the American Academy of Political and Social Science*, v. 636, July 2011, pp. 6–15, p. 7; Max Weber, *Economy and Society*, edited by G. Roth and C. Wittich (Berkeley: University of California Press, 1978), pp. 231–2.

[18] Useful overviews include the articles in the special issue of the *Annals of the American Academy of Political and Social Science* (v. 636, July 2011) edited by Mounira M. Charrad and Julia Adams; and Ann Pitcher, Mary H. Moran, and Michael Johnston, "Rethinking Patrimonialism and Neopatrimonialism in Africa," *African Studies Review*, v. 52, no. 1, April 2009, pp. 125–56. Discussions of the applicability of these concepts to Eurasian politics include Marlene Laruelle, "Discussing Neopatrimonialism and Patronal Presidentialism in the Central Asian Context," *Demokratizatsiya: The Journal of Post-Soviet Democratization*, v. 20, no. 4, Autumn 2012, pp. 301–24; and Richard Pipes, *Russia under the Old Regime* (New York: Collier, 1974).

[19] H. E. Chehabi and Juan J. Linz, *Sultanistic Regimes* (Baltimore: Johns Hopkins University Press, 1998), p. 4.

particular, it posits that patrimonial phenomena need not be in opposition to bureaucracy and could instead "coexist with, and suffuse" it.[20] But still problematic for present purposes is that it is designed to characterize a *form of "rule"* while patronalism is intended to characterize a broader *pattern of social relations.* Moreover, because neopatrimonialism characterizes a form of rule and was initially developed to characterize nondemocratic regimes, it has become widely equated with authoritarianism, though more recent scholarship has begun to theorize nonauthoritarian forms of neopatrimonial rule.[21] The concept's Weberian origins also imply that neopatrimonialism is a *legitimate* form of rule, raising a variety of questions associated with this problematic concept. Thus while the notion of neopatrimonialism could reasonably be broadened still further to capture patterns of social relations rather than just patterns of rule, a move that would have the benefit of connecting more directly with much excellent scholarship, the present author has concluded that this benefit would not outweigh the problems that would result from stretching the term further than it already has been stretched and from the risk that the term's preexisting usages would confuse more than clarify the concepts central to this book's argument. All neopatrimonialism involves patronal politics, but not all patronalism is neopatrimonial in the specific ways the term has generally been used.

"Uncivicness" or "Lack of Social Capital"

Patronalistic societies might be described as having low levels of "social capital." The latter term, however, is already used with a variety of meanings, so not only would adopting its opposite ("a lack of social capital") be terminologically awkward, but it would again risk confusing rather than clarifying the concept of patronalism.[22] Perhaps the most famous use of the concept of social capital is Robert Putnam's work on "civicness," which implies broad acceptance of abstract norms of reciprocity and generalized trust rather than dependence on personalized and hierarchical relationships. Putnam does describe how a state of lacking civicness can be a kind of social equilibrium, one that

---

[20] Michael Bratton and Nicolas van de Walle, *Democratic Experiments in Africa: Regime Transitions in Comparative Perspective* (New York: Cambridge University Press, 1997), p. 62. Other works productively using this approach include Gero Erdmann and Ulf Engel, "Neopatrimonialism Reconsidered: Critical Review and Elaboration of an Elusive Concept," *Commonwealth and Comparative Politics,* v. 45, no. 1, February 2007, pp. 95–119; Aleksandr A. Fisun, *Demokratiia, neopatrimonializm i global'nye transformatsii* (Kharkiv: Konstanta, 2007); Richard Snyder, "Explaining Transitions from Neopatrimonial Dictatorships," *Comparative Politics,* v. 24, no. 4, July 1992, pp. 379–99.

[21] Erdmann and Engel, "Neopatrimonialism Reconsidered"; Pitcher, Moran, and Johnson, "Rethinking Patrimonialism and Neopatrimonialism."

[22] A collection of perspectives on social capital by leading theorists can be found in Partha Dasgupta and Ismail Sarageldin, eds., *Social Capital: A Multifaceted Perspective* (Washington, DC: World Bank, 2000).

sounds much like patronalism as described here.[23] The concepts of civicness and patronalism, however, are not exact opposites. While patronalistic societies tend to be uncivic places, uncivic places are not necessarily patronalistic. For example, a perfectly atomized society is completely uncivic but also not patronalistic because it lacks the extended networks of actual acquaintance that are central to the concept of patronalism. Uncivicness, therefore, is not necessarily patronalistic, and in any case treating patronalism as something "un"-civic would cast on it a negative value connotation that is not intended. One might usefully think about patronalism, however, as one of multiple possible states of the social world that are alternatives to civicness or that feature low social capital in the sense described by Putnam. Indeed, since the literature currently lacks a good nonnegative term for such a state of the world, "patronalism" would seem to be a strong, intuitive candidate.

Informal Politics

As was noted in Chapter 1, an important and relevant literature has emerged on *informal politics*, which generally refers to behavior that is not explicitly codified and considered official.[24] While much of patronal politics is informal, including many phenomena that will be discussed later in this volume, it is also true that patronalistic behavior can be formally codified in law without becoming less patronalistic and less important. Moreover, informal collective behavior need not be patronalistic, as with unofficial coordination to support an ideology that is not organized by networks of actual acquaintance but effected by a common focal point or impersonal mass communication. Thus while there is overlap between the behaviors captured by the categories "informal politics" and "patronal politics," it is only partial and neither term subsumes the other.

Concepts Related to Corruption and the Rule of Law

A variety of other concepts are also related to the notion of patronalism, but are much more specific and so are best seen not as alternatives but as subsets of the larger set of phenomena that can be called patronalistic. One such example is *corruption*. Analysts have long observed, for example, that essentially the same practices can be considered normal, accepted behavior in one society but corruption in another for the sole reason that they are legalized and codified in the former but outlawed in the latter. A classic example is the practice of lobbying in the United States, which is legal and accepted there but much of which is not in many other countries.[25] Much of this behavior involves extended networks

---

[23] Robert Putnam, *Making Democracy Work* (Princeton, NJ: Princeton University Press, 1993).

[24] For an overview and framework, see Gretchen Helmke and Steven Levitsky, "Introduction," in Gretchen Helmke and Steven Levitsky, eds., *Informal Institutions and Democracy: Lessons from Latin America* (Baltimore: Johns Hopkins University Press, 2006), pp. 1–30.

[25] James C. Scott, "The Analysis of Corruption in Developing Nations," *Comparative Studies in Society and History*, v. 11, no. 3, June 1969, pp. 315–41, pp. 315–19.

of actual acquaintance and thus falls under the category of patronalism. But it is the underlying practices, not their status in formal law, that are important for the argument made in this volume. And of course the vast bulk of patronalistic behavior is perfectly legal and hence not "corrupt." For the same reason, the level of *rule of law* is also not coterminous with patronalism even though patronalistic societies tend to feature low levels of it. Similar examples of much narrower concepts that tend to involve patronalism include *machine politics* and *political monopolies*.[26]

Overall, one may say that highly patronalistic societies are prone to feature patrimonial/neopatrimonial forms of rule and legitimate domination, pervasive clientelism, high levels of "corruption," widespread machine politics, low civicness, weak rule of law, and the frequent dominance of informal politics over formal politics.[27] At the same time, we should not equate the concept with any one of these rough covariates since it tends to be broader than each of them except for low civicness (of which patronalism can be thought of as one important type) and informal politics (which overlaps imperfectly with patronalism). We can, however, reasonably use these covariates to help us identify highly patronalistic societies where empirical measures of the covariates exist.

Finally, it is worth emphasizing the strong positive case that can be made for the terminology in its own right. For one thing, it gives us a simple way of describing an important kind of social equilibrium that this volume will argue has extremely important implications for how politics works in a majority of the world's countries, one not captured fully by existing concepts. In addition, it avoids negative value connotations that are widely associated with other terms, such as corruption and patrimonialism. And perhaps most importantly from the perspective of terminology, "patronalism" has certain semantic benefits. In particular, it flows in a satisfying way from the concept of patron-client relations. And in characterizing the relationship between patrons and clients, if anything, it emphasizes the power of patrons more than that of the clients and does not limit consideration to any particular form of power. This is appropriate given that the inequalities these societies feature tend to favor patrons relative to clients, as will be discussed further later, though the terminology leaves open (and indeed frames) the question of whether this is true (and if so to what extent) in any given case.

---

[26] Respectively: James C. Scott, "Corruption, Machine Politics, and Political Change," *American Political Science Review*, v. 63, no. 4, 1969, pp. 1142–58, and Jessica Trounstine, *Political Monopolies in American Cities: The Rise and Fall of Bosses and Reformers* (Chicago: University of Chicago Press, 2008). On other related concepts (and some of those just discussed), see the useful anthology Steffen W. Schmidt, James C. Scott, Carl Lande, and Laura Guasti, eds., *Friends, Followers, and Factions* (Berkeley: University of California Press, 1977).

[27] Research indicating that these features tend to vary together includes Bo Rothstein, "Trust, Social Dilemmas, and Collective Memories," *Journal of Theoretical Politics*, v. 12, no. 4, 2000, pp. 477–501.

Patronalism in World Historical Context

When thinking about patronalistic phenomena, a natural impulse for many raised in the West is to treat them as a deviation from normal and more desirable social conditions. This impulse is misguided in a very important sense: Patronalism is in fact the *norm* throughout all recorded human history, with only a small number of large-scale societies having managed to break out of it to a significant degree, and even this only in the last two hundred years and only among a fraction of the world's population.

Upon reflection, this makes sense. The original human communities were very small hunter-gatherer groups that had no need for reliance on anything other than personal relationships. When the agricultural revolution produced the first large-scale settlements some five to ten millennia ago, the natural way to organize and lead them was to build on these established patterns.[28] Georgi Derluguian and Timothy Earle colorfully characterize the political systems that typically emerged as *handcrafted* rule by "chieftains" who worked through personal relationships. This general form of rule proved understandable, effective in establishing a modicum of social order and protection, and flexible enough to adapt to the myriad new circumstances in which human society found itself as millennia passed. It has thus been reproduced quite pragmatically in countless guises straight through the establishment of today's states.[29]

Nobel Prize–winning economist Douglass North and his colleagues John Wallis and Barry Weingast show how what this book would call patronalism in polity and society has reproduced itself through the present day, constituting what they dub the "natural state" of human society, a concept that they refer to as the "default social outcome."[30] This might also be called a highly patronalistic society. Because patronalism involves the kind of vicious-cycle equilibrium described previously (as in *The System Made Me Do It!*),[31] it has proven extremely hard to for societies to escape.[32] North and his colleagues,

---

[28] Douglass C. North, John Joseph Wallis, Barry R. Weingast, *Violence and Social Orders: A Conceptual Framework for Interpreting Recorded Human History* (New York: Cambridge University Press, 2009).

[29] Georgi Derluguian and Timothy Earle, "Strong Chieftaincies Out of Weak States, or Elemental Power Unbound," *Comparative Social Research*, v. 27, 2010, pp. 51–76, prepublication draft. See also Allen W. Johnson and Timothy Earle, *The Evolution of Human Societies: From Foraging Group to Agrarian State*, 2nd ed. (San Jose, CA: Stanford University Press, 2000).

[30] North, Wallis, and Weingast, *Violence and Social Orders*, p. 13.

[31] Karklins, *The System*.

[32] Barbara Geddes, *Politician's Dilemma: Building State Capacity in Latin America* (Berkeley: University of California Press, 1994). All this does not mean that certain "spheres of impartiality" or formality cannot be created by determined individuals or even organizations (such as monastic orders) within patronalistic societies, as Sverker Gustavsson pointed out to the author in a personal communication. As Juliet Johnson illustrates in a paper on central banking, however, such spheres can also be very vulnerable to the larger patronalistic context, as her case study of Kyrgyzstan shows. See Juliet Johnson, "From Monetary Independence to State Control: Central Banking in the Kyrgyz Republic, 1993–2010," paper presented at a PONARS Eurasia

in fact, report that escape has been achieved by only a fraction of the world's countries today, mostly in North America and Western Europe, and only as a result of a long chain of fortuitous circumstances that could have been broken at numerous junctures.[33] The endurance of patronal politics as a general phenomenon, then, owes primarily to pragmatism in the context of a tenaciously embedded social equilibrium, though the human imagination has constructed myriad specific ways in which patronalism can be practiced.[34]

Because the present book is about politics in patronalistic countries and not in the countries that have escaped it, it will not go into the chains of circumstances that drastically reduced patronalism in much of the West and produced there what North, Wallis, and Weingast call "open access orders."[35] It will, though, be important to show how patronalism managed to reproduce itself through major historical junctures in this volume's region of focus, Eurasia. This will help us understand how this deep social context interacts with formal institutions (and other factors), leading formal institutions to operate there in ways different than in the less patronalistic West. This will be accomplished in Chapter 3. For now, we must delve deeper into exactly what patronal politics is.

The Sinews of Patronal Power

Because the logic of patronalism is that of patrons and clients, patronalistic societies are distinguished more by what we might call "vertical" than "horizontal" political organization.[36] That is, rather than equal citizens selecting a primus inter pares to represent them impartially in the political arena, patronalism tends to generate powerful political patrons who sit atop (roughly) hierarchical networks of clients. Sometimes the patrons operate out of state institutions, and contemporary states' chief executives are frequently patrons of particular puissance, as were Zaire's President Mobutu Sese Seko and Azerbaijan's President Heydar Aliyev. In other cases, patrons can be barons of business or the bosses of territorially circumscribed political machines,

workshop in Bishkek, Kyrgyzstan, June 2011. At the same time, there is research indicating that there are conditions under which such spheres can spread, including Bo Rothstein and Daniel Eek, "Political Corruption and Social Trust: An Experimental Approach," *Rationality and Society*, v. 21, no. 1, February 2009, pp. 81–112. All of this is one reason why we empirically do not see a clear division of societies into two sets, one in a pure patronalistic equilibrium and one in a pure nonpatronalistic equilibrium. It is also a reason why escape, when it happens, often takes place by a gradual expansion of such enclaves and factors that sustain them rather than a sudden all-encompassing tip. See also North, Wallis, and Weingast, *Violence and Social Orders*.

[33] North, Wallis, and Weingast, *Violence and Social Orders*.

[34] This is why ethnic identity, for example, is much more easily constructed and changeable than patronalism as a broad phenomenon.

[35] North, Wallis, and Weingast, *Violence and Social Orders*, p. 2.

[36] Please refer to Figure 2.1 and the associated note of interpretation on the more precise nature of these networks.

as were, respectively, Russia's Mikhail Khodorkovsky (Yukos chairman and Russia's richest man until 2003) and America's Boss Tweed (patron of New York City's storied Tammany Hall).

In almost all cases, however, the most important patronalistic networks extend far beyond any single formal institution. Mobutu's and Aliyev's networks, for example, radiated out from state institutions to permeate virtually all lucrative business endeavors in their countries. Khodorkovsky, when Russian President Vladimir Putin's authorities jailed him in 2003, was by many accounts in the process of advancing his patronal network in parliament and, he hoped, into the presidency. Tweed wielded power not only as head of New York City's Democratic Party organization, but as a major property owner and business mogul. Some powerful patrons do not even hold the top formal positions in their organizational base. Deng Xiaoping, for example, dominated Chinese politics long after he gave up the nominal title of Communist Party chief. Vladimir Putin remained the most powerful man in Russia during 2008–12 despite ceding the presidency to his longtime underling Dmitry Medvedev and assuming the formally subordinate post of prime minister.

The chief collective actors in patronalistic dramas, then, are neither the formally defined institutions that typically structure comparative textbook descriptions of all countries' political systems nor imagined communities like "ethnic groups," "right-wingers," or "the rich and the poor." Instead, they are informal, generally though not strictly hierarchical networks.[37] It is thus these informal networks we have in mind when talking about "the Kremlin," "oligarchs," "the Kuchma team," "the presidential administration," or "regional political machines," to take some examples from former Soviet countries. Thus while there is some risk such terms will be interpreted too narrowly, they must be used because full descriptions of the complex networks they are intended to connote would be impossibly unwieldy for use in most scholarly analysis beyond these descriptions themselves. Descriptions of individual networks will, however, be provided in the case studies.

---

[37] This builds on a number of works that explicitly interpret politics in post-Soviet and other countries in terms of networks. For example, see Gerald M. Easter, *Restructuring the State: Personal Networks and Elite Identity* (New York: Cambridge University Press, 2000). Thomas Graham, "Novyi rossiiskii rezhim," *Nezavisimaia Gazeta*, November 23, 1995; Mustaq H. Khan, "Markets, States and Democracy: Patron-Client Networks and the Case for Democracy in Developing Countries," *Democratization*, v. 12, no. 5, December 2005, pp. 704–24; Vadim Kononenko and Arkady Moshes, eds., *Russia as a Network State: What Works in Russia When State Institutions Do Not?* (New York: Palgrave Macmillan, 2011); Duncan McCargo, "Network Monarchy and Legitimacy Crises in Thailand," *Pacific Review*, v. 18, no. 4, December 2005, pp. 499–519; Gulnaz Sharafutdinova, *Political Consequences of Crony Capitalism inside Russia* (South Bend, IN: Notre Dame University Press, 2010); Dan Slater, *Ordering Power: Contentious Politics and Authoritarian Leviathans in Southeast Asia* (New York: Cambridge University Press, 2010); and Idil Tuncer-Kilavuz, "Political and Social Networks in Tajikistan and Uzbekistan: 'Clan', Region, and Beyond," *Central Asian Survey*, v. 28, no. 3, September 2009, pp. 323–34.

What Binds Patronalistic Networks Together?

What holds these patronalistic networks and coalitions of networks together, and what prevents the patrons from being overthrown by other people who would rather be on the top of the hierarchy than the bottom? Classic studies in anthropology, sociology, and political science have generally emphasized two factors: (1) the patron's continued access to valuable *resources* for rewarding loyal clients and (2) the patron's power of *enforcement*, his ability selectively to deliver punishments to the disloyal.[38] A newer literature inspired by rational choice theory has added one more broad factor to this list: (3) the patron's capacity to *monitor* clients and "subpatrons," those figures who have clients of their own but who also are themselves the clients of more powerful patrons. That is, a patron with voluminous resources and a vast arsenal *still* may not be able to hold together his network if he has no way of finding out who deserves a reward and who a punishment. This new research, then, as well as the older research focusing on enforcement power, places the emphasis overwhelmingly on a patron's resources and organization.[39]

Some studies also cite the importance of ethnic or other bonds, such as shared ideology or the loyalties developed by units in combat, that are said to generate network cohesion.[40] Reference to such bonds, however, does not by itself get us very far beyond the literature's overwhelming focus on resources and organization as the key to network cohesion. For one thing, patronalism and its associated political networks constitute a much more general phenomenon that does not reduce to bonds of identity or ideology, leaving us much still to explain. Even in the limited realm where networks appear to correspond

[38] Jonathan Fox, "The Difficult Transition from Clientelism to Citizenship: Lessons from Mexico," *World Politics*, v. 46, no. 2, January 1994, pp. 151–84; Carl H. Lande, "Networks and Groups in Southeast Asia: Some Observations on the Group Theory of Politics," *American Political Science Review*, v. 67, no. 1, March 1973, pp. 103–27; Andrew J. Nathan, "A Factionalism Model for CCP Politics," *China Quarterly*, January–March 1973, pp. 34–66; James C. Scott, "Patron-Client Politics and Political Change in Southeast Asia," *American Political Science Review*, v. 66, no. 1, March 1972, pp. 91–113.

[39] That is, this literature recognizes an important principal-agent problem, whereby one cannot assume that agents who get orders share the same interests in obeying those orders as do the "principals" who give them. See Herbert Kitschelt and Steven I. Wilkinson, "Citizen-Politician Linkages: An Introduction," in *Patrons, Clients, and Policies: Patterns of Democratic Accountability and Political Competition* (Cambridge: Cambridge University Press, 2007), pp. 1–49; Susan Stokes, "Perverse Accountability: A Formal Model of Machine Politics with Evidence from Argentina," *American Political Science Review*, v. 99, no. 3, 2005, pp. 215–25.

[40] Steven Levitsky and Lucan A. Way, *Competitive Authoritarianism: Hybrid Regimes after the Cold War* (New York: Cambridge University Press, 2010), pp. 60–6, thus locate "the highest levels of cohesion" in bonds that they claim *generally* produce loyalty: common ethnicity, common ideology, and solidarity borne of violence. On solidarity borne of violence, see Steven R. Levitsky and Lucan A. Way, "Beyond Patronage: Violent Struggle, Ruling Party Cohesion, and Authoritarian Durability," *Perspectives on Politics*, v. 10, no. 4, December 2012, pp. 868–89. Older works examining these ties include Carl H. Lande, "Networks and Groups ...""; Rene Lemarchand, "Political Clientelism and Ethnicity in Tropical Africa: Competing Solidarities in Nation-Building," *American Political Science Review*, v. 66, no. 1, March 1972, pp. 68–90.

with such presumed sources of loyalty, however, voluminous research has accumulated over the past several decades to discredit generally the notion that ethnicity and other identity divides (even during violent conflict) can be assumed to generate coherent groups or networks.[41] Stathis Kalyvas, for example, documents how disunity among group members is actually quite common even at the height of civil war.[42] As for ideology, surely one can also come up with numerous examples of people sharing common ideologies behaving in extremely disunified ways, as with the highly fractious world of Marxist movements in tsarist Russia before a small one gained the levers of the state to impose its version of the ideology on others.[43]

We thus still need to explain why ethnicity or ideology sometimes produces coherent networks and sometimes not.[44] And on this specific question, seminal studies by James Fearon and David Laitin have found that what may outwardly appear to be loyalties maintaining group or network coherence can actually be the result of group *organization*. That is, group coherence is produced by informally institutionalized practices such as "in-group policing" and other efforts conducted by elite members of the group to raise or lower the costs that individual group members bear if they engage in behaviors unwanted by core group members.[45] Citing identity, ethnicity, or conflict as a source of network loyalty, then, leaves much to be explained and often seems to lead us back to the same old focus on organization and resources.

---

[41] To use the jargon of the subfield, such "primordialist" assumptions have been generally debunked by extensive "constructivist" scholarship. The most comprehensive statement is Kanchan Chandra, *Constructivist Theories of Ethnic Politics* (New York: Oxford University Press, 2012).

[42] Stathis Kalyvas, *The Logic of Violence in Civil War* (New York: Cambridge University Press, 2006).

[43] An outstanding recent account on how ideology can produce organizational unity is Stephen E. Hanson, *Post-Imperial Democracies: Ideology and Party Formation in Third Republic France, Weimar Germany, and Post-Soviet Russia* (New York: Cambridge University Press, 2010), though the ideology of which Hanson writes is explicitly a nonpatronalistic tie. This means that truly ideological parties are not likely to behave according to the logic of patronal politics. Indeed, the countries where he finds strong ideologies are France and Germany, while patronalistic post-Soviet Russia is a negative case where ideology is largely absent in big politics. He also defines ideology in a nonstandard way, as a view about who should be included in society, which essentially boils down to an identity question.

[44] An account of recent research findings from psychology and other social sciences on ethnicity and conflict-based group orientations can be found in Henry E. Hale, *The Foundations of Ethnic Politics: Separatism of States and Nations in Eurasia and the World* (New York: Cambridge University Press, 2008), chapters 2–3. On more general group solidarity, see Michael Hechter, *Principles of Group Solidarity* (Berkeley: University of California Press, 1987).

[45] James D. Fearon and David D. Laitin, "Explaining Interethnic Cooperation," *American Political Science Review*, v. 90, no. 4, December 1996, pp. 715–35; David D. Laitin, *Identity in Formation* (Ithaca, NY: Cornell University Press, 1998). A powerful more general argument based on wide-ranging research can be found in Andreas Wimmer, *Ethnic Boundary Making* (New York: Oxford University Press, 2013).

Let us now focus more intently on organization and resources as bases of network cohesion. A concentration on resources also proves far from satisfactory by itself. For one thing, patronal relations tend to exist even in the poorest of polities, including in the very earliest human societies.[46] This strongly suggests that not much in the way of resources is necessary to maintain a patronalistic hierarchy. More important may be whether the patron controls a significant *proportion* of what a society has, even if what a society has is very little. Moreover, if we are interested in patronal power linked to the state, as we most often are in this volume, the state almost always controls at least some resources that are valuable in the context of these societies, even if these resources are nothing other than state jobs or land. Indeed, such resources can be *especially* vital in the poorest of countries, where the state may in fact be the single most reliable employer and the richest source of scarce resources.[47] Whether a network holds together, therefore, should depend less on *absolute* amounts of resources than on *relative* resourcefulness, or more specifically, whether or not alternative patrons arise who can credibly offer more resources to potential clients. But even where the state is the only significant source of resources, we still cannot take it for granted that the state network sticks together. That is, what prevents the officials who actually handle the wealth from challenging state leaders by starting their own networks, cutting out those at the top so as to gain more for themselves? This gets us back to organization, according to the emergent common wisdom: Whether a credible alternative can arise will depend on the original patron's organizational capacity to prevent it.[48]

To claim that organization is what holds patrons and clients together in a single network, however, raises two crucial questions. First, is not a patron's organization made up of various clients? And, second, does not the patron's ability to reward and punish depend on at least some of these clients themselves actually carrying out the orders to monitor, reward, and punish? Since

---

[46] See Timothy Earle, *How Chiefs Come to Power: The Political Economy of Prehistory* (Stanford: Stanford University Press, 1997).

[47] In fact, much of the earlier literature on clientelism focused on poor or largely rural countries. For example, see John Duncan Powell, "Peasant Society and Clientelist Politics," *American Political Science Review*, v. 54, no. 2, June 1970, pp. 411–25.

[48] This organizational perspective lies behind a growing body of important new works on authoritarianism, hybrid regimes, and democratization. Among the most influential have been Jason Brownlee, *Authoritarianism in an Age of Democratization* (New York: Cambridge University Press, 2007); Jennifer Gandhi and Adam Przeworski, "Authoritarian Institutions and the Survival of Autocrats," *Comparative Political Studies*, v. 40, no. 11, November 2007, pp. 1279–1301; Jennifer Gandhi, *Political Institutions under Dictatorship* (New York: Cambridge University Press, 2008); Barbara Geddes, "What Do We Know about Democratization after Twenty Years?" *Annual Review of Political Science*, v. 2 June 1999, pp. 115–44; Levitsky and Way, *Competitive Authoritarianism* (especially pp. 37–83); Milan W. Svolik, *The Politics of Authoritarian Rule* (New York: Cambridge University Press, 2012) Lucan A. Way, "Authoritarian State-Building and the Sources of Regime Competitiveness in the Fourth Wave: The Cases of Belarus, Moldova, Russia, and Ukraine," *World Politics*, v. 57, January 2005, pp. 231–61. A classic work in the same vein is Samuel P. Huntington, *Political Order in Changing Societies* (New Haven, CT: Yale University Press, 1968).

the answer to both questions is clearly yes, we are face to face with a tautology: The patron is able to secure the loyalty of the clients when the clients loyally carry out the will of the patron.

The Great Power of Expectations

The way out of this circular reasoning, as counterintuitive as it may initially sound, is to recast the tautology as a self-fulfilling prophecy. Specifically: Clients obey patrons when they expect other clients to do so. This is far from a trivial statement because it shifts the focus from clients' organization to clients' *expectations*. And many considerations besides organization can shape clients' expectations. Expectations, in fact, turn out to be a more fundamental determinant of patrons' power than either resources or organization. Moreover, it is expectations that determine when these other factors are likely to work at all. And in order to work, these other factors must first influence expectations.[49]

This claim is grounded in a powerful logic of collective action that is in fact quite familiar. Perhaps most familiar is the idea of the "bank run." Since banks make money by lending out the money people deposit in their accounts, they never actually have all depositors' deposits lying in their vaults at once. And this is not usually a problem: Only a few people are likely to demand all of their deposits back on any given day. But occasionally something happens to shake people's confidence in the bank, sometimes something as simple as a groundless rumor that the bank is about to go under. The irony is that if everybody mistakenly believes this groundless rumor and demands their deposits back on the same day, the bank *actually will* go under because it will not be able to call back its loans in time to prevent defaulting. A bank run, then, is an example of a powerful self-fulfilling prophecy: A belief (expectation) that a bank will collapse, even if based on completely false premises, in fact causes the bank to collapse.

Economist Mancur Olson, the intellectual father of collective action theory, showed in 1990 how a similar logic can apply to regimes that depend not on some kind of belief in the regime, but instead on personalized benefits – the same kind of benefits that are stock in trade for patronalistic polities. He had in mind the communist regimes of East Central Europe, each of which had amazingly elaborate mechanisms in place for monitoring, sanctioning, and rewarding individual clients from top officials all the way down to ordinary individuals. The state hierarchy, through the command economy, held a nearly complete monopoly on virtually all resource flows in the country that could be used for blandishment or punishment. The logic of organization and resources predicts that such regimes should endure.[50]

---

[49] Indeed, the title of this book was originally going to be *Great Expectations*.

[50] For example, this would have been the prediction derived from virtually all of the theories cited in footnote 48.

So what changed in 1989? Not resources or organization. The state retained a nearly complete monopoly on resource distribution while the highly refined and brutally repressive apparatus remained essentially unchanged.[51] What did change, Olson argued, were the expectations of regime clients all the way down the hierarchy, including those crucial clients on whom regime leaders depended to carry out their orders of personalized reward and punishment. Witnessing perestroika in the USSR, having Gorbachev actively encourage it in their own states, and seeing him refuse to prop up any of the "brotherly" socialist regimes when they were challenged, these clients (including policemen, bankers, and politicians) quickly reached several simultaneous conclusions: Their own regimes were doomed; the odds were good that today's patrons would not be in place tomorrow to punish the disloyal; and, therefore, other clients were unlikely to obey any orders that the old regime's patrons might give to crack down on a massive scale. There was thus no reason for them themselves to obey the patrons any longer, and in fact it might now be *risky* to do so since a new patron could one day hunt down old regime loyalists.[52] Thus in a flash, virtually all of the organizational might and redistributive capacity of these communist regimes vanished into thin air, the victims of a self-fulfilling prophecy. Because external events had caused their various elites to expect that their regimes would collapse, these regimes did collapse. This was a "bank run" on the state.[53]

While Olson depicts a single large patron-client network that permeated a whole country, his logic of expectations can account for the coherence of patronalistic networks on all levels. For any patron to control her network, her most fundamental need is for her clients to continue carrying out her orders, especially when it comes to the dishing out of rewards and punishments. These clients, on the other hand, have no reason to carry out such orders if they do not think they themselves will be rewarded in the future for loyal behavior or punished for disloyal behavior. The network thus coheres thanks to a self-fulfilling prophecy: If each client believes that other clients will carry out the patron's orders to punish and reward, then each individual client will herself carry them out, and this in turn means that they actually will be carried

---

[51] See Stephen Kotkin (with a contribution by Jan T. Gross), *Uncivil Society: 1989 and the Implosion of the Communist Establishment* (New York: Random House, 2009).

[52] Mancur Olson, "The Logic of Collective Action in Soviet-type Societies," *Journal of Soviet Nationalities*, v. 1, no. 2, Summer 1990, pp. 8–27. One important part of this process was that each actor, with each act of defiance by others, also became confident that his personal dislike of the regime was widely shared. See Timur Kuran, "Now Out of Never: The Element of Surprise in the East European Revolution of 1989," *World Politics*, v. 44, no. 1, October 1991, pp. 7–48; Susanne Lohmann, "The Dynamics of Informational Cascades: The Monday Demonstrations in Leipzig, East Germany, 1989–91," *World Politics*, v. 47, no. 1, October 1994, pp. 42–101.

[53] Steven Solnick employs a similar logic, explicitly using the language of a bank run to explain the demise of the USSR in Steven L. Solnick, *Stealing the State: Control and Collapse in Soviet Institutions* (Cambridge, MA: Harvard University Press, 1998). Kotkin (*Uncivil Society*) also employs this terminology to account for European communism's collapse.

out, resulting in the coherence of the network. This also means that individual clients are unlikely to try to challenge the leadership of the patron: Without expecting other clients to join their rebellion, to attempt one would only seem to invite punishment or the loss of potential rewards. When clients *believe* their network is strong, therefore, it *is* strong.

This same logic helps us understand why individuals would choose to join some networks over others. Individuals join those networks they expect to give them the greatest payoffs once they have taken into account networks' various capacities to reward and punish. But what makes a network capable of generating the greatest payoffs? One crucial factor is the very fact that individuals join it – at least, enough individuals to give it the capacity to mobilize resources and impose punishments. Once again, we find ourselves facing a self-fulfilling prophecy. And this one lands individuals squarely in a coordination dilemma: Which network is best for a person to join depends on which networks *other* people join, but each of these other people faces exactly the same choice. How, then, do they all decide? *There is a crucial problem of coordination at the heart of power in patronalistic societies*, and how people coordinate depends on what they *expect* other people to do. Whoever or whatever can direct expectations, then, can wield extraordinary power in patronalistic societies.[54]

What prevents people from constantly switching from network to network with every little fluctuation in expectations? While plenty of switching does take place, networks in reality are "sticky," with some people adhering to their own networks more strongly than others. This is because people have different degrees of investment in networks, which impacts their expected gains from staying or leaving. Investment has several forms. Sometimes it reflects the sheer amount of time one has already been part of the network, or the density of interactions with other network members. Over time and with dense interaction, one can develop assets that enhance the gain one can expect from a network, assets like trust, reputation, clout, mutual understandings, and knowledge about how best to induce the different personalities in the network to do what you want them to do. This also means that one might expect the core of many networks to be groups of people with long-standing and intense personal ties. This is thus one reason why networks are often associated with groups of relatives, classmates, or neighbors. Ethnic commonality has also been found to lower interpersonal communication costs and to facilitate the easy demarcation (coordination) of network membership, giving individuals a greater level

---

[54] Coordination is of course not unique to patronalistic societies. As Paul D'Anieri helpfully pointed out in a discussion of an earlier draft of this manuscript, much of American electoral politics is also about coordination around expected potential winners and losers. For example, see Gary W. Cox, *Making Votes Count: Strategic Coordination in the World's Electoral Systems* (New York: Cambridge University Press, 1997). The key differences lie in how coordination in the pursuit of power is reached, as is discussed in what follows and developed further in Chapter 4.

of investment in networks with coethnics.[55] Investments can also reflect sunk costs, resources (such as a loan given to another network member or a favor done) that one would lose upon switching but that could produce a future reward (payment with some kind of interest or a favor returned) if one remains in the network.

Switching to another network can mean losing some of these investments and starting from a weaker position. Moreover, the new network might be less willing to trust a switcher who has large investments in the old network than a switcher who retains few such ties, making the highly invested switcher's position in the new network more tenuous. As people increasingly expect one network to dominate another, therefore, the first clients to defect to the rising network will generally be those who are least invested in the declining one, ceteris paribus.

The logic of expectations now helps us come full circle, explaining why it is that other theories have identified network coherence with factors such as organization, resources, and bonds of ethnicity and kinship. Indeed, this logic does not deny these factors any role. Instead, it assigns them an important complementary part – just not the lead. Ethnicity and kinship are therefore sometimes at the core of networks not because they supply some kind of primordial glue holding them together, an idea discredited by volumes of social science research, but because they reflect important investments that individual members sometimes have in the relationships at the heart of these networks.[56] Networks are thus mostly ethnically diverse, and one frequently sees "ethnic groups" divided among multiple important, often rival networks. "Ethnic" networks also often suffer membership defection when expectations as to their relative fortunes change, just as do other kinds of networks, even those based on kinship relations.

Organization and resources are thus not independent explanations for network coherence, but themselves result from expectations and in turn influence network coherence *primarily by influencing expectations*. For example, to say that a patron's poor organization produces a weak network is to say that his inadequate arrangement and tasking of clients in the network lead key clients to expect they can escape punishment for disloyalty or to fear that they will not be rewarded for loyalty, resulting in behavior deviant from the interests of the patron or the network as a whole. Similarly, to say that a network weakens with a decline in resources is to say that this drop in resources leads clients to expect they might do better by leaving (or ignoring) the network. But all the while, the expectations remain more fundamental. This is clear because changes in expectations can occur for exogenous reasons and have direct

[55] The state of current research is well discussed in Chandra, *Constructivist Theories.* Innovative experimental evidence is found in James Habyarimana, Macartan Humphreys, Daniel N. Posner, and Jeremy M. Weinstein, "Why Does Ethnic Diversity Undermine Public Goods Provision?" *American Political Science Review*, v. 101, no. 4, November 1997, pp. 709–25.
[56] See Hale, *The Foundations.*

effects on network coherence without any change in organization or resources whatsoever, as Olson's argument about the collapse of communist regimes and Stephen Kotkin's elegant rendering of these events illustrate.[57] Research into the role of organization and resources in producing network coherence, therefore, should be carefully couched in a logic of expectations and should not lead us to lose sight of other factors capable of radically changing expectations without significant change in resources and organization.

Conclusion

Naturally, all societies feature some elements of patronalism, in particular the pursuit of political and economic goals through personalized exchange of concrete rewards and punishments. Some societies, however, experience such phenomena in much greater measure than others. This is generally reflected in a variety of global indices of phenomena that tend to be correlated with patronalism, such as low social capital, weak rule of law, and high levels of corruption, as will be discussed later in this volume. Thus we would generally expect the regime dynamics described in this book to be stronger where patronalism is more pervasive, and weaker (though not necessarily absent) where it is less prominent. Some characteristic features of such polities include the central role of extended networks of actual acquaintance, the importance of coordination of such networks in pursuit of access to resources, and the power of expectations (often influenced by, but more fundamental than, resources or organization) in driving network coordination and hence power relationships in what often amount to self-fulfilling prophecies of network strength and weakness. The logic of patronalism, therefore, directs scholarly focus to the factors that drive such expectations as the key to understanding who and which networks control the state, the extent to which dominant networks are challenged by other networks or confronted with defections from within their own, and when regimes change and states collapse.

Chapter 3 illustrates this perspective by showing its power to reinterpret big patterns of politics over a thousand years of Eurasian history, including how patronalism reproduced itself throughout this period and left in place multiple new yet still highly patronalistic states by the start of 1992. Chapter 4 then develops the logic of patronal politics further to show how it can illuminate a range of more specific important regime dynamics that later chapters will argue have become prominent features of politics throughout the former USSR.

---

[57] Kotkin, *Uncivil Society.*

3

Eurasian History as Patronal Politics

The patronalistic soil in Eurasia is as rich as its Black Earth. In this sense, Eurasia features what might be called a typically patronalistic social context for politics, quite in line with much of the world outside the developed West throughout recorded history. While we must keep in mind that patronalism does not reduce to corruption, we would generally expect that highly patronalistic societies would also score high on measures of corruption. Figure 3.1 maps the most prominent such measure (Transparency International's Corruption Perceptions Index) onto a flattened view of the globe for the year 2013. Darker hues identify countries where citizens, experts, and international businesspeople regard corruption to be particularly pervasive; here the post-Soviet world looks strikingly shady, as does most of the rest of the world.[1] Measures of other concepts that the previous chapter discussed as likely to be correlated with patronalism produce similar portraits of Eurasia, such as the World Bank's finding that post-Soviet countries have consistently scored quite low on its measures of the rule of law.[2] All this reflects a reality long expressed in local popular culture, perhaps most famously through the joke – repeated over some two centuries of Russian history – that the severity of the country's laws is tempered by the fact that you need not actually obey them.[3]

---

[1] Figures can be viewed at Transparency International's Web site, http://cpi.transparency.org/cpi2013/results/#myAnchor1, accessed January 13, 2014.

[2] Daniel Kaufmann, Aart Kraay, and Massimo Mastruzze, "Governance Matters VII: Aggregate and Individual Governance Indicators 1996–2007," report dated June 2008, available at http://www-wds.worldbank.org/external/default/WDSContentServer/IW3P/IB/2008/06/24/000158349_20080624113458/Rendered/PDF/wps4654.pdf, access date August 21, 2009.

[3] The earliest reference to a version of this joke of which I am aware attributes it to the foreign ministry official Petr Poletika (1778–1849). See P. A. Viazemskii, *Zapisnye knizhki (1813–1848)* (Moscow: USSR Academy of Sciences, 1963), p. 24. I am grateful to Andrei Rogachevskii for calling this source to my attention.

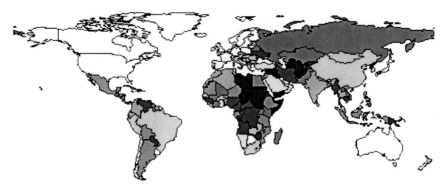

FIGURE 3.1. Levels of perceived corruption by country 2013.

Note: Darker shades represent higher levels of perceived corruption according to Transparency International's Corruption Perception Index 2013, data available at http://cpi.transparency.org/cpi2013/results/#myAnchor1, accessed January 13, 2014. The map is made with public domain Natural Earth map data, naturalearthdata.com, accessed January 14, 2014. The figure was created using Stata 11 with assistance from Eric Lawrence and students in his George Washington University class Visualizing and Modeling Politics, to whom the author is grateful.

The present chapter begins to show how the core logic developed in Chapter 2 can help us understand politics in highly patronalistic societies like those in Eurasia and illustrates patronalism's dynamic long-run staying power by reinterpreting a millennium of Eurasian political history – in broad strokes, of course. It traces the emergence of the first large-scale polities in Eurasia and demonstrates how they were (naturally) characterized by patronal patterns of politics, an approach that enables us along the way to reconcile sides in long-standing debates among historians on the nature of authoritarian rule in the region (for example, how powerful was the tsar?) and to cast certain major events, such as the 1917 Bolshevik Revolution and the breakup of the USSR, in new light. The chapter, which takes us through the disintegration of the USSR, shows how the region's patronalistic social-political equilibrium withstood even the most herculean of reform efforts. This sets the conceptual and empirical stage for the book's remaining chapters, which (Chapter 4) spin out more specific implications of patronalism for anticipating regime dynamics and then (Chapters 5–10) show how this plays out in practice in post-Soviet Eurasia over the near quarter century since the Soviet Union's demise. It also serves the important purpose of relating Eurasia's patronalistic social context to the rest of the world as summarized through different measures in the figures and tables that bookend the chapter. This helps us understand some of the political differences that scholars have long noted between post-Soviet and other, more westerly postcommunist countries.

Patronalism in Eurasia: From Prehistory to 1917

The long prehistory of Eurasian patronalism need not concern us here, as its origins are essentially the same as virtually everywhere else in the world: Societies found it natural to extend their forms of handcrafted rule through personal networks as they grew in scale from the original, small-scale communities where everyone knew everyone else, and conquerors such as the Mongols imported similarly patronalistic forms of rule.[4] Accordingly, historians of Russia almost all agree that what we are calling patronalism has been a fixture of the region's politics from the time its very first major polities appeared.[5] The same can be said for historians of the ethnically diverse territories to the south and southeast now known as Central Asia and the South Caucasus.[6]

As their domain expanded around Muscovy and to the east, Russian rulers connected their own central networks to local elites, sometimes working

---

[4] Georgi Derluguian, "Five Centuries of Russia's Modernizations," longer earlier draft (provided by the author) of Derluguian, "The Sovereign Bureaucracy in Russia's Modernizations," chapter 3 in Piotr Dutkiewicz and Dmitri Trenin, eds., *Russia: The Challenges of Transformation* (New York: New York University Press, 2011), pp. 73–86.

[5] See J. Arch Getty, *Practicing Stalinism: Bolsheviks, Boyars, and the Persistence of Tradition* (New Haven: Yale University Press, 2013); David Ransel, "Character and Style of Patron-Client Relations in Russia," in Antoni Maczak, ed., *Klientelsysteme im Europa der Frühen Neuzeit* (Munich: Oldenbourg, 1988), pp. 211–31. Richard Hellie ("Edward Keenan's Scholarly Ways," *Russian Review*, v. 46, no. 2, April 1987, pp. 177–90) argues that there is "very little evidence" of any "client-patron dynamic" in premodern Muscovy, but has in mind a narrow and somewhat formal definition by which long chains of subordinates can be observed following a patron as the patron moves from formal post to formal post. Thus he nevertheless also writes of the importance of patronage politics much as we describe patronalism in its broad sense in Chapter 2. The chief historical debates have thus been over how specifically to characterize it, what logic drove it, and whence it first arose. See also Edward L. Keenan, "Muscovite Political Folkways," *Russian Review*, v. 45, 1986, pp. 115–81; Richard Pipes, *Russia under the Old Regime* (New York: Collier, 1974); Marshall Poe, "The Truth about Muscovy," *Kritika: Explorations in Russian and Eurasian History*, v. 3, no. 3, Summer 2002, pp. 473–86. Interestingly, some of the arguments made by scholars of Eurasia as to the origins of what we here call patronalism in the region (e.g., Keenan, "Muscovite Political Folkways") cite some of the very same factors (such as geographically dispersed populations and harsh climate) that historians of other countries such as Sweden sometimes cite as leading to their escape from patronalism (e.g., Simona Piattoni, "Clientelism in Historical and Comparative Perspective," in Simona Piattoni, ed., *Clientelism, Interests, and Democratic Representation: The European Experience in Historical and Comparative Perspective* (New York: Cambridge University Press, 2001), pp. 1–30, p. 20), making a better explanation the one presented in the present volume (Chapter 2). The author is grateful to Georgi Derluguian for pointing this out in a personal communication.

[6] Adrienne Lynn Edgar, *Tribal Nation: The Making of Soviet Turkestan* (Princeton, NJ: Princeton University Press, 2004), pp. 20–3; Anatoly Khazanov, *Nomads and the Outside World* (New York: Cambridge University Press, 1984); Lawrence Krader, "Feudalism and the Tatar Polity of the Middle Ages," *Comparative Political Studies in Society and History*, v. 1, no. 1, October 1958, pp. 76–99; Virginia Martin, *Law and Custom in the Steppe* (Surrey: Curzon, 2001); Olivier Roy, *The New Central Asia: The Creation of Nations* (New York: NYU Press, 2000), pp. 5–11; Jeff Sahadeo, *Russian Colonial Society in Tashkent, 1865–1923* (Bloomington: Indiana University Press, 2007); Steven Sabol, *Russian Colonization and the Genesis of Kazak National Consciousness* (New York: Palgrave Macmillan, 2003), especially p. 15; Svat Soucek, *A History of Inner Asia* (New York: Cambridge University Press, 2000); Ronald Grigor Suny, ed., *Transcaucasia: Nationalism and Social Change: Essays in the History of Armenia, Azerbaijan, and Georgia* (Ann Arbor: University of Michigan Press, 1983).

with preestablished authorities there and sometimes putting new ones into place. These local elites could not be directly controlled, but they could be kept loyal and made to deliver the needed resources through selective rewards and punishments targeted at these individual elites. Some would be punished conspicuously in case of disloyalty, and for a time, nobles could even be publicly whipped. The far more common practice, however, was for these early rulers to co-opt local elites through a whole series of temptations that an emerging central authority could offer.[7] Indeed, in an impoverished society like Muscovy, the central authority (protostate) was effectively the only vast concentration of resources that a person could tap other than the Orthodox Church. And the church worked largely in tandem with the rulers. This pattern of extending territorial rule by expanding patronal relationships eventually produced what we now know as the Russian Empire.

When the Russian Empire grew still further, overrunning the diverse polities of Central Asia and the South Caucasus, its leaders resorted to similar tactics of governing through a combination of demonstrative selective punishment and co-optation of local patronage networks. For this reason, after the initial conquests of these lands in the eighteenth and nineteenth centuries and except for some instances when rebellions had to be quashed, the Russian Empire gave many of its southern acquisitions – particularly in Central Asia – considerable room to govern their own affairs through centrally sanctioned local patrons.[8] Governors were installed to keep an eye on regional politics, but they generally worked not to destroy local patronage networks and instead to take these patrons on as subpatrons in the new, larger imperial system. Formal titles sometimes changed, administrative boundaries were sometimes altered, and the Russian leaders were sometimes selective in whom they privileged locally, but the core patronalistic principles of local governance persisted.[9]

---

[7] Hellie "Edward Keenan's Scholarly Ways," p. 179.

[8] Russian rule did entail some major economic and demographic changes, including a strong orientation to Russian markets, first and foremost increasingly supplying Russia with more and more cotton and coming to depend more on Russian grain. A substantial influx of ethnic Slavs also settled the region after Russian conquest. See Elizabeth E. Bacon, *Central Asians under Russian Rule: A Study in Culture Change* (Ithaca, NY: Cornell University Press, 1980); Soucek, *A History of Inner Asia*, p. 203. Especially in areas with the largest Slavic in-migration, the changes could be very disruptive to local social and political organization. See Sabol, *Russian Colonization*.

[9] Different perspectives on this process include Seymour Becker, *Russia's Protectorates in Central Asia: Bukhara and Khiva, 1865–1924* (New York: RoutledgeCurzon, 2004); Daniel Brower, *Turkestan and the Fate of the Russian Empire* (New York: RoutledgeCurzon, 2003); Daniel R. Brower and Edward J. Lazzerini, eds., *Russia's Orient: Imperial Borderlands and Peoples, 1700–1917* (Bloomington: Indiana University Press, 1997); Edgar, *Tribal Nation*; L. H. Rhinelander, "Viceroy Vorontsov's Administration of the Caucasus," in Ronald Grigor Suny, *Transcaucasia: Nationalism and Social Change. Essays in the History of Armenia, Azerbaijan, and Georgia* (Ann Arbor: University of Michigan Press, 1983), pp. 109–40; Peter L. Roudik, *The History of the Central Asian Republics* (Westport, CT: Greenwood, 2007), chapter 5; Sahadeo, *Russian Colonial Society in Tashkent*, pp. 18–21, 230–1. The general process of expanding Russian

Politics in Muscovy and the Russian Empire it eventually became were thus pervasively patronalistic, despite some professionalization of the state bureaucracy that occurred prior to the 1917 revolution.[10] The grand princes of Muscovy and the tsars of imperial Russia sat at the center of a ruling elite consisting of noble families and, increasingly, leading bureaucrats without hereditary title. In fact, through painstaking research of the period 1689–1825, John LeDonne documents that much of imperial Russian politics revolved around the struggle for spoils between two extended family networks, the Miloslavskys and the Naryshkins. This, of course, took place *within* the larger patronalistic hierarchy of which the tsar was the chief patron, and in fact the competition between noble families often involved efforts to get closer to the tsar and his immediate family.[11] While kinship ties and political marriages defined the networks at the top, each major network extended downward to an ever-broadening array of subpatrons and clients, reaching into all classes of society, virtually all fields of endeavor, and all across the country's great expanse. Stretching beyond kin, these broader networks sustained themselves by doling out all kinds of patronage and punishments, sharing the spoils of political authority.[12] As one went down the hierarchy, the networks' membership became less fixedly defined and more contingent in nature, with elite families often mobilizing lower level clients through strings of personal connections as the need arose. The system, then, resembled the kind of hierarchy depicted in Figure 2.1, though with only one unrivaled pyramid in existence, headed by the tsar. Such arrangements are called in this volume a single-pyramid system, a concept that will be developed further in the next chapter.

Several studies have found that Russia's most influential extended networks within the tsarist pyramid seemed to be bound together by little other than pragmatic self-interest. Ideas, policies, and class all played secondary roles at best.[13] The patronage they plied involved everything from jobs to appointments, loans, debt cancelations, help with court cases, and direct transfers of

control over new territories by working through patronalistic relationships with local elites has also been found to apply to Muscovy's expansion in the territory we today call the Russian Federation, as with its absorption of the Kazan Khanate. See Edward Louis Keenan Jr., "Muscovy and Kazan: Some Introductory Remarks on the Patterns of Steppe Diplomacy," *Slavic Review*, v. 26, no. 4, December 1967, pp. 548–58.

[10] On such prerevolutionary "modernization," see Derluguian, "Five Centuries of Russia's Modernizations."

[11] John P. LeDonne, "Ruling Families in the Russian Political Order, 1689–1825," *Cahiers du Monde russe et Sovietique*, v. 28, nos. 3–4, July–December 1987, pp. 233–322.

[12] Donald Ostrowski, "The Façade of Legitimacy: Exchange of Power and Authority in Early Modern Russia," *Comparative Studies in Society and History*, v. 44, no. 3, July 2002, pp. 534–63, p. 537; Keenan, "Muscovite Political Folkways."

[13] Robert O. Crummey, *Aristocrats and Servitors: The Boyar Elite of Russia, 1613–1689* (Princeton, NJ: Princeton University Press, 1983); Nancy Shields Kollmann, *Kinship and Politics: The Making of the Muscovite Political System* (Stanford, CA: Stanford University Press, 1987); LeDonne, "Ruling Families."

money or other assets.[14] While formal law generally recognized these highly individualized transactions as improper, the historical record teems with examples of just how commonplace they were.[15] Brian Davies even documents an instance when the service community of Kozlov actually filed a formal complaint against its governor because he was *not corrupt enough*! By not accepting bribes, community members opined, the governor was failing them, effectively eliminating a pathway by which they could influence the state. Beset by constituents trying to leave gifts at his door, he resorted to literally fending them off with a cudgel, but to no avail. This poor honest soul was driven out of town as the classic "sucker," a victim of patronalism's vicious cycle of expectations.[16]

Thinking of Russian politics as patronal politics helps us understand why some of the most eminent scholars of Muscovite and imperial Russian history can disagree vociferously on one of the most basic questions of all: Just how powerful was the tsar?[17] Lay readers will most likely be familiar with the most established view, that the tsar was a despot who dominated the nobles and did whatever he[18] pleased to his subjects. This has been the interpretation of Russia's own most authoritative historians, codified by Richard Pipes in his famous theory of the "patrimonial state." The state – and indeed the entire country with all the people in it – was viewed as the patrimony of the tsar, Pipes argues, entirely at the sovereign's disposal.[19] By these lights, periods of civil war like the early seventeenth century Time of Troubles and the 1917 Russian Revolution show that the country functioned poorly when the tsar was weak.[20]

Pipes's colleague Edward Keenan, however, spawned a research program that supports nearly the opposite conclusion: The tsar was essentially a figurehead meant mainly for foreign consumption, with the nobles around him wielding the real power.[21] Autocracy was a "façade," and oligarchy the reality.[22] The Keenan school finds, among other things, that the tsar generally needed broad noble agreement to enact major decisions such as legal codes or

---

[14] Ostrowski, "The Façade of Legitimacy," p. 551; David L. Ransel, *The Politics of Catherinian Russia* (New Haven, CT: Yale University Press, 1975).

[15] Brian L. Davies, *State Power and Community in Early Modern Russia: The Case of Kozlov, 1635–1649* (New York: Palgrave Macmillan., 2004), especially pp. 207–48.

[16] Unpublished paper cited in Valerie Kivelson, *Autocracy in the Provinces: The Muscovite Gentry and Political Culture in the Seventeenth Century* (Stanford, CA: Stanford University Press, 1996), p. 161.

[17] For simplicity of discussion, by "tsar" we here refer not only to the rulers who had this formal title, but also those monarchs of Muscovy with the title of grand prince.

[18] Or, during certain periods, she.

[19] Pipes, *Russia under the Old Regime*. See also Ransel, "Character and Style."

[20] Nikolai Karamzin, "A Memoir on Ancient and Modern Russia," in Richard Pipes, ed., *Karamzin's Memoir on Ancient and Modern Russia* (New York: Atheneum, 1986), p. 110.

[21] Keenan, "Muscovite Political Folkways."

[22] Nancy Shields Kollmann, "The Façade of Autocracy," in Marker Kaiser, ed., *Reinterpreting Russian History: Readings 860–1860's* (New York: Oxford University Press, 1994).

foreign treaties, that the nobles had quite a good deal of autonomous power (including property rights), that nobles acting collectively actually forced one tsar (Peter III) to abdicate for trying to make decisions on his own, that they may have killed off other tsars, that impressions of a tsar's strength often primarily reflected strong noble consensus, and that Russia's periods of turmoil resulted not from the weakness of the tsar but attempts by the tsar to step beyond noble-set bounds on his personal authority.[23]

Supporters of the older view quickly united to denounce this interpretation, reporting many important instances when the tsar seemed to operate quite independently and noting that the tsar often directly attacked noble interests and got away with it (for example, Peter the Great). The Pipes school acknowledges some exceptions and admits that routine governing did not always put the tsar and nobles at odds, but contends that the system was geared toward sovereign dominance.[24]

How to reconcile these views?

The key is to recall the logic of patronal politics. The chief patron in such a system (the tsar) does in fact depend on his clients (the nobles) to carry out his orders, so in a very real sense he is quite beholden to them. But it does not make sense for any individual noble to betray the tsar so long as he expects other nobles to carry out the tsar's orders to punish the betrayal. This has the following implication: In order for the noble elites to exercise their power over the tsar, they must have confidence that something like a majority of them will *act collectively*. Yet this is no small matter: It can be extremely risky to stick one's neck out to initiate such collective action, especially where nobles are competing for influence and where one might seek to use the other's attempt to initiate collective action as a way to get the initiator punished or eliminated as a rival. The default expectation of each noble, therefore, is likely to be that other nobles will obey the tsar. The tsar does not face this problem of collective action because his role is precisely to be a focal point around which the nobles coordinate their expectations as to what other nobles (and the whole range of other officials in the bureaucracy and military) will do.

---

[23] Keenan, "Muscovite Political Folkways"; Kivelson, *Autocracy in the Provinces*; Kollmann, "The Façade of Autocracy"; Ostrowski, "The Façade of Legitimacy"; Daniel Rowland, "Did Muscovite Literary Ideology Place Any Limits on the Power of the Tsar?" *Russian Review*, v. 49, no. 2, April 1990, pp. 125–55; Cornelia Soldat, "The Limits of Muscovite Autocracy: The Relations between the Grand Prince and the Boyars in the Light of Iosif Volotskii's Prosvetitel'," *Cahiers du Monde russe*, v. 46, nos. 1–2, January–June 2005, pp. 265–76; George Weickhardt, "The Pre-Petrine Law of Property," *Slavic Review*, v. 52, no. 4, 1993, pp. 663–79.

[24] Robert O. Crummey, "The Silence of Muscovy," *Russian Review*, v. 46, no. 2, April 1987, pp. 157–64; Richard Wortman, "'Muscovite Political Folkways' and the Problem of Russian Political Culture," *Russian Review*, v. 46, no. 2, April 1987, pp. 191–7; Richard Hellie, "Why Did the Muscovite Elite Not Rebel?" *Russian history: Histoire russe*, v. 25, nos. 1–2, 1998, pp. 155–62; Marshall T. Poe, *"A People Born to Slavery": Russia in Early Modern European Ethnography, 1476–1748* (Ithaca, NY: Cornell University Press, 2001).

This logic thus explains how the elites, in those rare instances when they did manage to unite against the tsar, could be so powerful as to remove that tsar, as the hapless Peter III evidently discovered. But it also explains why this was in fact so rare and why, indeed, key scholars in the Keenan school have found noble "consensus" to have formed so readily around tsarist policies and to have coincided with apparent peaks in the monarch's power.[25] In fact, as some in the Pipes school – including Pipes himself – have noted, the tsars paid great attention to making it difficult for any elites ever to coordinate against them, regularly playing one group against the other in a strategy of divide and rule.[26] But this, as the Keenan school observed, meant neither that the tsars were all-powerful nor that the nobles were weak. Both the Pipes and Keenan schools were right, and the logic of patronalistic collective action helps us see how both tsar and nobles can be both strong and weak at the same time. Prerevolutionary Russian politics, then, is quite arguably well described as a patrimonial system, though "patrimonial" should be understood more as Max Weber understood it (an understanding more consistent with this book's notion of patronalism) than as the kind of pure despotism that Pipes and some of his followers have sometimes seemed to depict.[27]

Once it had evolved, the tsar's patronalistic single-pyramid system readily reproduced itself through its relative effectiveness in coordinating elite and mass expectations as to who would be chief patron in the future. For one thing, the dynastic tradition of primogeniture that was operative for most of the Russian Empire's last few centuries provided a modicum of insurance against the kind of uncertainty that can arise when a tsar dies.[28] That is, it defined an heir in terms meant to be (mostly) objective and indisputable and thus served as a stabilizing self-fulfilling prophecy. Generating coordinated expectations as to who was likely to be in charge in the future even should something happen to the tsar, the principle greatly complicated the task of any would-be challengers hoping to convince others that they had a chance to take the throne themselves even if the tsar were to be removed, and this in turn promoted expectations of continued stability in the system. Struggles for the throne were certainly not eliminated entirely, as the principle could still be challenged, manipulated, or even changed by the tsars themselves. And it did create some temptation for those who could make a case to be in the line of succession, as made clear in the successful elite plot led by the wife of Peter III to remove him and install

[25] Ostrowski, "The Façade of Legitimacy"; Kollmann, *Kinship and Politics*; Kollman, "The Façade of Autocracy."

[26] Hellie, "Edward Keenan's Scholarly Ways"; Hellie, "Why Did"; Pipes, *Russia under the Old Regime*.

[27] Max Weber, *Economy and Society*, eds. G. Roth and C. Wittich (Berkeley: University of California Press, 1978), pp. 231–2.

[28] Keenan, "Muscovite Political Folkways," pp. 140–3. Theoretical underpinnings for this function of monarchy are discussed in Gordon Tullock, *Autocracy* (New York: Springer, 1987).

herself, eventually becoming known as Catherine the Great.[29] But the principle at least served to narrow significantly the set of people expected to be potentially serious pretenders to the throne and thereby served as a stabilizing device, especially since the Romanovs were blessed with a regular spawn of royal heirs from the moment they first occupied the throne at the dawn of the seventeenth century. Russia's single-pyramid tsarist system was also fortunate in that for centuries it did not face the kind of external shocks that have brought down many similar systems in history, shocks such as defeat at the hands of a foreign conqueror. And this relative stability at the top ensured that there was no major challenge to the broad patronalistic equilibrium that characterized society more generally.

In the end, to topple Russia's imperial "pyramid" of patronal power, it took a losing war, acute mass grievances, and the dominance of nonabsolutist ideologies in the European system. These developments fostered the expectation among Russian elites and masses that monarchies like Russia's might not be long for this world. Once this expectation took root, intensifying with every loss on the front, the tsarist regime essentially just disintegrated in early 1917, a process that culminated in the tsar's abdication. Right down to the mass desertion of soldiers, this process greatly resembled Olson's description of the collapse of East Central Europe's communist regimes in 1989. One might even call this a political bank run on the tsarist regime. Several months then ensued in which multiple centers of power competed for authority, none able to generate a consensus expectation that it would eventually dominate, especially as German armies proceeded to advance toward Moscow, seemingly unhindered.

The Failed Antipatronalist Revolution

For true believers, communism represented in part a genuine effort to smash the patronalism of the tsarist period that was thought to be corrupt and inherent to capitalism and feudalism. This was, from their perspective, an attempt not just to invert the patronal pyramid, but ultimately to level it so that all would enjoy equal power, wealth, and opportunity. If patronalism had been the lifeblood of Russian society, the communists were planning a full transfusion. The irony is that the Bolsheviks wound up pragmatically resorting to patronal politics in order to stay in power once they gained it, in essence subverting communist ideals in the name of promoting them in the long run.[30]

---

[29] On uncertainties and changes in Russia's dynastic principle and some of the succession struggles the monarchy experienced, see Richard S. Wortman, *Scenarios of Power: Myth and Ceremony in Russian Monarchy from Peter the Great to the Abdication of Nicholas II* (Princeton, NJ: Princeton University Press, 2006), especially pp. 33, 52–5, 87–9.

[30] Getty, *Practicing Stalinism*. In this sense, the Russian Revolution represents a "signal juncture" when the enduring pattern of patronalism was challenged strongly but the process by which this challenge was defeated ultimately confirms the enduring strength of the patronalistic norm. On signal junctures, see Chris Rhomberg, "A Signal Juncture: The Detroit Newspaper Strike and

This foreshadows a dynamic that we will later see when we talk about not communism but democracy.

When Vladimir Lenin's Bolsheviks first started to fill the power vacuum in late 1917, they sought to exorcise patronalism from the body politic. They called for government by formal and generally applicable ideological guidelines, personnel practices based not on personal connections but on class background, individual merit according to explicit ideological criteria (such as demonstrated commitment to the cause), formal institutions such as the Communist Party, and uncompromising brute force for anyone (even their own relatives or friends) standing in their way or violating party rules.[31] Lenin, indeed, had spent years of his life debating the minutiae of Marxism, suffered exile rather than give up his views, passionately advocated a strong formal party organization as the key to socialist success, and had little truck with those who would disagree. This may have even been part of the Bolsheviks' public appeal, which was significant by late 1917. While elements of political opportunism, careerism, and even looting clearly played central roles for certain figures and at certain times, the Bolshevik Revolution still stands out in historical perspective for the sharp break with the patronal politics of tsarism that Lenin and his colleagues initially effected. Debates on how to apply Marxism in Russia's underindustrialized society were earnest, the effort to develop formal party organization was real, and the most prominent Bolsheviks initially paid strikingly little mind to building up their own client networks and practicing patronage, or tended to treat these phenomena as something to be overcome.[32]

It was just this lack of attentiveness, however, that proved to be their undoing by giving Joseph Stalin his opportunity. The odds surely seemed to be against him. The revolution's brightest light had always been Lenin, and when he died in 1924, the charismatic Leon Trotsky, goateed commander of the victorious Red Army, was widely considered his natural political heir. And no one would have called Stalin the party's leading ideologist, a reputation that belonged instead to Nikolai Bukharin, late-coming champion of the liberalizing

Post-Accord Labor Relations in the United States," *American Journal of Sociology*, v. 115, no. 6, May 2010, pp. 1853–94.

[31] For general accounts of the early Soviet period, see the classic works Jerry F. Hough and Merle Fainsod, *How the Soviet Union Is Governed* (Cambridge, MA: Harvard University Press, 1979) and Ronald Grigor Suny, *The Soviet Experiment: Russia, the USSR, and the Successor States* (Oxford: Oxford University Press, 1998), especially chapters 3 and 5. Lenin's description of his vision can be found, in part, in Vladimir I. Lenin, *What Is to Be Done?* (1902) and *State and Revolution* (1917), both translated in Robert C. Tucker, ed., *The Lenin Anthology* (New York: Norton, 1975), pp. 12–114 and 311–98. For a sense of the idealism involved for many, see John Reed, *Ten Days That Shook the World* (New York: Penguin, 1977).

[32] On the revolution and early Soviet state building, see sources in the previous footnote as well as Orlando Figes, *A People's Tragedy: The Russian Revolution 1891–1924* (New York: Penguin, 1996); Sheila Fitzpatrick, *Education and Social Mobility in the Soviet Union 1921–1934* (Cambridge: Cambridge University Press, 1979); Richard Pipes, *The Russian Revolution* (New York: Vintage, 1991); Adam Ulam, *The Bolsheviks: The Intellectual and Political History of the Triumph of Communism in Russia* (New York: Collier, 1965).

and successful "New Economic Policy" (NEP) that Lenin had launched.[33] Even worse for Stalin, Lenin had actually warned on his deathbed against considering his Georgian colleague as a successor, branding him too "rude" and even dangerous. Contemporaries compared Stalin to a "grey blur" who left little lasting impression. Not seen as having the right stuff for high-profile posts such as the one held by Trotsky, Stalin thus occupied a series of relatively low-profile positions in the Communist leadership after the revolution. One of these, which he acquired in 1919, was de facto head of the Communist Party's Organizational Bureau (Orgburo), seen then as a technical body in much the way a human resources department is seen today in a modern institution.[34]

Stalin's genius was to recognize that, for a power-hungry individual in a society where patronalistic practices were familiar and fresh in mind, this was precisely the position to occupy. Using his position to influence who was appointed to lower-level party posts, each relatively unimportant in its own right, Stalin systematically advanced people he believed would support him in the future, thereby constructing a large network of political clients within the party and the state that it dominated. When nationwide party congresses or meetings of the more elite Central Committee would convene, these were increasingly filled with his clients as delegates, and as Stalin's power grew it was increasingly risky for them to dare oppose him even if they did not consider themselves loyal to him personally. And it was these nationwide organs that had the power to decide who was in or out of the party leadership. This patronalistic mechanism constituted what Robert V. Daniels later called the great "circular flow of power" that essentially decided Communist Party leadership disputes and solved succession crises from Stalin straight through to Gorbachev. The power to influence lower-level appointments was concentrated, though still largely seen as a technical matter, with the creation of the post of general secretary in 1922, a post Stalin was in a perfect position to occupy, and he did.[35]

By first invoking this patronalistic "circular flow of power" mechanism, Stalin caught his rivals almost completely unawares. Naively in retrospect, they had instead been seeking to capture the early Soviet leadership by winning ideological or policy debates. To eliminate Trotsky, therefore, Stalin aligned his emerging political machine with Bukharinite liberals to brand the target as a left opposition. With Trotsky out of the party leadership, he reversed gear, backing more radical communists against what he now lambasted as Bukharin's right deviation. By the late 1920s, before other potential rivals fully grasped what was happening, Stalin had become the USSR's unrivaled political leader.[36]

[33] Stephen F. Cohen, *Bukharin and the Bolshevik Revolution: A Political Biography 1888–1938* (New York: Oxford University Press, 1980).

[34] Hough and Fainsod, *How the Soviet Union Is Governed*, p. 112–15.

[35] Robert V. Daniels, "Soviet Politics since Khrushchev," in John W. Strong, ed., *The Soviet Union under Brezhnev and Kosygin: The Transition Years* (New York: Van Nostrand Reinhold, 1971); Hough and Fainsod, *How the Soviet Union Is Governed*, pp. 112–33.

[36] Hough and Fainsod, *How the Soviet Union Is Governed*, pp. 128–46; Barrington Moore Jr., *Soviet Politics: The Dilemma of Power* (Armonk, NY: M. E. Sharpe, 1950), pp. 146–72. Research

Stalin quickly established the most brutal form of patronal politics Eurasia had ever seen, one based to an extraordinarily large degree on coercion and fear. Initially careful to gain the consent of key subpatrons, he moved to eliminate almost anyone who could possibly challenge his status atop a single-pyramid system, going even so far as to chase down Trotsky in Mexico with an icepick-wielding assassin. As his own preeminence became more established, he personally orchestrated the infamous purges and became the ultimate practitioner of "divide and conquer" in domestic politics.[37] Hailing the boy Pavel Morozov as a hero for exposing his own father's treachery, Stalin endeavored even to make sharing one's doubts about the regime within nuclear families a risky form of "sticking your neck out."[38] With death so readily doled out to dissenters, expressing any doubts about the regime – not to mention acting on them – was perilous indeed. Stalin accompanied this consolidation of power with an effort that left few nonstate resources in the hands of anyone: his reversal of Lenin's NEP, the collectivization of agriculture, and the massive industrialization campaign.[39] One result, along with millions of deaths, was to put almost all economic assets in the direct hands of the state in the form of the command economy.

Each successive leader altered the formal and informal rules somewhat, and the most acute forms of terror passed away with Stalin, but straight through Gorbachev each Soviet leader relied heavily on the patronalistic circular flow of power to gain and stay in office. After Stalin died in 1953, Nikita Khrushchev used his position in charge of party personnel appointments to defeat rivals who at the time seemed to hold more prominent and potent formal positions: Lavrenty Beria (head of the secret police) and Georgy Malenkov (head of state). He was ultimately unseated in 1964 by the person whom he himself had tapped to manage his personnel appointments, then–second secretary of the Communist Party Leonid Brezhnev. And Gorbachev, then the youthful hope of a gerontocratic regime, secured the party leadership in 1985 after initially gaining power over cadre appointments under the ailing Konstantin Chernenko and aligning with the machine that had put the dying Yury Andropov in power just before that.[40] None of this means that policy goals were absent, and even

currently in progress by Christopher Monty may challenge at least part of the common wisdom regarding Stalin's use of local party secretaries against his rivals, though he reports data are incomplete. This according to his presentation of a draft paper, "Stalin, Local Party Secretaries, the Politics of the Lenin Succession, 1922–27," at the Annual Meeting of the Association for Slavic, East European, and Eurasian Studies (ASEEES), November 22, 2013, Boston.

[37] Perhaps the most authoritative recent account of Stalin's ascent to total power is Oleg V. Khlevniuk, *Master of the House: Stalin and His Inner Circle* (New Haven, CT: Yale University Press, 2009).

[38] Orlando Figes, *The Whisperers: Private Life in Stalin's Russia* (New York: Metropolitan Books, 2007).

[39] Khlevniuk, *Master of the House*, p. 8.

[40] Robert V. Daniels, *The Rise and Fall of Communism in Russia* (New York: Macmillan 2007); Jerry F. Hough, *Democratization and Revolution in the USSR 1985–1991* (Washington, DC: Brookings Institution, 1997), chapter 3.

Stalin sought to achieve something, not simply to stay in power.[41] But it does mean that patronal politics proved consistently crucial for any leader who sought to get things done.

Interestingly, we find that Western scholars vigorously debated just how powerful the Communist Party leader was throughout these general secretaries' eras in a way that almost exactly mirrors the aforementioned historians' dispute over just how powerful the tsar was. On one side, we observe many advocates of the famous Totalitarian Model, a conceptualization of Soviet politics regarding the party leader as virtually all-powerful, ruling at his whim over other leading party officials and the whole of society.[42] On the other side are scholars who see in Soviet politics a constant competition among Kremlin clans, fierce battles that took place behind the scenes but whose results could be detected by tracking who stood next to whom on Lenin's Mausoleum during the May Day parade, who was promoted or passed over, or other minutiae of regime output. Against the simple version of the Totalitarian Model, these scholars advocated the "conflict model" or related concepts that characterized this competition in various ways, such as "institutional pluralism."[43]

It is also interesting that some of the scholars in the Keenan-Pipes debate on the tsar, including Keenan and Pipes themselves, also engaged the debate on the power of the party leader and did so in just the way one might predict: Pipes was a leading proponent of the Totalitarian Model and Keenan directly compared the USSR to Muscovy as a form of "oligarchic" rule.[44] Both saw continuities in Russian "political culture," but they interpreted what they saw in radically different ways.

The logic of collective action once again helps us understand how two sets of intelligent, well-informed scholars can reach two such different conclusions:

[41] See Khlevniuk, *Master of the House*.

[42] E.g., Karl J. Friedrich and Zbigniew K. Brzezinski, *Totalitarian Dictatorship and Autocracy* (Cambridge, MA: Harvard University Press, 1956); Martin Malia, *The Soviet Tragedy: A History of Socialism in Russia, 1917–1991* (New York: Simon & Schuster, 1995); Richard Pipes, *Russia under the Bolshevik Regime* (New York: Vintage, 1995).

[43] See "Conflict and Authority," discussion with Carl Linden, T. H. Rigby, and Robert Conquest, *Problems of Communism*, v. 12, no. 5, September–October 1963, pp. 27–46; "How Strong Is Khrushchev?" discussion with Carl Linden, T. H. Rigby, and Robert Conquest, *Problems of Communism*, v. 12, no. 6, November–December 1963, pp. 56–65; Robert V. Daniels, "Russian Political Culture and the Post-Revolutionary Impasse," *Russian Review*, v. 46, no. 2 April 1987, pp. 165–74, p. 169; Jerry F. Hough, *The Soviet Union and Social Science Theory* (Cambridge, MA: Harvard University Press, 1977); H. Gordon Skilling and Franklyn Griffiths, eds., *Interest Groups in Soviet Politics* (Princeton, NJ: Princeton University Press, 1970). Importantly, not all considered ideas such as institutional pluralism (a term coined by Hough) to be incompatible with the Totalitarian Model, instead considering the former a description of how the latter worked in practice, as did Hough in his many writings on these themes.

[44] Keenan, "Muscovite Political Folkways"; Pipes, *Russia under the Bolshevik Regime*. A Keenan protégé, Nancy Shields Kollmann (*Kinship and Politics*, p. 147), even coined the term "patrimonial pluralism" to describe Muscovy, a term evoking Hough's famous usage of institutional pluralism to characterize the USSR.

The USSR's primary "subpatrons" (top Communist Party officials) did in fact wield resources that, if pooled, could have unseated any party leader, and the party leader did in fact depend on these other officials to put his orders into practice. In this, it actually made little difference whether the resources they controlled were recognized formally as private or state property. But the problem of subpatron collective action remained: They had to act in concert in order to exercise this power while the chief patron (the party leader) did not because he was the default (institutionalized) focal point that determined how each individual elite expected the others to behave.

Seeking to take advantage of this, general secretaries frequently fostered rivalries among their own closest associates following the familiar divide-and-rule logic. Thus the aging Stalin kept around Khrushchev, Beria, and Malenkov just as the young Gorbachev drew into the Politburo the reputedly conservative Yegor Ligachev along with the radical Aleksandr Yakovlev and the ambitious Boris Yeltsin. Political competition in the USSR, then, was very real. But it generally revolved around rival subpatron networks' efforts to acquire spoils, curry favor with the party leader, and work to position themselves for the succession, not usually actual opposition to the sitting party leader.[45]

Communist in Form, Patronal in Content

Soviet patronal networks, far more intensely than tsarist era ones, stretched broadly downward into society through the state, which after Stalin was pretty much everything. All swearing loyalty to the party boss, the networks would typically extend both through the USSR's functional ministries and state committees (that is, through the state-owned economy and its administrative-coercive apparatus) and into territorial branches of the party. There was a party first secretary for fourteen of the Soviet Union's fifteen constituent union republics, ranging from the Ukrainian Republic (the most populous and important after Russia itself) to the tiny occupied Baltic republics.[46] The only exception was the Russian Republic, denied a full-fledged party subpatron for fear that any such person could rival the party leader as a result of the republic's enormous size and economic importance. Indeed, republic first secretaries had great opportunity to add clients to their personal networks by influencing local party and state appointments (including incorporation into the infamous

---

[45] A rare exception was the 1957 "Anti-Party Group" move against Khrushchev, who appealed to his clients in the Central Committee and won a contested vote, thereby confirming the Central Committee as the operational locus of ultimate power in the USSR. Another example also involved Khrushchev after Brezhnev effectively deprived him of his Central Committee majority, ousting him in 1964.

[46] The formal title of the union republics was "Soviet Socialist Republic" or SSR, but for the sake of convenience the term "republic" is used here instead (that is, "Ukrainian Republic" instead of "Ukrainian SSR"). Similarly, the term "Russian Republic" is used instead of Russian Soviet Federated Socialist Republic or RSFSR.

nomenklatura), and it was no coincidence that both Khrushchev and Brezhnev had histories partly in the largest non-Russian republic, Ukraine.[47]

Republic party bosses were directly in charge of regional (oblast, *krai*, autonomous republic) party secretaries, the famous "Soviet prefects" (as Jerry Hough dubbed them), who played extremely important roles in coordinating economic activity and making up for the natural dysfunction of the command economy through creative wheeling and dealing.[48] Indeed, it was the regional first secretaries who were the critical local hubs in the most important networks, collecting and cultivating vast arrays of informal relationships with anyone who might be willing to trade favors when the need arose. These relationships, known in the Russian vernacular cumulatively as *blat*, might reach through family, childhood friends, or close-knit school cohorts (*odnokashniki*) into factories, universities, repair shops, banks, bakeries, farms, resorts, energy suppliers, trade unions, transport managers, and other parts of the state. They were famous for concocting enormous barter chains, sometimes involving dozens of institutions, to compensate for the failures of supply and misallocated resources that were endemic to the Soviet economy.[49] Informal transactions and the "second economy" reigned to such an extent that vodka was studied by economists as a de facto black market currency.[50]

Whereas the Great Terror kept these networks fragile and highly dependent on Stalin personally, and Khrushchev's incessant institutional reshuffling complicated their operation, they flowered under Brezhnev's "stability in cadres" policy. Knowing that Brezhnev was not inclined to interfere in local affairs so long as they maintained stability, paid symbolic fealty, and supplied resources to the central government, republic bosses were able to extract vast spoils from the state and to plow much of this into local patronage networks, which then came to stand at the core of increasingly personalized political machines. Much of republic-level politics across the Soviet Union thus revolved around competition between regional networks, and powerful Brezhnev era bosses tended to govern by establishing the dominance of networks associated with themselves.[51] John Willerton's careful research in Azerbaijan and Lithuania shows it is possible to track patronal networks in the non-Russian republics rather precisely, as clients' careers tended to rise and fall in lockstep with the political fortunes

---

[47] Hough, *Democratization and Revolution*, p. 101.

[48] Except for the Russian Republic, where regional party secretaries reported to the Central Committee since there was no Russian Republic party boss.

[49] Jerry F. Hough, *The Soviet Prefects: The Local Party Organs in Industrial Decision-making* (Cambridge, MA: Harvard University Press, 1969); Heinz Kohler, *Comparative Economic Systems* (Glenview, IL: Scott, Foresman, 1989); Alena V. Ledeneva, *Russia's Economy of Favours: Blat, Networking, and Informal Exchange* (Cambridge: Cambridge University Press, 1998).

[50] Gregory Grossman, "The Second Economy of the USSR," *Problems of Communism*, v. 26, no. 5, September–October 1977, pp. 25–40.

[51] Pauline Jones Luong, *Institutional Change and Political Continuity in Post-Soviet Central Asia* (New York: Cambridge University Press, 2002).

of their republic subpatrons.[52] This process played out in different ways in different republics.[53] In Uzbekistan, Communist Party chief Sharof Rashidov established the preeminence of his own Samarkand network for twenty-four years while balancing powerful networks based in Tashkent and Ferghana.[54] Similarly, during 1969–82, Heydar Aliyev built a strong political machine in Azerbaijan relying heavily on cadres from his own native Nakhichevan region and Azerbaijanis with roots in Armenia.[55] In Kyrgyzstan, politics tended to center around rivalry between the more Russified and industrialized North and the more "Uzbek," Islamic, and agricultural South.[56]

System Breakup

The system-reinforcing, self-fulfilling expectations that underpinned Soviet power came unhinged as Gorbachev (in what scholars widely agree was his own contingent initiative)[57] pushed through a series of major reforms that dramatically altered the nature of the system. Most importantly, he introduced contested elections for republic parliaments and communicated that he would not use coercion to enforce Communist Party dominance. While he never put himself up for direct election, he did hold contested elections for many of the seats in a new national parliament in 1989 and gave this parliament the right to choose the country's leader. All this disrupted previously stable political expectations in society and gave explicit sanction to ambitious politicians who

---

[52] John P. Willerton, *Patronage and Politics in the USSR* (Cambridge: Cambridge University Press, 1992). See also research tracing regional-clan politics in Central Asia in Jones Luong, *Institutional Change*.

[53] To help maintain unity among these rivalrous networks while also ensuring the dominance of his own, several of these Brezhnev era republic first secretaries actually anchored their machines in the symbolism of moderate Islam and ("titular") ethnicity, even to the point of subtly promoting this symbolism. Likewise, first secretaries in Armenia and Georgia drew substantially on their titular groups' long-standing identification with Christianity. In ethnically divided Kazakhstan, however, where a stress on any religious tradition would likely have alienated about half or more of the population, religious symbolism was deemphasized. See James Critchlow, *Nationalism in Uzbekistan: A Soviet Republic's Road to Sovereignty* (Boulder, CO: Westview, 1991); and Mark Saroyan, *Minorities, Mullahs, and Modernity: Reshaping Community in the Former Soviet Union* (Berkeley: University of California Press, 1997).

[54] Donald Carlisle, "Islom Karimov and Uzbekistan: Back to the Future?" in Timothy J. Colton and Robert C. Tucker, eds., *Patterns in Post-Soviet Leadership* (Boulder, CO: Westview Press, 1995), pp. 191–216; James Critchlow, "Prelude to 'Independence': How the Uzbek Party Apparatus Broke Moscow's Grip on Elite Recruitment," in William Fierman, ed., *Soviet Central Asia: The Failed Transformation* (Boulder, CO: Westview Press, 1991), pp. 131–58.

[55] Ronald Grigor Suny, "On the Road to Independence: Cultural Cohesion and Ethnic Revival in a Multinational Society," in Ronald Suny, ed., *Transcaucasia, Nationalism, and Social Change* (Ann Arbor: University of Michigan Press, 1996), pp. 377–400.

[56] Jones Luong, *Institutional Change*.

[57] E.g., Archie Brown, *The Gorbachev Factor* (New York: Oxford University Press, 1997); Stephen Kotkin with a contribution by Jan T. Gross, *Uncivil Society: 1989 and the Implosion of the Communist Establishment* (New York : Random House, 2009).

wanted to develop new pyramids of power under their own patronage as well as to those who also genuinely wanted to create a different system altogether, one that was truly democratic and not based on patronalism. The result was a dramatic opening of the political space in the USSR and the emergence of what might be called a *competing-pyramid* arrangement of patronal networks in place of the single-pyramid system.

The particular nature of the new pyramids that emerged to compete with the central pyramid proved to be of paramount importance. Gorbachev's introduction of elections bestowed new autonomy and authority on the leaders of precisely those institutions in the USSR that had controlled the greatest formal and informal power but had previously been subordinate to the central leadership: the union republics. This was not necessarily a problem: Federal states – those combining democracy with territorial autonomy – have only rarely collapsed in world history, even in highly patronalistic contexts and even when federal lines overlap with ethnic lines. India is a prime example. This is largely because the central leadership usually retains both the power to divide and conquer and the capacity to induce regions to remain in the union through selective threats or "payoffs" to individuals positioned to undermine a separatist effort.[58]

But the emerging Soviet federation as Gorbachev democratized it contained a fatal design flaw that turns out to have been present in every single instance of ethnofederal breakup since at least World War II: a single federal region that overshadowed the others in population.[59] This "core ethnic region" was the Russian Republic, covering a seventh of the world's land mass and more than half the union's population. It is fascinating that Communist Party leaders ever since Lenin had sensed quite correctly that this particular republic, not the ethnic minority territories, constituted the greatest threat to the stability of the system. By denying the Russian Republic – and the Russian Republic alone – its own party first secretary and party organization, they expressed their fear that once this republic acquired a chief subpatron, she would inevitably control so much of the chief patron's (USSR party leader's) network that any challenge she posed to the central leadership could be credible enough to draw other elite supporters, creating uncertainty as to the expected future leadership of the country and thereby destabilizing it.

The events of 1990 and 1991 showed this fear was well founded. Gorbachev allowed elections for a new Russian Republic parliament (the Congress of People's Deputies), and then permitted it to elect the Russian Republic's formal leader. Boris Yeltsin won election to this Russian parliament and became its

---

[58] Henry E. Hale, "Divided We Stand: Institutional Sources of Ethnofederal State Survival and Collapse," *World Politics*, v. 56, no. 2, January 2004, pp. 165–93. For a different view that does not explicitly address the argument made in the former piece, see Philip Roeder, *Where Nation-States Come From* (Princeton, NJ: Princeton University Press, 2007).

[59] Hale, "Divided We Stand."

first chairman, whereupon he almost immediately used his own patronalistic authority to chip away at the links in Gorbachev's vertical network of authority, luring some elites over to himself, removing others, and creating new ones who would support him. Since Russia was such a huge block in the Soviet power pyramid, its effective removal by Yeltsin undercut Gorbachev's ability to carry out threats and make credible promises to stop the networks in charge of the minority republics from seceding. Russia's size also made Yeltsin, as its formal leader, a natural focal point for rallying elite and mass opposition to Gorbachev and the union itself once Yeltsin began challenging the Soviet leadership.

Yeltsin aimed more to replace Gorbachev as chief patron than to destroy the union, and so did not actually remove Russia from the USSR. But his uncertainty-creating actions as opposition focal point ultimately fractured the union irreparably. A group of hard-liners attempted to stop him by force in an August 1991 coup but botched it badly, in no small part because many Soviet elites now expected that Yeltsin would ultimately win any power struggle and accordingly dole out rewards and punishments based on who showed loyalty or deference to him at this crucial moment. Since the coup momentarily incapacitated the Soviet coercive apparatus at the same time that it confirmed the existence of a long-term risk to remaining in the union, it is little surprise that many minority republics' chief patrons who most feared Yeltsin's dominance seized the window of opportunity to exit the USSR entirely and thereby gain the opportunity to become chief national patrons themselves, albeit in smaller systems. Yeltsin could do little to stop it, and what he did do (including threatening Ukrainian territorial integrity should it secede) sometimes just exacerbated the fears in other republics.[60] A cascade of elite defections from the central to republic-based networks ensued, making Gorbachev's own resignation in December 1991 a mere formalization of a power transfer that had already occurred. By the start of 1992, therefore, the USSR had fallen victim to a bank run on the state just as had Russia's tsarist regime in 1917 and the East Central European communist regimes in 1989.[61]

The sudden disappearance of so many Soviet institutions that had been so all-encompassing for so many decades radically unhinged the expectations of elites as to the *very nature of power*. Formal and informal institutions in polity, economy, and society (while often continuing to exist) were all called into question, generating tremendous opportunity for entrepreneurial spirits both within and outside the state to forge new networks, invent new methods for gaining influence, and find new ways to obtain wealth.[62] The preceding sentence should

---

[60] On the Soviet breakup and the role of the Russian Republic, see Hale, *The Foundations*; and Henry E. Hale, "The Makeup and Breakup of Ethnofederal States: Why Russia Survives Where the USSR Fell," *Perspectives on Politics*, v. 3, no. 1, March 2005, pp. 55–70.

[61] Kotkin, *Uncivil Society*; Steven L. Solnick, *Stealing the State: Control and Collapse in Soviet Institutions* (Cambridge, MA: Harvard University Press, 1998).

[62] On the process by which Soviet era personal capital was translated into new outcomes during the USSR's demise, see Georgi Derluguian, *Bourdieu's Secret Admirer in the Caucasus: A World Systems Biography* (Chicago: University of Chicago Press, 2005).

not be read as meaning that all institutions at all levels vanished without a trace, producing a clean slate for the post-Soviet period. Far from it. Indeed, the formal institutions that constituted the newly independent states themselves were repurposed survivals from the Soviet period. And as will be detailed in Chapter 5, also carrying over were a wide range of structures at the meso or micro levels, including extended networks of friends, family, and acquaintances that had been forged during the Soviet period as well as certain concentrations of material and organizational resources, such as factories and work collectives. These holdover structures, however, fell into radical discoordination as expectations regarding future power were themselves discoordinated, and for many this also meant that their future was called into question. The structures that survived, along with some new ones that were created, became the building blocks for the new orders that emerged after 1991.[63] In social science terms, this period represented a *critical juncture*, a point in time when existing power arrangements are in flux, meaning that sunk costs in the old system are largely lost and greater opportunities for new arrangements are thereby created.[64]

This sudden unhinging of political expectations in fifteen newly independent states and four unrecognized de facto statelets (Abkhazia, Nagorno-Karabakh, Transnistria, and South Ossetia) affords us an outstanding natural laboratory in which to study how these new patronalistic regimes emerged and to understand the dynamism they have displayed over the nearly quarter century since 1991, and the collapse of less patronalistic polities in East Central Europe provides us with additional leverage to understand what the patronalistic context itself means. The initial period of uncoordinated post-Soviet expectations, as Chapters 5 and 6 will show, was to last some half a decade before elites eventually converged on an understanding of power, an understanding that proved to be remarkably uniform across the non-Baltic parts of the former USSR. One reason for this uniformity is that this new understanding did not emerge from scratch: The legacies of Eurasian patronalism turn out to have had crucial implications that laid the foundation for political regularities defining regime dynamics in Eurasia for at least the next quarter-century.

Conclusion

Patronalism emerged as the "default" state of affairs in Eurasia much as it did throughout the rest of the world, and understanding its logic helps us reinterpret the broad sweep of the region's political history in a way that reconciles

---

[63] The term "recombinance" nicely captures this process. See Anna Grzymala-Busse and Pauline Jones Luong, "Reconceptualizing the State: Lessons from Post-Communism," *Politics & Society*, v. 30, no. 4, December 2002, pp. 529–54.

[64] On critical junctures, see Ruth Berins Collier and David Collier, *Shaping the Political Arena: Critical Junctures, the Labor Movement and Regime Dynamics in Latin America* (Princeton, NJ: Princeton University Press, 1991); and Seymour M. Lipset and Stein Rokkan, "Cleavage Structures, Party Systems, and Voter Alignments: An Introduction," in Lipset and Rokkan, eds., *Party Systems and Voter Aligments: Cross-National Perspectives* (New York: Free Press, 1967), pp. 1–64.

sides in long-standing scholarly debates and sheds light on just what is new today and what is age-old. While patronalism as a phenomenon persistently reproduced itself from prehistory straight through 1991, the most important feature that has carried over has not been the specific dominant networks themselves. The Miloslavskys and the Naryshkins that competed within the tsarist single-pyramid system for more than a century were long gone (or completely marginalized) by the time of Stalin's rise and had nothing to do with the chief subpatrons in the Soviet dictator's single-pyramid system, such as Khrushchev, Malenkov, and Beria. Similarly, the Brezhnev and Gorbachev networks also fell by the wayside after the USSR ended. Conspiracy theories that a vast network of Soviet operatives retained control over the region straight through the union's breakup and into the independence period remain nothing more than conspiracy theories, notwithstanding the rise to power of former KGB operative Vladimir Putin in Russia.

The most important continuity over the centuries has instead been a social equilibrium of expectations, expectations that patron-client relationships were an often-unpleasant but necessary fact in this world, that the state was the chief source of patronage, and that one was likely to wind up a sucker (or worse) if one eschewed opportunities to use these relationships for the benefit of oneself, one's family, one's network, or the authorities. The Bolshevik Revolution in some sense was the exception that proved the rule, a daring and brutal attempt to subvert patronalistic tsarist ways that was ultimately undone by someone who figured out how to meld the old ways and the new, infusing the socialist experiment with patronalistic content that ultimately displaced almost everything else, genuine ideological belief included.[65] Some would also see in the Soviet breakup another failed attempt to escape the patronalistic ways that had been redeveloped so cruelly under Stalin and that had flourished under Brezhnev. Here, however, the succeeding authorities were for the most part not antipatronalistic revolutionaries as the Bolsheviks had been in seizing power from outside the state but rather subpatrons who had long been part of the old Soviet system. Those hoping for a quick and automatic transition to a Western style "open access order" (in the sense discussed by North and his colleagues)[66] were soon sorely disappointed as patronalistic practices proved highly profitable to those who exercised them, especially when creatively adapted to the new post-Soviet environment. Patronalism thus reproduced itself in new forms as Russia and other post-Soviet polities evolved, primarily by offering

---

[65] Intriguingly, Gorbachev himself appears to have been one of the few exceptions, a rare heartfelt Leninist in the late Soviet period (though he was also a master of Soviet-style patronal politics). On this and the Russian Revolution as truly revolutionary, see Stephen E. Hanson, *Time and Revolution: Marxism and the Design of Soviet Institutions* (Chapel Hill: University of North Carolina Press, 1997).

[66] Douglass C. North, John Joseph Wallis, Barry R. Weingast, *Violence and Social Orders: A Conceptual Framework for Interpreting Recorded Human History* (New York: Cambridge University Press, 2009).

up opportunities for power and enrichment that smart leaders could recognize and that few could stand to forgo. As we will see in future chapters, this continues to be a common theme throughout Eurasia today.

In fact, one of the most important legacies that "communism" left in the former Soviet world may actually be a legacy of patronalism with roots as old as human community itself.[67] Indeed, the perspective on offer here helps us understand certain broad patterns of politics that have previously been regarded as the products of different "communist legacies."[68] In a groundbreaking collaborative study, one group of specialists based in the United States and East Central Europe classified the USSR's legacy as one of "patrimonial communism," a form of communism with especially high degrees of what we here have called patronalistic content. They identified this form, in particular, with the USSR, Albania, Bulgaria, Macedonia, and Romania, noting that the patronalistic (patrimonial) element was only slightly weaker in the Baltic republics and Serbia.[69] Other postcommunist states are categorized as having experienced a more "formal-rational" form of communism (notably the Czech Republic, East Germany, Poland, Hungary, Slovenia, and Croatia).[70] It bears noting that this latter category includes states that had, prior to the onset of communist rule, spent significant periods under Habsburg domination or were otherwise more tightly connected to processes of escaping what North and his colleagues have called "the natural state" of deeply embedded patronalism during the preceding century or so.[71] Strikingly, this very general typology offered up by Herbert Kitschelt and his coauthors accords nicely with the index of corruption perceptions summarized in Figure 3.1 as well as the World Bank's study of the rule of law that was also cited in the introduction to this chapter.

A full historical accounting for these broad differences among countries is well beyond the scope of this volume, but to the extent that they are documented by others they do provide important bases for developing theoretical predictions as to what kinds of patterns are likely to prevail in which places. We would thus expect the patterns characteristic of patronal politics to be more pronounced in

---

[67] In an even more specific sense, patronalism turns out to be a "critical antecedent" for many critical junctures explaining divergences in post-Soviet regime dynamics examined later in this book. See Dan Slater and Erica Simmons, "Informative Regress: Critical Antecedents in Comparative Politics," *Comparative Political Studies*, v. 43, no. 7, July 2010, pp. 886–917.

[68] For a complementary approach to identifying legacies that can actually be pinned to the communist period, see Grigore Pop-Eleches and Joshua A. Tucker, "Communism's Shadow: Postcommunist Legacies, Values, and Behavior," *Comparative Politics*, v. 43, no. 4, July 2011, pp. 379–408. On important legacies of the perestroika period, see Eric McGlinchey, *Chaos, Violence, Dynasty: Politics and Islam in Central Asia* (Pittsburgh: Pittsburgh University Press, 2011).

[69] Also Slovakia, despite the extent to which it shared the Czech lands' history.

[70] Herbert Kitschelt, Zdenka Mansfeldova, Radoslaw Markowski, and Gabor Toka, *Post-Communist Party Systems: Competition, Representation, and Inter-Party Cooperation* (New York: Cambridge University Press, 1999), pp. 23–27, 39.

[71] North, Wallis, and Weingast, *Violence and Social Orders*.

TABLE 3.1. *Legacies of Patronalism at the End of Communist Rule*

Most Patronalistic	Moderately Patronalistic	Least Patronalistic
Albania	Estonia	Croatia
Armenia	Latvia	Czech Republic
Azerbaijan	Lithuania	East Germany (DDR)
Belarus	Serbia	Hungary
Bulgaria	Slovakia	Poland
Georgia		Slovenia
Kazakhstan		
Kyrgyzstan		
Macedonia		
Moldova		
Romania		
Russia		
Tajikistan		
Turkmenistan		
Ukraine		
Uzbekistan		

Source: Adapted from Herbert Kitschelt, Zdenka Mansfeldova, Radoslaw Markowski, and Gabor Toka, *Post-Communist Party Systems: Competition, Representation, and Inter-Party Cooperation* (New York: Cambridge University Press, 1999), p. 39.

countries with the strongest "patrimonial communist" legacies as identified by Kitschelt and colleagues and as summarized in Table 3.1. Chapter 12 directly addresses the postcommunist countries outside the former USSR and finds that this prediction is in fact borne out, with important implications for how we interpret politics across the postcommunist region. Chapter 4 now turns to what some of these implications might be that can help us understand the nearly two and a half decades of politics in post-Soviet countries and politics elsewhere as well.

4

Constitutions, Elections, and Regime Dynamics

As Chapter 2 argued and Chapter 3 illustrated, patronalism is a social equilibrium whereby individuals organize their political and economic pursuits more around the personalized exchange of concrete rewards and punishments than around abstract, impersonal principles such as ideological belief or categorizations that include many people one has not actually met in person.[1] It can be conceived of as a kind of collective action problem, a vicious cycle whereby individuals understand politics as an arena of personal wealth redistribution and targeted coercion and therefore reproduce these very practices themselves for fear of being the "sucker," the feckless soul who acts on principle but only succeeds in impoverishing one's family, marginalizing oneself, and accomplishing nothing. For individuals in highly patronalistic societies, what matters most for one's material welfare is belonging to a coalition that has access to – and hence can pay out – resources. But which coalitions are capable of this depends on who else joins. There is thus a very important process of *coordination* at the core of political competition in patronalistic societies, as discussed in the previous chapter: The strength of networks depends on the support of individuals, but which side individuals support depends very strongly on which side these individuals expect other individuals to support – or, more precisely, on which side they do not expect to wind up losing access to resources for patronage and coercion as a result of a lack of support.[2] Power, then, becomes a kind of self-fulfilling prophecy whereby those who are *expected* to become powerful (for whatever reason) can *become* powerful by virtue of these expectations. And they can lose power just as easily for the

---

[1] Recall Chapter 2's elaboration on this definition and discussion of how it relates to similar concepts such as clientelism, neopatrimonialism, and social capital.

[2] This dynamic is obscured in selectorate theory as elaborated by Bruce Bueno de Mesquita, Alastair Smith, Randolph M. Siverson, and James D. Morrow, *The Logic of Political Survival* (Cambridge, MA: MIT Press, 2003), though it can be interpreted as an extension of it.

opposite reason. This is the great power of expectations in highly patronalistic societies.[3]

To explain and predict regime dynamics in highly patronalistic societies, therefore, we would do well to focus on what shapes such expectations. A good starting point is to assume that *expectations about the future distribution of power among networks tend to reflect the current distribution of power*, at least as perceived through the various ways in which networks visibly exercise power. And when one network defeats another in a head to head context, thereby revealing at that moment the real distribution of power between them, the expectation is likely to be that the victorious network will also be the more powerful in the moment of time that immediately follows that victory. That "next moment" influences the following moment, and so on, and so on. Would-be clients who have no other reason for preferring one network to the other thus have incentive to hitch their fortunes to the victorious one not only during but after its victory.

If current balances of power were the sole generators of expectations regarding future power, however, we would never see any change in how networks arrange themselves. They would never expect anything to change in the future, having no aspirations, no hopes, and no fears.

Where, then, might dynamism originate? Generally speaking, there are at least four sources. One is perceptible change in factors that are beyond the patron's own control but that are widely believed to underpin her power, as when Gorbachev's decision to end Soviet support for East European communist regimes in 1989 triggered a fast-moving self-fulfilling prophecy that these countries' chief patrons were doomed, as Chapter 2 described.[4] Second, a dominant patron (or coalition of patrons) might initiate changes (as in formal or informal institutions or de facto property control) that she expects to strengthen her and that indeed lead others to share this expectation, as with Yeltsin's moves to claim more authority for his Russian Republic in 1990–1, described in Chapter 3. Third, these same powerful patrons might miscalculate or might lack complete information. For example, they may create institutions that they think will augment their power but that actually wind up facilitating the expectation that their power will diminish. Many see Gorbachev's granting more autonomy to the Russian Republic and the other union republics in just this light, as a move that was meant to placate republic-based networks but that actually fostered expectations that the center would lose even more power,

---

[3] "Highly patronalistic" communicates the idea that the more pervasive ("higher") are levels of patronalism, the more pronounced and observable the dynamics discussed in this volume should be and the more these dynamics should overpower other forces that might impact the outcomes of interest here.

[4] Stephen Kotkin with a contribution by Jan T. Gross, *Uncivil Society: 1989 and the Implosion of the Communist Establishment* (New York: Random House, 2009); Mark Kramer, "The Collapse of East European Communism and the Repercussions within the Soviet Union," *Journal of Cold War Studies*, v. 5, no. 4, 2003, pp. 178–256.

as discussed in Chapter 3.[5] And fourth, the powerful might intentionally allow for uncertainty (adopting changes they know entail some risk of weakening their position) as part of a trade-off that would get them something else they desire more than they fear the uncertainty. Many interpret Gorbachev's decision to start democratizing the USSR, discussed in the previous chapter, as just such a conscious decision to accept some short-term risk of ouster and instability as part of an effort to make his system more prosperous and stable in the long run.[6] The fact that all of the examples given here are from the perestroika period makes the point that the four sources of dynamism in expectations can interact, countervailing or reinforcing each other.

This volume trains attention on how constitutions and contested elections shape expectations and regime dynamics through these four sources. Constitutions and elections are singled out not because they are all that matters, but because they are *among* the most important factors as well as the most misunderstood. Thus despite the focus on elections and constitutions, the volume agrees all the while that the most important driver of expectations remains current perceived balances of power. To gauge the impact of constitutions and contested elections, therefore, the volume must explain how they emerge out of existing power balances in such a way that they can still have independent effects, and then demonstrate that they influence political outcomes in ways that do not simply boil down to the power balances that produced them.[7] The book also makes clear that regardless of constitutions and elections, individual leaders can drastically shape expectations about their future power through their own actions. This might be through a voluntary decision to leave power, a charisma that makes them seem irreplaceable, or dramatic mistakes that alienate key supporters and raise doubts about their prospects to survive for long in office. Nevertheless, the book shows that elections and constitutions help produce regularities that stand out despite individual agency and that tend systematically to magnify or dampen its effects.

One conclusion is that the most important effects of elections and constitutions in highly patronalistic countries are different than they are widely assumed to be in the West. Contested elections are important *not* because of any assumption they produce an accurate measure of the public's opinion of its leaders. Similarly, constitutions are important not because anyone assumes they

[5] Mark R. Beissinger, *Nationalist Mobilization and the Collapse of the Soviet State* (New York: Cambridge University Press, 2002)

[6] Archie Brown, *The Gorbachev Factor* (New York: Oxford University Press, 1997).

[7] This is especially important concerning formal constitutions, as some major studies explicitly argue that they have no significant causal effect of their own on major regime dynamics since they are essentially epiphenomenal or a by-product of the forces of informal politics that really drive changes in regimes. Two of the strongest such claims can be found in Jose Antonio Cheibub, *Presidentialism, Parliamentarism, and Democracy* (New York: Cambridge University Press, 2007); and Steven Levitsky and Lucan A. Way, *Competitive Authoritarianism: Hybrid Regimes after the Cold War* (New York: Cambridge University Press, 2010).

are generally "followed" or "obeyed." Such assumptions, rejected here, seem to underlie the most sweeping claims that constitutions and elections have little real effect in nondemocratic countries.[8] Indeed, official election results are typically manipulated or falsified and constitutions routinely violated or ignored. Instead, paradoxically, elections and constitutions can have major effects in highly patronalistic societies by shaping the ways in which the formalities of these very same formal institutions are *disregarded, violated, and manipulated*. This is because they supply focal points for patronal network coordination and other information about future network prospects that can produce different dynamics in the configuration of patronal networks.[9] Different constitutional and electoral arrangements, therefore, can produce different dynamics in how patronal networks coordinate their power-related activities. They can also interact differently with other factors that can impact expectations, one of the most important of which will be shown to be public opinion.

These dynamic patterns of network configuration are conceived as movement along a broad spectrum between two ideal-type configurations: In one, a country's main networks are glommed together to constitute a single "pyramid" of authority under a chief patron who is usually regarded as the country's leader, and any networks remaining outside this pyramid are systematically marginalized, widely regarded as unable to pose a credible challenge to the authority of the dominant group. We can call this a *single-pyramid* arrangement (see Figure 4.1).[10] The second is a *competing-pyramid* configuration, whereby a country's patronal networks arrange themselves in multiple distinct pyramids where no one clearly dominates the others and where each has strong incentive to compete for power and resources (see Figure 4.2).[11] What is important

---

[8] E.g., Levitsky and Way, *Competitive Authoritarianism*, pp. 79–80, on constitutions.

[9] Thus while the conclusions about how constitutions matter diverge from common wisdom, the logic presented in this chapter is quite consistent with some of the most prominent work on the origins of constitutions, which focuses on their role in facilitating coordination by influencing expectations of future power and future collective action among elites. See Douglass C. North and Barry R. Weingast, "Constitutions and Commitment," *Journal of Economic History*, v. 49, no. 4, December 1989, pp. 803–32; John M. Veitch, "Repudiations and Confiscations by the Medieval State," *Journal of Economic History*, v. 46, no. 1, March 1986, pp. 31–6; Barry R. Weingast, "The Political Foundations of Democracy and the Rule of Law," *American Political Science Review*, v. 91, no. 2, June 1997, pp. 245–63.

[10] It is important not to construe "single-pyramid system" as rule by a single monolithic network, a phenomenon that is exceedingly rare. More typically the "single pyramid" consists of multiple distinct networks that are part of or aligned with the patron's larger network that compete for position with respect to the chief patron (as did the different nobles in the tsar's court described in Chapter 3), as is depicted in Figure 4.1.

[11] As Serhiy Kudelia has pointed out, this does not exclude that the competitors can conclude pacts to keep their competition within a certain framework or even organize a kind of cartel – that is, competition does not have to be unruly or no-holds-barred. See Serhiy Kudelia, "Institutional Design and Elite Interests: The Case of Ukraine," unpublished paper presented at the DC Area Postcommunist Politics Social Science Workshop, George Washington University, January 4, 2012. Of course, at the far end of such a scenario, the coalition can essentially become a single

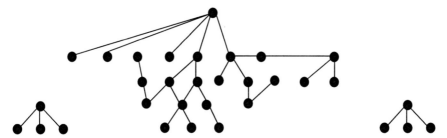

FIGURE 4.1. Example of an ideal-type single-pyramid system.

Note on interpretation: Dots represent individuals and lines indicate different mixes of coercive and mutually beneficial relationships, with vertical positioning indicating relative power. The tiny pyramids to each side represent marginalized networks. Interconnected sets of dots with distinct connections to the chief patron (the dot with highest vertical positioning) represent different patronal networks with distinct identities within the larger network that constitutes the single pyramid.

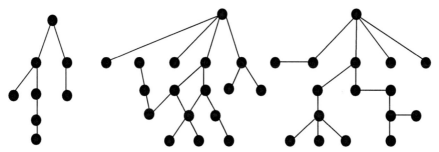

FIGURE 4.2. Example of an ideal-type competing-pyramid system.

Note on interpretation: Dots represent individuals and lines indicate different mixes of coercive and mutually beneficial relationships, with vertical positioning indicating relative power in the relationships.

about these arrangements is the possibility of movement between them – the dynamism that will be in focus in this volume – not the arrangements themselves as any kind of end point in a regime transition.[12] Indeed, as we will see, different drivers of expectations can produce cyclic as well as linear movement toward or away from single- and competing-pyramid configurations. And this movement, which involves complex shifts in coordination, does not take place instantly or automatically with every change in current power perceptions, constitutions, or elections. Instead, it represents a *process* that takes time. Evidence

pyramid of its own where all rivalry among the components ceases and network patrons are in perfect coordination.

[12] Thus when the term "single-pyramid system" is used, it does not imply that the arrangement is static, self-reinforcing, or even stable, just that there is a coherent logic to how this arrangement of networks functions and that its existence is more than fleeting.

for the importance of these patterns, and how they are shaped by constitutions and elections, is presented in the detailed case studies of regime dynamics in subsequent chapters.

The Origins of Contested Elections and Constitutions in Patronalistic Polities

To suggest that contested elections and constitutions have independent effects raises the question of where they come from. We must establish that the factors producing them do not also create the effects attributed to them. Since neither elections nor constitutions spring forth randomly from nature, but instead must be somehow adopted and accepted by human communities, the baseline assumption should be that dominant patrons or coalitions of patrons adopt electoral practices and constitutions that they believe serve their interests.[13] When there is a single dominant network capable of institutional change on its own, we would expect it to attempt to codify, legitimate, reinforce, or strengthen its dominance. When there is a coalition of separate networks (as when a stalemate produces a deal for joint rule), one would expect it to adopt electoral institutions and constitutions that support the balance among coalition partners, an outcome that can also involve willingness to support the position of third networks as potentially balancing coalition partners.[14]

Why, then, would we ever see a hybrid regime? That is, why would there ever arise a political system in which a dominant network allows at least some genuine opposition to run against it in elections? For some, the answer is simple: Leaders who allow such competition on the ballot must be too weak to prevent it. This is the logic of what Thomas Carothers has called "feckless pluralism" and Lucan Way has dubbed "pluralism by default."[15] This notion has its place, particularly in the very early years after a far-reaching collapse of state institutions, as Chapter 6 will show. It is unconvincing, however, in accounting for most hybrid regimes of the world that have lasted much more than a couple of years.[16] For example, it strains credulity to argue that Russia's

---

[13] Jack Knight, *Institutions and Social Conflict* (New York: Cambridge University Press, 1992).

[14] There is a large literature supporting such claims as to the relationship between balances of power and formal institutional change involving constitutions or elections. Along with Knight, *Institutions and Social Conflict*, see also Timothy Frye, "A Politics of Institutional Choice – Post-Communist Presidencies," *Comparative Political Studies*, v. 30, October 1997, pp. 523–52; Cynthia McClintock, "The Prospects for Democratic Consolidation in a 'Least Likely' Case: Peru," *Comparative Politics*, v. 21, no. 2, January 1989, pp. 127–148; Adam Przeworski, *Democracy and the Market* (New York: Cambridge University Press, 1991); Dankwart Rustow, "Transitions to Democracy: Towards a Dynamic Model," *Comparative Politics*, v. 2, April 1970, pp. 337–63.

[15] Thomas Carothers, "The End of the Transition Paradigm," *Journal of Democracy*, v. 13, no. 1, January 2002, pp. 5–21; Lucan A. Way, "Pluralism by Default in Moldova," *Journal of Democracy*, v. 13, no. 4, October 2002, pp. 127–41, p. 131.

[16] Way's full case in book form is still under construction, however, so his most definitive statement is yet to come.

Vladimir Putin, who has long controlled an impressive security apparatus and a massive political machine, faces opposition representatives on the ballot because he is unable to get rid of them.

More convincing is a growing body of research establishing that dominant patrons in fact derive *benefits* from allowing at least some genuine electoral competition, and that in return for these they can be willing to accept the modicum of risk entailed by allowing opposition participation in elections. "Modicum" is used because these regimes frequently develop a sophisticated arsenal of tactics designed to minimize the uncertainty that contested elections create, thereby hoping to reap the benefits from such competition while minimizing the risks. These tactics, which Andreas Schedler dubs the "menu of manipulation," will be elaborated later and their practice discussed throughout this volume.[17]

The *benefits* of contested elections for dominant patrons are counterintuitive, and research has found that they take many forms. Perhaps the most fundamental reason for potential autocrats to allow contested elections is developed by Graeme Robertson, advancing certain insights of Charles Tilly. Very importantly, establishing contested elections can be "a way to manage the disunity and disorder that threaten all authoritarian political regimes."[18] That is, world experience makes clear that regimes that do not allow regular, contested elections do face crises and revolutions, but these tend to be highly unpredictable for the ruler. The collapse of East European communism in 1989 and many of the Arab uprisings in 2011 are just two of the best known sets of examples. Moreover, such unexpected ousters can lead to quite dire consequences for the old elites should they occur. This risk gives rulers an interest in channeling public challenges through more predictable mechanisms. In so doing, rulers structure the political struggle according to ground rules that they themselves design, that enable them to prepare long in advance, and that reduce the chances losing power will involve the most catastrophic loss of property or even life. Brilliant research by Tilly on Great Britain thus finds that with the rise of parliament during the eighteenth and nineteenth centuries, "popular contention" became progressively *less* violent, *less* randomly timed, and *less* aimed at forcibly settling a claim immediately (as in a grain seizure or mob attack on an authority figure). Instead, "contentious issues and the actual periodicity of collective claim-making came to depend much more closely on rhythms of parliamentary elections and decision-making."[19] These more predictable patterns of contention also involved crowds' becoming more likely to mobilize against the state's repressive apparatus – precisely where the state

---

[17] Andreas Schedler, "The Menu of Manipulation," *Journal of Democracy*, v. 13, April 2002, pp. 36–50.

[18] Graeme B. Robertson, *The Politics of Protest in Hybrid Regimes: Managing Dissent in Post-Communist Russia* (New York: Cambridge University Press, 2011), pp. 12–13.

[19] Charles Tilly, "Parliamentarization of Popular Contention in Great Britain, 1758–1834," *Theory and Society*, v. 26, 1997, pp. 245–73, p. 265.

was best prepared to meet it – rather than points of greater ruler vulnerability. Parliamentary elections also provided occasions for the rulers to mobilize *supporters*, who were also in a position to help shore up the regime.[20]

On top of this larger benefit of being able to design the playing field for political contestation, potential dictators stand to reap a series of more specific, short-term gains from holding contested elections even as they seek to manipulate their outcomes. For one thing, elections can provide a useful mechanism for co-opting other networks, distributing patronage, or facilitating power sharing among the most important elite groups.[21] Electoral competition itself can be useful in producing information about impending crises, generating new ideas for solutions that it can adopt and call its own initiative, test the quality of new cadres to staff the authoritarian system, discover new potentially valuable cadres, maintain other links with the public that it can draw on later, and find out who is willing to cooperate with the leadership and who is not.[22] Others have found that patrons derive legitimation even from unfair elections.[23] And defeating an opponent soundly, even (or perhaps especially) by fraud, can send a clear message to others that resisting is futile, promoting demobilization.[24] Scholars have also long observed that powerful international actors have in recent decades explicitly linked to democracy a variety of potential benefits that rulers may want, benefits ranging from legitimacy to economic assistance to membership in prestigious or powerful international clubs. Moreover, leaders have generally discovered that allowing just *some* opposition competition on the ballot is enough to get them much of what they want from international actors (including avoiding the worst sanctions) even though these elections are highly manipulated.[25]

---

[20] Ibid.

[21] Lisa Blaydes, *Elections and Distributive Politics in Mubarak's Egypt* (New York: Cambridge University Press, 2013); Jennifer Gandhi, *Political Institutions under Dictatorship* (New York: Cambridge University Press, 2008); Jennifer Gandhi and Ellen Lust-Okar, "Elections under Authoritarianism," *Annual Review of Political Science*, v. 12, 2009, pp. 403–22; Ellen Lust-Okar, "Elections under Authoritarianism: Preliminary Lessons from Jordan," *Democratization*, v. 13, no. 3, 2006, pp. 456–71; Milan W. Svolik, *The Politics of Authoritarian Rule* (New York: Cambridge University Press, 2012).

[22] Nikolay Petrov, Maria Lipman, and Henry E. Hale, "Three Dilemmas of Hybrid Regime Governance: Russia from Putin to Putin," *Post-Soviet Affairs*, September 2013. A supporting argument is in Robert W. Orttung and David Rainbow, "How Do Authoritarian Leaders Stay in Power? Media, Information, and the Opposition in Russia," unpublished manuscript, 2011.

[23] Nathan Brown, "Dictatorship and Democracy through the Prism of Arab Elections," in Nathan Brown, ed., *Dynamics of Democratization* (Baltimore: Johns Hopkins University Press, 2011), pp. 48–51.

[24] Beatriz Magaloni, *Voting for Autocracy: Hegemonic Party Survival and Its Demise in Mexico* (New York: Cambridge University Press, 2006); Alberto Simpser, *Why Governments and Parties Manipulate Elections: Theory, Practice, and Implications* (New York: Cambridge University Press, 2013); Robertson, *The Politics of Protest*, pp. 12–13.

[25] Robert Bates, "The Impulse to Reform in Africa," in Jennifer Widner, ed., *Economic Change and Political Liberalization in Sub-Saharan Africa* (Baltimore: Johns Hopkins University Press,

We would thus expect potential autocrats to allow or institute contested elections when they calculate that the risk of losing power in elections (a risk that is quite real) is outweighed by the combination of two considerations: the benefits they hope to reap from holding such elections and the risk of a more catastrophic loss should they not hold elections and lose power through more violent, less institutionalized means. That is, such leaders are *knowingly* accepting a certain risk of ouster by election. Of course, they typically do also hope that they can find some way to minimize this risk through the menu of manipulation or genuine popular support, which many nondemocratic regime leaders are convinced they wield in great measure (arguably because nondemocratic rule distorts the information they receive, dampening bad news). In deciding whether the benefits of contested elections outweigh the risks, we would expect autocrats to be most likely to take the risks involved in trying something new when their autocratic institutions have already ruptured most completely for exogenous reasons.[26]

One very important implication of all this is that by taking the *calculated risk* of introducing elections, a leader is opening up the door for elections to have effects on expectations and hence regime dynamics that are *independent of the factors that led the patron to institute or tolerate the contested elections.* And by the time a leader suspects he or she may have lost the bet, it is usually too late since such realizations tend to occur only after expectations have shifted and key elements of the patron's coalition have become unhinged, as subsequent chapters will show.

Constitutions are also examples of institutions well documented often to reflect preexisting balances of power.[27] Since observed power balances themselves are a key and direct driver of expectations for the future, we must be careful not to assume that constitutions are driving expectations that actually have deeper roots in the balances of power that produce the constitutions. But as discussed previously, there are multiple ways in which constitutions can have independent effects. The most obvious way is that they can have unintended consequences, generating expectations among other elites that the leader does not anticipate until these expectations make it too late to "fix" the constitution.[28] This is more likely when constitutions are adopted in haste

---

1994), pp. 13–28; Susan D. Hyde, "International Dimensions of Elections," in Nathan Brown, ed., *Dynamics of Democratization* (Baltimore: Johns Hopkins University Press, 2011), pp. 266–82. Giving this factor special weight is Levitsky and Way, *Competitive Authoritarianism.*

[26] This is, of course, a logic of path dependence. See Douglass C. North, *Institutions, Institutional Change and Economic Performance* (New York: Cambridge University Press, 1990).

[27] Gerald Easter, "Preference for Presidentialism: Postcommunist Regime Change in Russia and the NIS," *World Politics*, v. 49, no. 2, January 1997, pp. 184–211; Frye, "A Politics of Institutional Choice"; Knight, *Institutions and Social Conflict.*

[28] Nathan Brown, *Constitutions in a Nonconstitutional World: Arab Basic Laws and the Prospects for Accountable Government* (Albany, NY: SUNY Press, 2002). While not explicitly focusing on constitutions, see Robert G. Moser, *Unexpected Outcomes: Electoral Systems, Political Parties, and Representation in Russia* (Pittsburgh: University of Pittsburgh Press, 2001).

because of contingent situations. In addition, there is research establishing that factors other than power balances can have influence on constitutional choices. Such other factors can include inheritance of particular forms from a preexisting colonial ruler or union state or a time-specific or region-specific belief as to what form a constitution should take.[29]

Even when they do fully reflect current power balances and when leaders do accurately understand their consequences, formal constitutions can still have effects independent of their origins. For one thing, as with contested elections, patrons can understand that different constitutions involve trade-offs between different kinds of risk and can willingly accept one form of risk to avoid another. One of the most important of these can involve time horizons: Patrons might fully understand, for example, that concentrating power in a single post can make the problem of succession more acute, but can prioritize the short-term need to concentrate power and figure they will take their chances in the long term, or let their successors deal with the instability after they themselves die of old age in office. Trade-offs involving time horizons can also be consciously made in the case of term limits, the inclusion of which in a constitution may help the currently dominant patron win allies in the short run, leaving the battle to extend or eliminate the term limits until later in the hope that the patron will be in a better position to win it when the time comes.[30]

While constitutions are in some cases changed frequently, changing them can be no simple task even for a powerful patron. This is because it typically requires a great deal of mobilization of patronalistic strength, including the costly securing of allies in parliament or, in the case of a referendum, coordination of clients and the distribution of resources across the country as a whole. This means constitutions are at least somewhat "sticky," not changing perfectly fluidly to reflect every momentary change in a leader's thinking.[31] And when expectations turn against a patron, this can also deprive the patron of the power needed to change the formal constitution at the very moment when

---

[29] Jose Antonio Cheibub, Zachary Elkins, and Tom Ginsburg, "Latin American Presidentialism in Comparative and Historical Perspective," *Texas Law Review*, v. 89, no. 7, 2011, pp. 1707–39.

[30] Svolik, *The Politics of Authoritarian Rule*, pp. 92–4. For example, Zein El Abidine Bin Ali, after defeating Tunisia's old dictator in a coup, "felt it necessary to begin by ingratiating himself with the Tunisian elite by introducing a three-term limit to the presidency, in contradistinction to [old president] Bourguiba's presidency for life, before spending the next eight years creating a mechanism that would allow him to introduce a plebiscite for an amendment that would, in turn, allow him to stand more for more [sic] than three terms after all," according to Roger Owen, *The Rise and Fall of Arab Presidents for Life* (Cambridge, MA: Harvard University Press, 2012), p. 54.

[31] This logic thus involves more than path dependence (North, *Institutions, Institutional Change*), which can also operate to make constitutions sticky. For perhaps the most thorough recent treatment of the question of constitutional change, see Zachary Elkins, Tom Ginsburg, and James Melton, *The Endurance of National Constitutions* (New York: Cambridge University Press, 2009).

the change is needed, and indeed an effort to amend the constitution to shore up obviously decaying power can provide a focal point for resistance among elites who are so inclined. All of these factors create space whereby even a constitution that initially purely reflects power balances can have independent effects. Indeed, if constitutions had no such effects, one would be hard-pressed to explain why leaders would ever bother to change or adopt them.

The key to establishing the effects of constitutions and contested elections in patronalistic polities, of course, will be research designs that allow us to understand their origins and then to isolate their effects from the effects of their causes. This will be accomplished in subsequent chapters through carefully chosen case comparisons and process-tracing analysis. The rest of this chapter now focuses on what we would expect the independent consequences of contested elections and formal constitutions to be in highly patronalistic societies.

Contested Nationwide Elections

For smaller networks trying to determine collectively which more prominent network among several to coordinate around, the most direct way to judge their relative future strength would be to witness the most recent outcome of direct competition between them. Throughout human history, this is effectively what has happened, with competition taking such forms as wars, feuds, conquests, rebellions, mutinies, protests, coups, and intrigues. The ultimate outcome would express itself in the holding of state power, around which patronal networks have tended to coordinate in a single-pyramid arrangement until something shook the coordinated expectations of continued dominance. The examples of the Russian Empire and the USSR from Chapter 3 are to the point. Contested elections tend to channel such contests into a framework that is more predictable and potentially less costly, which even dominant chief patrons in a country can be expected to desire.

The formal institution of contested nationwide elections (by which we imply elections for the most powerful formal executive and legislative offices in the country as a whole) is an explicit legal requirement that in order to hold state office, a patron must be able to produce a formal election victory over an opponent. This does not mean that the victory must reflect a free and fair contest with ballots honestly counted. To the contrary, elections in typical patronalistic polities are often quite crooked affairs, as people living in Huey Long's Louisiana or Nursultan Nazarbaev's Kazakhstan could attest. Patrons competing for office mobilize their media clients to burnish their own image and tarnish their opponents. They assign their clients in regulatory agencies to hit opposition offices (and the premises of their supporters) with unexpected fire, health, and safety inspections, which of course can result in shutdowns or fines. They direct their clients in law enforcement to investigate or prosecute opposition figures for tax evasion, corruption, or embarrassing crimes with the intention of humiliating and discrediting them. They deploy "dirty tricks" teams to threaten opponents directly or otherwise disrupt, discredit, and intimidate. Where patrons control money, they direct their clients to buy votes. And, of course, patrons with clients in election commissions may ultimately lead them to falsify the ballot count.[32]

None of this is a reason to ignore official election results in patronalistic societies. Instead, this is precisely *why they matter*. Pulling off a victory in contested nationwide elections is a herculean feat, one that requires massive mobilization of the leadership's extended client network and resources. Such victories tell everyone that the officially winning patron in fact has the raw power to do all this, creating incentives for a society's networks to coordinate around the winner's network in what over time can become a single-pyramid arrangement. This effect is magnified to the extent that at least some real opposition is actually allowed into the race. Conversely, a loss communicates to both clients and outsiders that a patron lacks this power, that his network is not capable of defeating a rival patronal network in a head-to-head contest that it sought to win. If a single opposing network is the clear winner, one would expect a cascading of elites from the old ruling network to the winner. But for as long as elections do not clearly indicate the dominance of any one network, one would expect a competing-pyramid arrangement to predominate as different elites either hedge their bets or pin their hopes on different networks in an uncoordinated fashion.

Contested national elections, therefore, powerfully shape the expectations of actual and potential clients about who is likely to win future battles, about which patronal networks will be able to follow through on their promises to reward and their threats to punish people in the future. This, in turn, alters people's calculations as to whether to join, ignore, or actively oppose different networks, and shapes smaller networks' decisions as to which alliances will be the most profitable in the future. And this impacts the strength of the networks themselves in another example of the kind of self-fulfilling prophecy discussed in Chapter 2, promoting movement toward or away from single-pyramid or competing-pyramid arrangements. Thus while one can be forgiven for concluding in disgust that patronalistic elections are nothing but a "sham" and therefore meaningless, in fact exactly the opposite is true.

This helps explain why such elections are so hard fought, why incumbent authorities go to great lengths and spare no expense to suppress and dominate opposition networks even when the latter clearly could not defeat them in a free and fair contest. It explains why relatively popular patronal leaders such as Belarus's Aliaksandr Lukashenka, Azerbaijan's Heydar Aliyev, and Kazakhstan's Nursultan Nazarbaev – each of whom could surely have won

[32] Henry E. Hale, "Hybrid Regimes: When Democracy and Autocracy Mix," in Nathan Brown, ed., *Dynamics of Democratization* (Baltimore: Johns Hopkins University Press, 2011), pp. 23–45; Schedler, "The Menu of Manipulation."

fully democratic races – all still have put their political machines in high gear to manufacture whopping official victories of at least 70 percent of the vote each time they have sought reelection. What they are doing is sending a message about the power of their networks, cultivating the expectation that they – and only they – must be reckoned with when it comes to politics. And these expectations generate incentives for other networks in society to coordinate around their authority, thereby underpinning single-pyramid politics.

In so shaping expectations, however, even dirty contested national elections do something surprising: They actually empower the people.[33] Because an official election result becomes the key to holding state office and signaling one's power, and because these results are at least formally interpreted as the actual counts of actual votes, and because ordinary people actually do cast ballots, a patron's *ability to win real votes* becomes a valuable resource. For one thing, the more people genuinely support a patron, the fewer rewards and punishments are needed to induce them to cast the desired ballots. Likewise, if an opposition wields true popular support, it is easier to convince people to resist rulers' threats and lures. Moreover, it is more costly to falsify an election the more ballots need to be eliminated or added. It is also more risky: If falsification flies blatantly in the face of public opinion, individual voters will be more willing to take to the streets in outrage when the opposition patrons (or their senior clients) call on them to do so. The more people who go out into the streets, the harder they become to suppress. And people who are genuinely committed to a cause will be much less likely to give up and go home at the authorities' first show of force.

In fact, Joshua Tucker has shown how competitive national elections actually make street protests more likely when authorities attempt to falsify an election result. When an election is clearly and outrageously stolen, and when a patron relies solely on coercive methods to "win" a vote, the time that results are announced provides something crucial for individuals considering whether to stick their necks out against the rulers: a single obvious moment for protest, a point when grievances against the incumbents are crystallized in a single issue (the election result), an instant when these individuals can "obviously" expect to find some safety in numbers. At such moments, these individuals also have before them a self-evident alternative to the incumbent authorities: the opposition candidate or candidates.[34] This is one reason protests have been so common almost immediately after crooked elections in patronalistic polities everywhere from the color revolutions in 2003–5 to Zimbabwe in 2007 to Iran in 2009, protests that often quite surprised observers in their scale and impact,

---

[33] This concurs with James C. Scott, "Patron-Client Politics and Political Change in Southeast Asia," *American Political Science Review*, v. 66, no. 1, March 1972.

[34] Joshua A. Tucker, "Enough! Electoral Fraud, Collective Action Problems, and the '2nd Wave' of Post-Communist Democratic Revolutions," *Perspectives on Politics*, v. 53, no. 5, 2007, pp. 537–53.

sometimes seeming to appear out of nowhere. This is part of the calculated risk that hybrid regime leaders accept when allowing elections to take place with opponents on the ballot.

This leads to a crucial observation: Because contested national elections give the masses this modicum of power, public opinion itself becomes an important influence on the expectations that lie at the heart of patronal strength. Popular support becomes one measure of a patron's power, of his potential to generate an official victory in important nationwide elections. This will not only influence whether voters will respond to a patron's promise that the right ballot today will be rewarded tomorrow and that the wrong one will land future punishment. It will also impact whether the patron's clients will actually carry out orders to put the political machine in motion in the first place. And the more people doubt that the machine will be put in operation, the fewer expect that it will win, thus making it in fact less able and less likely to win. In short, changes in public opinion, which can occur for all kinds of reasons exogenous to the power of the patron, become one of the factors capable of causing dynamism in expectations regarding a patron's future power, as discussed at the outset of this chapter. Contested elections, therefore, can greatly amplify the importance of public opinion in patronalistic polities despite the fact that these elections are routinely manipulated and falsified, and this amplification takes place primarily through public opinion's impact on the expectations of people in the polity.[35]

This sheds light on why the biggest of bosses – leaders whose brute machine power would seemingly obviate any need for it – so often appear obsessed with monitoring and bolstering their own public support.[36] Russia's Kremlin, for example, paid such close attention to measuring President Putin's public opinion ratings during the peak of his power in the 2000s that one Russian analyst memorably branded the regime itself a *ratingocracy*.[37] This term, of course, connotes that Putin's "ratings" were the central element in his own power despite the vast coercive apparatus developed and wielded by the former KGB colonel. And there is a great deal of evidence that it is in fact elections that make this attention to public support so acutely necessary in Russia just as it is in patronalistic polities as far away as Africa.[38]

---

[35] This contrasts, for example, with the much more limited role assigned to public opinion by Bueno de Mesquita et al., *The Logic of Political Survival*.

[36] While all rulers depend to some degree on popular support (Barbara Geddes, "What Do We Know about Democratization after Twenty Years?" *Annual Review of Political Science*, v. 2, June 1999, pp. 115–44), the argument here is that it plays a special role in patronalistic polities with contested national elections.

[37] Aleksandr Shmelev, in the roundtable discussion published as "Perspektivy avtoritarizma v Rossii," *Otechestvennye zapiski*, no. 6, 2007, pp. 41–61, p. 55. The Russian term he invented was *reitingokratiia*.

[38] Andrew Konitzer, *Voting for Russia's Governors* (Baltimore: Johns Hopkins University Press, 2005); Staffan I. Lindberg, *Democracy and Elections in Africa* (Baltimore: Johns Hopkins University Press, 2006).

In fact, much of public politics in patronalistic societies with contested elections is about creating both real popularity and, critically, the *impression* of popularity. Real popularity can be generated in relatively obvious ways, including providing tangible benefits (especially patronage and economic growth), connecting on the basis of common ideas, cultivating a personalistic appeal, and biasing media coverage.[39] Creating the impression of popularity can be accomplished through such techniques as the falsified opinion poll, forced displays of loyalty, and, again, biased media.[40] Mass rallies tend to play a special role, frequently being organized by both incumbent and opposition patrons as a way of signaling their ability to mobilize mass support.[41] At the same time, each side tends to portray the other's public demonstrations as paid-for rent-a-riots, not actually reflections of public opinion.

Impression management has its limits, however. At very low and very high levels, a patron's popularity becomes obvious in society, in which case attempts to claim otherwise will not be credible. And people are not infinitely manipulable by media. The Communist Party of the Soviet Union provides just one example: It completely monopolized major mass media but this did not stop overwhelming mass disaffection with its bosses leading up to Gorbachev. Thus while public opinion can be manipulated to some degree, the aspects that cannot be fully controlled by leaders remain an important independent driver of regime dynamics in patronalistic societies.

It is one thing to find that public opinion matters, but it is entirely another to understand where it comes from. This book is limited to the former task, showing how patterns and trends in public support for their leaders can shape expectations and hence regime dynamics, an effect that owes largely to the formal institution of contested elections. The pages that follow, therefore, will concentrate mainly on reporting evidence regarding the levels of leadership

---

[39] Timothy J. Colton and Henry E. Hale, "The Putin Vote: Presidential Electorates in a Hybrid Regime," *Slavic Review*, v. 68, no. 3, Fall 2009, pp. 473–503; Ellen Mickiewicz, *Television, Power, and the Public in Russia* (New York: Cambridge University Press, 2008); William Mishler and John P. Willerton, "The Dynamics of Presidential Popularity in Post-Communist Russia: Cultural Imperative versus Neo-Institutional Choice," *Journal of Politics*, v. 65, no. 1, February 2003, pp. 111–41; Daniel S. Treisman, "Presidential Popularity in a Hybrid Regime: Russia under Yeltsin and Putin," *American Journal of Political Science*, v. 55, no. 3, July 2011, pp. 590–609; Nicolas van de Walle, "Meet the New Boss, Same as the Old Boss? The Evolution of Political Clientelism in Africa," in Herbert Kitschelt and Steven I. Wilkinson, eds., *Patrons, Clients, and Policies: Patterns of Democratic Accountability and Political Competition* (Cambridge: Cambridge University Press, 2007) pp. 50–67, p. 56.

[40] Vaclav Havel, "The Power of the Powerless," in Paul Wilson, ed., *Open Letters: Selected Writings, 1965–1990* (New York: Vintage, 1992); Timur Kuran, "Now Out of Never: The Element of Surprise in the East European Revolution of 1989," *World Politics*, v. 44, no. 1, October 1991, pp. 7–48; Lisa Wedeen, "Conceptualizing Culture: Possibilities for Political Science," *American Political Science Review*, v. 96, no. 4, December 2002, pp. 713–28, p. 723.

[41] Paul D'Anieri, "Explaining the Success and Failure of Post-Communist Revolutions," *Communist and Post-Communist Studies*, v. 39, 2006, pp. 331–50; Graeme Robertson, "Managing Society: Protest, Civil Society and Regime in Putin's Russia," *Slavic Review*, v. 68, no. 3, Fall 2009, pp. 528–47.

popularity over key periods of time in each country and on showing how these relate to regime dynamics. Thus to some degree public opinion will be treated as an exogenous variable impacting these dynamics. Where possible, of course, the book will draw on existing research or local observers' reporting to explain why public support for given leaders is higher or lower, rising or falling, and to show that this variation does not derive from the very outcomes public opinion is being used to explain. But it leaves the task of finding systematic explanation of public support for future research.

This decision is based on the presumption, grounded in research in many countries of the world, that public opinion is in fact highly complex and cannot be explained with reference to one or two factors that would be easily measurable for the purposes of this volume. At the same time, this research also indicates that public opinion about leaders is not likely to be strongly endogenous to the other factors at the center of this book's attention, which, as will become clear later in this chapter, include the type of constitution and associated factors such as term limits. Instead, we expect public opinion to be related to such factors as the economy, campaigning, leadership performance, personal qualities of leaders, patterns of socialization, and ideational connections, just to name some.[42] Chapter 11 will return to an explicit discussion of what we have learned about public opinion, including an evaluation of whether this book is ultimately justified in treating mass support as an independent variable in its own right.

Constitutions

Just as elections have distinct meanings in highly patronalistic contexts, so too do constitutions play roles different from those they are widely understood to play in the West, even when on paper they look identical.[43] Classic social science research on political regimes tends to view constitutions as documents that stipulate a division of power that should then be followed, and debates center around whether that division has good or bad consequences or why this division might be observed or ignored in a given context.[44] Confronted with

---

[42] For example, on the complexity of American public opinion when it comes to voting, see Warren E. Miller and J. Merrill Shanks, *The New American Voter* (Cambridge, MA: Harvard University Press, 1996). There is little reason to expect post-Soviet peoples to be any less complex.

[43] Some of this section draws from Henry E. Hale, "Formal Constitutions in Informal Politics: Institutions and Democratization in Eurasia," *World Politics*, v. 63, no. 4, October 2011, pp. 581–617."

[44] Some classics in this voluminous literature include the exchange on constitutional design in the *Journal of Democracy*, republished in Larry Diamond and Marc Plattner, eds., *The Global Resurgence of Democracy* (Baltimore: Johns Hopkins University Press, 1996); M. Steven Fish, "Stronger Legislatures, Stronger Democracy," *Journal of Democracy*, v. 17, no. 1, January 2006, pp. 5–20; Linz and Stepan, *Problems of Democratic Transition*; Matthew Soberg Shugart and John M. Carey, *Presidents and Assemblies: Constitutional Design and Electoral Dynamics* (New York: Cambridge University Press, 1992); Cindy Skach, *Borrowing Constitutional Designs: Constitutional Law in Weimar Germany and the French Fifth Republic* (Princeton, NJ: Princeton University Press, 2005).

countries where constitutions are routinely disobeyed or changed by state leaders themselves, researchers sometimes understandably conclude that they have little effect or are even irrelevant.[45]

In highly patronalistic societies, however, constitutions can sometimes have their most powerful effects not by being formally observed, but instead by influencing expectations regarding how informal (nonconstitutional) politics is organized. Perhaps most importantly, they can shape the expectations of political elites as to who will *informally* (really) be the chief patron or patrons in the polity – even when the actual formalities of the constitution are regularly violated. Having particular impact is what the constitution signals regarding where the most power is likely to be concentrated.[46] We focus in particular on *presidentialist constitutions* (those formally stipulating a directly elected president as the most important source of executive power), *parliamentarist constitutions* (those giving an elected parliament the exclusive right to select the holders of significant executive power directly), and *divided-executive constitutions* (those that formally enshrine a balance between parliamentary and presidential power, assigning formally *independent* and roughly counterbalancing executive authority to each).

Because these different constitutional types matter most not by actually being followed, but by sending certain "signals" that shape how networks engage in constitution-disregarding as well as constitution-regarding behavior, one must not conflate these types with other typologies that might appear similar on the surface but that are developed for more formalistic studies of constitutions' effects. Most importantly, the idea of a divided-executive constitution does *not* boil down to widely used notions like "semipresidentialism" or even subtypes like "premier-presidentialism." A divided-executive constitution is something quite specific: Formal executive power not only is divided roughly equally between (usually) a president and prime minister, but (crucially) the prime minister is neither nominated/appointed nor removed by the president, instead serving formally at the sole pleasure of parliament, which is not readily subject to dissolution by the president.[47] That is, the key property of a divided-

---

[45] Levitsky and Way, *Competitive Authoritarianism*, pp. 79–80.

[46] No claim is made that this is the only way constitutions impact elite expectations with consequence for regime dynamics. The extent to which other institutions grounded in formal constitutions (such as judiciaries or parliaments) can play similar roles should be a subject for future research. On the judiciary in patronalistic societies, see Nathan Brown, *The Rule of Law in the Arab World: Courts in Egypt and the Gulf* (New York: Cambridge University Press, 1997); Tom Ginsburg and Tamir Moustafa, eds., *Rule by Law: The Politics of Courts in Authoritarian Regimes* (New York: Cambridge University Press, 2008); Maria Popova, "Political Competition as an Obstacle to Judicial Independence: Evidence from Russia and Ukraine," *Comparative Political Studies*, v. 43, no. 10, 2010, pp. 1202–29; and Alexei Trochev, *Judging Russia: Constitutional Court in Russian Politics* (New York: Cambridge University Press, 2008). On parliaments, see Gandhi, *Political Institutions under Dictatorship*.

[47] Or the president is severely constrained in this regard such that he or she effectively lacks this formal power, as when a constitution requires that the president nominate for prime minister the candidate chosen by the party that wins parliamentary elections, or when the president can

executive constitution is that the prime minister is chosen by parliament (which has a source of popular authority independent of the president) without significant formal dependence on the president for nomination, appointment, or staying in office. A semipresidential constitution, on the other hand, only stipulates that formal executive authority be divided between two offices (again, typically a president and prime minister).[48] Thus a constitution can be "semipresidential" even if the president has the power to nominate whomever she likes for prime minister and to fire the prime minister. The latter scenario clearly connotes that the president is the dominant figure, which the subsequent pages will show is crucial in the logic of patronal politics, and so such constitutions are classified simply as "presidentialist" by the present volume. Some might suspect that the subtype of semipresidentialism often called "premier-presidential" (by which the president cannot unilaterally remove ministers) might be essentially the same as a divided-executive constitution, but this is also not the case. Not only can premier-presidential systems include constitutions under which the president selects the prime minister, but "typically, presidents in premier-presidential regimes have the power to dissolve the assembly."[49] By the logic detailed later, such powers are quite likely to signal presidential dominance, which, as will be described, is crucial for understanding the effects of constitutions in patronalistic polities.

Presidentialist Constitutions

To understand how formal constitutional provisions – isolated from the conditions that gave them rise – can meaningfully shape informal political configurations, let us consider a hypothetical country that has two large, rival patronal networks perceived by all to wield equal informal power, plus some initially neutral elites (or smaller networks). Let us further assume that there is no history of a national government and no previous constitution, and then introduce to this mix a presidentialist constitution. At the moment the constitution is introduced, it is purely formal: There is nothing more behind the presidency than the piece of parchment on which it is described because the rival patrons' power is based solely on informal authority.

But as soon as it comes time to fill the office, even if the two networks intend the post to remain irrelevant, something interesting starts to happen: An *information effect* and a *focal effect* start to encourage the initially neutral elites in such a context to gravitate more to the presidency's occupant than

---

dissolve parliament but only under conditions that the president cannot generally create herself by virtue of formal presidential powers alone.

[48] Maurice Duverger, "A New Political System Model: Semi-presidential Government," *European Journal of Political Research*, v. 8, no. 2, June 1980, pp. 165–87; Steven D. Roper, "Are All Semipresidential Regimes the Same? A Comparison of Premier-Presidential Regimes," *Comparative Politics*, v. 34, no. 3, April 2002, pp. 253–72. See also Robert Elgie, *Semi-Presidentialism: Subtypes and Democratic Performance* (New York: Oxford University Press, 2011).

[49] Shugart and Carey, *Presidents and Assemblies*, pp. 23–4.

to its nonoccupant. The information effect essentially codifies the claim made earlier that institutions are likely to reflect current distributions of power in light of the fact that the presidency is an *indivisible good*, meaning that only one patron can occupy it.[50] If other elites are completely ignorant about the origins of the constitution, they will tend to assume that the network occupying it is at least marginally the more powerful one, and will tend to assume that others also make this assumption. The focal effect proceeds from the presidentialist constitution's conferral of the *symbolism* of supreme power upon its occupant. This – without assuming that the symbolism reflects *any* real power differential – can turn the presidency's occupant into a focal point[51] for elites who do not otherwise have any grounds for deciding whose network other elites will be most likely to support.

A presidentialist constitution's information and focal effects, then, can *resolve the coordination problem* for elites in generating a collective decision as to which of two otherwise equal patrons should be treated as the most powerful and hence accorded deference.[52] By deferring to the marginally stronger patron, each individual elite reduces her chances of winding up on the losing side and finding herself out of the richest patronage network. Recognizing that other elites are also likely to behave this way, each individual elite becomes less willing to challenge the president unless she faces some overriding other incentive to do so (such as knowledge of imminent excommunication from the patronal network for some exogenous reason). This, in turn, affords the patron who occupies the formal presidency an opportunity to manipulate it to her advantage, accumulating greater and greater informal power. Moreover, this greater informal power can then, if the president chooses, be directed by the president to enforce formal powers, including enforcement of the formal powers of the presidency and other laws that the president sees fit to support.[53]

As coordination dynamics play themselves out, then, the presidential patron can construct a system in which she dominates the polity by virtue of *both* formal and informal authority – usually in tight combination. Alternative "pyramids" of power under rival patrons generally face one of the following fates: liquidation, as their most marginal members progressively defect to the

---

[50] Juan Linz, "The Perils of Presidentialism," *Journal of Democracy*, v. 1, no. 1, Winter 1990, pp. 51–69; Alfred Stepan, Juan Linz, and Yogendra Yadav, *Crafting State-Nations: India and Other Multinational Democracies* (Baltimore: Johns Hopkins University Press, 2011), pp. 20, 199.

[51] Thomas Schelling, *The Strategy of Conflict* (Cambridge, MA: Harvard University Press, 1960).

[52] No claim is made that presidentialist constitutions are the only source of such effects. Formal statutes declaring a military dictatorship can do something similar for the top general, as can formal monarchic institutions for a monarch. Certain kinds of parliamentarist institutions can also have similar effects, as will be discussed later.

[53] On other ways in which informal institutions impact formal rules, see Anna Grzymala-Busse, "The Best Laid Plans: The Impact of Informal Rules on Formal Institutions in Transitional Regimes," *Studies in Comparative International Development*, v. 45, no. 3, September 2010, pp. 311–33; and Keith Darden, "The Integrity of Corrupt States: Graft as an Informal State Institution," *Politics & Society*, v. 36, no. 1, March 2008, pp. 35–60.

dominant network; co-optation into the larger pyramid; or operation at the margins of the system. The ultimate result is a single-pyramid system approaching the ideal type depicted in Figure 4.1.

Very importantly, this does not happen instantly or automatically as one would expect if constitutions worked by actually being followed. Instead, it reflects a complicated process of *coordination* among elaborate extended networks that takes significant *time* and effort as well as the leadership will and skill necessary to organize and manage it all. Moving too fast, attempting to exercise power before expectations regarding the president's future power and the role of each important network within it are sufficiently coordinated, can result in what might be called *authoritarian overreach*. That is, it can provoke a backlash by an aggrieved network that can quickly gain enough allies among those not yet integrated into the single-pyramid system to become politically lethal for the president. Over time, we would expect leadership to become more skilled at such coordination and management through processes of both learning and "natural selection." The nature of a given society's main networks is also likely to influence the rate and process by which the tendency to single-pyramid politics plays out as well as the specific form each single pyramid ultimately takes. The task of identifying and explaining different *types* of single-pyramid systems is not the focus of this volume, so is left for future work.

Divided-Executive Constitutions

Where presidentialist constitutions tend to encourage single-pyramid arrangements of patronal networks around the president, divided-executive constitutions complicate them and in fact promote network coordination in competing-pyramid arrangements (recall Figure 4.2). This effect is most powerful when separate networks occupy the two major executive posts. In terms of the information effect, the fact that one network occupies the presidency no longer signals that network's relative strength over all others, and in terms of the focal effect, it supplies no obvious way for elites to determine what other elites are likely to do and thereby coordinate their actions. Moreover, the divided-executive constitution provides a specific *alternative* focal point (the prime minister) around which patronalistic actors can coordinate, should they not be satisfied with any "deal" offered by the presidential network.

This, in turn, can have a multiplier effect by creating maneuvering room for "third" networks to become powerful by playing off one network against the other. And this provides cover for both opposition politics and simple honest work by professional journalists, political analysts, and pollsters, though it is likely that most of these will still succumb to the blandishments of one of the political machines. And because a wider range of information is more freely available, public opinion is likely to play a more direct and autonomous role in shaping elite expectations and hence political outcomes. Incumbent authorities have less incentive to attempt massive fraud because opposition pyramids control real resources that can be used to thwart it. The system resembles democracy more than presidentialist single-pyramid systems by virtue of vigorous competition and political openness, though the competition is typically fought by patronalistic means and is thus highly corrupt and far from the liberal ideal.[54]

These elite coordination problems engendered by a divided-executive constitution could be resolved if we assume a single person occupies both executive posts; the information and focal effects would again induce individuals and elites to orient themselves to the network that controls these two posts as opposed to one that controls neither. But if we remember from Chapter 2 that patronalistic networks are not unitary actors and instead consider that subpatrons may have their own ambitions to become top dog, it is not hard to imagine how the divided-executive constitution can work to promote divisions between a president and a prime minister (assuming they are separate people) even when they begin as part of the same network. Most importantly, the one who is subordinate within the network's informal hierarchy gains resources (an information effect that he may be the most powerful "subpatron" and focal status as a potential alternative patron) should he eventually decide to form his own network either from scratch or by splitting others off from his original network. The probability of such a schism in the dominant network will depend greatly on the personal characteristics of the two leaders and their mutual relationship, as well as the mechanisms holding the original network together. But some incentives are there for a split, and its likelihood will probably grow over time as relationships can sour under the various pressures and shocks that all such regimes face and as the top subpatron has time subtly to cultivate his own distinct patronalistic following.

Parliamentarist Constitutions

It is not the case, however, that constitutions providing still more formal powers to parliament generally create even more open configurations of patronal politics. Instead, parliamentarist constitutions occupy a certain middle ground between presidentialist constitutions (which tend to promote single-pyramid arrangements) and divided-executive ones (which tend to promote competing-pyramid arrangements). If a parliamentarist constitution creates a single top executive post, as many parliamentarist constitutions do, the network controlling it will have at its disposal nearly the same information and focal effects that arise from presidentialist constitutions and can be expected to promote single-pyramid politics. Only the formal means by which dominance is established is changed.

These distinctly parliamentarist formal means for establishing the dominance of a network, however, do tend to moderate the tendency toward single-pyramid politics by slightly altering presidentialist constitutions' information and (sometimes) focal effects. To win the top post under a

[54] Popova, "Political Competition"; Gulnaz Sharafutdinova, *Political Consequences of Crony Capitalism inside Russia* (South Bend, IN: Notre Dame University Press, 2010).

parliamentarist constitution, a patron must not only somehow gain a controlling majority of seats in the parliament for her allies, but then orchestrate a *separate* formal vote (this one in parliament) filling the chief leadership post. This modifies what elites perceive occupying the top spot to mean (information effect): Subpatrons within the dominant network and any alternative networks capable of acquiring some seats are expected to have additional opportunities to bargain with the chief authorities during this second formal vote. The result is likely to be that the resulting single pyramid will be perceived as somewhat less dominated by the chief patron and a bit more rewarding for autonomous activity. This "single-pyramid-loosening" effect of parliamentary constitutions is magnified to the extent that they also provide for additional powerful executive posts in addition to the prime minister (for example, a parliamentary speaker, a president elected by parliament, or ministers answerable directly to parliament rather than to the prime minister personally) that can be distributed (and bargained for) so as to seal power-sharing deals among networks credibly. The occupants of these posts can then serve as focal points for elites looking to coordinate efforts around other potentially powerful patrons. All this makes parliamentarist politics less a winner-take-all affair than is typically the case in the kind of presidentialist system discussed previously.[55]

Nonlinear Regime Dynamics

So far, we have primarily considered how contested elections and constitutions can induce linear regime dynamics: Unified-executive constitutions and decisive election victories tend to promote single-pyramid configurations of patronal networks while divided-executive constitutions and election stalemates create incentives for competing-pyramid network arrangements. But much of the dynamism in patronal politics is nonlinear. The conceptual framework developed so far helps us see that this nonlinear dynamism often reflects regular (sometimes cyclic) patterns, not just "chaos" or "instability."

Patronal Presidentialism

Let us take as a starting point a situation of *patronal presidentialism*, a useful term for an institutional framework in which a directly elected president is constitutionally established as a country's dominant political figure, but where the president's powers are not only formal but also informal, as is typical of highly patronalistic polities.[56] Let us also specify for starters that the patronal presidential system in question includes contested direct presidential elections. For reasons described previously, such systems tend to feature single-pyramid

---

[55] The theoretical logic of "patronal parliamentarism" will be elaborated in Chapter 10, where the case of Moldova is examined in depth.

[56] See Henry E. Hale, "Regime Cycles: Democracy, Autocracy, and Revolution in Post-Soviet Eurasia," *World Politics*, v. 58, no. 1, October 2005, pp. 133–65," on which some of the following discussion is based.

arrangements of patronal networks. Crucial to what follows is to recall that the president depends on elites (the subpatrons and most important clients in her network) to exercise her power since they are the ones who must first implement, enforce, and/or abide by presidential decisions. This means that – at least in principle – the elites could decide together to disobey the president, refusing to carry out her orders. In theory, they could even gang up and remove her from office. The elites face a tremendous barrier in any attempt to do this, though: They must act *collectively* since no one elite acting alone could hope to succeed in such an endeavor. The president is generally more powerful than the other elites precisely because she does not face such a collective action problem in her effort to stay in power. In fact, the president is powerful because the patronal presidency is an *institutionalized focal point* for determining elite expectations and thus directing elite collective action. So long as a president is regarded as firmly established in office, what she says and does determines what elites *expect* other elites to do, and the president can almost always be expected to direct elite collective action toward support of the existing regime.

The patronal presidency is not only a focal point for coordinated elite behavior, however. It is also an extraordinarily powerful weapon that can be used by its occupant to "divide and conquer" elites both within and beyond her closest set of clients, preventing almost any collective elite opposition action and thereby ruling successfully over them. The means used are very familiar to residents of these societies.[57] Appointed officials can be fired. Elected officials can be challenged or disqualified from the ballot when seeking reelection. Business elites can be denied licenses, deprived of state-linked business partners, or subjected to crippling inspections, fines, and closures at the partial hands of tax police, fire inspectors, health authorities, or other state agencies controlled by the president's network. Judicial elites can often be deprived of income or housing and can sometimes be removed from office. And, of course, everyone can be offered a bribe, prosecuted, or simply humiliated. So long as most presidential clients expect her other clients to follow instructions to engage in such regime-supporting activity, therefore, few tend to think it worthwhile to make themselves vulnerable by displeasing the president.[58] Thus even when allowed on the ballot, opposition parties and politicians frequently disappear from television news, encounter all kinds of technical and legal difficulties when running for office, and find it nearly impossible to locate companies or wealthy individuals willing to support their activities.

---

[57] For example, see the book by scholar-insider Mikhail N. Afanas'ev, *Klientelizm i Rossiiskaia Gosudarstvennost'* (Moscow: Moscow Public Science Foundation, 1997).

[58] Some elites nevertheless do challenge such presidents despite overwhelming odds. See Barbara Junisbai, "Market Reform Regimes, Elite Defections, and Political Opposition in the Post-Soviet States: Evidence from Belarus, Kazakhstan, and Kyrgyzstan," doctoral dissertation in political science, Indiana University, 2009.

The Single-Pyramid-Disrupting Effects of Lame Duck Status
The seemingly all-penetrating dominance of the single pyramid and the near-complete absence of significant organized opposition, however, obscure the fact that all this can change almost overnight the moment the elite expectations that underpin it change in a coordinated fashion. It often happens that elites come to expect a patronal president's imminent departure from power, and this can undermine the president's capacity to shape elite expectations as to how other elites in the system will behave even before the president actually leaves office. Elites anticipating the change begin thinking about a future without the old president, a future when the old president may not be capable of deciding who is punished and who is rewarded. The value of presidential promises and the gravity of her threats start to dissipate. The president can become a "lame-duck."[59]

Expectations of a patronal president's imminent departure can arise for any number of reasons. Sometimes, presidents fall gravely ill. Others simply grow so old that the end seems nigh.[60] Still others announce credible plans to leave their posts or face term limits that lead others to expect them to retire. A president can also suffer a massive drop in popularity (due to economic crisis, a highly damaging scandal, a loss in war, or major political missteps) that fosters expectations of faltering power.[61] We will return to these factors later in this chapter, discussing in more detail how they shape expectations.

This sort of "lame-duck syndrome" can generate tremendous centrifugal pressures within the dominant patronal network in advance of the anticipated moment of succession, pressures undermining presidential control and fraught with revolutionary potential. First, because the presidency is an indivisible good, different networks within the larger presidential network have great reason to start struggling openly against each other because only one of them can attain this large prize and the losers risk being cut out entirely by the winners. Second, while elites want most of all to wind up on the side of the person who wins any succession struggle, it may not be at all clear who this winner will be. The logic of single-pyramid rule in fact promotes this kind of uncertainty because presidents often intentionally divide and conquer elites precisely by creating some kind of balance among the main networks within the single pyramid.

---

[59] On connections between succession and revolution, see also Charles Tilly, *European Revolutions, 1492–1992* (Oxford: Blackwell, 1993), e.g., p. 18.

[60] Bueno de Mesquita et al., *The Logic of Political Survival*, pp. 312–13.

[61] While the East European communist regimes described in Chapter 3 were not presidentialist systems, their downfall nevertheless indicates that a patronal president's lame-duck syndrome can be brought on not only by issues related to succession, but also by external factors (such as changes in an outside patron state like the USSR under Gorbachev) that can create a sense a particular regime or regime type is doomed. Thus while this logic is *largely* about succession politics, it is not exclusively so.

An outgoing patron may try to put this uncertainty to rest by anointing a successor, but this is far from certain to work. Any networks not anointed are bound to fear that the heir, once in the presidency, will cut them off from power and wealth in an effort to establish his dominance and autonomy (a fear well grounded in world history). The president might offer them a power-sharing deal, but because the patronal presidency is an indivisible good, there is no position these networks could be given that would guarantee the security of their interests under the new leadership. In considering whether to back a sitting president's hand-picked successor, then, potential elite challengers must weigh the possibility of punishment for failing to do so against (a) the possibility that they would be punished anyway by the chosen successor even if they remained loyal and (b) the possibility that they could defeat the anointed one in a challenge and claim a greater share of state spoils for themselves. Anointing an heir, therefore, does not in and of itself solve the problem of succession.

Phases of Competing-Pyramid Politics

So long as the outcome is not already obvious, periods leading up to a specific point when patronal presidential succession is strongly anticipated (such as an election at the end of a president's expected final term in office) become increasingly likely to feature the breakdown of single-pyramid politics and the emergence of competing-pyramid arrangements of patronal networks. Weapons that once acted in unison to bolster the president – ranging from biased television news coverage to regional political machines to financial flows generated by corporate giants – can start to be directed by the different networks that control them against each other or even increasingly against the president. Other elites, uncertain about the ultimate outcome, are likely to find ways to hedge their bets, further undermining the presidential pyramid of power.

With the president losing control of the system's "political machinery," public opinion can become decisive in helping elites coordinate their expectations as to who is likely eventually to win a succession struggle. This is because victory requires orchestrating an official national election result, and for the reasons described earlier in this chapter, producing such a result is easier for candidates who can generate large numbers of actual, heartfelt votes. Elites seeking to back a winner – including potential defectors from within the presidential pyramid – are likely to see genuinely popular candidates as promising potential victors in a succession struggle. Such defectors, often having administrative or financial resources, can use these tools of patronalistic politics to shore up their candidate's popularity and to combat attempts by incumbent authorities to manipulate or fabricate an election outcome.

Street rallies frequently (though not always) become a prominent feature of such phases of competing-pyramid politics. Mass demonstrations can physically counter the machine tactics of rivals, create a crucial appearance of enthusiastic popular support, and demonstrate a network's power to mobilize resources.[62] And all this, in turn, can create a sense of likely victory, which will lure more elites to one's side and can then produce actual victory. It is not uncommon, therefore, for all major sides in a competing-pyramid interlude to rally people to the streets, and it is just as common for each side to belittle its rivals' demonstrations as being bought. Thus while protests and civic activists are often highly visible and can appear to be the lead actors, this logic suggests that they may well be playing a secondary role to that of elite network competition and coordination.[63]

Importantly, such periods of competing-pyramid politics typically start to emerge some time *before* the actual moment of anticipated succession. In this context, if a presidential election constitutes the actual moment when succession is expected, *other* kinds of elections occurring during the final presidential term can provide crucial tests of rival network strength that actually bring the struggle to a head. Where these produce a clear winner, they can resolve the problem of elite coordination that sustains the competing-pyramid situation, resulting in a cascade of elite defections to the winner. This helps explain why parliamentary elections are often very hotly contested even when the parliaments in question are widely perceived to be powerless. Such contests, in the apt term coined by Olga Shvetsova, essentially function as "elite primaries," preliminary contests that tell elites who has a serious chance to win the real prize, the presidential election.[64]

Such dynamics call into serious question standard approaches that treat "opposition strength," "civil society strength," or "elite unity" as independent factors impacting prospects for regime "transition," "transformation," "stabilization," or "consolidation." Rather than being exogenous factors, opposition, political civil society, and elite unity can become extremely strong or extremely weak almost overnight as changes in expectations generate cascades of elite defection from one side to another and create new spaces and new incentives for mass mobilization. These phenomena, then, are more likely to be *reflections* of fundamental regime dynamics than they are to be drivers of them in highly patronalistic polities.[65]

Another major implication is that revolutionary situations are far from unusual in patronal presidential systems. Instead, they are a natural result of this system's normal functioning.

---

[62] Robertson, *The Politics of Protest.*

[63] This is not to say they never play a lead role. But this book argues that it is far less often than some accounts would have it.

[64] Olga Shvetsova, "Resolving the Problem of Pre-Election Coordination: The 1999 Parliamentary Election as Elite Presidential 'Primary,'" in Vicki Hesli and William Reisinger, eds., *Elections, Parties and the Future of Russia* (New York: Cambridge University Press, 2003).

[65] On the endogeneity of opposition, mass protest, and public organization strength, see Robertson, *The Politics of Protest*, p. 12, and similarly Kuran, "Now Out of Never"; Douglass C. North, John Joseph Wallis, and Barry R. Weingast, *Violence and Social Orders: A Conceptual Framework for Interpreting Recorded Human History* (New York: Cambridge University Press, 2009), p. 128.

Regime Cycles

Caught up in the drama and even euphoria of such events, observers have frequently called them "democratic breakthroughs" when they result in the ouster of a sitting patronal president or her chosen heir. This is usually a mistake, because there is a strong tendency for a new single-pyramid structure that is just as "authoritarian" as the old one to arise. This is because a simple change in leadership does not remove the key elements that created the single-pyramid system in the first place: Society remains patronalistic, and the constitution remains presidentialist. Unless the change in leadership is accompanied by major constitutional change, therefore, we are likely to see a repetition of the dynamics that were described previously as being typical under presidentialist constitutions. Depending on how thoroughgoing the elite rupture is, the reemergence of single-pyramid politics will likely take time as various networks jockey for position in the new system and the new leadership gains its bearings, finds ways to remove its most threatening rivals (for example, in an "anticorruption" drive), and sorts out all the other complicated issues involved in establishing relations with other networks and organizing its own control (or is replaced in the event of overreach by a more competent patron).

This return to a single-pyramid system is likely even when the revolutionary winners and the masses that backed them genuinely hold democratic values. For one thing, so as to have a chance to win a power struggle in a patronalistic system, even true democrats usually find it necessary to make at least tactical alliances with "defectors" from the previous single-pyramid system whose commitment to democracy is questionable at best but whose interests are served by a change in power. Such nondemocratic allies are likely to resort to old methods once in power so as to ensure that they remain there. Lower-level elites, long accustomed to operating in a patronalistic hierarchy, are likely to be quite comfortable in complying, seeing the change at the top mainly as just a change in patron. Sincerely democratic presidents can also think they will be able to use the patronalistic weapons newly at their disposal "in the service of good" instead of evil. Why not use all means necessary to impose difficult reforms aimed at democracy, economic prosperity, and an end to corruption? Even in democracies, presidents rarely like having their reforms thwarted by opponents, and revolutionary leaders are more likely to regard their opponents as illegitimate, undeserving of democratic treatment because of their past service to a corrupt and authoritarian regime.

What we find, then, is that patronal presidential systems, so long as they include contested national elections, tend to produce *regime cycles*.[66] That is,

---

[66] The nonlinear or even cyclic dynamics of some regimes have also been observed by Guillermo O'Donnell, "Delegative Democracy," *Journal of Democracy*, v. 5, no. 1, January 1994, pp. 55–69; Charles Tilly, *Democracy* (New York: Cambridge University Press, 2007); and Sten Widmalm and Sven Oskarsson, eds., *Prometokrati: Mellan Diktatur och Demokrati* (Lund, Sweden: Studentlitteratur, 2010).

they take on strong authoritarian features as a single-pyramid system emerges, then appear to be democratizing as a lame-duck syndrome induces a competing-pyramid configuration of networks at a time of incumbent unpopularity, then revert to more authoritarian features with the reappearance of a single-pyramid network arrangement, which becomes vulnerable again as the next moment of anticipated succession approaches, and so on and so on. And all the while the *regime* itself, as "political regime" is defined in Chapter 1, has not fundamentally changed.

Regularity and Predictability of Regime Cycles

To the extent these cycles are regular, they become reasonably predictable, and regularity depends on the factors that drive expectations regarding the patron's potential future in power. Not all such drivers promote regularity, and some are probably best treated as exogenous and temporally arbitrary, generating cyclic phases of effectively random length. This tends to be the case for exogenous shocks that induce a lame-duck syndrome, as with Gorbachev's impact on East European communist regimes. Incapacitating illness can gradually or suddenly befall a sitting president, unexpectedly spawning expectations of his political demise. Leaders' own egregious missteps, or their voluntary decisions to leave power early, can also bring on lame-duck syndromes in an arbitrary fashion. Timur Kuran has also shown how some outbreaks of massive protest can be inherently unpredictable, dependent on individual thresholds for participation that are essentially unknowable in advance and that can combine quickly in chain reaction after essentially random triggers.[67] And protests that are large enough and that are widely understood to reflect broad opposition to the regime can potentially erode confidence in a leader's ability to survive long in office.[68] Such sources of lame-duck syndromes can facilitate irregular rather than regular regime cycles.

But many drivers of expectations tend to produce important regularities in patronal presidential regime cycles, and in fact there is good reason to expect them to dominate (though not entirely eliminate) the sources of irregularity. Elections, especially when combined with expectations of succession, turn out to be among the most important sources of regularity. One such combination would be an election in which an incumbent president makes clear in advance that he will not run. Potentially even more important, introducing even more regime cycle regularity, is the combination of elections with formal presidential term limits.[69] This is because term limits tend to generate at least some uncertainty

[67] Kuran, "Now Out of Never."

[68] Michael Bratton and Nicolas van de Walle, *Democratic Experiments in Africa: Regime Transitions in Comparative Perspective* (New York: Cambridge University Press, 1997).

[69] This corresponds with empirical findings reported in Alexander Baturo, *Democracy, Dictatorship, and Term Limits* (Ann Arbor: University of Michigan Press, 2014). This is surprising, however, for selectorate theory, which posits that formal term limits are irrelevant in nondemocratic regimes because they cannot be enforced (Bueno de Mesquita et al., *The Logic of Political Survival*, p. 319).

as to the president's staying in office beyond a certain point.[70] Crucially, the uncertainty generated by term limits is likely to rise in combination with other reasons people might expect a president to go. Indeed, term limits facilitate the *coordination* of any suspicions appearing for other reasons that the president might depart office but that do not involve a concrete point in time at which the departure is expected (and expected to be expected by others). They do this by providing a precise temporal focal point around which dissatisfied networks can coordinate activity aimed at removing the leader and by potentially opening up greater possibilities for themselves to gain the top office one day.[71]

It is important to recognize that the effects just described have little to do with any inherent legal power of term limits over presidents in patronalistic polities. While some patronal presidents observe them, others manage to extend or eliminate them as they approach. But so long as the president has not changed them, they not only suggest that the president may leave (disrupting presidentialist constitutions' information effect), but crucially pinpoint a *time* when this would happen (disrupting the focal effect of presidentialist constitutions that tends to promote single-pyramid systems). Formal presidential term limits can thus serve as focal points around which elites coordinate their expectations as to when *precisely* an unpopular, ill, aging, weary, or otherwise faltering president is most likely (a) to leave office voluntarily, (b) to be most vulnerable to ouster by other elites, and/or (c) to face other elites' attempts to oust him.[72] They also heighten presidential vulnerability to mass protest that may be ongoing. For similar reasons, we would expect that presidents facing other sources of vulnerability, such as low popularity, would be less able to remove formal term limits than would those not facing these other sources of vulnerability. That is, an attempt by an otherwise vulnerable patron to escape a formal term limit could itself become the focal point for coordinated elite defection. Formal term limits therefore serve to promote regularity among the

---

[70] Thus Tom Ginsburg, James Melton, and Zachary Elkins argue that, when established, term limits become the "default" expectation, though one that can be overcome by a variety of factors. Their potency owes largely to their clarity and simplicity, which the authors write make them a useful focal point for coordinated enforcement by other elites. Their comparative global study thus finds that term limits frequently have staying power, even in nondemocratic systems. See Tom Ginsburg, James Melton, and Zachary Elkins, "On the Evasion of Executive Term Limits," *William and Mary Law Review*, v. 52, no. 6, 2011, pp. 1807–73.

[71] Svolik (*The Politics of Authoritarian Rule*, pp. 92–4) argues (without specifying the precise mechanism) that formal term limits somehow make it more possible for other elites to monitor and thereby enforce power-sharing arrangements made with a dictator. The process he describes in the case of China, however, is compatible with the notion that term limits supply a focal point for coordinating the resistance of networks within the single pyramid that are dissatisfied with the prospect of the incumbent remaining in power.

[72] This very much recalls Tilly's analysis of how parliamentary elections served to coordinate previously randomly distributed contentious activity (which itself had a variety of causes) around specific points in time in Great Britain. Recall the earlier discussion of Tilly, "Parliamentarization of Popular Contention."

sources of lame-duck syndromes that would otherwise tend to occur irregularly or even randomly.

Another source of regime cycle regularity is likely to be the human life span, especially where term limits are not in place for the top executive posts. Reaching advanced age is widely associated with a decline in leadership capacity and the approach of the inevitable. The older a leader becomes when term limits are not in place, networks in a single-pyramid system are more likely to anticipate a nearing moment of succession. Age is a less precise generator of regime cycle predictability than term limits, however, because the exact date of a patron's decline or death is not known. This absence of an exact temporal focal point complicates coordinated succession-related elite defection. But what can be said is that as age advances, the chances rise that any given event will serve as a focal point for such coordination, ceteris paribus. Such events can include unexpectedly massive protests triggered by events that somehow happen to inspire emotion and capture the imagination, as per Kuran's logic.[73] Old leadership age can also raise the likelihood that any given election (even one not involving a term limit) can provide a focal point for coordinated network defection. While perceptions of what constitutes "old" are highly culturally specific, one would expect round numbers well beyond a country's official retirement age like seventy or eighty to be particularly potent. If term limits thus might be thought of as promoting regular "short regime cycles" that may last five to ten years, the human life span can be understood as a factor helping define regular "long regime cycles" that can (depending on when leaders initially take office) last for two or more decades.

All this generates some concrete predictions, each of which can be tested. Where term limits are established we would expect to find evidence of regular short regime cycles. Where they are not in place, we would expect to see signs of regular long regime cycles. To be sure, not all cycles will be of the regular sort even when term limits are in place. But the regular is likely to be more prominent than the irregular because term limits, elections, and the human life span serve to regularize many of the irregular sources of lame-duck syndromes. Moreover, this logic would also predict that the dominance of regularity over irregularity would not emerge *immediately* in the wake of state collapse on the scale of that described in Chapter 3, but would do so only after the initial turmoil has largely subsided. One reason is that current power is one of the most important sources of expectations of future power (as was discussed earlier), yet state collapse of the magnitude of the USSR's demise can create uncertainty even about what constitutes power in the first place. Until initial battles are won and lost, the nature of power is likely to remain unclear, giving more scope to all kinds of essentially random events in undermining network coordination around a leader. In addition, leaders with little experience to draw from under

---

[73] This will be discussed further in Chapter 12, with particular reference to the 2011 Arab uprisings and what were perceived as democratic breakthroughs in Africa in the early 1990s.

the new order are more likely to overreach or make other missteps that can effectively render them lame-ducks. As time passes, we would expect leaders to learn and those who do not learn to be increasingly eliminated through something like a natural selection process. We would therefore expect to find regime cycle regularity coming to dominate irregularity more clearly after the initial turmoil of a thoroughgoing state collapse subsides and after the first political battles are won and lost.[74]

At the same time, we must keep in mind that presidential networks experiencing a lame-duck syndrome do not always fall from power. Public opinion is still likely to decide which side wins succession-related struggles for reasons already described. And very high public support can nip any struggle in the bud. When the sitting incumbent is so popular that whomever he endorses would almost certainly win even a free and fair election, or when that endorsee has her own independent source of vast popularity, even that endorsee's rivals have incentive to avoid a hopeless rebellion and instead try to ingratiate themselves to the new leadership. When succession is not on the table, high popularity can make it seem even more pointless than usual to challenge the leadership in the name of democracy, since actual democracy would still result in the leadership's victory. Very high patronal presidential popularity, therefore, serves to reinforce elite coordination around the president and therefore to strengthen the single-pyramid system and make a regime seem more authoritarian.[75]

We thus arrive at some additional concrete predictions. One is that high presidential popularity should tend to extend the "closure" phase of a single-pyramid system. Another is that patronal presidents should be more subject to ouster when they are unpopular and facing an election that is associated with either a term limit or the president's own decision (for whatever other reason) not to run. If the patterns predicted in this section are not detectible, then the theory elaborated in the present chapter would be falsified.[76]

Regime Dynamics under Divided-Executive and Parliamentarist Constitutions

The regime cycles just described are those typical of highly patronalistic polities with presidentialist constitutions. Regime dynamics are likely to differ under divided-executive constitutions, which tend to promote competing-pyramid systems that will not generally experience strongly cyclic swings to and from states of political closure. Or, more precisely, *every* national election cycle is likely to

---

[74] One might even venture that this process represents the emergence of a political *regime* in the sense described earlier in this chapter.

[75] On the relationship between popularity and regime features, see also Daniel S. Treisman, *The Return: Russia's Journey from Gorbachev to Medvedev* (New York: Free Press, 2011).

[76] Or, at best for the theory, one could say that the incentives described by the theory tend to be overpowered by others to such an extent that they are not major drivers of regime dynamics, rendering the theory trivial.

involve significant levels of real political competitiveness and some expectation that an incumbent patron could be forced out of office, with a more direct role for public opinion in the process. Should one of the rival patrons in a competing-pyramid system attempt to usurp or cling to power by falsifying an election, a powerful opposition resistance effort is quite likely to occur and quite likely to succeed because there will be multiple sides with powerful political machinery at their disposal. "Revolutions" in such systems, therefore, will not be linked so closely with issues of succession, but will have more to do with ordinary and contingent attempts by leaders to steal or usurp power and efforts by oppositions to resist them by coordinating through elections.[77] Because of this, rather than a cyclic dynamic, one would expect to see fewer attempts to steal elections over time as would-be authoritarians learn how risky this can be.

As discussed, parliamentarist constitutions have many varieties that yield many different effects depending on the degree to which they concentrate executive power in a single post. "Unified-executive" parliamentarist systems, such as Great Britain's Westminster system, might be expected to facilitate regime cycles much as do presidentialist constitutions, though in a somewhat moderated form since the different networks in the single pyramid are likely to retain more autonomy for reasons described previously. This means that we would expect chief patrons to be more vulnerable to "revolutionary" ouster, meaning that popularity levels may not need to be as low for their downfall and that out-of-cycle revolutions may be somewhat more likely. That is, the amplitude and periodicity of the cycles could be shortened relative to presidentialism. At the same time, parliamentarist systems are less likely to have term limits, meaning that once a single-pyramid system does arise, it may lack this particular potential focal point for concerted elite action to subvert it. When parliamentarist constitutions create multiple roughly equal executive posts, they are more likely to be filled by different networks as part of a coalition, which could underpin competing-pyramid politics much as divided-executive constitutions do and thereby facilitate only weak cyclic dynamics.

The Dangers of Public Support

While contested elections ensure a strong role for public opinion in driving political outcomes in highly patronalistic societies, and while low support for patronal leaders can contribute strongly to their ouster, we must face the uncomfortable reality that *high* popular support for patronal bosses can pose a serious threat to political openness under all three kinds of constitutions.[78] This chapter has already discussed how high levels of leadership popularity

---

[77] On what kinds of opposition strategies are most likely to succeed in such settings, see Valerie J. Bunce and Sharon L. Wolchik, *Defeating Authoritarian Leaders in Postcommunist Countries* (New York: Cambridge University Press, 2011).

[78] For an example, see Cynthia McClintock, "Peru's Fujimori: A Caudillo Derails Democracy," *Current History*, v. 92, no. 572, March 1993, pp. 112–20. The author is grateful to Paul D'Anieri for calling his attention to this point at a conference discussion.

can enable a patronal presidency essentially to escape regime cycles, sustaining a single-pyramid system at a higher level of political closure. It turns out the high popularity is also a threat to political openness under other kinds of formal constitutions.

Under divided-executive constitutions, where public opinion regularly plays a strong role in determining electoral outcomes, a leadership popular enough to win control of both executive posts can potentially use this power to restore a single-pyramid system. This can be accomplished temporarily without a change in constitution so long as the network's two occupants of the two chief posts remain committed to the network and to the avoidance of splits. But such leaders are also typically in a strong position, at least at the moment when they capture both posts, to secure a change in the constitution to a presidentialist one just as presidentialism often arises out of strong leaders' seeking to consolidate their positions.

Under parliamentarist constitutions too, an overwhelmingly popular network can also capture a supermajority in a parliament, enabling it to build a single-pyramid system without any concessions made to other networks and also even potentially to change the constitution to reinforce its dominance. In fact, this is one of the great unrecognized perils of parliamentarism relative to divided-executive constitutions: A single election can result in one network's capture of all major executive posts. Under divided-executive constitutions, to capture all major executive posts, a network must typically win both a presidential and a parliamentary election, a task that can be even more difficult to the extent that they are held at different points in time. Overall, strong and enduring public support for a country's leaders can stabilize patronalistic polities, though this can often be a stability of political closure and a tyranny of the majority.

Conclusion

Patronal politics is dynamic. This dynamism cannot be dismissed as mere instability, but instead features significant degrees of regularity, even predictability, with the ultimate result the continuity of the underlying political regime. The key to this regularity is to understand patterns of expectations that can lead patronal networks to arrange themselves in different ways at different times. Some factors are inertial, as preexisting power arrangements can be expected generally to foster expectations of their own continuation as well as institutions that reflect those same power balances. But there are many sources of dynamism. Leaders frequently take calculated risks, and here we have emphasized the adoption of contested elections, which provide benefits to the regime but also open the door for not-completely-manageable public opinion to influence expectations and hence outcomes. Patrons are also not always in a position to alter formal constitutions, which are typically at least somewhat sticky and thus can have independent effects. In particular, we found that presidentialist constitutions tend to promote the gradual arrangement of patronal networks into single-pyramid patterns while divided-executive constitutions encourage competing-pyramid configurations, with different kinds of parliamentarist constitutions facilitating either single- or competing-pyramid arrangements depending on various circumstances.

Patronalistic regime dynamics are not limited to linear movement, however: Patronal presidentialism encourages movement toward the single-pyramid ideal type only so long as the chief patron is not expected to be leaving power anytime soon. These dynamics can dramatically reverse course when the sitting president becomes a lame-duck at the same time that he or his chosen heir does not clearly wield enough popularity to win a free and fair election if one were to occur. Succession-related uncertainty, typically occurring toward the end of formal constitutional term limits or toward the end of rulers' personal life cycles, though sometimes appearing for essentially random reasons, can produce a rapid transition to competing-pyramid politics. But this new state of affairs also cannot be expected to be long-lasting and is instead likely to be followed by a gradual restoration of a single-pyramid arrangement of networks under whoever wins the competition so long as a presidentialist constitution remains. Competing-pyramid situations underpinned by divided-executive constitutions can have more staying power, but they are also vulnerable to reversal if one network proves popular enough to capture both the presidency and the prime ministership. "Patronal parliamentarism" can also feature regular regime cycles akin to those associated with patronal presidentialism, though the extent to which this is the case depends heavily on the specifics of formal institutional design and the distribution of public support across the different networks in society.

The following chapters employ this logic of patronal politics to help solve some of the great puzzles of nearly a quarter-century of regime dynamics in Eurasia. Chapter 12 concludes with a discussion of patterns elsewhere in the world.

5

The Emergence of Networks and Constitutions

The most important actors in post-Soviet politics are not formal institutions such as "parliament," "political parties," or even "the KGB." Nor are they well-defined social collectivities like "ethnic groups." They are not even individual politicians, strictly speaking. Instead, the lead roles go to extended and loosely hierarchical networks led informally by powerful patrons. These patrons usually do boast prominent formal titles. They are the presidents and prime ministers of countries, the heads of prestigious state agencies, the owners of corporate mega-conglomerates, the elders of "clans," and the governors of provinces. But these titles, and the organizations to which they refer, do not define their networks.

Instead, their networks stretch far beyond and across formal institutional and identity boundaries. Ukraine's "oligarchs," formally businesspeople, spread their tentacles throughout society and the state, often claiming clients in all three branches of power through ties of family, friendship, and, of course, finance. The bosses of Russia's regional machines, formally governors, often controlled major shares of their regions' economies through kin or crony well into the 2000s. Top Azerbaijani ministers, formally civil servants, manage vast economic empires that often have little to do with their jurisdictions as listed on paper. Even networks frequently referred to as "clans" in Central Asia are neither coextensive with nor actually limited to kinship or ethnicity, a point that is frequently misunderstood by outsiders who take the local slang too literally.[1] The collective "actors" that actually wield the most influence in these countries, then, are precisely these extended informal networks, networks that

---

[1] This point is persuasively made through empirical research by Fredrik M. Sjöberg, "Competitive Elections in Authoritarian States: Weak States, Strong Elites, and Fractional Societies in Central Asia and Beyond," PhD dissertation, Department of Government, Uppsala University, Uppsala, Sweden, 2011; and Idil Tuncer-Kilavuz, "Political and Social Networks in Tajikistan and Uzbekistan: 'Clan', Region, and Beyond," *Central Asian Survey*, v. 28, no. 3, September 2009, pp. 323–34.

constitute institutions in their own right – just informal rather than formal ones. These networks are the building blocks of which post-Soviet Eurasia's power pyramids are made, the stuff of its *vertikals* of authority, the moving parts in its regime dynamics. For illustrative purposes, Figure 5.1 provides a stylized example of one such patronal network that will be discussed later in this volume, that of Moscow Mayor Yury Luzhkov as it was widely reported to exist circa 1998–9, on the eve of its challenge to Boris Yeltsin's incumbent network based in the Russian presidency.

No formal blueprints guide the actual assembly of these building blocks. Constitutions are not blueprints because the details of what they stipulate are not generally what come into being. In fact, in patronalistic societies constitutions are more likely to be ignored altogether than heeded for their own sake. But as the previous chapter demonstrated, one thing constitutions actually do is to influence the configuration of networks in a given country by shaping networks' expectations as to future power relationships, thereby resolving problems networks typically have in deciding how to coordinate their activities. That is, different constitutions tend to make it easier or harder for would-be chief patrons to assemble society's main networks into single-pyramid arrangements – almost as by endowing these networks with magnetic charges that can either repel or attract.

A crucial stage of our story, and the central subject of this chapter, is thus the emergence of the main networks and the initial constitutions that went on to influence Eurasian regime dynamics for more than two decades since the Soviet Union disintegrated. This disintegration, explained at the end of Chapter 3, provided the critical juncture that set these dynamics in motion – a moment of great flux when opportunities for creating new institutional arrangements were far greater than usual and when the opportunity costs of change were dramatically lowered because many old institutions had already been weakened or destroyed.[2] It did so by thoroughly shaking loose existing networks' expectations not only about where power lay in the larger polity, and not only about what the larger polity would even be, but about what the future was of these very networks themselves. Individuals who had invested years or even decades in particular patronal networks suddenly found themselves floating precariously freely, unsure whether there was much to be gained or lost by sticking with old hierarchies and able to join or form new ones without incurring much risk of punishment or the loss of sunk costs (though sometimes not knowing for sure whether sunk costs had already been lost). This was not a "clean slate" situation, but it was a moment of thoroughgoing uncertainty and discoordination.

---

[2] Ruth Berins Collier and David Collier, *Shaping the Political Arena: Critical Junctures, the Labor Movement and Regime Dynamics in Latin America* (Princeton, NJ: Princeton University Press, 1991); Seymour M. Lipset and Stein Rokkan, "Cleavage Structures, Party Systems, and Voter Alignments: An Introduction," in Lipset and Rokkan, eds., *Party Systems and Voter Alignments: Cross-National Perspectives* (New York: Free Press, 1967).

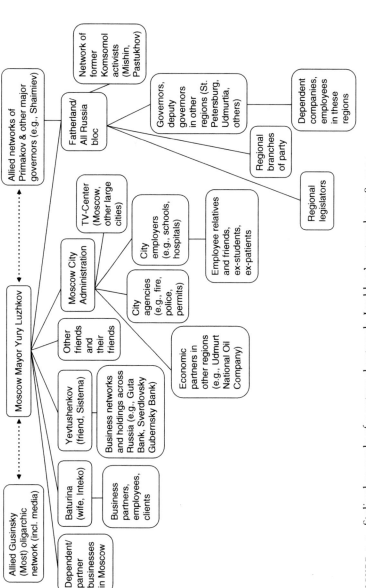

FIGURE 5.1. Stylized example of a patronal network: Luzhkov's network 1998–1999.

Note: This representation is for heuristic purposes only in illustrating the range of actors and some relationships that can be involved in patronal networks. It is thus not meant to be complete, and the categories and relationships depicted are in reality not so clear-cut or mutually exclusive. For example, the Sistema group was widely regarded to be a key backer of the Fatherland–All Russia electoral bloc effort, with the corporation's top leadership directly involved in the party's leadership, a relationship that is not captured by the stylized mapping of the network here. The simplification is for heuristic reasons: Including lines representing all relationships among all of the actors mentioned here would be extraordinarily messy.

While many fell into despair, creative entrepreneurs recognized opportunities to build something new out of the shaken networks, resources, and relationships that remained.[3] They thus sought to mobilize whatever personal "capital" they themselves possessed to string together new networks or mobilize old ones for new purposes, whatever these happened to be.[4] Some of these networks rose through business, others through state authority. Some emerged "from below" as the craftwork of start-up entrepreneurs or regional nabobs, while others were the spawn of central authorities, intended from the start to be individual pieces in a larger nationwide power pyramid. This same process ultimately produced new or amended constitutions in each state as the leaders who happened to be in place in the early 1990s scrambled to deal with immediate problems and figure out what was in their long-run interest so they could shore up their power.

Despite much diversity in the substance of the networks that emerged and the freedom that they in fact had to put their countries on very different tracks, a common process can be observed across most of the post-Soviet space: Emergence from Soviet rule meant a process in which economic power often fell into the grip of oligarchs, regional power consolidated under local machine bosses, state officials developed hierarchies able to influence national politics far beyond their narrow official mandates, and presidentialist constitutions became the nearly universal (if formal) law of the land. Radical market reformers and federal countries of the former USSR wound up with oligarchs, regional bosses, maverick state agencies, and (for the most part) presidentialist constitutions just as did the antimarket, unitary ones. What varied from country to country was nuance: whether the process was led from above or below, the form that the networks took, patterns of mesolevel alliance and aggregation of networks, the specific nature of their subordination to the state, and how and when (with rare exception) presidentialist constitutions came about. But nuance, it turns out, was not very consequential in driving the larger picture of regime dynamics in Eurasia, as subsequent chapters will show. It is important, then, not to let the nuances – interesting as they may be – distract us from the more fundamental process at work across virtually the whole post-Soviet space after independence.

The Formation of Corporate Conglomerates (Oligarchs)

Post-Soviet economic transition in almost every Eurasian country produced a set of business barons popularly known as "oligarchs," tycoons whose networks extended far beyond business and ran deep into politics. Some of these

---

[3] Anna Grzymala-Busse and Pauline Jones Luong, "Reconceptualizing the State: Lessons from Post-Communism," *Politics & Society*, v. 30, no. 4, December 2002, pp. 529–54.

[4] Georgi Derluguian, *Bourdieu's Secret Admirer in the Caucasus: A World Systems Biography* (Chicago: University of Chicago Press, 2005).

"oligarchic" networks were based in the private sector; others developed and operated primarily out of official state positions.[5]

The earliest private-sector oligarchs got their start by exploiting loopholes (nay, gaping lacunae) in the USSR's first efforts to reform property rights and liberalize the economy. Their breakthrough occurred with the revolutionary 1988 Law on Cooperatives, which legalized non-state-owned business in industry, commerce, and banking. Some began innocuously enough. Seeing opportunity and little regulation, mathematician Boris Berezovsky turned himself into a used car dealer, traveling to Western countries to buy up foreign cars, transport them back home to Russia, then resell them at huge markups. Others made their first fortunes by taking advantage of their positions in Soviet institutions. Mikhail Khodorkovsky, for example, put his position in the Communist Youth League (Komsomol) to good use, using it as cover and as a source of connections for a variety of money-making schemes that began with a disco and youth café and ultimately led to the founding of his bank, Menatep. A third path to initial riches was the insider deal. Vladimir Gusinsky, for example, plied his connections to Moscow city hall to win lucrative rights for his Most Bank to manage municipal accounts in place of the state banks that had previously handled them. Similarly, midlevel trade official Vladimir Potanin started Interros, a foreign trading company.[6]

These and analogous figures across the Soviet Union then found themselves in prime position to buy up even more valuable assets after 1991, when many of the newly independent governments started selling them off or giving them away and began market reforms in earnest. Russia's moguls were the most (in)famous, reaching the political stratosphere with the "loans-for-shares" scheme: They lent Yeltsin a reported $1 billion for his desperate 1996 reelection campaign in return for the right to organize auctions for some of Russia's most lucrative assets, including those in oil and metals. The bankers were then reported to have essentially rigged the auctions and walked away with the property. In the process, Khodorkovsky acquired Yukos (Russia's second-largest oil company), Berezovsky got the Sibneft oil concern, and Potanin, who had already used his family connections in the government to score his bank a monopoly on processing Russian customs payments in the early 1990s, won Norilsk Nickel, the world's largest nickel producer. Some accumulated major media assets, as Berezovsky gained 49 percent of Russia's biggest television channel and Gusinsky founded NTV, an independent television network, and a

---

[5] Henceforth, following popular usage in most of these countries, we will use the terms "oligarch" and "oligarchic" without quotation marks to refer simply to a big businessperson with reputedly important political connections, influence, or aspirations.

[6] Juliet Johnson, *A Fistful of Rubles: The Rise and Fall of the Russian Banking System* (Ithaca, NY: Cornell University Press, 2000); David Remnick, *Resurrection: The Struggle for a New Russia* (New York: Random House, 1997); David Hoffman, *The Oligarchs: Wealth and Power in the New Russia* (New York: PublicAffairs, 2002).

few owned whole stables of newspapers and magazines.[7] These business-based networks began penetrating political organs as soon as the opportunity arose. Indeed, it was a common practice for political parties to take corporate representatives onto their electoral candidate lists in return for donations, and some business figures won elections directly as territorial representatives in both local and national legislatures.[8] Even the Communist Party proved capable of attracting money from both Khodorkovsky's Menatep and Potanin's Interros after demonstrating its electoral clout in 1995.[9] Other ties involved the construction of mutually convenient personal relationships with those in power, as with Berezovsky's reputed relationship with President Yeltsin's daughter, Tatiana Diachenko, though surely the tightness of this relationship should not be exaggerated, as has often been done in the public imagination.[10] Some state- or partially state-owned enterprises also emerged at the center of important corporate-based networks by the end of the 1990s, including the gas giant Gazprom, the major oil concern LUKoil, and the electricity monopoly Unified Energy Systems. The result was a series of sprawling corporate networks that spanned many industries, formal institutions, and territories within Russia, each competing with the other for power, privilege, and resources.

Several other former Soviet republics resembled Russia in that oligarchs rose through the private sector in collaboration with arms of the state to create powerful political networks that reached through different economic sectors, mass media, parties, and state institutions. One of Ukraine's most famous, Yulia Tymoshenko, got her start creating a network of video salons in late Soviet Dnipropetrovsk by exploiting the connections of her father-in-law, a senior city party official, and working closely with Serhy Tihipko, the region's Komsomol chief. Tihipko resembled Russia's Khodorkovsky in turning his Komsomol capital into a highly successful bank, Pryvat Bank, with partner Ihor Kolomoisky.[11] The real money, however, was in trading energy-related products. This included gas from Russia obtained through complex barter arrangements, taking advantage of the crisis of nonpayments among state enterprises that had resulted

---

[7] Henry E. Hale, *Why Not Parties in Russia: Democracy, Federalism, and the State* (New York: Cambridge University Press, 2006); Johnson, *Fistful of Rubles*, p. 121; Jerry F. Hough, *The Logic of Economic Reform in Russia* (Washington, DC: Brookings, 2001), p. 41. For a somewhat different interpretation of the loans-for-shares deal, see Daniel S. Treisman, *The Return: Russia's Journey from Gorbachev to Medvedev* (New York: Free Press, 2011).

[8] Hale, *Why Not Parties in Russia*.

[9] Sergei Kolmakov, "The Role of Financial Industrial Conglomerates in Russian Political Parties," *Russia Watch* (Harvard University), no. 9, January 2003, p. 16.

[10] As is well demonstrated by Timothy J. Colton, *Yeltsin: A Political Life* (New York: Basic Books, 2008), pp. 422–5.

[11] Sergei Zhuk, *Rock and Roll in the Rocket City: The West, Identity, and Ideology in Soviet Dniepropetrovsk, 1960–85* (Washington, DC: Woodrow Wilson Center Press, 2010), pp. 298–301. Zhuk further points out that Tymoshenko and Tihipko, as with many other highly successful post-Soviet politicians from Dnipropetrovsk, were initially part of a "discotheque mafia" devoted to obtaining access to Western cultural production, especially rock music.

in part from IMF-backed budget strictures.[12] Tymoshenko thus mobilized her salon capital to become head of Ukraine's United Energy Systems, earning the unofficial title of Ukraine's "gas princess."[13] Tihipko's and Kolomoisky's Pryvat made fortunes trading in oil products; Viktor Pinchuk's Interpipe in gas and oil-and-gas products; the "Kyiv clan" of Hryhory Surkis, Viktor Medvedchuk, and (Russian citizen) Konstantin Grigorishin in oil products and privatized regional electricity monopolies; and Rinat Akhmetov's Donetsk-based System Capital Management in coal and gas.[14] These initial fortunes typically led to expansion in a variety of other sectors. For example, the Industrial Union of the Donbass (ISD), founded by metallurgist Serhy Taruta and Donetsk Deputy Governor Vitaly Haiduk in 1995, gained a local gas supply monopoly in 1996 and later translated it into massive metals industry holdings. Some began outside the energy sector, of course: Kyiv-based Petro Poroshenko, for example, became the country's candy king and later controlled a large business network that prominently included a bank and the all-news Fifth Channel television station.[15]

As in Russia, these figures became popularly known as "oligarchs," whose informal networks penetrated a whole range of formal institutions far beyond their economic holdings. Ukrainian political parties, even more than Russia's, were widely understood as the political vehicles for specific oligarchic groups. The Party of Regions, as perhaps the most prominent example, grew out of Akhmetov's Donetsk-based "clan."[16] It is important to recognize that the rise of Ukraine's oligarchs was not a purely spontaneous process, but as in Russia also involved close collusion with elements of the state, primarily under Leonid Kuchma during his time as prime minister and later president.[17]

Differentiated networks similarly developed out of economic interests in Kazakhstan, Kyrgyzstan, and Armenia, though in each case with stronger roles for the president's own relatives. Kyrgyzstan's President Askar Akaev cites Polish free-marketeer Leszek Balcerowicz as his inspiration in launching a major privatization initiative in the early 1990s, but paid at least as much attention to ensuring his personal control over the resulting economic networks.[18] Whereas in Russia it was Yeltsin's close political ally, Anatoly Chubais, who put state

[12] Igor' Guzhva and Yuriy Aksenov, "Deti gaza i stali," *Ekspert* (Russia), October 11, 2004; Heorhii Kas'ianov, *Ukraiina 1991–2007: Narysy novitn'oii istorii* (Kyiv: Nash Chas, 2008), pp. 71–4. On the causes of such barter arrangements, see David Woodruff, *Money Unmade* (Ithaca, NY: Cornell University Press, 1999)

[13] Zhuk, *Rock and Roll*, p. 301.

[14] Kas'ianov, *Ukraiina 1991–2007*, pp. 71–4.

[15] Guzhva and Aksenov, "Deti gaza i stali."

[16] Andrew Wilson, *Virtual Politics: Faking Democracy in the Post-Soviet World* (New Haven, CT: Yale University Press, 2005), pp. 134–40.

[17] Kas'ianov, *Ukraiina 1991–2007*, pp. 76, 172; *Zerkalo Nedeli*, no. 5, February 11, 2006.

[18] Askar Akaev, *Trudnaia doroga k demokratii* (Moscow: Mezhdunarodnye otnosheniia, 2002), pp. 136–7.

property into private hands, in Kyrgyzstan it was Askar Sarygulov, cousin of President Akaev's wife.[19] A variety of relatives soon monopolized many sectors, from real estate to media, it was widely reported. And what they did not initially own, presidential family members over time gained a reputation for acquiring by making "offers" that the original owners could not refuse.[20]

Not all emerging oligarchs were Akaev relatives, however. Some rose to the economic elite by using other ties to the state.[21] One of the most important bases for political-economic networks in Kyrgyzstan was the set of massive bazaars that attracted traders from all around Central Asia. For instance, Askar Salymbekov and Kubatbek Baibolov, former Komsomol and KGB men, founded Bishkek's Dordoi bazaar, with Salymbekov (also variously serving as governor of Naryn and mayor of Bishkek) diversifying into construction materials, textiles, bottled water, and other products and services.[22] Others had economic origins in organized crime. Wrestler Bayaman Erkinbaev, as one of the most important reputed examples, got his start as a strongman racketeer, eventually becoming Kyrgyzstan's main "drug baron" (an enormously lucrative enterprise connecting Afghan poppy with Eurasian markets), primary owner of mainstream assets like the profitable Karasuu bazaar in southern Kyrgyzstan (through its privatization in the mid-1990s), and a member of parliament.[23] Kyrgyzstan's governments kept some of the biggest potential sources of cash and patronage in state hands during the 1990s, however, including the country's hydroelectric industry.[24] State-appointed heads of these enterprises could also play important political roles, however, so Akaev generally tried to put in these places people he believed he could trust. Thus his in-law Dastan Sarygulov became head of Kyrgyzstan's single most lucrative enterprise, the state-owned gold company Kyrgyzaltyn, during the 1990s.[25]

Kazakhstan's most extensive economic empires grew primarily out of its vast energy complex, metals, and banking. But unlike Russia's, which created a large set of domestic energy barons in the private sector, Kazakhstan's leadership sold rights to its various oil and gas fields primarily to major foreign corporations, such as Chevron (after an initial period when a state company

[19] Martha Brill Olcott, *Central Asia's Second Chance* (Washington, DC: Carnegie Endowment for International Peace, 2005), p. 112.

[20] Olcott, *Central Asia's Second Chance*, pp. 106–12.

[21] Usenaly Chotonov, *Suverennyi Kyrgyzstan: vybor istoricheskogo puti* (Bishkek: Kyrgyzstan, 1995), pp. 118–19.

[22] Gul Berna Ozcan, *Building States and Markets: Enterprise Development in Central Asia* (Houndmills: Palgrave Macmillan, 2010), p. 112.

[23] Alexander Kupatadze, *Organized Crime, Political Transitions, and State Formation in Post-Soviet Eurasia* (New York: Palgrave Macmillan, 2012), especially pp. 145–8; Regine Spector, "Securing Property in Post-Soviet Kyrgyzstan," *Post-Soviet Affairs*, v. 24, no. 2, April–June 2008, pp. 149–76, p. 169.

[24] *TsentrAziia*, February 23, 2009, 08:13.

[25] Olcott, *Central Asia's Second Chance*, pp. 106–12.

held these assets).[26] This meant that Kazakhstan's initial oligarchs emerged not in energy production itself, as did many in Russia, but in the industries that serviced it, especially banks, as well as the mining sector, where materials could be smuggled for big profits to China, and commerce. It also meant that state leaders and their relatives reaped huge gains relative to other Kazakhstan entrepreneurs in the form of income (both on and off the books) paid by the foreign companies to the state for these rights, not to mention income from those state shares in the industry that remained. This, in turn, enabled them to snap up a wide variety of other economic holdings for themselves during extensive privatization conducted in the 1990s.[27]

By the end of the 1990s, therefore, two of the most powerful oligarchic networks were led by President Nursultan Nazarbaev's family members, his son-in-law Timur Kulibaev (who started in banking before managing major energy-related enterprises in both the state and private sectors), and the team of the president's daughter, Dariga Nazarbaeva (who by one count controlled four-fifths of all television and radio outlets and many newspapers in the country), and her husband, Rakhat Aliev (Kazakhstan's "sugar king," who led the financial police during 1997–9 and held other lucrative assets in vodka sales and leisure).[28] Major bank-centered networks with vast industrial holdings and political connections by the end of the 1990s included Aleksandr Mashkevich's Eurasia Bank Group (banking, metals); Nurzhan Subkhanberdin's Kazkommerts group (banking, oil processing); Mukhtar Abliazov's Astana-Holding (banking, metals, media); and Bulat Abilov's Butia group (trading).[29] Most of these figures were also tightly tied to Nazarbaev, and some served in government themselves, as did Abliazov as minister of energy, industry, and trade.[30] Among those building up substantial wealth while rising to occupy top state posts under Nazarbaev during the 1990s was former Kazakhstan Komsomol leader

[26] Pauline Jones Luong and Erika Weinthal, *Oil Is Not a Curse: Ownership Structure and Institutions in Soviet Successor States* (New York: Cambridge University Press, 2010).

[27] Jones Luong and Weinthal, *Oil Is Not a Curse*; Sebastien Peyrouse, "The Kazakh Neopatrimonial Regime and Its Actors: Balancing Uncertainties among the 'Family,' Oligarchs and Technocrats," *Demokratizatsiya: The Journal of Post-Soviet Democratization*, v. 20, no. 4, Fall 2012, pp. 345–70; Scott Radnitz, "The Color of Money: Privatization, Economic Dispersion, and the Post-Soviet 'Revolutions,'" *Comparative Politics*, v. 42, no. 2, January 2010, pp. 127–46.

[28] Alexandra George, *Journey into Kazakhstan: The True Face of the Nazarbayev Regime* (Lanham, MD: University Press of America, 2001), pp. 34–5; Barbara Junisbai, "A Tale of Two Kazakhstans: Sources of Political Cleavage and Conflict in the Post-Soviet Period," *Europe-Asia Studies*, v. 62, no. 1, March 2010, pp. 235–69, pp. 248–9; Sebastien Peyrouse, "The Kazakh Neopatrimonial Regime."

[29] George, *Journey into Kazakhstan*, pp. 34–6; Junisbai, "A Tale of Two Kazakhstans," pp. 248–9; Barbara Junisbai and Azamat Junisbai, "Democratic Choice of Kazakhstan: A Case Study in Economic Liberalization, Intraelite Cleavage, and Political Opposition," *Demokratizatsiya: The Journal of Post-Soviet Democratization*, v. 13, Summer 2005, pp. 373–92; Martha Brill Olcott, *Kazakhstan: Unfulfilled Promise* (Washington, DC: Carnegie Endowment, 2002), pp. 136–8, pp. 157–8, 282.

[30] Olcott, *Kazakhstan*, pp. 138, 158.

Imangali Tasmagambetov.[31] Thus even in formal terms, the distinction between state-based and private-sector-based oligarchic networks was a fuzzy one in Kazakhstan.[32]

Armenia's first president, Levon Ter-Petrossian, presided over extensive privatization policies that created oligarchs in banking, beverage production (including the country's celebrated cognacs), and the food industry. The central role played by personal ties is nicely illustrated by the fact that two presidential brothers (Telman, the oldest, and Petros, the second-oldest) served as top officials on privatization commissions, and Telman was himself a factory director known for his influence over the economy.[33] Through this privatization process, Khachatur Sukiasian, a young factory director who entered the car wash and auto parts business in 1989, created the massive SIL Concern with assets in banking, brewing, construction, dining, and manufacturing.[34] Others, such as Gagik Tsarukian, who started his business career in the early 1990s in agriculture, reached new heights in the latter 1990s (in his case, expanding into alcoholic beverages, chemical production, and other manufacturing and services).

Despite delays and complications owing to territorial conflicts, powerful economic elites similarly arose through the state-private sector nexus in Moldova, its breakaway region of Transnistria, and de facto independent Abkhazia (de jure part of Georgia). Like many other post-Soviet states, Moldova had opened up its economy broadly to private enterprise in the 1990s, though not privatizing what Charles King calls the "mammoth Soviet-era factories" that were formally part of the republic. These wound up in separatist Transnistria, which independent Moldova has never controlled.[35] The result in Moldova was a pool of individuals with moderate holdings who were soon overshadowed by such figures as Anatol Stati, who founded the highly lucrative oil trading business ASCOM with assets in Central Asia's energy sector, or those with strong connections to the state who later accumulated significant private sector holdings, such as the son of President Petru Lucinschi, Chiril.[36] Particularly important in highly rural rump Moldova was also a large network of agricultural elites (including many former Communist Party officials connected with the

[31] Sebastian Schiek and Stephan Hensell, "Seeing like a President: The Dilemma of Inclusion in Kazakhstan," in Susan Stewart, Margaret Klein, Andrea Schmitz, and Hans-Henning Schroder, eds., *Presidents, Oligarchs, and Bureaucrats: Forms of Rule in the Post-Soviet Space* (Burlington: Ashgate, 2012), pp. 203–22, pp. 208–9.

[32] John Schoeberlein, "Between Two Worlds," *Harvard International Review*, v. 22, no. 1, Winter 2000, pp. 56–61; *TsentrAziia*, February 23, 2009, 08:13.

[33] Nora Dudwick, "Political Transformations in Postcommunist Armenia: Images and Realities," in Karen Dawisha and Bruce Parrott, eds., *Conflict, Cleavage, and Change in Central Asia and the Caucasus* (New York: Cambridge University Press, 1997), pp. 69–109.

[34] *Kommersant-Den'gi*, March 31, 2003; Olga Vlasova, Gevorg Davtian, and Gevorg Mirzaian, "Desiat' dnei na ploshchadi Svobody," *Ekspert*, No. 10, March 10–16, 2008, pp. 26–8.

[35] Charles King, *The Moldovans: Romania, Russia, and the Politics of Culture* (Palo Alto, CA: Hoover Institution Press, 2000), p. 207.

[36] *Financial Times*, FT.com, May 29, 2009, 03:00; *Nezavisimaia Moldova*, February 4, 2009.

agricultural complex) that became represented in the formal party arena as the Agrarian Democratic Party.[37] Two of this network's most visible representatives with clear agrarian roots were Mircea Snegur, Moldova's first president, and Andrei Sangheli, a future prime minister, while others, including future president Lucinschi, were connected primarily through shared high-level service in the Moldovan Communist Party, of which Lucinschi had been first secretary 1989–91.[38]

After Moldova began allowing Transnistrian firms to export a certain amount of goods to world markets through Moldova, Transnistria's economy enjoyed a boom and its authorities launched a process of privatization, boosting the development of two major oligarchic networks in the breakaway region.[39] Longtime Transnistria President Igor Smirnov controlled one, which included the territory's Gazprombank and a cluster of other businesses run by Smirnov's family, including his son, Oleg.[40] The other was the Sheriff group, with its own media, supermarket chain, network of gas stations, telecommunications firm, soccer team, and a collection of privatized enterprises that would grow over the next decade. Sheriff was founded soon after Transnistria broke with the rest of Moldova and owned by two former Soviet officers initially friendly with President Smirnov, Viktor Gushan and Ilia Kazmaly.[41] By some accounts, much of its initial fortune arose from illegal trade during the 1990s, including contraband shipped to Ukraine, in collusion with the president's family.[42]

Despite President Eduard Shevardnadze's own relatively clean reputation, Georgia followed a similar path, right down to prominent involvement of immediate presidential family members in the economy. The "Shevardnadze clan" included nephew Nugzar (oil imports, casinos) and his connections through the Komsomol, and the networks of in-laws from the Akhvlediani

---

[37] Igor Botan, executive director of the analytical center ADEPT, author's interview, Chisinau, Moldova, June 30, 2009. See also ADEPT, "Agrarian Party of Moldova," http://www.parties.e-democracy.md/en/parties/pdam/, accessed June 20, 2012.

[38] William Crowther, "Moldova: Caught between Nation and Empire," in Ian Bremmer and Ray Taras, eds., *New States New Politics: Building the Post-Soviet Nations* (New York: Cambridge University Press, 1997), pp. 316–52, pp. 323–4.

[39] Kimitaka Matsuzato, "Nepriznannye gosudarstva v makroregional'noi politike chernomorskogo poberezh'ia," in Matsuzato, ed., *Pridniestrov'e v makroregional'nom kontekste chernomorskogo poberezh'ia* (Sapporo: Slavic Research Center, 2008), pp. 5–21, p. 19; expert at Pridniestrovsky State University, author's interview, Tiraspol, March 26, 2009.

[40] Rebecca Chamberlain-Creanga, "Politics without a 'State': Electoral Reform and Political Party Formation in Secessionist Transnistria – and Its Implications for Conflict Resolution," paper presented at the Annual Meeting of the American Association for the Advancement of Slavic Studies, 2007, p. 3.

[41] Margarita M. Balmaceda, "Privatization and Elite Defection in de Facto States: The Case of Transnistria, 1991–2012," *Communist and Post-Communist Studies*, v. 46, no. 4, pp. 445–54, especially p. 449; Chamberlain-Creanga, "Politics without a 'State,'" pp. 3–4; Daria Isachenko, "Hyperreality of Statebuilding: The Case of Transdniestrian Region of Moldova," draft paper presented at the International Studies Association Annual Convention, 2008, pp. 7–8.

[42] Isachenko, "Hyperreality of Statebuilding," p. 7.

(export-import, the Poti port, and reputedly also energy) and Jokhtaberidze (telecommunications) families.[43] Some of Georgia's other most important emerging oligarchic networks were similar to the Armenian ones, extending out of the Caucasus's rich array of consumer products and services through privatization or other forms of close collaboration with state officials after the wars of the early 1990s.[44] Thus Levan Gachechiladze converted a late Soviet career in commerce to found the giant Georgian Wines and Spirits (GWS) corporation in 1993, and medical doctor David Gamkrelidze started the insurance company Aldagi in 1991, three years later persuading the government to grant it a lucrative monopoly on corporate fire and automobile insurance (required by law) as well as commercial transit within Georgia.[45] Other oligarchs operated out of the state, as was the case most notoriously with the vast shadow economic empire run by Kakha Targamadze from the Ministry of Internal Affairs – an empire reputedly involving everything from drugs to fuel to sports, not to mention various forms of rent seeking involving the exploitation of formal police powers.[46] Georgia's two richest oligarchs, however, both made their initial fortunes in Russia before becoming involved in Georgian politics much later. Badri Patarkatsishvili, a former mechanic, started on the road to riches in Russia's car sales business as part of Berezovsky's oligarchic network (by some accounts supplying links to organized crime) before returning to Tbilisi in 2000. He bought aggressively into the Georgian market, most prominently founding the Imedi media empire.[47] Similarly, the almost fanatically private Bidzina Ivanishvili made his way to wealth by importing computers and other electronics into Russia and then used initial earnings to cofound Rossiiskiy Kredit Bank, which became the center of his business empire in Russia, with the Cartu Group later taking on that role for him in Georgia.[48]

While it may be tempting to draw a sharp line between the set of countries that underwent substantial privatization and those that did not, in practice the distinction can often be quite fuzzy. This is because in highly patronalistic societies, even state-owned corporations can have significant informal room for maneuver in how they dispose of their resources at the same time that the state can also exert a very strong degree of informal control over enterprises that are formally in the private sector. The degree of centralization of control,

[43] Jonathan Wheatley, *Georgia from National Awakening to Rose Revolution: Delayed Transition in the Former Soviet Union* (Burlington, VT: Ashgate, 2005), pp. 112–13.

[44] Privatization generally benefited former Komsomol leaders and enterprise directors. See Vladimir G. Papava and Teimuraz A. Beridze, *Ocherki politicheskoi ekonomii postkommunisticheskogo kapitalizma* (Moscow: Delo i Servis, 2005), pp. 154–5.

[45] Jaba Devdariani, "Georgia: Rise and Fall of the Façade Democracy," *Demokratizatsiya: The Journal of Post-Soviet Democratization*, v. 12, no. 1, Winter 2004, pp. 79–115, 98, 114 (fn18); International Republican Institute's Georgia Web site, "Personalities" page, http://www.iri.org. ge/en/georgia/personalities, accessed April 1, 2011.

[46] Wheatley, *Georgia*, pp. 113–5.

[47] Daan van der Schriek, "A 'Gangster' at Large," *Transitions Online*, March 1, 2004.

[48] Wendell Steavenson, "The Good Oligarch," *Prospect*, July 21, 2010.

as we will see in discussing the dynamics of post-Soviet regimes over more than two decades, has had at least as much to do with structures and practices of informal control as with formal property rights, though this is not to deny any effect to the formalities, as we will also see.

Thus it is important to recognize that even in the heavily nonprivatized countries, distinct networks did often (though not always) develop at the intersection of the state and the economy and the formal and the informal. In Belarus and Turkmenistan, this intersection was dominated by the president's own network of cronies, with the president taking care through constant reshuffling and seemingly arbitrary prosecutions to ensure that no one figure or grouping other than his own could establish any sort of stable claim on economic flows in any specific sector. This does not mean that there are no economic interests in these countries other than the president's own, just that these have not been allowed to institutionalize around persons outside the presidency itself or the president's own family members. While privatization in Belarus had begun in the early 1990s, it was largely reversed by Aliaksandr Lukashenka after he won the presidency in 1994. Thus before his rise, as Andrew Wilson puts it, "Would-be Belarusian 'oligarchs' were still relative small fry."[49] Of these, the most important was Aliaksandr Pupeika, whose PuShe network grew out of selling everything from cars to electronics and also held assets in banking and food processing.[50] In Turkmenistan, privatization was very nearly nonexistent.[51]

In other countries with limited privatization, however, significant oligarchic figures emerged within formal state structures themselves. While the presidents' innermost circles certainly claimed their share of sources of rents, distinct but allied networks were able to build economic empires and even exercise some significant autonomy over long periods via control of both state-owned companies and state institutions more generally, especially the most lucrative ministries. In Olivier Roy's apt terminology, the state was "effectively leased to networks of power."[52]

This is quite evident in Azerbaijan, its breakaway Nagorno-Karabakh region, Uzbekistan, and Tajikistan. In Azerbaijan, typically for this set of polities, privatization took place mainly for small and medium-sized businesses and not for such "blue chip" assets as oil and gas, air travel, railroads, or mining.[53] The chief fortunes to be made, then, primarily resulted from some kind of state

---

[49] Andrew Wilson, *Belarus: The Last Dictatorship in Europe* (New Haven, CT: Yale University Press, 2011), p. 164.

[50] Wilson, *Belarus*, p. 164. See also Kimitaka Matsuzato, "A Populist Island in an Ocean of Clan Politics: The Lukashenka Regime as an Exception among CIS Countries," *Europe-Asia Studies*, v. 56, no. 2, March 2004, pp. 235–61; Vladimir Rovdo, "Spetsifika i evoliutsiia politicheskogo rezhima Respubliki Belarus'," *Acta Slavica Iaponica*, v. 21, 2004, pp. 144–80.

[51] Sebastien Peyrouse, *Turkmenistan: Strategies of Power, Dilemmas of Development* (Armonk, NY: M. E. Sharpe, 2011), esp. pp. 73–5.

[52] Olivier Roy, *The New Central Asia: The Creation of Nations* (New York: NYU Press, 2000) p. 184.

[53] Author's expert interview, Baku, October 2, 2010.

connection. One of the first oligarchic networks to arise in Azerbaijan was that of Rasul Guliyev, using his position as head of the country's major oil refinery during the transition from communism to accumulate massive wealth and build a large network of political supporters.[54] The families of Azerbaijan's presidents – unlike in many other countries – were not during the 1990s particularly prominent in the economy, and even when President Heydar Aliyev's son, Ilham, was named vice president of the country's national oil company SOCAR in 1994, the junior Aliyev maintained a relatively low profile and was not seen as an oligarch, lacking his own evident and expanding set of business holdings.[55] Other important networks operating from within the state, however, were able to build up large economic empires largely uninterrupted throughout the 1990s. For example, brothers Rafiq and Farhad Aliyev (not related to President Aliyev), the latter a prominent minister, controlled AzPetrol Holding, which included the energy transportation company AzerTrans.[56] Another important example is Kamaladdin Heydarov, who gained status as a wealthy private- and public-sector oligarch while heading the revenue-rich Customs Committee in the Aliyev regime during the 1990s.[57]

Likewise, as Islom Karimov rose to the presidency in Uzbekistan, a prominent network linked to his home Samarkand region acquired economic opportunities by controlling ministries dealing with gold and energy, while a major Tashkent-based network gained trade and finance ministries.[58] In separatist Nagorno-Karabakh, former automobile repairman Samvel Babaian emerged as the highest-profile warlord during the region's fight for independence from Azerbaijan and then became defense minister in 1993, a combination enabling him to manage virtually all armed forces in the republic with impunity. This proved useful for making money, as he gained control of a large share of the territory's most lucrative businesses and became its chief oligarch.[59] Another prominent Karabakh network rose out of the local Communist Youth League

---

[54] Svante Cornell, *Azerbaijan since Independence* (Armonk, NY: M. E. Sharpe, 2011), pp. 107, 175–6.

[55] Cornell, *Azerbaijan since Independence*, pp. 101–3.

[56] Samuel Lussac, "The State as an 'Oil' Company? The Political Economy of Azerbaijan," *GARNET Working Paper* No. 74/10, February 2010.

[57] *Azadliq Radiosu*, July 2, 2006; Hannes Meissner, "Informal Politics in Azerbaijan: Corruption and Rent-Seeking Patterns," *Caucasus Analytical Digest*, no. 24, February 11, 2011, pp. 6–9.

[58] Alisher Ilkhamov, "The Limits of Centralization: Regional Challenges in Uzbekistan," in Pauline Jones Luong, ed., *The Transformation of Central Asia* (Ithaca, NY: Cornell University Press, 2004), p. 179; Radnitz, *Weapons of the Wealthy*, p. 58.

[59] On Babaian and political-economic networks in Nagorno-Karabakh more generally, see Pal Kolsto and Helge Blakkisrud, "Living with Non-recognition: State- and Nation-building in South Caucasian Quasi-states," *Europe-Asia Studies*, v. 60, no. 3, May 2008, pp. 483–509, pp. 491–2; Kimitaka Matsuzato, "From Belligerent to Multi-Ethnic Democracy: Domestic Politics in Unrecognized States after the Ceasefires," *Eurasian Review*, v. 1, November 2008, pp. 95–119, pp. 101–2; Razmik Panossian, "The Irony of Nagorno-Karabakh: Formal Institutions versus Informal Politics," *Regional & Federal Studies*, v. 11, no. 3, 2001, pp. 143–64, p. 150.

branch, supplying many chief mobilizers of the territory's national movement. These included Robert Kocharian and Serzh Sargsyan, both of whom would later cross the formal state border and go on to become presidents of Armenia.[60]

Tajikistan followed the same general pattern, though it exemplifies several ways in which oligarchic networks could rise in such a system.[61] Islamic clergyman and former opposition warlord Hoji Akhbar Turajonzoda, as one example, obtained management of a cotton processing enterprise and a department store as part of a state effort in the 1990s to gain control after the civil war by providing tangible rewards to commanders who would lay down arms.[62] Representing another pathway, Gaffor Mirzoev used his position as presidential guard chief to "acquire for himself or his family a meat processing factory, the Olimp bank, Jomi Jamshed casino, and over thirty apartments in Dushanbe."[63] In other cases, officials gained control over ministries that would generate a stream of income that they could then capture for themselves. In a few instances, whole state agencies were actually formally privatized in the officials' names, as happened when minister Sayfuddin Turayev presided over the transition of a ministry of industry, consumption, and services into what became the Khizmat company, which he then ran.[64] Some officials, of course, had their own economic enterprises running even before entering the formal economy, often reputedly trading in drugs.[65] The major formal enterprises in Tajikistan generally remained formally in state hands until the late 2000s, as the private sector constituted less than half of the country's GDP as late as 2007.[66] But as Martha Brill Olcott's extensive case study of Tajik Aluminum illustrates, in part on the basis of details revealed through public-record court cases in London, these were not initially controlled directly by the president or an impartial state bureaucracy, and those who managed them on the basis of management contracts (in this case, Avaz Nazarov and Abdukadir Ermatov) could enter into sharp conflict with sitting authorities and even resist presidential efforts to wrest away control.[67]

[60] Georgi Derluguian, "On ne Mandela," interview in *Ekspert*, No. 10, March 10–16, 2008, pp. 26–8.

[61] On economic reform there, see Olcott, *Central Asia's Second Chance*, p. 114.

[62] John Heathershaw, *Post-Conflict Tajikistan: The Politics of Peacebuilding and the Emergence of Legitimate Order* (London: Routledge, 2009), p. 122. An excellent detailed discussion of how Turajonzoda expanded his network to become one of the country's chief patrons during the civil war is Idil Tuncer-Kilavuz, "Understanding Civil War: A Comparison of Tajikistan and Uzbekistan," *Europe-Asia Studies*, v. 63, no. 2, March 2011, pp. 263–90, pp. 283–4.

[63] Heathershaw, *Post-Conflict Tajikistan*, p. 123.

[64] Roy, *The New Central Asia*, p. 184.

[65] Heathershaw, *Post-Conflict Tajikistan*, pp. 136–7.

[66] Martha Brill Olcott, *Tajikistan's Difficult Development Path* (Washington, DC: Carnegie Endowment, 2012), p. 101.

[67] Olcott, *Tajikistan's Difficult Development Path*, pp. 181–210.

Even in the smallest breakaway territories, among them Abkhazia and
South Ossetia, one finds distinct and significant economic networks at the core
of high politics despite the ravages of war, a dearth of major industry, and very
limited privatization.[68] In South Ossetia, money was made chiefly through controlling the flow of goods through the territory and related black market activity.[69] Among the most important local oligarchs were brothers Jambulat and
Ibragim Tedeev, who controlled the flow of goods through the Roki Tunnel, a
key ground transportation link between the Caucasus and Russia that Georgia
allowed to function (permitting relatively free travel between South Ossetia and
the rest of Georgia) despite the "frozen conflict."[70] In Abkhazia, Beslan Butba
gained initial capital in Russia before buying assets in Abkhazia, while other
politician-businessmen arose by converting their clout into business operations
upon leaving government office, as did Sergei Bagapsh, who became head of
the state corporation Chernomorenergo after leaving the prime ministership
in 1999.[71]

Overall, some sort of oligarch appeared in virtually all post-Soviet states
and statelets, and even this same term itself (*oligarkh*) became widely used to
refer to them locally. There were variations on this theme, of course, with some
arising out of the private sector and others out of the state. But very importantly, the formal difference between "private" and "state" in the post-Soviet
context should not be overestimated.[72] Even private-sector oligarchs generally
achieved their rise through some kind of close collusion with important state
actors, often using state or former Communist Party resources as their initial
capital, and they usually remained highly dependent on state structures (for
sustenance, protection, or license) straight into the 2010s for those who survived. Likewise, state-owned corporations and even ministries proved capable
of having their own parochial interests and in many cases became the center of
economic networks that generated private profits for their bosses and played
influential and somewhat autonomous roles in politics for extended periods.

Regional Networks

One of the most basic units to emerge in virtually all post-Soviet countries was
the regional political machine, which in this context generally means a con-
glomeration of local networks organized around the formal head of regional
state executive power in the next official territorial governance unit below the

---

[68] Charles King, "The Benefits of Ethnic War: Understanding Eurasia's Unrecognized States,"
World Politics, v. 53, no. 4, July 2001, pp. 524–52; Kolsto and Blakkisrud, "Living with Non-
recognition," p. 497.
[69] King, "The Benefits of Ethnic War."
[70] Kolsto and Blakkisrud, "Living with Non-recognition"; *Kommersant*, May 23, 2009.
[71] *Ekho Abkhazii*, April 1, 2004, p. 1.
[72] Also making this point explicitly are Heathershaw, *Post-Conflict Tajikistan*, pp. 80–1, p. 122;
and Roy, *The New Central Asia*, p. 184.

level of the country as a whole,[73] though powerful machines could also emerge in lower-level units like cities or under patrons who did not hold formal state posts (especially at the lowest levels, as in villages). At the largest subnational level (the regional level), the machine bosses were often called "governors" though the executives sometimes took on a variety of titles ranging from the grandiose "president" to the more technical "head of administration."[74] The chief distinction between types of regional machines as political actors across the post-Soviet space involves whether there was a significant bottom-up aspect to their development. That is, did the regional political machine have noteworthy local origins and play a highly autonomous political role (at least initially), or did it develop mainly from the top down, being primarily created by central state leaders in an attempt to assert political control over their territories?

Russia represents the clearest case of bottom-up regional political machines. The USSR was also noted for strong provincial power brokers, the regional Communist Party bosses that Jerry Hough famously dubbed the Soviet prefects. But it is crucial to recognize that Russia's regional political machines of the 1990s in fact bore little connection to these earlier figures.[75] Instead, they tended to be the new creations of political entrepreneurs who skillfully took advantage of a critical juncture to reassemble resources left by the crumbling USSR and combine them with new resources made valuable in the emergent political environment. Indeed, the post of governor was itself a creation of the transition, not a Soviet legacy. When Gorbachev first held competitive regional elections in the USSR in 1990, these were for soviets (councils, legislatures) that would then select the chief regional executives. The Communist Party bosses would only remain regional bosses if they could win control of the regional soviets. But while some won in 1990 and became governors, many others demonstrated their inability to control politics under the new conditions. Proreform intellectuals Gavriil Popov and Anatoly Sobchak, for example, thus won the leadership of Moscow and Leningrad (soon renamed St. Petersburg).

As the USSR dissolved and the new Russian state emerged, the strongest regional soviet chairmen in some ethnic minority republics, including Tatarstan and Bashkortostan, began creating new directly elected "presidencies." They calculated that these new posts would consolidate their own control locally while giving them more authority in negotiations with the central government

[73] For larger post-Soviet countries, the units correspond to what had been oblasts, krais, autonomous republics, autonomous oblasts, or autonomous districts in the USSR as well as cities of national status such as Moscow and St. Petersburg in Russia or Kyiv in Ukraine. In the smallest countries or de facto quasi-states, the units being discussed in this section generally correspond to Soviet era *raions* (districts) as well as to the capital city. Lumping all these together, this volume refers to the largest subnational units in a country as "regions" or, sometimes, "provinces."

[74] Those calling themselves "presidents" were usually the heads of ethnically designated autonomous territories, such as the Republic of Tatarstan in Russia.

[75] Jerry F. Hough, *The Soviet Prefects: The Local Party Organs in Industrial Decision-making* (Cambridge, MA: Harvard University Press, 1969).

over autonomy and subsidies. A few nonethnic regions followed suit, with Moscow and St. Petersburg moving to elect mayors directly.[76]

In the majority of Russia's eighty-nine regions, however, it was President Boris Yeltsin who initially created the governorship.[77] Upset that many regional councils had backed the hard-line Soviet coup plotters of August 1991, Yeltsin sought to wrest executive power from them by establishing the position of regional "head of administration." While he declared that these posts were to be filled by direct election, he also announced that he would personally appoint them for a transition period that was supposed to last until 1993, but in most cases wound up continuing until 1996.[78] Sometimes these appointees were Yeltsin associates with little experience in the regions to which they were assigned. In other cases they were from the local political milieu.

The figures who did somehow wind up in the governors' seats often found they had a great deal of opportunity to amass the kind of political and economic resources necessary to build a powerful political machine.[79] For one thing, the regions began with strikingly little managerial oversight from Moscow. Looking for allies anywhere they could in their late Soviet struggle for power, Mikhail Gorbachev and Boris Yeltsin (after becoming leader of the Russian Republic in 1990) had both competed for regional favor by promising provinces more autonomy. Gorbachev offered the ethnic minority republics in Russia a seat at the table alongside full-fledged union republics such as Ukraine and even Russia itself in negotiations to reconstitute a Soviet Union. Yeltsin, for his part, traveled the countryside calling on them to "take as much sovereignty as you can swallow."[80]

His victory over Gorbachev consolidated, Yeltsin soon found himself in competition with his own parliament in 1992–3, a situation that gave regional leaders further room to maneuver by playing one side against the other. To gain their political support as the 1990s progressed, Yeltsin concluded a series of "bilateral treaties" with nearly half of them that included a wide range of autonomy provisions. Even more importantly, however, Yeltsin's far-reaching economic reforms granted governors significant control over the privatization of local enterprises. In some cases, as in the ethnic region of Bashkortostan, local bosses opted to keep most major assets in state hands. In many others, the

---

[76] On Moscow, see Timothy J. Colton, *Moscow: Governing the Socialist Metropolis* (Cambridge, MA: Harvard University Press, 1998), pp. 683–5.

[77] Russia had eighty-nine regions in the 1990s. Some were merged after Putin came to power, and there are currently eighty-three (not including Crimea and Sevastopol, which are not internationally recognized as being part of Russia).

[78] Hale, *Why Not Parties in Russia*, pp. 34–5; Kathryn Stoner-Weiss, *Local Heroes: The Political Economy of Russian Regional Governance* (Princeton, NJ: Princeton University Press, 1997), pp. 56–89.

[79] Except where other source citations are given, the discussion of Russia in this section draws on Henry E. Hale, "Explaining Machine Politics in Russia's Regions: Economy, Ethnicity, and Legacy," *Post-Soviet Affairs*, v. 19, no. 3, July–September 2003, pp. 228–63.

[80] *Izvestiia Bashkortostana*, October 12, 1993, p. 3.

governor was able to manipulate the privatization process so as either to retain an influential state stake in the local economy or to ensure that the regional leader's close associates (or at least people thought to be controllable) gained ownership. For example, Yury Luzhkov, who had succeeded Popov as Moscow mayor in 1992, orchestrated a complex privatization scheme that enabled the city to control much of the capital's highly complex economy through a holding company, Sistema.[81] This helped him build the important political network depicted in Figure 5.1.

Russia's regional leaders also enjoyed autonomy when it came to designing or influencing local institutions, which could be crafted or co-opted by governors to maximize their own local control. One set of very important formal institutions involved local law-enforcement and regulatory powers: With police, prosecutors, and inspectors (fire, tax, health) as well as licensing authority under their influence or sometimes direct control, governors had a toolbox full of implements that could be applied informally to pressure or deter opponents.[82] Regional leaders were also frequently in position to sway local election legislation and the timing of elections and often gained control over local election commissions. This put them in a strong position to dominate gubernatorial elections, which some regions had held since 1991 but that did not begin in others until 1996 or later.[83]

The result of these transitional processes in Russia was a class of very powerful regional political machines that not only dominated local politics across much of Russia, but also became crucial power brokers and desired coalition partners in federal-level political struggles. By the end of the 1990s, it was widely acknowledged that for a candidate seeking election to almost any office in most regions, it mattered far more whether the governor was supportive than whether that candidate enjoyed any kind of party, corporate, or even direct Kremlin support.[84]

Russia's governors varied quite widely in their ability to take advantage of these opportunities to establish regional political dominance. Moscow's first post-Soviet mayor, Popov, represents one of the most dramatic flameouts, resigning in frustration a tumultuous year after winning the city's first

---

[81] Robert W. Orttung. "Business and Politics in the Russian Regions," *Problems of Post-Communism*, v. 51, no. 2, March–April 2004, pp. 48–60.

[82] Afanasiev, *Klientelizm i Rossiiskaia Gosudarstvennost*'; Brian Taylor, *State-Building in Putin's Russia: Policing and Coercion after Communism* (New York: Cambridge University Press, 2011), pp. 124–6.

[83] Grigorii V. Golosov, "Russian Political Parties and the 'Bosses': Evidence from the 1994 Provincial Elections in Western Siberia," *Party Politics*, v. 3, no. 1, 1997, pp. 5–21.

[84] E.g., Yitzhak Brudny, "Continuity or Change in Russian Electoral Patterns?" in Archie Brown, ed., *Contemporary Russian Politics* (New York: Oxford University Press, 2001), pp. 154–78; Golosov, "Russian Political Parties"; Steven L. Solnick, "Russia's 'Transition,'" *Social Research*, v. 66, Fall 1999, pp. 789–824; Kathryn Stoner-Weiss, "Central Weakness and Provincial Autonomy," *Post-Soviet Affairs*, v. 15, no. 1, January–March 1999, pp. 87–104.

direct mayoral election. That his immediate successor, Luzhkov, turned out to be one of Russia's most powerful regional machine politicians, as depicted in Figure 5.1, illustrates the importance of leadership skill during this transition period. The necessary abilities were not those of Soviet era party first secretaries, whom systematic analysis has shown to have been among the weaker political machine leaders during the Russia of the 1990s. For would-be political machine builders, what mattered far more than Communist pedigree was a general entrepreneurialism, managerial skill, and either a broad range of connections across the region or ties to specific institutionalized regional constituencies (such as a locally dominant ethnic group or a large collective farm network) that could provide a core of support. Over time, through a kind of "survival of the fittest" dynamic, the weaker leaders tended to be replaced by stronger ones as regional machines generally became more and more powerful during the 1990s.

Almost everywhere else in the former USSR, central executives appointed regional executives in attempts to establish "vertical" control over locally powerful networks, which had often gained strong representation in regional and local legislatures through the nationwide elections Gorbachev had orchestrated in 1990. In some cases, there were nuances that on paper would give a legislature power. According to a 1997 law in Abkhazia, for example, the president was required to pick the regional head from among existing regional council deputies. As Kimitaka Matsuzato points out, however, in practice this requirement was easily circumvented as the president could arrange a by-election to have anyone elected to the council whom he wanted to appoint head of the region.[85] The primary exceptions to the pattern of top-down appointment of regional executives outside Russia were the heads of ethnic enclaves (notably Georgia's autonomous republic of Ajara and Gagauz-Yeri in Moldova) or mayors of capital cities (such as Moldova's Chisinau and Ukraine's Kyiv), which in a few instances were elected directly by the population.

Even the direct appointment of governors did not necessarily give central authorities unambiguous control over regional networks, however. Especially during the turbulence of the early 1990s, central government oversight could be far from perfect, allowing considerable room for local officials to play their own games. Moreover, central authorities often feared that imposed outsiders would not be familiar enough with local networks and problems to be effective, leading them frequently to appoint governors from within the regional elites. This was especially likely to be the case if regional networks controlled sufficient resources to impose costs on central governments should their interests not be taken into account. Such costs could take many forms, right up to violent riots. Some, for example, interpret the major student uprising of 1992 in Uzbekistan as an attempt by the most powerful Tashkent-based network to

---

[85] Kimitaka Matsuzato, "Patronnoe prezidentstvo i politika v sfere identichnosti v nepreznannoi Abkhazii," *Acta Eurasica*, no. 4, 2006, pp. 132–59.

flex its muscle and stave off Karimov's effort to consolidate national power at its expense.[86]

This calls attention to the fact that local networks were often in position to exert considerable influence over early post-Soviet central authorities even when they were subjected to a system whereby a president appointed the regional heads of the executive branch. This frequently proved to be the case in Central Asia, where the USSR leadership had governed by essentially giving regional party bosses carte blanche to manage local economies (especially cotton) through the cultivation of extensive patronage networks. These regional networks quickly seized the opportunity of the transition to gain control over new aspects of the economy, such as nascent private enterprise, as well as subsidies on which their economies depended heavily. While they faced challenges from rivals and defectors in their own regions, the most powerful ones penetrated the economy and society extensively and vertically enough to be a force to be reckoned with for their countries' initial presidents.[87] Local networks gained special power during periods of civil war, when warlords could establish either violent control or protective patronage over particular pieces of territory completely independently of any central government, as in Tajikistan for much of the 1990s and parts of Georgia during the early 1990s.[88]

Two Crucial Caveats on the Nature of Post-Soviet Networks

The discussion up to this point helps us highlight two key points. One is that categorizing networks as "economic/oligarchic," "state-based," or "regional/local" makes sense only as a simplification that helps communicate the different ways patronal networks can emerge and exert power. That is, shorthand in this book like "oligarchs" and "regional political machines" should not be read as reifying networks and implying that they are limited to only one source of authority that can be easily identified. Instead, it is a major point of this volume that such networks are in fact quite fluid and tend to penetrate and embody

---

[86] Carlisle, "Islam Karimov and Uzbekistan," p. 198; Idil Tuncer-Kilavuz, "Understanding Violent Conflict: A Comparative Study of Tajikistan and Uzbekistan," dissertation in Central Eurasian Studies, Indiana University, Bloomington, 2007, chapter 4.

[87] Ilkhamov, "The Limits of Centralization"; Jones Luong, *Institutional Change*, chapters 3–4; Marlene Laruelle, "Discussing Neopatrimonialism and Patronal Presidentialism in the Central Asian Context," *Demokratizatsiya: The Journal of Post-Soviet Democratization*, v. 20, no. 4, Autumn 2012, pp. 301–24; Lawrence P. Markowitz, "The Sub-national Roots of Authoritarianism: Neopatrimonialism and Territorial Administration in Uzbekistan," *Demokratizatsiya: The Journal of Post-Soviet Democratization*, v. 20, no. 4, Fall 2012, pp. 387–408; Peyrouse, *Turkmenistan*, pp. 80–2.

[88] John Heathershaw and Edmund Herzig, "Introduction: The Sources of Statehood in Tajikistan," *Central Asian Survey*, v. 30, no. 1, March 2011, pp. 5–19; Stephen F. Jones, "Georgia: The Trauma of Statehood," in Ian Bremmer and Ray Taras, eds., *New States, New Politics* (New York: Cambridge University Press, 1997), pp. 505–43; Darrell Slider, "Democratization in Georgia," in Karen Dawisha and Bruce Parrott, eds., *Conflict, Cleavage, and Change in Central Asia and the Caucasus* (New York: Cambridge University Press, 1997), pp. 156–98.

a variety of different sources of power and authority, often having multiple bases. Thus we have seen that what are often called "regional" networks in Uzbekistan, for example, usually have *both* regional *and* economic dimensions that are important, yet at the same time are not limited to the single region by whose names they are referred to commonly.

Similarly, when the introduction to this chapter mentions "state agencies" as a network base distinct from "oligarchs" and "regional political machines," it is almost always the case that these networks are not limiting themselves to the exercise of administrative power, and certainly not to their formal powers as prescribed on legal documents, but are also highly involved in business and often have ties to particular regions. For example, the network of Azerbaijan's Heydarov (former Customs Committee head) was reported to play an influential role in Azerbaijani politics directly through his Emergencies Ministry (which controls its own troops) in the second half of the 2000s, though his family had significant business holdings as well as a reputed base of loyalty in the Qabala region, in which his family invests heavily.[89]

The second key point highlighted by the preceding discussion concerns popular misconceptions regarding the role of "clans" and "ethnic groups" (and sometimes, "regions"). Some accounts, especially in popular media, tend to treat these as gigantic, unified networks in and of themselves, as if elites falling into clan or ethnic categories were actually all linked to each other and acting in concert for their clan's or ethnic group's interests under the coordination of a recognized leader.[90] This interpretation has been rather decisively debunked in a large number of studies in different countries, virtually all of which reach several findings. One is that "clan" and "ethnic group" are not actually organized patronal networks, but categories of belonging that: do not necessarily command the loyalty of any given individual; often contain diverse positions on important issues; and in fact routinely contain multiple patronal networks that are often in competition with each other.[91] While patronal networks may include concentrations of members of one ethnic group or clan, they are not usually limited to members of these groups and frequently include many others. In the post-Soviet context, these others might be coworkers, former classmates, or neighbors.[92] The term "clan," in addition, is widely used in the

---

[89] *Azadliq Radiosu*, July 2, 2006; Meissner, "Informal Politics in Azerbaijan"; author's field notes, Qabala and Baku, Azerbaijan, 2010.

[90] E.g., Liz Fuller, "Azerbaijan: Former Presidential Advisor Discusses Regionalism in Politics," *RFE/RL News Analysis*, April 27, 2007. Among prominent scholarly works, Kathleen Collins, *Clan Politics and Regime Transition in Central Asia* (New York: Cambridge University Press, 2005), may come closest to this, though her account is in fact more nuanced.

[91] Directly establishing this against competing hypotheses is Sjöberg's impressive survey work in Kyrgyzstan, a case where "clans" are frequently described as prominent political actors. See Sjöberg, *Competitive Elections*.

[92] Muriel Atkin, "Tajikistan: Reform, Reaction, and Civil War," in Ian Bremmer and Ray Taras, eds., *New States, New Politics* (New York: Cambridge University Press, 1997), pp. 602–33; Ilkhamov, "The Limits of Centralization"; Edward Schatz, *Modern Clan Politics: The Power of "Blood" in Kazakhstan and Beyond* (Seattle: University of Washington Press, 2004).

jargon of many post-Soviet countries to refer loosely to any sort of patronal network, often without any actual connotation that members are literally relatives. Thus while it can be a useful shorthand to refer to certain networks as the "Nakhichevan clan," the "Tashkent clan," or even the "Chubais clan," we must bear in mind that these descriptions are just shorthand. It is probably more accurate, therefore, to follow Idil Tuncer-Kilavuz in referring more generally to "political-economic networks."[93] This terminology also has the effect of working against a tendency to exoticize Central Asian politics, aligning research on this part of the world more directly with prominent work on other countries that interprets politics in terms of networks.[94] The more general term "patronal network" also works well, of course.

Again, this is not to say that networks do not sometimes feature concentrations in a particular ethnic group, an extended family, or a particular region. And surely it is the case that networks possessing concentrated interests in the same region or having many members from the same ethnic community share certain important interests. For example, distinct networks based in the mining or metals of Ukraine's East may all oppose policies that could hurt Soviet era heavy industry, making them seem united in certain struggles. Thus the distinct Akhmetov (mining) and Haiduk-Taruta (metals) networks based in Ukraine's eastern Donbass region found common cause in supporting former Donetsk governor Viktor Yanukovych for president in 2004 over an opponent who advocated a smaller state role in propping up heavy industry, Viktor Yushchenko. And rival networks based in Kyrgyzstan's southern Uzbek community (such as those of Davron Sobirov in Osh and Qodirjon Botirov in Jalalabad) would also be expected jointly to oppose nationalistic policies originating in Bishkek that discriminate against Uzbeks and would thus hurt each of these networks' economic or political prospects, as they seem to have done since Kyrgyz nationalism became more prominent in 2010.[95]

But what the preceding analysis *also* means is that such commonalities are likely to have much more to do with the concrete material or political interests of the individual networks themselves (and the individuals within and especially at the helm of them) than to any "bonds" of loyalty to ethnic group,

---

[93] Tuncer-Kilavuz, "Political and Social Networks." See also a good analysis in Alisher Ilkhamov, "Neopatrimonialism, Interest Groups and Patronage Networks: The Impasses of the Governance System in Uzbekistan," *Central Asian Survey*, v. 26, no. 1, March 2007, pp. 65–84.

[94] E.g., Gerald M. Easter, *Restructuring the State: Personal Networks and Elite Identity* (New York: Cambridge University Press, 2000); Mustaq H. Khan, "Markets, States and Democracy: Patron-Client Networks and the Case for Democracy in Developing Countries," *Democratization*, v. 12, no. 5, December 2005, pp. 704–24; Vadim Kononenko and Arkady Moshes, eds., *Russia as a Network State: What Works in Russia When State Institutions Do Not?* (New York: Palgrave Macmillan, 2011); Duncan McCargo, "Network Monarchy and Legitimacy Crises in Thailand," *The Pacific Review*, v. 18, no. 4, December 2005, pp. 499–519; Gulnaz Sharafutdinova, *Political Consequences of Crony Capitalism inside Russia* (South Bend, IN: Notre Dame University Press, 2010).

[95] Brent Hierman, "Sources of Inter-ethnic Trust and Distrust in Central Asia," doctoral dissertation in Political Science, Indiana University, Bloomington, 2011, chapter 5.

region, or clan.[96] Thus such networks frequently wind up making alliances with, recruiting new members from, or even joining networks based in the supposedly "opposing" clan/group/region. Returning to the examples just given, the ethnic Uzbek Botirov was thus perfectly willing to align his network with that of the northern-based ethnic Kyrgyz President Akaev when it was profitable to do so, and the eastern Ukrainian Haiduk joined the western-Ukraine-based Yushchenko's presidential administration in 2006 when the chance to exert influence and gain a state-based competitive advantage presented itself.[97] This applies even to bonds of religion, which is sometimes portrayed as central to high politics in Tajikistan as the Islamic Renaissance Party (IRP) featured prominently in the country's opposition and then gained a place in the postwar coalition. Thus, without denying that the IRP has a strong religious component, it is also important to understand that it also initially mobilized partly through the regional network of its leader, Abdullo Nuri, and through the larger network of mullahs spanning different regions of the country (though it certainly did not represent the whole Muslim establishment).[98]

The Prevalence of Presidentialist Constitutions

As with the patronal networks described previously, post-Soviet constitutions generally emerged from the interaction of old-regime legacies and political opportunities served up by the transition from the USSR's dictatorship. Comparative research has demonstrated that constitutions are often the product of political forces that in fact cause many of the effects we attribute to the constitutions themselves.[99] This turns out to be true of the post-Soviet world as well, for reasons discussed in the previous chapter. This is not to say that constitutions do not matter. Once created, they can have independent effects, and indeed leaders pay attention to shaping them precisely because they suspect they can have such effects. This is what we find in Eurasia, a process by which leaders – recognizing that constitutions would have an impact on future power relationships but without complete certainty – struggled to influence these basic documents as part of their more general efforts to accumulate power. The process of initially creating directly elected presidencies in Eurasia, however, was

---

[96] On the role of ethnicity and identity more generally in politics, see Henry E. Hale, *The Foundations of Ethnic Politics: Separatism of States and Nations in Eurasia and the World* (New York: Cambridge University Press, 2008).

[97] Hierman, "Sources of Inter-ethnic Trust"; Adam Swain, "Yushchenko Plays His Donbass Card," *Kyiv Post*, November 16, 2006, as circulated in *The Ukraine List (UKL)*, no 405, compiled by Dominique Arel, November 21, 2006.

[98] Idil Tuncer-Kilavuz, "Understanding Civil War," pp. 269, pp. 283–4. For a broader history of political Islam in the region, see Sebastien Peyrouse, "The Rise of Political Islam in Soviet Central Asia," in Hillel Fradkin, Husain Haqqani, and Eric Brown, eds., *Current Trends in Islamist Ideology* (Washington, DC: Hudson Institute, 2007), pp. 40–54.

[99] Jose Antonio Cheibub, *Presidentialism, Parliamentarism, and Democracy* (New York: Cambridge University Press, 2007); Gerald Easter, "Preference for Presidentialism: Postcommunist Regime Change in Russia and the NIS," *World Politics*, v. 49, no. 2, January 1997, pp. 184–211.

very rapid, primarily a phenomenon of the waning years of the USSR's existence shaped by the peculiarities of the Soviet dissolution. It is thus largely exogenous to the events that followed in the independence period, though with some prominent exceptions that will be discussed in this volume.

The USSR up until 1990 had never had the post of president. Instead, as described in Chapter 3, it was the country's Communist Party boss who ruled, and he did so through what was formally a parliamentarist system in which a parliament elected a head of government who was formally head of state. Gorbachev set in motion the process of change that eventually led to the presidentialization of most post-Soviet polities. As a way of drawing new allies into politics and starting to chip away at his dependence on Communist Party structures, Gorbachev initially created a new parliament, a massive Congress of People's Deputies that would meet periodically and choose a smaller Supreme Soviet, which would be in session during the intervals. With the implementation of this reform in 1989, parliament was for the first time filled mostly through contested territorial district elections, though a third of the seats were reserved for representatives of certain institutions that were expected to vote for establishment candidates. The Congress then elected Gorbachev its chairman. But the executive authority that this chairman officially wielded turned out to be very cumbersome. As Jerry Hough writes of Gorbachev in this post:

Officially he had to consult with the forty-two members of the Presidium of the Supreme Soviet to take such an action as introducing troops to quell riots in Azerbaidzhan. This was a satisfactory arrangement if the Communists in the parliament were subject to party discipline, but it left the leader with few effective levers of executive power if party discipline weakened.[100]

Gorbachev's team quickly realized this was a "mistake."[101] Thus desiring more authority to deal with challenges from ethnic republics, central hard-liners, and even more radical reformists in early 1990, and additionally needing to create a new executive structure that could supplant the authority of the Communist Party, Gorbachev persuaded the Congress to create a new position of USSR "president."[102] While the position was stipulated to be directly elected, the reform made the first president an exception, so Gorbachev was chosen instead by a Congress vote in March 1990.

Gorbachev's creation of a Soviet presidency set in motion a chain reaction by which almost all of the country's union republics and many of the lower-level autonomous ethnic regions followed suit in adopting some kind

---

[100] Jerry F. Hough, *Democratization and Revolution in the USSR 1985–1991* (Washington, DC: Brookings Institution, 1997), p. 269.

[101] See the memoirs of a key Gorbachev adviser, Georgiy Shakhnazarov, *S vozhdiami i bez nikh* (Moscow: Vagrius, 2001), p. 349.

[102] Archie Brown, *The Gorbachev Factor* (New York: Oxford University Press, 1997), pp. 198–9; Mikhail Gorbachev, *Zhizn' i reformy*, book 1 (Moscow: Novosti, 1995), p. 483.

of "presidency."[103] While imitation does appear to have played some role, the cascade to presidentialism reflected a number of considerations that faced all republic leaders at the same time. For one thing, with Gorbachev actively undermining the authority of the Communist Party, which had provided the administrative backbone of the country for seven decades, republic leaders had strong incentive to construct new executive authority structures of their own that could either replace or reinforce the old party one, and Gorbachev's moves supplied an obvious model. Moreover, Gorbachev also announced plans to renegotiate the basis of the union around the same time, and many republic leaders came to believe that their republic's (and hence their own) interests would be best defended by a single leader capable of exercising authority on the republic's behalf and sitting as an "equal" with "President" Gorbachev (and with other republic "presidents" as they appeared).[104]

Another important factor driving the creation of directly elected presidencies was the desire of incumbent republic parliamentary chairmen to strengthen their own already strong positions, with Gorbachev's institutional moves providing a handy blueprint for how this might be done. Thus in each of the non-Baltic union republics that created an indirectly elected presidency in 1990 except Kyrgyzstan, it was the sitting chair of parliament who got himself chosen for the formally even more powerful post – with only one exception. In the exceptional Kyrgyzstan case, it appears that parliamentary chairman and republic Communist Party boss Absamat Masaliev simply overreached. Having alienated other networks by too overtly favoring his own based in Osh, and having failed to prevent deadly rioting in Osh just months before, Masaliev lost the support of many members of the newly elected parliament in the run-up to the October 1990 vote in parliament to choose the republic's first president. Thus while he presided over the creation of a presidency, he failed to win the majority of parliament members' votes required to occupy this post. While no other candidate won a majority, his parliamentary colleagues had hidden a mine for him in the presidential election law: If no candidate received a majority, the election had to be held again with an *entirely new slate of candidates*. Masaliev was out. Kyrgyzstan's parliament eventually agreed on republic Academy of Sciences head Askar Akaev, regarded as a neutral figure despite his northern Kyrgyzstan roots, a renowned physicist who had spent a great deal of time outside Kyrgyzstan and had risen to prominence through academia

---

[103] The term here is *prezident*, which was introduced to connote the stronger executive authority the new post wielded relative to that enjoyed by the preexisting posts of *predsedateli* (chairmen/chairwomen) of the parliaments. See Brown, *The Gorbachev Factor*, p. 198.

[104] These considerations are reflected, for example, in memoirs later published by republic leaders involved in creating the posts, such as Kazakhstan President Nursultan Nazarbaev, *Bez pravykh i levykh* (Moscow: Molodaia Gvardiia, 1991); Ukrainian leader Leonid Kravchuk, *Maemo te, shcho maemo: spohady i rozdumy* (Kyiv: Stolittia, 2002), p. 111. On Russia and Ukraine, respectively, see also Hough, *Democratization and Revolution*, pp. 404–20; and Kataryna Wolczuk, *The Moulding of Ukraine: The Constitutional Politics of State Formation* (Budapest: CEU Press, 2001), pp. 75, 79–82.

rather than as a party apparatchik.[105] Becoming the indirectly elected president, Akaev was then able to join every other indirectly elected union republic president in instituting a directly elected presidency and winning that post for himself during 1990–1. Where there was initially no indirectly elected president and the republic went straight to a directly elected one under Gorbachev, it was in every case the sitting chairman of parliament who won the first direct presidential elections. The lone exception was Belarus, which did not adopt a presidency until 1994, for reasons discussed in the next chapter.

Importantly, these patterns did not usually boil down to the Communist Party's simply changing its stripes to hold on to power.[106] While the first directly elected presidents had been the republics' Communist Party first secretaries in some republics (Azerbaijan, Kazakhstan, Tajikistan, Turkmenistan, and Uzbekistan), in several cases they had been secondary Communist figures who had leapfrogged their former party bosses (Kyrgyzstan, Moldova, Russia, and Ukraine), and in other instances they had been longtime opponents of the Communist Party, often from the intelligentsia (Armenia and Georgia). The creation and occupation of presidencies were related to power, not communism.

Overall, the proliferation of Eurasian presidencies occurred very rapidly, with every non-Baltic state having one *already* by the time the USSR finally dissolved at the end of 1991 except Belarus.[107] Thus following Gorbachev, Azerbaijan, Moldova, and all of the Central Asian republics adopted presidencies in 1990, though Turkmenistan was the only one of these to have established a directly elected presidency in this year, and parliaments elected the presidents in the rest. In 1991, all of the non-Baltic republics of the USSR adopted directly elected presidencies except Belarus, which alone retained a purely parliamentarist system at the time the USSR officially expired in December 1991.[108] Among the territories that would later become unrecognized separatist enclaves, Transnistria was the only one to institute a directly elected presidency in 1991, with Nagorno-Karabakh, Abkhazia, and South Ossetia retaining parliamentarist systems without a presidency until at least well into the 1990s.[109] The creation of a formal presidency did not mean whoever occupied it was all-powerful, however, and the struggle for power between presidents and their rivals is the central subject of the chapter that follows.

[105] Collins, *Clan Politics*, pp. 125–7; Eugene Huskey, "Kyrgyzstan: The Fate of Political Liberalization," in Karen Dawisha and Bruce Parrott, eds., *Conflict, Cleavage, and Change in Central Asia and the Caucasus* (New York: Cambridge University Press, 1997), pp. 242–76, pp. 250–3.

[106] The primary exceptions are Uzbekistan and Turkmenistan, as will be discussed later in this volume.

[107] This does not mean that the republic constitutions were already *strongly* presidentialist.

[108] For details, see the chapters on each non-Baltic post-Soviet country in Ian Bremmer and Ray Taras, eds., *New States New Politics: Building the Post-Soviet Nations* (New York: Cambridge University Press, 1997).

[109] Author's interview, expert in Tiraspol, March 26, 2009; Matsuzato, "From Belligerent"; Yu. D. Anchabadze and Yu. G. Argun, *Abkhazy* (Moscow: Nauka, 2007), p. 113; Kolsto and Blakkisrud, "Living with Non-recognition."

Conclusion

Overall, the late Soviet and early post-Soviet periods saw the rise of a wide variety of forms of patronal networks that we will demonstrate later became crucial moving parts in the regime dynamics that characterized post-Soviet political systems well beyond the first two decades of their existence. Only in rare cases were these direct holdovers from the Soviet period. Instead, they almost always reflected the outcome of political entrepreneurs' making the most of their own personal starting "capital" (accumulated during the Soviet period) to assemble in new ways resources and smaller-scale structures left by the crumbling Soviet state, often combining them with new resources that appeared during the transition itself.[110] Corporations and holding companies centered around "oligarchs" constituted one very important form of patronal network that appeared in this way, and another took the form of regional political machines, often centered around local heads of state administration (governors).

It was during this period too that the striking pattern of post-Soviet presidentialism started to emerge. Gorbachev provided the initial flap of the butterfly's wings, setting off a kind of chain reaction by which the most powerful actors in post-Soviet republics tended to create presidencies for themselves – sometimes first having the presidency be elected by parliament but usually by the end of 1991 having converted the post into a directly elected office. These constitutions then helped shape how the various networks described here came to be arranged and rearranged in each country after it became independent. How this played out is the subject of the next chapter.

[110] Derluguian, *Bourdieu's Secret Admirer.*

6

The Building of Eurasia's Great Power Pyramids

The political history of Eurasia since 1991 can be understood as a process in which the patronal networks described in the previous chapter, like building blocks, were formed, reformed, split, combined, arranged, and rearranged (or, in some cases, destroyed). To understand the patterns that eventually emerged in this process, it is crucial to keep in mind that they did not appear instantly or automatically. Instead, the Soviet collapse produced a situation of extreme institutional flux with all the economic and social turmoil one might expect to accompany it. Not only was it often unclear where the new loci of power would be, but it was not even clear what constituted power itself – either in the moment at hand or for the future. Old institutions that had once seemed permanent disappeared at the same time that new ones – both formal and informal – could appear and disappear like flashes in the pan. This applied to networks as well, so one makes a grave mistake assuming that any networks in the post-Soviet period were simply holdovers from the Soviet period. But even once networks were newly formed or revived with new meaning as described in the previous chapter, politicians' expectations regarding their relative power remained highly uncertain in the initial post-Soviet period. Indeed, this was not something anyone there had experienced before. The post-Soviet political context was completely new, leaving both old and new networks and network entrepreneurs essentially to duke it out and gradually establish a stable set of expectations over time through a process of trial and error.

In this context of great initial uncertainty, presidentialist constitutions – through the focal and information effects described in Chapter 4 – worked in mutually reinforcing conjunction with prior power balances to produce Eurasia's first post-Soviet single-pyramid systems almost everywhere by the end of the 1990s. Typically, as described in Chapter 5, the initial presidencies were created and occupied by the chairmen of Soviet republic parliaments, who by virtue of having won the USSR's first competitive republic-level elections in

1990 tended to be either the most powerful patrons or "compromise" figures chosen to solidify power-sharing deals among coalitions. The first presidents, therefore, tended to have at least one of two starting advantages over potential rivals: (1) raw patronal power that was initially greater than that of rival networks and/or (2) the focal and information effects of the formal presidentialist constitutions that had emerged by the end of 1991. Of course, with thoroughgoing uncertainty about the nature of power in the new post-Soviet environment and the lurching social and economic upheavals in this environment that characterized the wake of the USSR's demise, the presidential advantage was far from self-evident at any given time. It was thus subject to major challenges from other patrons – especially prime ministers and parliamentary chairmen.

Thus while the first postindependence presidents usually had the advantage of a stronger starting position and a presidentialist constitution, there was room for certain other factors to influence the outcome of the initial power struggles – particularly in the first half of the 1990s as coordinated understandings of the nature of power in the post-Soviet context were only emerging. One of the most important is of course the degree of institutional flux and uncertainty inherited from the Soviet breakup. In the two countries where the Communist Party structure was not fundamentally disrupted during the transition to independence, Turkmenistan and Uzbekistan, it provided a convenient mechanism for rule that did not involve the costs and risks of attempting to construct a hybrid regime.[1] The chief patrons of the other newly independent states did not have this option, making the construction of a hybrid regime with its attendant benefits for rulers (as discussed in Chapter 4) a preferable option to the even greater costs and risks involved in trying to create a new mechanism for fully autocratic rule. Thus only in the single-pyramid systems of Turkmenistan and Uzbekistan was all genuine opposition snuffed out after only a brief interlude, consistently kept off the ballot for the country's most important formal offices.

Also influential was whether the initial chaos of the post-Soviet period happened to produce a break from Soviet era election rules by which parliamentary deputies were chosen at least partly in single-member-district (SMD) elections. Outside the Baltics in the former Soviet space, only in Moldova did a switch to a purely proportional-representation system of parliamentary elections take place, a move that complicated its presidents' efforts to subdue the national legislature by co-opting or dividing and conquering its deputies.[2] Thus Moldova supplies the only instance when the legislature wound up winning the

---

[1] That is, the decision to stick with the old structure where it still exists makes sense through a logic of path dependence (Douglass C. North, *Institutions, Institutional Change and Economic Performance* [New York: Cambridge University Press, 1990]). Where the old structure has already been seriously disrupted or destroyed, the cost-benefit calculus in favor of trying something new rather than applying resources to attempt to restore the old improves (Collier and Collier, *Shaping the Political Arena*).

[2] Erik S. Herron, *Elections and Democracy after Communism?* (New York: Palgrave Macmillan, 2009), p. 34.

battles between parliament and president that were nearly a universal feature of politics in the wake of the USSR's dissolution. The result was the non-Baltic post-Soviet world's lone purely parliamentarist constitution.

Leadership will and skill also strongly influenced the outcomes of struggles between post-Soviet patronal networks in the 1990s, though their effects were felt more in the short run of the early 1990s than the longer run of the entire decade.[3] The presidential advantage could be used to great effect by skilled actors, but it could also be easily squandered, destroyed in a heartbeat with a major blunder, miscalculation, or inaction that could redirect actors' expectations as to which patrons had the most or least promising futures. As time passed, however, the importance of will and skill began to matter less and less for the big picture that interests us here. Unskilled, less ambitious, or more fickle presidents tended to fail quickly, whereupon their successors either learned from their mistakes or were the survivors of a natural selection process that weeded out the least fit.[4] And presidents with all kinds of backgrounds – from Communist Party boss to anti-Soviet dissident – proved remarkably consistent in their ability and willingness to use both formal and informal power to arrange oligarchic, regional, and other networks around the presidency in a single pyramid of power that dominated all other patronalistic hierarchies in politics. Leadership – a source of irregular regime dynamics – remained significant, but was increasingly overshadowed by factors promoting regularity in the sense described in Chapter 4.

The construction of single-pyramid systems during the 1990s, it turns out, did not hinge decisively on many other factors commonly said to make it easier or harder for leaders to behave in an authoritarian manner. Such systems thus emerged in the 1990s among impoverished as well as hydrocarbon-rich states, among ethnically homogeneous societies as well as those beset with deep and even violent identity divides, among states that began with relatively unified political elites as well as highly fractious ones, and among polities that adopted extensive market-oriented reform as well as among those clinging to economic statism.[5] These factors surely influenced the particular *character* of the single-

[3] Works stressing the role of leadership skill and values in regime change or political machine building include Giuseppe Di Palma, *To Craft Democracies: An Essay on Democratic Transition* (Los Angeles: University of California Press, 1990); Henry E. Hale, "Explaining Machine Politics in Russia's Regions: Economy, Ethnicity, and Legacy," *Post-Soviet Affairs*, v. 19, no. 3, July–September 2003, pp. 228–63; Michael McFaul, "The Fourth Wave of Democracy and Dictatorship: Noncooperative Transitions in the Postcommunist World," *World Politics*, v. 54, no. 2, January 2002, pp. 212–44; and Lucan A. Way, "Deer in Headlights: Incompetence and Weak Authoritarianism after the Cold War," *Slavic Review*, v. 71, no. 3, Fall 2012, pp. 619–46.

[4] Similarly, Levitsky and Way (Steven Levitsky and Lucan A. Way, *Competitive Authoritarianism: Hybrid Regimes after the Cold War* [New York: Cambridge University Press, 2010], p. 82) posit that for the subset of regimes they study, leadership mattered more in the short run than the longer run.

[5] Important works emphasizing these factors include M. Steven Fish, *Democracy Derailed in Russia: The Failure of Open Politics* (New York: Cambridge University Press, 2005); Lucan A.

pyramid systems and the *details* of how they operated, including the nature of political contestation they allowed at their peaks. But the focus here is on the bigger picture, the larger pattern by which *some form* of single-pyramid system developed in almost every non-Baltic post-Soviet state and quasi-state by the end of the 1990s. Indeed, no claim is made here that these systems were identical or featured exactly the same level or type of contestation. Kazakhstan's single-pyramid system in 1999 was much more closed than was the single-pyramid system in Ukraine, and the types of networks of which they were composed differed. But what was common by the end of the former USSR's first decade was the establishment of presidential networks' dominance and, even in the case of the more loosely constructed pyramids like Ukraine's, the ability of the presidential network to rally other networks to its cause when challenged and increasingly to marginalize the rest.

Without denying diversity in the details, then, this chapter (and volume) trains attention on the larger process these polities had in common in roughly the first decade after independence. The pages that follow thus trace how patronal presidents established their capacity to rally the most important patronal networks to their cause in decisive political struggles (especially their own reelection) and to render those that refused to cooperate in such instances increasingly irrelevant. This process tracing shows how this same basic process took place in all but one non-Baltic post-Soviet state or quasi-state, a pattern also found in year-by-year expert ratings that show a rise in levels of each polity's political closure beginning as the initial transitional chaos subsided. This took place nearly everywhere despite the great diversity in leaders' will, skill, resource endowments, and social, cultural, institutional, and economic contexts. The exception of Moldova will be shown to prove the rule, for reasons already mentioned. These 1990s struggles and their outcomes, in turn, contributed strongly to the emergence of a new "common sense" among elites as to what political power was, a new coordination of actors' expectations. This common sense – remarkably consistent across the Eurasian space – in turn came to inform the workings of patronal politics in the region through at least the present day.

Accordingly, this chapter also bears out a large-scale implication of the logic presented in Chapter 4. As understandings of power became more coordinated and as leaders either learned or were "selected out" through early battles during the decade following the USSR's demise, the sources of regularity in patronal presidential regime cycles gradually started to dominate the sources of irregularity. Chapter 7 then picks up the story where the present chapter leaves off, showing that these regularities give us an extraordinary ability to anticipate and explain some of the most important events in Eurasian politics, the ousters of patronal presidents.

Way, "Authoritarian State-Building and the Sources of Regime Competitiveness in the Fourth Wave: The Cases of Belarus, Moldova, Russia, and Ukraine," *World Politics*, v. 57, January 2005, pp. 231–61.

The Short-Term Importance of Leadership Will and Skill

In politics as in construction, not all builders are successful. So when it came to the construction of Eurasia's power pyramids, a leader's experience and skill as well as his[6] intentions, values, and propensity for risk taking mattered. This is evident in some spectacular failures by leaders with intelligentsia backgrounds and little previous administrative experience, leaders whose actions frequently undermined their own public support and shook the faith of their most important allies in their ability to rule, resulting in their downfall.

One of the major flameouts was Georgia's Zviad Gamsakhurdia, an academic who traded on fiery rhetoric to head the republic's main nationalist movement.[7] Leading the Round Table–Free Georgia bloc to a crushing defeat of the local Communist Party in 1990 elections – the first since Soviet troops massacred twenty people on the streets of Tbilisi – Gamsakhurdia went on a nationalist bender. Campaigning for ethnic purity and excluding non-Georgian "settlers" from political and economic power, he created a National Guard in late 1990 designed to be independent of Soviet control and appointed his friend Tengiz Kitovani, an artist, commander. Gamsakhurdia attacked other "guards" that sprang up outside his control, ultimately arresting the leader of the largest, the notorious Mkhedrioni ("horsemen") led by the former art historian Jaba Ioseliani, which traded in all kinds of criminal activities. In May 1991, he won the republic's first direct presidential election. But despite this mandate and his earlier bravado, just three months later he bizarrely seemed to cave in to the August 1991 Soviet coup plotters, ordering his friend Kitovani to turn over his weapons to the Interior Ministry. His increasingly "former" friend refused. Growing fretful for his rule, Gamsakhurdia systematically alienated many former allies by hastily firing or arresting them – often accusing them of plotting against him – instead of more pragmatically building alliances and cultivating patronage relationships that he could later exploit. After militia fired on a crowd of antigovernment protesters, Georgia's internal political conflicts turned violent. In September 1991, Gamsakhurdia declared a state of emergency and banned most political organizations, whereupon the artist-warlord Kitovani allied with Gamsakhurdia's former prime minister, Tengis Sigua, to resist with force. In January 1992, this opposition joined with recently escaped warlord Ioseliani to form a Military Council that claimed power, ultimately forcing Gamsakhurdia to flee. He then launched a civil war to retake power but failed, costing Georgia dozens more lives, culminating with his own (apparently by suicide) in early 1994.[8]

---

[6] All post-Soviet presidents through 2014 have been male except for Roza Otunbaeva's short transitional rule in Kyrgyzstan.

[7] Georgi Derluguian, *Bourdieu's Secret Admirer in the Caucasus: A World Systems Biography* (Chicago: University of Chicago Press, 2005), p. 61.

[8] Derluguian, *Bourdieu's Secret Admirer*, p. 61; Stephen F. Jones, "Georgia: The Trauma of Statehood," in Ian Bremmer and Ray Taras, eds., *New States, New Politics* (New York:

Azerbaijan's Abulfez Elchibey personified another intelligentsia debacle, albeit in the very difficult circumstances of war with Armenia over separatism in Nagorno-Karabakh. A history professor who won the presidency in June 1992 as leader of the country's main nationalist movement, he proved personally unwilling to exploit the opportunities he had to build authority using patronalistic methods. However admirable this may have been, the problem was that he developed no other mechanism for controlling the various elite groups in the country, including in his own administration. He also drove many away through his own policies. Declaring that Azerbaijani was a form of Turkish more than a proper language of its own and requiring its use in all state business, he alienated many within the broader republic elite. Ordering a counteroffensive to retake Nagorno-Karabakh, he moved before developing a command structure and loyal officer core, action that led to a series of disastrous losses and Armenian occupation of large swaths of Azerbaijani territory, even outside the separatist enclave. Losing control over law enforcement, the Interior Ministry became a rogue force, its minister reported to have personally assaulted an opposition editor before the president finally fired him. With Elchibey leading Azerbaijan conspicuously out of the Commonwealth of Independent States, Russia was more inclined to assist Armenia in its conflict with Azerbaijan. Thus when forced to withdraw its military forces from the country, Russia left its cache of arms in the hands of a particularly unruly Azerbaijani warlord, Surat Huseynov, who happened to be near the main Russian base. In Svante Cornell's wording, Elchibey "botched" an attempt to take the weapons under government control, giving Huseynov a pretext to use the arsenal to march on Baku and demand Elchibey's resignation. Elchibey refused to resign but nevertheless fled, heading to his native Nakhichevan autonomous republic in June 1993 for a long period of internal exile. Azerbaijan's parliament dealt him the coup de grace, first impeaching him and then organizing a referendum that returned a 97 percent vote of no confidence in him before ordering elections for a new president.[9]

The intelligentsia, however, had no monopoly on the production of incompetent leaders, as old regime experience was also no guarantee of success. Elchibey's immediate predecessor, Ayaz Mutalibov, demonstrated this quite clearly. Gorbachev had installed Mutalibov as Azerbaijani Communist Party first secretary as part of his effort to quash the local nationalist movement

---

Cambridge University Press, 1997), pp. 505–43; Darrell Slider, "Democratization in Georgia," in Karen Dawisha and Bruce Parrott, eds., *Conflict, Cleavage, and Change in Central Asia and the Caucasus* (New York: Cambridge University Press, 1997), pp. 156–98; Jonathan Wheatley, *Georgia from National Awakening to Rose Revolution: Delayed Transition in the Former Soviet Union* (Burlington: Ashgate, 2005), pp. 41–66.

[9] This account is drawn primarily from Svante Cornell, *Azerbaijan since Independence* (Armonk, NY: M. E. Sharpe, 2011), pp. 67–80, but see also Shireen T. Hunter, "Azerbaijan: Searching for New Neighbors," in Ian Bremmer and Ray Taras, eds., *New States, New Politics* (New York: Cambridge University Press, 1997), pp. 437–72.

and stop local ethnic violence. In January 1990, after attacks on Armenians in Baku had left more than five dozen dead, Gorbachev sent in Soviet troops to restore order, killing 150 in the process and replacing the old party boss with Mutalibov. This temporarily crushed Azerbaijan's nationalist movement, and Mutalibov won the republic's first presidential elections unopposed in September 1991. He was not able to maintain control during the transition to independence, however. Despite violent Azeri attempts to prevent it, the Armenian population of Nagorno-Karabakh voted overwhelmingly in a December 1991 referendum for independence from Azerbaijan. While Mutalibov sought to enforce Azerbaijani control over the region, he had not built a national army that had a good chance of doing so, in dramatic contrast with Armenia and Nagorno-Karabakh itself. The armed struggle quickly turned in the breakaway republic's favor, tragically symbolized for Azerbaijanis in the Armenian forces' capture of Khojaly and the killing there of hundreds of Azerbaijanis. The opposition lambasted him for this defeat, accusing him of having deliberately delayed the creation of a national army out of excessive loyalty to Moscow – indeed, there had been no such delay in Armenia – and Mutalibov made matters even worse by trying to downplay the events. With thousands protesting in the streets, Mutalibov resigned in March 1992, just three months after the USSR had dissolved. Elchibey won the presidential election that followed in July 1992.[10]

The most tragic of all post-Soviet failures to build a patronal monopoly on power, however, can be pinned to another former Communist Party boss, Rakhmon Nabiev, the republic first secretary 1982–5 and Tajikistan's first directly elected president as of November 1991. Nabiev began as one might expect a would-be pyramid builder to begin, restricting freedoms of press and assembly, harassing the main opposition parties, targeting a few opposition figures for conspicuous arrest, drawing on supporters from historically important regionally based networks (especially the dominant groups in Kulob and Khujand/Leninobod). Matters started to go badly wrong for him, however, when he arrested Dushanbe Mayor Maqsud Ikromov, who had irked the former Communist establishment by removing the city's most prominent Lenin statue and opposing Nabiev's return to power immediately after the August 1991 coup attempt in Moscow shook up local politics. Various opposition forces rallied to Ikromov's cause and mobilized more general opposition to Nabiev, bringing tens of thousands out into the streets. Nabiev's response would pave the way to civil war: Not only did he seek to counter the demonstration by busing in supporters from Kulob for a large counterdemonstration, but after this did not resolve the standoff, he distributed automatic weapons to them and dubbed them a "Presidential Guard" under the leadership of Sangak Safarov, described by leading academics variously as a "career criminal," "crime boss," and "multiple murderer." They then killed dozens in trying to drive out the

[10] Cornell, *Azerbaijan since Independence*, pp. 60–4; Hunter, "Azerbaijan."

opposition protesters, but only succeeded in outraging the opposition and alarming some of Nabiev's own associates, including his main military adviser, Bahram Rahmanov, who joined the opposition. Having failed to restore order, Nabiev sought cover in the KGB building, where he hid out until agreeing to cede the emergency powers he had claimed, to disband the Presidential Guard, and to form a coalition government. The disbanded "Guard" then took their weapons back to Kulob and began purging their network's local opponents, launching from there a brutal war to gain full control of the country. The Tajik Civil War, which did not finally end until 1997, is estimated to have killed up to 100,000 people and displaced about seven times that number. As for Nabiev himself, he was captured by the opposition in September 1992 and forced at gunpoint to resign, eventually to die a quiet death by heart attack in 1993.[11]

Far less disastrous, but still unable to form a single-pyramid system under his leadership, was the former longtime Communist Party official Leonid Kravchuk. Kravchuk was a savvy spinner of ideological nuance and a shrewd practitioner of political double-speak, which served him well in navigating his transition from Communist Party second secretary to parliamentary speaker to the first president of independent Ukraine, winning the country's first direct election to this office in December 1991. But he lacked the instincts of a machine politician. The challenges he faced were in many ways similar to those faced by more successful leaders like Russia's Boris Yeltsin, including unruly regional authorities and a parliament that still held the power to change the constitution unilaterally – all in the face of a precipitous economic collapse. Some of Kravchuk's responses would also resemble those of Yeltsin, notably pushing parliament for greater presidential powers to consolidate statehood and manage the economy, imposing appointed "presidential representatives" as the heads of regional executive power (governors), and granting significant resources to the most restive regions in a bid to retain their support.[12]

Yet Kravchuk demonstrated a remarkably hands-off attitude toward managing executive power, and little resolve in struggling for presidential power. Kataryna Wolczuk describes how he rejected calls from his allies to use his local powers more actively, and paid little attention to legislation after his first

[11] On the details of these events, see Muriel Atkin, "Tajikistan: Reform, Reaction, and Civil War," in Ian Bremmer and Ray Taras, eds., *New States, New Politics* (New York: Cambridge University Press, 1997), pp. 602–33, pp. 610–16; John Schoeberlein-Engel, "Conflict in Tajikistan and Central Asia: The Myth of Ethnic Animosity," *Harvard Middle Eastern and Islamic Review*, v. 1, no. 2, 1994, pp. 1–55, pp. 36–42; and Idil Tuncer-Kilavuz, *Power, Networks and Violent Conflict in Central Asia: A Comparison of Tajikistan and Uzbekistan* (New York: Routledge, 2014). An account stressing structural conditions making Tajikistan more vulnerable to such state failure than Uzbekistan is Lawrence P. Markowitz, *State Erosion: Unlootable Resources and Unruly Elites in Central Asia* (Ithaca, NY: Cornell University Press, 2013).

[12] Robert S. Kravchuk, "The Quest for Balance: Regional Self-Government and Subnational Fiscal Policy in Ukraine," in Taras Kuzio, Robert S. Kravchuk, and Paul D'Anieri, *State and Institution-Building in Ukraine* (New York: St. Martin's, 1999), pp. 155–212, pp. 162–5; Kataryna Wolczuk, *The Moulding of Ukraine: The Constitutional Politics of State Formation* (Budapest: CEU Press, 2001), pp. 110–19.

months in office as his "focus drifted away from domestic affairs" and turned to establishing Ukraine's standing in international affairs. When his allies urged him to seize control of the government, he replied that he would not "act like Boris Yeltsin and, apart from being the head of state, he will not perform the function of the head of government."[13] Thus when his first prime minister resigned in the wake of the economic crisis that had been ongoing since the USSR's demise, he nominated a little known industrialist from the dominant network in Dnipropetrovsk, Yuzhmash missile factory director Leonid Kuchma, and let him have his way entirely in appointing ministers and structuring the government.[14] In contrast, Kuchma proved to have the fire in the belly that Kravchuk lacked, moving quickly to augment and use prime ministerial power, even convincing the parliament to give him emergency powers (in return for accepting more formal parliamentary oversight) that included temporarily transferring to him the formerly presidential authority to issue decrees with the force of law on key economic issues. Only when Kuchma requested a renewal of these powers for two more years in 1993 did Kravchuk begin to resist seriously, eventually prompting Kuchma to brand the president an obstacle to economic improvement and to resign.[15]

The primary question was how to get out of the deadlock that had emerged among parliament, prime minister, and president. Kravchuk had originally concurred with the parliament to hold a referendum, but they disagreed on whether this should be a vote of (no) confidence in president and parliament (the parliament's choice) or a referendum on whether presidential powers should be transferred to the government (Kravchuk's choice).[16] But just days after a similar referendum won by Yeltsin in Russia had led Yeltsin to order the dissolution of his parliament and call early elections there, Kravchuk decided that the referendum could be skipped. He convinced parliament to resolve the crisis by holding early elections for both parliament and president in 1994. In his memoirs, Kravchuk called this move a "mistake," and indeed he realized too late that his neglect of building the machinery of power meant that he did not have the pieces in place to win an election.[17] Indeed, Kimitaka Matsuzato's research has shown that Kravchuk had been quite inattentive to pressuring his appointed governors to build up their local political machines and to remain loyal, removing only one governor for political reasons prior to February 1994 and only three more prior to the presidential voting.[18] And as

[13] Wolczuk, *The Moulding of Ukraine*, p. 114.
[14] Wolczuk, *The Moulding of Ukraine*, pp. 114–15.
[15] Paul D'Anieri, *Understanding Ukrainian Politics: Power, Politics, and Institutional Design* (Armonk, NY: M.E. Sharpe, 2007), p. 81; Wolczuk, *The Moulding of Ukraine*, pp. 116–18.
[16] Heorhii Kas'ianov, *Ukraiina 1991–2007: Narysy novitn'oii istorii* (Kyiv: Nash Chas, 2008), p. 48.
[17] Leonid Kravchuk, *Maemo te, shcho maemo: spohady i rozdumy* (Kyiv: Stolittia, 2002), p. 224.
[18] Kimitaka Matsuzato, "All Kuchma's Men: The Reshuffling of Ukrainian Governors and the Presidential Election of 1999," *Post-Soviet Geography and Economics*, v. 42, no. 6, September 2001, p. 424.

of mid-1994, the oligarchic networks that later became very important parts of Ukraine's national political machine were only beginning to emerge, meaning that they were not available as a major resource for Kravchuk even if he had tried aggressively to mobilize them. And because Kuchma had played the dominant hands-on role in the economy for most of 1993, he was in just as good a position to claim their loyalty as was the president.

Evidently reflecting this sense that he could not win, Kravchuk himself reports that he actually drafted a decree to dissolve parliament and postpone elections indefinitely, preparing an announcement to this effect for January 11, 1994. Kravchuk decided against the move only at the last minute, when his interior minister (in office since 1991) told him that he would not support the measure, a fact Kravchuk accepts in his memoirs as his failure as president to install loyal, reliable figures in such critical institutions. He also writes that he has grounds to suspect this minister was motivated by secret collaboration with the president's rivals.[19] The president then publicly declared in an interview that he would not seek reelection at all so as to preclude becoming a scapegoat for all the problems facing the country and a focal point for criticism, but then reversed himself the following week, allowing that he might run while also hinting that the presidential elections might need to be postponed.[20]

After all this waffling, Kravchuk entered the summer 1994 presidential race quite unprepared. This was a major problem because the main challenge was from an ambitious recent prime minister who had considerable appeal in Ukraine's East. Kuchma thus called for improved relations with Russia (largely severed by Kravchuk but vital for networks based in eastern heavy industry) and more competent economic management (having resigned blaming Kravchuk, he was not tainted by the ongoing economic crisis nearly as much as was Kravchuk). While Kravchuk in the end sought to muster what patronal strength he had, including manipulating mass media coverage and even temporarily shutting down the First Ukrainian television channel, which had been backing Kuchma, he wound up losing a narrow contest to the coalition built by Kuchma, who became Ukraine's second president.[21] The election was strikingly divided along east-west lines in terms of both voting patterns and elite network support, with Kuchma dominating in the East and Kravchuk overwhelmingly winning the West.

Stepping back to look at the larger picture, something other than leadership skill appears in the foreground. Indeed, it is striking that even where blundering presidents initially failed, new ones eventually emerged who did virtually the same thing all across the post-Soviet space: successfully construct a single-pyramid system of some kind by the end of the 1990s. These successors

---

[19] Kravchuk, *Maemo te, shcho maemo*, pp. 228–31.

[20] *RFE/RL*, no. 37, February 23, 1994; *RFE/RL*, no. 40, February 28, 1994. See Kravchuk's own later interpretation in Kravchuk, *Maemo te, shcho maemo*, pp. 231–2.

[21] D'Anieri, *Understanding Ukrainian Politics*, pp. 82–3; Kas'ianov, *Ukraiina 1991–2007*, p. 54.

either were better machine politicians or simply learned from the mistakes of their predecessors. Thus while leadership skill (a source of irregular regime dynamics) can account for short-run variation, the larger pattern that emerged over the course of the 1990s is best explained with reference to the incentives created by the region's combination of strong patronalism, the emergence of the kinds of patronalistic networks described in Chapter 5 at the intersection of historical legacy and post-Soviet transition, and the formal institutional design that emerged as the USSR dissolved, in particular presidentialist constitutions. Indeed, these factors created the opportunity to build strong political machines that ambitious leaders found hard to resist as a way of pursuing whatever it was that they wanted to pursue, be it corrupt personal wealth, market reform, stability, or simply power.

The Near-Universal Eurasian Tendency to Single-Pyramid Politics in the 1990s

There were variations on the general theme of how patronal presidentialism and the single-pyramid systems of the 1990s were built. Some presidents were more willing to use violent methods, such as deploying military might against a rebellious parliament or arresting or even killing one's political opponents or critics.[22] Others displayed more tolerance of risk, especially on the question of whether and what opposition should be allowed to compete in elections. And the timing of the consolidation of presidential power sometimes varied, usually depending on the peculiarities of the early struggles or the context in which they took place (for example, the separatist wars in Azerbaijan and Georgia). Nevertheless, patronal presidents ultimately established single-pyramid systems of some kind in nearly all fragments of the former Soviet space by the 1990s. And the significance of this pattern is rendered especially stark when one recognizes the wide variety of contexts in which this occurred and of leaders who carried it out. The following subsections lay out some of these patterns, showing that they developed in countries varying quite widely on other factors often thought to be important, including leaders' backgrounds, natural resource wealth, economic development, market reform, identity divides, initial violence, and elite fragmentation.

Democrats as Pyramid Builders: Armenia and Russia

Perhaps strongest testimony to the power of post-Soviet transitional incentives in driving the construction of patronal single-pyramid systems is that even leaders initially believed by many to be democrats and reformers built them. Moreover, some built them successfully regardless of how strong their

---

[22] Deadly violence was used much more extensively in such struggles in many African cases, as Will Reno has pointed out (personal communication), framing an interesting puzzle for future research beyond the scope of this volume.

antiauthoritarian backgrounds were and how weak their starting political position was. Thus while leaders' values may influence large-scale regime dynamics at the margins, the pull of the environment and the temptation to use all available mechanisms at one's disposal to achieve whatever goals one has can be strong indeed, evidently quite overpowering. Russia and Armenia are discussed here as examples where leaders regarded by many as personally inclined to more democratic outcomes became single-pyramid builders in the 1990s, though Georgia and Kyrgyzstan could just as easily have been included under this heading (they will be discussed later to highlight a different point).

One of the most prominent examples is Boris Yeltsin. While there were always questions about his democratic credentials, even as his blasting of Soviet rule reached fever pitch, Yeltsin appealed in part because he called for radical liberalizing reform in both the economy and the polity. Nevertheless, eager to drive home the reforms he had launched and to stay in power, he instituted three major changes that laid the foundation for a single-pyramid system in Russia. First, the privatization process and economic restructuring created a series of very large corporate conglomerates that could powerfully intervene in politics and that depended heavily for their wealth on the beneficence of different parts of the state, as described in the previous chapter. Second, he presided over the construction of potent regional political machines across many regions of Russia, as was also described earlier. The most innovative and proactive among governors used the authority he gave them not only to alter electoral institutions in ways that reinforced their own advantage, but also dramatically to shape the privatization process locally and to politicize sources of authority such as licensing powers or the ability to fine or suspend a company's operations through tax or fire inspections.[23]

Third, Yeltsin himself forcibly converted Russia from a system in which the Congress of People's Deputies had the formal authority to amend the constitution unilaterally to a strongly presidentialist system that was widely dubbed "superpresidential."[24] When parliament resisted, sending armed men out to seize important sites, the president literally ordered tanks to fire on the parliament building (widely known as the White House) in late 1993 and in the wake of the carnage held a snap referendum on a new strongly presidentialist constitution. The Duma on paper was not completely powerless, at least when controlled by opposition forces as it was for part of Yeltsin's presidency, but Yeltsin and his associates quickly built a tremendous degree of informal power around various presidential structures, especially a massive administration

[23] Mikhail N. Afanas'ev, *Klientelizm i Rossiiskaia Gosudarstvennost'* (Moscow: Moscow Public Science Foundation, 1997).
[24] Stephen Holmes, "Back to the Drawing Board: An Argument for Constitutional Postponement in Eastern Europe," *East European Constitutional Review*, v. 2, no. 1, Winter 1993, pp. 21–5.

that some characterized as a second, less publicly accountable government that often controlled what the real government did.[25]

While the moving parts of Russian politics (especially oligarchic networks and regional political machines) initially gyrated rather wildly, often taking the country in directions Yeltsin did not like, the key moment in Russian post-Soviet political history occurred in 1996. It was then when Yeltsin for the first time vigorously deployed his arsenal of sticks and opened his cornucopia of carrots to mobilize regional political machines and major financial-industrial groups into a nationwide pyramid of patronal networks capable of defeating a major political opponent in the presidential race of that year. The Communist Party's Gennady Zyuganov was in fact initially far ahead in public opinion polls, so far ahead that even some oligarchs donated money to his campaign so as to gain favorable treatment should the Communist candidate win.[26] In effect, while Zyuganov had ideational appeal, he also controlled his own power pyramid. Zyuganov's pyramid pulled together some relatively reluctant support from banks and combined it with strong backing from some struggling industrial enterprise networks, a large collection of parliamentary deputies, and a good number of "red governors" in rural or industrial regions who regarded Yeltsin's policies as ruinous for them and who thus were unwilling to place their bets on the incumbent.

The 1996 contest proved to all that Yeltsin's presidential pyramid was superior. Networks increasingly peeled off Zyuganov's pyramid as Yeltsin plied his formal and informal presidential powers. He supplied important transfers of resources to key regions at strategic moments, threatened the same regions with the denial of such funds should they not comply, and provided corporate leaders with highly favorable privatization opportunities in return for campaign financing and decidedly biased television news coverage on the channels they controlled. Regions like Bashkortostan, where a plurality vote had gone to Zyuganov in round one, suddenly supplied a majority to Yeltsin in round two.[27] The result was a resounding two-round victory despite the fact that Yeltsin's ratings had been in the single digits earlier that same year and despite a massive heart attack that caused him to disappear from public view before the runoff occurred. So effective had been this machine that Boris Berezovsky is said to have then declared (one suspects

---

[25] Timothy Colton and Cindy Skach, "The Predicament of Semi-Presidentialism," in Alfred Stepan, ed., *Democracies in Danger* (Baltimore: Johns Hopkins University Press, 2009); Fish, *Democracy Derailed in Russia*.

[26] Sergei Kolmakov, "The Role of Financial Industrial Conglomerates in Russian Political Parties," *Russia Watch* (Harvard University), no. 9, January 2003, p. 16.

[27] Juliet Johnson, *A Fistful of Rubles: The Rise and Fall of the Russian Banking System* (Ithaca, NY: Cornell University Press, 2000); Daniel S. Treisman, "How Yeltsin Won," *Foreign Affairs*, v. 75, no. 5, September–October 1996, pp. 64–77.

only half in jest if true) that he and the Kremlin could even get a "monkey" elected president.[28]

Armenia supplies an even clearer-cut case of an originally antiauthoritarian leader who became a patronal president and soon built a single-pyramid system around himself. Its first president was Levon Ter-Petrossian, a philologist with great oratorical prowess that carried him to the leadership of the Armenian National Movement (ANM) and then the parliament when it was first elected more or less freely in 1990.[29] Despite emerging as a prominent advocate for democratization and possessing impeccable antiestablishment credentials, having even been jailed as a dissident during the Soviet period, he soon realized the political value of political machine building for operating in Armenia's patronalistic environment and saw the transitional opportunities to do so, with his ANM providing a formal structure for his team. Administering the privatization process gave him ample opportunity to foster extended economic networks, for example, in his forging close ties over time with the emerging oligarch Khachatur Sukiasian and his SIL concern, described in Chapter 5. Indicating how central this was to Ter-Petrossian's rule, not only did his second-oldest brother, Petros, lead a privatization commission in the construction industry, but his oldest brother, Telman, was deputy chair of the Commission on Privatization and Denationalization for a time as well as the longtime director of the industrial enterprise Hrazdanmash. By one account, he was "the man who controls Armenian industry."[30] His Interior Minister Vano Siradeghian became notorious for orchestrating a racket generating payments through tax inspectors, customs officials, and police, which "regulate trade and transportation in and out of Armenia."[31] A similar scheme was reportedly organized by the Defense Ministry. Such arrangements created opportunities for illicit political influence that could potentially be directed from the very top.[32]

The only parliamentary elections to be held under Ter-Petrossian (in 1995) were widely interpreted as "competition between patron-client networks," though they were also manipulated by central authorities, with many opposition candidates disqualified in district contests that tended to be dominated by patronalistic "campaign" techniques (the parliament was mostly district-elected). Candidates allowed in included many business representatives, seeking influence and (by some accounts) immunity from prosecution, meaning

[28] *Sovetskaia Rossiia*, March 23, 2000.
[29] Ronald Grigor Suny, "Elite Transformation in Late-Soviet and Post-Soviet Transcaucasia, or What Happens When the Ruling Class Can't Rule?" in Timothy J. Colton and Robert C. Tucker, eds., *Patterns in Post-Soviet Leadership* (Boulder, CO: Westview, 1995), pp. 141–68.
[30] Nora Dudwick, "Political Transformations in Postcommunist Armenia: Images and Realities," in Karen Dawisha and Bruce Parrott, eds., *Conflict, Cleavage, and Change in Central Asia and the Caucasus* (New York: Cambridge University Press, 1997), pp. 69–109, quotation from p. 91.
[31] Dudwick, "Political Transformations in Postcommunist Armenia," quotation from p. 91.
[32] Dudwick, "Political Transformations in Postcommunist Armenia," pp. 91–8.

that Ter-Petrossian could influence their votes by impacting their pocketbooks when need be.[33] At the same time as the 1995 parliamentary elections were held, Ter-Petrossian organized a referendum on a strongly presidentialist constitution and mobilized state control over mass media to influence the vote, which ultimately went in the proposed constitution's favor. This gave him influence over the appointment of nearly all major state offices, including governors and courts.[34] With this highly presidentialist constitution passed, Ter-Petrossian pulled together his machine to win reelection in September 1996 against a vigorous challenge from a major opposition candidate (former prime minister Vazgen Manukian) despite virtual economic collapse and transitional chaos, though with the glow of victory in the Nagorno-Karabakh war. Manukian's supporters protested the result, even assaulting the parliamentary speaker in the legislature's building, and acquiesced only after Ter-Petrossian sent in police, called a state of emergency, and banned public protests.[35] This power *vertikal'* of a virulently anticommunist "democrat" had withstood a tough test indeed.

The Pyramids of Privatizers: Kyrgyzstan and Kazakhstan

Single-pyramid systems have emerged not only where leaders were initially thought to be democrats, but even where they were also generally regarded as being among the country's most avid marketeers and privatizers. Kyrgyzstan's President Askar Akaev provides a good example, initially enjoying a reputation as Central Asia's lone democratic and promarket leader due to his scholarly profile, lack of a party apparatchik past, pronouncements in favor of democracy, market-oriented reforms, and opening to the West, and, importantly, his standout refusal to bend to hard-line Soviet coup plotters in August 1991.[36]

But while still allowing more freedom than did his neighbors, Akaev began using his powers as president to build a strong power *vertikal'* beginning in the mid-1990s, initially formalized in the moderately presidentialist constitution of 1993.[37] Through his position as patron in chief, Kyrgyz authorities prosecuted or shut down several opposition newspapers (achieving fairly strong control of Kyrgyzstan's media space)[38] and followed Uzbekistan's Karimov in establishing a system of presidentially appointed regional administrators (*akims*) in 1995 to

---

[33] Dudwick, "Political Transformations in Postcommunist Armenia," pp. 91–8.

[34] Dudwick, "Political Transformations in Postcommunist Armenia," pp. 92–4.

[35] Dudwick, "Political Transformations in Postcommunist Armenia," pp. 103–5; Liz Fuller, "Democracy or Oligarchy?" *RFE/RL Newsline*, September 22, 1997.

[36] Eugene Huskey, "Kyrgyzstan: The Fate of Political Liberalization," in Karen Dawisha and Bruce Parrott, eds., *Conflict, Cleavage, and Change in Central Asia and the Caucasus* (New York: Cambridge University Press, 1997), pp. 242–76, p. 242.

[37] Usenaly Chotonov, *Suverennyi Kyrgyzstan: vybor istoricheskogo puti* (Bishkek: Kyrgyzstan, 1995), p. 62.

[38] Shairbek Juraev, "Kyrgyz Democracy? The Tulip Revolution and Beyond," *Central Asian Survey*, v. 27, nos. 3–4, September 2008, pp. 337–47.

reduce the autonomy of regional patronage networks and to become centers of patronage activities themselves. Putting this *akim* system to work right away, Akaev managed to orchestrate the dissolution of the parliament and elect a new one through single-member districts that were largely dominated by the *akims* and local business representatives.[39] The parliament elected in 2000 similarly gave him a majority formed largely through the patronalistic manipulation of district-elected deputies.[40] And business was increasingly dominated by Akaev's inner circle, which strongly influenced patterns of privatization, as was described in Chapter 5, and wielded significant regulatory and enforcement capacity. Kelly McMann's careful research conducted in the early 2000s shows how effective could be this power *vertikal'*, uniting major economic actors and local authorities to squelch political competition almost completely in some regions and significantly hindering opposition politics in others.[41] Akaev also exerted considerable effort to establish control over state revenues: For example, in a December 1998 government reshuffle as the 2000 election approached, he left in power those responsible for spending money already accumulated but replaced those in charge of collecting it.[42] He also devised clever ways to channel foreign aid, which started flowing in copiously after independence, to buy off parliamentarians.[43] He also explicitly stated on at least one occasion that a criterion for naming someone prime minister was whether the candidate would attempt to use the post to angle for the presidency. In all, he appointed eight prime ministers in the dozen years after 1990.[44] While he did permit real opposition candidates to compete against him in the December 1995 presidential election, others (such as Feliks Kulov and Topchubek Turgunaliev) were barred or jailed, and most media effectively campaigned in his favor, helping him generate a victory with 72 percent of the vote.[45]

In his 2002 memoirs, Akaev complains constantly about the limitations on presidential power, lamenting that in 1995 Kyrgyzstan's president was the equivalent in potency of "the Queen of England."[46] He thus orchestrated successive referenda in 1994, 1996, and 2003 to augment presidential authority. Not all of his attempts were successful; parliament did reject a September 1995 referendum initiative that would have extended his term by an extra

[39] John Anderson, *Kyrgyzstan: Central Asia's Island of Democracy?* (Amsterdam: Harwood, 1999) p. 41; Huskey, "Kyrgyzstan."

[40] Gulnara Iskakova, *Vybory i demokratiia v Kyrgyzstane: Konstitutsionnyi dizain prezidentsko-parlamentskikh otnoshenii* (Bishkek: Biyiktik, 2003), pp. 417–19.

[41] Kelly M. McMann, *Economic Autonomy and Democracy: Hybrid Regimes in Russia and Kyrgyzstan* (New York: Cambridge University Press, 2006).

[42] Iskakova, *Vybory i demokratiia v Kyrgyzstane*, pp. 311–12.

[43] Eric McGlinchey, *Chaos, Violence, Dynasty: Politics and Islam in Central Asia* (Pittsburgh: Pittsburgh University Press, 2011), chapter 4.

[44] Iskakova, *Vybory i demokratiia v Kyrgyzstane*, pp. 311–12, p. 315.

[45] Anderson, *Kyrgyzstan*, p. 53; *RFE/RL Newsline*, November 18, 1997; *RFE/RL Newsline*, November 30, 1998; *RFE/RL Weekday Magazine*, February 10, 2000.

[46] Akaev, *Trudnaia doroga k demokratii*, p. 218.

year. Akaev, however, also writes that he could have gotten the referendum by signature collection, circumventing parliament, had he really wanted it badly.[47] And when he did want something badly, he was generally able to get it. The 1996 referendum, just after his own reelection as president in December 1995, expanded his powers as president (for example, giving him the right to disband parliament if it thrice rejected his nominee for prime minister) and secured a Constitutional Court ruling that allowed him a third term in office on the grounds that his first term was initiated under the pre-1993 constitution and thus did not count toward the two-term limit.[48] Another referendum in February 2003 extended his constitutionally final term, delaying the time he was required to leave office until 2005.[49] Thus while Kyrgyzstan remained much more open politically than its Central Asian neighbors, Akaev had successfully constructed a single pyramid of patron-client ties based in the presidency that largely dominated national Kyrgyz politics, keeping alternative patrons weak and their own pyramids localized.

In Kazakhstan as well, relatively extensive privatization did little to hinder single-pyramid construction under President Nursultan Nazarbaev. While Gorbachev had ushered Nazarbaev into power in Kazakhstan much as he had Karimov in Uzbekistan, the Communist Party organization that Nazarbaev led during the Soviet period was – unlike in Uzbekistan – formally dissolved after the failed Soviet coup of August 1991, with two successor parties emerging in its place, the Socialist Party and the Congress Party. While Nazarbaev allies initially led both, the president, having rent the party organization that had sealed the balance among networks and withdrawn himself as the leader of that single party organization, soon lost control of both. Congress Party leader and famous writer Olzhas Suleimenov even displayed presidential ambitions as he reportedly gained access to wealth through metals trading.[50] An important early victory for Nazarbaev was convincing the parliament to adopt a new presidentialist constitution in January 1993, though this document did impose important limitations, including a two-term limit.[51] The new parliament did not prove fully pliable, however, blocking some of his economic initiatives and seeking control over the executive by collecting "compromising data on the executive elite."[52] Nazarbaev then "invited" the parliament to update the body's legitimacy by dissolving itself, a request some interpreted as a threat to do

---

[47] Akaev, *Trudnaia doroga k demokratii*, p. 180–2.

[48] Anderson, *Kyrgyzstan*, p. 54; *RFE/RL Newsline*, July 13, 1998.

[49] Pauline Jones Luong, "Politics in the Periphery: Competing Views of Central Asian States and Societies," in Jones Luong, ed., *The Transformation of Central Asia: States and Societies from Soviet Rule to Independence* (Ithaca, NY: Cornell University Press, 2003).

[50] Sally N. Cummings, *Kazakhstan: Power and the Elite* (London: I. B. Tauris, 2005), pp. 24–5; Martha Brill Olcott, *Kazakhstan: Unfulfilled Promise* (Washington, DC: Carnegie Endowment, 2002), pp. 93–5.

[51] Olcott, *Kazakhstan*, p. 96.

[52] Cummings, *Kazakhstan*, p. 25.

what Yeltsin had done just two months earlier in violently disbanding Russia's Congress in a similar standoff. Parliament obliged, calling new elections.[53] The new parliament was also not fully compliant, however, voting no confidence in the government in a nonbinding protest against continuing economic decline in May 1994 and actually overriding Nazarbaev's veto on two economic bills in July 1994.[54]

Nazarbaev, however, was gradually building up the ability to strike back through his cultivation of informal authority. Voucher privatization was part of this process rather than an obstacle to it. Beginning in April 1994, it produced some of the oligarchic networks described in the previous chapter (such as Bulat Abilov's Butia Capital) that were linked to Nazarbaev's political interests and could begin to direct new resources to political ends, with other oligarchs arising during this period with state or presidential assistance.[55] Similarly, the 1993 constitution had given Nazarbaev the power to appoint and control regional governors (called *akims* in Kazakhstan), who over time began establishing authority in their regions over the resistance of local legislatures.[56] With his informal and formal presidential power growing, the Constitutional Court (in a move many assumed was orchestrated by Nazarbaev) issued a surprise ruling in March 1995 that the parliament had been elected illegally and that all of its powers were thus null and void, with the president assuming virtually unfettered powers until new elections could be held in December.[57] The president used this interlude to good effect, ordering one referendum in April that extended his own presidential term until the year 2000 and a second in August that passed a new, even more strongly presidentialist constitution that essentially turned parliament into a "consultative body."[58]

Winning control of a new parliament that finally proved pliable, it went on to eliminate age and term limits on the presidency, extend the length of presidential terms to seven years, then call snap presidential elections for January 1999 that caught Nazarbaev's opponents off guard. The candidate thought most likely to be able to pose a challenge, former prime minister Akezhan Kazhegeldin, was arrested for an unsanctioned campaign demonstration then disqualified with reference to this "criminal record," while another rival was

[53] Cummings, *Kazakhstan*, p. 25.
[54] *RFE/RL*, May 30, 1994; Martha Brill Olcott, "Democratization and the Growth of Political Participation in Kazakhstan," in Karen Dawisha and Bruce Parrott, eds., *Conflict, Cleavage, and Change in Central Asia and the Caucasus* (New York: Cambridge University Press, 1997), pp. 201–41, p. 222.
[55] Olcott, "Democratization," pp. 217–18.
[56] Olcott, *Kazakhstan*, p. 96.
[57] Olcott, "Democratization," pp. 226–7.
[58] Olcott, *Kazakhstan*, pp. 110–12; Olcott, "Democratization," pp. 230–1; Ian Bremmer and Cory Welt, "The Trouble with Democracy in Kazakhstan," *Central Asian Survey*, v. 15, no. 2, 1996, pp. 179–99, p. 192.

co-opted by an appointment as Almaty governor.[59] Nazarbaev defeated the remaining contenders handily. He followed up on this victory in March 1999 by overseeing the creation of the new propresidential Otan Party (a party of power that would finally stick) and orchestrating early parliamentary elections later that same year, which Otan won handily despite a Communist Party challenge. Among the presidential tactics reportedly used were the creation of a variety of proregime "virtual parties" to divide the field and crowd out potential rivals, as well as simple fraud.[60] By the year 2000, then, Nazarbaev had built an evidently sturdy patronal-presidentialist single-pyramid system, though the great scale of this dominance masked the fact that he had had to win a significant post-Soviet struggle in order to wind up firmly on top.

From Feckless Elite Fragmentation to Single-Pyramid System: Belarus

Deep initial fragmentation among the elite also proved to be no lasting barrier to the emergence of single-pyramid systems once patronal presidentialism was in place, as the case of Belarus illustrates. Belarus, alone among former union republics, resembled South Ossetia and Nagorno-Karabakh in retaining a parliamentary constitution well into the 1990s. And once a presidency was created in 1994, Belarus became the only union republic where the leader under the parliamentary system did not successfully translate this into a direct presidential election victory when such elections were instituted. This reflected what was at first Belarus's highly fragmented political scene.[61] While the old guard had retained control of the parliament during the perestroika-era elections, choosing Viacheslau Kebich as prime minister, after the failed Soviet August 1991 coup it made physicist and former Belorussian State University prorector Stanislau Shushkevich, regarded as a reformer, its speaker as a kind of political counterweight to Kebich.[62] Neither side clearly dominating politics, the parliament drafted a new constitution with a presidency in late 1991, but declined to adopt it.[63] While Kebich pushed through some limited privatization, the republic was bogged down in political gridlock and economic crisis as most other post-Soviet republics were during this time. Uniquely to Belarus, however, a highly charismatic figure emerged to challenge the establishment. Aliaksandr

[59] Olcott, *Kazakhstan*, p. 119–21.

[60] Cummings, *Kazakhstan*, pp. 24–5; Olcott, *Kazakhstan*, pp. 93–5.

[61] Vitali Silitski, "Explaining Post-Communist Authoritarianism in Belarus," in Elena Korosteleva, Colin W. Lawson, and Rosalind J. Marsh, eds., *Contemporary Belarus: Between Democracy and Dictatorship* (New York: RoutledgeCurzon, 2003), pp. 36–52.

[62] Verena Fritz, *State-Building: A Comparative Study of Ukraine, Lithuania, Belarus, and Russia* (Budapest: Central European University Press, 2007), p. 212; Jan Zaprudnik and Michael Urban, "Belarus: From Statehood to Empire?" in Ian Bremmer and Ray Taras, eds., *New States, New Politics* (New York: Cambridge University Press, 1997), pp. 276–315, p. 290.

[63] Roy Medvedev, *Aleksandr Lukashenko: Kontury Belorusskoi modeli* (Moscow: BBPG, 2010), p. 85.

Lukashenka, a former collective farm chairman, won election to the parliament in 1990 and headed an anticorruption commission, which he then used to sublime effect in bolstering his own political cause while destroying the reputation of rivals with Howitzer force. The first major victim was Shushkevich, who came under fire for alleged corruption and was overwhelmingly voted out of the parliamentary chairmanship by his colleagues.[64]

Kebich, believing he now had a clear shot to the presidency, moved to institutionalize his advantage by ushering a strongly presidentialist constitution to adoption (which took place in March 1994) and arranging for presidential elections later that summer.[65] Kebich confirms in his memoirs that he expected to win the new presidency he was instituting himself, citing his many years of experience in both party and government and his election team and noting his control over the executive organs of power.[66] Yet a large number of parliamentary deputies had voted no confidence in Kebich himself, and even according to polls he himself cites, he had the support of only 13 percent of the population in the presidential race as of April 1994, so it would certainly appear that Kebich was overconfident.[67] Indeed, Lucan Way makes a strong case that the ineptitude of Kebich and his team wound up costing him the presidential election, for example, by allowing Lukashenka to take over the anticorruption committee in the first place and even letting him use offices that the government controlled in central Minsk until almost the start of the election.[68] To be sure, Lukashenka trained his anticorruption pronouncements intensely on Kebich during the campaign.[69] Kebich himself blames his own campaign staff, which he calls incompetent and passive to the point that he suspects they actually worked for Lukashenka.[70] Thus just as the uncertainty of the early post-Soviet transition made initial advantages easy to squander everywhere, so too did this occur in Belarus, where Kebich did not even have the advantage that Kravchuk and others had of already being a president and indeed proved unable to build his own strong power *vertikal'*. Instead, it was the only candidate who virtually all observers agree lacked significant administrative resources who won the 1994 presidential contest, a victory Kebich later called a "shock."[71] Observers cite Lukashenka's highly popular appeals against

---

[64] Fritz, *State-Building*, p. 213.
[65] Kebich writes that Belarus created a presidential system because it was necessary to concentrate power for policy-making purposes and because it was "trendy" (*modno*), making it necessary for Belarus's representative to have the same status as his counterparts in negotiations among former Soviet republics. Viacheslav Kebich, *Iskushenie vlast'iu: Iz zhizni prem'er-ministra* (Minsk: Paradoks, 2008), pp. 402–3.
[66] Kebich, *Iskushenie vlast'iu*, pp. 404, 408, 419.
[67] Zaprudnik and Urban, "Belarus," p. 312; Kebich, *Iskushenie vlast'iu*, p. 413.
[68] Way, "Authoritarian State-Building," p. 251; Way, "Deer in Headlights."
[69] Fritz, *State-Building*, p. 213.
[70] Kebich, *Iskushenie vlast'iu*, pp. 408–20.
[71] Kebich, *Iskushenie vlast'iu*, p. 433.

corruption, for restoration of the USSR, and for ending economic chaos and decline through a simple but herculean exertion of presidential will.[72]

Having smashed the establishment, Lukashenka moved quickly to pull the country's most important elite networks around him in a tight pyramidal power structure and to eliminate or marginalize the rest. His initial strategy was to promote old associates to key positions, particularly those from the Mahileu region, where he had particularly strong political roots.[73] This went along with the creation of what was called his "presidential *vertikal'*," inducing parliament to institute a system of presidentially appointed governors and lower-level executives, stripping elected councils of influence over them, on the grounds that this was necessary for reforms.[74] Choosing to rule over local networks rather than through them, Lukashenka regularly rotated governors so that they could not build up personal power there as even appointed governors had often done in Russia and Ukraine, where rotation as such was rare.[75]

Rather than governing by playing oligarchs off against each other as Yeltsin and Kuchma had done, Lukashenka placed existing ones directly under presidential control. Among other things, he nationalized the few major private corporations (including banks) that had already been partially privatized and established control over other financial flows.[76] In this process, he made a useful example of the oligarch Pupeika described in Chapter 5, issuing a warrant for his arrest and prompting him to seek Polish asylum in 1998.[77] It has been widely said since Lukashenka's rise that there are no oligarchs as such in Belarus. Business outside the state remained small and generally loyal, with many of his original business backers winding up in key state positions later.[78] Even in the state sector, Lukashenka frequently purged officials who might be in position to institutionalize and then politicize a source of personal power or income, including ministry officials and state corporation chiefs.[79] Only his own inner circle was allowed such privilege, and this circle was narrow indeed.[80] He used the frequent purging as a crucial source of populist strength, often giving

---

[72] Kimitaka Matsuzato, "A Populist Island in an Ocean of Clan Politics: The Lukashenka Regime as an Exception among CIS Countries," *Europe-Asia Studies*, v. 56, no. 2, March 2004, pp. 235–61, p. 243; Vladimir Rovdo, "Spetsifika i evoliutsiia politicheskogo rezhima Respubliki Belarus'," *Acta Slavica Iaponica*, v. 21, 2004, pp. 144–80.

[73] Olga Belova-Gille, "Difficulties of Elite Formation in Belarus after 1991," in Elena Korosteleva, Colin W. Lawson, and Rosalind J. Marsh, eds., *Contemporary Belarus: Between Democracy and Dictatorship* (New York: RoutledgeCurzon, 2003), pp. 53–67, pp. 60–1.

[74] Rovdo, "Spetsifika i evoliutsiia," p. 157; Zaprudnik and Urban, "Belarus," p. 301.

[75] Matsuzato, "A Populist Island," p. 238.

[76] Fritz, *State-Building*, pp. 213–17.

[77] "Oligarkhicheskie tendentsii v Belarusi: proshloe i nostoiashchee," analytical report dated July 2006 given to author in Minsk, December 11, 2008; Andrew Wilson, *Belarus: The Last Dictatorship in Europe* (New Haven, CT: Yale University Press, 2011), p. 164.

[78] Wilson, *Belarus*, pp. 164–5.

[79] Fritz, *State-Building*, pp. 213–17.

[80] Matsuzato, "A Populist Island," pp. 238–9.

major firings great publicity so as to appear the crusading champion of the popular will against an avaricious elite, striking fear in the elite and winning such popular support that few thought they had a chance to defeat him even if he were somehow to allow a free and fair election.

The intensity of all this activity picked up markedly after Lukashenka decisively defeated initial resistance from parliament and sealed the victory with a new, even more strongly presidentialist constitution in 1996. Indeed, his initial centralizing moves had generated resistance in parliament – especially after 1995 elections had returned an uncooperative set of deputies – and produced a situation some have compared with the Russian standoff between Yeltsin and the Congress. Lukashenka never had to resort to tank fire, however. First, he circumvented parliament by holding a May 1995 referendum that reinstated some Soviet-era symbols (for example, flag colors), raised the status of the Russian language, backed economic integration with Russia, and supported strengthening presidential rule. With this mandate in pocket, he called another referendum to amend the constitution accordingly. In this way, he won the adoption of an extremely presidentialist basic law in late 1996 that among other things lengthened his first term in office to seven years and enabled him directly to appoint half the Constitutional Court and its chair and the entire Supreme Court. To seal the referendum victory, his presidential guard went to the Central Election Commission chief's office and forced him to resign. The fact that the new constitution created a bicameral parliament gave him a way to subdue parliament without provoking the existing deputies into united opposition: After the dissolution of the old parliament, the new upper house was filled with presidential appointees and regional officials (generally under the president's thumb thanks to the regional reforms) and the lower house was then to consist of a subset of deputies from the old one that he himself selected. Naturally, the lucky chosen few tended to be his loyalists. Unsurprisingly, this largely new parliament worked in close harmony with the president.[81]

It was shortly after this period that Lukashenka undertook the bulk of his renationalization campaign and held frequent "show trials" of senior elites accused of corruption, trials that were often broadcast on live television and that even hit Mikhail Chigir, who had been Lukashenka's own prime minister 1994–6 before offering resistance.[82] These served to reinforce Lukashenka's already existing populist appeal, which itself was a crucial resource supporting his nearly complete patronal monopoly. While opposition parties and

---

[81] Fritz, *State-Building*, p. 212, p. 213; Medvedev, *Aleksandr Lukashenko*, pp. 89–92; Zaprudnik and Urban, "Belarus"; Stephen White and Elena Korosteleva, "Lukashenko and the Postcommunist Presidency," in Stephen White, Elena Korosteleva, and John Lowehardt, eds., *Postcommunist Belarus* (Lanham, MD: Rowman & Littlefield, 2005), pp. 59–78; Wilson, *Belarus*, pp. 181, 185.

[82] Matsuzato, "A Populist Island," p. 244.

politicians continued to function and even run for the highest offices, unlike in Turkmenistan and Uzbekistan, they were in no position to pose significant risk to Lukashenka of losing power.

Overall, therefore, we see how one of the post-Soviet region's strongest political machines developed even where back in the early 1990s intraelite chaos and conflict had reigned. And Lukashenka pulled it off without prior administrative resources upon which to build and without creating a strong presidential party, as he consistently resisted calls from among his own supporters to launch one.[83] Instead, his own popularity was the decisive resource he wielded at the start in conjunction with the formal presidency, enabling him to subdue emerging networks and ensure they either merged fully with his power pyramid or essentially disappeared from influential political life.

Single Pyramids in Divided Societies: Ukraine under Kuchma

It is sometimes argued that the consolidation of authoritarian rule is more difficult in countries riven by deep identity cleavages, and Ukraine is often cited as a prime example.[84] Indeed, experts have long demonstrated the enduring political salience of a divide between its more russophone and Russia-oriented East and its more Ukrainian-speaking and Western oriented West.[85] While such divides surely shaped the particular path by which post-Soviet patronal presidents built single-pyramid systems during the 1990s and perhaps even the specific form these systems took, they did not significantly hinder the construction of these systems more generally – at least, not any more than did the myriad other challenges that the first post-Soviet patronal presidents faced. The case of Kyrgyzstan discussed earlier represents a good example, strongly divided between a somewhat more Russified and industrialized North and the South with its large ethnic Uzbek minority, yet also developing a single-pyramid system by the end of the 1990s.[86] The same basic

---

[83] M. F. Chudakov, A. E. Vashkevich, S. A. Alfer, M. K. Plisko, and A. O. Dobrovol'skii, *Politicheskie partii: Belarus' i sovremennyi mir*, 2nd ed. (Minsk: Tesei, 2005), pp. 174–5.

[84] Vladimir Ia. Gel'man, "Uroki ukrainskogo," *Polis*, no. 1 (84), February 2005, pp. 36–49; Taras Kuzio, "Democratic Breakthroughs and Revolutions in Five Postcommunist Countries: Comparative Perspectives on the Fourth Wave," *Demokratizatsiya: The Journal of Post-Soviet Democratization*, v. 16, no. 1, Winter 2008, pp. 97–109; Levitsky and Way, *Competitive Authoritarianism*.

[85] Timothy J. Colton, "An Aligning Election and the Ukrainian Political Community," *East European Politics & Societies*, v. 25, no. 1, February 2011, pp. 4–27; D'Anieri, *Understanding Ukrainian Politics*; Keith Darden, *Resisting Occupation: Mass Literacy and the Creation of Durable National Loyalties* (New York: Cambridge University Press, forthcoming); Lowell W. Barrington and Erik S. Herron, "One Ukraine or Many? Regionalism in Ukraine and Its Political Consequences," *Nationalities Papers*, v. 32, March 2004, pp. 53–86.

[86] Pauline Jones Luong, *Institutional Change and Political Continuity in Post-Soviet Central Asia* (New York: Cambridge University Press, 2002), pp. 74–82; Maxim Ryabakov, "The North-South Cleavage and Political Support in Kyrgyzstan," *Central Asian Survey*, v. 27, nos. 3–4, September 2008, pp. 301–16.

process also developed in Ukraine, where the less resolute and less skilled Kravchuk was replaced by a more competent and determined machine politician in 1994, as described.[87]

After Kuchma won his close presidential race with Kravchuk in a runoff, with elites and voters dividing roughly along east-west lines, he set in motion a number of processes designed to build a "vertical" authority structure that in the end simply overpowered his country's identity divide. Until he could secure a presidentialist constitution, he trod carefully in exercising presidential muscle in overt political battles, even accepting some limitations on his power. For example, in its effort to weaken Kravchuk, the parliament had mandated that governors be directly elected rather than presidentially appointed, and the first such elections had been held at the same time as the 1994 presidential election. While the president retained the right to remove these elected governors, he was careful at first not to do so without reasonably legitimate cause.[88] He also continued to oversee privatization, in effect supervising the creation of the class of oligarchs described in Chapter 5, most of whom started to become wealthy and politically influential during the first half of the 1990s. Kuchma himself was once asked whether most of this process was conducted fairly, to which he replied, "Of course not! In what country have you ever seen honest privatization?"[89]

While parliament was reluctant to grant Kuchma a strongly presidentialist constitution, Kuchma found a way to change its collective mind in the summer of 1996. He suddenly called a referendum that would put to a popular vote a new constitution drafted by a Constitutional Commission that he dominated. He thus threatened parliamentary deputies that if they did not pass a constitution to his liking by legislative means, he would institute one by referendum that would not incorporate their input. Putting teeth in this threat, Kuchma was careful to gain prior approval for holding a referendum from his National Security and Defense Council.[90] He also promised that groups supporting him would be rewarded with state appointments, which would be firmly at his disposal in the event of his victory.[91] Rada Speaker Oleksandr Moroz then conceded, and deputies stayed up all night to finalize and approve it on June 28, 1996.[92]

Now with a strongly presidentialist constitution ratifying his status as top Ukrainian patron, he moved quickly to consolidate a full-blown single-

---

[87] For a fuller treatment of the role of identity divides in shaping regime dynamics in patronal politics, see Henry E. Hale, "Identity Divides as Authoritarian Resource: Post-Soviet Cases over Twenty Years," paper prepared for presentation at the Association for the Study of Nationalities annual meeting, April 19–21, 2012, Columbia University, New York.

[88] Matsuzato, "All Kuchma's Men," pp. 424–5.

[89] Kas'ianov, *Ukraiina 1991–2007*, pp. 76, 172; *Zerkalo Nedeli*, no. 5, February 11, 2006.

[90] Kas'ianov, *Ukraiina 1991–2007*, pp. 60–3.

[91] Matsuzato, "All Kuchma's Men," p. 425.

[92] Kas'ianov, *Ukraiina 1991–2007*, pp. 60–3.

pyramid system.[93] The new constitution restored Kuchma's formal right to appoint governors (ending gubernatorial elections), and as Matsuzato documents, the very next month after the new constitution was adopted Kuchma began aggressively firing and appointing governors primarily on the basis of their effectiveness in delivering the vote for his preferred candidates. This process involved not just the replacement of governors who were causing problems for his administration (including the major centers of Donetsk, Kyiv, and Kyiv Region) with his own loyalists, but also the rewarding of parties who had supported his push for the new constitution.[94] The oligarchic class fully flowered during this period, influencing politics through the media and material resources they controlled. Because of their dependence on the state for continued access to profits, Kuchma could count on them not to challenge his rule so long as they expected him to be the dominant player in the future. In the media realm, this control was formalized in the early 2000s through the infamous *temnyky* system, which sent what might be called "recommendations one cannot refuse" to media outlets as to how (or whether) they should cover certain stories. One indication of how close Kuchma's relationship to the oligarchs became is that one of them, Viktor Pinchuk, in the early 2000s even became Kuchma's son-in-law. As revealed in secret tapes later released by a member of his own security guard, Kuchma's team also systematically encouraged his top associates to engage in graft (some of it involving oligarchic payments for favors) to reward them and make them more vulnerable to punishment should they display disloyalty.[95] He also used state surveillance organs to blackmail key elites so as to ensure their loyalty and effectiveness in serving his political needs or, failing that, to punish them.[96]

The March 1998 parliamentary elections proved to be a crucial moment in Kuchma's establishment of a single-pyramid arrangement of political-economic networks with him perched at the top. For one thing, he used these contests as a testing ground for his subordinates: Those delivering weak showings for propresidential parties were typically removed, sometimes despite performing well in the realm of the economy. Accordingly, 15 of 27 governors were fired after these elections.[97] The 1998 contests also marked the large-scale entry

[93] On the formal constitution and its powers, see Charles R. Wise and Volodymyr Pigenko, "The Separation of Powers Puzzle in Ukraine: Sorting Out Responsibilities and Relationships between President, Parliament, and the Prime Minister," in Taras Kuzio, Robert S. Kravchuk, and Paul D'Anieri, eds., *State and Institution Building in Ukraine* (New York: St. Martin's, 1999), pp. 25–55; and Wolczuk, *The Moulding of Ukraine.*

[94] Matsuzato, "All Kuchma's Men."

[95] Keith Darden, "The Integrity of Corrupt States: Graft as an Informal State Institution," *Politics & Society,* v. 36, no. 1, March 2008, pp. 35–60.

[96] Keith Darden, "Blackmail as a Tool of State Domination: Ukraine under Kuchma," *East European Constitutional Review,* v. 10, nos. 2–3, Spring/Summer 2001, pp. 67–71. See also Dominique Arel, "Kuchmagate and the Demise of Kuchma's 'Geopolitical Bluff,'" *East European Constitutional Review,* v. 10, nos. 2–3, Spring/Summer 2001, pp. 54–9.

[97] Matsuzato, "All Kuchma's Men," p. 425.

of oligarchs into the parliamentary realm, with many appearing on the lists of several parties created to be their vehicles. These groupings became a key source of the MP votes that Kuchma used to control parliament. To shore up this control, he also fostered a series of "virtual parties" that could usher into parliament key interest groups or divide or confuse certain opposition constituencies.[98]

Kuchma demonstrated the dominance of his political machine with his 1999 reelection. He began from a weak position in public opinion, by the end of 1998 ranking only fourth and by March 1999 having the support of only 22 percent of the people.[99] He nevertheless found that the patronal presidency gave him considerable tools other than public support that he could use to defeat the opposition. A carrots-and-sticks strategy, for example, worked to neutralize National Bank Chairman Viktor Yushchenko, who was considered a possible challenger: Kuchma promised him the prime ministership while pressuring him with an SBU (former KGB) investigation into his activities at the bank, an investigation that was dropped when Yushchenko accepted and became head of Kuchma's government.[100]

Kuchma nicely demonstrates how identity alone was no match for the patronal presidency, which proved powerful enough to produce a complete reversal of presidential positioning along Ukraine's vaunted "east-west divide" between Kuchma's election in 1994 and his reelection in 1999. Kuchma had originally defeated Kravchuk in 1994 with support in the relatively pro-Russian East, but found it tactically useful to base his appeal this time in the West. To eliminate other West-based rivals, Kuchma's team employed a wide range of tactics to divide and conquer them. Lacking control over central television, the leading West-oriented party (Rukh) split after at least one faction within it started received funding from the presidential network. In the first round of the election, western votes were divided among multiple candidates, at least one of whom (former prime minister Yevhen Marchuk) wound up with a major state job after the election.[101] The western Ukrainian politician Viacheslav Chornovil, the country's most prominent nationalist leader, never made it to the ballot, perishing in a car crash a few months before the election. Using the agenda-setting power available to him through control over the media and the ability to set policy, Kuchma co-opted much of the western-based parties' core agenda, including unwavering support for Ukrainian independence, continued skepticism of any CIS institutions potentially tying Ukraine more closely to Russia, and a policy of integration into Western economic and political

---

[98] Andrew Wilson, *Virtual Politics: Faking Democracy in the Post-Soviet World* (New Haven, CT: Yale University Press, 2005).

[99] Kost' Bondarenko, *Leonid Kuchma: Portret na fone epokhi* (Kharkiv: Folio, 2007), p. 280.

[100] Bondarenko, *Leonid Kuchma*, pp. 276–7.

[101] Taras Kuzio, "Ukraine: Muddling Along," in Sharon L. Wolchik and Jane L. Curry, eds., *Central and East European Politics: From Communism to Democracy* (Lanham, MD: Rowman & Littlefield, 2008), pp. 339–67, p. 349; Wilson, *Virtual Politics*, pp. 42, 154–5.

structures. Kuchma also adopted resource distribution policies that favored western regions.[102]

All this resulted in exactly what Kuchma wanted: His main rival in his 1999 reelection effort became Communist Party of Ukraine leader Petro Symonenko, someone who had little hope of winning a majority and would make Kuchma seem to be the lesser of evils despite his difficult public opinion standing. After replacing several governors where first-round election returns had disappointed him, Kuchma handily defeated Symonenko in a runoff by winning every western region and many in other parts of Ukraine.[103] Using the power of the patronal presidency, Kuchma had thus completely reversed his relationship to the country's east-west divide, becoming a candidate of primarily western support as he easily two-stepped to reelection. Kuchma's single pyramid reigned supreme and identity politics proved just as capable of succumbing to patronal presidential power as did other bases of opposition appeals.

Single Pyramids Born of Civil War and State Failure: Azerbaijan and Georgia

Patronal presidents were even able to build single-pyramid systems when identity divides involved outright civil war and what was widely assessed as state failure. Azerbaijan's Heydar Aliyev provides an excellent example, having inherited a republic torn by civil war after the previous president (Abulfez Elchibey) had fled, unable to cope.[104] The career KGB officer Aliyev had served as Azerbaijan's party boss for nearly the entire Brezhnev era, 1969–82, a fact assuring that he was well practiced in the arts of patronage politics, and then served on the Politburo until Gorbachev fired him in 1987.[105] Eventually, he returned to his native Nakhichevan autonomous republic, from whose dominant network he had drawn heavily while in charge of Azerbaijan's Communist Party organization a decade earlier. After his return, he won election to the autonomous territory's legislature and became its chairman in 1991.[106] President Elchibey himself – facing Surat Huseynov's armed insurrection and major defeats in the war over Nagorno-Karabakh – then called on Aliyev to return to Baku to help resolve the crisis. Aliyev did so, whereupon Elchibey promptly fled the capital. The parliament quickly named the former party boss its chairman. The peculiar formality making this possible was that, as chairman of the Nakhichevan legislature, Aliyev also held the status of ex officio

[102] Stephen Bloom, "Which Minority Is Appeased? Coalition Potential and Redistribution in Latvia and Ukraine," *Europe-Asia Studies*, v. 60, no. 9, November 2008, pp. 1575–600.

[103] Bondarenko, *Leonid Kuchma*, p. 329; Matsuzato, "All Kuchma's Men."

[104] Another good example discussed later is Tajikistan's Rahmon.

[105] Ronald Grigor Suny, "On the Road to Independence: Cultural Cohesion and Ethnic Revival in a Multinational Society," in Ronald Grigor Suny, ed., *Transcaucasia, Nationalism, and Social Change* (Ann Arbor: University of Michigan Press, 1996), pp. 379–82.

[106] Gafar Aliev, *Osnovopolozhnik, spasatel' i sozidatel' sovremennogo Azerbaidzhana* (Baku: Shams, 2008), p. 110.

second deputy speaker of the national parliament. The parliament then called new presidential elections, which Aliyev won in 1993.[107] Remiz Mehdiyev, Aliyev's long-serving chief of administration, later wrote of the ensuing time that "a choice had to be made between aspirations to build an effective state management system where the authorities could steer processes, or to let everything drift so that so-called 'democratization' itself would establish the order of mutual relationships within society," making clear that the latter was considered too costly.[108]

Accordingly, Aliyev moved quickly to reestablish lines of patronal authority. Even before the presidential election, he cleverly neutralized the rebelling Huseynov by naming him prime minister, thereby detaching him from his militia and setting him up to be easily dispatched later.[109] In 1995, he defeated a mutiny by the head of special services police, Rovshan Javadov, mobilizing the army and police against him.[110] The next year, the oligarchic network led by parliamentary speaker Rasul Guliyev was forced out after becoming increasingly critical of the president. Guliyev was charged with embezzlement, fled the country, founded the opposition Democratic Party of Azerbaijan, and became one of Aliyev's most vocal critics from abroad.[111]

Aliyev then steadily rebuilt his own coalition of networks around the presidency, drawing in a heavy contingent of cadres and longtime associates from his native Nakhichevan as well as others from his KGB networks and Azeris with former residential ties to Armenia (known among insiders as the "Yeraz" or "Western Azerbaijani" network) – the same basic networks on which he had largely relied as republic first secretary.[112] The plum posts, by the account of one insider, were reserved for his personal network from Nakhichevan (for example, making academic Mehdiyev his chief of staff), though Yeraz representatives were given the parliamentary speakership as well as several lucrative ministries (for example, reputed Yeraz network patron Ali Insanov was made health minister).[113] Other figures appointed during the 1990s who remained at the core of the system until his death included prominent minister-oligarchs described in Chapter 5 such as Kamaladdin Heydarov and Farhad Aliyev. The system worked in part by allowing each major grouping in government opportunities to "manage" certain sectors. Insanov, arrested after Heydar Aliyev's death in a mid-2000s purge, essentially admitted his own complicity while characterizing a system in which "each minister had his own sector where their relatives had

[107] Cornell, *Azerbaijan since Independence*, pp. 66, 77–9.
[108] Remiz Mehdiyev, *Azerbaijan – 2003–2008: Thinking about Time* (Baku: Sharq-Qarb, 2010), p. 159.
[109] Cornell, *Azerbaijan since Independence*, p. 78.
[110] Cornell, *Azerbaijan since Independence*, p. 166.
[111] Cornell, *Azerbaijan since Independence*, pp. 106, 175–6.
[112] Cornell, *Azerbaijan since Independence*, p. 83.
[113] Liz Fuller, "Azerbaijan: Former Presidential Advisor Discusses Regionalism in Politics," *RFE/ RL News Analysis*, April 27, 2007.

all the benefits."[114] Aliyev also invested considerable effort into party building, making the Yeni Azerbaijan Party (YAP), founded prior to Aliyev's accession to power and containing much of his core team, the new party of power.[115]

Aliyev then formally anchored his patronal presidential single-pyramid system with the adoption of a decidedly presidentialist constitution in 1995.[116] The YAP dominated single-member-district parliamentary elections of 1995, giving Aliyev solid control over the legislature, though opposition representatives were allowed to win a significant minority of seats.[117] Aliyev also tolerated some significant media autonomy, including even some independent television.[118] Bolstering Aliyev's rule was his strong reputation for having saved Azerbaijani statehood as well as favorable domestic reaction to his concluding of what became known as "the Contract of the Century," which involved selling foreign companies the right to exploit vast Azerbaijani oil reserves in 1994 together with Azerbaijan's state oil company. The income generated by hydrocarbons, including massive foreign investment, served to grease the patronage machine.[119] Aliyev also negotiated a cease-fire to the Nagorno-Karabakh war in 1994 that bought him time and gained him support by at least ending the bloodshed so that the country could regroup to try to regain the territory in the future. By 1998, he was already in position handily to orchestrate a formal reelection victory.[120]

Georgia's Eduard Shevardnadze started in an even weaker position than did Aliyev because the people who called the former in to take over the badly failed state expected him to serve essentially as a figurehead. Succeeding first president Gamsakhurdia's debacle, it initially seemed that Shevardnadze had everything stacked against him. Not only had he lived outside the republic since 1985, having served as Gorbachev's pro-Western foreign minister, but he was enlisted by the Military Council in March 1992 mainly to present a familiar face to the international community, where he was something of a star, and to seal a de facto power-sharing arrangement between the country's two dominant warlords, Ioseliani and Kitovani. Moreover, Shevardnadze arrived just as Kitovani decided to launch the 1992–3 war with Abkhazia, which resulted in a disastrous loss and spurred civil war within Georgia as Gamsakhurdia's loyalists attempted a restoration.[121] Shevardnadze did have some resources to put

---

[114] Rovshan Ismayilov, "Azerbaijan: Ex-Minister's Trial Creates Political Sensation," *Eurasianet*, March 5, 2007, 8:00 pm.
[115] Author's interview, senior Yeni Azerbaijan Party official, Baku, October 3, 2008.
[116] Cornell, *Azerbaijan since Independence*, pp. 90–1.
[117] Cornell, *Azerbaijan since Independence*, p. 91.
[118] Eldar Namazov, President of the Public Forum for Azerbaijan and a former top aide to Heydar Aliyev, author's interview, Baku, October 4, 2008.
[119] Leila Alieva, "Azerbaijan's Frustrating Elections," *Journal of Democracy*, v. 17, no. 2, April 2006, pp. 147–60.
[120] Cornell, *Azerbaijan since Independence*, pp. 95–6.
[121] Jones, "Georgia"; Slider, "Democratization in Georgia," pp. 164–7.

on the table, however, such as personal popularity and the skills and networks he had developed as the republic's KGB chief and then, starting in 1972, its Communist Party boss, a post in which he served until being promoted to the Politburo and called to Moscow by Gorbachev in 1985.[122]

Perhaps most important, however, is that he proved to be a clever politician, wise enough to bide his time and to understand how he could rebuild a personal power network and ultimately create a single-pyramid system around it to anchor his rule. Top initial priority was to stay friendly with the warlords who recruited him, Ioseliani and Kitovani, rivals who could be played one off against the other when the time was right. Also imperative was to end the fall 1993 civil war, which he did at the cost of leading Georgia into the CIS in return for Russian military assistance putting down the uprising. As the presidency had been eliminated in the wake of the Gamsakhurdia disaster, another step was to hold elections for a new parliament (84 district seats and 150 proportional representation seats) in October 1992 and to become its chairman, starting the process of turning his formal power into informal power. Aiming for the next elections, he created a party, the Citizens Union of Georgia, that could serve as an institutional vehicle for his coalition in this parliament. Emphasizing his own centrality, he also threatened to resign, prompting parliament (fearing more chaos) to grant him additional formal powers and even to suspend its own activities for a period.

Also very importantly, Shevardnadze sought other powerful allies and gave each reason to be invested in his rule. One move was striking up working relations with Aslan Abashidze's regional machine in the autonomous region of Ajara, effectively letting it rule while giving it a prominent role in central Georgian politics. He also made representatives of two powerful Mingrelian and Svan regional-ethnic networks his prime minister and deputy premier, respectively. The shadow economy business operations of Kakha Targamadze's Interior Ministry also flourished. The presidential family's own network became an essential part of this system, expanding holdings in a wide range of sectors. Overall, he was essentially farming out key state functions to various networks, which then had de facto license to pursue their own private political or economic interests through these formal state structures in what Jonathan Wheatley has described as a "feudalization of power."[123]

In May 1993, he was confident enough to remove Kitovani as defense minister and in early 1995 jailed him after he attempted a new effort to reconquer Abkhazia. In August 1995, Shevardnadze presided over the signing of a new presidentialist constitution. In what appears to have been an attempt

[122] Suny, "On the Road to Independence," pp. 379–83.
[123] The quotation is from Wheatley, *Georgia*, pp. 109–10, though for other information in this paragraph, see also Jones, "Georgia"; Lincoln Mitchell, *Uncertain Democracy: U.S. Foreign Policy and Georgia's Rose Revolution* (Philadelphia: University of Pennsylvania Press, 2009); Slider, "Democratization in Georgia."

to derail this process (and a reflection that local powerful actors understood that a presidentialist constitution could have an important effect of weakening nonpresidential rivals), a bomb narrowly missed killing Shevardnadze and was linked to Ioseliani's Mkhedrioni. After winning both the presidential and parliamentary elections of 1995, Shevardnadze had Ioseliani arrested, a moment that essentially marked the rebuilding of Georgia's state and the establishment of a dominant pyramid of power.[124] The 1995 elections were also notable for Shevardnadze's introducing new blood to the parliamentary leadership as part of his party machine, including a group known as "young reformers" that most prominently included Zurab Zhvania, who became parliamentary chairman. Zhvania soon recruited into Shevardnadze's party of power Mikheil Saakashvili, who eventually became Shevardnadze's justice minister, and Nino Burjanadze.[125]

The Georgian version of a single-pyramid system under Shevardnadze was much looser than, say, Belarus's under Lukashenka in that more media freedom was allowed and Shevardnadze exercised less personal dominance, with various "cogs" in the machine often operating relatively autonomously and without micromanagement from the president himself. But the system was still quite recognizable in his machine's ability to mobilize considerable patronalistic resources when needed to pull together enough networks to win elections, effectively marginalizing all other major networks. This was on full display in the parliamentary elections of 1999 and the presidential contest of 2000, which Shevardnadze won handily.

Pyramids of the Resource-Poor: Tajikistan

While many have linked much post-Soviet authoritarianism to a "resource curse," plenty of post-Soviet patronal presidents successfully developed single-pyramid systems without having the benefit of oil or gas wealth either to fuel or to lubricate the construction process. Tajikistan is one of the most telling examples in this regard, especially since it began not only with grinding poverty, but also with a terrible civil war (cathected with an identity divide involving fragmented, armed elites) and virtually complete state collapse – all of which would seem to have made the construction of a single-pyramid system quite unlikely.

Tajikistan's civil war produced a highly regionalized pattern of politics in which dominant networks in key regions were often able to purge local oppositions and, at times, take vengeance on anyone from rival regions without stopping to figure out whether they were in fact part of a hostile network there. That is, the civil war had produced an unusually high degree of congruence between patronal networks and territorially defined

---

[124] Jones, "Georgia"; Mitchell, *Uncertain Democracy*; Slider, "Democratization in Georgia."
[125] Irakly Areshidze, *Democracy and Autocracy in Eurasia: Georgia in Transition* (East Lansing: Michigan State University Press, 2007), p. 41.

populations.[126] Consolidating power thus meant establishing one network's dominance even in regions that were overwhelmingly hostile, on top of the problem that the civil war victors constituted a coalition of multiple networks, notably the dominant ones from Kulob and Khujand. Reflecting that the armed core of the winning coalition was the aggressive Kulob network that failed president Nabiev had initially armed, as described earlier, the patron emerging from the carnage on top was Imomali Rahmonov, who in return ceded certain other key posts to the historically dominant Khujand group. Having largely defeated the opposition coalition, the winners began struggling among themselves.

Rahmonov established his relative dominance first by removing his Khujandi prime minister Abdumalik Abdullojonov in late 1993, then defeating him in the country's first presidential election since the war had started (in 1994), then charging him with corruption. At the same time, he imposed a referendum that confirmed a new, strongly presidentialist constitution.[127] Rahmonov also forged a People's Democratic Party of Tajikistan to be his political vehicle, the core of which consisted of supporters from his Kulob network.[128] Notably, Rahmonov formally joined the party itself, lending it his personal authority.[129] While the Khujand network was sidelined, Rahmonov's political machine was still quite weak, with significant other power pyramids competing for influence. For one thing, armed groupings from the winning coalition outside Kulob in many cases refused to give up their arms and thus kept tight control over their territories, meaning that the president's control over them was highly contingent.[130] Additionally, opposition units continued to mount resistance under cover of the country's mountainous terrain and taking advantage of neighboring Afghanistan's own civil war going on at the same time. Nevertheless, Rahmonov's win in the 1994 presidential contest established his network as the most powerful one, gradually enabling him to win others to his side (including former opposition commanders) by creating the expectation of his eventual dominance, beginning the process of forming a single-pyramid system.[131]

[126] Atkin, "Tajikistan," pp. 614–16; Schoeberlein-Engel, "Conflict in Tajikistan"; Idil Tuncer-Kilavuz, "Understanding Civil War: A Comparison of Tajikistan and Uzbekistan," *Europe-Asia Studies*, v. 63, no. 2, March 2011, pp. 263–90.

[127] Atkin, "Tajikistan"; Shahram Akbarzadeh, "Geopolitics versus Democracy in Tajikistan," *Demokratizatsiya: The Journal of Post-Soviet Democratization*, v. 14, no. 4, Fall 2006, pp. 563–78, p. 565.

[128] Kathleen Collins, *Clan Politics and Regime Transition in Central Asia* (New York: Cambridge University Press, 2005), pp. 282–3.

[129] Sayfullo Safarov, former deputy leader of the party and Rahmonov adviser, author's interview, Dushanbe, June 16, 2011.

[130] Muriel Atkin, "Thwarted Democratization in Tajikistan," in Karen Dawisha and Bruce Parrott, eds., *Conflict, Cleavage, and Change in Central Asia and the Caucasus* (New York: Cambridge University Press, 1997), pp. 277–311, p. 301

[131] Jesse Driscoll, "Commitment Problems or Bidding Wars? Rebel Fragmentation as Peace Building," *Journal of Conflict Resolution*, v. 56, no. 1, February 2012, pp. 118–49; Jesse Driscoll, "Inside Anarchy: Militia Incorporation as State-Building," unpublished paper, February 10,

The process accelerated after Rahmonov concluded a 1997 cease-fire that included a power-sharing deal with the opposition, one involving the merging of armed forces rather than the dissolution of one side.[132] It also allowed Abdullo Nuri's Islamic Renaissance Party, which had fought with the opposition, not only to be legally registered but to become one of the country's main political parties. Charismatic opposition leader and Islamic religious figure Turajonzoda not only was allowed to return to the country, but gained the post of deputy prime minister.[133] Importantly, the Khujand network was not included in the negotiation process.[134] Thus by including opposition parties with roots in other regions like Garm and the capital Dushanbe, Rahmonov was essentially replacing one dominant coalition with another that included multiple weaker networks as partners instead of the country's historically ruling network. Indeed, the opposition joining the coalition was only able to negotiate 30 percent of government positions for itself, and even these were not fully allocated.[135] Through parliamentary elections in 1998 and 2000 and a new presidential race in 1999, Rahmonov was steadily able to edge out competitors, establishing clear parliamentary dominance in the primarily district-elected parliament, with district-based deputies as a core of his support.[136] Dividing and conquering from an initially weak but focal position as president, Rahmonov was able to establish a patronal presidential single-pyramid system even in what had just a few years before been considered one of the world's failed states.

Pyramid Building in Separatist Quasi-States

Dov Lynch has argued that in the breakaway territories establishing de facto independence from their internationally recognized post-Soviet states, separatist wars gave a special impulse to the concentration of power around a single executive, where the fear of being militarily defeated caused a rally-round-the-leader effect and justified "security based on force." The separatist leaders traded on this fear to marginalize rival networks and institutionalize their control, this account goes.[137] The argument, however, fits better in Abkhazia and Transnistria than Nagorno-Karabakh and South Ossetia, where significant network rivalries flared up in full public view during the 1990s. Nevertheless, with the separatist wars becoming "frozen" as the 1990s progressed, we see some of the same processes developing in these unrecognized polities as we do in the independent countries of Eurasia.

Abkhazia's Vladislav Ardzinba and Transnistria's Igor Smirnov certainly reaped a great deal of elite unity thanks to their identification with their territories'

2009, p. 30; John Heathershaw and Edmund Herzig, "Introduction: The Sources of Statehood in Tajikistan," *Central Asian Survey*, v. 30, no. 1, March 2011, pp. 5–19, p. 11.

[132] Driscoll, "Inside Anarchy"; Heathershaw, *Post-Conflict Tajikistan*, pp. 118–26.

[133] *RFE/RL Newsline*, December 15, 1997.

[134] Akbarzadeh, "Geopolitics versus Democracy in Tajikistan," p. 565.

[135] Collins, *Clan Politics*, p. 286.

[136] Akbarzadeh, "Geopolitics versus Democracy in Tajikistan"; Collins, *Clan Politics*, p. 280–4.

[137] Dov Lynch, "De Facto 'States' around the Black Sea: The Importance of Fear," *Southeast European and Black Sea Studies*, v. 7, no. 3, September 2007, pp. 483–96, pp. 487–90.

independence struggles and the purging and sorting of elites and populations that accompanied them. The historian Ardzinba thus went from directing the Abkhaz Institute for Language, Literature, and History to winning election as chairman of the republic's legislature in 1990 to leading it to victory in war against Georgia in 1993, whereupon most of the republic's ethnic Georgian plurality fled.[138] The glow of victory left him largely unchallenged, and in a pattern reminiscent of what happened in the USSR's union republics during 1990–1, the district-elected parliament he led moved quickly to create an indirectly elected presidency and to install him in it in 1994.[139] While this was accompanied by parliament's passage of a new, strongly presidentialist constitution, it was only as the situation stabilized by 1999 that (simultaneously) a referendum confirmed it and Ardzinba won the unrecognized republic's first direct presidential elections uncontested.[140] One local party attempted to nominate former prime minister Leonid Lakerbai as an opposition candidate, but the Central Election Commission disqualified him on a technicality, and indeed the parliament introduced a number of requirements designed to rule out potential challenges.[141] District-based parliamentary elections had been held in 1996, further strengthening Ardzinba's position and setting the stage for direct presidential elections.[142]

Transnistria's Smirnov, an industrial manager, coordinated a series of strikes and protests that eventually propelled him to the forefront of a movement to detach his heavily industrialized zone from Moldova and keep it in the USSR during its waning days.[143] As the chairman of the territory's first self-proclaimed legislature (district-elected), he orchestrated the adoption of a highly presidentialist constitution by referendum in 1991 citing the need to concentrate power in the struggle with Moldova.[144] Handily winning the first presidential race that same year, contested nominally by a prominent parliamentarian representing a different part of the territory, Smirnov engineered adoption of new constitutions in 1996 and 2001, with the latter featuring even stronger presidential powers.[145] The interests of the networks of Smirnov and the massive Sheriff oligarchic group were tightly aligned, and in any case Sheriff was controlled by people regarded as his allies, as was noted in the previous chapter. The result was a political system that Oleh Protsyk reports greatly resembled others in the former Soviet Union, a kind of "managed pluralism" where some opposition

---

[138] Yu. D. Anchabadze and Yu. G. Argun, *Abkhazy* (Moscow: Nauka, 2007), pp. 102–4; Matsuzato, "Patronnoe prezidentstvo i politika v sfere identichnosti v nepreznannoi Abkhazii," *Acta Eurasica*, no. 4, 2006, pp. 132–59.

[139] Anchabadze and Argun, *Abkhazy*, p. 113.

[140] Matsuzato, "From Belligerent," p. 100; Matsuzato, "Patronnoe prezidentstvo."

[141] Matsuzato, "Patronnoe prezidentstvo."

[142] Matsuzato, "From Belligerent."

[143] Charles King, "The Benefits of Ethnic War: Understanding Eurasia's Unrecognized States," *World Politics*, v. 53, no. 4, July 2001, pp. 187–9.

[144] N. V. Babilunga, S. I. Beril, B. G. Bomeshko, I. N. Galinskii, E. M. Guboglo, V. R. Okushko, and P. M. Shornikov, *Fenomen Pridniestrov'ia*, 2nd ed. (Tiraspol: RIO PGU, 2003), p. 21.

[145] Author's interview with local expert, Tiraspol, March 26, 2009.

was allowed to exist but where the president dominated politics using political machine methods.[146]

The cases of Nagorno-Karabakh and South Ossetia demonstrate, however, that even war and imminent military threat are no guarantee that leaders will not experience challenges from rival networks as they attempt to build single-pyramid systems. Nagorno-Karabakh may constitute the most surprising case of the construction of a patronal presidential single-pyramid system only through fierce struggle between competing pyramids in the face of imminent threat. After declaring independence from Azerbaijan as the USSR broke down, it was engaged in civil war straight up until the 1994 cease-fire. The territory remained parliamentary in structure throughout this initial period, without a presidency of any kind. During the war, in 1992, its legislature created a State Defense Committee to run the entity and named as its head the former engineer and Communist Party official Robert Kocharian, who had become a member of the region's legislature and a key leader of the secession movement. With the end of the war in 1994, the legislature passed a law creating an extremely strong presidency, able to appoint the prime minister without any parliamentary approval, and named Kocharian to this post while setting direct elections for 1996.[147] During this period, when society was highly united against a common enemy, the primary task in consolidating presidential power was dealing with other powerful warlords. In this case, the main potential challenger was the network of Samvel Babaian, regarded as playing one of the leading roles in the armed conflict, as discussed in Chapter 5. Kocharian struck a deal that essentially yielded all of the force agencies to Babaian, making him defense minister and army commander and his brother, Karen Babaian, interior minister. Babaian was satisfied with this arrangement, which allowed him to pursue business opportunities behind the scenes, and supported Kocharian in the 1996 presidential elections.[148] Kocharian then won these with 89 percent of the official vote against two other candidates; he left the next year to become prime minister of Armenia.[149]

Kocharian's "close ally" Arkady Ghukasian (a former military journalist and territory foreign minister) succeeded him, winning election in 1997 with virtually the same percentage of the vote Kocharian got, but then entered into conflict with Babaian over political issues linked to business, such as how the city of Stepanakert should be rebuilt. Ghukasian managed gradually to edge Babaian out, calling for the "demilitarization" of the district as necessary for economic development, a call clearly aimed at those dissatisfied with Babaian's

[146] Oleh Protsyk, "Representation and Democracy in Eurasia's Unrecognized States: The Case of Transnistria," *Post-Soviet Affairs*, v. 25, no. 3, 2009, pp. 257–81.

[147] Matsuzato, "From Belligerent," pp. 101–2.

[148] Pal Kolsto and Helge Blakkisrud, "Living with Non-Recognition: State- and Nation-Building in South Caucasian Quasi-States," *Europe-Asia Studies*, v. 60, no. 3, May 2008, pp. 483–509, pp. 491–2; Matsuzato, "From Belligerent," pp. 101–2.

[149] Matsuzato, "From Belligerent," p. 101.

forceful commercial empire. One by one, Babaian associates were ousted from key posts, with Babaian himself removed as defense minister in August 1999. Kocharian, now president of Armenia, had backed Ghukasian's move, as had Armenian Prime Minister Vazgen Sargsyan, and some analysts have linked this to a gruesome attack that occurred two months later in Armenia's parliament, where gunmen burst in and killed several top Armenian officials, including the prime minister and parliamentary speaker. The next month, Ghukasian removed Babaian as army chief and in 2000 arrested him on charges of an attempted assassination of the territory's president.[150] Only in 2006 did the breakaway region adopt what it called a constitution, having delayed while waiting for Armenia to settle on its own constitution, which did not happen until 2005.[151] Thus Nagorno-Karabakh did not technically have a patronal presidentialist system until 2006, though with the 1996 Law on the Presidency serving a similar function, its politics followed much the same pattern as in other post-Soviet territories.

The initial post-Soviet transitional chaos also took longer than usual to play out in South Ossetia, forestalling the appearance of a robust single-pyramid system until the early 2000s. This had to do with a number of circumstances that delayed institution building. These included not only its war with Georgia, but the facts that South Ossetia had only been an "autonomous region" in the USSR – meaning having a less robust set of state institutions than the "union republics," whose independence was internationally recognized[152] – and that Georgia had earlier abolished even this autonomous status, gutting or eliminating some key institutions. South Ossetia gained de facto independence not because it had achieved any conflict-driven state building, but because Russia intervened on its behalf and Georgia – riven by violent domestic conflict in its own capital city and in Abkhazia – did not want to risk going to war with Russia.[153] By the account of its future first president, South Ossetia as late as 1993 was a polity without a system of courts and prosecutors, without an armed police force, and without even a jail.[154]

Exacerbating all this was that South Ossetia emerged from its early-1990s independence war with much more leadership instability than the other post-

---

[150] Stephan Astourian, "Killings in the Armenian Parliament: Coup d'Etat, Political Conspiracy, or Destructive Rage?" *Contemporary Caucasus Newsletter*, no. 9, Spring 2000, pp. 1–5, 19; Kolsto and Blakkisrud, "Living with Non-recognition," p. 501; Matsuzato, "From Belligerent," pp. 101–4.

[151] Kolsto and Blakkisrud, "Living with Non-recognition," p. 501; Matsuzato, "From Belligerent," p. 101.

[152] Nagorno-Karabakh was also an autonomous oblast, while Abkhazia had the slightly higher status of autonomous republic. Transnistria, upon becoming de facto independent, lacked any such autonomous status.

[153] Svante E. Cornell, "Autonomy as a Source of Conflict: Caucasian Conflicts in Theoretical Perspective," *World Politics*, v. 54, no. 2, January 2002, pp. 245–76, pp.267–8.

[154] Liudvig A. Chibirov, *O vremeni, o liudiakh, o sebe (zapiski Pervogo Prezidenta Respubliki Iuzhnaia Osetiia)* (Vladikavkaz: Ir, 2004), p. 142.

Soviet unrecognized states, even Nagorno-Karabakh. The parliamentary speaker to emerge from its 1990 legislative elections was school director and formerly disgraced party official Torez Kulumbegov, but in January 1991 he was captured and jailed by Georgian authorities. When the USSR dissolved at the end of that year, then, the republic's leader was his successor as parliamentary chairman, the Communist Party regional first secretary Znaur Gassiev. Gassiev ceded the post to Kulumbegov when the latter was released in 1992.[155] Kulumbegov proved unable to gain control of the region upon his return, ultimately resigning in the face of criticism in September 1993, whereupon the legislature replaced him with history professor and local university rector Liudvig Chibirov.[156] While the legislature was unanimous, Chibirov later wrote that only some deputies were true supporters, as many saw him as either a compromise or a temporary choice.[157] Chibirov did start to build up the polity's state institutions, united its force agencies into a single ministry,[158] and presided over the adoption of South Ossetia's first post-Soviet constitution, which retained the preexisting parliamentarist system in which the parliament selected the executive branch and retained the right to adopt or amend the constitution.[159]

The legislature created a presidency in 1996, but in contrast with the other polities examined in this volume, this presidency emerged more out of the incumbent parliamentary leader's weakness than his strength. After what appeared to be a political murder by a Chibirov in-law and a series of deadly explosions in the capital city of Tsinkhvali in early 1996, opposition to Chibirov swelled and many in parliament demanded his resignation.[160] Chibirov won a narrow vote of confidence but appeased his opponents by agreeing to create a presidency that they would have a chance to compete for themselves in elections to take place by the end of the year.[161] Chibirov later justified the creation of a presidency as having been necessary for restoring order and for aligning South Ossetia's status with that of other countries.[162] Nevertheless, the new presidency was regarded as having limited powers and was considered by many to

[155] *Information Agency Res* (Republic of South Ossetia), September 17, 2009, 10:51; *Iuzhnaia Osetiia*, February 2, 2011, p. 3; E. Dzh. Kokoity et al., "On stoial u istokov rozhdeniia respubliki," *Iuzhnaia Osetiia*, October 4, 2006, p. 2.

[156] Liudvig Chibirov, interview in *Nezavisimaia Gazeta*, September 10, 1998.

[157] Chibirov, *O vremeni*, p. 141.

[158] Chibirov, *O vremeni*, p. 145.

[159] Text of the 1993 South Ossetia Constitution, as published in *Iuzhnaia Osetiia*, December 8, 1993, as published by the Tbilisi-based Regionalism Research Center, http://www.rrc.ge/law/konstOSET_%201993_11_03_r.htm?lawid=1378&lng_3=ru, accessed May 7, 2011; *Voenno-promyshlennyi' kur'er* (Russia), December 10, 2008, p. 10.

[160] Chibirov, *O vremeni*; Dmitrii Sanakoev, former South Ossetia prime minister, *Ostaius' optimistom – ia Osetinskii patriot!* (Tbilisi, 2008) pp. 58–60.

[161] Sanakoev, *Ostaius' optimistom*, pp. 58–60.

[162] Chibirov, *O vremeni*, pp. 172–6.

be a stopgap measure until a truly new constitution could be adopted.[163] It was this presidency that Chibirov managed to win in 1996.

Chibirov's experience as South Ossetia's first president bears at least some resemblance to the feckless first presidents in other post-Soviet polities like Kravchuk in Ukraine described in the previous chapter, except that the de facto republic's first directly elected presidency was instituted later than elsewhere (only in 1996) and that he managed to last in this office through his entire first term, until his first reelection attempt. Reflecting the perception of the current institutions as stopgaps until a truly new constitution could be adopted, both president and parliament became embroiled in a struggle to tailor the anticipated new basic law to their own liking. While the region's Communist Party had backed Chibirov for president in 1996, they soon had a falling out as the economy failed to improve and they expressed different preferences on the division of executive powers, appointments, and property. With the 1999 parliamentary election, the Communists gained the upper hand by winning a near majority and capturing the speakership for its leader, Stanislav Kochiev. Both sides created bodies to draft a new constitution, and Chibirov failed in his effort to induce parliament to vote no confidence in Kochiev in 2000.[164] Over Kochiev's objections, Chibirov then bypassed the legislature and resorted to a referendum to institute his own version of the constitution – now clearly presidentialist – in April 2001.[165]

But with presidential elections scheduled for just a few months away and Chibirov having been revealed as vulnerable by defeats at the hands of Kochiev as recently as 1999 and 2000, the presidential contest of 2001 wound up being highly competitive as Kochiev and the Communists spearheaded the charge to bring Chibirov down and claim the new, strong presidency for themselves lest Chibirov obtain it and use it against them. Chibirov's vulnerability was heightened by what some judged to be a decline in his popular support brought about, according to his own prime minister's later memoirs, by a general fatigue with his leadership, a lack of improvement in the economy, rising inflation, pervasive corruption, "constant interruptions in electricity supply" due to the inability to pay Russian suppliers, and the arbitrary actions of a rogue branch of the security forces controlled by Chibirov's son, Aleksei.[166]

In seeking reelection, Chibirov claims in his memoirs not to have used "administrative resources" and implies this was a cause of his defeat,[167] though other accounts indicate he was not without a significant bag of tricks. For one

---

[163] Stanislav Kochiev, interview, *Pravda*, March 13–14, 2001, p. 3; Kolsto and Blakkisrud, "Living with Non-recognition," p. 504; *Nezavisimaia Gazeta*, April 12, 2001, p. 5; *Ossetia.ru*, November 21, 2007, 00:00.

[164] Stanislav Kochiev, interview, *Pravda*, March 13–14, 2001, p. 3

[165] *Iuzhnaia Osetiia*, April 10, 2010, p. 1; *Nezavisimaia Gazeta* April 12, 2001, p. 5.

[166] Sanakoev, *Ostaius' optimistom*, pp. 69–71.

[167] Chibirov, *O vremeni*, p. 275.

thing, the constitution he pushed through by referendum in 2001 stipulated that a president had to have lived in the republic for the past 10 years, which ruled out several promising Chibirov rivals, including two former prime ministers and his chief opponent from 1996.[168] Chibirov also was accused of inducing a schism in the Communist Party in a time-honored patronal presidential divide-and-rule tactic,[169] and secured support from Russia, reportedly including the Kremlin as well as North Ossetian authorities closer to home.[170]

His primary opposition arose from the networks of parliamentary chairman Kochiev and the Tedeev brothers, Jambulat and Ibragim, South Ossetians who were based in Russia and as shadow economy oligarchs controlled illicit trade through the Roki Tunnel between Russia and much of the South Caucasus through South Ossetia. Themselves barred from running by the residence requirement and following a strategy common in patronal politics, the Tedeevs were reportedly pushing two candidates for president. Their main candidate was Rezo Khugaev, but he was charged with a criminal offense shortly before the voting and the election commission refused to put him on the ballot. This moved to the fore a candidate who had initially just been their backup option, who was only in the race lest something happen to the main candidate. This backup candidate was Eduard Kokoity.[171] As a backup, the former midlevel communist official, former deputy to the legislature, and businessman was not considered a strong contender in his own right and was even judged by a major Russian publication just before the election to have had "political weight clearly insufficient for the achievement of victory."[172] Kokoity did, however, have close personal ties with the Tedeevs, even sharing with Ibragim a background in wrestling as well as business.[173] Kochiev and Kokoity both also took harder lines on Georgia than did Chibirov: While Chibirov emphasized the need for peace and stability and had pursued negotiations with Georgia over some form of new political association, his main opponents called sharply for South Ossetian independence and sovereignty.[174] On the campaign trail, they also charged that Chibirov was colluding with Georgia for the sake of corrupt business interests, claimed this put him in the pocket of Georgia, and further implied his pro-Georgian stance meant Russia wanted to get rid of him and preferred Kokoity.[175] And even as one major Russian newspaper discounted Kokoity's chances of winning, it did note his campaign's "great activeness."[176]

---

[168] *Nezavisimaia Gazeta*, April 7, 2001, p. 5; *Nezavisimaia Gazeta* April 12, 2001, p. 5.

[169] *Pravda*, September 27, 2001, p. 4.

[170] Sergei Markedonov, "Iuzhnaia Osetiia posle vyborov: vremia na razdum'ia," *Ossetia.ru*, November 15, 2006, 4:01; *Nezavisimaia Gazeta*, November 22, 2001, p. 7.

[171] Sanakoev, *Ostaius' optimistom*, p. 68.

[172] *Nezavisimaia Gazeta*, November 13, 2001, p. 4.

[173] *Kommersant*, May 23, 2009; *Ossetia.Ru*, November 5, 2007, 10:08.

[174] *Kommersant*, November 20, 2001, p. 10; Sanakoev, *Ostaius' optimistom*, pp. 70–1.

[175] *Nezavisimaia Gazeta*, April 7, 2001, p. 5; Sanakoev, *Ostaius' optimistom*, p. 71.

[176] *Nezavisimaia Gazeta*, November 13, 2001, p. 4; *RFE/RL Newsline*, November 26, 2001.

The official result appears to have shocked Chibirov, who finished third behind both Kochiev and Kokoity and thus did not even qualify for a runoff election. Chibirov's son, Aleksei, then took his armed special unit to the parliament building and reportedly demanded that Kochiev drop out (so that his father would be in the runoff) or "blood will flow." But he soon backed down, recognizing the hopelessness of the situation, especially after a large contingent of police special forces showed up to defend Kochiev.[177] Beyond this effort, Chibirov's network accepted its defeat.

It was only with Kokoity, then, that South Ossetia experienced the rise of a true single-pyramid system, with the systematic marginalization of opposing networks along the typical pattern of posttransition patronal presidents. He initially appeared to play his role as a Tedeev puppet, giving members of their network key posts, including the office of Security Council chief to Ibragim and minister of defense to their cousin, Valera Tedeev. But he soon found ways to edge them out, ultimately liquidating the Security Council and thus leaving Ibragim Tedeev without a job. The brothers were forced to leave South Ossetia and began financing Kokoity opponents, but the month before Kokoity was to stand for reelection in 2006, Ibragim was shot dead in the North Ossetian city of Vladikavkaz, across the border in Russia.[178] Kokoity then managed to pull his new political machine together with enough effect to deliver him a whopping 95 percent of the official vote to claim reelection in the 2006 presidential contest, defeating two of his own lower-level officials and an unemployed man, with the outcome reportedly never having been in doubt.[179] Jambulat Tedeev resided in Moscow, and other figures were reportedly harassed or arrested if they did not accommodate the Kokoity machine.[180] Reinforcing Kokoity's machine was strong support for his hard-line anti-Georgian stance in the face of intensifying Georgian efforts to regain control of the territory after the 2003 Rose Revolution.[181] According to one report, formally there was no opposition to Kokoity as of November 2007.[182]

Turkmenistan and Uzbekistan: The Implications of Lesser Transitional Disruption

The process of establishing single-pyramid systems went the quickest and furthest in the two countries where the dissolution of the USSR involved the least

---

[177] *Nezavisimaia Gazeta*, November 22, 2001, p. 7; *Kommersant*, November 30, 2011, p. 8.

[178] *Kommersant*, May 23, 2009; Sanakoev, *Ostaius' optimistom*, pp. 80–1.

[179] *Civil Georgia*, November 7, 2006, 16:59; *Kavkazskii Uzel*, www.kavkaz-uzel, November 19, 2008; *Nezavisimaia Gazeta*, October 19, 2006; Varvara Pakhomenko, analyst at the Demos center (for the support of conducting research on civil society), "Uroven' nedovol'stva vlastiu v Iuzhnoi Osetii ochen' vysok," *Polit.Ru*, May 29, 2009, 10:58.

[180] *Kavkazskii Uzel*, November 11, 2008; *Kavkazskii Uzel*, November 19, 2008.

[181] Markedonov, "Iuzhnaia Osetiia posle vyborov."

[182] *Ossetia.ru*, November 5, 2007, 10:08.

disruption of preexisting dominant patronal networks. More specifically, this was where the republic-level branch of the Communist Party of the Soviet Union – which during the Soviet period had often served to institutionalize balances of power among different networks – did not break apart under the pressure of the USSR's demise. In these cases, Turkmenistan and Uzbekistan, Soviet authorities had invested considerable effort ushering in new leaders in the second half of the 1980s. They had also carefully struck balances among the major political-economic networks described in Chapter 5 within the Communist Party framework rather than either leaving the republic networks to sort matters out among themselves in the waning years of the USSR (as in Kyrgyzstan) or actively promoting liberalization and proreform factions within the party (as in Ukraine).[183] The old regime leaders themselves thus had incentive to continue relying on these structures and to forgo the benefits and risks of allowing at least some real electoral contestation, leading to a rapid reconsolidation of full autocracy with little actual disruption in patterns of rule and balances among networks from the Soviet period.[184]

This process was smoothest in Turkmenistan, where the old Communist Party machine was essentially just renamed and conducted political business as usual.[185] Saparmurat Niyazov, who had been republic party chief from 1985 straight through 1991, never once allowed a contested presidential election, almost immediately took economic levers into his own hands, and exerted direct control over regional governments.[186] This situation was ratified in a new, post-Soviet presidentialist constitution adopted in 1992, the first in Central Asia.[187] The core of his rule was a personal security guard led by Akmurad Rejepov, who had begun serving Niyazov when the latter became republic party boss. Rejepov was reputed not to trust ethnic Turkmen people to staff his unit of some two thousand men, instead enlisting Slavs, Arabs, north Caucasians, and

---

[183] Research indicates that the reason for such Moscow intervention had more to do with a belief that these regions were more prone to dangerous destabilization as a result of "clan" or "tribal" fractionalization rather than less prone to destabilization, so it does not appear that prior stability was what led to the decisive Moscow interventions. On Uzbekistan and Kyrgyzstan, see McGlinchey, *Chaos, Violence, Dynasty*. On Turkmenistan, see Slavomir Horak, "The Elite in Post-Soviet and Post-Niyazow Turkmenistan: Does Political Culture Form a Leader?" *Demokratizatsiya: The Journal of Post-Soviet Democratization*, v. 20, no. 4, Fall 2012, pp. 371–85. McGlinchey (*Chaos, Violence, Dynasty*) argues that Kazakhstan received essentially the same treatment from Gorbachev; this case will be discussed separately later.

[184] Alisher Ilkhamov, "The Limits of Centralization: Regional Challenges in Uzbekistan," in Pauline Jones Luong, ed., *The Transformation of Central Asia* (Ithaca: Cornell University Press, 2004), p. 163; Sebastien Peyrouse, *Turkmenistan: Strategies of Power, Dilemmas of Development* (Armonk, NY: M. E. Sharpe, 2011), p. 70.

[185] Peyrouse, *Turkmenistan*, p. 70.

[186] Michael Ochs, "Turkmenistan: The Quest for Stability and Control," in Karen Dawisha and Bruce Parrott, eds., *Conflict, Cleavage, and Change in Central Asia and the Caucasus* (New York: Cambridge University Press, 1997), pp. 312–59.

[187] David Nissman, "Turkmenistan: Just like Old Times," in Ian Bremmer and Ray Taras, eds., *New States, New Politics* (New York: Cambridge University Press, 1997), pp. 634–53, p. 641.

Turks as enforcers. Niyazov purported to rule by being "above" tribal networks, and indeed Rejepov was not from the president's own Tekke tribe, one of the country's main five regional-tribal groupings.[188] By most accounts, however, being above tribe meant a careful balancing act, appointing representatives of different networks to various cabinet and territorial posts according to norms of equity, though also involving non-Turkmen prominently in his regime.[189]

If the vanity a leader can permit himself is a mark of success, then Niyazov was smashing, having dubbed himself Turkmenbashi (head of the Turkmen). The capital city of Ashgabat sported numerous golden statues of his likeness during the 1990s, with the most prominent (erected in 1998) rotating so that he always faced the sun.[190] By the end of the 1990s, Niyazov was named leader for life, not subject to even an unopposed election.[191]

The transition of Uzbekistan's institutionalized balance of networks from its late Soviet era Communist Party incarnation to its post-Soviet era form was a bit more rocky, but essentially followed the same pattern. Islom Karimov had, like Niyazov, been union republic party boss before the Soviet breakup, but Gorbachev had appointed him later than Niyazov, only in 1989, and then only as a compromise figure. Indeed, while Karimov hailed from Samarkand, home of one of Uzbekistan's strongest networks, he was at first an economic technocrat who had spent much of his career in Moscow working at Gosplan, the Soviet State Planning Agency. Until he became Uzbek finance minister in 1986, he had not held any party post and in fact had been demoted after a falling out with his republic-level boss.[192] In naming him republic first secretary, Gorbachev saw Karimov primarily as someone weak and therefore acceptable to the major political-economic networks based in Samarkand, Tashkent, and Ferghana that the party had traditionally balanced in the republic.

Karimov managed gradually to transform his status as compromise leader into that of dominant patron. One key move was to keep the republic Communist Party structure intact rather than to try to create his own new structure.[193] He then moved to align himself more strongly with the Samarkand network, to which he had the closest personal ties, and gradually began weakening the network that had been the most powerful at the time, the Tashkent network led informally by Shakarulla Mirsaidov. While

[188] John C. K. Daly, "Berdymukhamedov Moves to Eliminate Rivals after Foreign Policy Victories," *Eurasia Daily Monitor*, May 18, 2007.

[189] Slavomir Horak, "Changes in the Political Elite in Post-Soviet Turkmenistan," *China and Eurasia Forum Quarterly*, v. 8, no. 3, 2010, pp. 27–46; Ochs, "Turkmenistan," pp. 317–18.

[190] *The Times*, January 20, 2010.

[191] Bruce Pannier, "Turkmenistan's 'Gray Cardinal' Leaves Government," *RFE/RL*, January 23, 2009.

[192] Donald Carlisle, "Islom Karimov and Uzbekistan: Back to the Future?" in Timothy J. Colton and Robert C. Tucker, eds., *Patterns in Post-Soviet Leadership* (Boulder, CO: Westview Press, 1995), pp. 191–216, pp. 196, 200.

[193] Ilkhamov, "The Limits of Centralization," p. 163.

much of this maneuvering took place before Karimov won his first direct election to the presidency in December 1991, his decisive victory over poet Mukhammed Solih in that election emboldened him to strike. On January 8, 1992, he removed Mirsaidov as vice president, transferring him to a more subordinate position. About a week later, major student riots broke out in Tashkent decrying economic conditions, a protest many linked to Mirsaidov. Successfully putting down the riots, Karimov had now confirmed his position as the most powerful patron in the newly independent country and began gradually asserting more and more direct control.[194] One important move shortly after defeating the Tashkent network was to create a set of territorially defined political machines that were all beholden directly to him, formally subordinating regions to governors (*hokims*) whom he appointed as president starting in 1992. Karimov undergirded this in the early 1990s by constitutional reforms that codified a hyperstrong presidency, a crackdown on opposition politicians and parties, and the restoration of tight control over mass media.[195] His dominance throughout the 1990s, however, continued to hinge on balancing the interests of major regionally based patronal networks, which he controlled through a complex politics of patronage and divide and rule rather than simple diktat.[196] This practice represented a significant continuity from the Soviet period.

The Lone Eurasian Nonpresidentialist Patronal State: Moldova

It is remarkable that only one internationally recognized post-Soviet country outside the Baltic states, Moldova, emerged from the post-Soviet transition at the dawn of the 2000s without a single-pyramid system and with a parliamentarist constitution instead of a strongly presidentialist one. On one level this occurred because the battle between parliament and president – characteristic of most post-Soviet states in the first years after the USSR's demise – took longer to resolve itself and because it was only here where the parliament ultimately won this struggle. The deeper question is why the battle turned out this way only in Moldova. Of course, one cannot rule out pure chance: Even if we assume that post-Soviet conditions created a 90 percent probability of presidentialism – a strong causal effect indeed – we would expect at least one of the twelve non-Baltic countries to happen to adopt something else, and that could well be Moldova. Of course, we do have a specific historical path to trace that actually led to the parliamentarist outcome, and examining it is revealing of how patronal politics works.

To account for the Moldovan exception, the present analysis highlights a combination of the first presidents' personal dispositions and the republic

[194] Tuncer-Kilavuz, "Understanding Violent Conflict," chapter 4.
[195] Carlisle, "Islam Karimov and Uzbekistan"; Jones Luong, *Institutional Change*, p. 90.
[196] Ilkhamov, "The Limits of Centralization."

leadership's contingent early decision to get rid of district-based elections for parliament entirely. On one level, it is significant that both Moldova's first president, Mircea Snegur, and its second, Petru Lucinschi, in principle could have used force as had Yeltsin to subdue the parliament that both of them sought to control. To take such a step, however, would have had to have been considered extraordinarily risky in Moldova given that its military had not even been able to keep control over its territory (having lost Transnistria) and given that a Russian army unit sat in the separatist part of its territory across the river, adding peril to any local use of force. And while the Russian example from October 1993 demonstrated that this method could work, Yeltsin's shelling of the Congress had also reportedly cost more than a hundred lives, which even a patronal president might genuinely be unwilling to stomach, all the more so in a society just emerging from a bloody separatist war and longing for political stability. Indeed, asked directly whether force had been an option for him to establish a presidentialist system over parliamentary opposition, Snegur replied that it had not been possible because the memory of armed conflict was too fresh in the minds of Moldovans.[197] Lucan Way's interviews also indicate that Snegur had effectively lost control of the military to the parliament, which once refused to permit him to fire the top general.[198] Nevertheless, we have seen in other former republics that most presidents did not need to use violence to subdue parliament. And this leads us to the question of why two successive Moldovan presidents failed where presidents or their successors in virtually all the other fragments of the post-Soviet space discussed here eventually succeeded by the end of the 1990s in instituting strongly presidentialist constitutions and establishing some kind of single-pyramid systems.

Here we must begin with why the country's first president, Snegur, did not face down the parliament using nonviolent means, why he did not insist on a more strongly presidentialist constitution and force parliament to accept it, perhaps by threatening a referendum as Kuchma had in Ukraine. If we listen to Snegur himself, one factor was a personal preference on his part to "compromise" instead of entering into a showdown with parliament. It appears, though, that this consideration was shaped in part by his perception that other branches of formal power were held by other members of the same extended agrarian elite network. Indeed, during negotiations on Moldova's first post-soviet constitution, which was finally adopted in 1994, a more strongly presidentialist draft had been prepared that Snegur supported. He later wrote that he acquiesced to a "half-presidential, half-parliamentary" constitution, drafted by the parliament's Constitutional Commission under parliamentary chairman Lucinschi, in part because he, Lucinschi, and the bulk of MPs were all representatives of the same political party, the Agrarian Democratic Party, described in the previous chapter as the formal representation of a large

---

[197] Mircea Snegur, author's interview, Chisinau, Moldova, June 30, 2009.
[198] "Pluralism by Default in Moldova," *Journal of Democracy*, v. 13, no. 4, October 2002, pp. 127–41, p. 135.

network of elites with roots in the agricultural sector and associated former Communist Party structures. It was important to Snegur that major decisions for the country be reached by consensus among people in "one political boat," which resulted in their "mutual agreement" that it was "necessary to share power and establish a certain balance."[199] He thus believed at the time that both parliament and government supported his larger policy agenda, including economic reforms, which would have been jeopardized by a less compromising approach.[200] As one key figure in the constitutional reform process put it, unlike in the Russia of September–October 1993, in Moldova "there is not a confrontation between the legislative and executive branches. Our pain is within parliament itself,"[201] where the Agrarians faced opposition from an unruly minority that proved large enough to block many of their initiatives, facilitating support for new parliamentary elections and a new constitution in an effort to break the gridlock.[202] Snegur laments in retrospect, however, that he did not have an official presidential representative to look out for his own interests in parliamentary discussions on such reforms.[203]

In their memoirs, both Snegur and Lucinschi cite another factor promoting their agreement on constitutional reform, though Snegur calls it a secondary factor reinforcing his preference for compromise over conflict: international influence. The Council of Europe reportedly urged them to avoid a presidentialist constitution, and both leaders considered it important to become fully accepted by Europe. Snegur later boasted that this was not in vain: Moldova in 1995 became the first CIS country accepted into the Council of Europe.[204] At this early stage of Moldova's post-Soviet history, therefore, Snegur was led to compromise by a desire to please Europe and other personal factors, including his sense that parliamentary leaders were part of his own network as well as his preference for avoiding conflict.

The result of this compromise was a 1994 constitution that did feature a directly elected presidency and did give the holder of this office the right to nominate the prime minister. Thus this constitution was neither a parliamentarist nor a divided-executive constitution according to the definitions laid out in Chapter 4. It must thus be considered presidentialist. At the same time, both outside observers and local authorities perceived it as depicting a much weaker formal presidency than other post-Soviet constitutions. Concretely, the

---

[199] Mircea Snegur and Eduard Volkov, *Otkrovennye dialogi* (Chisinau: Draghistea, 2007), pp. 138–9.

[200] Mircea Snegur, author's interview, Chisinau, Moldova, June 30, 2009.

[201] Viktor Pushkash, deputy parliamentary chairman, interview, *Nezavisimaia Moldova*, October 12, 1993, pp. 1–2.

[202] William Crowther, "Moldova: Caught between Nation and Empire," in Ian Bremmer and Ray Taras, eds., *New States New Politics: Building the Post-Soviet Nations* (New York: Cambridge University Press, 1997), pp. 316–52, pp. 324–5.

[203] Snegur and Volkov, *Otkrovennye dialogi*, pp. 138–9.

[204] Petr Luchinskii, *Moldova i Moldavane* (Chisinau: Cartea Moldovei, 2007), pp. 327–8; Snegur and Volkov, *Otkrovennye dialogi*, p. 138.

bar set for parliamentary confirmation of the president's nominee for prime minister was set to a very demanding level: Not simply a majority was required (as in Russia or Ukraine at that time), but a three-fifths majority of all members. Importantly, this was a larger majority than the 54 percent majority the Agrarian Party had won in the elections that had preceded the adoption of the new constitution.[205] The president also lacked direct appointment power over regional officials, and the premier had more formal power in this regard.[206] The 1994 constitution, then, was not considered a presidential victory and not progress toward what observers regarded as presidential dominance.[207]

When Moldova's 1996 presidential election rolled around, then, Snegur had failed to establish expectations of his own future dominance in the country. This encouraged the ambitions of other leading members of the dominant agrarian/former-communist network, not content to be second fiddles and sensing that they could potentially use the resources at their disposal in key nonpresidential posts to displace Snegur as head of both the network and the country. The result was a fracturing of the Agrarian Democratic Party network that had controlled all three major posts in the country: president (Snegur), prime minister (Sangheli), and parliamentary chair (Lucinschi). But that the presidency was nevertheless seen as the most promising post to occupy was made clear from the fact that both Lucinschi and Sangheli challenged Snegur's reelection bid and ran for president in 1996.[208] With state administrative resources splintered and no presidential pyramid dominating, Lucinschi pulled off the victory in a free-for-all, defeating Snegur in a runoff.

As a new president with the dominant agrarian network fractured, Lucinschi essentially had to start from scratch in trying to build up his own presidential machine, and here he was hindered by another formal institutional feature differentiating Moldova from all other post-Soviet countries: In 1994, Moldova had become the lone former Soviet state to elect its parliament entirely through

---

[205] Eugene Mazo, "Post-Communist Paradox: How the Rise of Parliamentarism Coincided with the Demise of Pluralism in Moldova," *CDDRL Working Papers*, no. 17, Center on Democracy, Development, and the Rule of Law, Stanford University, August 27, 2004, p. 24.

[206] Way, "Pluralism by Default in Moldova," p. 135.

[207] For example, Steven D. Roper's analysis of formal presidential powers codes Moldova's presidency as stipulated in the 1994 constitution as having significantly weaker powers than other post-Soviet states. See Steven D. Roper, "Are All Semipresidential Regimes the Same? A Comparison of Premier-Presidential Regimes," *Comparative Politics*, v. 34, no. 3, April 2002, pp. 253–72. Snegur's autobiography, which takes the form of an interview, is also a colorful illustration of how the reform was seen with regard to presidential power: Snegur's interviewer presses him to explain televised episodes where "I see that you are sitting there behind your place at the presidium, and they are going article by article and clearly cutting your powers. Really?" Snegur curtly responds that this was done by "mutual agreement" and, lightly tapping his elbow on the desk, tells the interviewer to wrap up that discussion. Snegur and Volkov, *Otkrovennye dialogi*, p. 139.

[208] Snegur (author's interview, Chisinau, Moldova, June 30, 2009) attributed the presidency's relative attractiveness during this time as owing to its status as "head of state" along with the big responsibility that entailed.

party-list proportional representation (PR), as opposed to through a system with deputies elected in single-member districts (SMDs) or systems featuring a mix of both.[209] Reformers in countries like Russia that adopted a mixed system did tend to acknowledge that SMD elections might not promote party system development and thus thought that requiring some deputies to be elected on party lists through PR would promote political party development. The PR component would also provide a safe way to elect high-priority leaders atop a party list who might not be able to win a plurality in a district.[210] The designers of Moldova's 1994 constitution did take into account such considerations in supporting PR.[211]

But Moldova's reformers also added a pair of arguments for PR that featured less prominently in places that did not adopt it for filling their whole parliaments. For one thing, some deputies and their supporters argued that SMD elections would make it easier for existing authorities to use state levers on specific territories to shape electoral outcomes, including through vote buying, threatening the independence of parliament.[212] Deputies in other countries, including Russia, had also recognized this potential for district elections to be manipulated, and for presidential supporters such possibilities were sometimes considered a plus rather than a minus.[213] Since Moldova's was not the only parliament reluctant to grant a president more powers of manipulation, for example, as in Ukraine discussed earlier, it still remains unclear why Moldova would wind up the only country to adopt a fully PR system.

The largely unique consideration was as follows: With the effort to regain control over Transnistria front and center on the republic's political agenda, district elections would have meant that some districts' seats (those out of Moldova's control in Transnistria) would remain unfilled and the territory would not be represented in parliament. PR meant that each party list that was elected was in fact representing the entire country, including Transnistria.[214] All this led local views to resonate strongly with Council of Europe lobbying for fostering a multiparty parliament, a purpose that PR also served.[215] Thus in fall

---

[209] Several other post-Soviet states had mixed systems during the 1990s that nevertheless included sizable shares of district-elected deputies, but usually the party-list component did not constitute a majority of the seats.

[210] Jerry F. Hough, "Institutional Rules and Party Formation," in Timothy J. Colton and Hough, eds., *Growing Pains: Russian Democracy and the Election of 1993* (Washington, DC: Brookings, 1998), pp. 37–74, p. 54.

[211] *Nezavisimaia Moldova*, September 11, 1993, p. 2.

[212] Boris Marnan, "Komu budet vruchena vlast?" *Nezavisimaia Moldova*, September 14, 1993, p. 1.

[213] Hough, "Institutional Rules and Party Formation."

[214] Among many others interviewed, this reason has been cited as crucial by both Lucinschi (Luchinskii, *Moldova i Moldavane*, p. 327) and Snegur (author's interview, Chisinau, Moldova, June 30, 2009). Confirming is Crowther, "Moldova," pp. 324–5.

[215] Luchinskii, *Moldova i Moldavane*, p. 327. Some also suggest that Moldova was imitating Romania, but Snegur (author's interview, Chisinau, Moldova, June 30, 2009) points out that Romania's PR system was different, with regional party lists, a recipe that ran counter to the single countrywide party list option that was crucial for the Transnistria factor. Snegur thus

1993, when repeated standoffs within the parliament had convinced nearly all major political figures that some kind of change from the Soviet era all-SMD system and new elections were necessary, parliament agreed to dissolve itself and to be filled again according to a new all-PR election system. These new elections occurred on February 27, 1994, returning a majority of seats for the governing Agrarian Democratic Party coalition, which reelected Lucinschi as parliamentary chairman.[216]

Lucinschi strongly appears to have had much greater will and skill when it came to patronal politics than did Snegur, but the formal institutional changes enabled parliament ultimately to undermine his attempts to create either a single-pyramid system or a more strongly presidentialist constitution. Ironically, back when he was the legislature's chairman, Lucinschi himself had pushed through these very institutional changes that now hindered him.[217] Apparently recognizing the irony in retrospect, Lucinschi complained that soon after becoming president, he found himself unable to gain a stable parliamentary majority and enact policy, with parliament having had the upper hand.[218] Indeed, the presidential race had blown up the governing coalition that had produced constitutional agreement in 1994, as the Agrarian network's three leading figures (president, prime minister, and parliamentary speaker) had all run against each other and each still controlled significant deputy groups in the parliament. Instead of moving immediately to use his fresh electoral mandate to try to change the formal institutional rules to the president's favor, perhaps partly because he had played such a large role in creating the existing institutions and initially thought he could work through them, Lucinschi essentially hoped that the 1998 parliamentary elections would return a strong propresidential bloc. But without a mighty presidential machine in place to engineer a victory, 40 of the 101 parliamentary seats went to the surging Party of Communists of the Republic of Moldova (PCRM) and Lucinschi's loyalists failed to win a majority.

The president was able to have Dumitru Diacov, leader of a movement that Lucinschi had helped organize to support his presidential bid in 1996, elected speaker. But Diacov, once installed, proved less than pliable and in any case his parliamentary coalition contained a wide variety of networks that did not function as a coherent bloc, much less under presidential control. These included Snegur's remnant of the old Agrarian network and nationalist movement leader Iurie Rosca's Christian Democrats, which featured many from the

says that the Romanian example was not particularly influential, and that the consideration of Transnistria trumped suggestions for imitating Romania's system with regional PR party lists.

[216] On parliamentary elections in Moldova, see e-Democracy Web site, Association for Participatory Democracy ADEPT (run by Igor Botan), http://www.e-democracy.md/en/elections/parliamentary/, accessed May 9, 2011.

[217] On Lucinschi's role in the election system reform, see *Nezavisimaia Moldova*, October 16, 1993, p. 1.

[218] Luchinskii, *Moldova i Moldavane*, pp. 336, 340–1.

old independence movement.[219] Diacov and his allies report that Lucinschi in fact *promoted* fractiousness in the legislature in an attempt to divide and rule it, aiming to prevent Diacov or his party from gaining a strong enough parliamentary position to challenge the presidency.[220] This lack of control occurred despite Lucinschi's reportedly "aggressive" efforts to set up a "secret-police apparatus in order to harass foes and to collect compromising material (*kompromat*) on rivals."[221]

There is a strong case to be made that this was not simply a reflection of fragmented Moldovan society or of cronyism more generally.[222] Indeed, most post-Soviet societies were cronyistic and many were at least as politically splintered as was Moldova's at the time of the USSR's dissolution. Instead, Lucinschi's problems were the combined product of leadership tactics and, crucially, the institutional peculiarities noted previously. Tactically, Lucinschi did not move quickly to capitalize on his 1996 election victory to institute a more strongly presidentialist constitution, as might have been possible since he had defeated both the sitting president and prime minister to become elected president and so could have likely claimed a mandate to bolster his authority to get things done. Waiting allowed the impact of his presidential victory in signaling his likely future power to be diluted by myriad subsequent (if smaller) contests, which included some defeats at the hands of parliament, as Lucinschi himself notes.[223]

Most importantly – and a reason why he lost some of these smaller battles – the PR parliamentary electoral system in the 1998 elections deprived Lucinschi of the special opportunities single-member-district elections afforded other post-Soviet patronal presidents to manipulate electoral outcomes and subsequently influence individual deputies.[224] Even after mixed electoral systems were introduced in Russia and Ukraine, for example, the decisive basis for their first propresidential majority coalitions had been the district-elected deputies, many of whom were formally independents.[225] Scholars have long noted the fragmenting effects of presidential-PR systems.[226] But the effect at work

---

[219] Luchinskii, *Moldova i Moldavane*, p. 336.

[220] Dmitrii Topol' and George Movile, *Demokraticheskaia partiia: 10 let vmeste so strane* (evidently published by the Democratic Party in 2007 though publication information is not in the book; It was given to author by Democratic Party leader Dumitru Diacov on June 28, 2009, as a party history), pp. 7–8. Way's ("Pluralism by Default in Moldova") interviews concur.

[221] Way, "Pluralism by Default in Moldova," pp. 129–30.

[222] Arguments citing a general social fractiousness include Dmitry Furman, "Kommunisty i demokratiia," *Nezavisimaia Moldova*, May 4, 2009; and Way, "Pluralism by Default in Moldova."

[223] Luchinskii, *Moldova i Moldavane*, p. 336.

[224] Authors of the system indeed intended it to be resistant to presidential manipulation, as noted earlier. See Marnan, "Komu budet vruchena vlast?"

[225] E.g., Henry E. Hale and Robert Orttung, "The Duma Districts: Key to Putin's Power," PONARS Policy Memo, no. 290, September 2003. Recall also the discussion of other countries earlier in this chapter.

[226] Arend Lijphart, "Constitutional Choices for New Democracies," *Journal of Democracy*, v. 2, no. 1, Winter 1991, pp. 72–84, p. 77.

in Moldova is specific to highly patronalistic contexts featuring a high degree of political uncertainty and a relatively unpopular president unable to win majority support on the basis of his or her own appeal – features common in the early post-Soviet years. While all patronalistic deputies might be bought or otherwise influenced, those whose parliamentary position depended more directly on a local (district) power base could be more easily persuaded to defect from a central party leader than could deputies whose position and political future depended more directly on the party leader personally, all else equal. This is because executive power in the hands of a patronal president is likely to involve a hold on many levers (including state transfers and the capacity to intervene in local elections) capable of rewarding or punishing the local networks or machines on which district-elected deputies depend.[227]

The denouement occurred when Lucinschi finally gave up on the old institutional framework and attempted to ram a much more strongly presidentialist constitution through parliament in 1999. This reform would have also replaced the all-PR parliamentary election system with one where 70 percent of the seats were filled through SMD voting, leaving only 30 percent determined by PR. This indicates that Lucinschi himself saw that SMD would be a better basis for political machine building.[228] He called a consultative referendum, which in May 1999 produced a 55 percent vote in favor of presidentialism. But the parliament claimed that turnout had been too low for this to count as an expression of the popular will. Eventually, after Lucinschi created a commission to draft constitutional changes that would put this into effect and started pressuring parliamentary groupings to support it over the course of the ensuing year (for example, threatening to divide Diacov's originally pro-Lucinschi movement), nearly the whole parliament, including Diacov, turned against him.[229] For once almost completely united, on July 5, 2000, 90 of the 101 parliamentary deputies voted to change the constitution on the parliament's own terms, replacing direct presidential elections with the election of the president by the parliament, trimming some presidential powers, and preserving the all-PR method of electing the parliament.[230] Deputies generally cited the need to end what they saw as presidential usurpation of power, to create a more rational division of powers that would be less likely to result in political stalemate and more likely to produce stability, and to be in accord with European systems.[231]

---

[227] King, "The Benefits of Ethnic War," pp. 160–1.

[228] *Logos Press*, May 12, 2000.

[229] *Nezavisimaia Moldova*, summary of Lucinschi speech to parliament, July 21, 2000, p. 1; Iurie Rosca, author's interview, Chisinau, Moldova, July 7, 2010; Topol' and Movile, *Demokraticheskaia partiia*, pp. 29–40.

[230] Venice Commission, "Consolidated Opinion on the Constitutional Reform in the Republic of Moldova," CDL (2000) 95, Strasbourg, November 24, 2000, http://www.venice.coe.int/docs/2000/CDL(2000)095-e.asp, accessed May 9, 2011.

[231] See the useful summary of key leaders' positions in *Nezavisimaia Moldova*, July 7, 2000, pp. 1–2.

Lucinschi refused to sign the legislation, returning the bill to parliament on July 20 along with a counterproposal to hold a referendum on two alternative constitutional changes, the parliament's version and his own.[232] The parliament almost immediately rejected the president's offer and voted a second time for its own reform with an overwhelming majority, a move that now obligated the president to sign it into law.[233]

At this point, Lucinschi might have made a last stand by refusing to sign as the constitution required and then attempting to force a referendum. Indeed, he frequently objected in public appearances that the parliament's reform was diametrically opposed to the ballots of 55 percent of those who had voted for his presidentialist reform in the May referendum, and some of his allies warned that the people might rise up and force a referendum if the parliament ignored them.[234] As one Moldovan analyst reported at the time, however, a new referendum was unlikely to work in his favor even if he had forced one to occur. With the majority of significant political parties ready to campaign against the reform, including the rising Communists, who had won about 40 percent of the seats in the last election, the resources required to generate the required 50 percent of the vote and at least 60 percent turnout appeared to be beyond him, especially when the public was eager for an end to the political struggle and thus unlikely to back a presidential escalation of the battle. This left Lucinschi with the option of employing military force against the parliament as Yeltsin had. Diacov reports that this was considered a real possibility and that some were urging it, leading him to discuss the issue many times with Lucinschi, who promised he would not use force.[235] Diacov and others considered it a personal decision by Lucinschi not to go this route.[236] While one cannot rule out that he may simply not have been able to count on the military to follow through, Lucinschi in the end did accept his defeat, citing the need to obey the constitutional requirement that he sign the reform despite his own fundamental disagreement with it. He then dutifully resigned when his term ended.

Moldova thus became a parliamentary republic without ever having established a single-pyramid system, and starting in 2001 the parliament was scheduled to elect the president with a two-thirds vote among its members. The necessary supermajority of the sitting parliament that had enacted this reform could not be found to elect this new president, however. The Communists backed their leader, Vladimir Voronin, while Diacov's forces supported

[232] *Nezavisimaia Moldova*, July 21, 2000, p. 1.

[233] *Nezavisimaia Moldova*, July 27, 2000, p. 1; *Nezavisimaia Moldova*, July 27, 2000, p. 1.

[234] Anatol Plugaru, interview in *Nezavisimaia Moldova*, August 1, 2000, p. 2.

[235] Dumitru Diacov, author's interview, Chisinau, Moldova, June 29, 2009.

[236] V. Kirmikchi, "Parlament skazal svoe slovo. A chto predprimet prezident?" *Nezavisimaia Moldova*, August 3, 2000, p. 2.

Constitutional Court chairman Pavel Barbalat, an interesting choice that at least suggests that the parliamentary forces may also have arranged a quid pro quo with the court, which would have made Lucinschi's prospects for resisting even bleaker.[237] Since neither candidate secured the needed 61 parliamentary votes, Lucinschi undertook his presidential responsibility to dissolve the parliament and called new elections for February 25, 2001, after which the new deputies would elect the next president.[238] Lucinschi referred to this parliamentary victory as a "coup d'état."[239] In the terms of this volume, it represented the creation of the post-Soviet world's lone enduring instance of *patronal parliamentarism* in the 2000s, the implications of which will be examined in depth in Chapter 10.

Conclusion

The political history of Eurasia in the 1990s can largely be seen as the history of patronal presidentialism and the emergence of single-pyramid systems, and accordingly as the growing domination of regime cycle regularity over irregularity. Patronal presidentialism is an institutional arrangement that features a formally strong presidency that operates in a highly patronalistic context through great formal and informal powers. As the leaders who oversaw the creation of the presidencies usually won them, the first post-Soviet presidents were in general initially understood to be each republic's most powerful patron. This information effect, combined with the focal effects of presidentialist constitutions, gave patronal presidents an advantage over their parliamentary or prime ministerial counterparts in determining the expectations and hence the behavior of the main power-brokering networks. And this, in turn, gave them a marginal advantage in winning in the power struggles that characterized nearly every fragment of the post-Soviet space in the immediate aftermath of the USSR's breakup, enabling them to establish even more clearly presidentialist constitutions (usually in the early to mid-1990s) and then to build patronal monopolies for network coalitions they dominated. This advantage was still marginal, however: The upheaval of the transition generated tremendous uncertainty as to what constituted and was likely in the future to constitute power. This meant that the first presidents' advantage was unstable, capable of being squandered or otherwise upset by any variety of missteps or sometimes by simple bad luck. Therefore, leadership skill mattered a great deal in

---

[237] Diacov says the parliament did not control the court and that the court was itself worried about a presidentialist regime (Diacov interview 2009).

[238] ADEPT, "2000 Presidential Elections," ADEPT Web site, http://www.parties.e-democracy.md/en/electionresults/2000presidential/, accessed June 20, 2012.

[239] Luchinskii, *Moldova i Moldavane*, p. 343.

the first post-Soviet power struggles. Irregular sources of regime cycles were accordingly very prominent.

Over the course of a decade, however, regime cycle regularity started to become more prominent than irregularity. Patronal presidents eventually emerged almost everywhere who were both able and willing to build dominant political machines, either having learned what *not* to do from failed predecessors or having simply introduced more effective machine politics skills to the office. And what appears to have been important was indeed a more general kind of skill rather than a particular sort of background. We can conclude, for example, that patronal presidentialism was not simply a continuation of communist rule in a new guise. Only five of the successful patronal presidents (Aliyev, Karimov, Nazarbaev, Niyazov, and Shevardnadze), had been their republics' Communist Party first secretaries, and two of these (Shevardnadze and Aliyev) had long been out of office before being recalled to their republics' capitals to restore order. Plus, former Tajik Communist first secretary Nabiev was arguably the worst of all the failures, with Azerbaijan's Mutalibov not far behind. We can additionally conclude that success in building patronal presidential single-pyramid systems was not out of reach for intellectuals: While some like Gamsakhurdia and Elchibey failed spectacularly, Ter-Petrossian and Akaev were initially rather effective, at least enough to orchestrate their own reelection and marginalize other networks. Indeed, one should not underestimate the degree to which Soviet era academia itself was a major locus of patron-client relations, both in institutional hierarchies as well as in professional networks.

This chapter has also revealed some of the crucial importance of time in patronal politics that was discussed in Chapter 4. For one thing, we see that it indeed took time for leaders to manage the massive challenges of coordinating elite networks in post-Soviet society around a single pyramid of authority. Thus political closure tended to emerge only over a period of many years, and the process could be forced to start over when a sitting president failed and was ousted. Such initial setbacks for leaders, as well as the general chaos of the early post-Soviet period, also meant that the timing of political closure processes differed from place to place, with different bumps along the initial post-Soviet path causing delays or setbacks in some places and acceleration in others. Some have referred to such setbacks as instances of "feckless pluralism" or "pluralism by default."[240] To be sure, leaders in the early independence period could not simply seize all power immediately and assert full control at will, so to at least some degree pluralism is what initially resulted by "default." But to apply this concept more broadly to characterize these regimes is to miss the essential regime dynamic that was at work at the time across the whole region. Indeed,

---

[240] Thomas Carothers, "The End of the Transition Paradigm," *Journal of Democracy*, v. 13, no. 1, January 2002, pp. 5–21; Way, "Pluralism by Default in Moldova."

a. Polities Keeping CPSU Structure Intact with Transition to Independence:

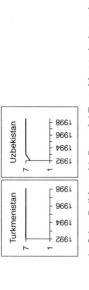

b. Other Polities with Peaceful Transition to Independence:

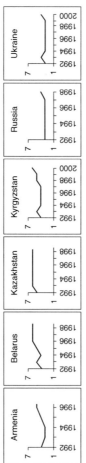

c. Polities Experiencing Civil or Separatist War During Transition to Independence:

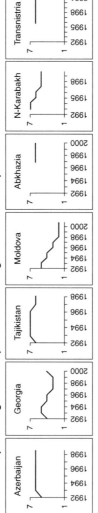

FIGURE 6.1. Levels of political closure in post-Soviet polities during emergence of initial single-pyramid systems. Specifically the vertical axis represents, Freedom House's Freedom in the World "Political Rights" index (freedomhouse.org), according to which a 7 refers to the least political rights, 1 to the most rights. The polities in category "c" are grouped separately because civil war counts as low political rights in Freedom House's scale. Thus the high values on the charts for these polities' early post-Soviet years often reflect civil war and extreme disorder rather than political closure, which high values after the wars' end tend to capture.

it turned out to be just a matter of time before virtually all of the Eurasian polities moved in the general direction of single-pyramid politics, with patronal presidentialism emerging as a dominant institutional type across most of the post-Soviet space by the year 2000. These patterns are broadly reflected in Figure 6.1, which shows a general movement in the direction of political closure during the periods discussed for each country.[241] This reflects the process by which patronal presidents gradually gained the capacity to mobilize other networks to their cause in the most important battles and increasingly to marginalize those that would not "play ball" when called upon.[242]

It was also around the end of the 1990s and early 2000s, however, that the first crisis points predicted by the sources of regime cycle regularity identified in Chapter 4 started to arise. These would make the overall picture of the 2000s look very different from that of the 1990s. These crisis points are the central subject of the next chapter.

---

[241] Figure 6.1 (and Figure 11.1, which will be presented later in this volume) report "political rights" index scores from Freedom House's annual Freedom in the World ratings. This index is intended to capture much of the variation in political openness and closure that this volume argues is associated with movement between single- and competing-pyramid systems. It focuses in particular on the openness of media and freedom of competition in elections, which should be greater when political networks are fragmented in a competing arrangement and should be lower when the country's main networks are arranged in a single-pyramid fashion. This index is imperfect for our purposes, however, because situations of extreme competition among networks (actual civil war) are also coded as a *lack* of political rights, meaning that these ratings cannot distinguish a situation of civil war (extreme discoordination of networks) from the tightest single-pyramid arrangement (a situation of high network coordination and extreme political closure). The present author approached Freedom House to obtain the subcomponents of this index so as to remove the component reflecting civil war and produce a purer indicator of political closure but was told that these were not available to be given out. Another imperfection in Freedom House's index for our purposes is that it only goes to 7 (the score of maximal closure) and can only rise or fall by increments of a whole point. This leaves little room to capture more subtle regime dynamics, though it does capture the larger trend, if in a rather clunky way.

[242] Some might suggest that Polity IV indices of democracy/autocracy are also reasonable indicators of the kind of political openness and closure considered in this volume. This is not the case. Polity IV is inappropriate because it is primarily concerned with capturing the extent of order, regulation, and institutionalization, as opposed to political openness and closure in the sense discussed here. For example, it codes the executive recruitment of a country as relatively "open" if "all the politically active population has an opportunity, in principle, to attain the position through a *regularized* process" (emphasis added). A careful reading makes clear that this is entirely different from what this volume has in mind by openness. Perhaps most strikingly, the Polity IV manual actually lists the *post-Stalinist USSR* as an *example* of *open* executive recruitment. Clearly, this is a radically different form of "openness" than is described in this volume and captured in Freedom House ratings. See Monty G. Marshall, Ted Robert Gurr, and Keith Jaggers, "Polity IV Project: Political Regime Characteristics and Transitions, 1800–2009: Dataset Users' Manual," Center for Systemic Peace, www.systemicpeace.org/polity/polity4.htm, p. 22.

7

Revolutions and Other Presidential Ousters

In late 2003, a dashing young Mikheil Saakashvili held high a red rose as he and a mass of followers chanted prodemocracy slogans and stormed the parliament during an address by President Eduard Shevardnadze. He literally drank the tea remaining in the president's cup, and Shevardnadze resigned the next day, a disgraced "autocrat." A year later, it was the star turn of Ukrainian opposition leader Viktor Yushchenko, his once-handsome face now green and pockmarked from eating a would-be assassin's dioxin-laced soup during the presidential campaign. Backed by nearly a million orange-festooned supporters camped for weeks in the November and December cold of Kyiv, he railed against the corruption and election fraud of the Leonid Kuchma regime and forced an unprecedented "repeat runoff" presidential election, which ultimately made the victim the victor. Overshadowed by this drama was a contemporaneous event in Abkhazia that was equally stunning to the few who were watching: Opposition leader Sergei Bagapsh rallied supporters to snatch power from an incumbent leadership backed by Vladimir Putin in this de facto Russian protectorate in Georgia, forcing them to recognize him as winner of the 2004–5 presidential election. Perhaps most amazing of all was the downfall of Kyrgyzstan's Askar Akaev, a president in a region that had up to that time been considered an impenetrable, culturally fortified bastion of authoritarianism. Demonstrators wielding tulips and yellow placards defied stereotypes of Central Asian docility and swelled up against him in March 2005. Bursting into his "White House" in the name of democracy, they forced the hapless "dictator" to flee to Moscow – by one account rolled up in a carpet.[1]

Observers in the West quickly dubbed the events in Georgia, Ukraine, and Kyrgyzstan "color revolutions" and leapt to brand them "democratic

[1] *TsentrAziia*, August 29, 2005, 12:43. Akaev supporters have denied this.

breakthroughs."[2] Democracy, rang out the refrain, was now again "on the march" in a chain of events that some traced back to the 2000 election defeat of Serbian President Slobodan Milosevic (dubbed by many the "Bulldozer Revolution") or even to the earlier defeats of incumbent leaders in Croatia, Slovakia, and Romania.[3] Local democracy activists and their Western supporters were fast to claim credit. Scholars generated long laundry lists of purported causes, and Western policy makers debated how they could best keep the new "democracy wave" going.[4] Russia's increasingly fretful leadership tried in vain to salt Westerners' heady drink, depicting instead a highly organized and well-financed American plot to dislodge inconvenient leaders and replace them with pro-Western ones, a view that did take root among many Eurasian analysts and even some Western observers.[5]

The notion of color revolutions as democratic breakthroughs, however, was quickly dashed against the hard rocks of subsequent post-Soviet events. Not only did the wave strangely fail to catch on in other countries where both foreign governments and civic activists tried hard, as in Belarus and Russia, but democracy quickly faltered in the post-Soviet revolutionary countries themselves. Freedom House's *Nations in Transit* ratings reflect this all too clearly: Both Georgia and Kyrgyzstan were less democratic in 2007 than they had been the year before their revolutions.[6] While Ukraine registered significant democratic improvement during the subsequent five years, as will be discussed in detail in Chapter 9, outside observers (and even more so domestic ones) widely came to view the Orange Revolution a failure as well, an event that left in place massive corruption, incessant self-serving political infighting, and policy paralysis. Then, in 2010, Kuchma's failed successor from 2004 amazingly returned to power through a relatively free election and began reversing many of the democratic gains that had been achieved.[7] At the same time, the notion

[2] Ariel Cohen, "Helping Kyrgyzstan's Democratic Revolution," Heritage Foundation WebMemo no. 701, March 24, 2005; Adrian Karatnycky, "Ukraine's Orange Revolution," *Foreign Affairs*, v. 84, no. 2, March–April 2005, pp. 32–52; Kuzio, "Democratic Breakthroughs"; Michael McFaul, Chingiz Mammadov, and Zamira Sydykova, "What's a Corrupt Election among Friends?" *Los Angeles Times*, October 23, 2005.

[3] Valerie J. Bunce and Sharon L. Wolchik, "Favorable Conditions and Electoral Revolutions," *Journal of Democracy*, v. 17, no. 4, October 2006, pp. 5–18.

[4] Prominent attempts to compile lists of factors can be found in Michael McFaul, "Transitions from Communism," *Journal of Democracy*, v. 16, no. 4, July 2005, pp. 212–44; Taras Kuzio, "Democratic Breakthroughs and Revolutions in Five Postcommunist Countries: Comparative Perspectives on the Fourth Wave," *Demokratizatsiya: The Journal of Post-Soviet Democratization*, v. 16, no. 1, Winter 2008, pp. 97–109; and Donnacha O Beacháin and Abel Polese, eds., *The Colour Revolutions in the Former Soviet Republics* (New York: Routledge, 2010).

[5] E.g., Natalia A. Narochnitskaia, *Oranzhevye seti: ot Belgrada do Bishkeka* (St. Petersburg, Russia: Aleteiia, 2008); Ian Traynor, "U.S. Campaign behind the Turmoil in Kiev," *The Guardian*, November 26, 2004.

[6] Jeannette Goehring, ed., *Nations in Transit 2008: Democratization from Central Europe to Eurasia* (New York: Freedom House, 2008), p. 44.

[7] Alexander J. Motyl, "The New Political Regime in Ukraine – toward Sultanism Yanukovych-Style?" Cicero Foundation Great Debate Paper, no. 10/06, July 2010.

that these revolutions reflected no genuine public outpouring and that the protesters were all paid off greatly strains credulity and flies in the face of a reality known by those whose friends or relatives took part in these events.[8]

This chapter shows that the post-Soviet color revolutions were neither democratic breakthroughs nor foreign plots, but instead a natural and even rather predictable product of patronal presidential systems. That is, they are well understood though the sources of regime cycle regularity that were discussed in Chapter 4. The color revolutions were in each case the outcome of a lame-duck syndrome where popular opinion played a key role in deciding a contest among patronal networks in favor of an opposition network. This account departs from many widespread interpretations of the color revolutions. In particular, it deemphasizes factors such as international diffusion (including demonstration effects, active international intervention, and transnational activist networks), state weakness, regime resources, leadership resolve, privatization, and opposition unity, strength, and strategy.[9] This is not to say none of these other factors has mattered at all. But it is to say that when such factors mattered, they tended to be of secondary importance in determining larger outcomes and of primary importance mainly in shaping the particular *forms* that these larger outcomes took. Indeed, one of the key arguments of Chapter 4 was that sources of regime cycle regularity like term limits and elections tend to *regularize* the impact of other factors that might tend to strengthen or weaken a president, determining when they are likely to have or lack impact.

This chapter goes even further, however. It shows that the entire realm of patronal presidential ousters in Eurasia after the point where Chapter 6 left off was much more a realm of regime cycle regularity than irregularity, as Chapter 4 led us to anticipate. In fact, just two factors – election-related expectations of impending succession and public opinion – go a surprisingly long way in determining not just whether, but when and even how any given incumbent network would be ousted in the patronal presidential systems of Eurasia. In nine of the ten instances when a presidential network has been ousted since the initial creation of a single-pyramid system in a polity through the time of this writing, the ouster took place when the incumbent was unpopular and was

---

[8] We now have systematically presented evidence to this effect in Mark R. Beissinger, "The Semblance of Democratic Revolution: Coalitions in Ukraine's Orange Revolution," *American Political Science Review*, v. 107, no. 3, August 2013, pp. 574–92 and Olga Onuch, "Why Did They Join *en Masse*? Understanding 'Ordinary' Ukrainians' Participation in Mass-Mobilization in 2004," *New Ukraine. A Journal of History and Politics*, v. 11, 2011, pp. 89–113.

[9] E.g., Mark R. Beissinger, "Structure and Example in Modular Political Phenomena: The Diffusion of Bulldozer/Rose/Orange/Tulip Revolutions," *Perspectives on Politics*, v. 5, no. 2, June 2007, pp. 259–76; Valerie J. Bunce and Sharon L. Wolchik, *Defeating Authoritarian Leaders in Postcommunist Countries* (New York: Cambridge University Press, 2011); McFaul, "Transitions from Communism"; Kuzio, "Democratic Breakthroughs"; O Beacháin and Polese, *The Colour Revolutions*; Scott Radnitz, "The Color of Money: Privatization, Economic Dispersion, and the Post-Soviet 'Revolutions,'" *Comparative Politics*, v. 42, no. 2, January 2010, pp. 127–46; Lucan Way, "The Real Causes of the Color Revolutions," *Journal of Democracy*, v. 19, no. 3, July 2008, pp. 55–69.

TABLE 7.1. *Patronal Presidential Network Ousters Occurring after the Initial Single-Pyramid Systems Described in Chapter 6 Were in Place through mid-2014*

Polity	Year	Ousted Network	Next President
Armenia	1998	Ter-Petrossian	Kocharian
Georgia	2003	Shevardnadze	Saakashvili
Abkhazia	2004	Ardzinba	Bagapsh
Ukraine	2004	Kuchma-Yanukovych	Yushchenko
Kyrgyzstan	2005	Akaev	Bakiev
Kyrgyzstan	2010	Bakiev	Otunbaeva
Transnistria	2011	Smirnov	Shevchuk
South Ossetia	2012	Kokoity	Tibilov
Georgia	2013	Saakashvili	Margvelashvili
Ukraine	2014	Yanukovych	Poroshenko

increasingly a lame-duck for one of the following reasons: being in his constitutionally final term in office (seven cases), opting not to run in an election when he formally had the chance (one case), and reaching the age of 70 and thus facing increasing speculation about his fitness to run and ability to serve long into the future (one case). Where and when the combination of low popularity and age- or election-related expectations of succession was not in place, presidential networks generally managed to hang on to power, as will be documented in the next chapter.[10] Whereas Chapter 6 documented that ousters arising from irregular sources of regime dynamics such as leadership incompetence were common in the early 1990s, the only case of an ouster in the last decade that was clearly due primarily to an irregular source was Ukraine's 2014 Euromaidan Revolution.[11] Even when one considers ambiguities in a few of the cases, as will be done in the concluding section of this chapter, the dominance of regularity in patronal presidential ousters over irregularity is impressive.

The present chapter demonstrates all this by examining every ouster of a patronal presidential network in every non-EU Eurasian polity but Moldova (which never developed patronal presidential single-pyramid system) since a single-pyramid system first emerged there.[12] A complete list is presented in Table 7.1. By examining all of these ousters, we gain confidence that the patronal politics logic outperforms rival logics, virtually all of which have been

[10] Statistical analysis of these patterns of patronal presidential ouster, confirming the theory econometrically, can be found in Henry E. Hale, "Why and When Do Patronal Presidents Fall from Power? A Quantitative Study of Eurasian Cases," paper prepared for presentation at the Annual Meeting of the Association for Slavic, East European, and Eurasian Studies (ASEEES), Boston, November 21–4, 2013.

[11] We would not expect irregular regime dynamics to disappear entirely, of course. Ongoing events in Abkhazia may ultimately constitute a second such case depending on the result of the next presidential elections there. Chapter 9 discussed this case as it stands at the time of this writing, in July 2014.

[12] That is, since the point at which Chapter 6 left off.

applied only to the three "classic" color revolutions (Georgia 2003, Ukraine 2004, Kyrgyzstan 2005). The chapter thus starts by demonstrating that the regime cycle theory holds in the most challenging cases for it, the two color revolutions that are the paradigmatic post-Soviet cases for alternative theories (Georgia 2003, Ukraine 2004). It then shows in detail how impending succession and low popularity combined to produce presidential network ousters not only there, but also in seemingly all kinds of other environments and situations that other theories would not see as conducive. These environments include where the opposition was fractured and civil society weak (as in Kyrgyzstan 2005); where politics was almost entirely isolated from international democracy diffusion processes (as in Abkhazia 2004–5); where Russia was considered dominant and backed the incumbent presidential network (as in South Ossetia 2011–12); where the incumbent had been widely credited with strengthening the state (as in Georgia 2013); where no mass protest was involved (as in Transnistria 2011); where an election result did not provide the catalyst (as in Armenia 1998); and where leaders showed bloodily repressive resolve (as in Kyrgyzstan 2010). Finally, the present chapter examines the last decade's lone case generated by what Chapter 4 called an irregular source of regime cycles, Ukraine's 2014 Euromaidan Revolution, an event that also tended to defy the logic of alternative theories. The cases that most clearly display regularity are discussed first, and the more ambiguous cases discussed later.

The chapter shows that the "regular" ousters did not occur until the combination of low popularity and a question of succession was in place, and that the particular mechanisms by which each ouster occurred were in line with the theory. For example, in almost every case, the supposedly democratic victor was a former high official in the old president's regime, usually a former prime minister. And by showing how oppositions often proceed from fecklessness to great apparent strength with the onset of a president's lame-duck syndrome, the following pages join Robertson in cautioning us against the widespread tendency in literatures on democratization and authoritarianism to treat "the opposition" and its "strength" as exogenous variables in patronalistic societies.[13] After Chapter 8 discusses countries where no patronal presidential network ouster has taken place, Chapter 9 examines what happens after such ousters, further confirming the patterns of regime cycles discussed in Chapter 4.

The Orange Revolution in Ukraine (2004)

It is useful to begin with the case that has been subjected to the most scholarly research, Ukraine's Orange Revolution. The previous chapter described how Ukrainian President Leonid Kuchma successfully built a patronal presidential single-pyramid system in Ukraine, dominating politics and marginalizing opposition by 1999, when he handily manipulated his way to reelection. After this victory, however, he experienced two developments that ultimately undermined

---

[13] Robertson, *The Politics of Protest*.

the elite coordination that underpinned his power pyramid: low popularity and a succession struggle brought about by the widespread expectation that he personally would not run for reelection.[14] The central event was the leaking of covert surveillance tapes (almost certainly originating from an elite source intent on damaging Kuchma's team) linking the president to the murder of journalist Hryhory Gongadze. This solidified Kuchma's association in the public mind with widespread corruption and government dysfunction that had increasingly stoked discontent and outrage in the country. As the scandal unfolded, Kuchma was also in the early phase of his second term as president under a constitution that allowed presidents only two consecutive terms. He repeatedly declared that he would not run for reelection and ultimately did not do so, even though the Constitutional Court found a technicality for him that would have made this formally possible.[15] The decision not to run combined with his low popularity to render him a classic lame-duck, prompting elites to jockey for position as the time drew nearer when Kuchma would no longer be able personally to carry out promises or threats made before leaving office.[16]

The most important such elite was Kuchma's own prime minister, Viktor Yushchenko. Kuchma had tapped Yushchenko for prime minister after his reelection in 1999, whereupon the former National Bank chief (1993–9) built up substantial popular support through his public rhetoric of market reform and a generally more Western orientation for Ukraine. It is important to realize that prior to his removal, Yushchenko was decidedly not seen as an opposition figure but instead was a key part of the Kuchma team. His pro-Western stance was largely in keeping with Kuchma's own reorientation to western Ukraine in the 1999 presidential election. Moreover, when Yushchenko's future partner in the Orange Revolution Yulia Tymoshenko teamed up with other opposition in 2000–1 to hold a series of "Ukraine without Kuchma" protests, Yushchenko joined Kuchma and the speaker of parliament in not only condemning the actions, but comparing the opposition to fascists.[17]

With Kuchma's popularity dropping in the wake of the Gongadze scandal and a succession election on the horizon, Yushchenko increasingly used his post as prime minister to blast official corruption, rhetoric that strongly resonated with public opinion inflamed by the Gongadze scandal but that threatened Kuchma personally. Kuchma thus opted not to promote Yushchenko as his successor,

---

[14] As of the start of 2004, some 80 percent of citizens did not want Kuchma to continue as president. See Dmitry Vydrin and Irina Rozhkova, *V ozhidanii geroia: Yezhenedel'nik goda peremen* (Kharkiv: Kankom, 2005), p. 19.

[15] Namely, that the constitutional change of 1996 meant he had in fact only served one full term toward his two-term limit under the existing version of the constitution and that he thus had the right to one more term. Sergei Danilochkin, "Ukraine: Kuchma Cleared to Run for Third Term," RFE/RL Features, December 30, 2003.

[16] Vydrin and Rozhkova, *V ozhidanii geroia*, pp. 193–4, 200, 220, 257.

[17] Kost' Bondarenko, *Leonid Kuchma: Portret na fone epokhi* (Kharkiv: Folio, 2007), p. 422; Paul D'Anieri, "Explaining the Success and Failure of Post-Communist Revolutions," *Communist and Post-Communist Studies*, v. 39, 2006, pp. 331–50, p. 343; Heorhii Kas'ianov, *Ukraiina 1991–2007: Narysy novitn'oii istorii* (Kyiv: Nash Chas, 2008), p. 259.

which would have represented a continuation of Kuchma's own "Western" strategy in the 1999 presidential race, and instead – after some fits and starts – landed on a strategy to try to ward off the threatening anticorruption campaign by politicizing identity instead. He did so by once again reversing his positioning vis-à-vis Ukraine's east-west identity divide, firing Yushchenko in 2001, nominating a prime minister who was very strongly associated with Ukraine's East and who would not campaign against presidential corruption, suddenly claiming more "pro-Russian" positions in foreign policy, and then trying to box Yushchenko into a narrow western Ukrainian base of support by portraying him in the media as a radical nationalist with fascist sympathies. The strategy was to induce people to vote more on the identity issue than against corruption, thereby cleaving the electorate in such a way that Yushchenko would win a big majority in the core western regions of Galicia but would lose big in the rest of the country. This would provide the public opinion foundation for a majority official vote count for Kuchma's designated heir.[18]

Before Kuchma had settled on his new strategy, Yushchenko responded to his firing by forming a new coalition of elite networks to contest the 2002 parliamentary (Rada) elections.[19] This race was widely seen as an "elite primary election" for the 2004 presidential contest, a test of strength for elites to determine who had the best chance to be the future president. By winning a significant minority of seats and assuming a clear lead in reliable presidential polls, Yushchenko confirmed his status as the most credible opposition "horse" to back for elites looking beyond the Kuchma era.[20] He was thus the obvious rallying point for networks that had been frightened by or disliked the direction Kuchma's network had taken. Thus even Tymoshenko, whose earlier opposition efforts Yushchenko had himself condemned while prime minister, joined his effort.

While the Kuchma team deployed a massive arsenal of administrative resources in the run-up to the 2004 presidential election as it had done in 1999, several conditions had changed since that time. Not only was Kuchma increasingly seen as an unpopular lame-duck, but many elites who had been loyal to Kuchma in 1999 were now fearful of being left out of a Ukraine run by Viktor Yanukovych, Kuchma's choice for prime minister and (he hoped) successor after the parliamentary elections in 2002. This fear arose because Yanukovych was associated with one particular set of pro-Kuchma oligarchic networks, first and foremost the Donetsk-based "clan" informally led by Ukraine's richest man, Rinat Akhmetov. Akhmetov was also in close alliance

[18] For more details on this strategy and its implications, see Henry E. Hale, "Identity Divides as Authoritarian Resource: Post-Soviet Cases over Twenty Years," paper prepared for presentation at the Association for the Study of Nationalities annual meeting, April 19–21, 2012, Columbia University, New York.

[19] Taras Kuzio, "The 2002 Parliamentary Elections in Ukraine: Democratization or Authoritarianism?" *Journal of Communist Studies and Transition Politics*, v. 19, no. 2, June 2003, pp. 24–54.

[20] Vydrin and Rozhkova, *V ozhidanii geroia*, p. 212.

with the Kyiv network of Hryhory Surkis and Viktor Medvedchuk, the head of Kuchma's administration during the campaign period. While Donetsk-based ISD oligarchs Serhy Taruta and Vitaly Haiduk had largely separated their assets from Akhmetov's by 2004, they also worked in close cooperation with this network for Yanukovych.[21] At the same time, it was not clear that Yanukovych had enough popular backing to win, especially since Yushchenko continued to mobilize support on the basis of his anticorruption appeals. This also raised the danger that anyone not on Yushchenko's side before the election might be subject to prosecution for corruption should Yushchenko manage to win.

Some elites who had long supported Kuchma but had simultaneously competed with the Donetsk group for the president's favor thus began to shift over to Yushchenko, supplying him with resources that would prove critical to his victory. A few oligarchs were so bold as to back Yushchenko openly from the start, including, most notably, candy king Petro Poroshenko.[22] Tymoshenko, who had also initially achieved prominence in big business as described in Chapter 5, was reputed still to control significant financial flows despite having gone into opposition. While most media treated Russian business as unanimously backing the more pro-Russian Yanukovych, in fact several major Russian financial groups associated with liberal leanings were reported to favor Yushchenko. These included Alfa group and the conglomerate of Aleksandr Lebedev, as well as Konstantin Grigorishin, a Russian businessman with major Ukrainian holdings.[23] Economic motives were clearly afoot in most cases. Alfa had been moving into the Ukrainian market, for example. And Grigorishin had formally partnered with Medvedchuk and Surkis, but had broken with them shortly before Medvedchuk became Kuchma's chief of staff. After that point, Grigorishin's business interests suffered, including losing control over all of his regional electricity monopolies.[24] Both thus had reason to think a bet on new authorities could pay off for them.

Outside Yanukovych's own Donetsk group and their core allies, however, the dominant oligarch strategy was at first to hedge bets. Such oligarchs tended to think Yanukovych might win and feared his powers of reprisal, but additionally also calculated that Yushchenko had a realistic chance to emerge victorious due to his popularity, his modicum of open elite support, and his suspected backing by the Western international community. They thus placed their eggs in both baskets in hopes of preventing a Yanukovych victory while

[21] Igor' Guzhva and Yuriy Aksenov, "Deti gaza i stali," *Ekspert*, October 11, 2004.

[22] See Serhii Leshchenko, "Petro Poroshenko v Inter'eri Kartyn i Kartynok," *Ukraiins'ka Pravda*, January 11, 2005, 19:36.

[23] Viacheslav Nikonov, "'Oranzhevaia' Revoliutsiia v Kontekste Zhanra," in Mikhail Pogrebinsky, ed., *"Oranzhevaia" Revoliutsiia: Versii, Khronika, Dokumenty* (Kyiv: Otima, 2005), pp. 95–105, p. 100; author interview with Mikhail Pogrebinsky, former campaign manager and adviser to Kuchma's administration, August 12, 2005; author interview with political analyst Dmitry Vydrin, Kyiv, August 12, 2005.

[24] Guzhva and Aksenov, "Deti gaza i stali."

not completely alienating his team in case it should win. Two such oligarchic networks were Ihor Kolomoisky's Pryvat (which had lost a series of privatization bids in disputed cases during Kuchma's second term in office)[25] and the team of Leonid and Andrei Derkach. The most surprising oligarch to wind up in this camp, however, was the president's son-in-law, Viktor Pinchuk. An influential insider in the Medvedchuk-Yanukovych camp reports that Pinchuk was in fact covertly providing support to Yushchenko at the same time he was overtly working for Yanukovych. This, the insider avers, was understood in the Yanukovych camp as Kuchma's personal effort to hedge his own bets, hoping thereby to avert threats to his own family's material and physical position in the event that Yanukovych lost.[26] The United States government accentuated the interest that some big business representatives had in bet hedging: Reports circulated during the campaign season that Pinchuk and several other major elites associated with Yanukovych would be denied visas to the United States because of their alleged corruption.[27] Even in Russia's business community, purportedly pro-Yanukovych conglomerates frequently played both sides in an effort to safeguard their interests regardless of which way the election went.[28]

Among the resources that two of these oligarchic networks supplied was television coverage. Poroshenko controlled the small opposition-oriented Fifth Channel and Andrei Derkach owned the Era television and radio networks. While Poroshenko's feisty Fifth Channel got most of the attention from outside observers, Era TV was also very important because it broadcast on a widely available channel (the First National channel) at times when many people watched, in the morning and later evening. While Era did not blatantly support Yushchenko as did Fifth Channel, it provided relatively objective information during the course of the Orange Revolution, giving people access to an opposition point of view.[29]

With Kuchma's heir designate so clearly tied to the interests of Donetsk and other parts of Russian-oriented "eastern" Ukraine, networks divided heavily along regional lines. Thus, those based in the more European-oriented western provinces feared their interests would be trampled in the event of a Yanukovych win.[30] Ukraine's elected regional legislatures thus tended to rally

---

[25] Guzhva and Aksenov, "Deti gaza i stali."
[26] Mikhail Pogrebinsky, "Kak Ukraina Shla k 'Oranzhevoi' Revoliutsii," in Pogrebinsky, ed., *"Oranzhevaia" Revoliutsiia: Versii, Khronika, Dokumenty* (Kyiv: Otima, 2005), pp. 106–18, p. 116. Also author interview with Pogrebinsky 2005; Vydrin and Rozhkova, *V ozhidanii geroia*, p. 227; author interview with Vydrin 2005.
[27] Vydrin and Rozhkova, *V ozhidanii geroia*, p. 387; Daniil Yanevsky, *Khronika "Oranzhevoi" Revoliutsii* (Kharkiv: Folio, 2005), p. 76.
[28] Nikonov, "'Oranzhevaia' Revoliutsiia v Kontekste Zhanra," p. 100.
[29] Taras Kuzio, "Yushchenko Victory to Speed Up Ukraine's Democratization and Europeanization," *Eurasia Daily Monitor*, December 17, 2004; Yanevsky, *Khronika "Oranzhevoi" Revoliutsii.*
[30] Dominique Arel has powerfully argued that the regional differences at work in the Orange Revolution most fundamentally reflect differences in national identity. See Arel, "Ukraina Vybyraet Zapad, No Ne Bez Vostoka," *Pro et Contra*, v. 9, no. 1, July–August 2005, pp. 39–51.

behind Yanukovych in the East whereas those in the West were often fiery supporters of Yushchenko. The country's religious establishment was similarly divided: Representatives of the eastern-based Ukrainian Orthodox Church subordinate to the Moscow patriarchate made some strong pro-Yanukovych statements, while Yushchenko found friendly attitudes among representatives of the more western-oriented Ukrainian Orthodox Church subordinate to the Kyiv patriarchate and of the western-based Ukrainian Greco-Catholic Church.[31] Ukraine's governors were a somewhat different story, as they had been appointed by Kuchma everywhere except Kyiv and Crimea and were tasked by the administration with backing Yanukovych. But so strong was popular and legislature support for Yushchenko in many western Ukrainian regions that a pro-Yanukovych insider reports that no serious attempts were made to use the governors there to win votes for him. The situation was seen as hopeless. Many regional administration officials were even believed to be covertly sympathetic to Yushchenko or co-opted.[32] This helps explain how Yushchenko was able to achieve massive majorities of the vote in many western regions even in the first round of presidential balloting, including an astonishing 89 percent in Ivano-Frankivsk.[33] This is especially striking, given that many of these same western elites had backed Kuchma in the 1999 presidential election. A full-fledged competing-pyramid situation had emerged.

The standoff between the two coalitions of networks gradually began to resolve itself after the first and second rounds of the election took place, giving elites who were hedging their bets more information about who was likely to win. While Yushchenko gained a few new allies after the first round, which resulted in a runoff with Yanukovych, it was this second round that generated the most decisive moments. The Central Election Commission (CEC) declared Yanukovych the winner by a narrow margin, reporting the results after great delay and in an irregular manner. At the same time, exit polls showed a decisive Yushchenko victory and many observers were reporting rampant fraud.[34]

Two key sets of "defections" from the Kuchma pyramid during this period were particularly important. One was the Kyiv political machine. This was a critical blow to Yanukovych because it effectively enabled the massive popular demonstrations that ultimately did in the incumbents. Kyiv Mayor Oleksandr Omelchenko had a long history of rivalry with Kuchma's chief of staff

[31] Aleksandr Litvinenko, "'Oranzhevaia Revoliutsiia: Prichiny, Kharakter i Rezultaty," in Mikhail Pogrebinsky, ed., *"Oranzhevaia" Revoliutsiia: Versii, Khronika, Dokumenty* (Kyiv: Otima, 2005), p. 13; Yanevsky, *Khronika "Oranzhevoi" Revoliutsii*, pp. 58, 64.

[32] Author interview with Pogrebinsky 2005.

[33] Table of official election results in Central Election Commission of Ukraine, *Vybory Prezydenta Ukraiiny 2004 Roku: Elektoral'na Statystyka* (Kyiv: Central Election Commission, 2005), pp. 496–7.

[34] Maksim Strikha, "Ukrainskie Vybory: Do i Posle," in Mikhail Pogrebinsky, ed., *"Oranzhevaia" Revoliutsiia: Versii, Khronika, Dokumenty* (Kyiv: Otima, 2005), pp. 150–64, p. 155. Exit poll results can be found in Vydrin and Rozhkova, *V ozhidanii geroia*, p. 391.

Medvedchuk and oligarch Hryhory Surkis, both of whom were positioned to reinforce their leading roles should Yanukovych win. Thus the city boss had at first hedged his bets during the campaign, avoiding support for Yushchenko but also finding ways to avoid helping Yanukovych too much. In a creative move, he declared his own candidacy for president. Omelchenko's candidacy was not a major concern for Yanukovych, since Kyiv city voters were seen as being more likely to prefer Yushchenko to Yanukovych. Yanukovych thus hoped Omelchenko would use his political machine to sap votes that would otherwise go to Yushchenko in Kyiv, and that the Kyiv mayor would then back Yanukovych in the anticipated runoff.[35] Omelchenko did not, however, deploy his political machine this time; rather, he effectively let the city's majority vote its conscience for Yushchenko. Moreover, as the runoff approached, the mayor's campaign office announced that it would support Yushchenko.[36]

The Kyiv mayor's most important act of defection, however, occurred after the first results of the runoff were out, when it was obvious that falsification had influenced them and that popular outrage was widespread. Omelchenko signed a decision of the Kyiv legislature appealing to the CEC to revoke its count.[37] Shortly thereafter, as pro-Yushchenko demonstrators were converging in massive numbers on Kyiv's central square and government buildings, the capital's administration and legislature ordered city agencies and companies to supply various kinds of support to the protesters. This included mobile toilets, medical care, hot drinks, meeting premises, and even many of the tents used by the demonstrators during their weeks of activity in the bitter cold.[38] Very critically, the city also intentionally took measures to undercut the possibility of a violent crackdown by the central authorities. Having received a direct order from Kuchma's administration shortly before the runoff to ban all demonstrations, the city administration did not immediately carry out the order – nor did it directly defy it. Instead, the city approached a court for sanction. The choice of court, however, was calculated: The Shevchenkivs'kyi district court was known by city officials to have bucked Kuchma's system. And as expected,

---

[35] Mykhailo Slaboshpyts'kyi, *Peizazh dlia Pomaranchevoii Revoliutsii* (Kyiv: Yaroslaviv Val, 2005), pp. 84, 86–8.

[36] Slaboshpyts'kyi, *Peizazh dlia Pomaranchevoii Revoliutsii*, pp. 86–8; Yanevsky, *Khronika "Oranzhevoi" Revoliutsii*, pp. 55–6.

[37] Kyiv State Rada, Rishennia 733/2143, "Pro Zahostrennia Suspil'no-Politychnoi Sytuatsii v Misti Kyevi, Iaka Sklalas'ia Pislia Proholoshennia Tsentral'noiu Vyborchoiu Komisieiu Rezultativ Povtornoho Holosuvannia po Vyborakh Prezydenta Ukraiiny," November 22, 2004, reprinted in Kiev State Administration, *Pomarancheva Revoliutsiia i Kyiivs'ka Vlada: Pohliad Kriz' Pryzmu Faktiv* (Kyiv: Kyiv State Administration, 2005), pp. 4–5; Yanevsky, *Khronika "Oranzhevoi" Revoliutsii*, p. 97.

[38] Kyiv State Administration, Rozporiadzhennia no. 2132, "Pro Zakhody Shchodo Zabezpechennia Hromads'koho Poriadku v Stolytsi Ukraiiny – Misti-Heroi Kyevi," November 24, 2004, reprinted in Kiev State Administration (fn. 64), 9–11; author interview with Oleksandr Petik, head of the Kyiv city administration's main directorate for internal politics, August 11, 2005; Slaboshpyts'kyi, *Peizazh dlia Pomaranchevoii Revoliutsii*, pp. 88–9.

it ruled that the demonstrations could not be banned and that police or other authorities would be violating the law to try to do so, thereby eliminating "enforcing the law" as a legitimate pretext for an early crackdown.[39] As the crowds in Kyiv swelled to unprecedented levels (and counts range anywhere from one hundred thousand to upward of a million at the peak), other networks began to sense the increased likelihood of a Yushchenko victory, the concomitant reduction in the likelihood that they would be punished for their insubordination, and the danger they might be punished later by new authorities if they failed to abandon Kuchma's ship in time. A sense of security in opposition grew as more people joined in. Also contributing to a growing sense Yanukovych might not win this struggle were the strong condemnations of the second round of elections from international observers (in particular the OSCE) and the U.S. government, which let it be known that it was now unlikely to consider a Yanukovych government to be legitimate.

The second set of momentous defections after the fraudulent runoff election was the most surprising: the security services, the military, and the police. Some contend Kuchma was simply too soft to order a crackdown, but in truth some in Ukraine's force agencies were highly sympathetic to Yushchenko while others simply started to anticipate that pro-Yushchenko forces might eventually prevail. The latter feared being punished later for shedding blood in the interests of a patron who was on his way out. Such forces were very unlikely to have implemented an order to crack down, especially once the crowds grew to such an immense size and once potentially legitimizing pretexts for state violence were removed.[40] Indeed, a Kyiv city administration official reports that the administration knew through regular contacts with military and police that the latter were wavering as to whether to obey a potential crackdown order and that the city's appeal to the Shevchenkivs'kyi court was partly intended to encourage a decision against violent intervention.[41]

In the end, as Paul D'Anieri observes, the security forces not only refused to fire, but "chose not to take a whole set of preventive measures" that such agencies routinely take in other instances to preempt protests so that they "do not need to be repressed."[42] Some high-ranking security service figures even appeared on stage encouraging protesters and provided information to opposition forces.[43] Ukrainian protesters thus found that in getting to the demonstrations in central Kyiv, not only were they unlikely to be punished, but public transportation was available, phone networks were working, and key roads and highways from around the country were open. As D'Anieri reports, "that

---

[39] Author interview with Petik 2005; Author interview with Pogrebinsky 2005; Yanevsky, *Khronika "Oranzhevoi" Revoliutsii*, pp. 82, 88.

[40] Arel, "Ukraina Vybyraet Zapad"; Taras Kuzio, "Did Ukraine's Security Service Really Prevent Bloodshed during the Orange Revolution," *Eurasian Daily Monitor*, January 24, 2005.

[41] Author interview with Petik 2005.

[42] D'Anieri, "Explaining the Success," p. 337.

[43] D'Anieri, "Explaining the Success," pp. 344–5.

this area could be shut down tightly had been demonstrated only two weeks earlier, when Vladimir Putin was among the dignitaries watching a military parade."[44]

The standoff between the two coalitions of networks was ultimately resolved through a negotiated compromise. Kuchma would not resist a fair repeat of the presidential election runoff in return for a constitutional change that greatly reduced presidential powers, giving Ukraine a divided-executive constitution (an important outcome that will be discussed in Chapter 9).[45] The Supreme Court, long considered to be in Kuchma's pocket, defected and invalidated the second round of elections, ordering a repeat runoff. The unprecedented "third round" of presidential voting ultimately took place under fairer conditions on December 26 and was won by Yushchenko. Yushchenko was officially inaugurated president in early 2005.

Overall, we see how a massive rupture of the networks constituting Kuchma's single-pyramid system, at a point of anticipated presidential succession under a highly unpopular president, generated a major opening for mass input in a country that just a few years earlier had been consigned by many to the camp of the hopelessly autocratizing. The result became widely known as the Orange Revolution.

The Rose Revolution in Georgia (2003)

Georgia's "Rose Revolution" followed a remarkably similar pattern, with a succession struggle and low leadership popularity combining to drive the process. Against a background of economic stagnation, sustained regular electricity blackouts, and the continued failure to regain control over Abkhazia and South Ossetia, incumbent President Eduard Shevardnadze's popularity was on the wane as he entered his constitutionally final second term after his relatively easy 2000 reelection.[46] These circumstances led some of Shevardnadze's own most ambitious allies to start planning to succeed him.[47] Chief among these was Mikheil Saakashvili. It is crucial to recall from Chapter 6 that Saakasvhili at this time was, like Yushchenko before 2001, not an opposition force but a key member of the incumbent president's team. Not only had Saakashvili

---

[44] D'Anieri, "Explaining the Success," p. 344.

[45] Serhiy Kudelia, "Betting on Society: Power Perceptions and Elite Games in Ukraine," in Paul D'Anieri, ed., *Orange Revolution and Aftermath: Mobilization, Apathy, and the State in Ukraine* (Washington, DC: Woodrow Wilson Center, 2010), pp. 160–89, pp. 183–4.

[46] See Lincoln Mitchell, *Uncertain Democracy: U.S. Foreign Policy and Georgia's Rose Revolution* (Philadelphia: University of Pennsylvania Press, 2009), chapters 2–3; and Cory Welt, "Georgia's Rose Revolution: From Regime Weakness to Regime Collapse," in Valerie J. Bunce, Michael A. McFaul, and Kathryn Stoner-Weiss, eds., *Democracy and Authoritarianism in the Post-Communist World* (New York: Cambridge University Press, 2010), pp. 155–88.

[47] Jonathan Wheatley, *Georgia from National Awakening to Rose Revolution: Delayed Transition in the Former Soviet Union* (Burlington: Ashgate, 2005), p. 110.

campaigned for Shevardnadze's reelection in 2000 as part of the party of power, Citizens Union, but he even became Shevardnadze's justice minister in October 2000. As the incumbent president's popularity sank, however, Saakashvili's continued to rise on the strength of his strong public relations work, anticorruption campaigning, and some major reforms that he led, including prison reform. His wife writes that after the 2000 election he "became more and more focused on the media, on communication, and that he couldn't live without his mobile phone anymore."[48]

Interestingly, as in Ukraine, the murder of a popular independent journalist dealt a critical blow to the incumbent president's popularity and, ultimately, expectations as to his continuation in office. In this case, the unfortunate media figure was opposition TV personality Georgy Sanaia, found dead in his Tbilisi apartment on July 26, 2001.[49] While no leaked audiotapes linked Shevardnadze to this event (as they had with Kuchma in Ukraine), it shocked the public and helped catalyze a drop in his popularity that was also rooted in the other difficulties Georgia faced that were described earlier. Shevardnadze was blamed at a minimum for not responding adequately. And not long after this event, in late summer 2001, he announced he would not attempt to change the constitution to seek reelection in 2005. This effectively confirmed his status as a lame-duck and accelerated the same kind of succession dynamics among elites that had undermined Kuchma in Ukraine. The news of this Shevardnadze announcement, according to one ITAR-TASS analyst writing at the time, "resounded like a gong for politicians: It is time to prepare."[50]

Thus while criticism had been building for a long time as Shevardnadze's popularity dropped and he entered his constitutionally final term, it was shortly after this announcement of his intent not to seek reelection that some of his most important elite allies positioned themselves clearly in opposition. Among them were the wine and insurance moguls Levan Gachechiladze and David

---

[48] Sandra Elisabeth Roelofs, the First Lady of Georgia, *The Story of an Idealist* (Tbilisi: LINK, 2010), p. 200.

[49] Host of the current events program *Kurieri* on Rustavi 2, he was regarded as a leader among a new breed of young journalists (Roelofs, *The Story of an Idealist*, p. 210). Saakashvili's wife also notes that her husband had long angled to become president and that this was a "very conscious process," though it "went faster than we had expected" (p. 9). This strongly indicates that the political opportunity served up by Shevardnadze's unpopularity and lame-duck status was crucial to Saakashvili's calculation that his presidential ambitions were no longer best served by aligning with Shevardnadze, but instead by entering into opposition. On the murder and investigation, see *Kavkazskii Uzel*, January 29, 2004, 17:55.

[50] Aleksei Aleksandrov, "Nasledstvo politicheskogo dolgozhitelia," *Ekho Planeta*, August 31–September 6, 2001. As another example of the expectations this promoted, *Nezavisimaia Gazeta*'s correspondent wrote of the announcement, "His current allies and opponents, anticipating the nearing of the desired moment, are preparing for a leap to the pinnacle of power. One can easily now predict an intensification of the struggle for power in the near future." This is from Nodar Broladze, "Eduard Shevardnadze tverdo nameren uiti vovremya," *Nezavisimaia Gazeta*, August 14, 2001.

Gamkrelidze, whose formerly pro-Shevardnadze New Rights Party turned against the president in late 2001.[51] The most momentous elite defections after Shevardnadze's announcement turned out to be parliamentary speaker Zurab Zhvania and Justice Minister Saakashvili, who began to work together as the most popular alternative to Shevardnadze. Saakashvili's own September 2001 resignation was a carefully planned media event for which he had arranged live coverage on the Rustavi 2 television channel. He had also timed it well: The parliamentary district he had once represented was holding a by-election the next month, allowing him to reenter parliament, this time clearly in opposition to the ruling authorities.[52] Notably resigning with Saakashvili was his Deputy Justice Minister Irakli Okruashvili, who would play a prominent role after the Rose Revolution.[53] Zhvania's resignation as parliamentary chairman soon followed in November 2001.[54]

In this context, the 2002 nationwide local elections and the 2003 parliamentary elections came to be seen as crucial tests of strength in the battle to succeed Shevardnadze. That is, they became elite primary elections, giving them far more significance than the actual offices at stake, being more about the future presidency than about the regional legislatures and the parliament themselves.[55] To contest these elections, Saakashvili founded the National Movement, a party that quickly gained the support of some key networks. These included more than ten early defectors from Shevardnadze's Citizens Union parliamentary delegation, who then helped Saakashvili form his own delegation in parliament.[56] Erosi Kitsmarishvili supplied favorable coverage on his independent Rustavi 2 television channel and joined Coca-Cola Georgia chief Temur Chkonia and Georgian Gas head David Bezhuashvili in providing financial support.[57] Other networks placed "eggs" in different or multiple baskets, or sought to remain neutral. Among Georgia's two wealthiest oligarchs, Bidzina Ivanishvili sustained a reputation for being out of politics, while Berezovsky associate Badri Patarkatsishvili backed Shevardnadze through biased coverage on his Imedi television channel, though he was rumored also to have been hedging his bets.[58] In the first of these two elite primaries, the nationwide local elections, Saakashvili's new National Movement performed well, enabling him to become chair of the Tbilisi city council atop an alliance

[51] Jaba Devdariani, "Georgia: Rise and Fall of the Façade Democracy," *Demokratizatsiya: The Journal of Post-Soviet Democratization*, v. 12, no. 1, Winter 2004, pp. 79–115, p. 98.

[52] *Civil Georgia*, September 25, 2001, 15:46; Roelofs, *The Story of an Idealist*, pp. 219–20, 224.

[53] *Civil Georgia*, September 25, 2001, 15:46.

[54] International Republican Institute Georgian Web site, http://www.iri.org.ge/ka/georgia/personalities/110-zhvania-zurab.html, accessed April 1, 2011.

[55] Irakly Areshidze, *Democracy and Autocracy in Eurasia: Georgia in Transition* (East Lansing: Michigan State University Press, 2007), p. 69; Georgi Kandelaki, "Georgia's Rose Revolution: A Participant's Perspective," *United States Institute of Peace Special Report*, no. 167, July 2006.

[56] Mitchell, *Uncertain Democracy*, p. 37.

[57] Radnitz, "The Color of Money," p. 136.

[58] Daan van der Schriek, "A 'Gangster' at Large," *Transitions Online*, March 1, 2004.

with another opposition party, the Labor Party.[59] This gave the young firebrand some influence over events in the capital city as well as a prominent position from which to campaign for the next round of elite primary elections, the parliamentary contest of 2003.

It was the parliamentary elections' status as a crucial elite primary that drove the timing of the Rose Revolution.[60] Polls showed that Shevardnadze's party could muster only a 6–9 percent level of popular support in the final weeks before the election.[61] But after a campaign in which incumbent authorities mobilized strongly against the opposition, official results were unveiled claiming that the authorities had won. This was contradicted by a parallel vote count and an exit poll publicized on Rustavi 2 television.[62] Instead, the parallel vote count showed Saakashvili's party had finished in first place with 27 percent of the ballots.[63] While 27 percent was far from an overwhelming figure, it signaled his victory in the elite primary. His network thus emerged as the one considered by others to be the *most likely* to win the upcoming presidential contest.

The parliamentary election, therefore, helped resolve the coordination problem faced by networks looking to ensure they wound up on the winning side in the anticipated succession struggle. Other major networks with their own opposition parties deferred to Saakashvili as the leading figure in a larger coalition against the sitting president, including those of Zhvania, parliamentary speaker Burjanadze, and Gachechiladze and Gamkrelidze. Saakashvili, Zhvania, and Burjanadze drew material and logistical support from business and other elite allies to bus people in from the provinces and otherwise support a twenty-day protest that featured sound equipment and trucks blocking riot police. Together they mobilized up to one hundred thousand people in Tbilisi's streets against the falsified results and Shevardnadze's efforts to enforce them, and ultimately led them in a takeover of the parliament building.[64] Shevardnadze's remaining loyalists were quick to give in lest they alienate the expected incoming patron any further. Crucially, this included even chief security figures such as Defense Minister Davit Tevadze. Unwilling to shed blood and risk their own futures for what they now saw as a likely losing cause, they disobeyed Shevardnadze's instructions to restore order.[65] With

[59] Roelofs, *The Story of an Idealist*, pp. 238–9.

[60] Mitchell, *Uncertain Democracy*, p. 43.

[61] Polls indicated it had only 6–9 percent popular support in the final weeks before the election (Welt, "Georgia's Rose Revolution," p. 160).

[62] Radnitz, "The Color of Money," p. 136.

[63] OSCE/ODIHR Election Observation Mission, Georgia, Parliamentary Elections 2003, *Post-Election Interim Report*, November 3–25, 2003.

[64] Radnitz, "The Color of Money," p. 136.

[65] Charles H. Fairbanks, Jr., "Georgia's Rose Revolution," *Journal of Democracy*, v. 15, no. 2, April 2004, pp. 110–24; Kandelaki, "Georgia's Rose Revolution"; Mitchell, *Uncertain Democracy*, p. 67.

his political machine disintegrating around him, Shevardnadze had no choice but to resign. Saakashvili confirmed his victory in early presidential elections in 2004, now winning an overwhelming majority of votes with support from almost all of the country's major networks.

The Tulip Revolution in Kyrgyzstan (2005)

Some influential accounts have treated Kyrgyzstan's 2005 "Tulip Revolution"[66] as a puzzling exception to patterns of postcommunist electoral revolutions. It possessed few qualities widely regarded as conducive to democratization (such as economic development or a "democratic neighborhood"), and its opposition was fractured and failed to employ the full range of coordinated strategies said to have led to the success of the Orange and Rose Revolutions. Such accounts tend to treat the Kyrgyz events either as a deviant case explained by ad hoc factors or as a result of pure demonstration effects, with the power of Georgia's and Ukraine's examples overwhelming the otherwise inhospitable environment.[67] A number of excellent accounts based on deep field research and focused primarily on Kyrgyzstan have provided other explanations for the Tulip Revolution, variously highlighting the country's relatively liberal political environment, the economic autonomy of local patron-client networks, the rivalry between northern and southern elites, and incumbent President Askar Akaev's own supposed weakness, softness, or unpopularity.[68]

Consistent with some but not all of these accounts, this section shows the Tulip Revolution can be well understood as the same class of event as the Orange and Rose Revolutions. That is, these events were a natural punctuation in regime dynamics defined by the combination of low presidential popularity and widespread elite expectations of upcoming presidential succession. Importantly, the patronal politics logic not only can explain the Tulip Revolution in a way consistent with the larger pattern of post-Soviet patronal presidential ousters, but also can account fairly precisely for when and how the revolution occurred.

Most fundamentally, Akaev fell victim to a cascade of defections from his own power *vertikal'* that took place after his popularity dropped and he fell into a lame-duck syndrome. The decline in Akaev's popularity gained steam toward the

---

[66] There was initial disagreement on how to "name" this revolution, with some early accounts associating it instead with the color yellow, borne by some of the youth activists involved. TOL, "A Second Round Beckons," *Transitions Online*, February 28, 2005; Cohen, "Helping Kyrgyzstan's Democratic Revolution."

[67] Beissinger, "Structure and Example"; Valerie J. Bunce and Sharon L. Wolchik, "Defeating Dictators: Electoral Change and Stability in Competitive Authoritarian Regimes," *World Politics*, v. 62, no. 1, January 2010, pp. 43–86, pp. 67–9.

[68] See, for example, Kevin D. Jones, *The Dynamics of Political Protests: A Case Study of the Kyrgyz Republic*, Ph.D. dissertation in Public Policy, University of Maryland, August 31, 2007, http://www.lib.umd.edu/drum/handle/1903/7431; Scott Radnitz, *Weapons of the Wealthy: Predatory Regimes and Elite-Led Protests in Central Asia* (Ithaca, NY: Cornell University Press, 2010) and the special issue of *Central Asian Survey*, v. 27, nos. 3–4, September 2008.

end of the 1990s after long years of economic difficulties and perceived corruption. While the economy experienced growth in 2001, unemployment remained high, as did inequality.[69] There was no major killing of a journalist to consolidate public opinion against Akaev, but a similar effect resulted from Akaev's decision to crack down on protesters in 2002 in the Aksy district, killing five. These "Aksy events," as they came to be known, dealt a severe blow to his legitimacy.[70]

On top of this, after his 2000 presidential victory, Akaev entered what the Constitutional Court had ruled must be his final term in office. Rather than attempt to orchestrate a referendum to try to extend his term or eliminate term limits, as some of his neighbors had done, Akaev announced in mid-2004 that he planned to leave office.[71] While some worried he nevertheless intended to find a way to stay on, Akaev publicly reiterated his intention to retire even as he cast his vote in the February 27, 2005, parliamentary elections, stating unambiguously that he would not change the constitution in order to extend his stay in office.[72] Aggressive accumulation of private resources for his family members had also alienated not only the public, but increasingly also the growing circle of elites cut out of crucial patronage networks.[73] Over the first years of the 2000s, all this created an expectation among increasing numbers of elites that there was a good chance Akaev himself might not be in a position much longer to punish those who defied him. And this meant that the risks of opposition activity got lower for elites at the same time that the chance they could wind up on the winning side by going into opposition grew.

Accordingly, one can observe increasingly brazen challenges to Akaev's authority developing during the years leading up to the time when he was scheduled to leave office. One of the most prominent was the uprising in the southern district of Aksy in 2002 that parliamentarian Azimbek Beknazarov mobilized to counter his arrest, the move that Akaev crushed in the bloody aforementioned crackdown that helped cement his increasingly negative reputation.[74] While Akaev suppressed the revolt, the show of force did not have the intimidating effect that is typical when people expect a leader to remain

---

[69] Emir Kulov, "March 2005: Parliamentary Elections as a Catalyst of Protests," *Central Asian Survey*, v. 27, nos. 3–4, September 2008, pp. 337–47, pp. 344–5; Transitions Online (editorial), "Kyrgyzstan's Dorian Gray," *Transitions Online*, March 25, 2002.

[70] Kulov, "March 2005," p. 345; Martha Brill Olcott, *Central Asia's Second Chance* (Washinton, DC: Carnegie Endowment for International Peace, 2005), p. 134.

[71] Osmonakun Ibraimov, *Ispytanie istoriei: Razmyshleniia i esse o sud'be Kyrgyzstana* (Moscow: Mezhdunarodnye Otnosheniia, 2008), p. 64.

[72] *RFE/RL Newsline*, February 28, 2005; Ibraimov, *Ispytanie istoriei*, pp. 63–4.

[73] Barbara Junisbai, "Improbable but Potentially Pivotal Oppositions: Privatization, Capitalists, and Political Contestation in the Post-Soviet Autocracies," *Perspectives on Politics*, v. 10, no. 4, December 2012, pp. 891–916; Eric McGlinchey, *Chaos, Violence, Dynasty: Politics and Islam in Central Asia* (Pittsburgh: Pittsburgh University Press, 2011); David Lewis, "The Dynamics of Regime Change: Domestic and International Factors in the 'Tulip Revolution,'" *Central Asian Survey*, v. 27, nos. 3–4, September 2008, pp. 265–77.

[74] *EurasiaNet*, March 19, 2002.

in continued control over such power.[75] Instead, Akaev's own prime minister, Kurmanbek Bakiev, resigned two months later and reemerged as a leading opposition figure, eventually becoming the coordinator of a coalition of largely southern-based networks seeking to replace Akaev in an increasingly open fashion. Many believe Bakiev had been forced out by Akaev as a scapegoat for the Aksy tragedy, though Bakiev himself claimed credibly to have resigned in protest and he in fact gained support not only in Kyrgyzstan as a whole, but in Aksy itself for this public stance.[76] As with Yushchenko and Saakashvili, Bakiev was certainly not regarded as being an opposition figure prior to leaving the government in 2002, but instead (also like Yushchenko and Saakashvili) moved into opposition politics during his president's expected final term in office and as that president was suffering a major decline in his public opinion standing. He did not play a major role in public politics between 2002 and 2005, but crucially during this time he established himself behind the scenes as the informal leader of some of the most influential local business and political networks in Kyrgyzstan's South.

In this situation, with the presidential election that would choose Akaev's successor slated for fall 2005, the February 2005 parliamentary elections became an elite primary much as the 2002 parliamentary elections had been in Ukraine and the 2003 parliamentary elections had been in Georgia, an event that would help elites decide both how much strength Akaev actually retained and who the real pretenders to the presidency were.[77] Thus when the first round of voting indicated that Akaev's supporters were winning far more seats than the regime's popularity level made credible, when major opposition figures like Roza Otunbaeva were disqualified, and when Akaev's own relatives (including son, Aidar, and daughter, Bermet) appeared to be headed to parliamentary seats and possibly even dynastic succession, losers of the formal counts rallied their forces and quickly joined efforts, with southern networks leading the way.[78] While Bakiev did not actually control each local initiative, he played a significant role coordinating them as they occurred and positioned himself as the chief southern-based politician who could claim to represent them in presenting demands to the authorities.[79] Protesters in the South, who Scott Radnitz shows were largely the mobilized clients of wealthy elites who had cultivated local

[75] Lewis, "The Dynamics of Regime Change," pp. 267–8.

[76] See Gulnara Iskakova, *Vybory i demokratiia v Kyrgyzstane: Konstitutsionnyi dizain prezidentsko-parlamentskikh otnoshenii* (Bishkek: Biyiktik, 2003), pp. 314–15, 423–4, 430; *RFE/RL*, September 14, 2007; Azimbek Beknazarov, interview, translation in *Ferghana.ru*, March 12, 2008, 11:10.

[77] Olcott (*Central Asia's Second Chance*), for example, describes these elections as "Akayev's testing ground" (p. 136). For a deeper analysis of the role of these elections in the revolution, see Kulov, "March 2005," especially p. 339.

[78] Radnitz, *Weapons of the Wealthy*; TOL, "A Second Round Beckons," *Transitions Online*, February 28, 2005.

[79] Temir Sariev, *Shakh Kyrgyzskoi demokratii* (Bishkek: Salam, 2008), p. 11.

bases there through patronage politics, soon overran government buildings and announced plans to take the movement to Bishkek.[80] With southern state structures in opposition hands, local media stopped toeing the Akaev line and began to engage in more neutral reporting or effectively to defect to the opposition.[81] A cascade of elite defections from the Akaev regime – their extended patronal networks in tow – had thus overtaken much of the South and increasingly spread to Akaev's native North.

Each new defection made it more and more clear to all that Akaev's days were numbered, thereby inducing more defections from people closer and closer to Akaev's innermost circle of supporters. Akaev's state secretary and "one of the president's closest allies,"[82] Osmonakun Ibraimov, later explicitly recalled a "syndrome of the leaving of power" setting off a succession struggle within Akaev's own elite during early 2005, including that "many members of [Akaev's] team had secretly agreed with the opposition so as to join with it and secure for themselves a place under the new authorities."[83] In fact, he went on to say that an internal analysis conducted by Akaev's inner circle in early 2005 showed that "almost the entire composition of the government and the whole governor-akim corpus" was ready to abandon their government responsibilities to join the elections.[84] These elite defections did not depend on any one opposition figure's becoming the obvious alternative to Akaev; there were at least three realistic pretenders to this status, and the key for defectors was primarily to gain a chance at winding up in or atop the winning coalition, which increasingly looked possible by defecting but unpromising by sticking with Akaev.[85] In keeping with the pattern noted in the Orange and Rose Revolutions, nearly all of the major pretenders had been former key subpatrons in Akaev's own single-pyramid system who had broken with him earlier, including not only Bakiev but former vice president Feliks Kulov (whom Akaev had jailed) and former foreign minister Roza Otunbaeva. Bakiev, however, remained a first among equals as a popular former prime minister with strong influence in the South. This status gained him recognition by most major opposition figures as leader of the People's Movement of Kyrgyzstan, a loose organization created in September 2004 to coordinate opposition forces from North and South.[86]

---

[80] Radnitz, *Weapons of the Wealthy*.

[81] Hamid Toursunof, "Tsunami in the Mountains," *Transitions Online*, March 25, 2005; Hamid Toursunof, "Celebrating, Not Looting," *Transitions Online*, March 29, 2005.

[82] Erica Marat, *The Tulip Revolution: Kyrgyzstan One Year After* (Washington, DC: Jamestown Foundation, 2006), p. 7.

[83] Ibraimov, *Ispytanie istoriei*, p. 64.

[84] Ibraimov, *Ispytanie istoriei*, p. 64.

[85] McGlinchey (*Chaos, Violence, Dynasty*) argues that each individual elite's chance of winding up in the winning coalition was enhanced in Kyrgyzstan by the country's relatively small pool of elites.

[86] Marat, *The Tulip Revolution*, p. 3.

The most momentous defections strongly appear to have been those of key Kyrgyz armed services. Akaev now claims the high ground, presenting himself as a peaceful figure who chose to sacrifice his own political career by leaving the country so as to prevent bloodshed, an interpretation later picked up by some outside analysts.[87] Political leaders representing antirevolutionary regimes in Russia and Kazakhstan have essentially concurred, stating publicly that one of Akaev's major mistakes was not acting tough enough, not ordering troops to fire on the crowd in order to restore order.[88] But there is substantial evidence, including from within Akaev's very innermost circle, that his decision not to order troops to fire on the crowds around key state buildings in Bishkek during the decisive days in March 2005 owed less to principled pacifism than to the knowledge (or at least a very strong sneaking suspicion) that key armed forces had essentially defected and that he could no longer count on them to obey him unquestioningly. Indeed, the 2002 events in Aksy show that Akaev was not averse to applying force to suppress a revolt against his rule. Moreover, as crowds descended upon Bishkek, he appointed a new interior minister with the status of vice prime minister, Keneshbek Diushebaev, who then warned the opposition that force would be used if the demonstrators attacked more state buildings.[89] In addition, one must pay very close attention to the specific explanation that Akaev himself; his daughter, Bermet; and his close associate and state secretary Ibraimov have each given as to why Akaev decided to avoid using force to stay in power. Crucially, their argument is *not* that restoring order was not worth bloodshed. Instead, they each argue that ordering troops to fire on the crowd would have caused "civil war." And this is an outcome one is likely to fear when one is aware that major parts of the armed forces may no longer be counted on to take the side of the president in a unified and decisive manner.[90]

Surprisingly, the most direct evidence that force agencies themselves ultimately defected from Akaev is supplied by his own daughter, Bermet. In her account of why the president opted to flee the country, she writes:

During the night of March 23–24, *a report came in that the leaders of the opposition had reached agreement with almost everyone responsible for law enforcement that there would be no resistance to the opposition forces.* Knowing that the organizers of the coup made his physical elimination from the political scene their goal, my father took the only right decision in such circumstances: to temporarily leave the country.[91] [Italics added]

---

[87] *RFE/RL Newsline*, April 8, 2005; Bunce and Wolchik, "Defeating Dictators," p. 69.

[88] See the report on comments by Russian President Vladimir Putin and Kazakhstan President Nursultan Nazarbaev in *RFE/RL Newsline*, March 25, 2005.

[89] Ibraimov, *Ispytanie istorii*, pp. 43–8; Toursunof, "Tsunami in the Mountains."

[90] Bermet Akaeva, *Tsvety zla: O tak nazyvaemoi "tiul'panovoi revoliutsii" v Kyrgyzstana* (Moscow: Mezhdunarodnye Otnosheniia, 2006), p. 35; Ibraimov, *Ispytanie istorii*, pp. 43–8; *RFE/RL Newsline*, April 8, 2005.

[91] Akaeva, *Tsvety zla*, pp. 35, 48.

That is, Akaev knew before he fled that those responsible for preserving order were now quite unlikely to follow his orders, that they had effectively determined that Akaev could not win and had thus thrown in their tacit support with the opposition. This also enables us to explain Akaev's otherwise puzzling statements shortly after the revolution, including his remark to the Russian newspaper *Kommersant* that he believed key figures in the police and security forces had been "in a plot with the opposition" (*v sgovore s oppozitsiei*).[92]

With the cascade of defections reaching key armed services and culminating in Akaev's own flight to Moscow, the opposition easily overran government buildings, freed Kulov from jail, and established its own power, completing what later became known as the "Tulip Revolution."[93] Akaev resigned effective April 5, 2005. Bakiev maneuvered to become acting president until new presidential elections could be held, coordinating closely with other opposition leaders, especially Feliks Kulov, who represented support from Kyrgyzstan's North that complemented Bakiev's own great authority in the South.[94]

Abkhazia's "Uncolored Revolution" (2004–2005)

The extensive literature on the color revolutions has generally neglected another important case, the ouster of the incumbent presidential network in Georgia's breakaway region Abkhazia through elections in late 2004 and early 2005.[95] Partly these events were simply overshadowed by the largely contemporaneous Orange Revolution, but it is also likely that they have been overlooked because they did not feature the outward trappings of prominent youth movements and prodemocracy rhetoric that so many analysts have held to be central to the color revolutions, plus transnational democracy promotion organizations were not involved. Yet this is precisely why the case of Abkhazia must not be overlooked: Here we have an instance of a successful electoral revolution that required none of these things, thus revealing that they are not essential causes. There was no significant borrowing of tactics from prior revolutions, no prominent prodemocracy activists or organizations leading the charge and advocating nonviolent resolution of the dispute, and no Western role supporting the opposition. Instead, what we find is the same sets of factors that this chapter has shown have been central to virtually all of the other ousters of patronal presidents in the post-Soviet space since the mid-1990s: expectations

---

[92] Askar Akaev, interview, *Kommersant*, July 11, 2005.

[93] For excellent interpretations of the "branding" or "framing" of this revolution, and why it became frequently identified as part of an internationally-led or transnational "wave of democratization" by Western analysts, see Juraev, "Kyrgyz Democracy?"; and Lewis, "The Dynamics of Regime Change."

[94] Scott Radnitz, "What Really Happened in Kyrgyzstan?" *Journal of Democracy*, v. 17, no. 2, April 2006, pp. 132–46, p. 134.

[95] The pioneering exception is Kimitaka Matsuzato, "Patronnoe prezidentstvo i politika v sfere identichnosti v nepreznannoi Abkhazii," *Acta Eurasica*, no. 4, 2006, pp. 132–59.

of a presidential succession combined with the low popularity of the incumbent regime.

The previous chapter described the construction of a single-pyramid system in Abkhazia in the 1990s under President Vladislav Ardzinba, who had led his territory to de facto independence from Georgia with Russian help in the early part of the decade. The single pyramid started to break down when three developments converged. First, with his uncontested reelection in 1999, Ardzinba entered his second and constitutionally final presidential term, with elections for a successor required in 2004. Second, as became visible in 2001–2, Ardzinba fell seriously ill, leading him to conclude and elites to understand that he could not well run for a third term even if he wanted to.[96] According to one top Abkhaz leader, during the last couple of years of his term Ardzinba did not even go into his office, meeting with top officials at his home when business had to be done.[97] Third, his own popularity and that of his close associates suffered a serious drop.[98] There were several reasons for this decline. For one thing the economy continued to suffer, isolated from most of the world with basic infrastructure remaining unrepaired from its separatist wars with Georgia. There was also a belief among some elites that Ardzinba's own inner circle, which Ardzinba had increasingly filled with relatives and businesspeople, had been taking advantage of their president's illness effectively to rule the country themselves so as to make themselves rich.[99] Others reported that a kind of fatigue with Ardzinba had set in, a feeling that he had fulfilled his national duty well by winning the war with Georgia but that he was inadequate to the crucial economic and state-building tasks that lay ahead.[100]

Ardzinba moved to designate a successor well before the 2004 election – on April 22, 2003 – by tapping former first deputy prime minister and current defense minister Raul Khajimba his prime minister. But the latter had not been well known in the republic before being appointed, and while reportedly being seen as young, energetic, modest, and honest, was not regarded as a strong politician and did not possess any particular charisma.[101] Khajimba himself refused to confirm his presidential ambitions until the campaign period had officially

---

[96] Alexander Skakov, "Abkhazia at a Crossroads: On the Domestic Political Situation in the Republic of Abkhazia," *Iran & the Caucasus*, v. 9, no. 1, 2005, pp. 159–85, pp. 159–60; *Polit. Ru*, March 4, 2010, 10:56.

[97] Nugzar Ashuba, speaker of parliament of Abkhazia, author's interview, Sukhumi, July 29, 2010.

[98] Skakov, "Abkhazia at a Crossroads," pp. 159–60. Note: Skakov submitted his article for publication in October 2004, before the "revolution" took place.

[99] Matsuzato, "Patronnoe prezidentstvo."

[100] This was the reason given by Sergei Shamba, foreign minister of Abkhazia at the time he started opposing the president's political ambitions. Shamba, author's interview, Sukhumi, July 29, 2010.

[101] *Ekho Abkhazii*, April 23, 2003, p. 1; Skakov, "Abkhazia at a Crossroads," p. 162. Khajimba served in the KGB then FSB during 1986–93, then in the Abkhaz SGB in 1993–5 before occupying government posts.

started just months before the election.[102] And during Khajimba's time as prime minister, he became associated with the lawlessness, corruption, and crime that had come to undermine the Ardzinba regime and was seen as "one who owes Ardzinba's clan a lot."[103] In short, Ardzinba lacked the public opinion standing to make his chosen heir the unquestioned favorite in the succession struggle, and the heir lacked the personal qualities to accomplish this. Ardzinba also complicated the situation still further by hedging his bets until just months before the October election: He retained Gennady Gagulia, Khajimba's rival for presidential favor and predecessor as PM, in the post of chief of his administration until June 2004, hamstringing Khajimba in his efforts to assert independent leadership strength and authority.[104]

This combination of impending succession and low regime popularity engendered a steady rise in the willingness of political elites to contest the Ardzinba regime's authority as they were compelled to envision a future when Ardzinba himself would not be in place to reward or punish them for what they did now. As one observer wrote in an Abkhaz newspaper as the 2004 presidential elections approached, "Literally before our eyes over the last five years, Abkhaz politics has been turned into an arena for an uninterrupted struggle for power and personal attacks."[105] In February 2000, the movement Aitaira (Revival) appeared, calling for reforms.[106] Ardzinba attempted to engineer a victory for his loyalists in the March 2002 parliamentary elections, with the Central Election Commission disqualifying several Aitaira candidates, leading this party to boycott the race.[107] Nevertheless, these elections returned a much less cooperative parliament than Abkhazia had ever before experienced, even to the point of its electing an opposition-oriented candidate to the speakership, big businessman Nugzar Ashuba. After this election, there were frequent clashes between president and parliament on legislation.[108] In spring 2003, the Amtsakhara movement representing veterans of the war with Georgia (a group previously loyal to the president who had led them to victory in that war) moved into radical opposition, first launching protests that forced out Khajimba's predecessor as prime minister, Gennady Gagulia, and then openly calling for Ardzinba to resign.[109] Its offices were bombed in April 2003.[110]

---

[102] See his interview in *Ekho Abkhazii*, February 11, 2004, p. 2, where he says it is "hard to judge" whether he will be the successor.

[103] Skakov, "Abkhazia at a Crossroads," p. 171.

[104] Skakov, "Abkhazia at a Crossroads," p. 172.

[105] Tomaz Ketsba, professor at Abkhaz State University and an NGO leader, "V situatsii 'mnimogo konstitutsionalizma,'" *Ekho Abkhazii*, May 26, 2004, pp. 1, 6.

[106] Matsuzato, "Patronnoe prezidentstvo."

[107] Matsuzato, "Patronnoe prezidentstvo."

[108] *Ekho Abkhazii*, February 4, 2004, p. 3.

[109] *Ekho Abkhazii*, February 4, 2004, p. 3; *Ekho Abkhazii*, March 17, 2003, p. 4; *Ekho Abkhazii*, April 23, 2003, p. 1.

[110] *Ekho Abkhazii*, April 23, 2003, p. 1.

This process culminated in a dramatic wave of major elite network defections to open opposition as the election neared in 2004. The most dramatic was the emergence of the new United Abkhazia Party, which grew out of a preexisting "Unity" faction in the parliament and held its founding congress on March 25, 2004.[111] This party initially positioned itself as a coalition of influential Abkhazian elites concerned about the future and interested in influencing who became president, but not yet as an open opposition force.[112] The impressive list of members who joined by summer 2004 included a huge share of the republic's power elite: parliamentary speaker Ashuba, former prime minister (until 1999) and current general director of the major state corporation Chernomorenergo Sergei Bagapsh, sitting Foreign Minister Sergei Shamba, parliamentarian and big businessman Beslan Butba, and former Sukhumi Mayor Nodar Khashba, among others.[113] While Ashuba and some of the parliamentarians had been in conflict with President Ardzinba over various points of policy over the prior two years, many of the other leading members had previously been decidedly loyal to the president or at least neutral, including Shamba, Bagapsh, and Khashba.

United Abkhazia quickly radicalized, however, spurred on by the shocking June 2004 murder of the Amtsakhara movement's executive secretary, Garri Aiba; large protests by his relatives and supporters; and the authorities' (including Khajimba's) weak response to the killing.[114] According to United Abkhazia's informal leader, parliamentary speaker Ashuba, this was the crucial event leading the previously highly cautious industrialist and former prime minister Bagapsh to join United Abkhazia and prompting the party to move to radical opposition.[115] Thus shortly after this murder, United Abkhazia joined with Amtsakhara in declaring no confidence in Khajimba's government and demanding its resignation, citing a litany of grievances ranging from its inability to reduce crime to its failure to normalize relations with Georgia.[116] President Ardzinba's own chief of administration, former prime minister Gagulia, then resigned, declaring that the president and his circle were planning a succession in which the next president would be a marionette in the hands of a mysterious "those who today rule the country."[117] In July, a coalition of United Abkhazia and Amtsakhara agreed to back Bagapsh for president, choosing history professor and former parliamentarian Stanislav Lakoba (Amtsakhara's favorite) to be his running mate.[118] This led Shamba, who had his own presidential ambitions,

---

[111] *Ekho Abkhazii*, April 1, 2004, p. 1.
[112] *Ekho Abkhazii*, June 30, 2004, p. 1.
[113] *Ekho Abkhazii*, April 1, 2004, p. 1.
[114] *Ekho Abkhazii*, July 7, 2010, p. 7.
[115] Ashuba interview 2010.
[116] *Ekho Abkhazii*, June 30, 2004, pp. 1, 3; Artur Mikvabiia, chair of the Council of the United Abkhazia movement, interview, *Ekho Abkhazii*, June 30, 2004, p. 3.
[117] *Ekho Abkhazii*, July 7, 2004, p. 7.
[118] *Ekho Abkhazii*, July 21, 2004, p. 1. The Abkhaz constitution provides for the post of vice president, with candidates for this office running in tandem with presidential candidates much as in the United States.

to leave the coalition and launch his own campaign for Abkhazia's top job, though this obviously meant that he too remained in opposition to Ardzinba.

The result was a pitched battle for the presidency in which both the main candidates, the opposition champion Bagapsh and the hand-picked presidential heir apparent Khajimba, had significant administrative resources (including media) with which to fight their battles due to the elite status of their coalitions. The opposition blasted Khajimba on the issues already mentioned and accused him of being a puppet for Ardzinba's circle. Khajimba felt compelled to deny this repeatedly, pleading that he would not be a "plastilene" president and averring that he was not a member of any "clan" other than the Khajimbas – and indeed he often appeared to be on the defensive.[119] In a major campaign move, Khajimba went to Russia and secured a widely publicized meeting with Putin, which was frequently interpreted (and advertised by Khajimba's supporters) as Putin's implicit endorsement.[120] Khajimba also argued that Bagapsh would be soft on Georgia because his wife was an ethnic Georgian, a tactic that Kimitaka Matsuzato notes actually garnered Bagapsh significant support in the Gali district, where a substantial number of Georgians still lived and voted despite a massive ethnic cleansing in the 1990s.[121]

Election day, October 3, unleashed a standoff in the streets that lasted for more than two months. The preliminary results gave Bagapsh a narrow majority of the votes, with particularly large majorities in the partly Georgian-populated Gali district and the Ochamchyrsky district, where he had once lived and worked.[122] Substantial irregularities, however, were reported in Gali, leading Khajimba to file for invalidation of the results and a repeat election on the grounds that no candidate won the majority of valid votes necessary to preclude a runoff. Bagapsh claimed victory outright. The CEC initially tried to strike a compromise, ordering a recount only in Gali. Predictably, this satisfied neither of the principal candidates. Khajimba, with President Ardzinba's backing, challenged the CEC's ruling and organized a series of protests in the capital, Sukhumi.[123] Bagapsh then also challenged the CEC's ruling, calling on it to recognize his victory.[124] While the Supreme Court appeared to stall for time while

[119] *Ekho Abkhazii*, September 7, 2004, pp. 1–2.

[120] *Ekho Abkhazii*, September 7, 2004, p. 6; Aslan Avidzba, "Vstrecha s V. Putinym – priznanie vyborov," *Respublika Abkhaziia*, September 25–6, 2004, no. 110, p. 5.

[121] Kimitaka Matsuzato, "From Belligerent to Multi-Ethnic Democracy: Domestic Politics in Unrecognized States after the Ceasefires" *Eurasian Review*, v. 1, November 2008, pp. 95–119, p. 110.

[122] Daur Arshba, member of parliament, deputy chair of FNEA (Forum of National Unity of Abkhazia), author's interview, Sukhumi, July 29, 2010; Kimitaka Matsuzato, "Mezhpravoslavnye otnosheniia i transgranichnye narodnosti vokrug nepriznannykh gosudarstv: Sravnenie Pridniestrov'ia i Abkhazii," in Matsuzato, ed., *Pridniestrov'e v makroregional'nom kontekste chernomorskogo poberezh'ia* (Sapporo: Slavic Research Center, 2008), pp. 192–224, pp. 214–15; *Respublika Abkhaziia*, October 7–8, 2004, no. 115, p. 1.

[123] *Respublika Abkhaziia*, October 9–10, 2004, no. 116, p. 1.

[124] *Respublika Abkhaziia*, October 12–13, 2004, no. 117, p. 1.

under pressure from both sides, the CEC declared Bagapsh the winner with 50.08 percent of the votes cast and Khajimba called on the prosecutor's office to investigate this decision and announced a street protest that would not end until a "lawful, legal decision" was adopted. Bagapsh supporters organized counter-rallies.[125] President Ardzinba himself then issued a decree condemning the CEC decision, warning of a coup in the works.[126] Parliament responded by issuing what it said was a legally binding interpretation of the law on presidential elections that would give the victory to Bagapsh.[127] The chairmen of both the Supreme Court and CEC resigned, and the Court complained that it could not find members of the CEC to provide the necessary information for a ruling.[128]

When the Supreme Court finally rendered a decision and found in favor of Bagapsh at 9:30 pm on October 28, Khajimba left the Court building crying that this was outrageous ganglike behavior (*bespredel*). His supporters let out a roar and stormed the building, marauding it.[129] Just five and a half hours later, at 3:00 am, the Supreme Court issued a new ruling that directly contradicted the previous one: The CEC declaration that Bagapsh had won was invalid, and new elections were now to be held within two months. President Ardzinba quickly followed up this second ruling with a decree requiring repeat presidential elections. One Supreme Court judge publicly declared that this second ruling was made under pressure, and Bagapsh refused to recognize it.[130] Crowds from both sides gathered around the building containing the president's offices until negotiations persuaded them to go home, though street protests from each side resumed as the crisis remained unresolved.[131] Battles to control major media ensued, with Bagapsh forces appearing to have taken over the primary government channel, which had been backing Khajimba.[132] A huge rally of Bagapsh supporters ultimately stormed and seized the state building that contained the offices of president, parliament, and government on November 12, overpowering Khajimba supporters in what President Ardzinba called an "armed coup d'état" that killed one person.[133]

With his supporters refusing to give up in the run-up to December 6, the day Bagapsh had officially been scheduled to take the oath of office under the original CEC ruling, Khajimba finally agreed to a deal that Bagapsh would also accept.[134] Some attribute this compromise to a Moscow role, and Putin's

[125] *Respublika Abkhaziia*, October 16–17, 2004, no. 119, p. 1.
[126] *Respublika Abkhaziia*, October 14–15, 2004, no. 118, p. 1.
[127] *Respublika Abkhaziia*, October 14–15, 2004, no. 118, p. 2.
[128] *Respublika Abkhaziia*, October 21–2, 2004, no. 121, p. 1.
[129] *Ekho Abkhazii*, November 2, 2004, pp. 1–2.
[130] *Ekho Abkhazii*, November 2, 2004, pp. 1–2; *Respublika Abkhaziia*, October 30–1, 2004, no. 125, p. 1.
[131] *Respublika Abkhaziia*, November 2–3, 2004, no. 127, p. 1.
[132] *Ekho Abkhazii*, November 2, 2004, pp. 1–2.
[133] *Respublika Abkhaziia*, November 16–17, 2004, no. 131, p. 1.
[134] *Ekho Abkhazii*, December 7, 2004, p. 1.

government notably did not oppose the settlement. But the two leaders' well-publicized trip to Moscow took place on November 1, well before the battle reached its head with Bagapsh forces storming presidential offices on November 12.[135] An alternative intepretation is that the key mediating role was played in back rooms by an informal council of elders (*sovet stareishin*), a traditional meeting of network leaders. This council reportedly convened, convinced the two sides to compromise so as to prevent bloodshed (especially worrisome since Abkhazia's population was heavily armed), and worked to assure Moscow this would not be against its interests.[136] A repeat election would be held, but this time Khajimba would run only as Bagapsh's running mate, for vice president. To make the vice presidency attractive, they signed a protocol stipulating that this office would be given control over the police, military, and security services, along with 40 percent of the budget and responsibility for 40 percent of cabinet posts. The pair also agreed to a new law granting Ardzinba, as the first president, immunity from prosecution as well as financial support.[137] This "tandem" handily won the January 2005 contest with 92 percent of the ballots, and Bagapsh was sworn in as president, with Khajimba as vice president, in February 2005.[138] An opposition had defeated a patronal presidential team in Abkhazia despite Putin's apparent support for the incumbents. Moreover, no media account of these events or interview with participants revealed any significant role whatsoever for youth activists, nongovernment democracy-promotion organizations, learning from previous revolutions (even the one in Georgia), special opposition strategies for defeating dictators, or Western support (the Russians having backed the incumbents). Directly asking whether such factors played roles evoked a bemused smirk in Sukhumi.[139]

Saakashvili's Downfall in Georgia (2012–2013)

In 2012–13, Georgia became the second country to experience a second patronal presidential ouster, though in stark contrast to the Rose Revolution this one did not require mass protests to force the president to leave. Chapter 9, which focuses on what follows patronal presidential ousters, will describe what happened after the Rose Revolution, though the short version is that it was followed by the emergence of a new single-pyramid system under Saakashvili. This new single-pyramid system involved a constitution that gave the president even greater formal powers than Shevardnadze had enjoyed, featured strong control over mass media, and showed its teeth in crushing a massive street protest in late 2007 in the prelude to Saakashvili's reelection. The present chapter,

---

[135] *Ekho Abkhazii*, November 2, 2004, pp. 1–2.
[136] Ashuba interview 2010; Shamba interview 2010.
[137] Matsuzato, "From Belligerent," p. 108.
[138] Ibid.
[139] Aleksandr Ankvab, then vice president and future president of Abkhazia, author's interview, Sukhumi, July 28, 2010.

however, is interested in how this single-pyramid system too broke down, resulting in the decisive loss of power by Saakashvili's network during parliamentary and presidential elections in 2012 and 2013. Its downfall is discussed here so that it can be considered together with the other instances of patronal presidential ouster, demonstrating that it followed the same basic pattern as the other ousters examined in this chapter.

With his 2008 reelection, Saakashvili entered his constitutionally final term in office with sagging popularity.[140] It was at this time that several major figures in his single-pyramid system opted to defect, positioning themselves for possibly succeeding him as chief patron. Defectors after the presidential election included parliamentary speaker Burjanadze, the widely liked senior diplomat Irakli Alasania, and businessman and former Saakasvhili prime minister Zurab Noghaideli. The latter two figures explicitly cited Georgia's bitter defeat in its August 2008 war with Russia over the breakaway territory of South Ossetia, which Saakashvili lost after being widely believed to have initiated the war in the first place in an effort to reestablish control over the region.[141] On the strength of targeted patronage and economic recovery after the 2008–9 financial crisis, however, the president's ratings had largely recovered by 2010. This helped stanch the outflow of defectors, assisting his party (now renamed the United National Movement) in decisively winning the elite primary of the Tbilisi mayoral election over Alasania in May 2010. This seemed to position it as the favorite to win the parliamentary elections scheduled for 2012 and the presidential contest slated for 2013.[142]

During this time, however, Saakashvili used his tremendous patronal presidential powers to push through a reform with major implications for patronal politics: He shifted Georgia to a divided-executive constitution. He whisked it through parliament in late 2010, after his popularity and authority had recovered. It was only to take effect in 2013, however, after he himself left presidential office and his elected successor assumed office. This reform dramatically weakened the formal powers of the president and stipulated that the prime minister would be elected by the parliament, with the party that won the most votes in the last parliamentary election having the right of nomination.[143] Thus the prime minister's government was declared the "supreme body of the

---

[140] Liz Fuller, "Georgian Presidential Ballot a Choice between Continuity and Radical Change," End Note, *RFE/RL Newsline*, January 4, 2008; *RFE/RL Newsline*, April 5, 2005.

[141] Irakli Alasania, interview in *RFE/RL*, January 5, 2009; *Civil Georgia*, June 27, 2008, in *Georgian Daily*, June 27, 2008; Molly Corso, "Georgia: Experts Believe There's Blood in the Water in Tbilisi," *Eurasianet*, Eurasia Insight, October 23, 2008; Zaza Jgharkava, "Election Gambit: Nino Burjanadze Leaves in Order to Come Back," *Georgia Today*, May 2, 2008.

[142] *Civil Georgia*, April 16, 2010, 13:37; *Civil Georgia*, May 31, 2010, 19:10; Matthew Collin, "Elections to Gauge Trust in Georgia's Democracy," *The Moscow Times*, May 24, 2010; *RFE/RL*, May 30, 2010, 17:04.

[143] See the list of changes in *Civil Georgia*, October 15, 2010, 18:59.

executive branch" and was to control the ministries directly, while the president would be deprived of any right to remove the prime minister without parliament initiating it first. Moreover, the prime minister gained several powers making his or her removal difficult or risky for the parliament. The president would be able to decide certain disputes that could arise between parliament and prime minister, and would retain control over the military, though the prime minister had to countersign appointment of officers.[144] The logic developed in Chapter 4 would anticipate that the passage of such a change would tend to weaken a single-pyramid system by complicating patronal network coordination around any single patron not only beyond 2013, but potentially prior to it: The focal and information effects of the new constitution should make elites less likely to believe that their future welfare would hinge on identifying and bandwagoning with a single patron who would be dominant after 2013. And this should work to amplify the discoordinating expectations resulting from a lame-duck syndrome and/or low popular support.

Accordingly, Saakashvili's constitutional move set off a great deal of speculation in Georgia as to his intentions, increasing uncertainty among elites as to what the future would hold. While some suspected he might be planning to occupy the new prime ministership and rule from there,[145] the constitutional change was also consistent with an intention actually to step down as patron in chief. Weakening the ability of his presidential successor to build a strong single pyramid of power would complicate any efforts by future presidents to persecute Saakashvili or his associates personally once he left office or to undo any of the reforms he might consider vital.[146] Saakashvili consistently made clear that he planned to leave office on constitutional schedule, but refused to say what he personally would do after leaving the presidency under the new constitution. This kept open the possibility that he might shift to the prime ministership and thus be in position to follow through personally on any preelection promises and threats he might make now. Indicating he indeed had this kind of logic in mind, he declared to media in Washington in January 2012, "The last thing I want to do is turn myself into a lame-duck by speculating about my own future."[147]

This set the stage for the most momentous defection to the opposition during Saakashvili's second term, that of megaoligarch Bidzina Ivanishvili, the world's 185th richest man in 2011 according to Forbes.[148] Ivanishvili had generally avoided public politics up until 2011, and after the Rose Revolution had even

---

[144] Cory Welt, "Georgia's Constitutional Reform," *CACI Analyst*, November 11, 2010.

[145] *Civil Georgia*, February 1, 2012, 13:49.

[146] Cory Welt ("Georgia's Constitutional Reform") suggests a third possible motive: to "assure his place in history as the last 'great man' of Georgian politics."

[147] *Civil Georgia*, February 1, 2012, 13:49.

[148] *Forbes.com*, "The World's Billionaires 2011," http://www.forbes.com/lists/2011/10/billionaires_2011.html, accessed January 4, 2013.

been "one of the main financial supporters" of Saakashvili's regime.[149] The
October 2011 announcement that a formerly quiet player with such resources
would use them to form a party opposing Saakashvili in the 2012 parliamentary elections sent shock waves throughout Georgia's political system. Over the
course of the next year, he became a center of gravity for key figures who had
defected much earlier when Saakashvili's popular support had still been low
(notably Alasania) as well as others looking to oust the incumbent.[150]

Selling off his massive Russian assets,[151] Ivanishvili named his new party
Georgian Dream and held a series of large rallies across the country, blasting Saakashvili for authoritarian behavior and recklessly initiating the August
2008 war. The war, Ivanishvili railed, had damaged Georgia's chances of ever
recovering the breakaway territories and had needlessly ruined economically
important relations with Russia. He promised to repair this damage as best he
could.[152] The oligarch stressed, though, that he was also still in favor of joining NATO and the European Union, as Saakashvili had been.[153] Ivanishvili
also made a number of concrete promises, such as hiking pensions, reducing
taxes on the poor, providing everyone with health insurance, and creating a
fund to invest in agriculture.[154] To help get this message out, he established
his own television channel (formally in his wife's name as majority holder)
by purchasing one that had a license to broadcast political programming[155]
and acquiring a share in another in the city of Gori to reach audiences in that
area. Named Channel 9, it began broadcasting in April 2012 and was for the
next few months available only by satellite dish through the Turkish Turksat
operator, via the Internet, or through the Global TV cable network, which his
brother coowned. No other cable companies would carry it.[156]

Unsurprisingly, this immediately attracted the attention of Saakashvili's
machine. Just four days after his announcement, the Ministry of Justice revoked
Ivanishvili's Georgian citizenship. The ministry argued that the businessman
also held French citizenship and that dual citizenship was not allowed, paying
no attention to Ivanishvili's saying he would renounce his French citizenship
in order to run for office.[157] After this strong-arm move to keep Ivanishvili off
the ballot proved unpopular domestically and generated heavy international

---

[149] Ia Antadze, "Next in Line? Saakashvili's Possible Successors as Georgian President," *RFE/
RL*, September 12, 2008; Georgi Kldiashvili, "The President in Opposition: Georgia's 2012
Parliamentary Elections," *Caucasus Analytical Digest*, no. 43, October 15, 2012, pp. 2–5, p. 2.
[150] *Civil Georgia*, February 6, 2012, 15:49.
[151] *Vedomosti*, May 10, 2012, 14:27.
[152] *Civil Georgia*, June 10, 2012, 20:24; *Civil Georgia*, June 13, 2012, 14:06; *Civil Georgia*, July
15, 2012, 22:52.
[153] *Civil Georgia*, February 7, 2012, 19:10.
[154] *Civil Georgia*, May 24, 2012, 17:40; *Civil Georgia*, June 17, 2012, 23:12.
[155] *Civil Georgia*, January 20, 2012, 14:08.
[156] *Civil Georgia*, April 30, 2012, 21:38.
[157] *RFE/RL*, December 27, 2011.

criticism, the ruling party changed tack. But rather than simply help bring Ivanishvili into compliane with the law and restore his Georgian citizenship, Saakashvili's parliamentary majority found a convoluted path that would let the oligarch run for office but still brand him a foreigner: It actually amended the constitution to allow Georgian-born citizens of European Union countries (such as Ivanishvili's France) to run for office in Georgia.[158] Insisting on reinstatement as a Georgian citizen, Ivanishvili refused to run for office as a noncitizen and instead had businessman and soccer star Kakha Kaladze lead the Georgian Dream party list for the 2012 election.[159]

The citizenship episode did not stop the Saakashvili political machine from trying to thwart Georgian Dream. Other forms of pressure were applied. A money laundering investigation was launched against Ivanishvili, and the state seized millions in assets from one of his banks.[160] A political finance monitoring body repeatedly investigated him, finding him in breach of campaign finance regulations.[161] An Education Ministry official who had just months before been publicly hailed as "a model of incorruptibility" was abruptly fired after her son participated in a Georgian Dream rally – prompting a wave of resignations from other ministry officials in protest.[162]

Ivanishvili was able to counter with his own media, though not without major resistance and harassment. The Global TV cable operator owned by Ivanishvili's brother and carrying his Channel 9 was asked by the country's two most popular channels, Rustavi 2 and Imedi (both Saakashvili-friendly), to stop carrying Channel 9. When the cable company refused, Rustavi 2 and Imedi pulled out of its cable package, citing business reasons, depriving Global TV of major channels its customers wanted.[163] In order to expand Channel 9's reach, Global TV launched a promotion to give out free satellite dishes to new subscribers. But the government responded by seizing the dishes, alleging that the antenna giveaway – financed by an Ivanishvili loan – amounted to a vote-buying scheme.[164] Essentially the same thing happened with the opposition-oriented Maestro TV channel, which was attempting to expand its audience beyond Tbilisi.[165] The parliament eventually relented, requiring all cable companies to carry all nonlocal channels with news content for 60 days leading up to election day. This significantly expanded voter access to Channel 9, but the fact that this requirement ended right before election day seemed aimed at limiting Ivanishvili's ability to rally public support in contesting official election results he might not like.[166]

[158] *Civil Georgia*, May 30, 2012, 13:07.
[159] *Civil Georgia*, April 11, 2012, 21:06; *Caucasus Election Watch*, September 2, 2012.
[160] *RFE/RL*, December 27, 2011.
[161] *RFE/RL*, March 20, 2012.
[162] *RFE/RL*, May 29, 2012.
[163] *Civil Georgia*, April 30, 2012, 21:38.
[164] *Civil Georgia*, June 21, 2012, 18:21.
[165] *Civil Georgia*, July 11, 2012, 19:51.
[166] *Civil Georgia*, June 29, 2012, 18:27.

Attempting to accentuate the positive, Saakashvili and his associates also got out their own message of Georgian modernization, economic development, state building, joining the West, and freeing the country from nefarious Russian influence. Indeed, Saakashvili even went so far as to compare himself to the historic Georgian leader David the Builder and essentially to brand his opponents tools of Russia and "mummies" from the Shevardnadze era, making use of the fact that Ivanishvili had made his fortune in Russia and saying he was trying to take Georgia back to the situation it had been in under Shevardnadze.[167]

Amid all the action, two developments in summer 2012 stand out from a patronal politics standpoint as being particularly important for the outcome. First, as the parliamentary election approached, Saakashvili made the surprise move of appointing his longtime high-profile Interior Minister Ivane (Vano) Merabishvili as his new prime minister. Merabishvili immediately announced a new government program to provide "more benefit to the people" from all the progress that he said had already been achieved.[168] This, according to the incoming PM, meant a large volume of handouts including health insurance for all, a hike in pensions, and major investment in rural areas. It even included actually giving people money: Each family would get a voucher "to solve its immediate problems" however it wished.[169] Taking a page from Newt Gingrich's 1994 Republican Party playbook, these promises were to be sealed by a "Contract with Georgia"[170] and the creation of a new post, state minister for employment.[171] All this created the impression that the regime was worried Ivanishvili's appeals were working in public opinion: Merabishvili's promises appeared almost to mirror those Ivanishvili had been making.

Making Merabishvili PM was also important for what it did to Saakashvili's status as a lame-duck. While other credible interpretations were available, by nominating such a strong and visible figure as prime minister at a time when the new constitution stipulated that the prime minister would be one of the two chief patrons in the future, Saakashvili sharply raised the odds that it would be Merabishvili rather than himself in the PM post under the new constitution. And because Saakashvili was generally believed to be leaving the presidency as he reached his two-term limit, this meant Saakashvili himself would not be holding a major position of formal executive power after the next presidential elections were over in 2013.[172] Indeed, Saakashvili had declared that the 2012 parliamentary election "will determine Georgia's development [for]

[167] *Civil Georgia*, January 11, 2012, 21:01; *Civil Georgia*, May 26, 2012, 23:54; *Civil Georgia*, June 16, 2012, 13:34.

[168] *Civil Georgia*, June 30, 2012, 21:27.

[169] *Civil Georgia*, July 2, 2012, 18:11.

[170] *Kavkazskii Uzel*, July 23, 2012, 04:15.

[171] *Civil Georgia*, July 2, 2012, 14:20.

[172] Thomas de Waal, "A Crucial Election in Georgia," post on Carnegie Endowment for International Peace Web site, September 11, 2012, http://carnegieendowment.org/2012/09/11/crucial-election-in-georgia/drlp, accessed January 4, 2012.

the next four years" and explicitly called Merabishvili's appointment a "new beginning."[173] Thus while Merabishvili's appointment was surely intended to reverse a downward trend in the ruling party's public support that was taking shape with Ivanishvili's aggressive campaigning, it also served to consolidate Saakashvili's status as a lame-duck. And this weakened his ability to direct the expectations and behavior of elites in his political machine as they sought to position themselves for the post-Saakashvili era.

Against this backdrop, the second major development in the 2012 campaign ultimately proved fatal for the Saakashvili regime: a major scandal that triggered a precipitous decline in support for the authorities. Less than three weeks before the election, the opposition-oriented Channel 9 and Maestro TV broadcast shocking video footage of state authorities beating and even torturing prisoners.[174] Saakashvili's United National Movement had been watching its lead over Georgian Dream gradually slip in polls commissioned by American agencies[175] ever since spring 2012. If it was besting Georgian Dream 47–10 percent in March 2012,[176] by July Ivanishvili's party had gained so that the UNM's lead was just 43–24 percent – with an ominous 19 percent undecided or refusing to answer.[177] By midsummer more people wanted Saakashvili not to assume the premiership (36 percent) after leaving the presidency than wanted him to shift to this position (33 percent), with another 30 percent undecided or refusing to answer.[178] And when it came to his successor as president, voters were almost evenly split between wanting a representative of Saakashvili's UNM (22 percent) and someone endorsed by Ivanishvili (20 percent), with a whopping 42 percent undecided or not answering.[179] The prison abuse scandal proved to be the dagger that Ivanishvili's forces drove into the heart of Saakashvili's public support, taking advantage of the fact that all cable television companies had to carry opposition channels for the immediate preelection period. With public outrage soaring, Saakashvili's interior minister resigned, but this did not allow the regime to escape blame. Instead, the scandal did irreparable damage to the United National Movement's reputation and credibility as a democratic force.[180] According to one analysis, the release of the prison videos shifted most of the large number of

[173] *Civil Georgia*, June 30, 2012, 21:27.
[174] Kldiashvili, "The President in Opposition," p. 4.
[175] The National Democratic Institute and the International Republican Institute. Results were generally not released by these organizations, but instead given to others, who leaked them to media.
[176] *Civil Georgia*, March 27, 2012, 13:47.
[177] *Civil Georgia*, July 25, 2012, 19:35.
[178] *Civil Georgia*, July 16, 2012, 11:07.
[179] *Civil Georgia*, July 16, 2012, 11:07.
[180] *RFE/RL*, September 20, 2012; *RFE/RL*, October 12, 2012. See also Cory Welt, "5 Things You Need to Know about Georgian Parliamentary Elections," post on Center for American Progress Web site, September 27, 2012, http://www.americanprogress.org/issues/security/news/2012/09/27/39492/5-things-you-need-to-know-about-georgian-parliamentary-elections/, accessed January 4, 2013.

undecideds to the opposition.[181] The judgment of RFE/RL shortly before voting day was that "most observers see the race as too close to call."[182]

The dramatic result was a decisive parliamentary victory for Georgian Dream in the October 1, 2012, elections. On election night, Saakashvili appeared to hold out hope that his campaign could still salvage a majority in the single-member-district part of the elections, where incumbent political machines are widely regarded as being most effective; however, the machine failed him and his party lost even there.[183] Still with the power to appoint the prime minister until the new constitution went fully into effect, the president acquiesced and named Ivanishvili to this post and vowed to fight another day, leaving open the possibility of new battles ahead as the 2013 presidential race started to near. New Prime Minister Ivanishvili, however, began an aggressive campaign charging former Saakashvili officials with crimes, even arresting Merabishvili. He also pledged that he would not run for president himself and would remain prime minister for only eighteen months, after which he would leave politics.[184] Thus by 2012, with Saakashvili rendered an unpopular lame-duck, Georgia emerged with a pronounced competing-pyramid situation.[185]

Presidential elections followed about a year later, on October 27, 2013, and confirmed the defeat of Saakashvili's power pyramid. A little-known man handpicked by Ivanishvili, former Education Minister Georgi Margvelashvili, handily defeated the United National Movement's minority leader in parliament to become president. Then, keeping his promise, Ivanishvili left the prime ministership in November 2013, handing over the government reins and leadership of Georgian Dream to thirty-one-year-old former Interior Minister Irakli Garibasvhili.[186]

South Ossetia's Revolution of 2011–2012

Chapter 6 described how Eduard Kokoity built up a closed single-pyramid system in South Ossetia starting in 2001 in the wake of first president Liudvig Chibirov's failure to do so. Kokoity's political machine, however, suddenly unraveled as he fell victim to low popularity and the approaching end of his constitutional two-term limit in 2011. The result was a dramatic defeat of his handpicked successor in the 2011 presidential elections under pressure from mass opposition mobilization – despite the candidate's having the evident

[181] Kldiashvili, "The President in Opposition," p. 4.
[182] *RFE/RL*, September 29, 2012.
[183] Central Election Commission of Georgia official Web site, http://results.cec.gov.ge/, accessed January 4, 2012.
[184] *RFE/RL*, October 25, 2012, 12:45.
[185] Scott Radnitz, "In Georgia, Two Machines Are Better Than One," *ForeignPolicy.com*, September 27, 2012; Cory Welt, "Can Georgia Become a Multiparty Democracy?" *Caucasus Analytical Digest*, no. 43, October 15, 2012, pp. 13–15.
[186] *Civil Georgia*, November 24, 2013, 16:24; *RFE/RL*, November 18, 2013.

backing of the Russian Federation's leadership. The ensuing standoff in the streets ultimately forced repeat elections in March 2012 that led to the victory of a Kokoity critic who proceeded to place longtime opposition figures in key government positions.

Kokoity's problems started to come to a head, ironically, with the August 2008 war that many ousiders considered would be seen as his greatest victory. On the surface, his power appeared to have strengthened as he took advantage of the moment to rid himself of opponents and strengthen his personal hold on the republic. Just days after the Georgian attempt to reestablish control over South Ossetia was defeated by a massive Russian military operation, Kokoity dismissed his government and introduced emergency rule.[187] Later in 2008, what one observer dubbed a "spy mania" overtook the territory as he reshuffled officials again, arrested or charged some with crimes, and pushed through a series of institutional reforms strengthening the presidency, including giving himself the right to dismiss judges without any parliamentary approval.[188] Some of the replaced officials were said to be Russian-backed, as Kokoity tried to wrest more direct personal control over financial flows into the republic from his large northern neighbor.[189] As the May 31, 2009, parliamentary elections neared, Kokoity pushed through a change in election law that eliminated single-member districts in favor of an entirely proportional representation party-list system,[190] and then stacked the deck heavily in favor of friendly parties. This was done by orchestrating a takeover of the opposition People's Party by his own loyalists, disqualifying the leader of the only other major opposition-leaning party (Fatherland) from the ballot, and seizing opposition literature.[191] The chairman of the Supreme Court, the ultimate formal arbiter of election outcomes, died in a car crash just under a month before the election.[192] When election day rolled around, the opposition Fatherland failed to win any seats while Kokoity's Unity Party won exactly half, with the raided People's Party and the allied Communist Party dividing up the other half.[193] In an expression of unity, he nominated Communist leader Kochiev to be chairman of the parliament.[194]

[187] *Kavkazskii Uzel*, August 18, 2008.

[188] *Kavkazskii Uzel*, November 11, 2008; *Kavkazskii Uzel*, January 1, 2009, 01:10.

[189] Some of the new officials were also from Russia, but were from outside Moscow's power center and thus widely seen as being in political bed with Kokoity pursuing their own interests. See *Civil Georgia*, October 22, 2008, 15:27; *Civil Georgia*, November 1, 2008, 16:48; *Kommersant*, December 5, 2008.

[190] *Civil Georgia*, August 18, 2008, 11:20.

[191] *Kommersant*, April 14, 2009; *The Moscow Times*, June 1, 2009; Varvara Pakhomenko, "Uroven' nedovol'stva vlastiu v Iuzhnoi Osettii ochen' vysok," *Polit.Ru*, May 29, 2009, 10:58; *Polit.Ru*, May 28, 2009, 13:21.

[192] *Ossetia.Ru*, May 2, 2009, 09:03.

[193] *Gazeta*, June 1, 2009.

[194] *Kavkazskii Uzel*, June 19, 2009, 22:00.

Despite the seeming impregnability of his political position and the abject weakness of the opposition at this time, the elements of a succession crisis were building up under the surface, setting the stage for his political machine to fall apart as the regularly scheduled 2011 presidential election approached. Most fundamentally, Kokoity was in his constitutionally final second term in office and he did not change the constitution to remove this limitation, ultimately trying to usher a handpicked successor into office. Many thought that the parliamentary victory he orchestrated was aimed at inducing the new deputies to vote to allow him a third term, and this formality was widely considered to be important – Kokoity could not simply ignore it. Thus Roland Kelekhsaev, whose People's Party was taken over by Kokoity forces, declared shortly before the election, "After term limits are removed, Eduard Kokoity will rise to a kingship (tsarstvo)."[195] Yet Kokoity repeatedly declared that he would neither run for a third term nor seek the right to do so, starting with such promises even before the parliamentary election.[196] In at least one instance after the 2009 parliamentary election (March 2010) he refused to deny unequivocally that he might consider a constitutional change and running for a third term,[197] though by July 2010 he was once again making repeated and quite forceful denials, including these words to a Unity Party Congress: "We do not intend to change the basic law of our republic for the benefit of anyone, and everything will be done in accordance with the constitution. There will not be any speculation on a third term."[198] He even rebuffed an armed group of his own supporters who had tried to force a referendum on the issue and then stormed parliament to demand a constitutional change to keep Kokoity.[199]

Some have speculated that Russia's leadership had applied pressure to prevent Kokoity from seeking a third term, having been dissatisfied with the South Ossetian leader's attempts to control resource and aid flows there and direct them to his own ends. But if Kokoity was acting disloyally to Moscow in trying to control such flows from his presidency, it would be odd if he were simultaneously acting loyally in leaving power, which would deny him the ability to benefit from the control he was seeking. Instead, others suspect him of attempting to do what Russia's Vladimir Putin did in 2008 (to be discussed in the next chapter): observe the formality of the constitution and become prime minister, governing from there after installing a weak president.[200] Kokoity's own declaration that leaving the presidency did not mean leaving politics, as well as a top Russian official's declaration that observing the letter of the constitution

[195] *Kommersant*, April 14, 2009.
[196] *The Moscow Times*, June 1, 2009; Eduard Kokoity, interview with *Gazeta.Ru* and *Kavkazskii Uzel*, published in *Ossetia.Ru*, May 29, 2009, 1:42 pm.
[197] Eduard Kokoity, interview, *Kommersant Vlast'*, March 22, 2010.
[198] *Kavkazskii Uzel*, July 2, 2010, 21:50. See also *Ossetia.Ru*, July 2, 2010, 21:27; *Kavkazskii Uzel*, August 5, 2010, 16:20.
[199] *Kavkazskii Uzel*, June 15, 2011, 22:30; *Kavkazskii Uzel*, November 27, 2011, 08:00.
[200] Sergei Markedonov, "The Unlikely Winners," *Russia Profile.org*, November 15, 2011.

was important, would be consistent with this interpretation.[201] In any case, Moscow's messages regarding Kokoity himself were mixed as his term ran out. On one hand, sharp words were exchanged at times over personnel questions in the government.[202] But on the other, Putin's United Russia Party established links with Kokoity's Unity, Russia's ministry that administered aid backed Kokoity against his critics, and Russia's formerly critical Accounts Chamber concluded there was ultimately no misuse of funds.[203]

Kokoity's bigger problem, however, was local. At the same time he was approaching a moment of expected presidential succession, his popular support dropped dramatically after the August 2008 war, with almost all accounts agreeing that dissatisfaction with his rule was "very high" in the republic through the year of expected succession, 2011.[204] For one thing, he was curiously invisible during the war itself, suggesting to many that he had fled and putting himself in a weak position to claim credit for the victory, which obviously owed primarily to the Russian military. More important, however, was that not only did victory and official recognition by Russia fail to produce rapid economic improvement, but the process of reconstruction of the war-damaged territory (including destroyed homes) was slow to the point of seeming nearly nonexistent and compensation payments promised to residents went into arrears.[205]

Starting a few months after the August war, a few major Kokoity allies turned against him, leveling charges that his corruption was responsible for the problems. Early defectors included Albert Jussoev (Kokoity's former adviser, owner of the republic's only private bank and head of a Russian Gazprom contractor building a major pipeline from Russia to South Ossetia) and Anatoly Barankevich (Kokoity's Security Council chief).[206] Barankevich's defection was particularly damaging to Kokoity's reputation, since as Security Council head, he had played a highly visible role defending Tsinkhvali against Georgian troops. He thus had local credibility when he publicly accused Kokoity of

---

[201] Eduard Kokoity, interview with *Gazeta.Ru* and *Kavkazskii Uzel*, published in *Ossetia.Ru*, May 29, 2009, 1:42.

[202] *Kavkazskii Uzel*, July 8, 2010; *Kommersant*, December 24, 2008; *Kommersant*, June 2, 2010.

[203] *Kavkazskii Uzel*, June 2, 2010, 13:31; *Polit.Ru*, February 16, 2009, 22:18; Jean-Christophe Peuch, "Georgia: Former Separatist Officials in South Ossetia Turn Against Regional Leader," *Eurasia Insight*, December 19, 2008.

[204] E.g., *Kommersant*, November 30, 2011, pp. 1, 8; Pakhomenko, "Uroven' nedovol'stva." An exception is a public opinion survey organized by Western geographers in November 2010. But because of Kokoity's sensitivity to the issue of his support, they report, they did not ask about him personally but about whether people had trust in the presidency, as two-thirds reported that they did. See Gerard Toal and John O'Loughlin, "Inside South Ossetia: A Survey of Attitudes in a De Facto State," *Post-Soviet Affairs*, v. 29, no. 2, 2013, pp. 136–72.

[205] *Kavkazskii Uzel*, March 13, 2009, 23:10; Markedonov, "The Unlikely Winners"; Pakhomenko, "Uroven' nedovol'stva."

[206] Peuch, "Georgia." On Jussoev, see also "Al'bert Dzhussoev," *Lentapediia*, lenta.ru/lib/14193521/, accessed October 9, 2012.

having fled the scene in his republic's moment of need and of having failed to organize the distribution of aid.[207]

Kokoity waffled in selecting his desired successor, and only at his Unity Party's September 2011 congress did he announce it would be Anatoly Bibilov, his emergencies minister.[208] While some speculated Kokoity chose Bibilov to be a weak successor whom Kokoity could manipulate from behind the scenes,[209] a focus on administrative resources and international factors should have made Bibilov a heavy favorite. Not only was he backed by Kokoity's presidential machine and his Unity Party, but Bibilov had the unequivocal support of Russia's top leadership. He was praised by Russian President Dmitry Medvedev, head of presidential administration Sergei Naryshkin, emergencies minister Sergei Shoigu, and head of the Duma's International Affairs Committee Konstantin Kosachev. Putin even delivered a personal message via Kosachev to a Unity Party congress organized to support Bibilov.[210] Bibilov could also claim to have won over some of Kokoity's elite critics, including Jussoev, Kelekhsaev (the leader of the real People's Party), and the Fatherland Party's leader (who had been disqualified from the 2009 parliamentary race), and enjoyed the Communist Party's backing to boot.[211]

Yet a classic competing-pyramid situation had already developed as the campaign season began, with Kokoity unable to prevent a major rupture in South Ossetia's elite and the emergence of a rival coalition of networks to challenge his machine. The central figures in the emergent rival pyramid were the oligarch Jambulat Tedeev (whom Kokoity had sidelined when consolidating power and was seeking a return to influence), former Security Council chief Barankevich, and Kokoity's former education minister and then Union of Women leader Alla Jioeva (who had fallen out with Kokoity in early 2008 and had been convicted of illegal business activity). Tedeev had sought to get on the ballot himself, with Jioeva as a low-profile backup candidate who would not likely raise much objection. The oligarch, however, was disqualified from the race for not meeting the residency requirement. This left Jioeva as the opposition coalition's main candidate. Kokoity does not appear to have taken her seriously.[212] Russia's leadership was reported to be opposed to the business group she represented.[213]

[207] Anatoly Barankevich, interview, *Kommersant*, December 4, 2008. On the 2008 events, see *Novaia Gazeta*, December 3, 2011.

[208] Before that, Kokoity had also publicly mentioned Prosecutor General Taimuraz Khugaev as a possible political heir. *Kavkazskii Uzel*, September 19, 2011, 10:40; Markedonov, "The Unlikely Winners."

[209] Markedonov, "The Unlikely Winners."

[210] *Ekspert*, November 21–7, 2011, p. 79; *Vedomosti*, November 29, 2011, p. 2.

[211] *Kavkazskii Uzel*, November 11, 2011, 22:00.

[212] On relationships among Jioeva, Tedeev, and Barankevich, see: *Nezavisimaia Gazeta*, November 29, 2011, p. 1; *Vedomosti*, November 29, 2011, p. 2. On Tedeev's disqualification from the ballot: *Kavkazskii Uzel*, September 30, 2011, 17:20. On Jioeva: *Kavkazskii Uzel*, April 30, 2010, 17:01; and November 4, 2011, 20:00.

[213] *Vedomosti*, November 29, 2011, p. 2.

But with Kokoity's machine weakened and Jioeva benefiting from the organizational and financial resources of heavy hitters like Tedeev and Barankevich, she was able to carve out political space to reach voters and capitalize on the widespread discontent with the incumbent authorities. Bibilov was accordingly on the defensive, attempting to distance himself from Kokoity. But in a campaign debate, Jioeva nailed him to his patron mercilessly: "You declare that you are not the candidate of the president. But at the same time, you are nominated by the Unity Party, the chairman of which is the current President Eduard Kokoity."[214] Bibilov was then forced to defend the party's and Kokoity's record and in turn accused Jioeva of being in cahoots with Georgia and played up his Russian endorsement, even using the Russian president's image on some of his campaign posters.[215] Strikingly, Jioeva turned Russian support around on Bibilov, accusing him of having too much visible support from it at the same time that she spoke positively about Putin.[216] The Bibilov campaign later cited its association with Kokoity as a potent factor working against it.[217] The first round of voting on November 13, 2011, featured 11 candidates and put Bibilov and Jioeva in a runoff, separated by only 14 ballots.[218] Jioeva attracted additional defectors prior to the November 27 second round, such as deputy foreign minister Alan Pliev.[219]

Jioeva's victory in the runoff vote count triggered a standoff in the street between the two competing coalitions of patronal networks. Both sides initially claimed victory. An exit poll organized by the reputable Russian Higher School of Economics indicated that Bibilov had won, but the Central Election Commission's count (with the commission reportedly being unanimous) held that Jioeva had won more votes.[220] After initially proclaiming the election democratic and transparent, Russian election observers reversed themselves and accused Jioeva supporters of illegal campaigning in polling places.[221] The Unity Party then appealed to the Supreme Court, which declared the results invalid, ordered a new election to be held, and barred Jioeva, whom it called the guilty party, from running in this new election.[222] This ruling was reported to be from the Court chairman alone, as all of the other judges refused to take part in the session that produced it. And the chairman, Atsamaz Bichenov, was regarded as a core member of Kokoity's network (the close friend from school days of

[214] *Kavkazskii Uzel*, November 27, 2011, 08:00.
[215] *Kavkazskii Uzel*, November 27, 2011, 08:00.
[216] *Kavkazskii Uzel*, November 27, 2011, 08:00.
[217] *Vedomosti*, November 29, 2011, p. 2.
[218] *Kavkazskii Uzel*, November 27, 2011, 08:00.
[219] *Kavkazskii Uzel*, November 27, 2011, 08:00.
[220] *Kavkazskii Uzel*, November 28, 2011, 07:27; *Kommersant*, November 30, 2011, pp. 1, 8; *Komsomolskaia Pravda*, December 1, 2011, p. 3; *Polit.Ru*, November 30, 2011, 17:20. On the exit poll, see: *Vedomosti*, November 28, 2011, p. 2.
[221] *Kommersant*, November 30, 2011, pp. 1, 8.
[222] *Kavkazskii Uzel*, November 28, 2011, 11:15, 11:30, 12:54; *Kommersant*, November 30, 2011, pp. 1, 8.

a Kokoity in-law).[223] Jioeva's supporters rallied in the streets on December 1, and some of her rival's erstwhile supporters defected to her side.[224] On the eve of the rally, she claimed to have been in touch with republic force agencies and been told they would not use force against her. In fact, the head of the republic's KGB declared it would not prevent the rally and police were seen allowing the gathering to take place, though they did intervene to prevent an attempt to break into the Central Election Commission building.[225] According to one account, the republic was on the brink of "civil war."[226] The example of the Orange Revolution was invoked after the fact in the republic, though as a pejorative, with Kokoity accusing Jioeva's backers of training with Ukrainian revolutionaries. Jioeva responded by promising to sue for "slander."[227]

Much as in Ukraine's Orange Revolution, however, the standoff ended in a compromise victory for the opposition rather than a total one. While the exact role of Russian mediation attempts is unclear,[228] Jioeva and Kokoity reached a deal on December 9 to resolve the election dispute: Kokoity would resign; Jioeva would lead her supporters from the main capital city square; repeat elections would be held but Jioeva would be able to run in them; the interim deputy prime minister should be from the opposition (Barankevich); and Kokoity should secure the resignations of the Supreme Court chairman and general prosecutor.[229] Thus Kokoity resigned the next day and sent parliament a request to remove the chief prosecutor and Supreme Court chair. Jioeva declared herself satisfied by December 11 that the deal was on track to be completely fulfilled.[230] But parliament, which still included many Kokoity supporters, rejected the resignation requests of the Supreme Court chief and general prosecutor, prompting Jioeva to declare the agreement breached, to revoke her signature from it, and eventually to announce plans to inaugurate herself president on February 10[231] (over the objections of Barankevich, who thought the deal was still the best option).[232] The day before her planned inauguration, police special forces raided her central offices and reportedly assaulted her personally, thwarting her assumption of the presidency and forcibly keeping her in a hospital.[233]

Despite this turn of events as the battle of political machines continued, the Kokoity power pyramid ultimately lost the new presidential elections in

[223] *Moskovskii Komsomolets*, December 2, 2011.
[224] *Kavkazskii Uzel*, November 29, 2011, 14:40.
[225] *Kavkazskii Uzel*, December 1, 2011, 15:26; *Kommersant FM radio* (Moscow), November 30, 2011, 08:50, author's notes; *Polit.Ru*, November 30, 2011, 11:19.
[226] *Kommersant*, December 1, 2011, p. 1.
[227] *Kommersant*, December 14, 2011, p. 7.
[228] *Kommersant*, December 2, 2011, p. 8.
[229] *Polit.Ru*, December 11, 2011, 16:54; *RFE/RL*, December 11, 2011.
[230] *Polit.Ru*, December 10, 2011, 18:35; *Polit.Ru*, December 11, 2011, 16:54.
[231] *Kavkazskii Uzel*, January 18, 2012, 13:12; *RFE/RL*, February 10, 2012.
[232] *Kavkazskii Uzel*, January 25, 2012, 10:05.
[233] *Kavkazskii Uzel*, February 10, 2012, 00:01; *Kavkazskii Uzel*, March 22, 2012, 02:16.

spring 2012 much as it had lost the original ones in 2011. While both Jioeva and Tedeev were barred from running, their coalition of networks coalesced around another decidedly anti-Kokoity candidate, Leonid Tibilov, former head of the republic's KGB.[234] On the campaign trail, Tibilov supported Jioeva, calling for her release and lambasting what he declared was a gross human rights violation.[235] Leading Jioeva backers supporting Tibilov included none other than Tedeev, Barankevich, and Pliev.[236] Jioeva refused to endorse anyone publicly so as not to recognize the denial of her 2011 victory, but it was widely believed she preferred Tibilov.[237] Other major networks also gravitated to Tibilov, including those of Jussoev and the original People's Party leader Kelekhsaev.[238] And while Communist leader Kochiev ran on his own, he also made statements in Jioeva's favor and backed Tibilov in the runoff election.[239] Tibilov's runoff opponent was one of two candidates linked closely to Kokoity, and even they were at pains to distance themselves from the person widely understood to be their patron (Tibilov, of course, energetically highlighted their links to Kokoity in debates and campaign appearances).[240] The runoff rival, David Sanakoev, however, was the only one not to support Jioeva openly.[241] Jioeva was finally released on the eve of the April 8 runoff, which Tibilov won with 54 percent of the vote.[242] Probably indicating where key backers resided, Sanakoev won the precinct for South Ossetian voters in Moscow.[243]

Tibilov's actions after assuming the presidency left little doubt that South Ossetia had, in fact, experienced an opposition victory. He replaced the government virtually wholesale and actually named Jioeva herself deputy prime minister.[244] His first prime minister, a South Ossetian who had worked for years in the Russian city of Samara, was backed by Jioeva herself.[245] Barankevich was made head of the government apparatus.[246] Pliev was given leadership of the capital city district.[247] Aza Khabalova, called one of Jioeva's "closest supporters," was named minister of finance.[248] One of her top campaign leaders, Rodion Siukaev, became state adviser on social issues.[249] Tibilov did throw some olive branches

---

[234] *Kavkazskii Uzel*, March 24, 2012, 18:10; *RFE/RL*, April 9, 2012.
[235] *Kavkazskii Uzel*, March 23, 2012, 07:35.
[236] *Kavkazskii Uzel*, April 4, 2012, 19:29; *Kavkazskii Uzel*, April 5, 2012, 20:56.
[237] *Kavkazskii Uzel*, January 25, 2012, 10:05.
[238] *Kavkazskii Uzel*, April 5, 2012, 20:56.
[239] *Kavkazskii Uzel*, March 23, 2012, 07:35; *Kavkazskii Uzel*, April 4, 2012, 01:19.
[240] *Kavkazskii Uzel*, March 21, 2012, 07:58; *RFE/RL*, April 9, 2012.
[241] *Vedomosti.ru*, April 9, 2012.
[242] *Polit.Ru*, April 19, 2012.
[243] *Kavkazskii Uzel*, April 8, 2012, 22:35.
[244] *Polit.Ru*, May 23, 2012, 20:54.
[245] *Civil Georgia*, May 24, 2012, 12:32.
[246] *Ossetia.ru*, May 24, 2012, 19:09.
[247] *Kavkazskii Uzel*, May 23, 2012, 21:31.
[248] *Kavkazskii Uzel*, May 19, 2012, 18:32.
[249] *Kavkazskii Uzel*, May 19, 2012, 18:32.

to former opponents, making Sanakoev his foreign minister and reappointing the defense minister.[250] But the clear majority of key posts went to people who had opposed Kokoity.[251] And this while a Russian court was actually extending the jail term of another Jioeva supporter who had been arrested in Russian North Ossetia during the December 2011 election standoff.[252] We thus see the powerful logic of regular patronal presidential regime cycles driving revolution and leadership turnover even where Russian influence was deemed to be at a maximum and where that of Western or transnational prodemocracy networks were regarded to be at a minimum – and in a war zone no less.

Transnistria's 2011 "Stunning Election"

As was described in Chapter 6, Transnistria's President Igor Smirnov had established a strong single-pyramid system by the end of the 1990s, winning three straight presidential elections in 1991, 1996, and 2001 with huge majorities, a process that included a successful amendment of the constitution prior to the 2001 elections to remove a two-term limit.[253] This clearly did not owe primarily to Moscow's political support. In the 2001 election, the Kremlin was reportedly seeking his replacement for geopolitical reasons and Russian media (accessible in the breakaway territory) were actually directed against Smirnov and instead favored one of his opponents, the former mayor of the city of Bendery.[254]

During the 2000s, however, some changes began to be felt in his single-pyramid system. Perhaps most important were the rapid growth and concomitant rise in political assertiveness of the massive business conglomerate Sheriff. In particular, it was a major beneficiary of an extensive privatization initiative Smirnov launched in the 2000s, obtaining such major assets as the Tiritex textile plant in 2004 and the Kvint cognac factory in 2005.[255] By the second half of the 2000s, so big was this network that it was reported to spend more on its own security than Smirnov's government did on the defense budget.[256] Sheriff also controlled media assets that rivaled those under direct control of the president, including newspapers and a television channel.[257] This growth also led it to seek more direct

---

[250] *Kavkazskii Uzel*, May 30, 2012, 19:59.

[251] *Kavkazskii Uzel*, May 25, 2012, 13:01.

[252] *Kavkazskii Uzel*, May 24, 2012, 01:45.

[253] Professor of the history of the PMR, Pridniestrovsky State University, author's interview, Tiraspol, March 26, 2009.

[254] Matsuzato, "From Belligerent," p. 111.

[255] Rebecca Chamberlain-Creanga, "Politics without a 'State': Electoral Reform and Political Party Formation in Secessionist Transnistria – and Its Implications for Conflict Resolution," paper presented at the Annual Meeting of the American Association for the Advancement of Slavic Studies, 2007, pp. 3–4.

[256] Matsuzato, "Nepriznannye gosudarstva v makroregional'noi politike chernomorskogo poberezh'ia," in Kimitaka Matsuzato, ed., *Pridniestrov'e v makroregional'nom kontekste chernomorskogo poberezh'ia* (Sapporo: Slavic Research Center, 2008), pp. 5–21, p. 16.

[257] Expert at Pridniestrovsky State University, author's interview, Tiraspol, March 26, 2009.

expression in public politics, with the Renewal (Obnovleniia) Party becoming a prominent part of the territory's electoral scene in the 2000s.[258] Fronted in politics by a charismatic young politician, Yevgeny Shevchuk, the Sheriff network actually gained a parliamentary majority with the 2005 election and secured the post of parliamentary speaker for him.[259] This victory also meant that nearly ten directors of major state or private enterprises in the extended network gained seats for themselves in parliament (out of a total of 43).[260] At the time, Sheriff was widely seen not as a clear opponent, but still mainly as a component of the Smirnov single-pyramid system.[261] Indeed, this powerhouse network consistently backed Smirnov for president in a collusive relationship straight through 2006, when Smirnov won another large election victory.

But despite the fact that Smirnov faced no formal term limit, tensions intensified after that 2006 victory as other factors helped create a sense that his time as republic leader was coming to an end and eroded his popular support. As of 2009, observers reported widespread perceptions – especially among younger upwardly mobile elites and businesspeople – that President Smirnov was getting too old, nearing his seventieth birthday and increasingly past his prime and unable to understand business.[262] Rumors started to circulate that the president would resign because of ill health, though Smirnov's office denied vigorously that he faced any fitness problems.[263] The global financial crisis also hit Transnistria very hard in late 2008 and 2009, causing the output of its heavy industry to plummet.[264] By its own government's account, nearly a quarter of its functioning enterprises were not producing at all during the first part of 2009.[265] Sentiment was also reportedly growing that because war with Moldova was no longer imminent, less centralization around Smirnov's authority was needed.[266]

By 2009, the Sheriff network became more openly aggressive in standing up for its own interests against those of Smirnov's personal network, though

[258] Margarita M. Balmaceda, "Privatization and Elite Defection in de Facto States: The Case of Transnistria, 1991–2012," *Communist and Post-Communist Studies*, v. 46, no. 4, pp. 445–54; Chamberlain-Creanga, "Politics without a 'State,'" pp. 3–4; Daria Isachenko, "Hyperreality of Statebuilding: The Case of Transdniestrian Region of Moldova," draft paper presented at the International Studies Association Annual Convention, 2008, pp. 7–8.

[259] Matsuzato, "Nepriznannye gosudarstva," p. 17; Vladimir Korobov and Georgii Byanov, "The 'Renewal' of Transnistria," *Journal of Communist Studies and Transition Politics*, v. 22, no. 4, December 2006, pp. 517–28.

[260] Anatoly Kaminsky, deputy chairman of the Supreme Soviet of Transnistria (later chairman) and head of the Renewal Party faction in the Supreme Soviet (parliament), author's interview, Tiraspol, March 26, 2009.

[261] Chamberlain-Creanga, "Politics without a 'State,'" p. 9.

[262] Matsuzato, "Nepriznannye gosudarstva," p. 16; Expert at Pridniestrovsky State University interview 2009.

[263] *Moldova Azi*, July 1, 2009, 19:08.

[264] Yevgeny Shevchuk, author's interview, Tiraspol, May 11, 2012.

[265] *Infotag*, May 20, 2009.

[266] Matsuzato, "Nepriznannye gosudarstva," p. 16; Expert at Pridniestrovsky State University interview 2009.

divisions also became visible within the Sheriff conglomerate over how far to go. For one thing, parliament – now controlled by Sheriff's Renewal Party – blamed Smirnov for inadequately responding to the financial crisis and failing to make satisfactory use of the resources the parliament had allocated to aid the population.[267] More dramatically, the parliament under Shevchuk's leadership started calling for constitutional reform that would cut presidential powers, prompting Smirnov to organize protests against the parliament and to advance a counterproposal that would strengthen his control over deputies.[268] By March 2009, the leader of the Renewal Party's parliamentary delegation, Anatoly Kaminsky, was comfortable enough to admit in an interview with a foreign scholar that there was "no love" between parliament and president.[269]

The precise details of what happened next remain murky, but what is clear is that divisions emerged between Shevchuk and others in the Sheriff network over how far to go in opposition, with Shevchuk taking the harder opposition line and resigning as parliamentary chairman during summer 2007 while blasting Smirnov's attempt to subjugate the parliament and other republic institutions.[270] Shevchuk soon made clear that he had defected openly from Smirnov, joining with his predecessor as parliamentary speaker (Grigory Marakutsa, described as recently as 2008 as a "close ally" of the president)[271] to lambast Smirnov for usurping power and call on him to resign.[272] Shevchuk was succeeded as parliamentary chair by first deputy chair and Renewal Party parliamentary delegation leader Kaminsky, who together with the majority of Sheriff-linked deputies in the parliament was not yet calling for Smirnov's ouster.[273] Kaminsky and the bulk of the Sheriff network, however, did push through constitutional reforms that weakened Smirnov's formal presidential powers, including creating a new post of prime minister that could be filled only with the approval of the parliament, though the president retained the right of nomination. This new post, according to Kaminsky, served as something of a counterbalance to the president.[274] Shevchuk, however, remained the formal head of Sheriff's Renewal Party, leading it to major victories in March 2010 city council

---

[267] See *Infotag*, July 16, 2009.

[268] Expert at Pridniestrovsky State University interview 2009; Oleh Protsyk, "Representation and Democracy in Eurasia's Unrecognized States: The Case of Transnistria," *Post-Soviet Affairs*, v. 25, no. 3, 2009, pp. 257–81, p. 260.

[269] Kaminsky interview 2009.

[270] *Infotag*, July 12, 2010. One interpretation is that Sheriff agreed with Smirnov to replace Shevchuk, seen as too far in opposition to Smirnov, as part of a deal to pass its constitutional reforms. See Vladimir Bukarskii, "Smena vlasti v Tiraspole: Pridniestrov'e obrelo legitimnogo prezidenta," *Win.ru*, December 29, 2012.

[271] Isachenko, "Hyperreality of Statebuilding," p. 8.

[272] *Lenta PMR*, November 18, 2009, 13:21.

[273] *Infotag*, July 12, 2010.

[274] Anatoly Kaminsky, chairman of Transnistria's Supreme Soviet, author's interview, Tiraspol, May 11, 2012.

elections in the territory's largest urban centers.[275] Nevertheless, Shevchuk lost the battle within the Sheriff network over positioning vis-à-vis Smirnov. He was thus replaced as formal chief of the Renewal Party in July 2010 by Kaminsky, with a source in the party reporting that under new leadership, it would work out a coalition with pro-Smirnov forces looking ahead to the December 2010 parliamentary elections.[276] Shevchuk responded with charges of "hypocrisy" and materialistic collusion.[277] This Sheriff strategy, including continued (if tense) collusion with Smirnov and the ouster of Shevchuk, appeared to be working in December 2010, when Renewal won a new majority in parliament under the leadership of Kaminsky, who was reelected parliamentary speaker.

Sheriff finally challenged Smirnov's core network directly for political primacy in the December 2011 presidential election, when the president was indeed already seventy years old and under renewed pressure from Moscow. The Russian government had taken a number of steps in 2010–11 that were widely interpreted as support for Smirnov's removal. These included a suspension of aid and an investigation of Smirnov's businessman son Oleg for misuse of Russian aid funds, a move that went so far as to close accounts of the younger Smirnov's Gazprombank.[278] Renewal leaders made efforts, including in the run-up to the 2010 local elections, to demonstrate they could work out a better relationship with Russia. The latter appeared more accommodating of requests from the Sheriff-controlled parliament than from Smirnov, granting new money for pensions after a visit by Kaminsky and Shevchuk in early 2010.[279]

Thus with age, low public support,[280] and the strikingly open opposition of the self-proclaimed republic's major patron (Russia) combining to create expectations that he was likely to leave power in the foreseeable future, Smirnov's power *vertikal*, fractured to produce a classic competing-pyramid situation.[281] This situation pit his personal network anchored in presidential administrative power against the Sheriff machine rooted in big business, large company towns, and the parliament with Kaminsky as its candidate. Kaminsky also had what most observers regarded as the obvious backing of Russian authorities.[282] Indeed, Kaminsky campaigned openly with images of Putin on his campaign

[275] *Infotag*, March 29, 2010.
[276] *AllTiras: Biznez Prindniestrov'ia*, July 1, 2010.
[277] *Infotag*, July 12, 2010.
[278] V. Diukarev, "Chernaia strategiia 'kandidata Moskvy,'" *Pridniestrov'e*, November 26, 2011, p. 2; *Infotag*, July 23, 2010.
[279] *Novaia Gazeta* (Transnistria), March 3, 2010, p. 1.
[280] His low levels of popular support were reported to have continued and even deepened by the end of 2011 owing to his old age, economic problems, visible corruption around him, and a general desire for change (expert at Pridniestrovsky State University, author's interview, Tiraspol, May 11, 2012). This was confirmed in a survey organized by Toal and O'Loughlin ("Inside South Ossetia") in 2010–11, which found the presidency was trusted by only 36 percent.
[281] Balmaceda, "Privatization and Elite Defection."
[282] *RFE/RL*, December 12, 2011, 08:52; *RFE/RL*, December 14, 2011.

billboards, trumpeted at least two trips to Moscow during the weeks prior
to the vote, ran television ads declaring he was the only candidate backed by
Putin's United Russia Party, and had a top United Russia leader attend the party
congress that nominated him.[283] Russian media broadcasting in the republic
were largely negative about the situation there, coverage that was expected to
play into the hands of Smirnov's opponents.[284] It would be a mistake to consider that the focus of the campaign was only about Russia, however. In his
speech to the Renewal Party congress that nominated him in September 2011,
Kaminsky blasted Smirnov for "stagnation" in organs of state power (evoking
images of the "era of stagnation" as Soviet leader Leonid Brezhnev aged) and
called for an end to corruption and economic change.[285] A newspaper advertisement he placed declared, "Anatoly Kaminsky: Together with Russia!" and
said that problems in the republic could no longer be blamed on nonrecogni-
tion.[286] Smirnov's allies responded by cautioning against too much Moscow
interference in Transnistrian affairs, warning that voters would not submit to a
candidate too subservient to Moscow.[287]

As is also typical of competing-pyramid situations, the intense competition between two rival centers of patronal power created room both for third
forces to operate with some degree of freedom and for public opinion to play
a more direct part in deciding the outcome. And here the main third force was
Shevchuk, his ties with the Sheriff network largely broken and widely regarded
as a hard-core opponent of Smirnov. Having formed a new movement of his
own called "Rebirth of Transnistria," Shevchuk called for change – including
ending business monopoly schemes – at the same time that he appealed for
people to vote their conscience without fearing political machines: "If you are
being threatened that there will be no pensions or stipends or that you will
be fired if you do not elect those whom today's authorities need, then clearly
the authorities need to be changed! Voting is secret! Come to the elections
and vote for a young team!" This particular newspaper campaign ad went on
to call for benefits to be provided to the people, "not only to the authorities
and monopolists," a not-so-subtle reference to both Smirnov and Sheriff.[288]
With the two primary centers of political machine power seeing each other as
the main contenders and not taking Shevchuk – now largely stripped of the
administrative power he used to wield – seriously as a candidate, Smirnov and
Kaminsky concentrated largely on defeating each other, essentially ignoring

---

[283] *Pridniestrov'e*, September 20, 2011, p. 1; *Pridniesrov'e*, September 29, 2011, p. 1; *Pridniestrov'e*,
   November 26, 2011, p. 1; *Pridniestrov'e*, November 30, 2011, pp. 1–2.
[284] *Pridniestrov'e*, November 18, 2011, p. 1.
[285] *Pridniestrov'e*, September 20, 2011, pp. 1.
[286] Paid advertisement for Kaminsky appearing in *Pridniestrov'e*, November 16, 2011, pp. 3. Video
   advertisements for Kaminsky could be seen on his official campaign Web site, which was still
   accessible as of October 11, 2012: http://www.kaminsky-pmr.ru/rus/video/.
[287] Diukarev, "Chernaia strategiia 'kandidata Moskvy,'" p. 2.
[288] Paid advertisement for Shevchuk appearing in *Dniestrovskaia Pravda*, December 3, 2011, p. 1.

Shevchuk. By at least one local expert account, this left Shevchuk looking clean and fresh, a reformer outside the realm of dirty politics. The other candidates realized their mistake only late in the game, when an illicit mudslinging campaign was reportedly launched that included homophobic insinuations regarding Shevchuk, a bachelor.[289] As one professor observed partly on the basis of what he saw of students, much of Shevchuk's support was believed to be from younger voters, to whom the articulate and hip forty-three-year-old candidate was appealing.[290]

The official first round vote count clearly was stunning to Smirnov.[291] By one account, he had been flattered by his advisers and was not aware of how unpopular he had become.[292] Despite wielding the powers of the patronal presidency, he had finished only in third place with about 25 percent of the vote, leaving him out of a runoff that would be required between the two top vote getters, Shevchuk (39 percent) and Kaminsky (26 percent).[293] Shevchuk declared particularly strong tallies in several of the territory's biggest industrial centers, including the capital city of Tiraspol and the Rybnitsky district.[294] Smirnov initially called foul, citing violations of election law and appealing to the Central Election Commission to invalidate the results.[295] But after a few days' delay, the commission reaffirmed the results and Smirnov let the runoff take place between his opponents Kaminsky and Shevchuk as scheduled without putting up a fight. Smirnov declared afterward that while the election had been dirty, he would not let the de facto republic's enemies have a civil conflict to exploit, and so conceded.[296] By at least one account, the republic's army had instructed soldiers to vote their conscience, and it along with the KGB refused to use force to salvage their boss's power, fearful that a bloody conflict could undermine their ambitions for Transnistrian statehood and, relatedly, alienate Russia even further.[297]

The result of the December 25 runoff strongly appears to be an instance of a competing-pyramid situation creating space for public opinion (and the genuine ability to appeal to it) to decide the ultimate outcome: Shevchuk crushed Kaminsky in a landslide with 74 percent of the official vote.[298] Kaminsky called this result a "shock" and elaborated on the puzzle himself when asked to explain it: His party had the largest membership, a majority

[289] *Pridniestrov'e*, November 26, 2011, pp. 1–2; Expert at Pridniestrovsky State University interview 2012.

[290] Expert at Pridniestrovsky State University interview 2012.

[291] "Stunning election" is Huntington's term for an election that an incumbent autocrat allows to happen and expects to win but loses convincingly. Samuel P. Huntington, *The Third Wave* (Norman: University of Oklahoma Press, 1991).

[292] Expert at Pridniestrovsky State University interview 2012.

[293] *RFE/RL*, December 14, 2011.

[294] *Dniestrovskaia Pravda*, December 20, 2011, p. 1.

[295] *Pridniestrov'e*, December 15, 2011, p. 1.

[296] *Pridniestrov'e*, December 29, 2011, p. 1.

[297] Expert at Pridniestrovsky State University interview 2012.

[298] *Polit.Ru*, December 26, 2011, 12:37.

in the parliament, majorities in the biggest cities' councils (including Tiraspol, Rybnitsa, and Bendery), and even access to administrative resources, but still lost.[299] He also clearly had the backing of the Russian authorities, as documented previously. Shevchuk lacked all of these assets, but what he did have was a much better connection with public opinion and significantly greater campaigning skills.

As was pointed out by local experts, Shevchuk absolutely destroyed Kaminsky in a campaign debate televised live just two days before the voting on the de facto republic's main channel.[300] Throughout this debate, an energetic, articulate, and stylish young Shevchuk pressed Kaminsky mercilessly for details of his economic plan for Transnistria that Kaminsky, speaking evasively, appeared unprepared to give. When pressed to state his ideas on a particular law enforcement issue, for example, Kaminsky complained that Shevchuk was giving him a test and asking provocative questions. When Shevchuk responded that the republic's citizens wanted to know his stand on their security, Kaminsky said it would take too long to describe it and offered to show him what it means after the debate, whereupon Shevchuk replied, essentially, "Is that a threat?" Shevchuk managed to lay out a clear vision for improving life in Transnistria by making government more effective, and through his responses created a strong impression that Kaminsky's plan was mainly just to throw money at the problem, with the money coming from Russia. While Shevchuk advocated good relations with Russia, he argued strongly that it was much more important to conduct a series of domestic reforms in Transnistria that he laid out. Kaminsky seemed on the defensive the whole time, was much less articulate, and often left Shevchuk's charges without a significant response. In one instance Shevchuk caught him apparently admitting a violation of campaign law during the debate: Kaminsky said in answer to a voter's question that he had ordered the parliament to put an issue on the agenda that very day, whereas by law during the campaign he was not supposed to be acting as parliament chairman.[301]

Kaminsky did not mention his debate debacle when asked by the author to explain his puzzling defeat, though he did begin his answer by modestly noting that he was a common man (*prostoi chelovek*). He went on to say that age was a major factor, as people preferred the youth of the forty-three-year-old Shevchuk to the seventy-year-old president and him, above age sixty. Kaminsky went on to assign great importance to his own strong association with the powers that be, having long held a leadership position in the parliament, noting that Shevchuk had effectively played the role of opposition to

[299] Kaminsky interview 2012.

[300] Two experts at Pridniestrovsky State University, author's interview, Tiraspol, May 11, 2012.

[301] Video of presidential election debate between Anatoly Kaminsky and Yevgeny Shevchuk broadcast live December 23, 2011, on the First Republican Television Channel (TV PMR), for the December 25, 2011, runoff election, posted on http://dniester.ru/content/videozapisdebato-vanatoliyakaminskogoevgeniyashevchuka on December 24, accessed October 11, 2012.

Smirnov, resigning as head of the parliament and Renewal Party. Saying that the defeat was cause for self-reflection, he also ventured that the Renewal Party had grown somewhat soft with its large organization and strong support, not running its campaign tightly or well.[302] Shevchuk, when asked to explain his victory, just said that this was a question for the voters, though when pressed he cited economic difficulties facing the territory and voters' desire for something new.[303] In the debate, however, Kaminsky also claimed that some big city administrations were backing Shevchuk using administrative methods, citing Rybnitsa as an example.[304]

Overall, Transnistria appears to be a good example of how factors other than term limits or a decision by incumbent presidents not to seek reelection can generate a lame-duck syndrome, creating centrifugal forces capable of irreparably rupturing a single-pyramid arrangement of patronal networks. Advanced age is perhaps the most important such additional factor here, very capable of working against an incumbent leader though less predictable because human health and life spans are less predictable and do not provide key temporal focal points in the way elections do. One implication may be that, as Chapter 4 suggested, the older a president who does not face term limits gets, the more likely it is that she will experience ouster as the next presidential election approaches if her popularity drops, as Smirnov's did both because of age itself and because of how hard the financial crisis hit the unrecognized state's industrial base. Indeed, the only post-Soviet patronal presidents to have reached at least the age of seventy between the mid-1990s and the early 2000s were Georgia's Shevardnadze (overthrown in the Rose Revolution) and Azerbaijan's Heydar Aliyev (who died shortly after handing off power to his son as described in the next chapter). The only others since the 1990s to reach this personal milestone in office did so around the same time as Smirnov, so they may yet fall victim, though Kazakhstan's Nursultan Nazarbaev has retained much stronger popular support than did Smirnov, and Uzbekistan's Islom Karimov has not allowed contested elections at all.[305] It also bears mentioning that Transnistria's network arrangement is striking in being highly bifurcated, with the presidential machine divided largely into Smirnov's family network and the megaconglomerate Sheriff, meaning that Sheriff's defection alone would deal a major blow to Smirnov's machine without having to organize any collective action with other networks, making its defection more likely. That said, the defection of Shevchuk even from Sheriff cautions us that we should not treat networks as somehow fixed in composition.

---

[302] Kaminsky interview 2012.
[303] Shevchuk interview 2012.
[304] Video of presidential election debate, December 23, 2012. On the situation in Rybnitsa, see Balmaceda, "Privatization and Elite Defection," p. 452.
[305] See Chapter 8.

Armenia's Palace Coup (1998)

The palace coup that removed Armenia's first president, Levon Ter-Petrossian, in 1998 has usually not been considered together with the color revolutions because this presidential ouster did not involve prominent mass protest, and existing theories of electoral revolution indeed cannot account for it. But the broader logic of patronal politics outlined here reveals that it is, fundamentally, the same class of event as the color revolutions, an instance when a patronal president facing low popularity and in his final constitutional term in office lost control of his political machine as key elites defected. The primary difference is that elites very quickly coordinated around a new top patron even before the struggle reached the realm of electoral politics, obviating the need for popular mobilization to be used as a battle weapon by competing patronal networks.

As described in Chapter 6, Ter-Petrossian had successfully constructed a patronal presidential single-pyramid system in the 1990s and mobilized it to secure reelection in 1996. This vote was widely considered fraudulent, but he was able to keep key elites (including those wielding control of the means of force) in line to put down protests forcibly.[306] After 1996, however, Ter-Petrossian faced two problems that proved his political undoing. First, he entered his second and constitutionally final term in office, which created grounds for speculating about a possible future succession. The second was the most fateful: Under international pressure to make concessions to bitter rival Azerbaijan so as to resolve the Nagorno-Karabakh conflict, Ter-Petrossian agreed in 1997 to pull Armenian forces out of occupied "buffer" regions around the disputed territory unilaterally as a confidence-building measure.[307] His public support plummeted, by one measure falling below 15 percent by the start of October 1997.[308]

To shore up his administration's nationalistic credentials prior to making this move, in 1997 he had named the former leader of Nagorno-Karabakh, Robert Kocharian, to be his prime minister. Being made prime minister, Kocharian secured his position as informal head of a large network of politicians and veterans from that territory who were in Armenia itself. Intended to bolster Ter-Petrossian's flagging support, appointing Kocharian to such a high post only accelerated the onset of the president's lame-duck status. For one thing, it meant that his own prime minister became the most potent critic of the concessions.[309] Even more fatefully, making the independent-minded and authoritative Kocharian head of his government sealed Kocharian's position as the obvious alternative for elites thinking that Ter-Petrossian was on his way out. This combination effectively undermined for Ter-Petrossian the ability

---

[306] Liz Fuller, "Democracy or Oligarchy?" *RFE/RL Newsline*, September 22, 1997.

[307] Emil Danielyan, "Armenian President's Resignation Likely to Cause Policy Changes," *RFE/RL Newsline*, February 5, 1998; *RFE/RL Newsline*, November 3, 1997.

[308] *RFE/RL Newsline*, October 2, 1997.

[309] Ronald Grigory Suny, as summarized in U.S. Institute of Peace, "Nagorno-Karabakh Searching for a Solution: Politics and Identity in Armenia and Azerbaijan," December 1998.

that patronal presidents typically have to divide and conquer elites or otherwise prevent them from coordinating strongly against the regime: He had provided both a personal focal point (Kocharian) and a temporal focal point (the Karabakh concession) around which elites could quickly coordinate to resolve the uncertainty surrounding the expected succession struggle before the struggle had a chance to break out into public politics.

Striking before his own popularity and likely successor status could be challenged, Kocharian wasted little time in using a series of events to induce the defection of key elites and their networks to his side against the president.[310] One of the most dramatic instances was what one observer called the "mass defections" from Ter-Petrossian's majority parliamentary coalition to a coalition representing veterans of the Karabakh war led by Defense Minister Vazgen Sargsyan.[311] Only a little more than a quarter of MPs remained with the president by early February 2008.[312] The most important defections following Kocharian, however, were of those elites who controlled the means of force, especially the defense minister himself and Minister of Interior and National Security Serzh Sargsyan.[313] The latter even intimated that these ministers would not obey if Ter-Petrossian ordered them to step down.[314]

Ter-Petrossian, recognizing his lack of both elite and mass support, ultimately resigned on February 3, 1998, rather than bother to take the battle to voters by attempting to fire Kocharian or promoting a successor other than Kocharian in the next elections through ballot box falsification or other machine political methods.[315] Ter-Petrossian, in effect, recognized the inevitability of Kocharian's victory and defected from himself, and this was in essence all that prevented Armenia from becoming the first post-Soviet electoral or color revolution. With Ter-Petrossian having resigned, the speaker of parliament, in line to be acting president in such an event, himself then stepped down as acting president to pave the way for Kocharian to assume that status.[316] Acting President Kocharian then won the early presidential election that followed later that year. Here we have a case, then, illustrating that mass opposition mobilization, youth movements, and other features frequently said to be linked to the color revolutions are in fact not essential for removing unpopular lame-duck patronal presidents from office.

---

[310] *RFE/RL Newsline*, v. 2, no. 23, February 4, 1998.

[311] Emil Danielyan, "'Velvet Coup' Promises Sweeping Changes in Armenia,' *Jamestown Foundation Prism*, v. 4, no. 4, February 20, 1998.

[312] *The New York Times*, February 4, 1998, p. A6.

[313] Emil Danielyan, "Armenian President's Resignation."

[314] Emil Danielyan, "'Velvet Coup.'"

[315] Paul Goble, "Why Ter-Petrossyan Fell," End Note, *RFE/RL Newsline*, February 6, 1998; Emil Danielyan, "Armenian President's Resignation"; *RFE/RL Newsline*, November 3, 1997; *The New York Times*, February 4, 1998, p. A6.

[316] *BBC World Service*, WBUR Boston, February 4, 1998, 9 am broadcast.

A Blood-Red Revolution in Kyrgyzstan (2010)

In 2010, Kyrgyzstan became the first post-Soviet republic to face a repeat convergence of the critical factors conducive to revolution in patronal presidentialist polities: an approaching succession and low leadership popularity. Chapter 9, which will examine what happens after patronal presidential ousters, will discuss in detail precisely how Kyrgyzstan under Bakiev came to reestablish a single-pyramid system during the course of his first five-year term in office. But for now, the most important points are that this happened and that the underlying cause was that the Tulip Revolution had not altered the fundamental sources of patronal presidentialism (pervasive patronalism and a presidentialist constitution). Instead, what the revolution changed was primarily the man at the top, who then presided over the creation of his own single-pyramid system in much the way Chapter 6 described so many other post-Soviet presidents doing.

In retrospect, having already observed that the country experienced two revolutions, analysts have called Kyrgyzstan a state so weak that it has been perennially vulnerable to even the least organized of revolutionary attempts, and Bakiev has been branded a weak or incompetent leader who crumbled as soon as the opposition mounted a challenge. This hindsight is belied, however, by a closer look at events during Bakiev's first term. Again leaving many of the details for Chapter 9, it is important to recognize that the opposition was constantly mobilizing street protests and other challenges designed to bring down Bakiev during his first term (2005–9), but he was able to beat them all back by crushing, co-opting, or dividing and conquering his opponents in the classic manner of patronal presidents who are not lame-ducks. This included an uprising that actually seized Kyrgyzstan's White House for a while in June 2005 in support of Urmat Baryktabasov;[317] a massive multiday protest during November 2006 aimed at forcing Bakiev to adopt a parliamentarist constitution;[318] former prime minister Kulov's April 2007 multiday uprising in central Bishkek aiming to force early presidential elections, which led to clashes with police;[319] the attempt by former Tulip revolutionary Azimbek Beknazarov to form a "Revolutionary Committee" to remove Bakiev in 2008;[320] and the subsequent high-profile efforts to end Bakiev's reign undertaken jointly by almost the entire spectrum of Kyrgyz opposition figures and out-of-favor elites under the banner of the United Popular Movement, including its attempt at a massive opposition rally in March 2009.[321]

[317] Sultan Jumagulov, "Bishkek in Turmoil Again," *Reporting Central Asia* (IWPR), no. 388, November 20, 2005.

[318] For an insider's account, see Sariev, *Shakh Kyrgyzskoi demokratii*.

[319] *AKIpress*, April 20, 2007, 11:39; *Polit.Ru*, April 20, 2007, 12:36; *RFE/RL Newsline*, April 27, 2007.

[320] *AKIpress*, September 16, 2008, 14:07.

[321] *AKIpress*, December 24, 2008, 13:33; *TsentrAziia*, January 13, 2009, 14:27.

And despite unprecedented unity leading into the race, the opposition attempt to defeat Bakiev in the July 2009 presidential elections also flopped quite spectacularly, securing only 15 percent of the officially counted vote (divided between their two main candidates, Almaz Atambaev and Temir Sariev) to Bakiev's 76 percent.[322] Efforts to mobilize street protests against this result across the country also fell stunningly flat and were easily put down by a show of presidential force.[323] Believed to have lost a struggle between his network and one linked to a brother of the president, Bakiev's chief of staff, Medet Sadyrkulov, resigned in early 2009 and was reportedly arranging to finance the opposition in return for backing his own presidential candidate, but died in a mysterious car accident later that spring and his preferred presidential candidate never made it onto the ballot.[324] Thus while there were good reasons to consider Kyrgyzstan a "weak state," during his first term Bakiev was more than capable of sustaining the dominance of his own power pyramid in the face of major opposition challenges.[325]

So what changed between July 2009 and April 2010, when suddenly Bakiev's regime crumbled in the face of the same kind of opposition efforts that had failed miserably so many times before? The comparative perspective supplied by the present volume calls attention to the fact that Bakiev had now entered into his second and constitutionally final term in office. While this need not have been a major impediment had he retained strong popular support, considerable evidence indicates that Bakiev's standing in public opinion had been falling precipitously. This occurred for a number of reasons. One was the deteriorating economy. While the president had secured a large Russian credit in the run-up to his reelection to stave off the worst effects of the 2008–9 global financial crisis until after the vote, by early 2010 the effects were clearly felt. Moreover, old economic problems continued to deepen, including the practice of rolling electricity blackouts, which were widely attributed to corruption in the electricity sector. Exacerbating all this was that while creating and maintaining a single-pyramid system typically requires care and time-consuming efforts to divide and conquer elites as described in Chapter 6, Bakiev overreached in his attempt rapidly to establish full control over the polity and economy for a very narrow circle of his closest associates, prominently including close relatives. This not only increased elite motivation to defect, but helped create a sense of "now or never" for Kyrgyz elites dissatisfied with the Bakiev "family's" increasing monopolization of the state, which facilitated their coordination in defiance of him without the need for an election as a focal point.

Several Bakiev moves combined to create this effect, generating widespread elite and mass disaffection while fostering a sense of urgency that he be

[322] Central Election Commission of Kyrgyzstan, official Web site, http://cec.shailoo.gov.kg/i-election.asp?ElectionID=93&DistrictID=1373, accessed January 13, 2012.

[323] *Fergana.ru*, July 29, 2009, 11:26.

[324] *Ekspert Kazakhstan*, February 2, 2009; *Svodka*, July 19, 2012, 15:11.

[325] McGlinchey, *Chaos, Violence, Dynasty*.

removed now before he could eliminate opposition altogether, gather all wealth in his inner circle's hands, and remain in power indefinitely. For one thing, in December 2009 a famous Kyrgyzstan journalist known for his criticism of the regime, Gennady Pavliuk, was fatally thrown from a sixth-floor apartment in Almaty with his hands and legs taped together. A Kazakh television station linked the killing to Kyrgyz special forces, though the latter categorically denied this.[326] In early 2010, Bakiev greatly accelerated his crackdown on mass media, shuttering, taking over, or blocking several television, radio, and Internet outlets.[327] Bakiev also undertook a number of economic policies after his reelection that consternated large parts of the population. These included "multifold increases in the prices for electricity, heating, and water" as well as a surcharge for every user of a mobile phone connection – that is, the vast majority of the politically active population.[328]

Further alienating elites and masses alike, Bakiev also greatly expanded his own family's control over the economy after his reelection.[329] One move was to make his son, Maksim, head of a new Agency for Investment and Economic Development, through which "most of the money coming into the Kyrgyz economy – including foreign investment and social and pension payments" – passed.[330] Russian media played an important role in calling negative attention to all this and helping amplify his lame-duck status. With the Kremlin reportedly upset Bakiev was not fully compliant in foreign policy, Russian television widely available in Kyrgyzstan aired a number of highly critical reports in March 2010 accusing Bakiev and son Maksim of corruption. Opposition leader Omurbek Tekebaev said that this and other indications of Russian displeasure were important because they signaled to state officials that Bakiev was on his way out, facilitating defections from key ministries under the opposition's assault.[331]

The ultimate catalyst for presidential ouster was, as in the Armenian case, not an election but another event that proved capable of resolving problems of elite coordination in opposing the regime. The opposition, much as it had done many times during Bakiev's first term, once again announced a large protest campaign against developments under the president. This one was to begin on April 7, 2010. The day before, opposition Ata-Meken Party activist Bolot Sherniiazov arrived in the northern Kyrgyz city of Talas to prepare for that

[326] *TsentrAziia*, March 31, 2010, 19:04.
[327] *Fergana.ru*, April 2, 2010, 14:54; *Polit.Ru*, March 12, 2010, 13:56; *Polit.Ru*, March 19, 2010, 12:02; *RFE/RL Press Release*, Prague, March 12, 2010.
[328] Venera Djumataeva, "The Roots of Kyrgyzstan's Uprising," *RFE/RL Commentary*, April 23, 2010.
[329] On the crucial importance of greedy presidential "inner circles" driving economic elites into opposition and promoting revolutionary dynamics even in strongly authoritarian regimes, see Barbara Junisbai, "Market Reform Regimes, Elite Defections, and Political Opposition in the Post-Soviet States: Evidence from Belarus, Kazakhstan, and Kyrgyzstan," doctoral dissertation in Political Science, Indiana University, 2009.
[330] Djumataeva, "The Roots."
[331] *The Washington Post*, April 12, 2010, online edition.

municipality's part in the planned protest. Police arrested him upon his arrival, sparking street protests by his supporters. A complicated set of events escalated, resulting in the protesters' seizure of the region's governor's office and other state buildings. Recalling how seizures of regional gubernatorial offices had launched the Tulip Revolution five years before, the fall of Talas sent shock waves throughout the political elite. When Bakiev responded by arresting a whole series of major opposition leaders, the result was only to enrage opposition forces further. The April 7 protests thus occurred as planned but took on new fervor, with people shouting in Bishkek, "Today or never!"[332] Protesters reportedly arrived with weapons of their own, though by most accounts police snipers began the killing by firing into the crowd around the Kyrgyz White House, with other police acting panicky and seemingly unsupervised. When the masses failed to disperse, Bakiev's apparatus crumbled, his top authorities fending for themselves and Bakiev himself fleeing first to his native southern Jalalabad and then on to Belarus, where he was given safe haven.[333] This time it was Roza Otunbaeva's turn to assume leadership of the new revolutionary government, once again producing a situation where a former senior member of the old regime (Otunbaeva had been Bakiev's foreign minister) became the leader of the new regime.

The bloody revolution of April 2010 thus differed from the other post-Soviet patronal presidential revolutions discussed so far in this chapter. Not only did it not involve an election as a focal point for elite coordination against the regime, but it was far more violent and took place with lightning speed rather than demonstrating the kind of gradual cascade of elite defections characteristic of the others. Indeed, Bakiev had effectively already forced many key elites out of his regime as he hastily tried to monopolize power and money in the republic. But the core drivers of post-Soviet patronal presidential revolutions remained central: Previously seeming invincible, Bakiev almost suddenly became vulnerable when he entered his constitutionally final term in office and then made a series of moves that damaged his public support and aggravated significant networks in his single-pyramid system, providing them with incentive to mobilize against him. With the next elections still a few years away, a clash in the city of Talas served to catalyze both opposition and the crumbling of the forces that kept him in power, providing a focal point for protest and defection. Elections and standard playbooks for defeating dictators, it once again turns out, are not the primary drivers of post-Soviet revolution. The logic of elite collective action in patronal presidential systems does a better job of accounting for both where and when these revolutions have taken place. [334]

---

[332] Djumataeva, "The Roots."

[333] Account compiled from numerous contemporaneous reports in *AKIpress*, *TsentrAziia*, *Polit.Ru*, and *The New York Times*.

[334] Readers should not mistake this discussion of Kyrgyzstan for an ad hoc extension of patronal politics logic developed after the fact. Instead, this sort of dynamic was anticipated in work

Ukraine's Euromaidan Revolution (2014)

Ukrainians could be forgiven for having a sense of déjà vu in early 2014. Not only did their country experience a second revolution with street protests on the same massive scale as those in 2004, but both revolutions denied the very same man the presidency. The aftermath of the Orange Revolution will be discussed in detail in Chapter 9, but for now what is important is that in 2010, Viktor Yanukovych finally won election to the presidency and restored patronal presidentialism after a five-year hiatus of competing-pyramid politics anchored by a divided-executive constitution.[335] As expected, new movement then began toward a single-pyramid system. As Chapter 9 will describe and as is documented in various monitoring reports by Freedom House and others, between 2010 and 2013 Ukraine experienced a significant political closure. This included tightening media control, diminishing oligarch willingness to support outright opposition, jailing of the most powerful rival network's chief patron (Yulia Tymoshenko), and other manipulations of the political process that increasingly marginalized anyone not willing to play ball with the president.[336]

The increasing media control, however, was unable to prevent a pronounced drop in public support for Yanukovych and his Party of Regions that was starkly evident already in 2011. The initial cause was not economic decline, as Ukraine's economy returned to growth in 2010 and appeared to recover from the 2008–9 financial crisis.[337] Instead, observers noted widespread feelings the president had broken campaign promises to improve people's lives.[338] By 2012, however, a stalling economy had indeed started to compound his problems, as growth dropped to just 0.4 percent.[339] Strikingly, he was losing large shares of supporters even in his political base of southern and eastern Ukraine. He remained Ukraine's most or second-most popular politician, but this said more about how widely disliked opposition forces were than about how much support he himself had. According to a reputable polling agency, by May 2013

published by the author even before Kyrgyzstan's 2010 revolution. This work argued that a patronal president reacting to previous color revolutions too strongly by dramatically accelerating repression could actually increase the chances of a nonelectoral and more bloody ouster. See Henry E. Hale, "Democracy or Autocracy on the March? The Colored Revolutions as Normal Dynamics of Patronal Presidentialism," *Communist and Post-Communist Studies*, v. 39, no. 3, September 2006, pp. 305–29, especially p. 322.

[335] While Yanukovych defeated incumbent president Viktor Yushchenko in this election, this did not constitute a patronal presidential ouster because Ukraine at the time did not have a patronal presidentialist system; see Chapter 9 for more details.

[336] For example, Oleksandr Sushko and Olena Prystayko, "Ukraine," *Nations in Transit 2013* (New York: Freedom House, 2013), pp. 579–97.

[337] According to the World Bank's World Development Indicators, growth rates were −14 percent in 2009, 5 percent in 2010, and 6 percent in 2011 (http://data.worldbank.org/datacatalog?display=default, accessed January 2, 2014).

[338] *RFE/RL*, March 7, 2012.

[339] Again, according to the World Bank.

only 14 percent of potential voters were willing to say that they would vote for Yanukovych if the first-round presidential election were held at that time.[340] While no opposition figure would have received much more support in the first round, surveys also consistently showed that Yanukovych would lose runoff elections to the jailed Tymoshenko, the boxer Vitali Klitschko, and the formal head of Tymoshenko's party, Arseny Yatseniuk. The incumbent's only hope of winning a fair count seemed to have been somehow to arrange for radical nationalist Oleh Tiahnybok, known among other things for anti-Semitic and anti-Russian rants, to be his second-round opponent.[341]

Yanukovych's troubles crystallized when he waffled on whether to sign an Association Agreement that would have entailed substantial deepening of economic relations with the European Union. While Yanukovych had expressed support in principle for this agreement, the EU had demanded in return (among other things) that Tymoshenko be released from jail as a sign of commitment to democratization. Finally, shortly before the November 2013 EU summit when the signing ceremony was to have taken place, Yanukovych balked, declaring that he would not sign at the present time. This triggered a sudden wave of pro-EU protests in public squares across the country, a movement that soon became known as the "Euromaidan" protests.[342] Numbers soon reached hundreds of thousands by some counts, with crowds rivaling if not exceeding those in the Orange Revolution. In Kyiv, multiple protest sites eventually converged on Independence Square, the main site of the Orange Revolution encampments.

The initial protests, large as they were, did not shake Yanukovych's emergent single-pyramid system, but the regime then made a series of ham-handed moves that time after time inflamed the protesters and alienated allies just as the protests appeared to be petering out. First, in the early morning of November 30, when just a few thousand people remained in Independence Square, special "Berkut" police stormed it. Brandishing clubs and firing tear gas, they left dozens bloodied and arrested others.[343] Outraged, protesters returned in huge numbers the next day, overrunning police, who surrendered the square to them. The main demands shifted beyond the Association Agreement to target the regime itself, now blamed for inflicting violence on its own people.[344] After a weak attempt to push protesters away without the use of live ammunition, police let the protesters peacefully occupy the square (and multiple state buildings they had stormed) for most of December and the first

---

[340] The survey was by KMIS, as reported in *Ukraiins'ka Pravda*, June 17, 2013, 12:11.

[341] E.g., *Ukraiins'ka Pravda*, October 21, 2013, 10:57.

[342] *Maidan* is the Ukrainian word for square. Anticipating in advance that such a protest might be possible among Ukraine's youth, see Nadia Diuk, "Youth as an Agent for Change: The Next Generation in Ukraine," *Demokratizatsiya: The Journal of Post-Soviet Democratization*, v. 21, no. 2, Spring 2013, pp. 179–96.

[343] *RFE/RL*, November 30, 2013; *Ukraiins'ka Pravda*, November 30, 2013, 05:05.

[344] Author's field observations in the Kyiv Euromaidan, December 2014.

part of January. During this period, the crowds started to grow thin, deflated in part after Yanukovych obtained a $15 billion economic bailout from Putin. Opposition leaders were increasingly giving up hope of forcing Yanukovych to resign and shifting focus to preparing to challenge Yanukovych in the next presidential election, scheduled for early 2015. The logic presented in this volume would predict that Yanukovych would have been in a good position to win such a contest, regardless of opposition resolve. Events seemed on track for a scenario in which Yanukovych could find a way to disqualify such major candidates as Klitschko and Yatseniuk, potentially paving the way to maneuver Tiahnybok (who could be expected to benefit politically from the street polarization around national identity issues) into a runoff against the incumbent president, maximizing the latter's chances. But amazingly, the regime once again overplayed its hand. On January 21, 2014, parliament adopted a series of laws greatly restricting freedoms and widely seen as paving the way for a crackdown on the protesters. Enraged, some in the crowd ignored entreaties by Klitschko and reacted violently. Police fired back, and the revolution had its first martyrs. For many protesters, no compromise was possible any longer that did not involve Yanukovych's immediate resignation.

The violence quickly escalated, with some radicals among the protesters (reportedly mostly Ukrainian ultranationalists) hurling Molotov cocktails at police and proregime thugs (widely called *titushki*) roaming the city and beating, kidnapping, and sometimes brutally torturing protesters. Opposition activists in several regions (mostly in western Ukraine) countered by seizing control of local government buildings and ousting regime authorities there, raising fears for many that Ukraine actually risked civil war or perhaps even state breakup. Yanukovych's coalition in parliament, as well as most of his single-pyramid system outside western Ukraine, generally did not break ranks until one final regime action that alarmed even his close allies in February 2014: Possibly provoked by militant opposition forces, police opened massive fire with live ammunition on protesters in one final attempt to drive them from the square on February 18. This battle, raging for some two days, wound up killing close to ninety people, a stunning number for a country that had experienced hardly any deadly political violence since independence. Not only did the protesters refuse to be cowed, but now key networks in Yanukovych's own coalition defected en masse, saying the regime had gone too far.[345] His majority in parliament evaporated. Quickly losing position, Yanukovych managed to strike a compromise deal on February 21 with the main opposition parties that would leave him in office until early elections later in the year. Hardcore protesters on the square, however, whistled down the party leaders when the deal was announced, demanding nothing less than the president's immediate resignation. Yanukovych then fled the country, eventually turning up in a

---

[345] For example, see reports on such defections in *Ukraiins'ka Pravda*, February 19, 13:31, 20:11, 23:29;

peripheral Russian region. Large numbers of former Yanukovych supporters in the parliament then joined opposition deputies to declare Yanukovych unfit to rule, to restore Ukraine's divided-executive constitution of 2004, to form a new government, and to call new presidential elections for May 2014.[346]

For reasons to be described in the next chapter, Russia responded with an intense campaign in media viewable in much of Ukraine branding the new Ukrainian authorities as something akin to genocidal fascists, using this as a justification to mobilize troops to arrange the secession and ultimately annexation of Ukraine's region of Crimea, home to an ethnic Russian majority. Pro-Russian movements suddenly mobilized in Donetsk and Luhansk as well, soon taking over local government buildings and orchestrating referenda on autonomy from Kyiv. Despite such dire circumstances, Ukrainian authorities managed to organize a presidential election on May 25, 2014. These were won overwhelmingly by the oligarch Petro Poroshenko on the strength of what many perceived to be his uncompromising leadership during the Euromaidan protests (he had been an early backer of the movement and was not part of the ill-starred compromise agreement of February 21) combined with what many anticipated would be a pragmatic ability to rebuild the country given his business experience and prior service as an official in Yanukovych's government. Separatist forces were able to disrupt at least some of the voting in Donetsk and Luhansk, however. Nevertheless, the May 25 election consummated Ukraine's second post-Soviet revolution, which like the first left Ukraine with a divided-executive constitution in place of a presidentialist one.

The Euromaidan Revolution differs from the other patronal presidential ousters discussed in this chapter in that it reflects clearly irregular rather than regular drivers of expectations. In this case alone, there was no question of term limits or elections involving succession. Instead, it was an EU summit that provided a temporal focal point for a mass outpouring of opposition to the highly unpopular Yanukovych, against which backdrop Yanukovych's own bungling alienated allied networks and eventually created immediate expectations that he would be unlikely to hang on to power and that his opponents would be more likely to win any ensuing political competition.

These events suggest several observations regarding irregular regime cycles of the type discussed in Chapter 4. For one thing, the fact that Yanukovych was not a lame-duck at the time it occurred (still having had the right to run for reelection in 2015 and potentially serve another five years after that) meant that despite his low popular support and despite facing protests of essentially

[346] Along with nearly minute-by-minute reporting by outlets such as *Ukraiins'ka Pravda*, useful English-language timelines of these events can be found in: Olga Onuch and Gwendolyn Sasse, "What Does Ukraine's #Euromaidan Teach Us about Protest?" post on "The Monkey Cage" blog, *The Washington Post*, February 27, 2014, http://www.washingtonpost.com/blogs/monkey-cage/wp/2014/02/27/what-does-ukraines-euromaidan-teach-us-about-protest/, accessed June 2, 2014; and *BBC.com*, May 29, 2014, http://www.bbc.com/news/world-middle-east-26248275, accessed June 2, 2014.

the same scale as the Orange Revolution, very few defections from his regime occurred during the entire first three months of the street standoff. This includes his broad parliamentary coalition, many of whom were not elected on the Party of Regions party list; it held together until the regime undertook the extremely unpopular action of killing many dozens of protesters. This stands in stark contrast with the Orange Revolution, when the unpopular Kuchma faced a large and growing number of major defections long before the biggest protests broke out in November 2004.

These events also demonstrate that authoritarian overreach did not cease to be a threat to single-pyramid building after the 1990s.[347] At the same time, it should also be noted that after five years of a lively and unruly competing-pyramid system (see Chapter 9), Yanukovych's task in building a power pyramid shared some of the difficulties that Eurasia's first pyramid builders in the mid-1990s faced. The five years under Ukraine's divided-executive constitution had radically discoordinated the country's elite networks, a situation that could not be undone overnight. Yanukovych's hasty, overly aggressive, and unpopular actions illustrate this well. Patience, leaders ranging from Kuchma to Putin could have told him, was important because successful coordination of patronal networks (including subtle games of divide and conquer and finding arrangements that effectively divide spoils) takes time.[348] By committing such violence and demonstrating incompetence as a patron in the process, all the while having very low public support, Yanukovych himself created expectations that he was a goner, punctuating a closure phase in what turned out to be an irregular regime cycle.

Conclusion

In short, a careful tracing of events in all ten instances when a patronal president has been ousted since the creation of his polity's first single-pyramid system through mid-2014 reveals that every case but one involved an incumbent president who was highly unpopular and facing a lame-duck syndrome. This is strong evidence for the growing dominance of regularity over irregularity in Eurasian regime dynamics. The lame-duck syndrome generally meant a president's being in his final constitutional term in office (seven cases) or opting not to seek reelection for a different reason (one case) or reaching the age of seventy and thus facing growing doubts about his ability to rule effectively much longer (one case).

---

[347] Anticipating how presidential overreach could lead to irregular revolution in patronal polities, see Hale, "Democracy or Autocracy on the March?", especially p. 322.

[348] Interestingly, Belarus President Aliaksandr Lukashenka – both a tough leader and a highly skilled patronal president – in fact said that Yanukovych could have and should have reached a deal with the Euromaidan protesters and avoided shedding blood. See *Nasha Niva*, April 13, 2014, 14:42.

These events sometimes did involve the outward trappings of democratic breakthroughs that had in fact occurred during the previous decade in some southeastern and east central European countries, trappings such as visible prodemocracy youth movements and NGOs explicitly borrowing tactics of regime replacement from previous breakthroughs. But these were not the driving forces of the color revolutions and vast bulk of the post-Soviet presidential ousters that followed. Oppositions described here were successful whether or not they adopted these tactics (as Abkhazia's uncolored revolution and Kyrgyzstan's bloody revolution demonstrate), whether or not they presented a clear united front against the incumbents (as Kyrgyzstan's Tulip Revolution illustrates), whether or not an actual election provided a focal point for concerted action (as Armenia's palace coup and Kyrgyzstan's bloody revolution show), whether or not a strong identity divide was there for them to mobilize against the authorities (as Georgia's two presidential ousters and Armenia's palace coup reveal), whether or not transnational prodemocracy forces intervened to support them (as Abkhazia's uncolored revolution and Armenia's palace coup establish), whether or not Russia backed the incumbents (as Abkhazia and South Ossetia illustrate), and, indeed, whether or not there was any mass mobilization at all (as Armenia's palace coup attests). Instead, what strongly appears to have mattered most was the combination of an election-related lame-duck syndrome and low incumbent popularity. Ukraine's Euromaidan Revolution was the lone exception, a holdover of regime cycle irregularity in an era of regularity.

When one moves from the broad patterns to the concrete details of how each ouster occurred, the logic of patronal politics is strongly borne out, though what precisely happened in a few cases remains less clear. In Georgia 2003, Ukraine 2004, Abkhazia 2004, Kyrgyzstan 2005, South Ossetia 2011–12, and Georgia 2012–13, a careful process tracing of events uncovers strong evidence of a "classic" short-cycle pattern. Single-pyramid systems collapsed as unpopular presidents were already widely expected to leave office, leading elites to think increasingly about uncertain futures when the president would not be around to punish or reward them for what they did today. The result in each case was a power changeover centered around an election result, when elites defecting from the old president's own ruling circle in anticipation of a succession wound up the victors, ultimately inducing others to their side with the help of popular support.

The role of expectations of succession is less clear for the ousters that did not involve an election result as the mechanism for presidential replacement. In Armenia 1998, the palace coup itself was carried out rapidly and without much public mobilization. Thus while there is strong evidence that incumbent President Ter-Petrossian had suffered a major drop in popularity, there is no smoking gun to confirm or deny that his mutineers were expecting him to leave anyway and that this emboldened them or helped them coordinate their actions. In Kyrgyzstan 2010, events took place very suddenly as incumbent

President Bakiev made a number of rapid moves after his election to seize control of the economy and polity and suffered a (not unrelated) major drop in popular support. The role of succession in this instance would thus seem to have been different from in the "classic" cases: Rather than seeing Bakiev as already on his way out, as in the other cases, the fact that he was in his constitutionally final term led elites to think that he was amassing power to try to escape this limit somehow. This contributed to the documented sense of "now or never" that spurred them to act collectively, even to the point of defying state-initiated violence, once the uprising in Talas provided a temporal focal point for coordinating their actions.

And finally, the case of Transnistria differs from the classic cases in that age was a chief source of the lame-duck syndrome. It functioned, though, only in combination with other factors that turned the 2011 elections into the chief focal event for coordinated elite defection.

Overall, the majority of the cases (six) are *strongly* consistent with the logic of short-term regime cycles outlined in Chapter 4, an additional one is *strongly* consistent with the logic of long-term regime cycles, and two more, where the evidence on mechanisms is less clear, are at a minimum still *consistent* with the logic of short-term regime cycles, in no way directly contradicting it. And only one presidential ouster examined here, the Euromaidan Revolution, clearly falls outside the realm of regime cycle regularity as described in Chapter 4. Taken together, this is an impressive finding for the argument that patronal presidential ousters are likely to be governed to a significant degree by regular shifts in expectations that are to a significant degree predictable on the basis of succession-related elections and public opinion. It also adds to the finding from Chapter 6 that after an initial period of transition-related turmoil, regularity in Eurasian regime dynamics became more prominent than irregularity as elections, term limits, and presidential age increasingly shaped when and how other threats to patronal presidential strength mattered.

The next chapter now turns to discussing in detail post-Soviet countries that have not experienced a patronal presidential ouster since the point at which Chapter 6 left off. This helps us establish still further that the logic of patronal politics outlined in Chapter 4 is at work and to rule out alternative explanations for the larger pattern identified in this book.

8

Nonrevolution in Post-Soviet Presidential Systems

The previous chapter has shown that once a single-pyramid system was initially built in a post-Soviet presidentialist polity, patronal presidents have fallen primarily as they simultaneously encountered a lame-duck syndrome and low popular support. The present chapter addresses post-Soviet presidentialist polities that have not so far experienced the ouster of their dominant presidential network. It shows they stand out from the bulk of cases in the previous chapter in at least one of three ways. First, some presidents have never become lame-ducks despite allowing at least some opposition to compete in the most important elections.[1] Second, others experienced a lame-duck syndrome and even a dramatic competing-pyramid situation but had presidents or handpicked successors who were popular enough to win the competition. Third, two countries emerged from the Soviet breakup as outright dictatorships rather than hybrid regimes. Full dictatorship does not make a regime immune to patronal presidential ouster, as discussed in Chapter 4, but does essentially keep elections from serving as key focal points that can facilitate coordinated defection among elites anticipating succession under an unpopular incumbent. Other focal points can arise in full dictatorships, but they are likely to be much fewer and farther between and less predictable in form and timing. In short, full autocracies are most likely to feature irregular regime cycles or regular "long regime cycles" linked to the age of the dictators.

These cases of presidential network nonouster provide telling control cases that reinforce our conclusions as to when revolution or other forms of dominant network turnover are likely in patronal presidential countries. Just as the previous chapter found a lame-duck syndrome and low popular support combining in every case of patronal presidential network ouster since the first single-pyramid systems were built after the Soviet breakup, so the present chapter

---

[1] A few are just now entering a lame-duck phase, the implications of which will be discussed.

shows that in the absence of either of these factors (popular support or a lame-duck syndrome) neither revolution nor any other kind of ouster was forthcoming. Moreover, as expected, we find that the countries in this set experiencing lame-duck syndromes did in fact often display succession-related tensions and sometimes even outbreaks of open elite contestation to influence it, but that patterns of popular support were important in ensuring victory for the incumbent networks. Thus when we train a higher-powered microscope on these cases of nonrevolution, we are able to frame a series of "microcomparisons" that further demonstrate the critical importance of a lame-duck syndrome and low popularity. For example, we can show that Tajikistan experienced a situation highly similar to that of Kyrgyzstan in 2005 in terms of factors most existing theories cite as being critical to the color revolutions, but that this situation did not go on to catalyze revolution because the incumbent president was not a lame-duck.

These cases of nonouster are also the ones that tend to drive what some observers have called the "authoritarian trend" of the 2000s and 2010s in the post-Soviet space, perhaps most prominently featuring developments in Russia under Vladimir Putin. The present chapter's analysis, however, reveals that this trend is much more contingent than is often assumed, and uncovers the central nature of popular support in underpinning the ability of these regimes to continue to appear and act authoritarian. In fact, when taken together with the discussion in Chapter 7, we discover that post-Soviet patronal presidential systems – despite their tendency to produce single-pyramid systems – do feature a significant and powerful accountability mechanism forcing their leaders to cater to and cultivate public opinion, a mechanism that sheds some light on Russia's decision in 2014 to annex Crimea. This mechanism, however, is less responsive than in democracies and works primarily through a messy, state-weakening process of revolution or forcible ouster rather than through the more orderly processes typical of democracies.[2] The pages that follow first discuss Eurasia's two actual dictatorships, then consider the hybrid regimes that have not experienced a lame-duck syndrome, showing that they have not generally faced serious threats of ouster since their single-pyramid systems were originally built. The chapter then turns to those hybrid regimes whose dominant networks experienced lame-duck syndromes but survived them, demonstrating that their remaining in power owed largely to their winning a struggle for actual popular support.

Full-On Dictatorships: Turkmenistan and Uzbekistan

A subset of post-Soviet regimes cannot be called hybrid and instead must be classified as full dictatorships for the whole period since at least the mid-1990s: Uzbekistan and Turkmenistan. Neither country during this period has allowed

[2] This fits with findings at the local level in Russia that regional political machines were systematically more vulnerable to losing control even in imperfect, manipulated elections when they failed to perform for the benefit of their populations (Hale, "Explaining Machine Politics in Russia's Regions: Economy, Ethnicity, and Legacy," *Post-Soviet Affairs*, v. 19, no. 3, July–September

any genuine opposition to compete for the most powerful formal office in the land and opposition figures are generally repressed far more thoroughly and brutally than in any other post-Soviet state. Opposition politicians are not only prevented from getting on the ballot. In these countries, they are systematically jailed, tortured, or exiled and, more generally, effectively denied any outlet whatsoever to publicize their views in openly circulated print or electronic media. Dissidents carry on activities only at great peril to themselves and their families. While some of the other patronal presidential systems examined in this volume feature closed polities and harass and occasionally either jail or (informally) exile their critics, even the most closed of them (such as Belarus) feature nothing approaching this level of systematic repression, which strongly resembles what existed in the USSR but without the communist ideology. This is not entirely by chance: As was discussed in Chapter 6, it was only in Turkmenistan and Uzbekistan that the Soviet Union's Communist Party structure remained intact during the last stages of perestroika and the local party bosses ruled through it during the transition to independence, effectively just renaming the party.

This extreme repression (regularly rated among the worst the whole world has to offer) has had two effects in terms of the patronal politics logic that is the subject of this book. First, it has meant that no president in these countries has faced a lame-duck syndrome other than that generated by his own human life expectancy. Islom Karimov, Uzbekistan's president since before independence, has never signaled he would leave office and has left little doubt he would do whatever necessary to stay in power if challenged. He was first elected in late 1991 in a contest that included one genuine opposition figure (the moderate nationalist poet Mohammed Solih). But this was the last time any true challenger would appear on a presidential ballot. In 1995, Karimov extended his term to 2000 by referendum. When the 2000 election rolled around, Karimov won with only one other candidate on the ballot, the academic Abdulkhafiz Djalalov, who hailed from a party Karimov created. A referendum in 2002 and constitutional change in 2003 extended presidential terms from five to seven years. In the 2007 presidential election, Karimov faced three others on the ballot, but all were clearly progovernment figures.[3] While exiled critics argued that 2007 represented the expiration of his constitutionally final second term, the Central Election Commission ruled (in a common post-Soviet practice) that the earlier changes to the constitution reset the term count, meaning he had the right to at least one more term.[4] Likewise, Turkmenistan's first president,

---

2003, pp. 228–63; Andrew Konitzer, *Voting for Russia's Governors* (Baltimore: Johns Hopkins University Press, 2005).

[3] Ironically, his substantive message was one of modernization and liberalization. Islom Karimov, speech to the November 6, 2007, 4th Congress of the Movement of Entrepreneurs and Businesspeople – Liberal Democratic Party of Uzbekistan, which nominated Karimov for president, published by *Pravda Vostoka* as the main Karimov preelection speech on November 27, 2007, reprinted by *Ferghana.Ru*, November 27, 2007, 11:40; *RFE/RL Newsline*, October 12, 1999; *RFE/RL Newsline*, December 27, 2007.

[4] *RFE/RL Newsline*, January 23, 2007; *RFE/RL Newsline*, November 26, 2007.

Saparmurat Niyazov, who renamed himself Turkmenbashi (which means "head of the Turkmen"), not only countenanced no notion that he would ever leave power, but ended the formality of presidential elections altogether. A second effect of full dictatorship has been that the actual physical elimination of real opposition parties or candidates from the political scene (not to mention the ballot) has greatly reduced the opportunity for elites to use the election process or mass protests to coordinate political activities against the incumbent president.[5]

One result has been a distinct absence of the *regular* revolutionary politics that previous chapters have shown is characteristic of patronal presidential polities. Thus when challenged by an uprising of a prominent business elite network in the Andijon province in 2005 that greatly resembled the kind of regionally concentrated uprising that sparked the Tulip Revolution in Kyrgyzstan and that in fact strongly appeared to be modeled on or inspired by those events, Karimov had full confidence that his officers and troops would obey his orders to fire on the crowd.[6] Each officer and soldier was sure that if he disobeyed the order, Karimov would be in place to punish him severely afterward. The result was a massacre that left, by some counts, close to a thousand dead.[7] Contrast this with Kyrgyzstan's Tulip Revolution, where a lame-duck syndrome and low presidential popularity led President Akaev's agents of state violence to defect and refuse to follow his orders after the outbreak of events, leaving him little option but to leave office and flee the country. Karimov then followed the Andijon bloodshed with a crackdown on what remained of autonomous civil society, expelling a number of foreign nongovernmental organizations, arresting opponents, and tightening media restrictions.[8] In general, to help prevent such uprisings from occurring and spreading, he has tended to reappoint regional leaders "every three years on average."[9] Some transformation has taken place in the nature of Uzbekistan's networks over time, as they have become decreasingly regionally based, with each of the most potent networks depending on important footholds in the capital city, usually formalized by some kind of state post or other connection to Karimov, and frequently developing assets and clients in a number of territories.[10]

---

[5] See the related discussion in Chapters 2, 4, and 12.

[6] On the origins of the Andijon network and what triggered its rebellion, see Lawrence P. Markowitz, *State Erosion: Unlootable Resources and Unruly Elites in Central Asia* (Ithaca, NY: Cornell University Press, 2013), pp. 117–23.

[7] Eric McGlinchey, *Chaos, Violence, Dynasty: Politics and Islam in Central Asia* (Pittsburgh: Pittsburgh University Press, 2011), chapter 4.

[8] *RFE/RL Newsline*, March 2, 2006; *RFE/RL Newsline*, March 7, 2006; *RFE/RL Newsline*, January 17, 2007.

[9] Alisher Ilkhamov, "Neopatrimonialism, Interest Groups and Patronage Networks: The Impasses of the Governance System in Uzbekistan," *Central Asian Survey*, v. 26, no. 1, March 2007, p. 77.

[10] Ilkhamov, "Neopatrimonialism," p. 77.

This is not to say that Karimov will not become vulnerable if he encounters a period of low popular support, as some indicate he already has.[11] But it is to say that cascades of elite defection are less likely to occur around elections because full dictatorship sharply reduces the potency of elections and formal term limits as focal points for their occurrence. What may be starting to increase the likelihood of other, essentially random events sparking mass protest and a downfall of the regime, however, is Karimov's age. With Karimov reaching 76 on January 30, 2014, elites have increasingly pressing cause to anticipate that a succession is nearing – they just do not know at precisely which age this will happen.

A succession struggle already strongly appears to be playing itself out. Experts have focused on several prominent networks vying to control the succession. One includes Prime Minister (since 2003) Shavkat Mirziyoyev and National Security Services head (since 1995) Rustam Inoyatov. Also important is a network under the patronage of Finance Minister Rustam Azimov.[12] A third network, however, has attracted much of the attention in recent years, that of Karimov's Harvard-educated elder daughter, Gulnara Karimova. Long speculated to harbor presidential ambitions, Karimova cultivated a high profile as not only a political figure (representing the country in the United Nations, among other things), but also a pop diva wannabe (under the stage name Googoosha)[13] and NGO leader (founding the Center for Political Research among other things). She was also widely reported to be the formal or informal patron of a large business network involved in everything from fashion to energy.[14] Some of the earliest signs of battle between these groups occurred when Karimov assigned Prime Minister Mirziyoyev to investigate leading businesses, soon after which an asset freeze was ordered on one of the firms reputed to be central to his daughter's business empire, Zeromax.[15]

After rumors circulated in March 2013 that Karimov had suffered a heart attack, which he and family members denied, a new phase of the succession struggle broke out spectacularly into the open – revealing that even the closest of kinship ties are not an absolute bond for patronal networks.[16] Shortly after the heart attack rumors, Gulnara Karimova appeared to go on the offensive, issuing multiple Twitter posts implying corruption on the part of Azimov.[17]

---

[11] McGlinchey, *Chaos, Violence, Dynasty.*

[12] Alisher Ilkhamov, "Uzbekistan Country Report," in *Bertelsmann Stiftung Transformation Index (BTI) 2012* (Gutersloh: Bertelsman Stiftung, 2012); Joanna Lillis, "Uzbekistan: Karimov Heart Attack Report Puts Succession in Spotlight," *Eurasianet*, March 26, 2013, 10:59.

[13] See http://realgoogoosha.com/.

[14] Farangis Najibullah, "Is Kyrgyzstan's Revolution Ready for Export?" *RFE/RL Features*, April 28, 2010; *TsentrAziia*, September 19, 2008, 18:47.

[15] Bruce Pannier, "Does PM's Rise, Energy Firm's Demise Shed Light on Uzbek Succession Question?" *RFE/RL Features*, May 20, 2010; Deirdre Tynan, "Zeromax's Woes in Tashkent: GooGoosha's Swan Song from Politics?" *Eurasianet*, May 20, 2010, 1:15.

[16] Lillis, "Uzbekistan."

[17] *CA-News*, March 27, 2013, 11:55; *CA-News*, April 2, 2013, 12:20.

Her fortunes soon began to turn for the worse, however. In July, after being named in a Swedish corruption scandal, she lost her post as her country's permanent representative to the United Nations in Geneva.[18] Then in September, her own younger sister, Lola Karimova-Tillaeva, told the BBC Uzbek-language service that her sister's chances of being elected president were "not great," adding that they had not met for more than twelve years because they were "completely different people."[19] In October, calamity struck: Uzbek authorities simultaneously shut down several television channels and then a series of radio stations understood to be under Gulnara's Terra Group's control – just before they were set to cover one of her highest-profile cultural events.[20]

Fascinatingly, Karimova fired back through her Twitter account, saying her father was being lied to, comparing him to Stalin, and even hinting strongly that her mother was involved in the occult.[21] Also on Twitter, she confirmed that one of her close associates had been arrested,[22] said that authorities were using coercion to prepare a corruption case against her Terra Group,[23] and posted video of prosecutors' raids of a chain of "Nirvana" stores owned by a close associate and rumored boyfriend.[24] Perhaps most remarkably, she openly accused Inoyatov of attacking her as part of his "struggle to become Uzbekistan's next president," saying he was frightened by her popular support. She went on to accuse security forces of torture, even posting a medical record of someone who she said had been a victim.[25] Karimova did not stop with that, also accusing Inoyatov's security services of being engaged in the smuggling of alcohol and cigarettes.[26] With her media shut down and key assets arrested, however, she soon relented. "I am not a politician," she now tweeted, saying that she instead preferred to be an "artist, poet, or photographer."[27] The presidency, she said in a show of humility, was for "strong men chosen by the people."[28]

Even with one contending network suffering a major battle loss, tensions among the others in Karimov's single-pyramid system remained as of the time

---

[18] *CA-News*, July 15, 2013, 14:21.

[19] Lola Karimova-Tillaeva, "Matbuotda meni 'diktatorning qizi' deiishlari shakhsiiatimga oghir botadi," *BBC O'zbek*, September 25, 2013, 15:37 GMT.

[20] Petr Bologov, "Doch' Islama Karimova stala zhertvoi semeinykh razdorov," *CA-News*, October 26, 2013, 09:58.

[21] *CA-News*, October 24, 2013, 09:44; *CA-News*, November 1, 2013, 11:42; *RFE/RL*, October 30, 2013.

[22] *RFE/RL*, November 13, 2013.

[23] *RFE/RL*, November 7, 2013.

[24] *CA-News*, November 5, 2013, 14:09.

[25] *RFE/RL*, November 5, 2013; *RFE/RL*, November 1, 2013.

[26] Gulnara Karimova, Twitter post, November 4, 2013, 9:06 am, https://twitter.com/GulnaraKarimova, accessed November 5, 2013.

[27] *CA-News*, November 6, 2013, 11:57; Gulnara Karimova, Twitter post, November 5, 2013, 5:24 pm, https://twitter.com/GulnaraKarimova/status/397897294739427329, accessed January 29, 2014.

[28] *CA-News*, November 6, 2013, 11:57.

of this writing. And without even semicontested elections to resolve a succession, the chances that any random event could serve as a focal point for coordinated elite defection rise with each year in office when significant popular support is absent. Uzbekistan, then, might be a strong candidate for a Tunisia-style revolution, catalyzed unexpectedly by something as seemingly random as a fruit vendor setting himself afire in an event that for some reason crystallizes local outrage and generates a cascade of mass protest that then serves as a temporal focal point for elite defection from the incumbent leadership.

In Turkmenistan, with presidential elections eliminated altogether under Turkmenbashi, competition among elite networks was of the most muted form, with the regime doing everything it could to keep conditions that way. The main attempt at a challenge to his rule appears to have been a mysterious 2002 assassination attempt, after which Niyazov presided over a wave of arrests and prosecutions.[29] Thus when the Turkmen leader died rather suddenly (without previously being known to be incapacitated) in December 2006, the absence of either elections or the possibility of organized domestic opposition meant that the ensuing power struggle among elites took place behind closed doors and among a very narrow circle of players, much as it had in the USSR after Stalin. This made possible the selection of Turkmenbashi's dentist (and illegitimate son, if some rumors are to be believed) from his own Tekke tribal network, Health Minister and Deputy Prime Minister Gurbanguly Berdymukhamedov. The dentist thus won out over the person who had been next in the formal line of succession, parliamentary speaker Ovezgeldy Ataev, who was jailed soon thereafter for allegedly driving his wife to suicide. This maneuver was reportedly orchestrated by Akmurad Rejepov, who had been head of Turkmenbashi's personal guard since 1985 and had become the top adviser to the president, as described in Chapter 6.[30] Thus there was a struggle for succession after the leader died, but unlike in the hybrid regimes with at least some sphere for public politics, it took place behind the scenes in the form of elite network intrigues rather than in the public arena. It also played itself out extremely quickly.

While Berdymukhamedov restored the formality of elections, he maintained his predecessor's policy of not brooking any opposition whatsoever, and has not experienced anything even close to revolutionary activity.[31] He thus won an uncontested presidential election that formalized his status as Turkmen leader in February 2007 and then, consolidating his own personal power, jailed Rejepov himself and began systematically filling the security services and other positions

---

[29] *RFE/RL Newsline*, October 18, 2006.

[30] Dmitry Glymskov, "Polet dantista," *Ekspert*, no. 7, February 19–25, 2007, p. 85; *RFE/RL Newsline*, February 28, 2007.

[31] Signaling the futility of any challenge, copies of the "confession" of one of the alleged plotters from the 2002 assassination attempt, former Foreign Minister Boris Shikhmuradov, could be seen prominently for sale on Turkmenistan state bookstore shelves as late as November 2010 (author's field observations).

with close personal associates, including from his own village.[32] A visit to the country by the present author in 2010 revealed what appeared to be a personality cult emerging around the new president. While golden statues of the "head of the Turkmen" were still quite numerous, a few had been dismantled and images of the new president were quite widespread, with his face (which indeed resembles a younger-looking Niyazov) gazing even upon lucky passengers seated in internal airline flights. In February 2012, Berdymukhamedov defeated seven other candidates to win a new term as president, though these seven were all reported to have "praised his leadership in their campaigns," helping him garner 97 percent of the officially counted ballots.[33] Formally multiparty parliamentary elections were allowed for the first time in December 2013, but both of the parties allowed to compete supported the incumbent president.[34]

Patronal Presidencies without Lame Ducks: Kazakhstan, Tajikistan, Belarus

A second set of patronal presidential cases includes those that have continued to allow at least some genuine opposition to exist and even compete in presidential elections, but have experienced no significant competing-pyramid phase after the establishment of patronal presidential institutions and their initial single-pyramid systems in the mid- to late 1990s. The leaders of these territories, including Belarus, Kazakhstan, and Tajikistan, have one important trait in common: They have never encountered the lame-duck syndrome since their patronal presidential systems were firmly established (at least, not until very recently). In fact, in each case, the incumbent presidents secured the elimination of term limits or significant extensions of their legal time in office by orchestrating referenda to remove or extend them well in advance of actually reaching the limits.[35] This appears to have been possible for them not just because they had the required patronalistic apparatus, but also because at the time of their attempts to escape term limits, they wielded high enough popularity that the prospect of their continued rule would not spur significant public resentment and thus would not encourage elites from within their coalition to risk defecting to oppose it and try to seize power themselves. And even more generally, these presidents consistently made clear that they had no plans to leave office. Accordingly, defection was seen by elites to be very risky and unprofitable, and few of them dared challenge these presidents.

[32] John C. K. Daly, "Berdymukhamedov Moves to Eliminate Rivals after Foreign Policy Victories," *Eurasia Daily Monitor*, May 18, 2007; *Polit.Ru*, July 31, 2007, 17:55; *RFE/RL Newsline*, February 14, 2007; *RFE/RL Newsline*, May 17, 2007.

[33] *Associated Press*, printed by *theguardian.com*, February 13, 2012, 07:02 EST.

[34] *RFE/RL*, December 15, 2013.

[35] Pauline Jones Luong, "Politics in the Periphery: Competing Views of Central Asian States and Societies," in Jones Luong, ed., *The Transformation of Central Asia: States and Societies from Soviet Rule to Independence* (Ithaca, NY: Cornell University Press, 2003).

Kazakhstan under Nazarbaev

Kazakhstan supplies a classic case where a patronal president has sustained high popularity, has shown no signs of preparing to step down soon, and has accordingly presided over tight elite network coordination around a single-pyramid system.[36] His popularity has been rooted in personal charisma, strong economic growth (driven largely by the country's natural resource wealth) that has produced a steady rise in living standards for average Kazakhs, and his careful balancing of policies designed to provide political and economic advancement for ethnic Kazakhs along with close ties to Russia that were popular among the country's large ethnic Russian population.[37] Nazarbaev has also been highly attentive to avoiding the lame-duck syndrome. Thus in 2000, he signed the Law on the First President of Kazakhstan, which would give him powers even after leaving office should he ever do so.[38] In 2007, he presided over a constitutional amendment that eliminated term limits for the first president of the republic (that is, him).[39] Going still further, parliament in 2010 bestowed on Nazarbaev the legal status of "leader of the nation," which would allow him to veto all policy initiatives even after leaving formal presidential office and would protect him from future prosecution or even investigation.[40] Too modest to sign this piece of legislation himself, he nevertheless let it go into effect by declining to block it.[41] Capping it all off, he has declared that he has no successor and will stay in office as long as the people want him and his health permits.[42]

Nazarbaev has also reinforced expectations of his own pyramid's dominance by refining and tightening the particular manner in which the country's major networks are coordinated around his own personal authority as chief patron. Thus while he had been able to control parliament for more than a decade as documented in Chapter 6, in 2007 he tightened his grip. He eliminated single-member-district elections, switched to holding parliamentary elections only by

---

[36] Nazarbaev's popularity throughout the 2000s has been documented by multiple agencies, including IRI-Gallup (Joanna Lillis, "Citizens in Kazakhstan Are High on Nazarbayev, Tepid on Democratization," *Eurasianet*, May 26, 2010, 1:32 pm), as well as local agencies and experts (*RFE/RL Newsline*, March 20, 2008; Association of Sociologists and Political Scientists of Kazakhstan, "Est' li u oppozitsii Kazakhstana Shansy na uspekh?" *Respublika* [Kazakhstan], May 30, 2008, posted by *Central Asian News*, June 2, 2008, 19:58).

[37] Henry E. Hale, "Cause without a Rebel: Kazakhstan's Unionist Nationalism in the USSR and CIS," *Nationalities Papers*, v. 37, no. 1, January 2009, pp. 1–32; Sebastien Peyrouse, "The Kazakh Neopatrimonial Regime and Its Actors: Balancing Uncertainties among the 'Family,' Oligarchs and Technocrats," *Demokratizatsiya: The Journal of Post-Soviet Democratization*, v. 20, no. 4, Fall 2012, pp. 345–70; Edward A. D. Schatz, "Framing Strategies and Non-Conflict in Multi-Ethnic Kazakhstan," *Nationalism & Ethnic Politics*, v. 6, no. 2, Summer 2000, pp. 71–94; Edward Schatz, "The Soft Authoritarian Tool Kit: Agenda-Setting Power in Kazakhstan and Kyrgyzstan," *Comparative Politics*, January 2009, pp. 203–22.

[38] *RFE/RL Newsline*, July 24, 2000.

[39] *Polit.Ru*, May 18, 2007, 19:02.

[40] *RFE/RL News*, May 13, 2010.

[41] *Polit.Ru*, June 15, 2010, 08:28.

[42] *TsentrAziia*, June 9, 2008, 10:32.

party list, became leader of the new Nur Otan Party, dissolved the old parliament, and then called new elections that resulted in this party's winning 100 percent of the seats.[43] In the sphere of the economy, he presided over a massive consolidation of the country's assets under the control of his closest associates, including relatives. One noteworthy development was the emergence of the massive holding company Foundation for National Well-Being Samruk-Kazyna, which controlled huge shares of the country's economy (including the lucrative hydrocarbon sector) and counted Nazarbaev son-in-law Timur Kulibaev among its top formal leadership.[44] By some calculations, this entity controlled as much as 45 percent of the country's GDP,[45] and Sebastien Peyrouse reports that "there are virtually no key sectors of the economy in which the fund does not intervene."[46]

None of this means that there have been no challenges to Nazarbaev's single-pyramid system. As Barbara Junisbai's research has shown, competition for power and assets by networks within dominant presidential pyramids is to be expected, and it can sometimes result in challenges from elite networks that fear being squeezed out by the president's closest associates.[47] But with expectations that he will remain the dominant force long into the future, such challenges have not been able to convince a critical mass of other elites in the system to disobey Nazarbaev and shake his machine.

Thus the president has been able to marginalize summarily even the most powerful of these challenges. One of the biggest was a group of several major oligarchic and state-based networks, including Mukhtar Abliazov's Astana-Holding network and that of Pavlodar governor Galimzhan Zhakiianov, united under the banner of the Democratic Choice of Kazakhstan Party in 2001 to call for reforms and oppose the aggressive expansion of the network of Nazarbaev son-in-law Rakhat Aliev.[48] The Nazarbaev machine quickly marginalized it by not only mounting a negative publicity campaign in media it controlled, jailing Zhakiianov and Abliazov on formally unrelated charges that provided legal

---

[43] Barbara Junisbai, "A Tale of Two Kazakhstans: Sources of Political Cleavage and Conflict in the Post-Soviet Period," *Europe-Asia Studies*, v. 62, no. 1, March 2010, pp. 235–69; *Polit.Ru*, June 20, 2007, 14:40.

[44] Nikolai Kuz'min, "Proshche prostogo," *Ekspert Kazakhstan*, October 27, 2008, no. 42; *TsentrAziia*, October 13, 2008, 23:31.

[45] Sebastian Schiek and Stephan Hensell, "Seeing Like a President: The Dilemma of Inclusion in Kazakhstan," in Susan Stewart, Margaret Klein, Andrea Schmitz, and Hans-Henning Schroder, eds., *Presidents, Oligarchs, and Bureaucrats: Forms of Rule in the Post-Soviet Space* (Burlington: Ashgate, 2012), pp. 203–22, p. 213.

[46] Peyrouse, "The Kazakh Neopatrimonial Regime."

[47] Barbara Junisbai, "Market Reform Regimes, Elite Defections, and Political Opposition in the Post-Soviet States: Evidence from Belarus, Kazakhstan, and Kyrgyzstan, doctoral dissertation in Political Science, Indiana University, 2009; Barbara Junisbai, "Improbable but Potentially Pivotal Oppositions: Privatization, Capitalists, and Political Contestation in the Post-Soviet Autocracies," *Perspectives on Politics*, v. 10, no. 4, December 2012, pp. 891–916.

[48] Barbara Junisbai and Azamat Junisbai, "Democratic Choice of Kazakhstan: A Case Study in Economic Liberalization, Intraelite Cleavage, and Political Opposition," *Demokratizatsiya: The Journal of Post-Soviet Democratization*, v. 13, Summer 2005, pp. 373–92.

pretexts for keeping them out of elections, complicating its efforts to get on the ballot (which it did only in a bloc with the Communist Party of Kazakhstan), and harassing its campaign for the 2004 parliamentary election, but also pragmatically "exiling" Aliev to be ambassador to Austria so as to remove the main concern that united them. Many of the new party's initial supporters thus quickly backed away, and it failed to win any seats in the 2005 campaign, an outcome that sparked little public protest and was quickly followed by a court order of the party's dissolution.[49] Higher-level defectors also proved unable to shake Nazarbaev's power pyramid. Thus parliamentary speaker and head of the main pro-Nazarbaev party Zharmakhan Tuiakbai did manage to rally those already in opposition to unite behind him by defecting in 2004, but received only 7 percent of the vote in the 2005 presidential election to Nazarbaev's 91 percent.[50]

The most surprising defection of all was in 2007 and came from Nazarbaev's own son-in-law Rakhat Aliev in the affair known widely as *Rakhatgate*.[51] While details are disputed, by most accounts Aliev (after returning from Austria) continued to display too much presidential and/or business ambition – and to have used tactics that were too brutal – and was thus exiled anew by Nazarbaev. Aliev then went into bitter opposition and, as a consequence, was charged by Nazarbaev's regime with kidnapping and corruption, effectively forced into real exile, stripped of his main assets, and divorced by Nazarbaev's daughter, who also lost some of her own key holdings.[52] The authorities, or at least some of the networks in the ruling coalition, have sometimes been accused of more deadly tactics, as when a former top government official who went into opposition in 2004 was ruled to have committed suicide despite dying from multiple gunshot wounds.[53]

Nazarbaev tightened his personal grip on the most important networks in his single-pyramid system in other ways during the 2000s as well. As Peyrouse reports, these included continuing his family's management of economic assets (with the president's brother, Bolat, gaining control in the mining sector) and even sports clubs, "important places for all sorts of trafficking" as well as effective structures for monitoring certain youth circles (with Kulibaev leading the Kazakh Boxing Federation).[54] Thus while some elite groups treaded the tightrope between opposition and loyalism, for example, the KazKommertzbank

[49] Anthony Clive Bowyer, "Parliament and Political Parties in Kazakhstan," *Silk Road Paper*, Central Asia-Caucasus Institute and Silk Road Studies Program, Johns Hopkins University SAIS, Washington, DC, May 2008; Junisbai, "A Tale of Two Kazakhstans," p. 251; OSCE ODIHR, "Statement of Preliminary Findings and Conclusions," International Election Observation Mission, Republic of Kazakhstan Parliamentary Elections, September 19, 2004; *RFE/RL Newsline*, February 23, 2004; *RFE/RL Newsline*, June 17, 2004; *RFE/RL Newsline*, January 19, 2005.

[50] Bowyer, "Parliament"; Daniel Kimmage, "Nazarbaev Landslide Obscures Future Problems," End Note in *RFE/RL Newsline*, December 8, 2005.

[51] Junisbai, "A Tale of Two Kazakhstans," p. 254.

[52] Junisbai, "A Tale of Two Kazakhstans," p. 254; *RFE/RL Newsline*, May 25, 2007; *RFE/RL Newsline*, May 29, 2007.

[53] *RFE/RL Newsline*, November 14, 2005.

[54] Peyrouse, "The Kazakh Neopatrimonial Regime."

network of Nurzhan Subkhanberdin, this position was regarded as precarious. Instead, tighter coordination around Nazarbaev was the norm throughout the 2000s and into the next decade for the major oligarchic networks not considered part of the presidential family, such as Aleksandr Mashkevich's and Vladimir Kim's.[55] State-based wealth holders such as Tasmagambetov did the same, in his case shifting from one top post to another, most recently becoming mayor of the capital city Astana in 2008.[56] Indeed, Nazarbaev regularly shuffled many of the most important figures among key state posts, allowing each one to retain opportunities for power and wealth while reducing the chances that any one of them could gain authority that might start to rival his own or become seen as a clear successor.[57] All this increasingly tended to give "family" network members the upper hand after 2000, with close Kulibaev associates allowed to hold on to the post of prime minister (Karim Masimov) for 2007–12 and again starting in 2014 and leadership of the National Bank of Kazakhstan (Grigory Marchenko) for most of the period from 1999 until October 2013.[58]

Perhaps as in Smirnov's Transnistria, however, the question of succession has been growing more acute as Nazarbaev grows older and approaches the inevitable.[59] But with Nazarbaev popular enough essentially to be a kingmaker, able to lend enough public support to whomever he chooses to make that person likely to win even in a free and fair election, much speculation in Kazakh elite circles has centered around whom he will designate as his heir and when. For a time, the object of such speculation was his daughter Dariga, who actually said at one point that she would not rule it out.[60] But it was she who was married to Aliev, and Rakhatgate removed her from the position of odds-on favorite.[61] The succession speculation has not disappeared, however, but largely transferred to others in Nazarbaev's inner circle, including Kulibaev and even the president's two grandsons through Dariga.[62]

Nazarbaev is caught in a difficult situation and clearly recognizes the danger. By tipping his hand about his preference for successor, he could render himself a lame-duck as elites rush to coordinate around the new rising leader and simultaneously catalyze desperate defections from those convinced there would be no place for them in the new leadership. This explains not only his emphatic statements that there is no successor, but also his amassing of personalized formal powers designed to last even if he leaves the presidency. His

---

[55] Peyrouse, "The Kazakh Neopatrimonial Regime."

[56] Schiek and Hensell, "Seeing Like a President," pp. 208–9.

[57] Schiek and Hensell, "Seeing Like a President," pp. 211–13.

[58] *CA-News*, October 1, 2013, 16:02; *RFE/RL Newsline*, January 11, 2007; Peyrouse, "The Kazakh Neopatrimonial Regime."

[59] Joanna Lillis, "Kazakhstan: PM Tops Ranking of Influential Kazakhs," *Eurasianet*, April 25, 2012, 5:20 am.

[60] *RFE/RL Newsline*, December 7, 2005.

[61] Farangis Najibullah, *RFE/RL* story reposted as "Central Asia: Ambition Often the Downfall of Powerful Presidential Relatives," *Eurasianet*, May 31, 2008.

[62] *Moskovskii Komsomolets*, November 21, 2008, reprinted in *TsentrAziia*, November 22, 2008, 08:20.

associates also recognize the danger of a succession crisis, moving in 2010 to stave it off by appointing him president for life, an initiative that Nazarbaev declined.[63] Elections are likely to become more and more risky for Nazarbaev's network as he ages or shows signs of ill health, especially if his popular support starts to wane. It remains to be seen whether this support will endure.

Perhaps starting to call Nazarbaev's popularity into question was the brutal 2012 crackdown by authorities on strikes in the resource-rich western oblast of Mangistau, reportedly opening fire on protesters. At least sixteen were said to have died in these clashes, with some claiming the toll was as high as seventy.[64] As the strikes had reflected long-simmering social problems there,[65] the crackdown sparked local outrage and fears within the regime that this could spread. This led authorities to suspend or shutter a set of media that reported independently on the events, to jail politicians and activists who supported or were involved in the protests, and even to shut down parties that did the same.[66] Nazarbaev son-in-law Kulibaev then lost his job as head of the megaholding Samruk-Kazyna, which manages the energy sector in the territory where the strikes occurred and whose leadership came under public criticism by the appointed new manager.[67] Several months later, his close associate Masimov was shifted out as prime minister, though made head of the president's administration and eventually returned to the post in 2014.[68] In another sign that the incumbent leadership was worried about the possibility of growing dissatisfaction, it called a snap parliamentary election for January 2012, with 81 percent of the official vote producing a parliamentary majority for the propresidential Nur Otan Party for at least one more legislative term.[69] This situation remained more or less unchanged through mid-2014.

Tajikistan under Rahmon(ov)

Tajikistan has also largely managed to avoid a lame-duck syndrome during the period in question (at least, until late 2013), though it started from conditions that were much more difficult than Kazakhstan's due to its civil war, which formally ended only in 1997. In the first part of the 2000s, Rahmonov's single-pyramid dominance was reinforced by the significant popular support he had won for having finally restored stability to Tajikistan and having successfully drawn a large share of even former opposition field commanders into a broad coalition government with international support.[70] Rahmonov

[63] *RFE/RL News*, June 3, 2010.
[64] *RFE/RL*, February 16, 2012; Robert Jones, "Kazakh Massacre Cover-Up," *The Moscow Times*, May 27, 2012.
[65] Nate Schenkkan, "Kazakhstan: Astana at a Turning Point," *Eurasianet*, March 26, 2012, 2:28.
[66] *RFE/RL*, November 22, 2012; *RFE/RL*, November 26, 2012.
[67] *RFE/RL*, February 16, 2012.
[68] *Polit.Ru*, September 24, 2012, 14:23.
[69] Joanna Lillis, "Kazakhstan: Genuine Pluralism Remains Elusive as Observers Slam Election," *Eurasianet*, January 16, 2012, 1:03 pm.
[70] On Rahmonov's perceived popularity, see Freedom House, *Nations in Transit 2004*, http://unpan1.un.org/intradoc/groups/public/documents/NISPAcee/UNPAN017051.pdf (accessed February 20, 2006).

traded on this popularity in 2003 to have constitutional amendments approved by referendum that not only increased the formal powers allotted to the president, but allowed the president two seven-year terms instead of one, which had been the agreement in the 1997 peace accords. Since the term count was only to begin with the *next* presidential election, scheduled for 2006, Rahmonov effectively secured himself the right to serve two more terms in office, meaning that he would not start to enter a lame-duck phase until after the presidential elections of 2013.[71] Expected to be firmly in place long into the future, Rahmonov was able to ensure that Tajikistan's most important elite networks generally coordinated their activities around him or were marginalized by the concerted action of other elites who did not want to wind up outside his favor.[72] He thus was able increasingly to integrate the most important former warlords of nearly all stripes into his regime and easily to divide and conquer those who tried to organize resistance, a process that Jesse Driscoll models formally with quantitative evidence.[73] For example, Rahmonov in 2005 arrested Yakub Salimov, one of his own former commanders with a power base in Dushanbe who had initially after the war been made interior minister and was later put in charge of state customs.[74] Likewise, Gaffor Mirzoev, who was from Kulob and as Chapter 5 noted had translated his warlord capital into positions as presidential guard chief and antidrug agency head, was jailed in 2004.[75] The fact that he was from Kulob as the president was indicates that regional identity (in the sense of an imagined community) was far from being the dominating feature of Tajik elite politics, with patronal politics much more important.

This account helps us understand what is otherwise a striking puzzle: Tajikistan held parliamentary elections on the very same day as did Kyrgyzstan in 2005 (February 27) and both elections were judged by the international community as having been unfair, but only Kyrgyzstan's elections sparked mass unrest and a revolution.[76] This is especially puzzling because with Tajikistan

---

[71] *Polity IV Country Report 2010: Tajikistan*, http://www.systemicpeace.org/polity/Tajikistan2010. pdf, accessed January 15, 2012.

[72] On the mix of incorporation and marginalization, see Markowitz, *State Erosion*, chapter 5.

[73] Jesse Driscoll, "Commitment Problems or Bidding Wars? Rebel Fragmentation as Peace Building," *Journal of Conflict Resolution*, v. 56, no. 1, February 2012, pp. 118–49. For more detail on the process and context, see John Heathershaw, *Post-Conflict Tajikistan: The Politics of Peacebuilding and the Emergence of Legitimate Order* (London: Routledge, 2009).

[74] Martha Brill Olcott, *Tajikistan's Difficult Development Path* (Washington, DC: Carnegie Endowment, 2012), p. 77.

[75] Olcott, *Tajikistan's Difficult Development Path*, p. 77.

[76] On the Tajikistan election, see Zafar Abdullaev and Kambiz Arman, "To the Rulers, Victory," *Transitions Online*, February 28, 2005, and the OSCE's final report, available at http://www. osce.org/documents/html/pdftohtml/14852_en.pdf.html (last accessed February 19, 2006); K. F. Boboev, *Politicheskie partii Tadzhikistana na vyborakh 2005 goda* (Dushanbe: Irfon, 2006), pp. 6–34. On the centrality of the election to Kyrgyzstan's revolution, see in particular work by Scott Radnitz ("What Really Happened in Kyrgyzstan?" *Journal of Democracy*, v. 17, no. 2, April 2006, pp. 132–46; *Weapons of the Wealthy: Predatory Regimes and Elite-Led Protests in Central Asia* [Ithaca, NY: Cornell University Press, 2010]) and works cited in the previous chapter.

still recovering from a civil war, it was widely regarded as at least as weak a state as was Kyrgyzstan at that time and at least as poor, isolated, and divided, with weak centralization giving local actors the potential to mobilize local resources in protest as in Kyrgyzstan had they chosen to do so. If revolutions are caused by state weakness and/or protest against corrupt elections, as many theories suggest, then, one should have expected these elections to have been more likely to generate an uprising in Tajikistan than Kyrgyzstan. This should have been especially the case if demonstration effects were at work causing the weakest regimes to succumb to color revolutions in light of the examples so recently provided by Serbia, then Georgia, then Ukraine.

A patronal politics perspective resolves this puzzle. Prior to these simultaneous elections, Kyrgyzstan's President Akaev not only was unpopular and thus unable to endow an heir with enough mass support to hope to win, but had announced he would abide by constitutional term limits and leave office later that same year. Rahmonov, on the other hand, faced no term limits anytime soon, was not widely expected to leave office for any other reason, and wielded greater public support than did Akaev at that time.[77] Tajikistan's elites, expecting to have to contend with Rahmonov as president long into the future, thus had much stronger incentive to toe the presidential line and not to stick their necks out against him. This left both the organized opposition and any discontented masses few resources and little opportunity to challenge the incumbent.

Indeed, firmly atop his presidential pyramid, sending no signals of planning to leave office, and not facing a constitutional end to his reign until 2020, Rahmonov (who renamed himself Rahmon in 2007, shedding the typically Russian ending "-ov") comfortably secured reelection in 2006 and continued to dominate parliament with his People's Democratic Party of Tajikistan. Following a pattern observed in many of these states in the 2000s, Rahmon's own relatives came to play increasingly prominent roles in the polity and economy. For example, by 2011 his brother-in-law (Hasan Sadulloev) was running Orienbank, the country's largest bank. Among his nine children, his daughter Ozoda had become deputy foreign minister and his son Rustam had served in the Dushanbe City Council, the Central Committee of the dominant party, and the State Customs Committee (heading an antismuggling department) and controlled a major Internet provider.[78] As a patronal logic of divide and rule can be useful even when it comes to disputes among relatives who might otherwise develop overly lofty ambitions, as both Kazakhstan and Uzbekistan demonstrate, Rahmon's status as anything but a lame-duck helped him weather even a scandal when son Rustam was widely rumored to have shot his maternal uncle Sadulloev,[79] by some accounts in a dispute over control of Orienbank.[80]

[77] TOL, "Sidelining the Opposition," *Transitions Online*, February 26, 2005; Freedom House, *Nations in Transit 2004*.

[78] *Kommersant – Vlast'*, no. 36, September 15, 2009; Olcott, *Tajikistan's Difficult Development Path*, pp. 5, 15, 94.

[79] *Eurasia Insight*, "Tajikistan: Who's in Charge?" May 16, 2008.

[80] Olcott, *Tajikistan's Difficult Development Path*, p. 15.

Instead, Rustam continued to acquire assets, including being tapped head of the country's soccer federation in early 2012.[81] Rahmon's network also managed finally to establish control over Tajik Aluminum after a hard-fought struggle with the network that had previously controlled it.[82]

While his family has increasingly become the core of the single-pyramid system, as of 2014 the system still involved other important networks. The most prominent other network in the system, in something of a rivalry with the networks based in the president's own family, is that of Mahmadsaid Ubaidulloev, who is, like Rahmon, from the Kulob region. Since 2000, he has chaired the upper house of parliament and simultaneously served as mayor of the capital city, with a hand in a variety of businesses believed by some to include involvement in narcotics trading.[83] Others kept lower profiles. Turajonzoda, the former Islamic leader and head of opposition forces during the civil war, who joined the pyramid after the 1997 peace settlement, held a seat in parliament but generally maintained a low profile,[84] content to remain financially well enough off to be listed by one estimate among the " 100 Richest Tajiks."[85]

The system as a whole greatly resembled the single-pyramid systems in other republics in several additional ways. The president is reported to appoint personally not only each head of regional administration, but also chief physicians at major hospitals and university rectors, among others.[86] Media, especially television and radio, not only remain tightly controlled, but are relatively sparse and provide very little coverage of politics at all, with few elites bothering to risk running afoul of the official line. This is even the case for newspapers, of which there did not even exist a daily as of 2012. Some opposition publications have consistently been allowed to function, as is typical in hybrid regimes, though under pressure.[87] Similarly, while Rahmon has not taken the Uzbek and Turkmen route of shutting opposition down or out of elections entirely, his regime has imprisoned some prominent rivals, including Mahmadruzi Iskanderov (Democratic Party of Tajikistan leader) and ex–Interior Minister Yakub Salimov – both in 2005, the year before Rahmon's reelection.[88] With others weeded out, the Islamic Renaissance Party became Rahmon's chief formally organized opposition, a situation that served his electoral interests since many in the country saw the specter of an Islamic state as more concerning

[81] *RFE/RL*, January 5, 2012.
[82] Olcott, *Tajikistan's Difficult Development Path*, pp. 181–210.
[83] Olcott, *Tajikistan's Difficult Development Path*, p. 16–17; *RFE/RL News*, April 23, 2010.
[84] Analyst, author's interview, Dushanbe, June 17, 2011.
[85] As rated by the news agency Avesta. See Farangis Najibullah, "In Tajikistan, Politicians and Their Friends Dominate '100 Richest' List," End Note, *RFE/RL Newsline*, April 11, 2008.
[86] Konstantin Parshin, journalist, author's interview in Dushanbe, June 16, 2011.
[87] Olcott, *Tajikistan's Difficult Development Path*, pp. 23, 36.
[88] Olcott, *Tajikistan's Difficult Development Path*, p. 32.

than his rule; the IRP thus functioned much as the Communist Party in Russia has done, as a seemingly conveniently "unelectable" opposition that could be safely allowed to maintain a certain prominence and to contest elections regularly.[89]

Expectations of his continued rule also helped Rahmon weather a subsequent major drop in his popularity and secure reelection in November 2013. The drop in popular support occurred during the later 2000s as economic and other problems mounted, including electricity shortages that combined with a rough winter in 2007–8 to contribute to "the illness and death of hundreds and possibly even thousands of elderly citizens, newborns, and young children."[90] Martha Brill Olcott reports (on the basis of a public opinion poll taken in the country by the International Foundation for Electoral Systems) that Rahmon's mass support had substantially recovered by 2010, largely because people still viewed the present period favorably in comparison with the time of civil war.[91]

Perhaps taking no chances, Rahmon for the first time stood for reelection without any true opposition on the ballot. The country's main opposition forces, including the Islamic Renaissance Party and the Social Democratic Party of Tajikistan, united in advance of the election and chose a prominent nonpolitician to represent them in the race, Oinihol Bobonazarova.[92] She pledged that if she won, she would not serve out her term, instead dismantling the authoritarian system and laying the groundwork for truly democratic elections.[93] In the face of obstacles set up by the regime, however, she failed to collect enough signatures to get on the ballot.[94] This left only a handful of minor figures on the ballot, none regarded as significant or true opposition.[95] Rahmon then went on a tour of the country's regions, concluded a long-term deal to keep a Russian military base in the country, and presided over reportedly widespread election violations, ultimately claiming 84 percent of the officially counted votes.[96] Almost immediately after his victory, he replaced the prime minister, shuffled other officials, and appointed his own son head of the Customs Service, a potentially

---

[89] Parshin interview 2011. Of course, the risk is that what once seemed unelectable could over time become electable, undermining the strategy.

[90] Quotation from Olcott, *Tajikistan's Difficult Development Path*, p. 6. On other information in this paragraph, see also *Kommersant*, May 28, 2008; David Szakonyi, "Tajikistan: Not Protesting Enough," *Transitions Online*, July 16, 2008; Christopher Walker, "East: The 'Leader for Life' Governance Model," *RFE/RL Features*, February 29, 2008.

[91] Olcott, *Tajikistan's Difficult Development Path*, p. 8.

[92] *RFE/RL*, September 9, 2013.

[93] *RFE/RL*, September 10, 2013.

[94] *RFE/RL*, October 14, 2013; David Trilling, "Tajikistan's Opposition Challenger Forced Out of Presidential Race," *Eurasianet*, October 11, 2013, 3:50 am.

[95] *RFE/RL*, November 7, 2013; Trilling, "Tajikistan's Opposition."

[96] *CA-News*, October 28, 2013, 11:26; *Polit.ru*, October 1, 2013, 11:20; Konstantin Parshin, "Tajikistan: Population Votes in One-Man Race," *Eurasianet*, November 6, 2013, 1:25 pm; *RFE/RL*, November 7, 2013.

very lucrative position in a highly patronalistic polity.[97] Appointments of more relatives to state posts continued through mid-2014.[98]

With his reelection in late 2013, however, Rahmon entered his constitutionally final term in presidential office. The logic of patronal politics would thus suggest he is likely to become a prime "candidate" for ouster, though most likely as the actual end of his seven-year term approaches. Of course, much is also expected to depend on whether he can sustain strong popular support; given Tajikistan's poverty, this might be a difficult proposition.

Belarus under Lukashenka

Aliaksandr Lukashenka's regime in Belarus, widely branded "the last dictatorship in the heart of Europe,"[99] has survived for nearly two decades despite major efforts by opposition and transnational democracy-promotion networks to orchestrate a "color revolution" there using essentially the same techniques that seemed to have worked elsewhere.[100] While this longevity surely owes in part to the series of political machine tactics that Vitali Silitski memorably branded "preemptive authoritarianism,"[101] underpinning the president's success in these measures has been that he has managed both to avoid a lame-duck syndrome and to remain quite popular, far more so than potential rivals.[102] Moreover, these circumstances have been sufficient even in the absence of a dominant "party of power," which he has consistently eschewed as unnecessary throughout his tenure.[103] His allies did, however, create a "White Russia" (Belaia Rus') movement in 2007 that some argued served as a kind of reserve structure, ready to be pulled off the shelf should he need it.[104]

Analysts have found his public support to draw on a wide variety of factors, especially his common-man personal charisma, relatively strong economic performance under his watch (including an economic recovery that started much earlier in the 1990s than it did elsewhere in the former USSR), rhetoric and symbolism playing on widespread sympathy with Russia and nostalgia for the USSR (though increasingly replaced by a nationally oriented symbolism), substantial wages and social transfers that are regularly paid, visible

---

[97] *CA-News*, November 30, 2013, 13:24.

[98] *RFE/RL*, May 15, 2014.

[99] Condoleezza Rice, quoted by the Associated Press, April 22, 2005, as posted by http://www.foxnews.com/story/0,2933,154146,00.html, accessed December 22, 2012.

[100] Elena Korosteleva, "Questioning Democracy Promotion: Belarus' Response to the 'Colour Revolutions,'" *Democratization*, v. 19, no. 1, February 2012, pp. 37–59.

[101] Vitali Silitski, "Preempting Democracy: The Case of Belarus," *Journal of Democracy*, v. 16, no. 4, October 2005, pp. 83–97.

[102] Emphasizing the importance of his consistent popular support in sustaining his regime's stability through at least 2011 is Korosteleva, "Questioning Democracy Promotion."

[103] Lukashenka is quoted at length on this subject in Roy Medvedev, *Aleksandr Lukashenko: Kontury Belorusskoi modeli* (Moscow: BBPG, 2010), pp. 121–3.

[104] Korosteleva, "Questioning Democracy Promotion," p. 44; *RFE/RL Newsline*, November 19, 2007.

campaigns against present or potential "oligarchs," and a sense that there is no alternative, a sense sustained by aggressive efforts to tarnish or politically eliminate potential rivals.[105] Independent surveys (including some conducted out of neighboring Lithuania) show that this has been remarkably consistent, with short-lived dips occurring mainly in the early 2000s before a new rise in wages and pensions kicked in and again in 2011 with a new drop in economic performance – though in neither case did his standing fall below 20 percent of the whole population, and he was still far ahead of all others during these periods.[106]

This public backing is supported not only by tight control over information and policy making, but crucially also by an elaborate method of preparing for each presidential campaign intended to make sure the regime is sustaining support by responding to the most acute social needs. Roughly a year in advance of the election, teams of several dozen officials (representing government, the intelligence organs, and his administration) are sent off to each district to work closely with local officials, listen to local complaints through public walk-in reception hours and other channels, monitor activities there, and prepare state actions to address these concerns in conjunction with pollsters. These generate recommendations that then shape long-term economic plans for the country that are a major part of Lukashenka's public politics.[107]

Lukashenka has avoided lame-duck status for two main sets of reasons. For one thing, he remains relatively young (born in 1954, he was less than forty when first elected), has been healthy (famously still playing hockey), and has never stated that he will not run for reelection, leading people instead to expect him to remain in office long into the future.[108] Also importantly, he has avoided the temporal focal point for coordinated elite actions in anticipation of a succession that term limits can provide. While the constitution he originally pushed through parliament in 1996 included a two-term limit, he moved to eliminate this constraint at a time when he still could claim the formal right to run in one more election[109] and when he still had substantial public support. He did

---

[105] Verena Fritz, *State-Building: A Comparative Study of Ukraine, Lithuania, Belarus, and Russia* (Budapest: Central European University Press, 2007), p. 214; Korosteleva, "Questioning Democracy Promotion," especially pp. 48–9; David Marples, "Outpost of Tyranny? The Failure of Democratization in Belarus," *Democratization*, v. 16, no. 4, August 2009, pp. 756–76; David Rotman, survey specialist, author's interview, Minsk, December 11, 2008.

[106] "Rezhim Lukashenko posle vyborov: chto dal'she?" report by a local independent analyst dated June 2006 given to author in Minsk, December 11, 2008; and IISEPS (Lithuania) data on intended voting in Belarus presidential elections, http://www.iiseps.org/trend.html, accessed December 22, 2012.

[107] Author's field notes, Minsk, December 2008. For example, see *Belorusskoe Telegrafnoe Agentstvo (BELTA)*, May 31, 2010, 07:07.

[108] E.g., his statement to AFP reported in *Ukraiins'ka Pravda*, November 27, 2008, 18:15.

[109] While the opposition contested this, many post-Soviet presidential term limits have been counted from the first full term after the constitution was adopted; that method would make Lukashenka's 2001 election his first under the constitution.

so by announcing only in September 2004 that a referendum would be held in October to remove term limits. Thus while his critics had little time to prepare a "no" campaign, his own backers successfully mobilized substantial support for the change, with proponents found by independent pollsters to outnumber opponents by the time of the vote.[110] The official vote of 88 percent of the whole electorate was widely considered fraudulent, though an independent exit poll did find that far more people had backed the measure than not (49 percent to 29 percent, with 12 percent not answering and 10 percent not voting). Formal approval required, however, that 50 percent of the whole electorate (not just those voting) back the measure, so this exit poll created some ambiguity, and its margin of error is not clear. In any case, with such credible independent sources showing that a large majority of the electorate was supportive, deferential, or indifferent, neither elites nor masses mounted a significant challenge. For good measure, Lukashenka soon drove the offending polling agency out of the country, forcing it to relocate to Lithuania.[111] This same agency, IISEPS, did also report in early 2005 that 77 percent of the country's elites (including even 53 percent in the nonstate sector) expected Lukashenka to be around for "at a minimum" one additional full term as president.[112]

Wielding clear popular support and widely expected to be in office in the future to follow up on threats and promises, Lukashenka was in strong position to brandish all the political weaponry for which his power pyramid has become known. Opposition parties were allowed to exist and operate but were marginal in importance, and new party initiatives have generally not been registered since 1996.[113] After Lukashenka was reelected in 2001, a whole series of popular independent newspapers were shut down,[114] and many that remained were dropped from the state distribution monopoly on subscriptions.[115] In general, many media that were not directly controlled exercised self-censorship to preclude running into trouble with the regime.[116] Even though little privatization had taken place and private business occupied a minor position in the economy,[117] businesses were cowed out of backing opposition parties as vehicles for exercising influence.[118]

---

[110] "Komanda A. Lukashenko nakanune prezidentskikh vyborov: osnovnye tseli i personalii," report by a local independent analyst dated February 2006 given to author in Minsk, December 11, 2008.

[111] *RFE/RL Newsline*, October 22, 2004; *RFE/RL Newsline*, December 2, 2005; Andrew Wilson, *Belarus: The Last Dictatorship in Europe* (New Haven, CT: Yale University Press, 2011), p. 207.

[112] "Prezidentskie perspektivy Belarusi: Mnenie elity," IISEPS report, January 2005, IISEPS Web site, http://www.iiseps.org/1-05-1.html, accessed December 22, 2012.

[113] Former vice-chair of an opposition party, author's interview, Minsk, December 11, 2008.

[114] Vladimir Rovdo, "Spetsifika i evoliutsiia politicheskogo rezhima Respubliki Belarus'," *Acta Slavica Iaponica*, v. 21, 2004, pp. 144–80, p. 160.

[115] *RFE/RL Newsline*, November 16, 2005.

[116] Stanislav Shushkevich, head of the Hramada Party and former leader of Belarus, author's interview, Minsk, December 12, 2008.

[117] Fritz, *State-Building*, p. 217.

[118] M. F. Chudakov, A. E. Vashkevich, S. A. Alfer, M. K. Plisko, and A. O. Dobrovol'skii, *Politicheskie partii: Belarus' i sovremennyi mir*, 2nd ed. (Minsk: Tesei, 2005), pp. 182, 190.

A new law in 2005 formalized the KGB's right to search offices or apartments freely without warrants and to embed secret agents at will, and anyone who exposed these agents could get a prison term.[119] Lukashenka was also able to direct money through a special nontransparent fund that was admitted to exist as well as through proceeds from selling off seized illegal imports.[120]

Most horrific was a death squad that a defector later confirmed to exist, reported to be led by Lukashenka's longtime Security Council chief Viktar Sheiman together with the interior minister.[121] It was widely held responsible for the sudden and permanent disappearances of a series of major opposition figures in 1999 as the 2001 presidential elections approached. These included Yury Zakaranka, a former interior minister, who became a corruption whistle-blower and defected to the opposition; Viktar Honchar, an uncooperative central election chief who was fired and went into opposition; and Anatol Krasowski, a Honchar business associate. Also disappearing, in 2000, was Lukashenka's personal television cameraman for official events, who was reported to have betrayed him.[122] In 1999, one of Lukashenka's most prominent potential rivals fell dead suddenly of a heart attack.[123]

A signature behavior of Lukashenka's style of single-pyramid rule was the regular purging and shuffling of high-level elites. During the 2000s, nearly two dozen state investigative structures existed that could collect kompromat on state officials and economic leaders, "dirt" that could be used to keep them in line.[124] With such material in hand, Lukashenka frequently shuffled people in and out of very high-level positions, ranging from the directorships of flagship state firms to the heads of the KGB and his own presidential administration. This could take place by means of appointments, firings, and in some cases arrests.[125] This contrasts significantly with Russia and Azerbaijan in the 2000s, where the "stability of cadres" was instead the dominant strategy of managing the single-pyramid system.

The main changes in the network structure of Lukashenka's power pyramid during the 2000s were an increased "oligarchization" of politics and the rise of a network closely associated with his eldest son, Viktar. One of the most important networks since the start of his regime, that of Sheiman, was increasingly reported to be involved in profitable operations through its control over the KGB (Stsiapan Sukharenka) and presidential administration (Henadz Niavylhlas) along with the country's energy complex.[126] This network's fortunes diminished, however, with the rise of Viktar Lukashenka, who began in the Border Troops, Foreign Ministry, and Defense Industry and

[119] *RFE/RL Newsline*, May 25, 2005.
[120] Fritz, *State-Building*, pp. 231–2.
[121] Wilson, *Belarus*, pp. 190–1.
[122] Wilson, *Belarus*, pp. 190–1.
[123] Rovdo, "Spetsifika i evoliutsiia," p. 165.
[124] Rovdo, "Spetsifika i evoliutsiia," p. 165.
[125] Fritz, *State-Building*, p. 217; Wilson, *Belarus*, p. 208.
[126] Wilson, *Belarus*, p. 223.

gained a prominent position in construction and development before being tapped a presidential aide for security in 2005 and a Security Council member in 2007.[127] It was shortly after this that several of his close associates replaced Sheiman network members in the key posts of KGB chief (Vadzim Zaitsaw) and presidential administration (Uladzimir Makei),[128] with Sheiman himself even being replaced in 2008 with a person linked to Viktar Lukashenka (Viktar Zhadobin) after a mysterious explosion rocked an independence day celebration and injured dozens of people.[129]

With his machine firmly in place and no challengers from within it, Lukashenka went on to win crushing official victories in all elections in the 2000s through the time of this writing. In the 2000, 2004, 2008, and 2012 parliamentary elections, each of which was conducted with an entirely single-member-district system, not one true opposition candidate obtained a seat.[130] The full array of administrative tactics discussed previously were used to manipulate the outcomes, and efforts to protest were summarily suppressed.[131] The opposition fared little better in local elections, with "deputies from anything resembling the opposition" winning only 10 seats anywhere in 2010, for example.[132]

Presidential elections were somewhat more contentious as they were generally the focus of concerted and explicit opposition and transnational efforts to orchestrate Lukashenka's ouster through either elections or postelection protests, as in the color revolutions. The initial such attempt occurred with Lukashenka's first reelection in 2001, when opposition and Western organizations adopted a set of tactics "near identical" to the one that was applied to topple Serbian leader Slobodan Milosevic in 2000 and that accompanied revolutions in Georgia and Ukraine.[133] Seeking openly to replicate the Serbian experience, opposition figures rallied around a single opposition candidate (former trade union leader Uladzimir Hancharyk) and mobilized a youth movement, Zubr. While the officially announced 76 percent of the vote for Lukashenka was far greater than an IISEPS poll's finding that he actually got about 57 percent, fraud seemed not to have changed the overall outcome and inspired no major defections from the regime. Post-election protests went nowhere. As Andrew Wilson reports, Zubr was penetrated and disrupted by regime agents

[127] *RFE/RL Newsline*, January 11, 2007; Wilson, *Belarus*, pp. 223–4.

[128] With management purges in the energy complex taking place around the same time.

[129] David Marples, "Assessing the Terrorist Explosion in Minsk," *Eurasia Daily Monitor*, July 22, 2008, 12:00; Wilson, *Belarus*, pp. 223–4.

[130] Fritz, *State-Building*, p. 214; Medvedev, *Aleksandr Lukashenko*, p. 139; *Polit.Ru*, September 24, 2012, 10:31; Wilson, *Belarus*, p. 192.

[131] Fritz, *State-Building*, p. 214; David Marples, "Little Chance for the Disorganized Opposition in Belarus Parliamentary Elections," *Eurasia Daily Monitor*, August 5, 2008; David Marples, "Belarus Pressures EU for Closer Ties," *Eurasia Daily Monitor*, October 2, 2008; *RFE/RL*, September 25, 2012, 06:07; Wilson, *Belarus*, p. 227.

[132] Wilson, *Belarus*, p. 229.

[133] Ian Traynor, "U.S. Campaign behind the Turmoil in Kiev," *The Guardian*, November 26, 2004.

and Hancharyk failed to shed his image as a holdover associated with the special privileges of his union's Soviet past.[134] Valerie Bunce and Sharon Wolchik call this failed attempt a revolutionary "dress rehearsal" of essentially the same type that preceded successful democratic breakthroughs in Serbia and other color revolution countries.[135]

The dress rehearsal in Belarus was not sufficient for future success, however. The next presidential election, in 2006, also involved a concerted transnational effort to apply "color revolution" tactics to oust Lukashenka but also failed. In retrospect, having already seen the failure, many concluded that the opposition must not have employed the same model for election-centered mobilization that had toppled presidents in Serbia and the color revolution countries. But in fact this model was generally in place in Belarus in 2006. Not only did Western organizations and governments devote considerable effort and resources to ridding Europe of its "last dictator," but the opposition managed to unite around a single candidate (Aliaksandr Milinkevich) and explicitly adopted the methods of prior successful revolutions and even trained with their activists.[136] And at least some Western analysts bold enough to make an assessment looking at the opposition *prior to* witnessing its failure saw it as well coordinated and on the rise rather than dysfunctional and lacking a plan.[137] Surely, had the revolutionary attempt succeeded, these elements would have been identified in retrospect by many as evidence that the "color revolution" model of transnational democracy promotion had worked again.

Instead, the would-be revolutionaries' failure had much more to do with Lukashenka's dominance as a highly popular and decidedly vigorous (certainly not lame) "duck," and a lack of public support for the opposition. This was not for the want of opposition efforts. Andrew Wilson writes that multiple focus groups in spring 2005 found Belarus lacked any one issue that the opposition could use to mobilize the population against the regime.[138] Milinkevich's message of freedom, delivered in his allotted campaign-period time on central television and through Internet and door-to-door campaigning, did not strike a chord.[139] Accordingly, independent polls – including from Gallup and the International Republican Institute – showed a consistently large Lukashenka lead over all potential contenders, even after the opposition united around

---

[134] Medvedev, *Aleksandr Lukashenko*, p. 92; Wilson, *Belarus*, pp. 195–8.

[135] Valerie J. Bunce and Sharon L. Wolchik, *Defeating Authoritarian Leaders in Postcommunist Countries* (New York: Cambridge University Press, 2011), p. 200.

[136] Korosteleva, "Questioning Democracy Promotion"; Jan Maksymiuk, "Can Belarus's Opposition Unite to Challenge Lukashenka?" End Note, *RFE/RL Newsline*, October 4, 2005; *RFE/RL Newsline*, May 16, 2005; *RFE/RL Newsline*, August 26, 2005; Wilson, *Belarus*, p. 211.

[137] Celeste Wallander, "Candles, Denim, and the 16th of February," CSIS Web site under "Recent Commentary," February 15, 2006, http://www.csis.org/ruseura/commentary.

[138] Wilson, *Belarus*, p. 211.

[139] *RFE/RL Newsline*, January 24, 2006; *RFE/RL Newsline*, February 13, 2006; *RFE/RL Newsline*, February 23, 2006.

Milinkevich.[140] Lukashenka did all he could to reinforce this situation, using the massive media and campaign resources at his disposal to stress his own economic achievements and managerial experience and to brand Milinkevich a foreign stooge.[141] He was also not short on tricks, some dirty. These included calling the elections earlier than expected so that Milinkevich had less time to try to rally support and apparently framing an NGO by preparing a fake exit poll and citing it as part of a plot to overthrow the government after the election.[142] Thus while the official result giving Lukashenka 83 percent was not generally believed, independent pollsters (including IISEPS) still indicated the incumbent had won by far the most votes.[143]

With in-system elites and opposition both expecting beforehand that Lukashenka would win and having good reason to believe afterward that he did win (and to believe that others believed he won), the protests could not hope for success even when they turned out as many as ten thousand on election night and as many as fifteen thousand several days later. Elites in Ukraine had reason to defect during the 2004 protest standoff because they thought it had a good chance of succeeding, as described in Chapter 7. But in Belarus, when protesters were attempting to camp out on the central October Square, politically savvy small businesses decided to shut down rather than supply them with basics like toilet access, blankets, and opportunities to shop.[144]

Thus while it is easy in retrospect to call Milinkevich timid for trying hard to avoid confrontation and telling NGO-mobilized protesters to go home instead of mobilizing them for a long standoff in the streets,[145] his behavior also bespeaks an underlying expectation of failure that was generated by the factors given central attention in this chapter: Lukashenka's popular support and expectations that he would remain in power. To get some people into the streets to protest Lukashenka's overclaiming was one thing, but to conclude from this that the regime had a real chance of collapsing was another step entirely, and this fact impacted the behavior of both opposition and regime elites. While Wilson writes of Milinkevich that "temperamentally, he was simply not a revolutionary,"[146] surely neither was Ukraine's Viktor Yushchenko

---

[140] "Komanda A. Lukashenko nakanune Prezidentskikh vyborov: osnovnye tseli i personalii," report by independent local analyst, February 2006, given to author in Minsk, December 11, 2008; *RFE/RL Newsline,* July 21, 2005; *RFE/RL Newsline,* January 25, 2006.

[141] Jan Maksymiuk, "The Peculiarities of Political Discourse in Belarus," End Note, *RFE/RL Newsline,* March 7, 2006; Wilson, *Belarus,* p. 215.

[142] Center for Political Education, "The Fading Pillars of Power in Belarus: 100 Days of Milinkevich," report, Minsk, February 2006; *RFE/RL Newsline,* March 1, 2006; Wilson, *Belarus,* p. 217.

[143] Wilson, *Belarus,* p. 218.

[144] Wilson, *Belarus,* pp. 219–21.

[145] Bunce and Wolchik, *Defeating Authoritarian Leaders,* pp. 207–8; Stanislav Shushkevich, *Belovezhskii konsensus i Belarus' (Zametki pervogo),* unpublished book manuscript, Minsk, 2011, provided by the author, chapter 12; Wilson, *Belarus,* p. 220.

[146] Wilson, *Belarus,* p. 221.

before he wound up in a revolutionary situation that involved an unpopular lame-duck incumbent giving him a real chance to win. Bunce and Wolchik also note the absence of local-NGO-organized exit polls as a deviation from the "electoral model" of opposition-driven revolution, but these would not have helped since they in all likelihood would have shown a Lukashenka victory, as already noted.[147] In the end, Lukashenka easily put down the protest and arrested five hundred to a thousand people, jailing Milinkevich for a month and another candidate for more than two years.[148]

The December 2010 presidential election led to a similar result. Some had thought Lukashenka would run into trouble due to economic problems and a rise in tensions with Russia, whose leadership wanted him to be more pliable. Indeed, not only had the global financial crisis of 2008–9 forced a major devaluation of his currency relative to the dollar,[149] but in 2010 the Russian NTV channel available in Belarus broadcast a four-part negative documentary about his reign called "Krestnyi Bat'ko," a play on words comparing him to a mafia godfather.[150] Lukashenka had responded to these problems early on by seeking a warming with the West, releasing virtually all of the main political prisoners and then allowing opposition candidates to register for the election with hardly any filtering.[151] This time, however, the opposition was not coordinated, leaving multiple candidates in the race. As before, independent polls going into the election showed him far ahead of the field.[152] Also as before, the official result showed a gigantic Lukashenka victory (80 percent) while independent polls showed that he received far less, though still far more than other candidates.[153] After some thirty thousand turned out to protest, Lukashenka dramatically ended the liberalization, harshly cracking down, jailing almost all opposition candidates and over six hundred more.[154] While some were eventually released, others remained in jail for years.[155]

Lukashenka's standing in presidential election polls quickly recovered from its low of about 20 percent in late 2011, steadily rising to 37 percent by June 2013 in step with a rise in individuals' average income levels and up to 40 percent by March 2014.[156] While this was still below the 50+ percent he enjoyed

---

[147] Bunce and Wolchik, *Defeating Authoritarian Leaders*, p. 205.

[148] Wilson, *Belarus*, p. 220.

[149] David Marples, "Belarus Devalues Its Currency," *Eurasia Daily Monitor*, January 12, 2009.

[150] Ekho Moskvy radio Web site, July 17, 2010, 13:05, http://www.echo.msk.ru/news/696147-echo.html, access date January 30, 2014.

[151] Medvedev, *Aleksandr Lukashenko*, p. 138, *Polit.Ru*, August 21, 2008, 09:41; Wilson, *Belarus*, pp. 231.

[152] *Polit.Ru*, January 21, 2010, 12:20.

[153] Wilson, *Belarus*, pp. 233–4.

[154] Wilson, *Belarus*, pp. 234–5.

[155] *RFE/RL*, December 19, 2011, 15:08; *RFE/RL*, April 15, 2012, 14:51.

[156] IISEPS, "Dinamika reitinga samogo poriadochnogo Evropeiskogo politika," July 5, 2013, http://www.iiseps.org/analitica/551, accessed January 30, 2014; IISEPS, "Krymskaia sostavliaiushchaia reitingov A. Lukashenko," April 19, 2014, http://iiseps.org/analitica/570, accessed June 3, 2014.

at times prior to the December 2010 elections, it was still far higher than the ratings of any potential political rival.[157] Still less than sixty years old as of midsummer 2014, Lukashenka gave little indication he would be leaving office anytime soon. Rumors have increasingly circulated since the late 2000s that he is grooming one of his sons to succeed him eventually,[158] though he has denied this and few expect him to try to orchestrate something like it in the near future.[159]

Surviving Lame-Duck Syndromes: Russia, Azerbaijan, Nagorno-Karabakh

Chapter 7 demonstrated that all but one of the non-Baltic post-Soviet patronal presidents who have been toppled since the first appearance of single-pyramid systems in their polities suffered this fate only after they were already in some sense lame-ducks, but not all presidential networks that faced a lame-duck syndrome were ousted. The present section considers these survivors, presidents who became lame-ducks but still successfully ushered their chosen heirs into presidential office. They generally had one important factor in common: Either the sitting president or the handpicked successor enjoyed genuine and broad-based popularity relative to his opponents, providing for the successor's victory.

Indeed, an expectation that a leader is on his or her way out does not *in itself* guarantee that the opposition will win; it just makes a hard-fought succession struggle much more likely by reducing the likelihood that the sitting president will be in a position later to follow through on threats and promises made today. Who wins this struggle, as was described in Chapter 4, depends most fundamentally on relative degrees of popular support. This is because popular support strongly influences who gains and who loses administrative resources as elites whose networks control these resources decide where to place their bets. Victory does depend secondarily on factors like opposition tactics, incumbent strategy, and preexisting distributions of administrative resources. But such factors have some of their greatest effects precisely *by influencing popular support*. To be sure, patterns of public support can change in the course of a single election campaign in patronal presidential systems just as they can in democracies, though the opportunities for oppositions to make this happen are fewer given their typical lack of control over television. The subsections that follow consider the cases of patronal presidential networks that have survived moments of succession from the late 1990s through mid-2014, specifically those in Russia (2000, 2008, 2012), Azerbaijan (2003), and the latter's breakaway region of Nagorno-Karabakh (2007).

[157] IISEPS, "Eroziia obraza 'sil'nogo lidera,'" 2012, IISEPS Web site, http://www.iiseps.org/press2. html, accessed December 23, 2012.

[158] *Kommersant – Vlast'*, no. 36, September 15, 2009.

[159] *Polit.Ru*, December 11, 2012, 17:52.

Russia's Phase of Competing-Pyramid Politics: The Centrality of Popular Support

Russia nicely illustrates how shifts in public support for a patronal president can drive regime dynamics and strongly influence who wins the struggles when single-pyramid systems break down and competing-pyramid situations emerge. The Russian case is particularly useful in this regard because regular, reliable public opinion polls have consistently been available that let us nail down the degree of presidential popularity at any given time with confidence. The current subsection shows how a highly unpopular and physically ailing Yeltsin, able to pull together a loose single-pyramid system for the first time in 1996 when he was not a lame-duck, saw it unravel into a new competing-pyramid situation as he approached his presidential term limit and the question of succession loomed large. It also demonstrates how it was Putin's dramatic rise in public support that resolved the resulting crisis in the Kremlin's favor. The next subsection describes how public support and firm expectations he would remain in power were crucial to Putin's careful construction of a much more closed single-pyramid system during the 2000s. The subsection that follows turns to a discussion of the 2008–12 "Tandem" arrangement, where Putin served as prime minister and Dmitry Medvedev as president. It shows how Putin's and Medvedev's popularity helped the regime weather some dangerous tensions within the Kremlin's single pyramid as Putin left the presidency and how the separation of formal and informal power (in effect creating two closely aligned centers of patronal power) sustained a certain ferment in the political system. The final subsection focusing on Russia then shows how the decision for Medvedev to leave the presidency, creating another moment of expected presidential succession, helped produce the massive 2011–12 protest wave that shocked the regime, forcing it into a new round of concessions. It then describes the regime's "comeback," resulting in a new phase of political closure after Putin anchored himself once again in presidential office, a comeback that helped set the stage for Russia's dramatic 2014 bid to annex Crimea and destabilize post-revolutionary Ukraine.

After the emergence of a loose single-pyramid situation during Yeltsin's 1996 reelection as president, the point where Chapter 6 left off, new uncertainty about his political future quickly emerged. Yeltsin faced not only constitutionally embedded term limits, but also debilitating illness. In fact, he had suffered a massive heart attack prior to voting day, a fact not revealed until after the ballots were counted. With the succession question on the horizon, Russia's most important networks did not wait long after 1996 to begin openly mobilizing to influence it. After a great deal of jockeying for position, a formidable opposition coalition of networks had emerged by late summer 1999. Calling itself the Fatherland–All Russia bloc, it was coled by Russia's most powerful regional boss (Moscow Mayor Yury Luzhkov) and a widely liked former prime minister sacked by Yeltsin for political reasons earlier in 1999 (Yevgeny Primakov). Primakov's substantial popular support sealed the coalition, which boasted many of Russia's most influential provincial machines and the active support of key oligarchic concerns, such as Vladimir Gusinsky's Most Group, which owned one of Russia's top three television networks, NTV. Yeltsin effectively countermobilized only in August 1999, surprising observers by appointing the little-known Vladimir Putin his prime minister and then proclaiming him his preferred successor. So unknown was Putin that he could boast only 2 percent support in presidential polls immediately after his appointment.[160]

Anticipating a point of patronal presidential power transfer, Russia's regional and business elites were feverishly jockeying to pick the "winning horse," and only some initially bet on Putin. In terms of the potential for a patronal presidential network ouster, the Russia of summer 1999 looked a lot more like Ukraine in 2004 than like Kazakhstan in 2004. Moreover, for many observers, the Primakov-Luzhkov coalition was the odds-on favorite. The contest that played out in Russia during the fall of 1999 turned out to be a strikingly balanced competition, with each side possessing major administrative assets, including mass media, large financial flows, and regional political machines – a classic competing-pyramid situation.

Importantly, public opinion wound up being decisive in tipping the scales of this elite struggle to the side of the incumbents' pyramid. It did so in complex, dynamic relationship with administrative resources and campaign strategy. That is, the major coalitions of networks used what resources they had to influence public opinion, and the side that won more support came out the victor in the competing-pyramid situation. Very importantly, public opinion in this instance was not simply a function of who controlled media, because both sides had some media (including television) effectively in their pockets. This meant that part of the battle was about campaign teams' skill in framing and attracting attention, much as in democratic elections anywhere. As it turns out, pro-Kremlin media proved more effective in using slanted news and analytical coverage than did media that favored Fatherland–All Russia. This superiority in savvy was perhaps most evident with the highly entertaining show hosted by Sergei Dorenko, whose exposés, dripping with irony, dramatically exposed what was portrayed as a seemingly endless array of corruption schemes linked to Luzhkov and by association Primakov.

Even more important, however, was Prime Minister Putin's aggressive and highly popular response to the savage bombings of two apartment buildings in Moscow and to two explosions in other cities that terrorized the Russian population in September 1999. Regardless of whether one thinks his allies actually orchestrated the bombings, his sending the military into Chechnya sent his standing in the presidential polls skyrocketing, raising him from his 2 percent in August to nearly 50 percent in November. Figure 8.1 portrays the dramatic

[160] According to an August 20–4, 1999, nationwide survey by the VTsIOM agency, reported in *Russian Election Watch*, no. 2, September 1999, p. 1.

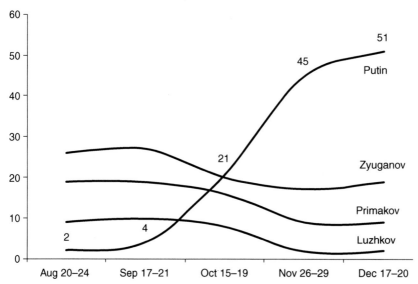

FIGURE 8.1. Late 1999 dynamics in electoral support (percentage of likely voters) for major presidential candidates in Russia.[161]

trend. With not even Luzhkov or Primakov at even half this level, surely thanks partly to Dorenko and his ilk, oligarchic and regional networks that had previously backed the Primakov-Luzhkov tandem began to have second thoughts. Ultimately, Fatherland–All Russia received a disappointing 13 percent of the vote in the 1999 parliamentary elections while the pro-Putin Unity bloc surged from nonexistence to 23 percent in less than three months. Yeltsin dealt the coup de grâce on New Year's Eve 1999 by resigning, bestowing the focal symbolism and formal powers of the patronal presidential office upon Putin, who became acting president pending early elections scheduled for March 2000. As all indicators pointed to a resounding Putin victory, virtually every major elite network returned to the Kremlin camp, which then waltzed to an easy victory.[162]

[161] The figures report the percentage of people who said they would vote for the given candidate if the presidential election were held at that time, calculated from the set of people who said they would vote. Data as reported by *Russian Election Watch* (a publication of Harvard University's Kennedy School of Government), September 1999 and January 2000 issues. *Russian Election Watch* obtained results directly from VTsIOM and from www.russiavotes.org.

[162] On these elections, see Timothy J. Colton and Michael McFaul, *Popular Choice and Managed Democracy* (Washington, DC: Brookings Institution Press, 2003); Henry E. Hale, "The Origins of United Russia and the Putin Presidency: The Role of Contingency in Party-System Development," *Demokratizatsiya: The Journal of Post-Soviet Democratization*, v. 12, no. 2, Spring 2004, pp. 169–94; Henry E. Hale, *Why Not Parties in Russia: Democracy, Federalism, and the State* (New York: Cambridge University Press, 2006); and very important work by Olga Shvetsova that deserves more attention than it has so far received, "Resolving the Problem of Pre-Election Coordination: The 1999 Parliamentary Election as Elite Presidential 'Primary,'"

A New Phase of Closure under Putin

Putin then developed and greatly strengthened the mechanism that Yeltsin had created and first mobilized to win reelection in 1996, using to tremendous advantage his new status as unrivaled patron with a fresh mandate and broad public support.[163] The most important change he made was in radically reducing the autonomy allowed to the subpatrons in the system and thereby tying them more tightly into the pyramid of power he established. In addition, one of Putin's first moves was to invest considerable resources in building up what would become Russia's first dominant party since the demise of the USSR. To understand why he put a priority on party building, we recall Putin's recent political experience: He had very nearly lost power to an opposition coalition of networks, and a key to his thwarting it had been to create an alternative party (the Unity bloc) that was able to beat it decisively in the "elite primary" that was the 1999 parliamentary election. Brilliantly confirming perceptions of his dominance, Putin built his new party not by simply developing Unity, but by merging it with the defeated elite network coalition represented in the Fatherland–All Russia movement. The result was the United Russia Party. With his own popularity higher than that of the party and not wanting the party to become so powerful he might one day not be able to control it, Putin opted not actually to become a member himself. But he strongly backed it in the 2003 Duma elections, helping it attain a deputy delegation large enough to change the constitution unilaterally and demonstrate his power pyramid's dominance in the lead-up to his 2004 reelection. The party also became his primary formal structure for reining in the major networks that had nearly ousted his own network in 1999–2000.[164]

One of the first sets of networks to be reined in was Russia's gaggle of regional political machines. Putin began almost immediately after his May 2000 inauguration, creating a set of seven federal districts (macroregions) led by his appointed envoys. The envoys were tasked with reducing the ability of governors to flout federal law and to bend local branches of federal agencies to their own will. By 2008, the center had largely eliminated regional laws that contradicted federal law (which by one estimate had been close to one-third of all regional laws at the start of his presidency) and reestablished a significant degree of federal control over local prosecutors, ministries, and courts in most regions.[165] Soon afterward, he stripped governors of their seats in the Federation Council, replacing them with a system of appointments in which the center wielded significant informal influence. This not only reduced the

in Vicki Hesli and William Reisinger, eds., *Elections, Parties and the Future of Russia* (New York: Cambridge University Press, 2003).

[163] A detailed case study of the system Putin created and performance implications in governance is forthcoming in a book in progress coauthored with Nikolay Petrov and Maria Lipman.

[164] Hale, *Why Not Parties in Russia?*

[165] Nikolai Petrov, ed., *Federal'naia Reforma 2000–2004, T. 2. Strategii, Instituty, Problemy* (Moscow: Moskovskii Obshchestvennyi Nauchnyi Fond, 2005); *Reuters*, May 14, 2000, Johnson's Russia List.

degree of governors' direct influence on federal politics as of 2001, but also denied them an important forum for meeting directly with each other in large numbers and coordinating their activities outside central initiatives. As of July 2003, another reform reduced the degree to which governors could get their own people elected to regional legislatures: At least one chamber of every region's legislature had to fill at least half of its seats through a competition of nationally registered parties' lists. Now governors had to reach agreement with a federal party to run their candidates under its label or lose control of those seats in the legislature. Accordingly, governors – previously reluctant to commit themselves to any one party – joined United Russia en masse and over the course of the 2000s orchestrated a majority for the party in every regional legislature.[166]

The most dramatic move against governors' independent power, however, occurred in the wake of the 2004 Beslan tragedy, after which Putin eliminated direct gubernatorial elections and replaced them with a form of appointment system. In this new system, the president's envoy nominated the candidate, who then had to be confirmed by a majority vote in the regional legislature. Partly because the center had made great headway in creating large United Russia Party fractions in the legislatures after the 2003 reform, no regional legislature ever rejected a Putin nominee during his first period as president. So powerful was the bandwagoning effect of Putin's growing power pyramid, driven by expectations of his future dominance, that the bulk of governors actually supported the very reform that stripped them of their direct electoral mandates.[167]

The result of all these reforms has been a radical reduction in the degree to which governors' networks can act autonomously to influence federal politics. One VTsIOM poll is telling of their reduced prominence: As of July 2008, only two governors were named by more than 4 percent of the Russian population as being best at solving key problems: Moscow Mayor Luzhkov and Kemerovo Governor Aman Tuleev.[168] By one count, all but one "red governor" by 2008 had been either replaced by more Kremlin-friendly individuals (for example, in Briansk, where the Communist Party's Yury Lodkin was replaced by United Russia candidate Nikolai Denin) or essentially turned into Kremlin loyalists (for example, Vladimir's Nikolai Vinogradov, who was ultimately expelled by the Communists). The lone Communist Party holdout as of early

[166] On the governors and United Russia, see Ora John Reuter and Thomas Remington, "Dominant Party Regimes and the Commitment Problem: The Case of United Russia," *Comparative Political Studies*, v. 42, no. 4, 2009, pp. 501–26.

[167] Donna Bahry, "The New Federalism and the Paradoxes of Regional Sovereignty in Russia," *Comparative Politics*, v. 37, no. 2, 2005, pp. 127–46; J. Paul Goode, *The Decline of Regionalism in Putin's Russia* (New York: Routledge, 2011); Gulnaz Sharafutdinova, "Gestalt Switch in Russian Federalism: The Decline in Regional Power under Putin," *Comparative Politics*, v. 45, no. 3, April 2013, pp. 357–76.

[168] *Kommersant*, July 24, 2008.

2008 was Volgograd's Yury Maksiuta, but he too succumbed before long.[169] As a result, virtually all gubernatorial networks were now firmly embedded in the Kremlin's own power pyramid and had much less will and ability than before to join any attempt to form a rival pyramid.[170]

The other set of major networks to be prodded into line much more strictly than before consisted of the oligarchs, with those controlling mass media coverage of politics among the first to be targeted. The major moves took place in Putin's first term. Initially, former Kremlin insider Boris Berezovsky, quite instrumental in Putin's rise to the presidency, was effectively forced to give up key assets (including control over the First Channel) and to leave the country for fear of prosecution. The next business network to fall was Vladimir Gusinsky's, which controlled the country's third-largest television channel (NTV) and had been a strong supporter of Fatherland–All Russia rather than Putin until the last stages of the 1999–2000 power struggle. A variety of charges led Gusinsky to flee Russia, and the partially state-owned Gazprom took control of NTV by calling in a Yeltsin era debt that NTV was unable to pay off. Business structures reputedly close to the Kremlin continued to acquire media assets under Putin's presidency far more often than they gave them up, by 2008 even owning relatively minor formerly independent outlets like REN-TV.[171] The press at this time remained relatively free despite the fact that many newspapers and magazines were acquired by Kremlin-connected business entities. But surveys showed throughout the 2000s that nearly 90 percent of all Russian citizens regarded television as their primary source of political information.[172]

Media were not the oligarchic networks' only source of influence, of course, and Kremlin forces accordingly took other steps to ensure that business worked in concert toward the national objectives set by the president. The most dramatic move was the highly visible October 2003 arrest of Mikhail Khodorkovsky, at the time Russia's richest man and chief of the Yukos corporate empire.[173] While the notion that his business had engaged in illegal activity (as with charges against Berezovsky and Gusinsky) was credible, observers were widely doubtful that Khodorkovsky and his circle were the only or even the most guilty parties. Those who acted in a more loyal fashion to the authorities were generally not facing such problems with law enforcement agencies.

[169] *Kommersant-Vlast*, January 21, 2008, p. 24.

[170] Grigorii Golosov, "The Regional Roots of Electoral Authoritarianism in Russia," *Europe-Asia Studies*, v. 63, no. 4, June 2011, pp. 623–39.

[171] Robert Coalson, "NTV's Past Points toward REN-TV's Future," End Note, *RFE/RL Newsline*, March 4, 2008.

[172] According to the 2008 Russian Election Studies (RES) survey, the figure just after the presidential election of that year was 89 percent. See Henry E. Hale and Timothy J. Colton, "Russians and the Putin-Medvedev 'Tandemocracy': A Survey-Based Portrait of the 2007–8 Election Season," *Problems of Post-Communism*, v. 57, no. 2, March/April 2010, pp. 3–20.

[173] See Richard Sakwa, *Putin and the Oligarchs: The Khodorkovsky-Yukos Affair* (London: I. B. Tauris, 2014). On the energy sector more generally, see Stefan Hedlund, *Putin's Energy Agenda: The Contradictions of Russia's Resource Wealth* (Boulder: Lynne Rienner, 2014).

In fact, the Khodorkovsky arrest was preceded by a number of other Kremlin moves designed both to cow and to coordinate business networks that could potentially become important players in politics. In 2000, for example, Putin was reported to have met with business leaders and, it was widely believed, promised to leave them in control of their assets so long as they did not operate against Kremlin wishes in politics. One theory is that it was this "pact" that Khodorkovsky broke, precipitating his arrest.[174]

Importantly, the Kremlin worked not only to prevent unwanted business support for opposition, but also to coordinate business political activity so that it was not divided among different Kremlin loyalists competing for influence under Putin's wing. In the run-up to the 2003 Duma election, the presidential envoys in the federal districts were very active in instructing business as to which pro-Kremlin candidates to back in the single-member-district Duma elections in an effort to preclude splits that could let an opposition candidate win.[175] United Russia served as an important structure for coordinating these elite efforts around specific candidates in all kinds of elections, district- and party-list-based.[176] Partly as a result of these actions and policies, business-based networks became generally unwilling (if not actually unable) to back opposition parties without the OK of the Kremlin.[177] But sometimes the Kremlin did give this OK. Yabloko Party representatives, for example, have claimed Putin personally gave Khodorkovsky the instruction to fund their party prior to the 2003 election, and that their sources of financing almost completely dried up after the Yukos chairman's arrest.[178] Even the business-friendly Union of Right Forces (SPS) claimed to have nearly completely lost its corporate donors after going into "hard opposition" against the Kremlin in the 2007 Duma campaign. This claim was lent credence by Russian Union of Entrepreneurs and Industrialists Vice President Igor Yurgens, who said that a version of SPS led by a person more capable of reaching agreement with the Kremlin (Leonid Gozman) would regain significant donations.[179]

Once efforts to coordinate gubernatorial and oligarchic networks around the structure of United Russia had demonstrated success in the party's landslide parliamentary victory of 2003, and after United Russia's ratings in the

---

[174] David Woodruff, "Khodorkovsky's Gamble: From Business to Politics in the YUKOS Conflict," PONARS Policy Memo no. 308, November 2003. Compare Sergei Markov, "The Yukos Affair and Putin's 2nd Term," *The Moscow Times*, July 29, 2003, circulated on Johnson's Russia List No. 7269.

[175] Hale, *Why Not Parties in Russia?*

[176] Regina Smyth, Brandon Wilkening, and Anna Urasova [Lowry], "Engineering Victory: Institutional Reform, Informal Institutions, and the Formation of a Hegemonic Party Regime in the Russian Federation," *Post-Soviet Affairs*, v. 23, no. 2, 2007, pp. 118–37.

[177] Natalia Morar', "Chernaia kassa Kremlia," *The New Times*, December 10, 2007, pp. 18–22.

[178] Senior Yabloko Party officials, author's interviews.

[179] Nikita Belykh, personal blog, http://belyh.ru, September 26, 2008, accessed September 27, 2008; *Vedomosti*, September 29, 2008.

polls indicated it would likely have at least as good a result in the future, Putin (as part of the 2004 post-Beslan reforms) felt confident enough to eliminate district elections entirely for the parliament and move to an all-party-list system of voting.[180] As discussed in Chapter 6 in the analysis of Moldova, SMD elections make deputies less dependent on their own parties' leadership and more dependent on local interests within their districts, which patronal presidents typically have many levers to influence. For a patronal president, then, a parliament full of SMD deputies from an opposition party is preferable to a parliament full of opposition PR deputies, who are not as easily manipulable and more dependent on the opposition parties' leaders. But when the presidential party can gain a majority for its own party, it is likely to prefer that its deputies be directly dependent on their own central leadership rather than on district-based interests. Thus while United Russia managed to forge a two-thirds supermajority in the Duma in the 2003 elections, this had required attracting a significant number of SMD deputies who had run as independents to the party's delegation. By eliminating SMD deputies from the Duma, then, Putin strengthened his direct control over the system (so long as he could ensure that his party would win a majority of the PR seats).[181] Just to be sure, the threshold for winning any seats in the Duma at all was raised from 5 to 7 percent of the vote, a bar few were thought able to cross.

Already by 2003–4 and without question by 2007–8, therefore, Putin had effectively combined virtually all major networks into a single patronal pyramid that was so tightly bound that few even thought a serious challenge was possible, marginalizing those who would not play along. Accordingly, a survey of elites and experts from across Russia conducted by the Institute for Public Planning and the journal *Ekspert* found that the number of politicians with a high level of influence in Russia had declined from around two hundred in 2002 to just about fifty in early 2007. Moreover, the list consisted mostly of state officials.[182]

Why was Putin so much more effective in turning Russia's political system into something that might be described as "one big political machine" than was Yeltsin? one obvious factor is that Yeltsin did the hard work of establishing the basic mechanism in the wake of the post-Soviet transitional chaos, leaving it for Putin to take it further. Indeed, while the 1999 election featured wild competition at the national level, the preceding period since the 1990s had featured a pronounced centralization of power *locally* in many regions as governors developed and perfected their own political machines. These machines were disunited at the federal level, populating the different "pyramids" of power that were competing for federal-level power, but many were increasingly dominant locally. This left Putin mainly the task of coordinating the country's

[180] *RFE/RL Newsline*, May 20, 2005.
[181] Erik S. Herron, *Elections and Democracy after Communism?* (New York: Palgrave-Macmillan, 2009), p. 43.
[182] Editorial, "Biurokratizatsiia Politiki," *Ekspert*, no. 6, February 12–18, 2007, p. 19.

regional political machines and encouraging the weaker ones to be more like the stronger ones.[183]

In explaining the difference between Yeltsin and Putin, one might also consider political style, or appetites for risky behavior. While a close examination of Yeltsin's record belies any claim that he was a true democrat, what we can say is that he was more tolerant of media criticism and, significantly, more inclined to trust in his own ability to mobilize forces to achieve an improbable victory against strong opponents than Putin has been. There is some evidence that Yeltsin even thrived personally on pulling off such political victories.[184] Thus while he was quite authoritarian in some of his methods of rule, he mainly sought to rein in opposition when a personal victory was most essential, as in the presidential contest of 1996 and the struggle leading up to his succession in 1999. Putin, on the other hand, has been a more cautious political actor when it comes to his domestic political position, leading him to take greater advantage of patronal presidential power to control the Russian political environment even when he could probably win handily even in a completely free and fair contest.

Putin also clearly benefited in this regard from his background in the KGB and FSB.[185] Especially as he proved willing to strike decisively against political opponents, those contemplating opposition were frequently intimidated and believed that he had both the power and will to detect and ruthlessly suppress it. Thus even when Putin actually did nothing, there seems to have been a great deal of self-censorship and self-suppression, especially in business and media. The regime has also proven very sophisticated in a variety of "postmodern" efforts to defuse or "manage" public displays of dissent.[186]

Finally, Putin's popularity was an essential part of his success in building Russia's power *vertikal'* and eliminating rival political *vertikals*, producing a single-pyramid system much more closed than Yeltsin's ever was. Potential political opponents surely understood that a challenge to Putin, who from the moment he took presidential office was rated favorably by more than a majority of the adult population, was unlikely to find much mass support. This is especially true since many of those few who actively disapproved of Putin's job performance were already committed to the Communists, who were also opposed by a clear majority of the population ever since the late 1990s. This, combined with the observed failure of opposition attempts from both left and right to mobilize mass support, served to disincline most major networks with something to lose to become very involved in opposition politics.

[183] Hale, "Explaining Machine Politics."

[184] Timothy J. Colton, *Yeltsin: A Political Life* (New York: Basic Books, 2008).

[185] Fiona Hill and Clifford G. Gaddy, *Mr. Putin: Operative in the Kremlin* (Washington, DC: Brookings, 2013).

[186] Graeme B. Robertson, *The Politics of Protest in Hybrid Regimes: Managing Dissent in Post-Communist Russia* (New York: Cambridge University Press, 2011).

Studies indicate Putin's popularity was based during this period on a variety of factors, factors not entirely dissimilar to what influences presidential popularity in other societies. Most obviously, Putin benefited in public eyes from a steadily growing economy.[187] In addition, he cultivated a sense of inevitability and stability about his rule that increased people's willingness to support him relative to the kinds of alternatives they could conceive as realistic.[188] He also took policy stands that were both recognized and supported by the wider public, including opposition to a socialist economy, and developed a personal style of leadership that people generally liked.[189] All this was increasingly reinforced by a macho, sometimes tongue-in-cheek tough-guy media image cultivated by his occasional use of gangland slang, displays of sporting acumen, and shirtless appearances in rugged natural settings.[190]

The 2008 Succession and the Resulting Two-Tipped Pyramid

As Putin's 2008 constitutional term limit approached, however, Russia once again saw a rise in uncertainty as to whether the president would remain in office beyond that year, with elites in particular increasingly beginning to expect he would actually leave office. As we know, Putin indeed opted not to attempt to change the constitution to permit himself a third term and consistently declared this would be the case all the way up to the 2007–8 election season.[191] The Duma, where United Russia's delegation controlled a supermajority, explicitly voted down a bill that would have created a way for him to gain a third term without amending the constitution.[192] The Central Election Commission rejected a referendum initiative to give Putin a third term.[193] All this occurred even as many called for him to stay on, seeing him as the linchpin of the system.[194] Opinion polls provided mixed signals: Putin remained highly popular, but the extent to which the public would back an effort to keep him in the presidency beyond his second term was less clear. Much depended on specifically how the question was framed. The state-run VTsIOM agency reported in spring 2007, for example, that a majority would support giving all Russian presidents (including Putin) the opportunity to run for three terms.[195] But the

---

[187] Daniel S. Treisman, "Presidential Popularity in a Hybrid Regime: Russia under Yeltsin and Putin," *American Journal of Political Science*, v. 55, no. 3, July 2011, pp. 590–609.

[188] Richard Rose, William Mishler, and Neil Munro, *Russia Transformed: Developing Popular Support for a New Regime* (New York: Cambridge University Press, 2006).

[189] Timothy J. Colton and Henry E. Hale, "The Putin Vote: Presidential Electorates in a Hybrid Regime," *Slavic Review*, v. 68, no. 3, Fall 2009, pp. 473–503.

[190] Julie A. Cassiday and Emily D. Johnson, "A Personality Cult for the Postmodern Age: Reading Vladimir Putin's Public Persona," in Helena Goscilo, ed., *Putin as Celebrity and Cultural Icon* (New York: Routledge, 2013), pp. 37–64.

[191] E.g., *RFE/RL Newsline*, April 12, 2005; *RFE/RL Newsline*, September 19, 2005; *Polit.Ru*, April 5, 2007, 10:55.

[192] *Polit.Ru*, June 29, 2005, 16:44.

[193] *Polit.Ru*, September 27, 2006, 13:56.

[194] *Polit.Ru*, April 5, 2007, 10:55; *RFE/RL Newsline*, August 23, 2005.

[195] *RFE/RL Newsline*, April 18, 2007.

independent Levada-Center found around the same time that an impressive 54 percent opposed making Putin president for life.[196]

This uncertainty regarding the succession increasingly induced visible centrifugal dynamics within the single-pyramid system despite Putin's efforts to prevent this. Indeed, the Kremlin was acutely aware in advance of this danger. Russian leaders were not only still spooked by the narrowness of their own victory in the 1999–2000 succession. They were also surely extra cautious because of the Orange Revolution in Ukraine (which had been a surprise for them) as well as protest potential they witnessed in their own country in early 2005. At that time, an unpopular economic reform had suddenly sparked a wave of spontaneous mass demonstrations across Russia, forcing the regime to back down on the policy.[197] Putin publicly acknowledged the uncertainty created by the succession expectations in May 2006, letting it be known that he would only name his preferred successor later: "Everyone is concerned about stability and [people] are wondering what will happen after 2008.... I have certain ideas about how to set up the situation in the country in this period of time so as not to destabilize it, so as not to scare people and business."[198]

One such idea was an attempt to lead rather than follow the anticipated division in the elite, thereby making it more manageable. Thus in November 2005, Putin strongly signaled he was primarily considering two main candidates to succeed him, each widely associated with a different group of Putin supporters. Putin then named both to roughly comparable senior government positions at the same time, making his former KGB colleague and ex-defense minister Sergei Ivanov deputy prime minister and naming presidential administration chief Dmitry Medvedev (a former law professor often portrayed as representing a "liberal" network of "St. Petersburg lawyers" in Putin's system) first deputy prime minister. Elites and mass media immediately began speculating as to which one Putin would choose and which one would better connect with the public. Media of all stripes dramatically increased the mentions of each, with the prime minister himself (seen as a technocratic figure) overshadowed by his two high-profile subordinates and the great expectations for one of them.[199]

This did not prevent succession-related intraelite tensions from showing signs of spinning out of control, however. Most dramatically, rival networks of force agents (the usually secretive *siloviki*, often mistakenly lumped together as a single network) began engaging in a strikingly public battle against each other. This included not only criticizing each other in major media, but also actually arresting each other's key members as well as those

[196] *RFE/RL Newsline*, May 7, 2007. A Levada survey in 2005 found that only 44 percent said they wanted him to have a third term, with more thinking he should either go (34 percent) or choose a successor (12 percent) (*RFE/RL Newsline*, October 5, 2005).

[197] Robertson, *The Politics of Protest*.

[198] *RFE/RL Newsline*, May 15, 2006.

[199] For a count of media mentions in 2006 compared to 2005, see *Kommersant-Vlast*, no. 3, January 29, 2007.

of other networks they did not like, such as the "liberal" deputy finance minister.[200] Richard Sakwa has impressively documented the strikingly byzantine battle, showing how the networks carried out their struggle throughout both business and the state and how the rivalry centered precisely around the expected 2008 succession because of the uncertainty these expectations had unleashed.[201]

With some of the bolts starting to pop off his political machine, Putin made a series of moves that well illustrate two things: how a leader can successfully manage ushering a protégé into office while keeping the single-pyramid system intact, but also how formal presidential succession can entail significant political risk even for the most popular of patronal presidents, risk that must be managed very carefully. One such move was to pay great attention to sustaining both Putin's and his possible successors' popular support. This meant everything from advertising major patronage giveaways known widely as the four Priority National Projects (on education, agriculture, housing, and health) to tightly controlling how political events were portrayed on the most-watched television channels. Putin's own broad support in the population created the impression among both elites and masses that whoever he endorsed would win. Independent opinion polls lent credibility to this belief, and indeed the eventual successor's standing in preelection polls immediately leapt to Putin's own levels after he was chosen.[202] This resource could conceivably have been used by Putin even if he had left politics entirely because (assuming his support would not immediately dissipate) he could announce a return to politics and possibly defeat a leader who had strongly diverged from his preferred course. The successor's own appeal was also important to establish, however. Polling done after the election indicates that Putin's endorsement would not have generated the same bump in support for just any old candidate, having little effect on candidates who were not credibly in line with the reasons why people supported Putin. For example, most said they would still have voted against the Communist Party's Gennady Zyuganov even had Putin for some reason endorsed him.[203] Thus Ivanov and Medvedev were both lavished with positive television coverage, and Medvedev was given the enviable responsibility of doling out funds for the socially oriented Priority National Projects after being named first deputy prime minister.

---

[200] See reports, for example, in *Polit.Ru*, December 6, 2007, 18:48; *Vedomosti*, October 10, 2007, p. 2.

[201] Richard Sakwa, *The Crisis of Russian Democracy: The Dual State, Factionalism, and the Medvedev Succession* (Cambridge: Cambridge University Press, 2011), especially chapter 6.

[202] *RFE/RL Newsline*, December 13, 2007; *RFE/RL Newsline*, December 27, 2007. After the election, the 2008 RES survey found that only half of the people who said they had voted for Medvedev would have done so had Putin not endorsed him. See Hale and Colton, "Russians and the Putin-Medvedev 'Tandemocracy,'" p. 14.

[203] Hale and Colton, "Russians and the Putin-Medvedev 'Tandemocracy,'" p. 14.

With both possible successors consistently leading all challengers in the presidential polls, even when both were included as possible competitors against each other, Putin made a second major move to keep the single-pyramid system together during the succession. In early fall 2007, he made the unprecedented announcement that he would personally lead United Russia's party list in the Duma elections later that year. It was unprecedented because no Russian president had ever even run for reelection as any party's nominee, much less anchored its party list in a parliamentary contest. This move accomplished two tasks simultaneously. First, it maximized United Russia's vote tally by making a vote for the party list a direct vote for Russia's most popular leader, and all seats were now to be filled by party-list rather than district elections. Putin thereby ushered as large a delegation as possible into the Duma, a delegation consisting of deputies who would each owe their seats to him personally. Second, this move demonstrated his electoral strength even outside the presidential election arena and even as his second term ended, proving to all that his popularity could overcome his status as a presidential lame-duck and thereby intimidating would-be challengers.

This proved a remarkable success. United Russia managed for the first time to claim a two-thirds supermajority in the Duma outright, and this set the stage for a third and fourth dramatic move designed to help him manage the succession. The third move was actually making the long-anticipated announcement that his successor was to be Medvedev, but making it so late in the game (December 2007) that those who did not like it had little time to countermobilize by the March 2008 presidential election.[204] The fourth move was for Medvedev almost immediately to invite Putin to be his prime minister. Putin accepted, creating what became widely known in Russia as the Tandem, with the political arrangement it engendered often called "tandemocracy."[205] Putin's decision to transfer to the post of prime minister sent the crucial signal to elites that he was still going to be in a position after the election to punish anyone who defected or acted too far out of line before or during it, establishing a powerful counter to the centrifugal pressures of the succession process. Putting the cap on this arrangement, Putin also arranged to become formal leader of the United Russia Party. Thus while he did not accept the parliamentary seat he won as the party's list leader in the 2007 election, becoming PM instead, his post as party leader gave him a formal basis on which to claim authority over the parliamentary supermajority he had led into office.

Very importantly, the decisions to become prime minister, head the United Russia party list, and chair the dominant party formally were mutually reinforcing. They combined to provide a formal check on presidential powers should Medvedev ever attempt to use the formal powers of the presidency against him. While the president had the right to appoint the prime minister according

---

[204] *Polit.Ru*, December 10, 2007, 14:22.
[205] Dmitrii Kamyshev, "Tandemokratiia," *Kommersant Vlast'*, March 10, 2008, p. 15.

to the Russian constitution, the Duma had to approve this appointment. And since United Russia ultimately achieved a two-thirds majority in the Duma thanks to Putin, few observers expected that this Duma would ever accept anyone other than Putin for prime minister unless Putin himself asked them to do so. And, of course, Putin took to this new position the considerable informal authority that he had accumulated as president.

This, then, was the essence of the Tandem period: By leaving the presidency, *Putin separated the informal power of the office from the formal power of the office*, instead investing the informal power he had accumulated as president into his new office, the premiership. His successor, Medvedev, inherited only the bare formal powers of the presidency, with minimal informal authority independent of Putin. Because Putin and Medvedev were part of the same core network, one might well refer to this situation as a "two-tipped pyramid," though still a single-pyramid system because the two were so clearly in the same network and never ruptured these ties.

A two-tipped pyramid arrangement in a highly patronalistic presidentialist system, with one tip supported mostly by formal power and the other by informal power, was bound to introduce some instability into the system relative to a simple single-tipped pyramid arrangement whereby the leader with the most informal power also occupies the presidency. This is because the situation served to disrupt the presidentialist constitution's expectations-coordinating effects, discussed in theoretical terms in Chapter 4. The greatest damage was done to the information effect of the constitution: Someone other than the president was now "obviously" the dominant figure informally, the chief patron of the system. At the same time, the fact that someone else occupied the presidency communicated the information that perhaps that person was destined to become the patron in the future, perhaps because he had Putin's backing to gain this status eventually. At the same time, the focal effect of the presidentialist constitution was still fully operative, giving any elites who otherwise had no idea how to read the situation marginal reason to pick Medvedev. Naturally, most people still saw Putin as dominant. But there was great uncertainty about his future intentions, with many speculating that he might either voluntarily hand off power to Medvedev or become less relevant (indeed, one might reason, why else would he ever have left the presidency when he easily could have found a way to have stayed?). Elites who were actually dissatisfied with Putin or their place in Putin's immediate circle also now had an alternative focal point in authority around which to orient themselves with little short-term risk to them and with the prospect of long-term gain if they wound up early on the side of the eventual patron. In such a situation, the stability of the (two-tipped) single-pyramid system required above all a nonconflictual relationship between the two patrons: Would the ties that bound them together in the same network remain stronger than incentives that might pull them apart, such as the temptation Medvedev might face to become supreme leader himself?

Analysts both inside and outside Russia devoted great attention to the question of whether a rift could be detected between Putin and Medvedev. Medvedev's public rhetoric stood out from Putin's by suggesting a plan to liberalize the political system, more boldly "modernize" the economy, and orient Russia more firmly toward the West. Some interpreted these as deep and real differences.[206] Overall, however, the ruling Tandem remained on the same page, as they themselves repeatedly stressed, when it came to major policy initiatives. Their differences remained mainly in the realm of rhetoric and style, or were not on fundamental issues. At times, they appeared to play a kind of "good-cop/bad-cop" strategy, with Putin appearing as the tough guy and Medvedev the "friendlier" front man who could hope to appeal more to Western policy makers and Western-oriented populations in Russia itself.

What the Tandem arrangement accomplished most of all, however, was to create significant uncertainty among both elites and masses during 2008–11 as to what the future held at the pinnacle of Russian power, creating a certain relaxation of the political environment that some even called a "thaw."[207] Most in the elite agreed Putin was the more powerful figure throughout Medvedev's presidency, but there were many who placed their reputational bets on Medvedev's eventually becoming chief patron one way or other.[208] The fact that anyone would consider such thoughts about Medvedev, even when Putin clearly overwhelmed him in informal power, is itself testimony to the power of formal constitutions to shape expectations of future power. Analysts have found considerable evidence that networks during this time were often able to maneuver between the two centers of authority, with two distinct and even rival coalitions coming to gravitate around Putin and Medvedev.[209] One effect

---

[206] E.g., Sakwa, *The Crisis of Russian Democracy*. The most dramatic instance when they were widely perceived to have genuinely disagreed was Putin's opposition to Medvedev's UN Security Council abstention on a resolution enabling American military force to be used in Libya in spring 2011. See Natalia Kostenko, "Rokirovka vo vlasti polozhila konets modern-izatsii," *Vedomosti.ru*, December 30, 2011.

[207] See poll results showing that only a minority were willing to say that Putin had more power than Medvedev in 2008, 2009, and 2010: *Polit.Ru*, August 1, 2008, 10:14; *BBC Russian Service*, April 22, 2009, 02:31; *The Moscow Times*, August 4, 2010 (though the latter reports an exception earlier in 2010).

[208] See, for example, the range of essays by leading Russian and Western experts on what Russia's political future held written as late as 2011 (though before Putin had resolved the uncertainty by announcing his return to the presidency): Maria Lipman and Nikolay Petrov, eds., *Russia in 2020: Scenarios for the Future* (Washington, DC: Carnegie Endowment, 2011). A backer of Medvedev's chief presidential rival from 2007 to 2008 also feared Medvedev would gradually accumulate power through the formal presidency: Aleksandr Prokhanov, interview on the show "Osoboe Mnenie," Ekho Moskvy radio, December 12, 2007, 19:00, author's observation.

[209] On Medvedev's building of some real authority and resulting discord within the elite, see Sakwa, *The Crisis of Russian Democracy*, especially pp. 343–50.

was strikingly new personal criticism of Putin from many who had previously been loyalists or at least politically quiet.[210]

The apparently liberalizing internetwork ferment at the top should not be confused with an actual policy of political liberalization, a few largely cosmetic changes notwithstanding.[211] In fact, prior to the crisis discussed in the next section, the Tandem presided over a series of reforms that seemed to be setting the stage for greater long-term tightening of the single-pyramid system once the uncertainty about who would lead it had resolved. One of the most important such reforms was a constitutional amendment – the first since the basic law was adopted in 1993 – that lengthened parliamentary terms from four to five years and presidential terms from four to six years, starting with the elections scheduled for 2011–12. Another very important development was Medvedev's dramatic replacement of more than half of Russia's governors, with thirty-nine removed prior to the 2011 Duma election.[212] Crucially, among these figures were the majority of Russia's "heavyweight" regional leaders, people who controlled some of the country's most vote-rich regional machines and whom the regime had not dared replace before. The highest-profile examples included Moscow Mayor Luzhkov, Tatarstan President Mintimer Shaimiev, and Bashkortostan President Murtaza Rakhimov. This paved the way for central authorities to install people more closely tied to Putin's own networks or more politically pliable for other reasons. New opposition party initiatives were regularly denied registration, FSB powers were augmented, and formal presidential control over the Constitutional Court was expanded.[213]

The Formal Presidential Succession of 2012, Putin's New Single Pyramid, and the Annexation of Crimea

Since he proved right in gambling that Medvedev was either too loyal or not bold enough to break decisively with him while in the presidency, the chief political risk Putin created in instituting the two-tipped pyramid was that it set up another presidential succession election in the event he decided to reunite formal and informal power by returning to the presidency. That is, in order to regain the presidency, he had to orchestrate a formal election victory while others who might not be satisfied with this arrangement occupied key positions around the presidency. Moreover, the lengthening of presidential terms to six years had the effect of significantly raising the stakes: Since Russian law allows a returning president (so long as he spent a period out of office) to sit for two

---

[210] For examples, see Nabi Abdullaev, "Putin's Teflon Image Takes Hit," *The Moscow Times*, December 23, 2008.

[211] An example of such cosmetic changes is the giving of small parties a few token rights, such as the ability to speak in parliament once a year: *Kommersant*, May 14, 2010.

[212] Olga Pavlikova, "Ne vyshel iz teni," *Profil*, November 28, 2011, pp. 11–14; *The Moscow Times*, April 28, 2012.

[213] E.g., the Party of Popular Freedom (PARNAS), *RFE/RL News*, June 22, 2011, 17:49. On the FSB, see *RFE/RL News*, July 16, 2010. On the Court, see *The Moscow Times*, May 25, 2009.

full terms, elites came widely to expect that if Putin returned, it could be for a full twelve years, a seeming eternity in Russian politics. The logic of patronal politics suggests that this would not prove to be a particular problem so long as Putin wielded the overwhelming popularity he had enjoyed since late 1999 and, as in 2007–8, avoided major blunders in managing the succession.

As it turns out, the 2011–12 election season proved to be another good illustration of the importance of public opinion in patronal presidential systems. We see how a significant decline (though far from a collapse) in support for the regime generated a major crisis for the authorities, forcing a temporary limited political opening before Putin eventually won out and presided over a new closure of the single-pyramid system. Multiple polling agencies registered a significant drop in public backing for Putin, Medvedev, and United Russia over the course of 2011, a change roughly on the order of 10 percent, though each still remained significantly more popular than any other potential alternative.[214] Most linked this to a longer-term decline in support owing to slowing economic growth in the wake of the 2008 global financial crisis combined with rising aspirations and fatigue with the leadership.[215] In addition, polls showed that nearly as many voters preferred Medvedev to Putin for president if forced to choose between them. According to the Levada-Center, in July 2011, Putin led Medvedev by only 5 percent.[216] In fact, there is an argument to be made that the rise of Medvedev in the Tandem had been helping stave off an even greater potential decline in support for the regime by adding to it a sense of freshness and expectations of change.

In this context, the regime's public opinion problems intensified when Medvedev announced on September 24, 2011, that Putin would return to the presidency, sucking the oxygen from the air of those who had hoped for something different. Making matters worse, Putin remarked that such a maneuver had been planned all along. This conveyed that they had essentially regarded the citizenry as dupes in portraying Medvedev as an autonomous president, ultimately pulling what might be called a political switcheroo. In Russian, the preferred description was "the castling," referring to the chess move. Resentment crystallized among many when Putin was dramatically whistled down (booed) on live television in November when he appeared on stage at Moscow's Olimpiisky Stadium to greet a large crowd after a mixed martial arts match. Putin's political "Teflon" appeared to be flaking off rapidly. The share of people declaring to pollsters that they would vote for Putin's dominant party,

---

[214] See the trends reported by both the independent Levada-Center and the Public Opinion Foundation, which worked closely with the Kremlin: Levada-Center, "Dekabr'skie reitingi odobreniia i doveriia," press release, December 22, 2011, http://www.levada.ru/22–12–2011/ dekabrskie-reitingi-odobreniya-i-doveriya, accessed January 16, 2012; Public Opinion Foundation, "Politicheskie indikatory," *Dominanty. Pole mnenii*, no. 50, December 15, 2011, pp. 2–7, http://bd.fom.ru/pdf/d5011.pdf, accessed December 10, 2012.

[215] E.g., Levada-Center director Lev Gudkov. See *Vedomosti.ru*, November 29, 2012.

[216] Levada-Center, "Dekabr'skie reitingi odobreniia i doveriia," press release, December 22, 2011.

United Russia, suffered a notable drop to just 36 percent of the population in November even according to the Public Opinion Foundation, which does much contract work with state structures.[217]

This drop in popularity threw a wrench into the Russian political machine at a critical moment before the "elite primary" 2011 Duma elections. Recognizing United Russia's declining ability to win genuine votes combined with their accountability for the performance of the party in their jurisdictions, local officials scrambled to find ways to pump up official ballot counts. This proved more difficult than one might expect. For one thing, Putin and Medvedev had almost wholesale removed the strongest governors during the Tandem period, leaving in place relative novices who often had weak ties to local elites. In addition, Russian state officials were not in fact well practiced in massive fraud. When Putin's and United Russia's popularity had been riding high, they had not needed to rely on the most intensive pressure tactics or outright ballot-count falsification, using them mainly at the margins or in extraordinary circumstances (a few "overachievers" in certain loyalist territories notwithstanding). Local officials' panicky efforts to manufacture or falsify a strong official vote total for United Russia were therefore often sloppy and careless, sometimes captured on video that was posted on the Internet for all to see. Reflecting some rather dramatic cracks in the single-pyramid system, it was often dissatisfied system insiders rather than opposition leaders who did this exposing.[218] This damaged the authorities' popular standing still further.

The problems with United Russia's regional political machines went beyond inexperience. Because they were now mostly appointed from the outside rather than elected after having risen up from within, many governors had little local public appeal to lend the party in its hour of need. So dire was this problem that United Russia – in dramatic contrast with 2007 – selected only 31 of the country's 83 governors to lead its regional party lists. In some cases, the party instead nominated federal officials and actually campaigned *against* its own unpopular governors.[219] Surely, such governors had at best mixed incentives when asked to put full effort into mobilizing their political machines for United Russia: A strong showing for the party would represent popular endorsement of the criticism directed against them.

The party's campaign suffered additional disarray because the September switcheroo arrangement also included an unpleasant surprise for United Russia: the newly emasculated Medvedev, not Putin, would head the party list. United Russia's campaign team had based its Duma election strategy on Putin's leading the party list, a decision that itself reveals the uncertainty regarding

---

[217] Public Opinion Foundation 2011.
[218] Tat'iana Garina and Dmitrii Kamyshev, "Razminka pered vbrosom," *Kommersant Vlast'*, November 28, 2011, pp. 15–18.
[219] *Vedomosti*, December 1, 2011, p. 2.

the future that the two-tipped pyramid arrangement had produced. Now the party had to scrap its campaign strategy at the last minute and create a new one oriented to Medvedev as party list leader.[220] Making a bad situation for the party worse, Putin distanced himself from the party even further in his rhetoric, not wanting United Russia's declining fortunes to damage his own further by association.[221]

Smelling blood, "virtual" as well as genuine opposition parties turned against United Russia, and even state-controlled media appeared to take at least some advantage of the drama for ratings purposes. Anticorruption blogger Aleksei Navalny had back in early 2011 coined the moniker "Party of Swindlers and Thieves" to refer to United Russia, and this caught on among a broader range of the party's opponents by the fall.[222] Most dramatically, even the formerly docile "A Just Russia" Party turned aggressively against United Russia. This was surprising because A Just Russia was led by a close Putin associate from St. Petersburg and had been created in 2006–7 with Kremlin support as a kind of receptacle for pro-Putin regional and other networks left out of United Russia, often being called a second party of power.[223] While the Kremlin blocked some of A Just Russia's critical ads, the party managed to have others aired that absolutely lambasted official corruption and pointedly averred that Russia did not need "swindlers and thieves."[224] If parliamentary campaign debates in 2007 had been rather sterile affairs broadcast at inconvenient times of day, in 2011 the state's Rossiia-1 channel treated them very differently. The channel slated debates for Moscow during prime time, broadcast them live, assigned the popular talk show personality Vladimir Soloviev to host them, and even advertised them in advance as dramatic viewing. At least one of these produced a significant moment in the campaign. The tenacious nationalist Vladimir Zhirinovsky managed to goad United Russia representative Aleksandr Khinshtein into bursting out, "Better to be a party of swindlers and thieves than a party of murderers, robbers, and rapists!"[225] Others picked up on this outburst to claim in later debates that United Russia had itself *admitted* it was a party of swindlers and thieves.[226] According to one measure, close to

---

[220] *Moskovskie Novosti*, November 25, 2011, p. 1.

[221] For more on the 2011 campaign, see Henry E. Hale, "The Putin Machine Sputters: First Impressions of Russia's 2011 Duma Election," *Russian Analytical Digest*, no. 106, December 21, 2011, pp. 2–5. Some very useful figures are also in this issue of *Russian Analytical Digest*.

[222] Liliia Biriukova, "Mitingi nachali diktovat' modu obshchestvennogo povedeniia," *Vedomosti.ru*, December 30, 2011.

[223] Luke March, "Managing Opposition in a Hybrid Regime: Just Russia and Parastatal Opposition," *Slavic Review*, v. 68, no. 3, Fall 2009, pp. 504–27.

[224] E.g., A Just Russia advertisement, run on First Channel, November 29, 2011, 07:25, after a campaign debate and just before "Dobroe Utro Rossii," a popular morning program.

[225] *Kommersant*, November 28, 2011, p. 2.

[226] E.g., the statement made by A Just Russia leader Sergei Mironov in his debate with United Russia representative Oleg Morozov broadcast on First Channel, November 29, 2011, 18:25.

a fifth of people watching TV at that time in Moscow had this debate on, and patterns were said to be similar across the country.[227]

The result in December was not only a dismal showing for United Russia, but the eruption of some of the largest mass protests Russia has seen since perestroika. Putin's party was not able even to manufacture a majority of the officially counted vote, claiming only 49 percent. It did get a slight majority of the seats, however, due to some parties' failing to clear the 7-percent threshold needed to win a parliamentary delegation. Adding insult to injury, many believed that even this result reflected substantial fraud, prompting tens of thousands (and by some estimates more than 100,000) of Muscovites to turn up at two massive protest rallies following the election on December 10 and 25.[228] The authorities did not attempt to prevent these rallies, a decision reached only after seeing that tens of thousands of individuals were willing to identify themselves on social media as committing to join the initial December 10 rally.[229] This indicates the Tandem understood the possibility of violence could pose a greater threat to their regime than the protests by further damaging their popularity, and that violence might not even succeed if enough troops refused to fire on the people with the political uncertainty caused by the moment of succession and the possibility the incumbents could be on their way out.

Clearly caught off guard, Putin and Medvedev quickly initiated a series of liberalizing political reforms designed to take away the opposition momentum generated by the protests, though they did not bow to the opposition's core call to repeat the Duma election. Concessions included installing webcams in polling places for the March 2012 presidential election, dramatically liberalizing political party registration such that only 500 members would be required instead of 40,000, and restoring direct gubernatorial elections, though with some major restrictions for getting on the ballot. In the new gubernatorial contests, candidates would have to obtain the signatures of a share of municipal legislators and mayors (usually controlled by United Russia), meet certain other requirements regional legislatures could set, and possibly consult the president at the latter's discretion.[230] State-controlled television also saw a major thaw, as suddenly some long-unwelcome opposition figures (such as Vladimir Ryzhkov) reappeared on political talk shows as guests and on news broadcasts as commentators after a lengthy absence.[231]

Along with making these concessions, the Kremlin launched a vigorous campaign that succeeded in restoring Putin's public standing. This campaign had two central parts, each strongly promoted by television news coverage

---

[227] *Kommersant*, November 28, 2011, p. 2.

[228] *Polit.Ru*, December 25, 2011, 17:59. Large rallies also occurred in other cities across Russia.

[229] *The New Times*, December 12, 2011, pp. 2–7.

[230] *RFE/RL*, December 15, 2011, 15:10; *RFE/RL*, March 23, 2012; *Polit.Ru*, April 27, 2012, 11:48.

[231] Author's field observations, Moscow, February 2012.

as well as events formally part of the campaign. First, it placed a new emphasis on Putin personally as "father of the nation," a peerless leader who had pulled Russia from the brink of ruin to a country on the rise economically and internationally. While Putin still ran as United Russia's formal nominee, the embattled party was deemphasized in his campaign. Second, Putin and his allies began stressing a set of "conservative values" themes that were quite popular with a majority but also divisive. The Kremlin had previously avoided relying much on such themes as they would have strongly alienated large parts of the population, especially in the major cities of Moscow and St. Petersburg. The 2011–12 protests, however, made clear that these groups were already quite alienated from the regime, which meant that adopting the new themes was no longer very costly and now possibly quite profitable politically. The Duma, dominated by United Russia, starting in 2012 churned out a ban on "homosexual propaganda" that might reach children, a prohibition on the adoption of Russian children by Americans, additional measures to prevent foreign homosexuals from adopting Russian children, and a measure making blasphemy a crime.[232] One of the first major signs of this "conservative turn" was the aggressive prosecution of the Pussy Riot art-rock collective for desecrating Moscow's Christ the Savior Cathedral to create an anti-Putin video to post online, for which two members served nearly two years in prison.[233] This new values-based approach also served to isolate supporters of the 2011–12 protest movement, painting them as advocates of Western liberal and moral degeneracy that threatened true Russian morality, stability, and culture.

The new appeals, combined with the tactical retreat in machine politics, worked. Putin handily claimed a majority of the official vote count in the March 2012 presidential election, and even independent observers mostly conceded that he had probably won a majority of the actual vote despite some fraud that they say supplemented his totals.[234] As of April 2012, a Levada-Center survey showed that he would have won 60 percent of the vote had a presidential election been held again then. This figure rose to 67 percent by the time of the February 2014 Winter Olympic Games in the Russian city of Sochi, an event Putin used domestically to promote the image of a great nation that was finally restoring lost glory after years of chaos and decline.[235] Even the ratings of the United Russia Party began to recover, being found likely to win 55 percent of the vote if a Duma election had been held in May 2012.

---

[232] *Kommersant-Online*, June 30, 2013, 16:11; *RFE/RL*, December 21, 2012; *RFE/RL*, June 21, 2013; *RFE/RL*, June 30, 2013.

[233] Regina Smyth and Irina Soboleva, "Looking Beyond the Economy: Pussy Riot and the Kremlin's Voting Coalition," *Post-Soviet Affairs*, December 17, 2013.

[234] For example, Golos: *RFE/RL*, March 5, 2012.

[235] Richard Arnold and Andrew Foxall, "Lord of the (Five) Rings: Issues at Sochi, 2014," *Problems of Post-Communism*, January/February 2014, v. 61, no. 1, pp. 3–12.

This figure was still over 50 percent as of 2014.[236] Surveys show that while United Russia lost some supporters between 2008 and 2012, those whom it gained to replace them tended to stand out primarily for their support for Vladimir Putin personally rather than for any particular ideas associated with the party.[237]

Putin's electoral ratings soaring once again, the country's major political networks recoalesced around him as the undisputed patron and he began using this opportunity to re-tighten his shaken single-pyramid system. Perhaps reflecting the replacement of the system's longtime chief strategist (first deputy head of presidential administration Vladislav Surkov), after the December 2011 debacle by Viacheslav Volodin, the new tightening took some new forms.[238] As Grigorii Golosov has noted, the "liberalizing" reforms now actually appeared to be strengthening the position of the incumbents. The "municipal filter" in gubernatorial elections allowed the Kremlin to select out unwanted candidates.[239] The liberalization of party registration led not simply to the registration of opposition parties long denied, but to a massive proliferation of parties of all stripes, including many created by regime supporters. By January 31, 2014, the Justice Ministry had listed no fewer than 75 registered parties.[240] Having many parties on the ballot in practice meant that those with the greatest name recognition like United Russia gained an advantage. In addition, the Kremlin could still foster the registration of multiple other parties designed to chip away votes from opposition forces strategically. For example, multiple leftist or nationalist parties now appeared on the ballot alongside the Communists.[241] And when Russia's rising opposition star Aleksei Navalny decided to join and register a party with his supporters called Popular Alliance, a political entrepreneur with ties to the Kremlin beat him to the punch, quickly rebranding one of his own new parties to take on the very same name, registering it with the government so that Navalny could no longer claim it.[242] A slew of criminal cases were brought against leading opposition figures and even some ordinary people involved in the 2011–12 protest wave, resulting

---

[236] Levada-Center, "Vozmozhnie rezul'taty prezidentskykh i parlamentskykh vyborov," press release, May 14, 2014, www.levada.ru/14-05-2014/vozmozhnye-rezultaty-prezidentskikh-i-parlamentskikh-vyborov, accessed June 3, 2014. See also *Kommersant*, February 24, 2012, p. 2; Aleksei Levinson, "Kuda krutit' gaiki," *Vedomosti.ru*, April 17, 2012, 00:31.

[237] Henry E. Hale and Timothy J. Colton, "Who Defects? Defection Cascades from a Ruling Party and the Case of United Russia 2008–12," unpublished paper, March 19, 2014.

[238] *Polit.Ru*, December 27, 2011, 17:46.

[239] Grigorii V. Golosov, "The 2012 Political Reform in Russia: The Interplay of Liberalizing Concessions and Authoritarian Corrections," *Problems of Post-Communism*, v. 59, no. 6, 2012, pp. 3–14.

[240] "Spisok zaregistrirovanykh politicheskikh partii," Ministry of Justice of the Russian Federation official Web site, http://minjust.ru/ru/nko/gosreg/partii/spisok, accessed January 31, 2014.

[241] Grigorii Golosov, "Dmitry Medvedev's Party Reform," *Russian Analytical Digest*, no. 115, June 2012, pp. 8–10.

[242] *Polit.Ru*, November 28, 2013, 12:57.

in several convictions as of mid-2014. Of special note was a five-year sentence given to Navalny for what many observers believed was an obviously trumped-up corruption case.

Already by fall 2012, observers were decrying a new wave of political closure. United Russia comfortably orchestrated wins in regional legislative elections and the first gubernatorial contests under the new law (held in five regions in October 2012). The party's overall results were generally better than what it was able to claim in December 2011.[243] Strikingly, these outcomes generated very little protest among either elites or masses, suggesting that the Kremlin had successfully weathered the political storm. It was thus little surprise when the Kremlin won all gubernatorial and regional legislative elections the following year, in September 2013. So confident were the authorities feeling that they even instructed United Russia local deputies to sign the necessary petition for Navalny to get on the ballot for Moscow mayor despite his criminal conviction, allowing him to challenge incumbent Sergei Sobianin, a close Putin associate. Navalny put up a brave fight, organizing a vigorous door-to-door campaign to get around the lack of objective major media coverage. While his 27 percent was respectable, it was not enough to prevent Sergei Sobianin from claiming an outright victory with more than 50 percent of the vote.[244] No major street protests followed this result. With the 2014 Sochi Olympics approaching and Russia moving into the worldwide media's attentive gaze, the regime made a number of small new gestures to political liberalization, including releasing Khodorkovsky a few months early rather than finding a way to keep him in jail; he promptly left the country. But the overall trend was strongly back toward political closure, though at the same time attempting to find new ways to make it more palatable than in late 2011, as with manipulated (rather than absent) gubernatorial elections.

Whether the Kremlin will be able to sustain Putin's popular support well into the future remains an open question. If Putin's ratings were to drop significantly, the logic of patronal politics would expect him to be in a strong position to claim reelection in the next scheduled election of 2018 should he decide to run, though he would then enter a lame-duck period likely to be very dangerous for him and his network, especially because he would be older by 2024 than was Andropov when he assumed leadership of the USSR. If Putin attempts to hand off the presidency in 2018 as he did in 2008, the result could be another tense election season, more acute the lower his support in the population becomes. The Euromaidan Revolution in Ukraine, however, reminds us as well as Russian authorities that not all patronal politics is regular, with irregular patterns of revolution potentially threatening even patronal presidents who are not lame-ducks.

[243] *Vedomosti.Ru*, October 15, 2012.
[244] Robert W. Orttung, "Navalny's Campaign to be Moscow Mayor," *Russian Analytical Digest*, no. 136, September 16, 2013, pp. 2–5.

Such considerations, combined with the imperative they place on leaders to sustain popular support, shed considerable light on Russia's behavior after Ukraine's Euromaidan Revolution. Coming shortly after Putin's moment in Sochi's sun, the Euromaidan Revolution – which unseated a leadership he had publicly backed – threatened to dampen his afterglow by dealing him an embarrassing defeat in his efforts to promote the idea of a Russia that is rising rather than declining in world and regional influence. To the extent the Kremlin feared a successful revolution in Ukraine could reinvigorate the 2011–12 protests at home, Putin also had a political interest in somehow spoiling it. He also had to consider that his domestic political opponents – especially on the more nationalist side of the political spectrum – may have used these events against him at home, chipping away at his public standing. The fact that economic growth was slowing again around this time was also cause for great Kremlin concern.

In this context, one can understand Putin's decision to annex Crimea and Sevastopol (formally separate administrative regions) as an attempt to overturn the political chessboard and force a new game in which the Kremlin regains the advantage of initiative. For one thing, the stealth seizure and absorption of these Ukrainian regions dealt a harsh blow to the new Ukrainian authorities, forcing them to preside over the loss of some of their country's most valuable territories and triggering great internal turmoil over how to respond. These moves also inflamed national tensions within Ukraine, providing Russia with a steady stream of intolerant rhetoric from fringe Ukrainian nationalists that it could use to justify its actions inside Russia. This also played into a stunning Kremlin media campaign to stir up fear in other Ukrainian regions (in many of which Russian television was quite popular) and justify domestically at least tacit support for new separatist or irredentist forces mobilizing in other regions of Ukraine, which in turn served to further destabilize the country. Surveys show that the intensely hostile Russian media interpretation of Ukrainian events, which can create the impression that something like a Western-backed anti-Russian genocide is in the making,[245] has been very effective in augmenting and deepening public support in Russia for Putin, who is now portrayed as the great Russian leader who not only protects Russians but is restoring Russian lands that were unjustly lost due to historical accidents. Indeed, this is a message that fits very comfortably with the more general conservative turn discussed above. In April 2014, Levada-Center polling found that Putin would win a hypothetical presidential election at that time with a whopping 81 percent of the vote. Even United Russia would now get 60 percent of ballots for the Duma.[246]

Having already learned that long-earned popularity can be squandered quickly, it is little surprise that Putin and his allies show signs of using this

---

[245] Author's field observations, Moscow, May 2014.

[246] Levada-Center, "Vozmozhnie rezul'taty prezidentskykh i parlamentskykh vyborov," press release, May 14, 2014, www.levada.ru/14-05-2014/vozmozhnye-rezultaty-prezidentskikh-i-parlamentskikh-vyborov, accessed June 3, 2014.

moment of broad and deep domestic support to tighten Russia's single-pyramid system still further, attempting to reduce the limited opportunities that exist for opposition mobilization even more. As of mid-2014, these efforts included increased pressure on the Internet (for example, blocking several websites featuring critical material at least temporarily and subjecting blogs with more than 3,000 readers to official media regulations), a law criminalizing interpretations of history that denigrate Russia's role in World War II, and a new wave of inspections of NGOs.[247] Russia's single-pyramid system, therefore, looks to be continuing on a path of closure, though this could change as inevitable moments of expected succession arise, especially if the regime does not find ways to sustain strong popular support once the glow from Crimea fades.

Dynastic Succession in Azerbaijan

Since Heydar Aliyev originally rose to power, Azerbaijan experienced one lame-duck period as father attempted to hand presidential power over to son, and that son has since managed to escape facing a lame-duck situation. As in Russia, here we also find that the expected moment of succession generated significant tensions among the country's most powerful political-economic networks. And also as in Russia, we find that the incumbent successfully navigated them thanks partly to significant public support as well as great skill displayed in orchestrating the succession process in a way that minimized the chances of coordinated elite actions against his choice. Despite being regarded as a political novice, the younger Aliyev then managed to oust some of the most powerful networks in his initial coalition and increasingly find a role for his own family's network, ultimately freeing himself from formal term limits while his popularity was still high and creating expectations that he would remain in power long into the future.

Some have argued that dynasty can provide a useful solution to the elite contestation that can mark succession processes. Hereditary succession, it is claimed, can supply a clear focal point for patronal network coordination and an expectation of continuity in old deals.[248] The prospect of hereditary succession, however, can also provoke conflict within the single-pyramid system when the ruler's family is seen as a growing and aggressive political-economic network in its own right that has designs on the resources controlled by other networks. Junisbai has shown how the expansion of family networks helped undermine both popular and elite support for two presidents in Kyrgyzstan and caused serious problems for others, such as Nazarbaev in Kazakhstan.[249] Dynasty thus cannot be treated as an explanation of succession success by itself,

---

[247] *BloombergBusinessWeek*, businessweek.com, May 1, 2014; *RFE/RL*, May 14, 2014; *The New York Times*, May 11, 2014; Steven Wilson, "The Logic of Russian Internet Censorship," Monkey Cage blog, *The Washington Post*, March 16, 2014.

[248] Jason Brownlee, "Hereditary Succession in Modern Autocracies," *World Politics*, v. 59, no. 4, July 2007, pp. 595–628.

[249] Junisbai, "Improbable but Potentially Pivotal Oppositions."

but it can resolve the coordination problem among rival patronal networks if buttressed by strong popular support and great skill in managing the handoff.

Heydar Aliyev supplied history with a useful example of how this can be accomplished. For one thing, he wielded great authority and broad popular support as the "savior" of the nation, having restored authority after the loss of a fifth of Azerbaijan's territory and the violent political turmoil that characterized the early 1990s in the country.[250] He did not face a term limit when he decided to hand over presidential power. The Constitutional Court had ruled that his service prior to the adoption of the 1996 constitution did not count toward the presidency's two-term constraint, making his 1998–2003 term technically his first.[251] He did, however, increasingly encounter a lame-duck syndrome as he advanced in age, reaching 80 prior to the October 2003 presidential election. The opposition figure who would become his chief opponent in that contest, Musavat Party leader Isa Gambar, later reported that there had been a sense that as long as Aliyev was alive, no change was possible, but that it would become possible once he was gone.[252] As 2003 approached, Aliyev was known to be in increasingly bad health, and Gambar recalls that as early as 1999 he and his associates figured he would not be likely to serve beyond 2003.[253]

It was around the time of Aliyev's visible health problems that he started the process of carefully preparing for his son to take over as president. Very importantly, prior to this time, the younger Aliyev was not regarded as an "oligarch" in his own right with designs on other networks' assets. Instead, Ilham Aliyev was seen more as a technocrat, a former instructor at the prestigious Moscow international relations university MGIMO who had returned to Azerbaijan and eventually became vice president (not even president) of the country's state oil company SOCAR in 1994. In 1999, Ilham was named one of five deputy chairs of the dominant Yeni Azerbaijan Party (YAP), and in 2000 he became the main public face on YAP posters in that year's parliamentary campaign, understood as a clear signal he was the designated heir.[254] The elder Aliyev then arranged a constitutional amendment in 2002 that made the prime minister the first in line of succession to the president rather than the head of parliament, and in August 2003 – while hospitalized in Turkey – appointed his son prime minister. After this appointment, sending a signal to key networks in the country's single-pyramid system, the younger Aliyev promised to maintain the economic policies of his father.[255] As added insurance against elite splits, the elder Aliyev registered as a candidate himself, nominated by his Yeni Azerbaijan Party, and "was regarded as the leading candidate for most of the

[250] On this period, see Thomas Goltz, *Azerbaijan Diary: A Rogue Reporter's Adventures in an Oil-Rich, War-Torn, Post-Soviet Republic* (Armonk, NY: M. E. Sharpe, 1998).
[251] *Eurasianet*, Azerbaijan Daily Digest, July 19, 2002, 14:35:26.
[252] Isa Gambar, Musavat Party leader, author's interview, Baku, August 7, 2010.
[253] Gambar interview 2010.
[254] Svante Cornell, *Azerbaijan Since Independence* (Armonk, NY: M. E. Sharpe, 2011), p. 102.
[255] *RFE/RL Newsline*, August 4, 2003.

campaign."[256] Ilham had been formally nominated only by a group of voters rather than the party. But Heydar withdrew in favor of his son less than two weeks prior to the vote, leaving little time indeed for elite machinations against his chosen political heir.[257]

With a credibly technocratic son in place promising to anchor continuity in Heydar Aliyev's "deal" among elite networks, with Heydar continuing to wield strong popular support, with his son also enjoying significant public backing (also having low negatives), and with the possibility open for most of the preelection period that Heydar himself was seeking reelection for himself, the most important networks in the single-pyramid system generally held ranks despite rumors circulating in advance that the elder Aliyev had already died.[258] This included key Yeraz network elites in Heydar's system, notably Ali Insanov and Farhad Aliyev, discussed in previous chapters, who reportedly were not happy with the continuing dominance of the Aliyev family's Nakhichevan network.[259] It also included Heydar's brother Jelal, who is reported to have seen the upstart Aliyev as a threat.[260] Thus the main opposition candidate linked to the Yeraz network, Etibar Mamedov, could muster only 3 percent of the official vote.[261] A leading Yeni Azerbaijan Party official credited the presence of this dominant party for supplying stability during this period and later.[262] The political machine accordingly functioned smoothly, employing a wide range of dirty tricks that hindered or discredited opponents, lavishing Ilham with positive media attention, and engaging in a range of abuses at polling places and in the vote tabulation process.[263] Some prominent candidates were filtered out through the registration process, including former parliamentary speaker Rasul Guliyev and former president Ayaz Mutalibov.[264]

The only opposition candidate with popular support potentially strong enough to rival Ilham Aliyev's was Musavat Party leader Gambar, who had been parliamentary chairman during the nationalist, relatively democratic, but ultimately disastrous Elchibey's presidency in the early 1990s. While he managed to win the support of a number of opposition groupings,[265] Gambar's efforts to

[256] OSCE/ODIHR Election Observation Mission Report, Republic of Azerbaijan Presidential Election 15 October 2003, p. 9.

[257] Ibid.

[258] *RFE/RL Newsline*, August 4, 2003.

[259] Scott Radnitz, "Oil in the Family: Managing Presidential Succession in Azerbaijan," *Democratization*, v. 19, no. 1, February 2012, pp. 60–77, p. 66.

[260] Cornell, *Azerbaijan since Independence*, p. 102.

[261] Unlike in 1998, when Yeraz officials in the regime reportedly backed him as Aliyev was still consolidating his hold on power. See Cornell, *Azerbaijan since Independence*, pp. 169–70.

[262] Siyavush Novruzov, deputy executive secretary of the Yeni Azerbaijan Party and member of parliament, author's interview, Baku, October 3, 2008.

[263] OSCE/ODIHR Election Observation Mission Report, Republic of Azerbaijan Presidential Election 15 October 2003.

[264] *RFE/RL Newsline*, July 22, 2003.

[265] *RFE/RL Newsline*, March 31, 2003.

induce splits within the ruling elite failed. As he later reported, some top officials (whom he did not identify) were willing privately to say before the election they would support him if he won, but did not provide material or public support, only some information. Business, Gambar averred, did not believe change was possible and so did not provide meaningful investment in him. Some midlevel bureaucrats, he said, were supportive, and he claimed that certain forces in the military and police favored change but did not want to get involved in political battles.[266] And in any case, Gambar did not have "regional" ties to the dominant Yeraz or Nakhichevan networks, himself being associated with the Karabakh network of Azerbaijanis.[267] A prominent politician who withdrew from the race to help unite the opposition, Azerbaijan Popular Front leader Ali Karimli, likewise reported that he had held negotiations with key figures in the regime and that some had said they would support the opposition if it could demonstrate the capacity to win. But opposition candidates' failure to unite, he reported, contributed to their sense that Aliyev was the probable victor.[268]

With elites expecting a successful succession and most evidence indicating Aliyev did in fact win more votes than Gambar,[269] the protests that mobilized against what appears to be grossly distorted official results (a 77 percent to 14 percent win for Aliyev) did not catalyze new divisions among the major power networks and were summarily put down. Of some ten thousand Gambar backers who rallied in Baku's central Azadliq square, one was killed, more than three hundred were injured, and some four hundred were arrested, including Gambar himself. Gambar was released after about a month, though others were held until spring 2005.[270] Many opposition leaders blamed the protests' failure on a lack of support from either the West or Russia.[271] Heydar Aliyev was officially pronounced dead on December 12, 2003.[272]

New President Ilham Aliyev then moved cautiously but decisively to anchor his position as patron by bolstering popular support, making his father's political machine his own. As described by the key strategist of his father's regime, political scientist and long-serving Presidential Administration chief Ramiz Mehdiyev, 2003 marked the start of a new model of state management in Azerbaijan, with an emphasis on "strong statehood" and economic growth.[273] Rapid economic

---

[266] Gambar interview 2010.

[267] Cornell, *Azerbaijan since Independence*, p. 169.

[268] Ali Karimli, Azerbaijan Popular Front Party leader, author's interview, Baku, August 10, 2010.

[269] Cornell (*Azerbaijan since Independence*, p. 107) weighs the various accounts. Gambar claims he won decisively in real votes.

[270] Radnitz, "Oil in the Family," p. 67; Anar Kerimov, "Opposition Scores Two Gains in Azerbaijan," *Jamestown Eurasia Daily Monitor*, March 29, 2005.

[271] E.g., Isa Gambar, Musavat Party leader, author's interview, Baku, August 7, 2010. See also Bunce and Wolchik, *Defeating Authoritarian Leaders*, p. 189.

[272] Radnitz, "Oil in the Family," p. 66.

[273] Ramiz Mekhtiev, *Na puti k demokratii: razmyshliaia o nasledii* (Baku: Sharq-Qarb, 2007), pp. 392–6 (quotation p. 396).

growth would indeed be possible thanks largely to the country's major oil and gas assets increasingly coming online, providing an ever larger pie for the country's networks to carve up. According to World Bank data, the country averaged economic growth rates of an astounding 15 percent between 2003 and 2010, even factoring in a sharp dip to just 4 percent after the 2008–9 financial crisis.[274] This growth was sufficient to accommodate a notable expansion of Ilham Aliyev's own family's network without stepping too heavily on other networks' toes. Relatives and associates through Ilham Aliyev's wife and daughters thus came to play greater roles in the economy (especially through the vast Pasha Holding group, which included Pasha Bank and Pasha Construction), in politics (e.g., Aliyev's wife, Mehriban's, serving in parliament and later in the YAP leadership), and in civil society (such as the Heydar Aliyev Foundation directed by Mehriban Aliyeva).[275] A decade after Heydar Aliyev's death, analysts widely regarded the Pashayev network and the Nakhichevan network as the two most powerful components of Azerbaijan's single-pyramid system, vying for position within it.[276]

Rapid economic growth also supplied some visible benefits to substantial parts of the population and thus served as one important basis for Aliyev's popular support. By 2010, while some areas were not evidently benefiting much (including many run-down parts of Baku), others (such as the Qabala region patronized by one of the machine's main oligarchs, Emergencies Minister Kamaladdin Heydarov) could boast a wide range of economic activity and major infrastructure developments, including well-paved central roads and nicely groomed parks.[277] Thus consistently in the second half of the 2000s, more people reported to survey researchers that their personal financial position had improved over the preceding six months than said it had worsened.[278] Perhaps more important was a widespread sense that the economy as a whole was improving. Throughout 2006–10, 63–71 percent thought the country was moving in the right direction, 48–54 percent believed the general situation in the country would soon improve, and 35–47 percent expected their own economic position to get better soon, with "no change" being by far the main alternative response instead of "get worse."[279] Ilham Aliyev has sought to bolster his own authority by presiding over what might be described as a cult of his father

---

[274] Calculation based on data from the World Bank, World Development Indicators, http://data. worldbank.org/data-catalog?display=default, accessed August 9, 2011.

[275] Mehriban is from the Pashayev family, very prominent among Soviet era intelligentsia and rooted largely in Baku. See *The Guardian* online, December 12, 2010, 16:30; Ulviyye Asadzade and Khadija Ismayilova, "Aliyev's Azerbaijani Empire Grows, as Daughter Joins the Game," *RFE/RL News*, August 13, 2010.

[276] See the analysis, for example, in Arastun Oruclu, interview, "Iqtidar daxilinda chox riskli bir proses mushahida olunur," *Gundam Xabar*, June 10, 2013, p. 7; and *Yeni Musavat*, June 8, 2013, p. 9;

[277] Author's field observations, Azerbaijan, July–August 2010.

[278] The one exception being when the financial crisis hit hard in early 2009.

[279] Rasim Musabayov and Rakhmil Shulman, *Azerbaijan in 2006–2010: Sociological Monitoring* (Baku: Friedrich Ebert Stiftung and Puls, 2010), pp. 8, 38.

to bask in, with billboards, portraits, statues, parks, and museums dedicated to the former president becoming seemingly ubiquitous in the country and continuing to spread.[280] The Yeni Azerbaijan Party headquarters in Baku was particularly lush with such works of art, ranging from a vase with Heydar's face on it to an indoor wall mural featuring Heydar's head in the upper right corner representing the sun, with rays emanating down to enlighten all around him, in particular his son, Ilham, depicted in the lower left corner looking up at Heydar to receive his wisdom and inheritance from among the people.[281] An uncompromising hard line on Azerbaijani possession of Nagorno-Karabakh is also an important element of Aliyev's appeal to public opinion,[282] with majorities consistently citing the Armenian-Azerbaijani conflict as the most important issue facing the country, more important than corruption, crime, poverty, and other problems.[283] As Svante Cornell sums up, Ilham Aliyev "has been able to build a relatively strong popular following, a task facilitated by windfall oil revenues, but he does not generate widespread enthusiasm either."[284]

Also important for the junior Aliyev in taking ownership of the political machine was to strike preemptively against some of the very networks that had been part of his father's team and had helped put him in power. This served as an example to any who might think the younger Aliyev could lack the resolve of the elder in enforcing loyalty. Ilham not only removed some smaller-scale figures in the system shortly after inauguration,[285] but in October 2005 – on the eve of the November 2005 parliamentary election – presided over the dramatic arrest of two of the most important figures in his own and his father's regimes, Ali Insanov (formally health minister but more importantly informal patron of the Yeraz network) and Farhad Aliyev (the economic development minister formerly in charge of privatization). Both wound up with long prison sentences. Their demise represented a substantial weakening of the Yeraz network, and indeed a series of others associated with it also lost position during this purge.[286] While a number of analysts find some credibility in the official accusation that Ali Insanov and Farhad Aliyev had been dissatisfied with Ilham Aliyev's accession and were plotting to remove him,[287] the main point is less the

[280] It has been spreading even beyond the borders of Azerbaijan with efforts to erect statues of Heydar Aliyev everywhere from Mexico City to Astrakhan, Russia.

[281] Author's field observations, Azerbaijan, June–August 2010.

[282] For example, "Azerbaijan Respublikasina Hizmet Edirem," broadcast on the AzTV (Azerbaijan Televisiyasi) television channel, August 1, 2010, 12:30, author's observation.

[283] Musabayov and Shulman, Azerbaijan in 2006–2010, p. 9.

[284] Cornell, Azerbaijan since Independence, pp. 174–5.

[285] For example, he replaced the ministers of foreign affairs, of communication and information technologies, and of national security (Cornell, Azerbaijan since Independence, p. 113).

[286] On these events, see Cornell, Azerbaijan since Independence, p. 114 Polit.Ru, October 21, 2005, 09:31; Radnitz, "Oil in the Family," p. 66.

[287] For example, Cornell, Azerbaijan since Independence; and Radnitz, "Oil in the Family." For a more skeptical view, seeing the 2005 purge as more about preemption than punishment, see Alieva, "Azerbaijan's Frustrating Elections."

pretext than the signal that the arrests themselves sent to the elite: The political machine was now firmly in Ilham's hands, and he would wield it decisively.

This purge was surgically targeted, however, and Ilham Aliyev in fact kept most of the patronal pillars of the single-pyramid system he inherited in place. In fact, there has been remarkable stability in key official cadres and state-based oligarchs in Azerbaijan since the Heydar Aliyev era. Mehdiyev, regarded as the regime's chief political strategist, has served as head of the president's administration from early in the Heydar era through the time of this writing in 2014, as has Interior Minister Ramil Usubov. Defense Minister Safar Abiyev served from Heydar's day until 2013. Natik Aliyev had served as SOCAR chief since 1993 before joining the government as industry and energy minister in 2005.[288] Kamaladdin Heydarov was chief of the potentially lucrative Customs Committee under Heydar before becoming minister of emergency situations under Ilham, with one of his associates assuming charge of Customs while he himself gained control of ministerial troops and other levers of power. Ziya Mammadov, whose Transportation Ministry manages much of the infra-structural boom in Azerbaijan as well as goods shipments, has also been in place since the Heydar Aliyev era.[289] Heydarov and Mammadov, in particular, remain visible as political-economic oligarchs in the country, their networks and dealings featuring prominently in the country's independent press, though the ambitions of networks led by others such as Usubov also get attention.[290]

Ilham also continued to refine a wide variety of mechanisms in his political machine through at least 2014. He continued to make the Yeni Azerbaijan Party a centerpiece of his rule, with one of its longtime leaders from the Heydar era averring that it has been important in preventing splits in the elite.[291] Some media remain independent, in particular Azeri-language newspapers, some of which publish all kinds of information on alleged corrupt schemes operated by senior government officials and oligarchs[292] and lambaste the regime as a dicta-torship.[293] But surveys indicate that even the highest-circulation newspaper of this sort reached only 5–7 percent of the population in the mid-2000s.[294] Some independent information is available on the Internet, and its use as a primary news information source was on the rise, reaching nearly 7 percent by 2010.[295]

[288] Radnitz, "Oil in the Family," pp. 69–70.

[289] *The Guardian*, December 6, 2010, 09:30.

[290] Mostly, such reports appear in the Azeri-language press. On these oligarchs' struggle to get associates into the new parliament in the 2010 elections, for example, see *Reytinq: Musteqil qazet*, August 1, 2010, pp. 1, 5.

[291] Novruzov (who is from Nakhichevan) interview 2008.

[292] E.g., *Yeni Musavat*, August 6, 2010, pp. 1, 7.

[293] E.g., Ilham Huseyn, "Vicdan azabi chakirikmi?" *Azadlıq*, June 1, 2013, p. 11.

[294] Rasim Musabayov and Rakhmil Shulman, *Azerbaijan in 2007: Sociological Monitoring* (Baku: Friedrich Ebert Stiftung and Puls, 2008), pp. 20–1. Poll by the PULS-R Sociological Service, managed by Musabayov and Shulman, N = 1000 across the country in 2008, past survey details not given.

[295] Musabayov and Shulman, *Azerbaijan in 2006–2010*, pp. 20–1.

But especially after the shuttering and "reprogramming" of the last relatively independent television station in 2006,[296] the rest of the media environment remains either highly docile or outright servile to the authorities. Those independent sources that remain tend to experience a great deal of pressure, with such journalists and bloggers running a risk of being jailed (sometimes on formally unrelated charges), defamed, blackmailed, or assaulted.[297] Opposition politicians and civil society activists who seek to constrain the authorities or hold the regime accountable to the public experience similar forms of pressure as well as more petty kinds of harassment and restraint.[298]

The November 2005 parliamentary election, Ilham's first after becoming president, proved particularly important in consolidating his position as single-pyramid patron. Opposition forces sought to build on the trial run of 2003 and mobilize a color revolution along the lines of those that had occurred during the previous two years in Georgia, Ukraine, and Kyrgyzstan. They borrowed explicitly from this recipe of techniques, including youth group activism (including the organizations Yeni Fikir and Yox!), uniting in a big bloc (Azadliq), and even adopting the color orange. By some counts, they were able to rally as many as fifty thousand people in the streets in the run-up to the election.[299] But even this concerted effort proved no match for the political machine of a relatively popular patronal president who was not a lame-duck, with its ability to bias media strongly, constrain opponents, shape policy strategically (for example, raising the minimum wage 20 percent prior to the voting),[300] and falsify election results.[301] The result was a major win for the Yeni Azerbaijan Party and regime-friendly independents, with opposition candidates winding up with just 8 of 125 seats.[302] Having anticipated and prepared for such an outcome, the opposition bloc was able to mobilize as many as twenty thousand to the streets after the vote to demand new elections.[303] These included many losing district

---

[296] Eldar Namazov, adviser to President Heydar Aliyev until 1999, president of the Public Forum "For Azerbaijan" as of 2008, author's interview, October 4, 2008.

[297] Some of the of many instances documented in Azerbaijani and international media can be found in *Azadliq*, June 1, 2013, p. 3; *Bizim Yol*, June 15, 2013, p. 2; *Kavkazskii Uzel*, May 2, 2012, 00:39; *Polit.Ru*, June 4, 2009, 16:22; *RFE/RL Newsline*, March 7, 2006; *RFE/RL Newsline*, May 30, 2007; *RFE/RL Newsline*, March 10, 2008; *RFE/RL Newsline*, March 14, 2008; *RFE/RL Newsline*, April 9, 2008; Shahla Sultanova, "Bull's Eye on Their Backs," *Transitions Online*, March 20, 2012.

[298] For example, occasional beatings and threats (*Gundam Xabar*, June 3, 2013, p. 3), jailing (*Gundam Xabar*, June 10, 2013, p. 6), restriction of rallies to remote locations (*Kavkazskii Uzel*, September 12, 2008), eviction from offices (Liz Fuller, "Azerbaijani Opposition Mulls Presidential Election Boycott," *RFE/RL*, August 2, 2008), and expulsion from university (*Eurasianet*, May 10, 2012, 2:28 pm).

[299] Alieva, "Azerbaijan's Frustrating Elections."

[300] *RFE/RL Newsline*, September 19, 2005.

[301] Alieva, "Azerbaijan's Frustrating Elections."

[302] Radnitz, "Oil in the Family."

[303] *RFE/RL Newsline*, November 14, 2005.

candidates, a category of politician Radnitz has shown were key players in Kyrgyzstan's Tulip Revolution.[304] But the regime, suffering no significant defections, easily disrupted and then put down the protests, with police preventing people from attending the rally through preemptive arrests and blocking roads from the country's provinces into the capital city even before using force to disperse them.[305] Seeking to explain their failure, some in the opposition blamed the United States and other powers for a lack of support.[306]

This crushing official victory by Ilham Aliyev's power pyramid strongly reinforced expectations that his regime was there to stay. Gambar, for example, reports that people came to think there was close to a zero chance of political change in the foreseeable future, an attitude that in turn led to demoralization and a rise in passivity within the ranks of the opposition.[307] The Azadliq bloc accordingly fractured.[308] Aliyev easily dispensed with one elite defection that occurred a year and a half later when Yeni Azerbaijan Party deputy chair Siruz Tebrizli called publicly for people to attend a rally organized by Gambar's Musavat and defended Insanov just after the latter had gone on trial.[309] The president also made clear soon after this election that he intended to be reelected, with the YAP announcing already in 2006 that it would back him in the 2008 presidential contest.[310]

This set the stage for an easy Aliyev win on October 15, 2008, touring the country's provinces, presiding over the opening of Heydar Aliyev museums in district after district,[311] and stressing themes of economic progress,[312] local infrastructural improvements,[313] preparation for war if necessary to regain Nagorno-Karabakh,[314] and a battle against corruption (arresting a member of his government).[315] The machine was also in full operation, including media biased heavily in favor of Aliyev[316] and election laws constraining the opposition even more than before. In the face of all this, the opposition was relatively quiet, not expecting a victory and thus dividing over whether to boycott the vote. With the major parties in the end deciding to boycott, the result was that only minor figures wound up on the ballot challenging the incumbent.[317]

---

[304] Radnitz, *Weapons of the Wealthy*; *RFE/RL Newsline*, November 18, 2005.

[305] Radnitz, "Oil in the Family"; *RFE/RL Newsline*, November 9, 2005.

[306] *RFE/RL Newsline*, December 6, 2005.

[307] Gambar interview 2010.

[308] *RFE/RL Newsline*, February 14, 2006.

[309] *RFE/RL Newsline*, March 19, 2007.

[310] *RFE/RL Newsline*, September 29, 2006.

[311] *Yezhednievnye Novosti* (Azerbaijan), September 26, 2008, p. 2.

[312] *Ekho*, September 27, 2008, p. 2.

[313] *Yezhednievnye Novosti* (Azerbaijan), October 3, 2008, p. 2.

[314] *Day.Az*, October 13, 2008, 18:58.

[315] *Kavkazskii Uzel*, August 7, 2008.

[316] *Kavkazskii Uzel*, October 12, 2008.

[317] Ayca Ergun, "The Presidential Election in Azerbaijan, October 2008," *Electoral Studies*, v. 28, no. 4, December 2009, pp. 647–51; Rovshan Ismayilov, "Azerbaijan: Officials Plan for

Aliyev refused to participate in televised debates himself, but did have a proxy make his case for him.[318] The Yeni Azerbaijan Party remained the basis of his campaign organization. Beginning a year and a half in advance, the YAP mobilized some thirty thousand people through party organizations in all districts, contacting people door to door and by phone and drawing in part on election training received by a chief official from democracy-promotion agencies in the United States.[319] Asked who might be able to pose a challenge to Aliyev, 59 percent in a nationwide poll said no one could, while his wife, Mehriban Aliyeva, got the most such "votes" in the survey with 7 percent and Gambar was named by 6 percent.[320] Aliyev claimed 89 percent in the final official vote count.[321] Examination of unusual digit patterns in officially reported results strongly indicated that this result reflected at least some fraud.[322] Other statistical analysis, while concurring there was at least some fraud, also found evidence that the official vote did in fact vary across regions to some degree in correlation with economic well-being.[323] No major protests ensued.[324]

Aliyev used his position of strength to start the process of removing term limits even before his 2008 reelection. Earlier, many had speculated that his wife, herself a parliamentarian and head of the Heydar Aliyev Foundation, could succeed him after his second term.[325] During July 2008, however, calls rose from the Yeni Azerbaijan Party leadership to hold a referendum on removing term limits for Aliyev, effectively linking this idea to his October 2008 reelection.[326] Parliament finalized these plans after the election, calling the referendum for March 2009. To maximize chances for approval by lowering the stakes, the change was limited in scope: The elimination of term limits was to apply only during situations of war, which Azerbaijan was officially in

'Problem-Free' Presidential Election," *Eurasianet*, May 21, 2008; Mina Muradova, "Azerbaijan: Opposition Mulls Presidential Election Boycott," *Eurasianet*, June 9, 2008.

[318] Presidential election candidate debate (Azeri language), ITV Channel, author's observation, Baku, October 2008.

[319] Novruzov interview 2008.

[320] Musabayov and Shulman, *Azerbaijan in 2007*.

[321] *TsentrAziia*, centrasia.ru, October 19, 2008, 18:41.

[322] Fredrik Sjoberg, "Autocratic Adaptation: The Strategic Use of Transparency and the Persistence of Election Fraud," *Electoral Studies*, v. 33, no. 1, March 2014, pp. 233–45. An analysis consistent with this finding is Erik S. Herron, "The Effect of Passive Observation Methods on Azerbaijan's 2008 Presidential Election and 2009 Referendum," *Electoral Studies*, v. 29, no. 3, 2010, pp. 417–24.

[323] Erik S. Herron, "Measuring Dissent in Electoral Authoritarian Societies: Lessons from Azerbaijan's 2008 Presidential Election and 2009 Referendum," *Comparative Political Studies*, v. 44, no. 11, November 2011, pp. 1557–83.

[324] Ron Synovitz, "Azerbaijan's Opposition Cries 'Foul' As President Reelected," *RFE/RL*, October 16, 2008.

[325] E.g., *Radio Svoboda*, December 19, 2008, translated into Russian by Zpress.kg, published in *TsentrAziia*, December 23, 2008, 12:23.

[326] Ali Akhmetov, executive secretary of the Yeni Azerbaijan Party, interview with *Ekho*, July 19, 2008, no. 130.

with Armenia. This also increased chances of success by linking its passage to success in the Nagorno-Karabakh conflict. Further diluting the debate, the term limit question was only one of more than forty referendum items appearing on the ballot at the same time.[327] To minimize the chances of protest, according to one account, the referendum was held on the eve of the major Novruz holiday.[328] Opponents publicly called the referendum initiative a move to "dictatorship and monarchy."[329] The regime responded that it was democratic in giving the people the option to reelect a leader they liked.[330] With the single-pyramid system showing no cracks, and in the wake of Aliyev's resounding presidential victory just a few months earlier, the official result was an overwhelming yes.

Presidential Administration chief Mehdiyev assured democracy advocates in a 2010 book that they did not have to worry. Azerbaijan, he wrote, was merely following the findings of scholars ranging from Seymour Martin Lipset to Raymond Duch to Samuel Huntington that democracy could not work until a high GDP per capita was achieved. And this, he averred, was Ilham Aliyev's top priority.[331] But despite rapid per capita economic growth well into the 2010s, there was little sign of political opening. If anything, developments appeared to be continuing to move in the opposite direction as few significant networks dared challenge his dominance. With restrictions on campaigning and pressure on independent media growing, the YAP cruised to victory in the 2010 parliamentary elections and the opposition could not mobilize a significant protest.[332]

Ilham Aliyev then went into the 2013 presidential election showing no intention to leave power, and at age 51 on voting day there was no reason to expect him not to remain vigorous in office long into the future. Some signs of discontent occasionally bubbled up in Azerbaijani society. Rioting in Quba against a governor linked to the oligarch-minister Mammadov took many by surprise in March 2012, but did not spread.[333] A similar local uprising involving discontent with the locally dominant oligarch's network (that of Labor and Social Security Minister Fizuli Alakbarov) broke out in Ismayilli in January 2013, but also did not spread and the authorities found it a convenient pretext to jail certain opposition leaders, including REAL chief Ilqar Mammadov.[334] Subsequent youth group attempts to mobilize a protest movement leading up to

[327] *Kavkazskii Uzel*, February 21, 2009, 23:27; Mina Muradova, "Azerbaijan: Referendum May Mark Demise of Civil Society," *Eurasia Insight*, March 17, 2009.

[328] Mina Muradova, "Azerbaijan: Grumbling over Referendum Results Continues in Baku," *Eurasianet Civil Society*, April 13, 2009.

[329] *Kavkazskii Uzel*, March 14, 2009, 16:23.

[330] Ali Valiyev, "High Hopes," *Transitions Online*, February 17, 2009.

[331] Mehdiyev, *Azerbaijan – 2003–2008*, p. 12.

[332] *Kavkazskii Uzel*, May 31, 2010, 19:24; *Kavkazskii Uzel*, June 18, 2010, 19:46.

[333] Shahin Abbasov, "Azerbaijan: Is Guba Protest Response a Harbinger of a Political Shift in Baku?" *Eurasianet*, March 6, 2012, 3:31; *RFE/RL*, March 1, 2012, 14:35.

[334] Khadija Ismayilova, "Azerbaijan: Examining the Economic Sources of Ismayilli Discontent," *Eurasianet*, January 31, 2013, 1:52 pm.

the election were persistent but did not generate broad participation or significant elite defections, and instead many activists were arrested.[335] A university rector's September 2012 release of videotapes implicating a YAP parliamentarian in bribery resulted in the latter's resignation, but the rector felt the need to remain abroad and the scandal did not appear to affect the public standing of the regime greatly.[336] The main opposition parties managed to unite and fielded historian Camil Hasanli as their candidate, and he blasted Aliyev personally for corruption during a live televised debate.[337] But his candidacy essentially suffocated under the weight of expectations that Aliyev would remain dominant, unable to mobilize significant business support or to compete with the lavish coverage of the president that the country's major television news programs had to offer. After the official tally gave Aliyev 85 percent of the vote, the opposition could mobilize only about ten thousand in protest of what it called fraud.[338]

In a display of dominance, only after his reelection did Aliyev bow to public opinion by removing some of the less popular figures in his government, such as Alakbarov, reputed to be the informal curator of Ismayilli.[339] Media also experienced new pressure, as first opposition and then all newspapers were barred from being sold in Baku Metro stations (though they could still be purchased freely in kiosks throughout the city).[340] The head of a prominent election watchdog organization was arrested in late 2013.[341] In Azerbaijan as of 2014, then, elite and mass expectations all pointed to a continued phase of political closure, with little prospect for the single-pyramid system to break down in the foreseeable future barring a grievous regime mistake or a dramatic turn of events such as presidential illness or new losses in the Nagorno-Karabakh war.

Succession in Nagorno-Karabakh

After Ghukasian inherited the presidency from Kocharian (who had departed to become Armenia's president) and eliminated his main rival (Babaian), Nagorno-Karabagh experienced a lame-duck period as Ghukasian reached the end of his second term in 2007. Ghukasian is reported by outside observers to have enjoyed strong popular support among the Armenian residents of Karabakh (the native Azeris there having been forced out long ago) as a kind of "peace dividend." Indeed, something resembling normalcy had returned to the unrecognized republic after the cease-fire with Azerbaijan and the elimination of most violent domestic contestation with the sidelining of Babaian's

[335] Saadat Cahangir, "Bir daha 'zavzayi oldurmak' haqqinda," *Azadliq*, June 1, 2013, p. 7.
[336] Shahin Abbasov, "Azerbaijan: Secret Videos Threaten Top Presidential Aide," *Eurasianet*, January 29, 2013, 4:17 pm.
[337] *Kavkazskii Uzel*, October 2, 2013, 01:58.
[338] *Kavkazskii Uzel*, October 12, 2013; *Kavkazskii Uzel*, October 27, 2013, 18:43.
[339] *Kavkazskii Uzel*, October 23, 2013, 13:05.
[340] *Kavkazskii Uzel*, November 15, 2013, 22:25.
[341] RFE/RL, December 18, 2013.

network of violent entrepreneurs. Thus while the opposition Dashnaktsutiun party was able to win about a third of the seats in the parliament in the 2000 elections, by August 2002 he had sailed to victory in the presidential election with the support of all of the main parties (his own ruling Union of Democratic Artsakh as well as the Dashnaks and Communists), claiming an 88 percent win in the official tally.[342] This did not mark the absence of opposition, however. With Ghukasian serving his second and constitutionally final term in office, the Dashnaks returned to opposition in 2003 and joined a new Movement-88 opposition party, which managed to win the direct mayoral elections in Stepanakert in 2004.[343] But with Ghukasian enjoying popularity, his lame-duck status did not translate into a strong opposition showing in the 2005 parliamentary elections: The bloc of these two opposition parties netted just 3 of the 33 seats up for election, with propresidential parties winning the rest.[344]

Ghukasian had promised when the new constitution was adopted in 2006 that he would recognize the two-term limit to apply to the two terms he had served since taking office, and he kept his word in the end.[345] In selecting a successor to endorse, he picked former National Security Service chief Bako Saakian, who reportedly had both Armenia and Russia in his corner as well.[346] Saakian could hope for public support among the Karabakh Armenians due to an aura of de facto victory in the independence war working in his favor since he had fought in it and could claim credit for helping to preserve its autonomy in his ministerial role. The Dashnaks (perhaps under pressure from their Armenian partner organization) refused to challenge Saakian, leaving Deputy Foreign Minister Masis Maiilian as his main election opponent. As Maiilian did not even hold the rank of minister, his candidacy represented only a minor crack in the republic's single-pyramid system and he was backed only by a breakaway faction of Movement-88.

The result was a major Saakian victory, with 85 percent of the official vote, in the 2007 presidential election.[347] This unity of the territory's main networks around Saakian continued into the 2010 parliamentary elections, when none of the competing parties openly opposed him.[348] Making no major missteps, the local economy growing, and reportedly very popular among the Armenians living

[342] Kimitaka Matsuzato, "From Belligerent to Multi-Ethnic Democracy: Domestic Politics in Unrecognized States after the Ceasefires," *Eurasian Review*, v. 1, November 2008, pp. 95–119; Pal Kolsto and Helge Blakkisrud, "Living with Non-Recognition: State- and Nation-Building in South Caucasian Quasi-States," *Europe-Asia Studies*, v. 60, no. 3, May 2008, pp. 483–509.

[343] Matsuzato, "From Belligerent," pp. 97, 105.

[344] Kolsto and Blakkisrud, "Living with Non-recognition," p. 502.

[345] That is, Ghukasian might have been able to claim that the new constitution of 2006 meant he could start counting terms toward his two-term limit afresh from that date and thus run for a new period in office in 2007. *RFE/RL Newsline*, February 22, 2007; *RFE/RL Newsline*, July 19, 2007.

[346] Kolsto and Blakkisrud, "Living with Non-recognition," p. 501.

[347] Matsuzato, "From Belligerent," pp. 105–6.

[348] *Kavkazskii Uzel*, April 29, 2010, 16:50.

in the territory, Saakian won reelection in the 2012 presidential contest stressing the need for continuity in pursuing independence and development.[349] While he faced a critic in that election, parliamentarian Vitaly Balasanian, the incumbent more than doubled the challenger's official vote total, 67–33 percent.[350] Saakian thus entered his own lame-duck term in office, though if he is able to sustain popular support (or at least select a popular heir), the logic of patronal politics would suggest he has good chances of ushering his pick into the presidency after him when the next presidential elections roll around.

Conclusion

This chapter has established two core findings. First, patronal presidents who became widely expected to leave office but did not suffer low popularity tended to be successful in their attempts to install hand-picked "heirs" in office to succeed them. At the same time, the chapter establishes that they did tend to experience crises of elite coordination during these moments of anticipated succession. Though a lame-duck syndrome typically works against the coordination of elite networks in a single-pyramid system, it need not be fatal to incumbent networks that can sustain or gain substantial public support. Second, those patronal presidents who were never widely expected to leave the presidency during a specific upcoming election also tended to be successful in resisting attempts to overthrow them, even when these attempts greatly resembled efforts that had been successful against lame-duck presidents.

Beyond these general observations are a number of more specific findings that help establish the usefulness of the patronal politics lens for understanding post-Soviet politics. For one thing, because the coordination process involved in the pyramid-building process takes time, we see power pyramids tending steadily to tighten, with interruptions primarily around moments of succession. Accordingly, we tend to see the tightest pyramids, those that are the most politically closed and most closely approximating autocracy, emerging in those regimes that have experienced the least disruption for the longest periods of time as a result of either high leader popularity or the avoidance of term limits, or both. The strongest cases in point include Uzbekistan and Turkmenistan, but Azerbaijan, Belarus, Kazakhstan, Nagorno-Karabakh, and Russia also well illustrate the point. At the same time, except for the countries that inherited the Communist Party infrastructure for full dictatorship intact when becoming independent, the political closure we have witnessed in the post-Soviet region has generally been asymptotic rather than linear. That is, it has generally approached but not actually crossed the crucial line separating a hybrid regime

---

[349] *Kavkazskii Uzel*, July 8, 2012, 06:10. A survey organized by Gerard Toal and John O'Loughlan ("Inside South Ossetia: A Survey of Attitudes in a De Facto State," *Post-Soviet Affairs*, v. 29, no. 2, 2013, pp. 136–72) in 2010–11 reportedly found overwhelming trust in the presidency.

[350] *Novosti-Armeniia*, July 23, 2012, 10:54.

from a full autocracy: the presence of at least some genuine opposition on the most important ballots, however unfairly the deck is stacked against them.[351]

This chapter's analysis also shows how term limits, among all of the other reasons why patronal presidents might come to be expected to leave office, tend to provide particularly important focal points around which elites can coordinate to remove unpopular leaders. In general, the cases considered in Chapters 7 and 8 suggest that those leaders who succeeded in attempts to remove term limits outright generally wielded substantial popular support at the time they made their moves (for example, Aliyev, Lukashenka, and Nazarbaev), whereas unpopular ones have not been guaranteed success (thus Kuchma succeeded, but Yeltsin failed) or found ways simply to delay when the limit applied to them (as did Akaev, Karimov, and Rahmonov). Tactics also may have mattered, or at least the leaders who successfully escaped term limits often behaved as if they had to tread delicately with the issue. Aliyev, therefore, essentially buried the term limit question in a hugely complex referendum on many different questions and found a formulation that made the removal of term limits not permanent (tying it to the state of war Azerbaijan was and remains in). We will return to this discussion in Chapter 11.

The detailed analysis in this chapter has also been important in establishing what is less essential for the ouster of a nondemocratic patronal president. For one thing, the set of "nonousters" examined here includes several cases where most if not all of the main "ingredients" of commonly cited opposition recipes for removing dictators have been in place. It turns out that these playbooks have tended to have little effect on regime survival when the incumbents either are not lame-ducks or wield substantial popular support. One can even go further: Not only are such "opposition toolkits" secondary causes of presidential ouster, but *whether or not these instructions are "fully adopted" is in fact largely endogenous to the logic of patronal politics*.[352] That is, we find that opposition forces are much more likely to adopt bold and ambitious strategies, to be united, to find and coordinate around a message that will resonate, to attract business support, and to have cracks in the system that enable credible parallel vote counts and exit polls when incumbent presidents are unpopular lame-ducks.

Likewise, we find that patronal presidents with significant public support and/or "healthy duck" status have been able to sustain their power pyramids and keep their own networks in power through all kinds of different methods and in all kinds of different circumstances that different analysts often posit are centrally important. Some constantly reshuffled elites (as did Lukashenka), while others did not, letting different ones build up substantial fiefdoms (as did

---

[351] Tajikistan's presidential election in 2013 appears to have crossed this line, though subsequent elections will show whether this was a contingent aberration or the actual traversing of a Rubicon. To date, at least, opposition parties in Tajikistan are still able to operate and contest other elections, in stark contrast with the situation in Turkmenistan and Uzbekistan.

[352] For an argument that these factors are not endogenous to other forces, see Bunce and Wolchik, *Defeating Authoritarian Leaders*, pp. 216, 243–5.

the Aliyevs). Some had precious little economic activity by presidential relatives (for example, Putin) while others allowed it to happen in spades (for example, Nazarbaev). Some presided over extensively privatized economies (as in Russia and Kazakhstan), while others' economies featured little privatization (as with Belarus and Uzbekistan). Some survived despite their polities' having experienced presidential ousters and great political violence in the past (as in Azerbaijan), while others have avoided turnover for the entire life span of their initial leaders (as in Turkmenistan). Some of their states are widely regarded as strong (such as Belarus) while others are seen as weak (such as Tajikistan). Some have relied on dominant parties (for example, Putin), while others have eschewed them (for example, Lukashenka). And some have enjoyed immense oil wealth (as has Azerbaijan), while others have had quite measly economic resources to draw on for their political machines (as has been the case in Belarus and Tajikistan).

Comparative analysis, then, suggests that much of what may appear significant in any one case is likely to be much more or much less significant depending on whether leaders are lame-ducks and are able to sustain significant public support because of, despite, or regardless of such factors. Now that we have explored what happens in countries that have not experienced patronal presidential ousters since at least the mid-1990s, the following chapter turns to an examination of what happens after such events have occurred.

9

After Revolution

To say that revolutions and other leadership ousters are normal regime dynamics in patronal presidential systems is to say that they are not likely to constitute or lead to true or sustained democratization. That is, they do not tend to constitute regime change in the sense that they do not change the fundamental set of rules (formal or informal) that tend to govern which individuals have access to the most important state positions, how such access is obtained, and how binding state decisions are made.[1] Once one side has won the political struggle and assumed the patronal presidency, even if the outcome at that moment was decided in a free and fair vote because of a rupture in the single-pyramid system, society's most important patronal networks have great incentive once again to start rallying around the new president so as to preclude falling out of favor. This is because of the information and focal effects of presidentialist constitutions in patronal polities that were described in Chapter 4 and documented in many countries by Chapters 6 and 8. Postrevolutionary patronal presidents, having just won a major contest of patronal network strength, often also benefit politically from this fresh and obvious information confirming their dominance. But even when such a president is not yet dominant, as can happen when she is a first among equals in a revolutionary coalition, the fact that she occupies the patronal presidency tends to confirm that she is indeed the most powerful of the lot and gives her focal status for elites otherwise unsure where to place their bets.

Realizing this tendency, incoming revolutionary presidents thus have incentive to encourage it and use it to their advantage. They can do so actively (through repression or reward) or passively (through overlooking the corruption of political allies or selectively ignoring pleas for resource transfers made by political opponents). Taking advantage of the opportunities provided by

---

[1] This refers to the definition of "regime" given in Chapter 1.

the presidentialist constitution, however, does require skill, sensitivity, and patience in order to avoid authoritarian overreach. To the extent that the revolution does not produce a single new leader acknowledged by all, more skill and patience are required because other prominent individuals and networks must be marginalized without provoking them into a coordinated challenge. More skill and patience are also required the more complete is the discoordination of the country's major networks at the outset. If the revolution represents only a last-minute break of one major network from the dominant power pyramid, for example, the single-pyramid system will be easier to put back together. But if the revolution is the result of a long, drawn-out struggle through which the country's main networks have badly damaged relationships or completely destroyed institutions that help bind them together in the previous political machine, then it will be much more difficult to induce them to work together for the new authority and more time-consuming to find ways of actually organizing them into a single pyramid of authority. The more sustained the competing-pyramid period, and the more it can be called a competing-pyramid *system*, the more time and skill it will take to restore a single-pyramid system.

The incentive to take advantage of patronal presidential authority is very powerful. Even well-intentioned, Western-oriented presidents who rise to power atop what they see as a prodemocracy movement are likely to find themselves resorting to machine tactics in an effort to overcome "stubborn," "obsolete," "corrupt," "unpatriotic," "pro-Russian," or "illegitimate" opposition to what they may actually see as necessary democratic or market reforms. The temptation patronal presidents face is to "impose reforms from above" through the existing (or potential) concentration of political machine power rather than to engage in the more uncertain process of building the broad-based coalitions that working within a competing-pyramid system can necessitate. Even in established minimally patronalistic democracies, few are the presidents who actually like the uncertainty democracy generates when it comes to getting something important done. Where presidents have the chance to build up greater authority, then, the result ironically can be a reversion to the same kind of authoritarian-style politics that had been the target of a new leader's criticism prior to assuming office. Of course, the tendency to restore the methods of single-pyramid politics is even stronger to the extent leaders make little pretense of supporting democratic norms.

This is not to say that actual, lasting democratization by overthrowing a patronal presidential network is impossible. There are at least two paths by which it might come about, and the key is whether the ouster actually changes the core conditions this book has identified as tending to generate single-pyramid politics. The most likely path (at least in the short term) occurs when the overthrow *also* produces a change in the formal constitutional framework, replacing a presidentialist constitution with a divided-executive one (or, under some conditions, a parliamentarist one). This might happen, for example, when a contestation phase in a patronal presidential country happens to result in a stalemate where both sides are uncertain about their ability to prevail. As a compromise and a hedge for their bets, these two sides might create institutions that reduce the stakes of the contest, promote opportunities for sharing power equitably, and provide some insurance against the possibility that whoever wins the presidency will, after having occupied the office, persecute the other side.[2] That is, they might agree to introduce a divided-executive constitution or some other formal arrangement that complicates the patronal network coordination dynamics at the heart of single-pyramid politics.

A less likely but still possible avenue by which a patronal presidential revolution might lead to true democratization would be if it empowers a truly committed democratic leader. Such a leader might ardently refuse to govern by machine methods. Steven Levitsky and Lucan Way note that determined leadership can produce a kind of contingent democratization, one that is likely to be reversed when a new leader is elected who lacks this commitment.[3] More promising for long-run democratization would be if this leader willfully pushes through herculean reforms designed to change the country's social equilibrium of patronalism, cleansing it from the proverbial stables of politics in a way that would be hard or impossible to reverse. While not outside the realm of reality, this is extraordinarily unlikely. Looking around the globe, one can identify only a handful of leaders who through sheer force of will appear to have radically purged a culture of patronalism (including phenomena often associated with it, such as corruption) during their lifetime. Singapore's Lee Kwan Yew and Chile's Augusto Pinochet are perhaps among the lonely examples, and neither can be considered a model democrat, to put it very mildly.

In the post-Soviet context, the leader is rare indeed (if existing at all) who is so committed to democracy that he or she is able to resist the siren's song of the patronal presidency. The patronal presidency is attractive as a seemingly all-powerful instrument for getting done whatever one wants to get done in a society where "no one" abides by the formal rules anyway, where attempting to do so oneself is likely to land one in the ash heap of history as an ineffectual ruler, and where it is common knowledge that to accomplish anything, one needs to do the dirty work. Reflecting for a moment on recent post-Soviet history shows how powerful these temptations can be. Who actually were the "decrepit autocrats" overthrown in the iconic post-Soviet color revolutions? Askar Akaev, long regarded in the West as the sole democratic leader in Central Asia? Eduard Shevardnadze, Gorbachev's pro-Western foreign minister who had resigned that post in early 1991 explicitly to warn presciently against an impending hard-liner coup? Even Ukraine's Leonid Kuchma was seen initially as a Russophilic technocratic manager rather than a dictator, and when he challenged Kravchuk, there was "no fear that he was not a democrat."[4]

---

[2] Timothy Frye, "A Politics of Institutional Choice – Post-Communist Presidencies," *Comparative Political Studies*, v. 30, October 1997, pp. 523–52.

[3] Steven Levitsky and Lucan A. Way, *Competitive Authoritarianism: Hybrid Regimes after the Cold War* (New York: Cambridge University Press, 2010), pp. 82–3.

[4] Paul D'Anieri, *Understanding Ukrainian Politics: Power, Politics, and Institutional Design* (Armonk, NY: M. E. Sharpe, 2007), p. 82.

The fact that even leaders with such strong apparent democratic credentials wound up succumbing to the call of the power pyramid, as did all of the other kinds of leaders described in Chapter 6, must tell us something about the dominance of its incentives over individual leaders' values when it comes to larger patterns in the patronalistic context.[5] Or at least, it tells us that leaders are frequently led to accept dirty means in pursuit of lofty and more distant ends. Thus with rare exceptions, we should generally expect revolutionary leaders' personal inclinations to matter only at the margins. Whether a particular leader is more or less risk-acceptant in domestic politics, for example, is likely to color the degree of tightness or looseness of the power pyramids she constructs. But such personal dispositions are unlikely to alter the fundamentals, the mechanisms of power that are exercised in highly patronalistic polities when the most important resources or goals are at stake. In the language of regime cycles, leadership values can shift their length or amplitude to some degree, but are unlikely to change the larger patterns fundamentally.

Post-Soviet, postouster history confirms these general predictions. Overwhelmingly, one sees that where patronal presidentialism remained in place after a leadership ouster (be it a color revolution or palace coup), single-pyramid politics reemerged much as it had originally developed in the 1990s. Georgia after the Rose Revolution represents the sole instance where it is plausible to argue that an exertion of patronal leadership went at least part of the way to reducing the degree to which patronalistic relations dominated the nexus of state, society, and economy. But this progress was partial at best, and in any case postrevolutionary developments featured the strong reemergence of a new single-pyramid system, if a more sophisticated version with a lighter touch than had existed before. Ukraine starting in 2004, however, represents a significant pattern of exceptions that proves the larger rule. During the Orange Revolution, the ouster of an incumbent presidential network also resulted in a dismantling of patronal presidentialism by means of constitutional change, accordingly leading to a period of remarkably open politics during 2005–10. Since then, we find three similar instances: The 2010 revolution in Kyrgyzstan, the ouster of Georgia's Mikheil Saakashvili in 2013, and Ukraine's Euromaidan Revolution in 2014 each came with a transition to a divided-executive constitution. The latter two events are too recent for us to judge the effects with confidence, but Kyrgyzstan since 2010 has experienced dramatically more open politics than before, and in a context that had initially led many to relegate the country to the realm of failed states.

This chapter begins by demonstrating the critical importance of whether presidentialist constitutions are changed in the course of revolution in determining whether the ultimate outcome of that revolution is likely to be genuine democratization (in the form of an enduring competing pyramid system)

---

[5] On the relatively low level of ideological commitment in former Soviet countries, see Stephen E. Hanson, *Post-Imperial Democracies: Ideology and Party Formation in Third Republic France, Weimar Germany, and Post-Soviet Russia* (New York: Cambridge University Press, 2010).

or a new cyclic movement toward a single-pyramid system. The chapter accomplishes this through a tightly focused "pair of paired comparisons"[6] involving Ukraine and Kyrgyzstan during two separate periods, 2005–10 and 2010–14. These two countries in these two periods give us special ability to isolate the effects of formal constitutional design on postrevolutionary patronal network arrangement because they are strikingly similar in nearly all relevant respects except for the factor of interest: whether a postrevolutionary power-sharing deal was anchored in the elimination of a formally presidentialist constitution. Kyrgyzstan had a presidentialist constitution while Ukraine did not during 2005–10, but the reverse was true for 2010–14. The effects in both of these periods in both of these countries are as we would expect.

The chapter then provides an in-depth discussion of Ukraine's 2010 presidential election to illustrate how democracy can function in highly patronalistic contexts, producing an essentially free and fair expression of genuine public sentiment despite rampant corruption and manipulated media. Sections on Abkhazia, Armenia, and Georgia after their presidential ousters then show how postrevolutionary regime dynamics there also fit the pattern anticipated by the patronal politics logic. The patronal presidential network ousters in South Ossetia and Transnistria, not to mention Ukraine's Euromaidan Revolution, occurred too recently for their effects to be clear and so their aftermath is not discussed here. But the logic of regular patronalistic regime dynamics would expect renewed closure in Transnistria and South Ossetia,[7] which continue to have presidentialist constitutions, and sustained competing-pyramid politics in Ukraine, which shifted back to a divided-executive constitution in 2014.

A Pair of Paired Comparisons: Ukraine and Kyrgyzstan 2005–2010 and 2010–2014

Ukraine and Kyrgyzstan during 2005–10 provide as good an opportunity as can be expected in the real world to deal with the "chicken and egg" difficulties that Chapter 4 mentioned can plague attempts to figure out what the effects of formal constitutions are on how patronal networks are arranged in a society.[8] Kyrgyzstan and Ukraine make for a good comparison because both

- have been enduringly highly patronalistic societies as defined previously and as indicated in the quantitative measures and qualitative discussion presented in Chapters 2, 3, and 5–7;

---

[6] Alexander L. George and Andrew Bennett, *Case Studies and Theory Development in the Social Sciences* (Cambridge, MA: MIT Press, 2005); Sidney Tarrow, "The Strategy of Paired Comparison," *Comparative Political Studies*, v. 43, no. 2, February 2010, pp. 230–59.

[7] With some chance of interruption by irregular regime dynamics.

[8] Some of the material on the 2005–10 period in this section draws from Henry E. Hale, "Formal Constitutions in Informal Politics: Institutions and Democratization in Eurasia," *World Politics*, v. 63, no. 4, October 2011, pp. 581–617, which also includes a rigorous discussion of alternative hypotheses (not reproduced here) to which readers are referred.

- had presidentialist constitutions from at least the mid-1990s up until their first revolutions, as was documented in Chapters 6 and 7;
- had single-pyramid systems dominated by a president relying on both formal and informal powers prior to these revolutions, as was also shown in Chapters 6 and 7.

Because these countries were so similar in regime and constitution prior to 2005, we cannot explain any dramatic post-2005 differences in regime or constitution by citing factors that did not change dramatically in either country in 2005, including religious heritage, historical legacy, extent of kinship-based politics, political culture, and structurally present patterns of international linkage and Western leverage.

Moreover, the specific events during and immediately following 2005 are strikingly similar in important details that help isolate the effects of formal constitutions. In each case:

- The old presidential network was ousted by an electoral revolution during the same span of a few months (late 2004 through early 2005), with each new president assuming the right to a five-year term in office in 2005;
- Emerging victorious was not a single leader but a "tandem" of leaders who each represented separate but allied patronal networks (Viktor Yushchenko and Yulia Tymoshenko in Ukraine and Kurmanbek Bakiev and Feliks Kulov in Kyrgyzstan);
- A deal was struck in which one member of each tandem became president (Yushchenko and Bakiev) and the other became prime minister (Tymoshenko and Kulov);
- The future president, unable to win the presidency outright, was forced to accept a power-sharing arrangement that involved transferring significant powers to the prime minister.

What crucially differentiates the two cases is that in Ukraine, the power-sharing arrangement was accompanied by the adoption of a *formal divided-executive constitution* that declared the prime minister to be roughly equal to and independent of the president, whereas in Kyrgyzstan the power-sharing deal was based only on the rough balance of *informal* power that each tandem mate wielded at the time of the revolution, without changing the presidentialist nature of the formal constitution.[9] At the time, Bakiev described his deal with Kulov thus: "This is not a legal document, but a political document. Of course, the word of a politician is worth nothing, but I gave my word as a man."[10]

But why is it that Ukraine's prime minister wound up with a constitutional change while Kyrgyzstan's got only a "word as a man"? It was certainly not

---

[9] Robert K. Christensen, Edward R. Rakhimkulov, and Charles R. Wise, "The Ukrainian Orange Revolution Brought More than a New President: What Kind of Democracy Will the Institutional Changes Bring?" *Communist and Post-Communist Studies*, v. 38, no. 2, June 2005, pp. 207–30; Feliks Kulov, *Na perevale* (Moscow: Vremia, 2008), pp. 199–200.

[10] *RFE/RL Newsline*, May 18, 2005.

that the future Ukrainian prime minister had stronger bargaining power within her tandem than did Kyrgyzstan's Kulov: Tymoshenko actually *opposed* this constitutional reform and during the negotiations pushed strongly for a fully powerful formal presidency for her tandem mate, Yushchenko. It was also not that Yushchenko was any weaker than Bakiev: Each one had agreed to accept reduced presidential power because each one was unable to win on his own. In Yushchenko's case, there was an unprecedented and extended street standoff between the eastern-based ruling authorities and up to a million of his more western-oriented supporters, and the Kuchma regime's price for conceding the presidency to Yushchenko was to weaken this presidency by transferring important formal powers to a prime minister.[11] Yushchenko feared the alternative was civil war.[12] Bakiev faced essentially the same fear and inability to win outright. The Tulip Revolution had begun in the South and its leading figure, Bakiev, was a southerner, while the ousted Akaev had his strongest base of support in the North.[13] When Akaev fled, northern networks and public opinion quickly rallied around the northern Kulov, whom Akaev had imprisoned but who was let out during the revolution and then took over security structures in the capital city.[14] Polls show a clear regional divide in Bakiev's and Kulov's support.[15] Perceiving a dangerous north-south split as likely in the event that the two campaigned against each other in the upcoming presidential election, Bakiev acquiesced to sharing power with Kulov.[16] It was not any special power advantage for either Tymoshenko or Bakiev, then, that explains why Ukraine wound up with a constitutional change and Kyrgyzstan did not.

Instead, the reason is that a fully developed constitutional reform bill transferring significant presidential power to a prime minister was *already available* – predrafted and ready to be pulled off the shelf to seal a deal – in Ukraine, unlike in Kyrgyzstan. After consistently working to strengthen presidential powers during the 1990s and early 2000s, incumbent President Leonid Kuchma had sensed a growing political vulnerability. His popularity was near rock bottom in the wake of the Gongadze scandal and his associates were starting to jockey to be his successor. He thus increasingly worried that he might become *personally* vulnerable *after* he left the presidency in 2004. Thus in August 2002, he reversed his earlier position for a stronger presidency and now proposed a constitutional reform that would have greatly weakened the presidency and thus reduced his own vulnerability to any successor. Importantly, he was not

[11] Serhiy Kudelia, "Betting on Society: Power Perceptions and Elite Games in Ukraine," in Paul D'Anieri, ed., *Orange Revolution and Aftermath: Mobilization, Apathy, and the State in Ukraine* (Washington, DC: Woodrow Wilson Center, 2010), pp. 160–89, pp. 181–4.

[12] Viktor Yushchenko, interview published in *Kommersant Ukraina*, April 15, 2009.

[13] Scott Radnitz, "What Really Happened in Kyrgyzstan?" *Journal of Democracy*, v. 17, no. 2, April 2006, pp. 132–46.

[14] Erica Marat, *The Tulip Revolution: Kyrgyzstan One Year After* (Washington, DC: Jamestown Foundation, 2006); *RFE/RL Newsline*, March 25, 2005.

[15] *RFE/RL Newsline*, April 13, 2005.

[16] Kurmanbek Bakiev, "Kurmanbek Bakiev," interview, *Gazeta.Kg*, June 28, 2005, 21:06.

only concerned that an opposition figure like Yushchenko would become president, but also did not fully trust the man he himself had handpicked to be his political heir, Prime Minister Viktor Yanukovych. The latter represented the ambitious eastern-based Donetsk network and had business and political interests in tension with those of some key Kuchma allies, including chief of staff Viktor Medvedchuk, the constitutional reform's major advocate within the administration.[17] But Kuchma's status as an increasingly lame-duck meant that he could not push the reform through parliament when he tried in 2004, defeated by the defection of key deputies. It was this "very same draft" that was then brought in to become the basis for the presidential power-sharing arrangement that ended Ukraine's standoff.[18] This essentially random reason why Ukraine's revolution immediately produced a constitutional change but Kyrgyzstan's did not went on to have major implications for their subsequent regime dynamics, as the following sections demonstrate.

Building on the 2005–10 comparison, it is also highly useful to compare the same two cases in the subsequent period 2010–14 because both countries in 2010 experienced a reversal in the main factor of interest here: Ukraine switched from a divided-executive constitution back to a presidentialist one, while Kyrgyzstan switched from its presidentialist constitution to a divided-executive one. This fact itself reinforces the conclusion that there are no deeper factors such as culture or history that are simultaneously causing different patterns of political closure *and* presidentialism in one case or the other: Both countries over the past dozen years have experienced both presidentialist and divided-executive constitutions, just at different times. This fact also enables us to test the argument presented here further: If the logic outlined in Chapter 4 is valid, then we should find that Ukraine after 2010 started to become more closed than it had been under its divided-executive constitution while we should also find that Kyrgyzstan has enjoyed a sustained political opening, being more open by 2014 than it had been under its presidentialist constitution. This is indeed what we find.

After Kyrgyzstan's Tulip Revolution: Patronal Presidentialism, Single-Pyramid Politics

That Kyrgyzstan would revert to its earlier levels of authoritarianism was not immediately or universally evident.[19] Indeed, many at the time hailed the revolution as a democratic breakthrough.[20] Bakiev himself declared he did not aim to reconcentrate power around the presidency.[21] But the fact that Kyrgyzstan

---

[17] D'Anieri, *Understanding Ukrainian Politics*, pp. 88–98; Kudelia, "Betting on Society," pp. 172–3; Andrew Wilson, *Ukraine's Orange Revolution* (New Haven, CT: Yale University Press, 2005), p. 80.

[18] Kudelia, "Betting on Society," pp. 172–3, 182.

[19] Radnitz, "What Really Happened in Kyrgyzstan."

[20] Compare McFaul, "Transitions from Communism," *Journal of Democracy*, v. 16, no. 4, July 2005, pp. 212–44; and Vitali Silitski, "Beware the People," *Transitions Online*, March 21, 2005.

[21] *RFE/RL Newsline*, July 13, 2005.

retained its presidentialist constitution turned out to have major consequences for the Kyrgyz political system. With the constitution conferring on Bakiev the symbolic attributes of power and communicating that because he occupied this post he was in fact the more powerful of the two partners, he proved better able than Kulov to attract clients, punish the disloyal, and gradually strip his rival of authority and clients by using both informal and formal powers. Kulov was maneuvered out of office by early 2007 and ceased to be considered a serious rival, with no other serious rivals rising to compete with Bakiev's single-pyramid system.

Bakiev accomplished this in a number of ways, sending signals through his use of formal and informal powers to induce network coordination around his personal and formal authority and to marginalize those who resisted. One of the first things he did was to use his formal powers of appointment to replace senior figures in the Interior Ministry, the secret police (SND), and territorial governments in both North and South.[22] The president also took a number of steps designed to establish control over financial operations and much economic activity in Kyrgyzstan, including issuing decrees to create both a Financial Intelligence Service (September 2005) and a new Financial Police Service (November 2005).[23] These formal personnel arrangements then structured the informal process whereby these agents acted contrary to law – providing legal pretexts or cover – to secure the transfer of key economic assets to Bakiev's own family members and close allies. This included but was not limited to many of those assets formerly controlled by the Akaev family, as has been documented in a number of studies.[24] Rents from an American military base were particularly important in this regard.[25]

Understanding the importance of good relations with the president, many business and other elites who had previously been loyal to Akaev sought accommodation with the new president. Detailed case studies of some of Kyrgyzstan's biggest businesses by Regine Spector describe a pattern by which, for example, the coowner of Kyrgyzstan's massive and rich Dordoi Bazaar, Askar Salymbekov, had carefully developed positive relations with Akaev's family during the prerevolutionary period but switched to cultivating ties with Bakiev's family network almost immediately after the revolution. Through a conscious business-preservation strategy of maintaining good relations with whichever president's family happened to be in place, Salymbekov thus managed to keep his business holdings despite not being related to the Bakievs. The fate of the other coowner, Kubatbek Baibolov, shows why this was a smart

[22] *Gazeta.Kg*, June 30, 2005, 19:59; *RFE/RL Newsline*, February 7, 2006; *RFE/RL Newsline*, January 30, 2006.
[23] *RFE/RL Newsline*, September 12, 2005; *RFE/RL Newsline*, November 29, 2005.
[24] Erica Marat, "Need for More Transparency in Kyrgyz and Tajik Energy Sectors to Avoid Future Crises," *Eurasia Daily Monitor*, December 19, 2008; Gul Berna Ozcan, *Building States and Markets: Enterprise Development in Central Asia* (Houndmills: Palgrave-Macmillan, 2010).
[25] Alexander Cooley, *Great Games, Local Rules: The New Great Power Contest in Central Asia* (New York: Oxford University Press, 2012), chapter 7.

business strategy: Refusing to seek accommodation, he went into political opposition and was consequently forced out of the business.[26]

During and immediately after the revolution, Bakiev had publicly supported constitutional amendments to formalize a weaker presidency,[27] but he kept stalling and by early 2006 was sounding a different note. After several clashes with parliament over the president's growing authority, Bakiev's administration reportedly began drawing up its own draft constitution independently of the parliament or civil society organizations that were originally promised a role. The document his inner circle was preparing would retain "all the powers that Akaev had," and a referendum was planned for November 2006.[28] Opposition forces rallied over the course of that year. A large pair of protests in April–May 2006 prompted Bakiev to reshuffle his cabinet and remove certain officials whose resignations the opposition demanded.[29] Such reshuffling simultaneously served the presidential purpose of dividing and conquering his own supporters, preventing any from becoming too entrenched in their posts. Bakiev was also on the offensive: Prominent opposition leader Omurbek Tekebaev was arrested in Warsaw for allegedly carrying drugs, an incident widely regarded as a setup arranged by the National Security Service (SNB), which just happened to be headed by the president's brother.[30] Once again, we see formal institutional arrangements linked to the formal presidency (in this case, the presidentially appointed SNB leadership) shaping arrangements of informal politics by disrupting rival networks (such as Tekebaev's) and arranging others in an increasingly tight hierarchical configuration dominated by the person at the top.

A set of events in November 2006 were revealing of how the formal constitution had over time rendered Kulov a figure not expected to be able to act independently of Bakiev. The events in question were those surrounding the opposition's last major attempt to force Bakiev to live up to his promise not to govern as Akaev had. In November 2006, a group of opposition figures under the banner of the "For Reforms" movement mobilized several straight days of protests in Bishkek to demand a constitution that reduced presidential power.[31] One of the chief rally organizers, Temir Sariev, reports in a memoir that Kulov made contact with him and other key opposition figures and communicated that he (the prime minister) was "in complete solidarity" with the opposition in making these demands and planning the rally. At the same time, Kulov puzzled organizers by doing this secretly and refusing to come out in public.[32] This was not the mark of a man who expected he could mobilize the government he

---

[26] Regine Spector, "Securing Property in Post-Soviet Kyrgyzstan," *Post-Soviet Affairs*, v. 24, no. 2, April–June 2008, pp. 149–76.

[27] E.g., *RFE/RL Newsline*, April 28, 2005.

[28] Stanislav Pritchin, "Vtoroi Akaev?" *Oazis*, no. 3 (23), February 2006.

[29] *RFE/RL Newsline*, May 11, 2006; *Polit.Ru*, May 10, 2006, 11:08, 10:01, 17:02.

[30] *RFE/RL Newsline*, September 11, 14, 25, 2006.

[31] *RFE/RL Newsline*, October 3, 2006.

[32] Temir Sariev, *Shakh Kyrgyzskoi demokratii* (Bishkek: Salam, 2008), pp. 71–2.

formally headed against a president he opposed. It was also in marked contrast to the behavior of Ukrainian prime ministers who were similarly dissatisfied with presidential attempts to usurp some of their authority, as we will see later in this chapter. And indeed, organizers report that no significant support arrived from Kulov. That is, Kulov as prime minister appears to have been unable (or unwilling because of his own dependence on Bakiev) to provide actual political cover for opposition politics and instead could only covertly suggest support while toeing the presidential line in public. Sariev's account also makes clear that Kulov was not expected to be any significant counterweight to Bakiev's presidential authority because of his position.

Bakiev ultimately used the opposition's November 2006 protest to deliver the coup de grace, forcing Kulov out. After complicated political intrigues on both sides, the opposition's massive protest went forward and convened a "Founding Assembly" that included members of parliament. This assembly then adopted a new constitution that met the protesters' demand for a weaker presidency. Facing sustained street protests, Bakiev agreed to sign it with only slight amendments in November 2006. The protesters dispersed, believing they had won.[33] But Bakiev had simply made a tactical retreat that in fact simultaneously persuaded the crowds to go home *and* gave him an opportunity to use the informal authority he had already accumulated to remove Kulov as prime minister and ram through a new presidentialist constitution with even greater formal presidential powers than before.[34] By one account, Bakiev in this process co-opted key members of the opposition, including parliamentarian and Social Democratic Party of Kyrgyzstan (SDPK) leader Almaz Atambaev, with promises of future rewards.[35] The president cut Kulov loose after some highly complex maneuvering, replacing him first with Azim Isabekov – a close Bakiev ally[36] – and then, less than two months later, indeed with Atambaev, thereby splitting the opposition and also providing a semblance of regional balance, as Atambaev was a northerner.

Kulov, now without his prime ministerial post, tried to mobilize popular resistance through what was left of his own network in a much-heralded April 2007 rally. But he enticed hardly any major figures from within the Bakiev power pyramid. Kulov was unable even to draw meaningful support from the government he had formally headed for more than a year. Bakiev's forces thus had little trouble putting down the protest with a decisive show of force. As a final humiliation, Bakiev in May 2008 offered Kulov a minor state post with lucrative patronage potential, head of the Directorate of the Project on Development of Small and Medium Energy. Acknowledging his own utter

---

[33] Sariev, *Shakh Kyrgyzskoi demokratii*, pp. 74–91, 97–100.
[34] Details on these complex events can be found in Kulov, *Na perevale*, pp. 229–33; *Polit. Ru*, December 30, 2007, 10:43, 12:38; *RFE/RL Newsline*, January 16, 2007; Sariev, *Shakh Kyrgyzskoi demokratii*; *Utro.ru*, December 19, 2006, 13:40.
[35] Sariev, *Shakh Kyrgyzskoi demokratii*.
[36] *Radio Svoboda*, January 26, 2007, 13:08.

defeat, Kulov accepted.[37] Kulov, then, became one of the starkest symbols of a major network being co-opted to Bakiev's side in recognition of the latter's dominance. Kulov had in essence been co-opted from himself.

Eugene Huskey's and Gulnara Iskakova's survey of opposition politicians in Kyrgyzstan in 2008 helps us peer into the minds of at least some Kyrgyz elites, demonstrating that Kulov's thinking in joining Bakiev even after having been blatantly betrayed by him in fact reflects a calculus common to elites, at least those in opposition. The interviewed elites at that time indeed regarded Bakiev's ability to dole out rewards and mete out punishments as a critical reason why opposition figures were unable to join forces to oppose the president effectively. Very interestingly, Huskey and Iskakova's survey finds that this perception of the centrality of state authority in dividing the opposition was decidedly highest among opposition figures who had previously served as executive branch officials.[38] This strongly suggests that this was not primarily a perception held by the opposition, but by elites more generally. Indeed, Huskey and Iskakova refer to a "long list of opposition politicians who have succumbed to the temptations of *vlast'* [power] and abandoned their colleagues in the opposition for high-ranking positions in government."[39]

Kulov's 2007 defeat consolidated the expectation that the power of the Bakiev network would not be effectively balanced by anyone in state executive power. Accordingly, that point in time marked an acceleration in the consolidation of a single-pyramid system around Bakiev's presidency. The elite expectations involved are explicitly articulated by a "veteran leader of the opposition" in Huskey's and Iskakova's 2008 elite interview project: After Kulov left the political scene and Atambaev was co-opted, there was a general perception that the "last chance to unite the opposition" was lost, and "people simply turned away in disgust, saying the opposition is no different from the government."[40]

With little coordinated elite resistance from inside or outside his regime, the consolidation of Bakiev's power pyramid was rapid. His loyalists passed an even more strongly presidentialist constitution by referendum, then forced early parliamentary elections in December 2007 and filled 71 of its 90 seats with a newly created propresidential party, the Ak Zhol ("True Path") Party.[41] Minority fractions went only to parties considered to be pliable, the Party of Communists and Atambaev's Social Democratic Party, and the territorial breakdowns of the vote were never released.[42] The Central Election Commission chief

[37] *AKIpress*, May 6, 2008, 13:15.
[38] Eugene Huskey and Gulnara Iskakova, "The Barriers to Intra-Opposition Cooperation in the Post-Communist World: Evidence from Kyrgyzstan." *Post-Soviet Affairs*, v. 26, no. 3, July–September 2010, pp. 228–62, p. 237.
[39] Ibid., 238.
[40] Ibid., 247–8.
[41] *RFE/RL Newsline*, October 24, 2007.
[42] *AKIpress*, December 18, 2007, 17:14; *RFE/RL Newsline*, December 27, 2007.

who legitimized these results later admitted to having been under unrelenting pressure from the president and his family to influence election results.[43]

Trying to catch the opposition off guard and win reelection before the effects of the 2008 financial crisis could hit hard, Bakiev secured a Constitutional Court ruling moving the election date from 2010 up to summer 2009. The opposition tried to unite, but Atambaev and Sariev both ended up running, the latter accusing the former of collaborationism. Neither managed to mobilize much elite or mass support, and Bakiev won the official count with 76 percent of the vote, far ahead of Atambaev's 8 and Sariev's 6 percent.[44] Postelection protests were easily put down, though mostly just ignored because they found few supporters among either the elite or the masses. Kulov campaigned for Bakiev.[45] This regression back to single-pyramid politics is clearly reflected in Freedom House ratings. Among other things, these show that after an initial opening in electoral process following the Tulip Revolution, the democratic quality of Kyrgyzstan's elections had become more closed by 2009 than prior to the revolution.[46]

After Kyrgyzstan's Bloody Revolution: Divided-Executive Constitution, Competing-Pyramid System

The developments that led to Kyrgyzstan's bloody April 2010 revolution do not need repeating (see Chapter 7), but what is important to highlight here is that this new revolution resembled the Orange Revolution in producing a shift to a divided-executive constitution. The new Kyrgyzstan constitution went even further in ensuring that the information and focal effects of the constitution complicated rather than strengthened the kind of network coordination necessary for creating a single-pyramid system. The president not only would be unable to appoint or remove the prime minister, with only parliament having this right, but would be limited to a single six-year term in office. Additionally, no party would be allowed to win a majority large enough to change the constitution unilaterally, and the law enforcement and budget committees would have to be chaired by opposition members.

Bakiev's victorious opponents, representing a variety of distinct networks ranging from Atambaev's and Sariev's northern-based ones to Tekebaev's southern-based one, intentionally designed the document this way to prevent the emergence of a single dominant source of executive power so as to prevent a repeat of the Akaev and Bakiev episodes and to preserve their own autonomy vis-à-vis the others. In short, their intent was to avoid a winner-take-all

---

[43] *AKIpress*, September 26, 2008, 10:19, 15:22, 17:17, 17:41, 18:50.
[44] *AKIpress*, July 21, 2009, 19:15.
[45] *AKIpress*, June 19, 2009, 14:23.
[46] Erica Marat, "Kyrgyzstan," in *Nations in Transit 2012* (New York: Freedom House, 2012), pp. 297–316, p. 297. Hale, "Formal Constitutions" shows that this pattern is also evident in other Freedom House ratings and other institutions' prominent projects that attempt to quantify levels of democracy or political rights.

system.[47] The one-term limit would reduce the stakes in allocating leadership posts since each member of the new leadership could hope for his or her own turn as president in the not-too-distant future as well as a stake in parliament that would have real influence. Facilitating their process of initial agreement, the interim president who had taken over right after the revolution, Roza Otunbaeva, would be excluded from running for the new presidency herself, and she legitimated her transitional authority through a referendum that explicitly limited her to a short interim period in office. The referendum on Otunbaeva was simultaneous with the referendum adopting the new divided-executive constitution, and it was held June 27, 2010.[48] Essentially, not only was the new constitution designed to generate focal and information effects complicating elite coordination in single-pyramid systems, but each president would also be rendered a lame-duck from the start. All of this created incentives directed strongly at supporting a competing-pyramid system and militating against the emergence of a single-pyramid system. At the same time, the drafters also explicitly kept in mind the Ukrainian experience that will be described later, seeking to craft the divided-executive constitution in a way that would still allow for effective governance and not lead to paralyzing elite conflict.[49]

Along with the new constitution, however, the violent April 2010 revolution unleashed one of the most tragic forms of competing-pyramid politics. This was an ethnically charged battle for position in southern Kyrgyzstan (especially in Osh) that left more than four hundred dead, many more injured, thousands of refugees, and entire neighborhoods burned to the ground.[50] With new uncertainty suddenly emerging and prior deals and power balances over property and influence suddenly thrown into question, various networks across the country scrambled to find ways to secure what they had and, in many cases, take advantage of the opportunity to gain more or eliminate rival networks. Eric McGlinchey writes that Otunbaeva's transitional government exacerbated the situation by immediately ordering the dissolution of the Bakiev era parliament. He argues the parliament had essentially been a mechanism for protecting the political and economic interests of key networks around the country, with many important patrons occupying these offices.[51]

---

[47] Erica Marat, "Kyrgyzstan: A Parliamentary System Based on Inter-Elite Consensus," *Demokratizatsiya: The Journal of Post-Soviet Democratization*, v. 20, no. 4, Fall 2012, pp. 325–44. See also statements by key figures in the drafting process: *CAnews*, April 19, 2010, 15:42; *AKIpress*, April 24, 2010, 16:49. This was not an elite consensus against presidentialism: Some prominent elites argued that presidentialism should be kept; see *AKIpress*, April 24, 2010, 12:46; *AKIpress*, April 26, 2010, 12:00.

[48] *RFE/RL News*, May 21, 2010, 18:56.

[49] Almazbek Akmataliev, former constitutional convention participant, Naryn governor, and rector of the State Academy of Management, author's interview, June 22, 2011.

[50] *AKIpress*, June 7, 2011, 18:55.

[51] Eric McGlinchey, "Exploring Regime Instability and Ethnic Violence in Kyrgyzstan," *Asia Policy*, no. 12, July 2011, pp. 79–98.

While some observers have described these events as a simple eruption of long-standing ethnic tensions, including Kyrgyz government representatives, who proceeded to blame local Uzbeks,[52] more credible reports based on more impartial investigative reporting have tended to uncover a complicated situation with its causes lying more clearly in patronal political economy than in ethnic tensions per se. In particular, the collapse of the Bakiev single-pyramid system led to a scramble for security and resources among networks generally associated with local Uzbeks and local Kyrgyz that quickly escalated.

Here one must be careful not to essentialize ethnic divisions. Some Uzbeks were known to be aligned with the most important Kyrgyz networks, and vice versa.[53] For example, some Uzbek networks such as Batyrov's in Jalalabad had largely been marginalized under the Bakiev political machine but now mobilized militias to help establish the authority of the new (predominantly Kyrgyz) government.[54] They hoped the Kyrgyz central authorities would offer them a better position and sought them as allies against opportunistic local networks that were also primarily rooted in Kyrgyz communities and that had been dominant locally under Bakiev. For their part, key southern networks that had previously been part of the Bakiev machine suddenly found their chief patron gone and saw these "Uzbek networks" as one of the most important local bases of support for the new central authorities they opposed.[55] The result strongly appears to have been that leaders of some southern (mainly Kyrgyz) networks wielding substantial means of force – including strong representation in local police who were witnessed participating in the violence – took matters into their own hands by launching a horrific pogrom, with most of the victims and the homes destroyed being Uzbek.[56] While there is a good case to be made for security dilemma dynamics being at root, there is circumstantial evidence that simple greed was also involved. For example, by some reports, many of the razed Uzbek neighborhoods in the city of Osh had been proposed for corporate development by the local strongman mayor Melis Myrzakmatov prior to the June 2010 pogrom.[57]

Despite this tragic episode, on June 27 the transitional government did manage to carry out and win its referendum confirming the new divided-executive

[52] *AKIpress*, August 17, 2010, 14:07.

[53] On an important Uzbek network working with the dominant Kyrgyz Bakiev network, see Sanobar Shermatova, "Kirgizskii Iug i uzbekskii vopros," *Fergana.ru*, June 8, 2010, 13:35 Moscow time.

[54] On these networks, see Brent Hierman, "Sources of Inter-ethnic Trust and Distrust in Central Asia," doctoral dissertation in Political Science, Indiana University, Bloomington, 2011, especially chapter 5.

[55] E.g., *AKIpress Fergana*, April 19, 2010, 09:46; David Trilling, "Ethnic Violence in Kyrgyzstan Presents New Test for Provisional Government,"" *Eurasianet*, May 19, 2010, 11:54; *The New York Times*, June 26, 2010.

[56] *EurasiaNet*, August 16, 2010, 10:46 am; *Fergana.ru*, May 5, 2010, 16:58; *RFE/RL News*, August 17, 2010.

[57] *Eurasianet*, August 19, 2010, 2:25 pm. Movement on these plans proceeded afterward as the mayor stayed in place: David Trilling, "Kyrgyzstan: Reconstruction Competes against Redevelopment in Osh," *Eurasianet*, July 26, 2011, 2:12 pm.

constitution and installing Otunbaeva officially as interim president.[58] Politics during the years since the bloody 2010 revolution have largely been in line with what Chapter 4 would lead us to expect, with the divided-executive constitution underpinning a highly contested competing-pyramid system, though one also featuring a competition between political machines with high degrees of reported corruption in politics.[59] The first parliamentary election held under the new constitution took place on October 10, 2010, and was widely considered the most free and fair election post-Soviet Central Asia had seen. The OSCE declared that voters had a "genuine choice of political alternatives," "parties were able to campaign freely," "fundamental freedoms … were generally respected," the atmosphere was "peaceful," and all contestants had access to the most important media, with few formal complaints being filed.[60] In the voting, which was all by proportional representation party list, three opposition parties won delegations (the southern-based pro-Bakiev and largely ethnically Kyrgyz Ata-Zhurt, Omurbek Babanov's Respublika, and Kulov's Ar-Namys) along with two parties from the transitional government (Atambaev's Social Democratic Party and Tekebaev's Ata-Meken). Other parties led by prominent businessmen-politicians who had been part of the transitional government, including Ak-Shumkar and BEK, failed to win seats. The eventual result was a three-party coalition: Atambaev became PM, Ata-Zhurt's Akhmatbek Keldibaev assumed the parliamentary speakership, and Respublika's businessman leader Babanov became deputy PM – all on the informal understanding that the PM and parliamentary chair should not be both from either South or North.[61]

Atambaev then won the October 30, 2011, presidential election, which reputable international observers also evaluated positively despite citing some flaws they said were unlikely to have impacted the outcome.[62] Indeed, while other Freedom House indicators of democracy such as corruption and governance remained high for the year of this election, as one might expect in a highly patronalistic environment, the organization improved its rating in "electoral process" to the best the country had seen since well before the Tulip Revolution.[63] With Atambaev shifting to the presidency and replacing Otunbaeva, the old government coalition in parliament fell apart and a new one was created with all the parliamentary parties except the pro-Bakiev Ata-Zhurt, which lost its hold over the parliamentary speakership. As a result, Respublika's Babanov became PM and Atambaev's SDP received the chairmanship of parliament.

[58] RFE/RL News, June 28, 2010, 07:53.

[59] Marat, "Kyrgyzstan: A Parliamentary System."

[60] OSCE/ODIHR Election Observation Mission Report, "Kyrgyz Republic Parliamentary Elections October 10, 2010," December 20, 2010, p. 2.

[61] Erica Marat, "Kyrgyzstan," in *Nations in Transit 2011* (New York: Freedom House, 2011), pp. 297–316, p. 307.

[62] Erica Marat, "Kyrgyzstan," in *Nations in Transit 2012* (New York: Freedom House, 2012), pp. 297–316, p. 299.

[63] Marat, "Kyrgyzstan," *Nations in Transit 2012*, p. 297.

Kyrgyzstan after 2010 was far from a model democracy; as with Ukraine 2005–10, it was clear that the complex single-pyramid system that constituted Bakiev's political machine had simply been broken up rather than society completely transformed. While the OSCE and others generally noted the increasingly open and competitive nature of elections as discussed earlier, they also tended to cite other important features that differentiate patronal democracy from ideal democracy. These include reports of direct payments or gifts for votes or places on party lists, little impartial analysis in the media as most reports and information were paid for or otherwise partisan, and highly personalistic campaigns that did not pay great attention to issues.[64] During the 2011 election period, live broadcasts from foreign television were temporarily banned so as to minimize Russian influence on the elections, and delayed broadcasts had to cut out any news coverage of Kyrgyzstan's election.[65] The temporary government was also quick to nationalize some key assets linked to the Bakiev family, including a large bank (AsiaUniversalBank)[66] and a big mobile phone company (Megacom),[67] and there were widespread suspicions that such assets were simply being appropriated by the new patrons.

Moreover, the lack of a single pyramid of power went to such an extreme that some regions were essentially not controlled by the central government at all, instead having local machines calling the shots. The most infamous example is the already-mentioned Osh Mayor Melis Myrzakmatov, who was installed under Bakiev and simply refused to leave after the April 2010 revolution. He made no secret of his opposition to the new authorities and of his ethnic Kyrgyz nationalism, which he helped increasingly to become a salient mobilizing set of ideas in the country in the wake of the 2010 tragedy.[68] Indeed, the postrevolution leadership remained highly sensitive regarding the June 2010 riots. Parliament even declared persona non grata the author of an international report implicating government forces in the violence. It also called for a ban on a Russia-based news Web site (*Fergana.ru*) that had been "exposing atrocities committed by security forces against Uzbeks during and after the June 2010 clashes."[69] Many ethnic Uzbek leaders were jailed, and some given harsh sentences.[70]

Importantly, however, such initiatives were no longer issuing from a single, united pyramid of power, but from different players in a competing-pyramid

[64] Marat, "Kyrgyzstan: A Parliamentary System," pp. 335–6; OSCE/ODIHR Election Observation Mission Report, "Kyrgyz Republic Parliamentary Elections October 10, 2010," December 20, 2010 (p. 16 on media).

[65] Marat, "Kyrgyzstan," *Nations in Transit 2012*, pp. 308–9.

[66] *RFE/RL News*, June 7, 2010.

[67] Cholpon Orozobekova, "Kyrgyzstan: Moscow, Riled over Nationalization, Fires Shot across Bishkek's Bow," *Eurasianet*, March 14, 2011, 2:28.

[68] *Polit.Ru*, July 29, 2010, 13:21; *RFE/RL News*, August 20, 2010, 12:24; *RFE/RL*, March 5, 2012.

[69] Marat, "Kyrgyzstan," *Nations in Transit 2012*, pp. 303–4.

[70] *Eurasianet*, June 30, 2010, 11:19 am.

system. Many actions of the parliament (such as the banning of *Fergana.ru*) were actually opposed by President Atambaev.[71] Some analysts identified efforts by Atambaev to use administrative resources, including pressuring certain journalists and only selectively prosecuting corruption.[72] Others interpreted a new 2012 law establishing presidential primacy in broad foreign policy making as an attempt to gain power at the government's and parliament's expense.[73] And the Ata-Zhurt opposition cried foul when one of its parliamentarians, oligarch and Bakiev's former mayor of Bishkek Nariman Tiuleev, was arrested for corruption in June 2012.[74] In late 2012, as opposition efforts to mobilize street actions against the regime picked up, three top Ata-Zhurt leaders were jailed on charges of attempted violent seizure of power after they tried to storm into the White House over its gates during a protest.[75] And in late 2013, central authorities finally succeeded in ousting the maverick Osh mayor, Myrzakmatov. The Respublika Party's Babanov was forced to resign as prime minister in 2012 and was succeeded by a member of Atambaev's party, Zhantoro Satybaldiev.[76]

But nothing resembling a crackdown occurred, and against the background of the 2010 state collapse, many of these moves also resembled simply a gradual reestablishment of at least some state authority. Many observers agreed that President Atambaev was mainly playing a role as "arbiter" among factions in a divided parliament, government, and society.[77] Shairbek Juraev observed the formation of a "more inclusive political power sharing system," calling this a "drastic difference" from the pre-2010 period. Helping sustain the balance were five parliamentary parties that were "relatively independent of each other" and possessed "a comparable number of seats."[78] Indeed, Atambaev undertook some actions to liberalize political activity, including signing a law facilitating exercise of the right of assembly in June 2012.[79] And during March and early April 2014, parliament replaced Prime Minister Satybaldiev (part of Atambaev's Social Democratic Party network) with Joomart Otorbaev, who had earlier run for parliament on Tekebaev's Ata-Meken Party list and was nominated by

---

[71] Almazbek Atambaev, president of Kyrgyzstan, interview with chief editor of Fergana.ru Web site, *24.kg*, March 29, 2012, 16:10.

[72] Asel' Otorbaeva, "Kyrgyzstan. Sto dnei Atambaeva," *24.kg*, March 7, 2012, 10:41; Chris Rickleton, "Kyrgyzstan: Is Corruption Controversy a Sign of Political Trouble Ahead?" *Eurasianet*, July 26, 2012, 1:33 pm.

[73] *AKIpress*, June 29, 2012, 11:22.

[74] *AKIpress*, June 25, 2012, 19:35.

[75] *AKIpress*, October 4, 2012, 10:58, 11:00, 12:12, 14. 12; *AKIpress*, October 3, 2012, 20:00.

[76] David Trilling, "Kyrgyzstan: Parliament Approves New Premier, Government," *Eurasianet*, September 5, 2012, 12:09 pm.

[77] Valentin Bogatyrev, "Segodnia glavnaia problema dlia Atambaeva – eto sam Atambaev," *AKIpress*, May 18, 2012, 15:57.

[78] Shairbek Juraev, "April in Kyrgyzstan," blog post, PONARS Eurasia Web site, April 16, 2013, http://www.ponarseurasia.org/article/april-kyrgyzstan, accessed April 17, 2013.

[79] *AKIpress*, June 4, 2012, 10:32.

Ata-Meken.[80] The president also repeatedly and unequivocally stated that he would not seek a way to remain in office beyond 2017, when his single constitutionally allowed term was up.[81] The moves against Myrzakmatov could also be interpreted as an attempt to establish central state authority in the South, where many regarded the government as being virtually powerless. At the same time, mighty struggles over potentially lucrative state posts and resources took place among key patronal networks that did not simply break down along regional lines.[82] The president himself said explicitly that he would have fired certain ministers and made other changes if he had enjoyed the power of a presidentialist constitution, but praised the parliamentary system as a whole as a necessary price to pay for transparency and preventing a repeat of the Akaev and Bakiev disasters.[83] Freedom House ratings already by 2011 registered improvement in the openness of elections and democracy more generally relative to the later Bakiev period. But at the same time, and as the logic of patronal politics would lead us to expect, no significant improvement was recorded in levels of corruption.[84] This was a fracturing of machine politics, not a reduction in it.

After the Orange Revolution: Divided-Executive Constitution, Political Opening

A detailed look at post-Orange revolution Ukraine presents a dramatic contrast with post-Tulip revolution Kyrgyzstan, a clear move to open, competing-pyramid politics. In fact, between the Orange Revolution and 2010, Ukraine became the only non-Baltic post-Soviet country ever to have been rated fully "free" by Freedom House's *Freedom in the World* index, a remarkable achievement that is reflected in strong showings in all the other major indices of levels of "democracy."[85] But here it is crucial to dig deeper into these indices to identify what precisely had changed. Freedom House's *Nations in Transit* reports that Ukraine made dramatic improvements in electoral process and media independence during the period of interest, reflecting the competitive and open nature of competing-pyramid politics, as described in Chapter 4. But crucially, this same report *also* records *no* significant improvement in levels of corruption and governance, reflecting that politics and society remained highly patronalistic.[86] Lest one distrust Freedom House, the *Economist Intelligence*

---

[80] *24.kg*, April 3, 2014, 07:20.

[81] E.g., *AKIpress*, October 9, 2013, 20:34; *CA-News*, October 17, 2013, 12:30; *RFE/RL*, September 27, 2012.

[82] See the struggles described, for example, in *AKIpress*, April 13, 2013, 16:29; "Den' 11 Oktiabria," *AKIpress*, October 11, 2013, 18:33; Chris Rickleton, "Kyrgyzstan: Parliament Failing Public-Faith Test," *Eurasianet*, June 13, 2013, 2:47 pm.

[83] *AKIpress*, August 31, 2013, 14:18.

[84] Marat, "Kyrgyzstan," *Nations in Transit 2012*, p. 297.

[85] Jeannette Goehring, ed., *Nations in Transit 2008: Democratization from Central Europe to Eurasia* (New York: Freedom House, 2008); for details, see Hale, "Formal Constitutions."

[86] Oleksandr Sushko and Olena Prystayko, "Ukraine," in *Nations in Transit 2009* (New York: Freedom House, 2009).

Unit similarly reveals Ukraine during 2005–10 to have been at the level of Switzerland and Ireland in terms of electoral process and pluralism, but at the level of Mali and Nicaragua when it came to the functioning of government.[87] Taken all together, this pattern strongly confirms what the logic described in Chapter 4 would lead us to expect from a divided-executive constitution and what we have also witnessed in Kyrgyzstan after 2010: What had changed after the Orange Revolution was *not* the level of patronalism in politics, but the *arrangement* of patronal networks, which had collectively taken on more open and competitive rather than closed configurations.[88] Ukraine's new divided-executive constitution complicated and ultimately undermined attempts by any one pyramid to emerge dominant by creating uncertainty as to who would dominate, promoting coordination around more than one patronalistic "pyramid," and incentivizing rivalry among these pyramids.

As discussed previously, the Orange Revolution's standoff in the streets resulted in a constitutional change that the team of outgoing President Kuchma forced Yushchenko to accept in return for a peaceful transition to the presidency in early 2005. The presidency Yushchenko won would be weakened as of January 2006, with the prime minister gaining direct control over key ministries (including the police) and, most importantly, becoming exclusively responsible to parliament instead of being nominated or removed at the whim of the president.[89] The fact that the new division of power formally took effect only in January 2006 helps us separate the "informal" effects of the constitutional reform from the formal effects. Despite the formality of Yushchenko's wielding the powers of Kuchma during 2005, the adoption of the constitutional reform to resolve the Orange Revolution standoff had already created the expectation that the president would not be the single dominant authority as of 2006. Thus Yushchenko did use his formal power to try to subordinate the prime minister after they clashed publicly, firing Tymoshenko in September 2005 and replacing her with the more pliable Yury Yekhanurov. But the constitutional reform meant that observers regarded Yekhanurov as a "caretaker" prime minister from the very start, expecting that the March 2006 parliamentary election would determine an independent prime minister and that the president might thus not be in as strong a position position after that point to follow through on promises or threats made before.[90]

Tymoshenko voiced (and sought to reinforce) these expectations rather dramatically just before the 2006 elections, saying the prime ministership was worth fighting for in the election because "under the new constitution, the

---

[87] Economist Intelligence Unit, "Index of Democracy 2008," http://graphics.eiu.com/PDF/Democracy%20Index%202008.pdf, accessed February 2, 2014.

[88] Yuri Matsievski, "Change, Transition, or Cycle: The Dynamics of Ukraine's Political Regime in 2004–2010," *Russian Politics and Law*, v. 49, no. 5, September–October 2011, pp. 8–33.

[89] Christensen, Rakhimkulov, and Wise, "The Ukrainian."

[90] *RFE/RL Newsline*, September 12, 2005.

president has practically lost all of his powers."[91] Despite the falling out with the president that had led to her dismissal, she ran for parliament in 2006 again as part of a "democratic" coalition with Yushchenko. This election returned the man Yushchenko had defeated in 2004, Viktor Yanukovych, to the premiership atop a new parliamentary coalition. This coalition was formed only after a key member of the "democratic" coalition, Socialist Party of Ukraine leader Oleksandr Moroz, defected in response to the presidential network's overreaching. Moroz had expected the third most powerful formal post (parliamentary speaker) in return for being the decisive and third largest partner in Yushchenko's winning coalition. But Yushchenko refused, insisting that this third post go to his own person. At this point, Yanukovych promised Moroz the post he desired if he switched sides and enabled Yushchenko's rival to form the governing coalition.

During the ensuing period, one finds all major political networks almost openly flouting formal rules and employing patronalistic practices to gain power at the expense of their rivals, using and claiming state executive authority wherever possible. Prime Minister Yanukovych wasted little time. One of his first and most creative moves was to claim the right to invalidate presidential decrees unilaterally by refusing to countersign them as required by procedural regulations.[92] Even more momentous was his 2006–7 push for a new Law on the Council of Ministers, which would have significantly augmented prime ministerial power at the president's expense. These determined moves, reportedly along with material blandishments, induced a growing stream of elites (especially parliamentary deputies) to defect from Yushchenko and join Yanukovych's coalition. The prime minister's allies bragged they would soon have the 300 parliamentary votes they needed to amend the constitution unilaterally, potentially emasculating or even eliminating the presidency. This led some to forecast a new single-pyramid *vertikal'* of power emerging out of the premier's office instead of the presidency.[93]

What stopped Yanukovych in 2007? Here we see a pattern that occurs repeatedly in the Ukraine of 2005–10 and is commonplace for polities with divided-executive constitutions: Efforts by one arm of the executive to flout formal rules and usurp power from the other were defeated by similarly patronalistic political practices undertaken in response by the occupant of the rival executive post. In this case, President Yushchenko became the focal point for opposition to Prime Minister Yanukovych. Renewing his alliance with Tymoshenko, he rallied her and other elites as he issued and enforced a decree of extremely dubious constitutionality in April 2007 to dissolve the parliament.[94] This decree was not simply "obeyed," but enforced through the

[91] *RFE/RL Newsline*, February 28, 2006.
[92] *Ukraiins'ka Pravda*, September 21, 2006, 13:31, 15:42.
[93] *Ukraiins'ka Pravda*, April 6, 2007, 17:10; *Korrespondent*, January 20, 2007, 20.
[94] The president's status as "guarantor of the constitution," he asserted, implied the duty to dissolve parliament if it acted in a way that the president unilaterally deemed unconstitutional. This

extensive coordination of informal networks around the president. The defense minister, who by Ukraine's divided-executive constitution was appointed by the president, quickly made clear that should Yanukovych attempt to resist by using force, "the army will only carry out orders from the commander in chief" (Yushchenko).[95] The parliamentary coalition behind Yanukovych nevertheless sought to block any new elections by passing a resolution to disband the Central Election Commission.[96] About a week later, with the eighteen-member Constitutional Court gearing up to decide the case, five Court justices linked to Yushchenko publicly accused "some well-known statesmen and political figures" of pressuring the Court into a ruling, forcing the Court's hearing to be delayed. When doing so, however, they seemed to back Yushchenko even before the deliberations had begun, calling his decree "within his presidential authority."[97] In early May, while the case was still being decided, Yushchenko issued decrees unilaterally removing three justices who had been appointed by his predecessor, Kuchma.[98] As the month went by, Yushchenko took direct control of antiriot police troops and then ordered more of them into the capital city. At that point, Yanukovych conceded, allowing new elections to be held in fall 2007. These restored Tymoshenko as premier in alliance with Yushchenko.[99]

Power grabs were not limited to Yanukovych, but were undertaken by Yushchenko as well. The most dramatic occurred in 2008. Shortly after she became prime minister, Tymoshenko and Yushchenko experienced another falling out as he sought to augment the power of the presidency at the prime minister's expense, especially in control over the economy. Yushchenko's team systematically issued bogus constitutional challenges so as to stall or undermine government decisions;[100] sought to revoke the citizenship of a prominent critic on the grounds he had falsified his application back in 1999;[101] pressured certain television outlets to influence political content (driving the famous

---

justification, to say the least, did not appear among the three circumstances that the constitution explicitly stipulated as the only grounds for the president to dissolve parliament. See Ukaz prezydenta Ukraiiny, "Pro dostrokove prypynennia povnovazhen' Verkhovnoi Rady Ukraiiny," in *Ofitsiinyi Visnyk Prezydenta Ukraiina,* April 2, 2007, no. 1, 3–5, made available online at http://www2.pravda.com.ua/news/2007/4/5/56948.htm, accessed April 26, 2011; Jan Maksymiuk, "Ukraine Faces Crisis as President Dissolves Parliament," End Note, *RFE/RL Newsline,* April 3, 2007.

[95] Maksymiuk, "Ukraine Faces Crisis."
[96] *RFE/RL Newsline,* April 3, 2007.
[97] *RFE/RL Newsline,* April 11, 2007; *Polit.Ru,* April 11, 2007, 11:28.
[98] For more details on these extraordinarily complex maneuverings and the general pervasiveness of patronalism in Ukraine's judiciary of this period, see Alexei Trochev, "Meddling with Justice: Competitive Politics, Impunity, and Distrusted Courts in Post-Orange Ukraine," *Demokratizatsiya: The Journal of Post-Soviet Democratization,* v. 18, no. 2, Spring 2010, pp. 122–47, p. 134.
[99] *RFE/RL Newsline,* May 29, 2007.
[100] N. Yatsenko, "Konstitutsiina 'balalaika,'" *Dzerkalo Tyzhnia,* July 19–August 1, 2008, pp. 1, 3.
[101] Pavel Korduban, "Ukrainian Prosecutors Target Self-Defense Leaders," *Eurasia Daily Monitor,* May 30; *Ukraiins'ka Pravda,* July 21, 2008, 19:31.

former Radio Liberty journalist Savik Shuster to leave one such channel);[102] and even ordered the Ukrainian Security Service (SBU) to open a case against Tymoshenko in 2008 for treason over an alleged secret deal with Russian President Vladimir Putin.[103] The culmination was Yushchenko's attempt to force a new dissolution of the parliament and new elections in 2008 so as to gain a new, more pliable government. Trying to enforce this move, the president team was found to have removed judges who had decided against him or were expected to do so,[104] dissolved an entire court that had ruled against him so as to get the desired decision from one of the two courts he created to replace it,[105] and sent state guard (UGO) troops under his authority to "protect" a court making a decision important to Yushchenko.[106] Interior Minister Yury Lutsenko, elected atop the party list that Yushchenko himself had supported, reported that the Presidential Secretariat had engaged in several phone calls to judges during the precise times of key court deliberations.[107]

President Yushchenko's power grab was rebuffed in much the same way Prime Minister Yanukovych's had been: The occupant of the opposite branch of executive power became a focal point for those networks interested in restraining the overstepper and accordingly was able to employ "political machine" tactics effectively enough to defeat the effort. This focal effect helped Prime Minister Tymoshenko coordinate efforts with some unlikely tactical allies. One was Yanukovych's Party of Regions. That Tymoshenko would join forces in any way with Yanukovych is surprising given how colorfully she had ruled out such an alliance just two years earlier: "Our bloc could only unite with the Party of Regions if a UFO abducts me onto its flying saucer, conducts illegal research on me and takes away my memory and reason."[108] But determined to prevent Yushchenko's presidency from becoming too powerful, she braved the aliens and joined her parliamentary forces with Yanukovych's to deny funding for the early elections Yushchenko had decreed. Tymoshenko's supporters also physically blocked the work of courts thought likely to rule in Yushchenko's favor.[109] The PM also went on the counterattack by entering negotiations with the Party of Regions on a plan to pool their parliamentary votes to amend the constitution and eliminate the directly elected presidency altogether, subordinating the office instead to parliament. Yushchenko, in turn, countered this

[102] Savik Shuster, interview, *Segodnia*, August 7, 2008, 7; *Segodnia*, July 30, 2008, 4; Mustafa Naiiem and Serhyi Leshchenko, "Oliharkhichni viiny: Khoroshkovskyi iak maska Firtasha?" *Ukraiins'ka Pravda*, July 30, 2008, 22:05.
[103] *Ukraiins'ka Pravda*, August 21, 2008, 11:50; *Ukraiins'ka Pravda*, February 11, 2009, 20:02.
[104] *Segodnia*, October 17, 2008, 3; *Kommersant Ukraiina*, November 24, 2008.
[105] *Ukraiins'ka Pravda*, October 17, 2008, 15:55.
[106] *Kommersant Ukraina*, October 15, 2008.
[107] *Ukraiins'ka Pravda*, October 16, 2008, 14:49.
[108] Serhy Leshchenko, "Yuliia Tymoshenko stala zaruchnykom svoho iazyka," *Ukraiins'ka Pravda*, September 5, 2008, 09:29.
[109] *Ukraiins'ka Pravda*, October 11, 2008, 16:08; *Segodnia*, October 17, 2008, 3; *Kommersant-Ukraiina*, November 24, 2008.

threat by warning he would call a referendum on the issue or even force early direct presidential elections before the change could be effected. He ultimately shelved the plan in 2009 as the regularly scheduled presidential election campaign took its course, with the voting scheduled for early 2010.[110]

The constitutionally underpinned expectations that there were two independent centers of executive power rather than just one, along with the constitutionally provided alternative focal points for elites dissatisfied with either center, gave elite networks of various kinds a great deal of latitude to pursue their own games by switching sides at opportune moments or playing one side against the other. Socialist Party leader Moroz, in playing one side off the other to become parliamentary speaker in 2006 as described previously, provides only one such instance. Major oligarchic business networks supply other examples. Ihor Kolomoisky and his Pryvat group went from being key Tymoshenko supporters to Yushchenko backers during 2005–10, while Petro Poroshenko (at one time part of Kuchma's coalition) began the year 2005 as a fiercely anti-Tymoshenko Yushchenko advocate but by 2009 had joined the Tymoshenko camp. Donetsk businessman Vitaly Haiduk had been Yanukovych's deputy prime minister in 2002–3 and backed him for president in the 2004 election. But after this loss, he switched to become Yushchenko's National Security and Defense Council secretary. The story did not stop there, however, as he later left Yushchenko following a policy dispute, ultimately winding up supporting Tymoshenko's 2010 presidential campaign.[111] Yanukovych's Party of Regions, when occupying neither the presidency nor the prime ministership, also played both sides against each other. Thus while it joined Tymoshenko to block Yushchenko's 2008 early election decree, it initiated a no-confidence vote in Tymoshenko earlier that same year. Tellingly, this no-confidence move was undermined by the formerly pro-Kuchma-and-Yanukovych Communist Party's delegation shortly before news emerged that two people connected to the party had received potentially lucrative posts in Tymoshenko's government.[112] With Yushchenko's popular support dropping and Tymoshenko emerging as the main expected alternative to Yanukovych leading in to the 2010 presidential election, Yushchenko's own parliamentary delegation NUNS (itself a coalition of networks) began to splinter. Defectors within the delegation came to outnumber loyalists, with the result being that NUNS as a parliamentary fraction effectively joined the Tymoshenko camp in the Rada.[113]

[110] *Ukraiins'ka Pravda*, May 27, 2009, 15:26; *Segodnia*, June 7, 2009, 12:30.

[111] *KyivPost*, January 22, 2010, 6–7; *RFE/RL Newsline*, May 14, 2007; *Ukraiins'ka Pravda*, October 10, 2006, 11:55; Stefan Wagstyl and Roman Oleachyk, "Ukraine Election Divides Oligarchs," *Financial Times*, January 15, 2010, circulated by The Ukraine List (UKL) #438, compiled by Dominique Arel, January 16, 2010.

[112] Pavel Korduban, "Tymoshenko Cabinet Survives No-Confidence Vote," *Eurasia Daily Monitor*, July 16, 2008; *Kommersant Ukraina*, July 25, 2008, p. 2.

[113] *Ukraiins'ka Pravda*, December 12, 2008, 18:57; Nikolai Martynenko, leader of NUNS fraction in Rada, interview, *Fokus*, no. 3–4, January 23, 2009.

This opportunity for business and political elites to switch sides, to find new political cover when one side ceased to be useful to them, was precisely what was missing in Kyrgyzstan after the Tulip Revolution, forcing "oligarchs" either to toe the official line or to surrender key assets to the president's circle. Just recall the contrast between the fates of Kyrgyz big businessmen Salymbekov and Baibolov discussed earlier.[114] Ukraine's divided-executive constitution, therefore, not only underpinned the existence of two centers of executive power, but created opportunities for a plurality of smaller "pyramids" to compete openly and fiercely using all the patronalistic means they could muster.

Case Study of a Democratic Election in a Highly Patronalistic Society

Some readers might wonder how patronal politics can actually be democratic. The answer depends, of course, on how one defines democracy.[115] If democracy requires a process completely free of vote buying, payoffs to journalists, employer pressure on employees, and politicization of the regulatory and enforcement apparatus of the state, then patronalism and democracy might well be incompatible. But most standard definitions of democracy do not require democratic perfection, meaning that countries can be considered to have passed a threshold of democracy so long as political competition is robust, entry into the political market is generally free, the information environment is open, and individual voters cast ballots that are honestly counted to produce an official result that reflects some aggregation of the popular will according to reasonable institutional rules. Indeed, as emphasized in Chapter 1, real-world democracy is historically often far from the idealized version one encounters in civics textbooks. This is abundantly clear from many episodes in the history of America and other countries widely considered democracies at the time.

To get a better idea of precisely how democratic elections can exist in a patronalistic environment under a divided-executive constitution, it is helpful to examine Ukraine's 2010 presidential contest as what might be called an "extreme case study." The case is extreme because the battle was much more pitched than need be the case, with bitter rivals employing nearly all the patronalistic tools at their disposal to influence the final formal result nationwide.[116] It thus nicely illustrates the full range of ways in which an election can

---

[114] Spector, "Securing Property"; and Ozcan, *Building States and Markets*.

[115] This section draws from Henry E. Hale, "The Uses of Divided Power," *Journal of Democracy*, v. 21, no. 3, July 2010, pp. 84–98.

[116] Patronal democracy does not always or even usually look as it did in Ukraine, even under a divided-executive constitution. The process can become more institutionalized in ways that eliminate some of the wildest uses of patronalistic methods, as appeared to be the case in Kyrgyzstan as of mid-2014. Ukraine's extremeness in 2010 likely reflects the work of at least three factors, which should be considered subjects for future research: (i) the extremely low and sinking popularity of the president at that time, which made him more desperate; (ii) the fact that Ukraine's competing-pyramid system had not yet been stabilized by institutionalization over time,

be fought by patronalistic means and nevertheless produce a genuine expression of popular sentiment that ultimately decides the official result, with the democratic aspects of the contest being crucially underpinned by a divided-executive constitution even as none of the actors behaved in truly democratic ways.

Ukraine's 2010 presidential election featured an intense competition between the chief wielders of formally divided executive power, President Yushchenko and Prime Minister Tymoshenko. Moreover, the roughly equal balance of formal and informal power between them served both to prevent either one from monopolizing authority and to create the political opening that Yanukovych needed to stage his political comeback. Out of executive power at the federal level after 2007, Yanukovych's network manipulated the competition between the prime minister and president to retain a measure of executive authority in eastern and southern Ukraine, including through directly elected mayors in such strongholds as Donetsk and Kharkiv. Regional "governors" at the time of the 2010 elections, though, had mostly been appointed by Yushchenko.

All three of these political figures, to the extent that they controlled any executive power capable of influencing the vote, vigorously sought to exploit the advantages of incumbency to win the 2010 presidential contest. Tymoshenko gave away apartments or small plots of land to families across Ukraine;[117] doled out new ambulances to Khmelnytska Oblast;[118] raised teachers' wages by 20 percent nationwide;[119] funded a program for miners in Luhansk;[120] and used economic-development agreements to slosh large streams of government money into various regions.[121] Yushchenko countered not only by using his "bully pulpit" to accuse her of everything from corruption to treason, but also by taking advantage of the executive power at his own disposal. Shortly after the August 2008 war between Georgia and Russia, for example, Yushchenko's

---

fostering uncertainty as to whether a single-pyramid system might not eventually reemerge; (iii) the personal willingness of the major networks and figures to engage in such a struggle without restraining themselves for the sake of stability. Similarly, Oleksandr Fisun ("The Dual Spiral of Ukrainian Politics after 2010," PONARS Eurasia Policy Memo no. 165, September 2011) cites the weakness of the presidential party in parliament, which hinged in part on low presidential popularity, and Serhiy Kudelia ("Institutional Design and Elite Interests: The Case of Ukraine," unpublished paper presented at the DC Area Postcommunist Politics Social Science Workshop, George Washington University, January 4, 2012) argues that fluctuating perceptions of each side's power undermined incentives for them to strike deals that would have prevented such costly competition. A good example of a highly patronalistic but institutionalized democracy might be India, though under a parliamentarist rather than divided-executive constitution.

[117] "Podrobnosti," Inter TV channel, January 23, 2010, 20:00, author's observation; "Fakty," ICTV, January 23, 2010, 18:45, author's observation.

[118] *Ukraiins'ka Pravda*, January 26, 2010, 20:29.

[119] *Weekly UA*, January 15–21, 2010, p. 11.

[120] Yuliia Mostova, "Pered ryvkom," *Dzerkalo Tyzhnia*, January 23–9, 2010, p. 2.

[121] *Ukraiins'ka Pravda*, January 26, 2010, 20:29. On the use of patronage in this campaign, see Serhiy Kudelia, "Clients' Revolt? Explaining the Failure of Government's Patronage in Ukraine's 2010 Presidential Election," paper presented at George Washington University workshop, April 2010.

Presidential Secretariat claimed to have evidence that Tymoshenko had struck a deal to back Russia in return for Kremlin help in financing her presidential campaign, as was described previously. Yushchenko also issued a slew of highly publicized honors to various constituencies during the final weeks before the vote.[122] While Yanukovych did not formally wield state executive powers, big-city mayors and city councils controlled by his Party of Regions helped him with positive coverage on state-influenced local media[123] and gave him considerable potential administrative resources of his own.[124]

While many of Ukraine's major oligarchic networks had shifted sides multiple times during the 2000s, the configuration in place by the 2010 election left each of the major power players – Yushchenko, Tymoshenko, and Yanukovych – with at least some such support. Counted among Yanukovych's chief oligarchs were gas-trading tycoon Dmytro Firtash and System Capital Management chief Rinat Akhmetov, still Ukraine's richest man and a native of Yanukovych's home region of Donetsk. Tymoshenko's reported bankrollers included Donetsk steel magnate Sergei Taruta, his former business partner Vitaly Haiduk, chocolate-confection king Petro Poroshenko, and iron-ore dealer Konstiantyn Zhevago. The latter three had been Yushchenko supporters before aligning with Tymoshenko as the president's reelection prospects dimmed. Several other oligarchs – including Pryvat conglomerate owners Ihor Kolomoisky and Gennady Bogoliubov as well as Kuchma's son-in-law, Interpipe group chief Viktor Pinchuk – were reportedly placing their financial eggs in multiple baskets, contributing to Yushchenko as well as others.[125]

Tymoshenko and Yanukovych had the best-financed campaigns. Each spent freely in order to win voters, but often not in ways reflective of ideal-type democracy. The chief editor of *Telekritika*, a journal devoted to monitoring media practices in Ukraine, reported that both campaigns concluded actual contracts with editors to buy positive reports as election day approached. Some such material would be marked explicitly as advertising, but much would not, being presented instead as news stories without any indication they were paid for.[126] Even a cursory reading of Ukrainian newspapers reveals a large number of stories that appear implausibly positive with respect to one candidate or another. Vote buying and rent-a-rally activity was also widely reported, with

---

[122] Pershyi Kanal (TV channel), December 20, 2009, 18:50, author's observation; "Vremia Novosti," Channel 5 TV, December 21, 2009, 22:37, author's observation.

[123] E.g., "Khar'kovskie Izvestiia," Channel 7 TV (Kharkiv), January 23, 2010, 20:30, author's observation; Viktor Yanukovych, interviewed on Channel 7 TV (Kharkiv), January 21, 2010, 20:20, author's observation.

[124] See the long list of Yanukovych supporters in positions of influence in each Ukrainian region in *Ekspert*, nos. 1–2, January 18–24, 2010, pp. 38–9.

[125] *Kyiv Post*, January 22, 2010, pp. 4, 6–7; Wagstyl and Oleachyk, "Ukraine Election Divides Oligarchs."

[126] *Kyiv Post*, January 15, 2009, 13.

the *Wall Street Journal* even finding a registered firm advertising services along these lines.[127]

The main candidates and their supporters also engaged in the practice of buying, or at least helping recruit and finance, "technical candidates" to run in the presidential contest as a way to manipulate the field and damage opponents' chances. Yanukovych, for example, was reportedly behind the nomination of his former Party of Regions associate Inna Bohaslovska, who was intended to weaken Tymoshenko by criticizing her during the campaign and by drawing away people looking for a female candidate. Analysts credibly linked Tymoshenko to two or more technical candidates, both aimed less at Yushchenko (whom she was confident of beating) or Yanukovych (who she hoped would be her opponent in a runoff election) than at the candidate who ultimately finished fourth, former foreign minister and parliament speaker Arseny Yatseniuk. Yatseniuk had rapidly gained popularity at Tymoshenko's expense after 2007 as a young "fresh face" – he had had to wait until his thirty-fifth birthday in 2009 to become eligible for the presidency. There were persistent reports that his candidacy was in fact covertly promoted by Yushchenko supporters precisely to undermine Tymoshenko and thereby give Yushchenko a better chance of making the runoff. As Yatseniuk's popularity peaked, one reputed Tymoshenko technical candidate, the little-known Uzhgorod mayor Serhy Ratushniak, caught media attention by branding Yatseniuk an "impudent Jew," a move some believe hurt Yatseniuk's standing among anti-Semitic voters in the Tymoshenko stronghold of western Ukraine.[128] By some accounts, third-place finisher Serhy Tihipko was another one of Tymoshenko's technical candidates. Tihipko, a former deputy prime minister and National Bank chief under Kuchma, had successfully refreshed his image by departing politics altogether from 2005 to 2009. Thus his "freshness" afforded him a chance to cut into Yatseniuk's support, while his ties to Kuchma and roots in eastern Ukraine gave him appeal in Yanukovych's eastern base.

One must be wary of the most conspiratorial interpretations, however. While such elaborate strategies of manipulating the candidate field are surely not beyond the pale in post-Soviet Ukraine, just as surely the "puppets" here were also using their "puppet masters" as a way to get funding for their own political ambitions. Both Tihipko and Yatseniuk clearly took on political lives of their own once their campaigns gained traction, so they cannot simply be regarded as marionettes.[129]

The presidential candidates also brazenly vied to influence courts whose rulings might impact election outcomes.[130] It was considered essential for analysts

[127] Richard Boudreaux, "Bucks Populi," *Wall Street Journal*, February 5, 2010.

[128] *Kyiv Post*, December 18, 2009, pp. 1, 14.

[129] Oleksii Mustafin, "Serhyi Tihipko: Vybir pislia vyboriv," *Dzerkalo Tyzhnia*, January 23, 2010, p. 3.

[130] Important works on the politicization of courts in Ukraine include Maria Popova, "Political Competition as an Obstacle to Judicial Independence: Evidence from Russia and Ukraine," *Comparative Political Studies*, v. 43, no. 10, 2010, pp. 1202–29; and Trochev, "Meddling with Justice."

to know which courts were in whose pockets. Experts reported that the Supreme Court and the Kyiv Appeals Administrative Court were in Tymoshenko's; the Supreme Administrative Court of Ukraine (VASU) was in Yanukovych's; and the Constitutional Court was in Yushchenko's (at least until his chief of staff, Viktor Baloha, resigned).[131] Indeed, competition for control over the courts was an essential part of all the major campaigns' strategy for 2010. For example, just before the February 7 runoff that pitted Yanukovych against Tymoshenko, Yanukovych's Party of Regions pushed in parliament to remove Supreme Court chief justice Vasyl Onopenko, who had previously been deputy leader of the Yulia Tymoshenko Bloc in parliament and thus was widely considered her political ally.[132] The Party of Regions alleged that Onopenko had improperly attempted to force out the Yanukovych-linked chief justice of VASU, the court with the power to rule on the validity of presidential-election results.[133] At one point, two justices claimed the chief judgeship of VASU at once, and one of them even absconded with the official stamp in an attempt to retain authority.[134] The struggle for control of the courts also helps explain why Tymoshenko would work closely with Viktor Medvedchuk, Kuchma's chief of staff during the Orange Revolution: During the 2010 campaign, he was an influential member of the Higher Council of Justice, which issued recommendations on the hiring and firing of judges.[135]

At the same time, Ukraine's 2010 presidential race also illustrates how informal politics can sometimes reinforce formal institutions (including formal laws).[136] Many of the patronalistic uses of power that have checkered Ukrainian political life – despite being aimed at aggrandizing particular factions – also had the positive side effect of countering abuses of power by rival factions. When the Tymoshenko Bloc pushed successfully to restrict the legal space permitted to at-home voting, for instance, it was simultaneously making a self-serving attack on one of Yanukovych's known advantages *and* putting a lid on a potential source of vote fraud.[137] The Tymoshenko Bloc's winning of a late-night, election-eve court ruling requiring medical documentation of need before anyone could legally cast a ballot at home was a first step. Next, Tymoshenko's cabinet (with the emphatic participation and support of her interior minister) ordered that any election commissioner who took a ballot box to

[131] Sergei Vysotskii, "Krepkii tyl," *Fokus*, January 22, 2010, pp. 16–19; *Ukraiins'ka Pravda*, January 28, 2010, 14:38.

[132] *Korrespondent.net*, May 22, 2006, 20:25.

[133] *Ukraiins'ka Pravda*, February 1, 2010, 14:32.

[134] *Ukraiinskyi Tyzhden'*, January 15–21, 2010, pp. 8–9.

[135] Vysotskii, "Krepkii tyl."

[136] As Anna Grzymala-Busse ("The Best Laid Plans: The Impact of Informal Rules on Formal Institutions in Transitional Regimes," *Studies in Comparative International Development*, v. 45, no. 3, September 2010, pp. 311–33), for example, has argued.

[137] Because they can escape the attention of election monitors present at most polling places, the mobile ballot boxes used for at-home voting are a notorious source of fraud across the former Soviet Union. In Ukraine, they were widely seen as tools that local officials friendly to Yanukovych could use to fabricate votes (*Kyiv Post*, January 22, 2010, p. 2).

the home of someone lacking proper medical permission would be billed for any expenses incurred (including pay and transportation) or face charges of misusing state resources.[138] In another move that both weakened her rivals and eliminated an opportunity for corruption, Tymoshenko struck a direct blow at one of Yanukovych's main financial backers, Dmytro Firtash, by cutting his gas-trading company out of Ukraine's lucrative energy deals with Russia in 2008.[139]

This was not a one-way street. Anything that smacked of self-dealing by Tymoshenko drew eager resistance from quarters of the state apparatus accessible to Yushchenko and Yanukovych. Yushchenko especially seemed to relish every chance to strike blows at Tymoshenko, even if they wound up helping Yanukovych. Thus when Tymoshenko replaced the head of the State Property Fund with a close supporter after accusing her of improprieties, Yushchenko issued a decree reversing the decision.[140] Citing concerns Tymoshenko had replaced Firtash's gas-trading arrangement with one favorable to her own cronies, Yushchenko's National Security and Defense Council ordered an investigation of the new deal.[141] Two days before the runoff, Yushchenko fired the governors of Kharkiv and Dnipropetrovsk, accused in media of misusing "administrative resources" and pressuring public employees to support Tymoshenko.[142] Even the Party of Regions was able to press its interests through national level state channels. Between the two rounds of presidential balloting, it found enough votes in parliament (including some legislators from Yushchenko's bloc) to dismiss the interior minister for politicizing the police, then managed to lift the limits Tymoshenko had won on home voting, calling it unfair to change the rules during a campaign.[143]

Strikingly absent from this picture of the 2010 presidential elections as an exercise in competitive patronalism,[144] however, is outright falsification of the results. Accusations of chicanery flew, but even many partisan observers conceded that any actual ballot-box fraud was too insubstantial to have made the difference between winning and losing in either the first or second rounds. International election monitors of all stripes concurred, as did analysis using sophisticated social science tools of fraud forensics.[145]

---

[138] *Ukraiins'ka Pravda*, January 16, 2010, 17:59.
[139] Anders Åslund, "Will the Real Gazprom CEO Please Stand Up?" *The Moscow Times*, January 28, 2009.
[140] *RFE/RL Newsline*, February 8, 2008.
[141] *Ukraiins'ka Pravda*, February 10, 2009, 16:32.
[142] *Ukraiins'ka Pravda*, February 16, 2010, 13:46.
[143] *Kommersant Ukrainy*, January 20, 2010, p. 2; *Ukraiins'ka Pravda*, January 28, 2010, 11:46, 12:27.
[144] This adapts the concept of "competitive clientelism" developed in Jennifer Gandhi and Ellen Lust-Okar, "Elections under Authoritarianism," *Annual Review of Political Science*, v. 12, 2009, pp. 403–22, p. 407.
[145] Erik S. Herron, "How Viktor Yanukovych Won: Reassessing the Dominant Narratives of Ukraine's 2010 Presidential Election," *East European Politics and Societies*, v. 25, no. 1, February 2011, pp. 47–67.

The major competitors used patronalistic methods to influence voters' hearts and minds, but in the end it was those hearts and minds (however influenced) that decided the winner. Accordingly, the same candidates who were wrestling for control over the courts, buying votes, and paying off the media were also working to prove they were better leaders with superior ideas about how to deliver the policies people desired. The final tallies, therefore, can be explained by three factors that typically influence voters in democracies: perceived incumbent performance, the quality of the campaigns and candidates themselves, and long-standing political preferences associated with different regions of the country.

Yushchenko's popular support had dropped steadily after he assumed the presidency, largely as a result of disappointment with his failure to eliminate corruption even from within his own administration and his constant squabbling with his erstwhile ally, Tymoshenko. Oligarchs were not prosecuted, including virtually all of the major figures widely believed complicit in the political crimes of the Kuchma era. These were facts that Tymoshenko was quick to point out as her rivalry with the incumbent president grew more heated. Yushchenko's standing rose slightly after he teamed up with Tymoshenko to force Yanukovych out as prime minister in April 2007. But in the parliamentary elections that September, not only did Yanukovych's Party of Regions come in first with 34 percent of the vote, but Yushchenko's broad coalition of parties (NUNS) finished a poor third with 14 percent. This was less than half the 31 percent that Tymoshenko's bloc won, making her the most credible challenger to Yanukovych and returning her to the premiership via a slim majority coalition comprising her bloc and NUNS. Although Yanukovych's party had won the most votes, its two allies only barely passed the 3 percent threshold that parties had to meet before they could win any seats, so a governing coalition lay out of reach.

Yushchenko's reelection effort consisted mostly of attacks on Tymoshenko. He would use his presidential powers repeatedly to block her policy moves as described previously – freezing privatization initiatives by challenging them in court on dubious constitutional grounds, for instance – and then accuse her of incompetence, corruption, and ineffectiveness.[146] The sitting president also aimed to drive a wedge between Tymoshenko and the voters in the country's more assertively ethnic-Ukrainian western region, which had been his stronghold during the Orange Revolution but which now backed Tymoshenko. This undercut Tymoshenko's efforts to make her appeal truly nationwide by stressing populist policies instead of the cultural issues that tended to split eastern from western Ukraine. Most prominently, when she refused to take a side early in the August 2008 war between Georgia and Russia over South Ossetia, Yushchenko quickly and loudly backed Georgian President Mikheil Saakashvili and branded Tymoshenko's more cautious response evidence of a treasonous

---

[146] E.g., *Ukraiins'ka Pravda*, January 30, 2009, 21:39.

deal with Moscow.[147] Averring throughout the campaign that the election was really about "values," Yushchenko lumped Tymoshenko and Yanukovych together as equally anti-Ukrainian and emphasized his own ardent support for ethnic Ukrainian culture, democracy, and a foreign policy that would steer Ukraine closer to Europe than to Moscow.[148]

For all his assaults on Tymoshenko, Yushchenko did make a few gestures at positive campaigning. One of the most prominent was a nationwide billboard and television advertising campaign touting major achievements of his presidency. These ranged from securing freedom of speech to winning the right to hold the 2012 European soccer championships in Ukraine and were accompanied by the phrase "We got it done." None of this proved enough to get Yushchenko's popular support out of the single digits, however, and his televised appearances – during which he seemed tired, preachy, humorless, and aloof – did not help.[149]

Tymoshenko's strategy going into the race was to build support nationwide, reaching beyond her base in western Ukraine through populist policy stances, personal appeal, and the downplaying of ethnocultural issues. In early 2008, this approach seemed promising: She was presiding over a growing economy; her campaign since the 2006 parliamentary races had successfully shed the explicitly "Orange" campaign symbols that had become anathema to many in eastern Ukraine, sporting instead a purer white symbolism that was frequently combined with national imagery and a red heart shaped to evoke a check mark; and the 2007 parliamentary elections had revealed she was gaining support in several eastern regions. And despite her appeal in western Ukraine, she herself was from Dnipropetrovsk and so could claim eastern roots.

In mid-2008, two developments combined to derail this strategy. The first and more important was the global financial crisis, which put her in an unenviable position as sitting premier during a severe economic downturn. Tymoshenko responded by arguing she had succeeded in preventing a steeper decline and blamed Yushchenko and the Party of Regions (with some credibility) for blocking her policies.[150] But she remained vulnerable to the simple contrast between her time as premier and the steady economic growth that had occurred under both Yanukovych governments (2002–4 and 2006–7). The second development was the South Ossetian war and the renewed fear of Russia it roused in western Ukraine. Her cautious response, in contrast with Yushchenko's unhesitating support for Saakashvili, started to give some traction to Yushchenko's charges that Tymoshenko was not a full-blooded defender of the Ukrainian

[147] E.g., *Segodnia* (Ukraine), August 13, 2008, p. 2. See also Taras Kuzio, "Strident, Ambiguous and Duplicitous: Ukraine and the 2008 Russia-Georgia War," *Demokratizatsiya: The Journal of Post-Soviet Democratization*, v. 17, no. 4, Fall 2009, pp. 350–72.
[148] *Dzerkalo Tyzhnia*, January 23–9, 2010, p. 1; *Fakty*, December 22, 2009, p. 4.
[149] Author's field observations, Ukraine, December 2009 and January 2010.
[150] *Fakty i Kommentarii* (Kharkiv area edition), January 22, 2010, p. 2.

nation. This forced her to moderate her appeals to eastern electorates lest she give the charges even more credibility.

When the official campaign period started in late 2009, Tymoshenko's chief goal was to make it to the second round because an outright victory in the first round seemed out of reach. She avoided criticizing Yushchenko and even Yatseniuk as intensely as she might have, hoping she could draw many of their voters in the second round. Instead, she emphasized image-based appeals and personal charisma. Particularly attention-grabbing was a nationwide billboard campaign that saw new designs appear progressively as election day drew near. Featuring a white background with only a traditional Ukrainian embroidery strip running down one side, the billboards included just a couple of lines of text and never showed Tymoshenko's face or even mentioned her name. The first read simply: "They are squabbling. She is working!" After these had been up for some time, new text appeared: "She will be victorious. 'She' is Ukraine." Having now implicitly identified Tymoshenko with Ukraine itself, an idea she had long sought to convey with her trademark hairstyle of traditional braids, the final installment read: "Ukraine will be victorious. 'Ukraine' is you." Celebrities endorsed her and even sang about her in a pop song.[151] To the extent she communicated a programmatic message, it was the need to restore order,[152] revive the economy,[153] and prosecute corrupt oligarchs.[154] An image released just prior to the first-round voting featured her beside a white tiger, a symbol of strength, capable of defending its motherland.[155]

What is bad for incumbents is often good for oppositions, and this proved to be the case in Ukraine in 2010. Yanukovych not only was the leading opposition figure at a time of economic crisis, but could also claim credit for the robust growth that had taken place during his two periods as prime minister.[156] Although he blamed the crisis on incumbent incompetence,[157] his

[151] Author's field observations, Ukraine, December 2009 and January 2010.

[152] *Ukraiins'ka Pravda*, January 30, 2010, 00:21.

[153] *Ekonomichna Pravda*, February 1, 2010, 21:18; *Fakty i Kommentarii* (Kharkiv area edition), January 23, 2010, p. 4.

[154] E.g., Tymoshenko's remarks on the television program *Shuster Live*, Ukraiina Channel, December 18, 2009, 21:30, author's observations.

[155] "White tiger" television advertisement for Tymoshenko widely broadcast during the campaign, e.g., Pershyy Kanal TV, December 21, 2009, and 5th Channel TV, December 22, 2009, 22:30, author's observations.

[156] Viktor Yanukovych, interviewed on *Shuster Live*, speaking Russian, Ukraiina TV Channel, January 29, 2010, video posted at http://shuster.kanalukraina.tv/ua/, accessed February 3, 2010. On the importance of economic factors more generally in this election, see Stephen Bloom and Stephen Shulman, "Interest versus Identity: Economic Voting in Ukrainian Presidential Elections," *Post-Soviet Affairs*, v. 27, no. 4, October–December 2011, pp. 410–28.

[157] Viktor Yanukovych, on Velyka Politika z Yevheniem Kyseliovym, Inter TV network, February 5, 2010, 21:30, online recording, http://politika.inter.ua/ru/episode/54, accessed February 7, 2010.

message remained largely positive. He promised change, which he said would include uniting the Ukrainian nation after years of internecine squabbling, restoring competence to government, and prioritizing the battle against poverty ("our biggest enemy")[158] over all else.[159] And while he called for restoring "normal" relations with Russia and hinted at raising the formal status of the Russian language, he also consistently reaffirmed Ukraine's basically European orientation, though without dropping his opposition to NATO membership.[160]

Despite much talk of Tymoshenko's charisma and campaign prowess, it was Yanukovych who in the end ran the better campaign in terms of both style and organization. If Yushchenko appeared arrogant and removed, and if Tymoshenko often seemed frenetic and defensive, Yanukovych managed to strike a personal tone in his televised appearances that communicated normality, a common touch, and even a certain likability.[161] Talking in calm and reassuring tones, avoiding angry language and expressions, and speaking almost always with a light smile that connoted bemusement with the rarified world of politics, he cast himself as something like an "uncle" who may not have been the best speaker, but who for all his foibles would at least be a comfortable and genuine choice for ordinary Ukrainians. While Yanukovych mounted a well-organized effort across the whole of Ukraine, Tymoshenko's campaign was surprisingly weak in many regions, sometimes with figures of dubious repute in positions of responsibility. Her campaign also seemed oddly inert almost up to election day in the first round, even in such crucial locales as the large city of Lviv near Ukraine's western border.[162]

When the ballots from the January 17, 2010, first round were counted, Yanukovych wound up on top with 35 percent of the vote, not nearly enough to avoid a runoff with Tymoshenko, who had finished second with 25 percent. Starting 10 percent behind her rival, Tymoshenko set her sights first on those voters who had supported Serhy Tihipko, the surprisingly strong third-place finisher. His late surge to a 13 percent total had been fueled by his calls for tough economic reforms, his avoidance of divisive ethnocultural issues, and campaign imagery that seemed to invoke the vigorous personal style of Russia's President

---

[158] Yanukovych quoted in *Khar'kovskie Izvestiia*, January 21, 2010, p. 3.

[159] Viktor Yanukovych, in "open letter" to fellow citizens, "Viktor Yanukovych nazval svoikh vragov," *Segodnia* (Kharkiv edition), January 22, 2010, p. 5; Yanukovych presidential campaign ad, aired on Ukraiina TV Channel, December 17, 2009, 18:30, author's observation.

[160] *Kyiv Post*, January 22, 2010, p. 10.

[161] Compare, for example, their contrasting manners while appearing on Yevgeny Kisilev's political talk show shortly before the first round: Yulia Tymoshenko, on *Velyka Politika z Yevheniem Kyseliovym*, Inter TV network, January 29, 2010, 21:30, http://politika.inter.ua/ru/episode/53, accessed February 7, 2010; Viktor Yanukovych, on *Velyka Politika z Yevheniem Kyseliovym*, Inter TV network, February 5, 2010, 21:30, http://politika.inter.ua/ru/episode/54, accessed February 7, 2010.

[162] Volodymyr Martyn, "Faktor Balohy," *Dzerkalo Tyzhnia*, December 19–25, 2009, p. 2; Mostova, "Pered ryvkom"; author's field observations.

Vladimir Putin – even down to his haircut and gait.[163] While Yatseniuk sank to fourth place after once challenging for second, thanks largely to a poor campaign and the rise of Tihipko, his 7 percent was also a prize for the second round, as was the 5 percent Yushchenko garnered, however humiliating that total may have been for him. The Communist Party's Petro Symonenko's 4 percent was expected to go to Yanukovych, and no other candidate received as much as 3 percent.

With the February 7 runoff looming, Tymoshenko pleaded with Tihipko, Yatseniuk, and Yushchenko to join her in a "democratic" alliance against Yanukovych, even promising to make Tihipko her replacement as prime minister if she won (despite the fact that as president under the divided-executive constitution, she would not have the power actually to appoint him).[164] These entreaties fell embarrassingly flat as Tihipko refused to endorse anyone while Yushchenko and Yatseniuk urged a vote "against all" in the runoff. Yanukovych also wooed Tihipko voters but refused to pander, saying only that he would find a way to oust Tymoshenko as premier and would consider Tihipko among others when deciding whom to endorse to replace her.[165]

Tymoshenko was left with a second-round strategy that leaned heavily on efforts to demonize Yanukovych while casting herself as "democratic" Ukraine's last hope. She and her supporters cited his past criminal conviction in claiming that he represented organized crime's rise to power in Ukraine. They further warned that a Yanukovych victory would mean the domination of the Donetsk region over all other regions (a charge that was particularly potent in western Ukraine); argued that a vote for him would put Ukrainian independence at risk; and cast the election as a choice between accepting or rejecting Europe.[166] Yanukovych largely ignored her change in tactics and stuck to his successful first-round strategy. As for his time in jail, he said in a live televised interview that it had been a "learning experience," which had helped him change his ways and left him with a keener sense of sympathy for those who fall into misfortune.[167] All this resonated with his chief campaign slogan, "Ukraine for the People," which was visible on billboards across the country.

Exit polls from the runoff reveal Tymoshenko drew most of those Yushchenko and Yatseniuk voters who showed up, while splitting the Tihipko vote more or

[163] Author's field observations, Ukraine, December 2009 and January 2010.
[164] *Fakty i Kommentarii* (Kharkiv edition), January 21, 2010, p. 2.
[165] Viktor Yanukovych, on *Shuster Live*, Ukraiina TV Channel, January 29, 2010, http://shuster.kanalukraina.tv/ua/, accessed February 3, 2010.
[166] For a sampling of her themes, see *Ukraiins'ka Pravda*, January 25, 2010, 20:27; *Ukraiins'ka Pravda*, February 1, 2010, 21:59; Tymoshenko television advertisement, broadcast on 5th Channel, February 1, 2010, 17:15, author's observation on live Internet broadcast of TV 5 at http://5.ua/live; Tymoshenko television advertisement, broadcast on 5th Channel, January 27, 2010, 17:10, author's observation on live Internet broadcast of TV 5 at http://5.ua/live.
[167] Viktor Yanukovych, interviewed on *Shuster Live*, Ukraiina TV Channel, January 29, 2010, author's observation via http://shuster.kanalukraina.tv/ua.

less evenly with Yanukovych.[168] This was only enough to gain her 45 percent, however, and Yanukovych took the prize with 49 percent of valid votes cast.

Although candidates were both found to have "bought" favorable media coverage as well as votes, in the end voters had a wide array of differing contenders, interpretations, and messages to weigh, and were able to make their choices as they saw fit. Big business stood just offstage employing its resources as it too saw fit, but all major candidates found ample campaign funding just the same. Thus while the environment was far from the democratic ideal, the problems ultimately did not stop voters from making an informed and reasoned choice that reflected their priorities and concerns. Ukrainian democracy during the 2009–10 election season was highly patronalistic indeed, but democracy nonetheless.

Ukraine 2010–2014: *Presidentialism Restored, Political Closure, Revolution*

One of the chief ironies of divided-executive constitutions and competing-pyramid systems is that the democratic election results they promote can also provide a window of opportunity for the victor to move toward single-pyramid politics and even to change the constitution itself. This is because, as Chapter 4 discussed, a victory in a head-to-head high-stakes contest between rival networks can be among the most powerful shapers of expectations as to which network is likely to be dominant in the future. For elites looking to wind up on the side of an eventual winner (crucial to maintaining or expanding access to power and resources), this gives incentive to coordinate their activities around the election victor rather than the loser. And while the information and focal effects of a divided-executive constitution will still be functioning to promote coordination around multiple centers of patronal authority, these decentralizing effects can be momentarily overpowered by the raw demonstration of network strength in the election.

This effect is generally "momentary" because as time passes, the election victory becomes a less reliable indicator of current and future network strength. This is especially true as expectations become complicated by changes in leaders' popularity or the outcomes of myriad subsequent low-stakes contests, giving new prominence to constitutions' information and focal effects. Thus without changing the divided-executive nature of the constitution, efforts to use election victories to build single-pyramid systems are less likely to last. But if the moment is used successfully to restore a presidentialist constitution, then this can reinforce a new tendency toward single-pyramid politics as elites increasingly coordinate around the victorious network.[169] Elections, then, can

---

[168] *Segodnia* (Ukraine), January 19, 2010, p. 3; "Velyka Polytyka z Yevheniem Kyseliovym, Nich Vyboriv," Inter+ TV network, 21:00, accessed live online through http://www.jumptv.com/en/node/88?MyJumpTV=1.

[169] In principle, this can happen with either a presidential or parliamentary election so long as the victory is decisive.

constitute moments of special vulnerability for competing-pyramid systems and divided-executive constitutions. Of course, such efforts may or may not be successful even if the moment is opportune; these moments are thus times of flux when leadership will and skill again are at the fore. And because constitutions are not automatically and instantly followed, but instead simply provide certain signals that facilitate difficult processes of elite network coordination, any new closure of the system will not be completed overnight but will take time, and its nature and success will depend partly on the will and skill of the patrons involved. And the more entrenched are divisions among the major networks before a presidentialist constitution is restored, the more challenging it will be for the new leader to build a new single-pyramid system successfully without overreaching and provoking collective resistance. This helps us understand events in Ukraine after the 2010 presidential election, including the gradual new closing of the political system that led up to the Euromaidan protests described in Chapter 7.[170]

Ukraine's return to a presidentialist constitution owes to the Yanukovych network's dramatic defeat of Tymoshenko's network in the highly competitive head-to-head patronalistic election just described, a victory that signaled his network's superiority. Crucially, after securing this win, Yanukovych moved with lightning speed to maneuver his close associate Nikolai Azarov into the prime ministership. He did this by inducing parliamentary deputies from the losing Tymoshenko and Yushchenko camps (still in disarray after their losses) to defect to his side. The key defection for influencing the prime ministership was that of parliamentary speaker Volodymyr Lytvyn, a partner in the parliamentary coalition that had undergirded Tymoshenko's government. Importantly, Lytvyn's initial political instinct was to balance rather than bandwagon: Shortly after the election, he said that "the victor cannot take all" and that he would support Tymoshenko to stay on as prime minister. At the same time, however, he warned that Tymoshenko should recognize Yanukovych's victory and avoid opposing him in ways that would divide the country and make it ungovernable, as by blocking important economic and other reforms.[171] Indeed, as Serhiy Kudelia has pointed out, democracy under a divided-executive constitution does not have to involve Hobbesian conflict among networks, but can also involve cooperation in important spheres that can be profitable to all groups.[172]

Tymoshenko, however, proved unrelenting, unwilling to recognize her loss or work with the new authorities, even vowing that she "never" would do so.[173] In an effort to mobilize the power of positive thinking during her

[170] For analysis of events through 2012, see Mykola Riabchuk, *Gleichschaltung: Authoritarian Consolidation in Ukraine 2010–2012* (Kyiv: K.I.S., 2012).

[171] *Ukraiins'ka Pravda*, February 14, 2010, 21:36.

[172] Kudelia, "Institutional Design and Elite Interests."

[173] *Ukraiins'ka Pravda*, February 8, 2010, 23:06.

election campaign, she had reportedly refused to draw up contingency plans for how to maintain her parliamentary coalition and remain prime minister should she lose. Thus after the election, she focused on contesting the result rather than sustaining her own coalition, which was demoralized and in disarray after the defeat. In Lytvyn's words, instead of creating a working balance between the prime minister and new president, Tymoshenko insisted on continuing what he called "relentless war against the elected president" that would produce more of the dysfunction that had plagued Ukraine for the previous five years. This, according to Lytvyn himself, led him to defect from Tymoshenko's coalition and set up her replacement by Azarov.[174] Indeed, some of the same experts who had said just prior to the February runoff that even Yanukovych's oligarchic supporters feared a new concentration of power under a single president reported after the election that there was also an elite consensus that the constant political battles between president and prime minister had to stop.[175]

The decisive moment of Lytvyn's defection to Yanukovych occurred when he used his position as speaker to orchestrate key and legally dubious changes in parliamentary rules (which he could have easily prevented) that made possible Tymoshenko's ouster and Azarov's confirmation as prime minister.[176] Asked about another reform that he helped pass a bit later that was expected to benefit Yanukovych, Lytvyn gave an answer that also sheds light on his initial defection: "I am a realist, and when you cannot stop a process, you must lead it. And make this process civilized."[177] Other deputies formally in Tymoshenko's or Yushchenko's camp followed Lytvyn's lead, ultimately voting to confirm Azarov as prime minister. This gave Yanukovych's network control over both of the country's key formal executive posts. One veteran political strategist described a key logic behind these parliamentarians' moves: Since it was inevitable that Yanukovych would get his man installed as PM, they were better able to make money off this by accepting offers to defect than by futilely attempting to resist.[178] The expectation of Yanukovych's dominance helped make him dominant.

With the capture of the presidency and prime ministership, a single network thus established itself as unrivaled and left no clear alternative focal point for dissatisfied networks to coordinate around in the future.[179] Observers quickly noted a reorientation of business-based elites, including key figures controlling

[174] Volodymyr Lytvyn, interview, *Kommersant Ukraina*, July 16, 2010.
[175] Author's interviews with experts on Ukrainian politics, Kyiv, January 2010 and August 2011.
[176] *Kommersant Ukraina*, April 9, 2010; *Ukraiins'ka Pravda*, March 2, 2010, 11:38; *Ukraiins'ka Pravda*, March 9, 2010, 18:45.
[177] *Ukraiins'ka Pravda*, June 22, 2010, 23:27.
[178] Dmytro Vydrin, author's interview, Kyiv, August 2, 2011.
[179] On the Donetsk network at the core of Yanukovych's power that includes Azarov, see Taras Kuzio, *Ukraine: A Contemporary History*, unpublished draft book manuscript, July 2011, chapter 11.

television, around Yanukovych.[180] Moving fast before any split could emerge between him and his prime minister, before his popular support could sink substantially, and before he might manage to lose smaller battles that could eat away at the sense of inevitability of his network's dominance, Yanukovych sought to change the divided-executive constitution to a presidentialist one so as to "lock in" his dominance as chief patron. Even at this point, however, the constitutional change was not automatic. Experts on different sides of the political fence prior to the runoff election had said that Yanukovych would be unlikely to muster the 300 parliamentary votes he needed to amend the constitution, and it appears they were in fact right: Parliament resisted the Party of Regions' effort to gain its sanction for a referendum to effect the change. Even after having facilitated Azarov's rise to PM, Lytvyn began stalling and sabotaging the constitutional initiative from his position as parliamentary speaker during summer 2010, arguing that repealing the 2004 reform would have negative effects and was illegal.[181]

But with no significant concentration of state executive power capable of stopping him outside his own network's hands, Yanukovych's Party of Regions simply sidestepped the parliament: Instead, the Constitutional Court invalidated the 2004 reform. Yanukovych's team had successfully packed the court in September 2010 by having four justices replaced. Then, just days later, the court ruled that the 2004 reform had been improperly established and was thus null and void, restoring the presidentialist constitution of 1996 – the same one Kuchma had enjoyed as patronal president.[182] According to one political expert and Yanukovych adviser, the key was not so much that the court was bought. Instead, it was engaging in its usual practice of reading the political winds, which in this case blew in the direction of Yanukovych's rising dominance and an end to the large-scale elite battles with which much of the elite was fed up.[183]

These events thus call attention to the importance of formal constitutions at the same time that they establish some of the limits of their effects. On one hand, these events do show that the signals about relative network power coming from the result of a head-to-head electoral contest can at least momentarily overpower the discoordinating effects of divided-executive constitutions before new battles and events introduce fresh uncertainty into these calculations. There is thus a constant interplay between the effects of constitutions and the effects of specific other events involving network contestation, such as but not limited to the formal institution of elections.

---

[180] E.g., *Segodnia*, May 15, 2010, 08:04; *Telekrytyka*, July 12, 2010.

[181] E.g., *Ukraiins'ka Pravda*, July 8, 2010, 14:54; *Ukraiins'ka Pravda*, July 8, 2010, 14:40.

[182] Alexei Trochev, "A Constitution of Convenience in Ukraine," *Jurist-Forum*, January 18, 2011, http://jurist.org/forum/2011/01/jurist-guest-columnist-alexei-trochev.php, accessed April 24, 2011; *Ukraiins'ka Pravda*, September 21, 2011, 11:01.

[183] Vydrin interview 2011.

But, on the other hand, the fact Yanukovych considered a constitutional change necessary does indicate he himself saw the divided-executive constitution as potentially complicating his consolidation of power and a presidential-ist constitution as facilitating it. Indeed, the very same Yanukovych tried twice under a divided-executive constitution to create his own single-pyramid system rooted in state executive power, once in 2006–7 and once in 2010, but was thwarted by constitutionally induced dynamics in the first of these tries. And the preceding pages showed how the formal constitution helped thwart similar attempts by both Yushchenko and Tymoshenko to coordinate the country's main networks around their own authority.

Regime dynamics in Ukraine after the adoption of the new presidentialist constitution are also in line with what the patronal politics logic would lead us to anticipate: a significant though gradual closing of the political space as elite groups began to coordinate around Yanukovych as chief patron.[184] A dramatic signal to the elite was the arrest and conviction of Tymoshenko on charges that she had abused her office in striking a gas deal with Russia,[185] a conviction that was soon followed by the jailing of others linked to her, including former Interior Minister Yury Lutsenko.[186] Businesses that had been part of her power pyramid during her presidential bid also suffered. Those of oligarch Konstantin Zhevago, former Kharkiv governor Arsen Avakov, and Tymoshenko's party's youth wing leader Yevgeny Suslov, for example, were all hit by a wave of searches and inspections from various executive and regulatory organs. Other business figures quickly realigned from Tymoshenko to Yanukovych,[187] with perhaps the most prominent example being the oligarch Petro Poroshenko, the erstwhile member of Kuchma's team who then became an early backer of Yushchenko before defecting to Tymoshenko in the run-up to the 2010 campaign.[188] In 2012, he became Yanukovych's minister of trade and economic development. Not everyone switched sides; Avakov held out and was arrested.[189] Politicians were also generally able to secure a new position in the Yanukovych power pyramid if they defected in a timely manner, as had former Yushchenko chief of staff Viktor Baloha, who became Yanukovych's emergencies minister.[190]

[184] See also Olexiy Haran, "Ukraine: Pluralism by Default, Revolution, Thermidor," *Russian Politics and Law*, v. 50, no. 4, July–August 2012, pp. 51–72; David J. Kramer, Robert Nurick, Damon Wilson, with Evan Alterman, "Sounding the Alarm: Protecting Democracy in Ukraine," Freedom House Report, April 2011; Alexander J. Motyl, "The New Political Regime in Ukraine – toward Sultanism Yanukovych-Style?" Cicero Foundation Great Debate Paper, no. 10/06, July 2010.

[185] See Serhiy Kudelia, "Why Yanukovych Did It: Explaining the Rationality of His Choice," blog post, PONARS Eurasia Web site, October 18, 2011, http://www.ponarseurasia.org/article/why-yanukovych-did-it-explaining-rationality-his-choice, accessed February 2, 2014.

[186] *RFE/RL*, April 6, 2012.

[187] *Korrespondent* (Ukraine), July 29, 2011, pp. 30–2.

[188] *Korrespondent.net* (Ukraine), "Petro Poroshenko," http://korrespondent.net/uastartup/1-poroshenko, accessed June 4, 2014.

[189] *RFE/RL*, January 31, 2012.

[190] *Dzerkalo Tyzhnia*, April 6, 2012, 21:50.

The networks in Yanukovych's emergent single-pyramid system, while all oriented now to the new patronal president's authority, remained configured in a relatively loose formation in this pyramid as 2013 drew to a close, with a great deal of open competition among them for assets and influence and extensive overlap of roles and interests within the political system. Indeed, after Ukraine experienced five years of competing pyramid politics anchored by a divided-executive constitution, Yanukovych's task of political machine building resembled that of Kuchma in the mid-1990s (and other patronal presidents of that decade described in Chapter 6) because the power *vertikal'* had to be reconstructed nearly from scratch, a process that takes a great deal of time to orchestrate and organize without suffering setbacks. By 2013, one could characterize Ukraine's organization of major patronal networks with reference to three categories. First, effectively marginalized were political-economic networks associated with Tymoshenko that did not accommodate themselves to the new patron. A second category included a wide range of networks that remained influential players within the Yanukovych system, but were not part of its inner core. These included networks like Kolomoisky's Pryvat and that of Kuchma son-in-law Pinchuk. Third, emerging at the core was a set of networks associated with the Party of Regions, which was increasingly used as a structure for organizing formal and informal power in the country.

The Party of Regions, however, was by no means unified, itself featuring strong intraparty "factional" competition among at least three networks during this period. According to Oleksandr Fisun's analysis, these included the famed Donetsk network informally led by Rinat Akhmetov and including such major figures as Prime Minister Azarov, parliamentary chairman Volodymyr Rybak, and National Security and Defense Council Secretary Andry Kliuev; the RosUkrEnergo network of the superwealthy Dmytro Firtash, which included Presidential Administration chief Serhy Liovochkin as well as big businessman, first deputy prime minister, and former SBU head Valery Khoroshkovsky (not formally a party member); and a network new to the height of power linked to Yanukovych's own family. Indeed, President Yanukovych's son, Oleksandr, was emerging as a major oligarch, with his own network considered to be one of the most important in politics.[191]

Just as the interests and activities of Ukraine's main political-economic networks were only loosely organized around Yanukovych by the end of 2013, so too did the media environment still feature significant political debates and a wide range of opinions even on television. To be sure, media were nowhere near as tightly controlled as in Russia or Azerbaijan at the same time, as

---

[191] Oleksandr Fisun and Oleksandr Polishuk, "Ukrainian Neopatrimonial Democracy: Dominant Party-Building and Inter-Elite Settlement in the Semi-Presidential System," paper presented at PONARS Eurasia workshop, Kyiv, November 3–5, 2012. The younger Yanukovych denies a connection between his rise to business prominence and his father's presidency: *Ukraiins'ka Pravda*, May 22, 2012, 13:03.

anyone watching a typical newscast on television in these countries could tell. Nevertheless, the trend was toward increased tightening of both control and message, much as happened when Eurasia's original single-pyramid systems were forming in the 1990s. The television channel with perhaps the most pronounced critical stance toward the Ukrainian authorities (TVi) was harassed by tax police.[192] The major opposition figure and former presidential candidate Arseny Yatseniuk was effectively kept off the main television political talk shows on one pretext or another starting in May 2010 and continuing well into 2012.[193] In general, television tended to downplays politics, presenting more anodyne programming instead.[194]

Despite these efforts to influence media, Yanukovych's public support went on the decline shortly after his 2010 election for reasons described in Chapter 7. This did not mean that his opponents were any more popular, however. The jailed Tymoshenko defied postelection predictions of her political demise and remained one of the top two opposition figures, the other being world heavyweight boxing champion Vitali Klitschko. These two figures were consistently the most popular rivals to Yanukovych, but neither had ratings higher than the incumbent straight into 2013, by most measures.[195] Klitschko founded the party UDAR, an acronym that in Ukrainian memorably meant "punch." Yatseniuk, who had pointedly refused to endorse Tymoshenko over Yanukovych in the 2010 election, now joined her and became the formal leader of her Fatherland (Batkivshchyna) Party while the former PM was in prison, though his ratings continued to trail Tymoshenko's. Rounding out the triumvirate of opposition parties was ultranationalist Oleh Tiahnybok and his Svoboda (freedom) Party. Svoboda had performed strongly in the late 2000s in some local elections in western Ukraine, and after 2010 it gained enough support potentially to win a delegation in parliament. Many experts in 2012 claimed he was being covertly supported by pro-Yanukovych forces as a conveniently unelectable political enemy who could cut into the western Ukrainian political base of the president's most feared rivals, Tymoshenko and Klitschko.[196] In April 2012, therefore, only 19 percent of potential voters said they would cast a presidential ballot for Yanukovych, but this was far more than the second-place Tymoshenko (11 percent), who was followed by Klitschko (8 percent), Yatseniuk (8 percent), and Tiahnybok (2 percent), with a few others between the latter two.[197]

With the October 28, 2012, parliamentary election approaching, the Party of Regions sought to buttress its public standing by stressing the restoration

---

[192] *Ukraiins'ka Pravda*, April 26, 2012, 12:05.
[193] *Ukraiins'ka Pravda*, June 29, 2012, 14:08.
[194] *Ukraiins'ka Pravda*, June 27, 2012, 17:38.
[195] *Ukraiins'ka Pravda*, April 1, 2012, 20:58; *Ukraiins'ka Pravda*, June 7, 2011, 15:28; *Ukraiins'ka Pravda*, March 14, 2013, 14:53.
[196] Author's field observations, Kyiv and Lviv, Ukraine, October and November 2012.
[197] *Ukraiins'ka Pravda*, April 28, 2012, 19:50.

of order, the raising of the status of Russian as a second state language (which provoked an actual fistfight in the Rada[198] as well as street protests)[199], and the improvement of the economy it promised to achieve.[200] The party and its representatives also advocated a wide range of concrete benefits, and provided some in advance. These ranged from higher pensions across the board[201] to packages of food handed out to individuals with deputies' pictures on them.[202]

But with Yanukovych's administrative capacity to win votes by patronage and pressure on the rise and his ability to generate them by genuine public support on the decline, another strategy proved more important in sustaining control over the parliament. In late 2011, the Party of Regions pushed through a reform of the parliamentary election system that restored the practice whereby half of the Rada seats would be chosen through single-member districts rather than nationwide proportional representation. Indeed, consistent with Chapter 6's discussion of Moldova and Chapter 8's analysis of Russia, Ukrainian insiders widely regarded district-based elections as making it easier for the authorities to manipulate outcomes when the regime had low levels of support and easier to influence the postelection behavior of deputies who happened to be elected on an opposition platform.[203] The strategy worked. Yanukovych's Party of Regions netted only 30 percent of the vote in the party-list half of the election but was able to woo enough of the district-based deputies and allies in the Communist Party of Ukraine to cobble together a parliamentary majority. Fatherland, UDAR, and Svoboda each won enough votes to form officially recognized opposition factions in the Rada.[204]

After the October 2012 parliamentary elections, political closure continued in Ukraine right up to the Euromaidan protests discussed in Chapter 7. Elections for Kyiv mayor and city council that the Party of Regions was likely to lose were indefinitely delayed.[205] The feisty independent TVi was finally taken over, with its new management announcing in May 2013 that it would stop "constant criticism of the authorities."[206] Subsequent monitoring detected a marked drop in its political balance.[207] In October 2013, the Rada changed laws in a way that would disqualify Klitschko from running for the presidency, barring anyone from the ballot who has permanent resident status in another country (Klitschko had this status in Germany).[208] In December, a

[198] *RFE/RL*, May 25, 2012.
[199] *RFE/RL*, June 5, 2012.
[200] *Ukraiins'ka Pravda*, July 6, 2012, 20:44.
[201] *Ukraiins'ka Pravda*, June 14, 2012, 19:50.
[202] *Ukraiins'ka Pravda*, May 23, 2012, 10:28.
[203] *Ukraiins'ka Pravda*, November 17, 2011, 19:31.
[204] See the breakdown provided by *Ukraiins'ka Pravda*: http://www.pravda.com.ua/articles/2012/10/29/6975859/, accessed January 1, 2013.
[205] *RFE/RL*, August 19, 2013.
[206] *Ukraiins'ka Pravda*, May 2, 2013, 14:14.
[207] *Ukraiins'ka Pravda*, June 11, 2013, 15:50.
[208] *Ukraiins'ka Pravda*, October 24, 2013, 13:11.

journalist reporting on a palatial residence being constructed for Yanukovych was savagely beaten and pushed along with her car into a ditch.[209] Not all developments were toward closure. For example, Yanukovych pardoned the opposition former interior minister Yury Lutsenko.[210] But the more important Tymoshenko continued to languish in jail. One early ominous sign for the regime involved Poroshenko, whose patterns of defection have been something of a belwether of Ukrainian political trends since the late 1990s: In 2012, after less than a year as minister, he left the government to become an independent parliamentary deputy and gradually drifted into opposition. Until 2014, however, his actions were the exception rather than the rule.

Overall, as the logic of regime cycles would predict, Ukraine under its newly instituted presidentialist constitution was clearly experiencing increasing political closure until the outbreak of the Euromaidan protests. Chapter 7 described these protests and showed how they resulted from irregular drivers of regime dynamics. As that chapter also described, the revolutionaries, in taking power away from Yanukovych, also revoked the presidentialist constitution, which by that time had become widely believed to be a source of authoritarian tendencies in Ukraine.[211] The logic outlined in Chapter 4 would lead us to expect this eventually to promote competing-pyramid politics in Ukraine, though it is far too early to tell as of mid-2014.

Regime Cycles in Abkhazia and Armenia

The preceding pair of paired comparisons demonstrates that revolutions do have a chance to break the cyclic regime dynamics characteristic of patronal presidentialism if they produce a divided-executive constitution, but that where presidentialist constitutions remain in place the result is likely to be the reemergence of single-pyramid politics. The fact that Ukraine and Kyrgyzstan both experienced both patterns in mirror-image fashion in two successive periods in time helps us rule out alternative explanations involving factors that did not similarly change in mirror-image fashion in 2005 and 2010.

The remaining pages of this chapter examine four other cases (in three different polities) that reinforce the larger conclusion that revolutions tend not to mean democratic breakthroughs unless they are accompanied by an elimination of the presidentialist constitution. The present section examines events following the presidential ousters in Abkhazia and Armenia that were described in Chapter 7. In both cases, we see that the ouster did not involve a move away from presidentialism and that, as expected, the result was new movement toward a single-pyramid system around the new president as the new patron. Armenia then went on to experience a new lame-duck phase of presidential leadership,

[209] *KyivPost*, December 25, 2013, 7:20 pm.
[210] *Ukraiins'ka Pravda*, April 7, 2013, 09:40.
[211] Author's personal observations of placards in the Kyiv Euromaidan and the comments of many protest leaders and supporters in December 2013.

resulting in a significant fissure in its elite and a major battle for power that turned violent in 2008. Reflecting the pattern theorized in Chapter 4 and documented in Chapter 8, however, the regime's relatively strong public support (and in this case, the relative unpopularity of the most prominent opposition figure) enabled it ultimately to survive in power, leading to a new reconsolidation of the single-pyramid system. The next section then considers two cases of postouster developments in a single country, Georgia. After the Rose Revolution, Georgia kept a presidentialist constitution and the outcome was as expected: the reemergence of a single-pyramid system under Mikheil Saakashvili. This occurred despite the optimism that many initially had regarding Georgia under the Western-educated Saakashvili and despite some real success he had in eliminating certain kinds of corruption. Saakashvili's removal, however, occurred with a transition to a divided-executive constitution, creating significant potential for a sustained competing-pyramid system in the years ahead.

Postrevolutionary Abkhazia: The Demise of Another Tandem

After Abkhazia's uncolored revolution, we find a reversion to single-pyramid rule that strongly resembles what happened in Kyrgyzstan after the Tulip Revolution. Specifically, the return to greater political closure occurred despite the fact that its revolution had resulted in a tandem of rivalrous leaders who had agreed to share power but whose power-sharing deal was not anchored in a formal constitutional change. As will be recalled from Chapter 7, to resolve the dangerous street standoff that the disputed 2004 first-round presidential election had produced, challenger Sergei Bagapsh agreed to rule in a tandem arrangement with his rival. Regime candidate Raul Khajimba would thus become his running mate and then vice president with substantial powers, including control of the budget and military. Also like Kyrgyzstan in 2005 – and unlike Ukraine in 2004 – the power-sharing arrangement between Khajimba and Bagapsh was not anchored in a formal divided-executive constitution, but instead in a nonconstitutional agreement between the two men. Undermining this arrangement was the presidentialist constitution. The election had revealed Bagapsh's to be the more powerful of the conflicting coalitions of networks, reinforced by the fact that Khajimba had to agree to a formally subordinate post – a concession that a divided-executive constitution could have enabled him to avoid. Widely expected to be the more powerful of the tandem, Bagapsh was able to sideline Khajimba speedily, never actually giving him the promised powers.[212]

Abkhazia's newly emergent single-pyramid system did retain a significant measure of pluralism, greater than even in many recognized post-Soviet states. Khajimba formed the basis for a new opposition grouping, the Forum of Popular Unity of Abkhazia, which included eight of thirty-five members of parliament. Local business mogul Beslan Butba was able to found an independent television station, Abaza-TV, in 2007, replacing the old independent Inter-TV.

---

[212] Kimitaka Matsuzato, "From Belligerent to Multi-Ethnic Democracy: Domestic Politics in Unrecognized States after the Ceasefires," *Eurasian Review*, v. 1, November 2008, pp. 95–119, p. 108.

While these covered only the capital city of Sukhumi and a neighboring region, this was a substantial portion of the republic's population, and in the most sensitive political center.[213] The opposition's opportunity for political advancement was limited, however, especially as the government applied pressure to opposition-oriented businesspeople through the tax system, making it risky for them to back political forces other than those sanctioned by Bagapsh.[214] Thus when Khajimba challenged Bagapsh in the 2009 presidential elections, Bagapsh decisively won. This enabled Bagapsh to dispose of Khajimba as vice president and install an ally with a strong following of his own, Aleksandr Ankvab. This effectively crowned the establishment of a loose but effective single-pyramid system.

Speculation about and jockeying for the succession were already under way soon after Bagapsh entered his constitutionally final second term in 2009.[215] During this period, support for the presidency was reportedly high.[216] Thus when Bagapsh died of cancer in 2011, the resulting early presidential election (held in August 2011) merely compressed the political contestation phase that had already been brewing in the unrecognized statelet. Each of its most prominent longtime presidential aspirants contested the race. This included not only opposition figures like former vice president Khajimba, but also multiple top officials from the Bagapsh regime, notably Vice President Ankvab (who became acting president after Bagapsh's passing) and Prime Minister Sergei Shamba. Ankvab won the resulting contest with 55 percent of the vote to Shamba's 21 percent and Khajimba's 20 percent. As one would expect when a polity's major power networks are divided and competing, Freedom House reports that this election was generally regarded as free and fair.[217]

Ankvab then moved into a phase where Chapter 4's theory of regular regime cycles would expect us to see the reemergence of a single-pyramid system. Some such moves were evident since that time. Perhaps most prominently, after the March 2012 parliamentary elections, Khajimba was decisively defeated in his effort to become speaker, with that office instead going to a more compliant figure who proclaimed that only "constructive opposition" would be welcome in the parliament.[218] At the same time, there were signs that Ankvab was struggling

---

[213] Sabrina Badger, "Democratisation in an Unrecognized State: Abkhazia, 1994–2007," M.Phil. thesis in Russian and East European Studies, Pembroke College, Oxford, 2008, p. 27. The source Badger cites is *Kavkaz Uzel*, June 25, 2007.

[214] Kimitaka Matsuzato, "Patronnoe prezidentstvo i politika v sfere identichnosti v nepreznannoi Abkhazii," *Acta Eurasica*, no. 4, 2006, pp. 132–59.

[215] Author's field observations, Abkhazia, July 2010.

[216] A survey organized by Gerard Toal and John O'Loughlin (Gerard Toal and John O'Loughlan, "Inside South Ossetia: A Survey of Attitudes in a De Facto State," *Post-Soviet Affairs*, v. 29, no. 2, 2013, pp. 136–72) reportedly found overwhelming trust in the presidency in Abkhazia not long before Bagapsh's death.

[217] *Kavkazskii Uzel*, August 27, 2011, 12:23; Freedom House, "Abkhazia," *Freedom in the World 2012*.

[218] *Civil Georgia*, April 3, 2012, 23:04.

in his efforts to master the political domain he inherited. Less than a year after taking office, in early 2012, his motorcade was hit by machine-gun and anti-tank fire, though the president survived. With the isolated quasi-state facing a major economic crisis, in early 2013 Ankvab's government announced the doubling of electricity rates, sparking protests that ultimately forced it to compromise.[219] Just a few months later, the top leadership of the United Abkhazia Party, which had backed Ankvab for president and had been the main party of power under the late President Bagapsh, announced opposition to what it said was growing authoritarianism and a failure to deal with the dire socioeconomic situation. In reaction, some parliamentarians and high-level officials renounced their party membership and confirmed their loyalty to Ankvab, though the damage to Ankvab was significant.[220] Ankvab recouped somewhat when the Amtsakhara movement declared it would turn itself into a party to back him.[221] A local newspaper editor, however, said that Ankvab needed to have developed his own dominant party earlier but failed to do so.[222] In late 2013, Ankvab fired his Security Council chief after the latter accused him of giving out passports too readily to ethnic Georgians who remained in Abkhazia.[223]

Most ominously for Ankvab, in early 2014 Khajimba teamed up with Shamba, Butba, and a long list of other elites to demand the resignation of the government, citing the region's paralyzing unemployment levels (a stunning 70 percent by some reports) and what they said was the misspending of Russian aid on pointless projects such as a sports stadium.[224] In late May 2014, this opposition mobilized in the streets and stormed the presidential administration building as negotiations with the president were in process, now demanding he resign immediately. Ankvab fled the building. A parliamentary majority then voted in support of his resignation. With Russia sending in mediators to help end the political crisis, in early June 2014 Ankvab agreed to step down and allow early presidential elections.[225]

The ultimate outcome of this crisis was unknown at the time this book manuscript was submitted for production in mid-2014. Observers in Abkhazia tended to agree that Ankvab was unlikely to run in the early presidential elections himself, though at this point this could not be ruled out, and it was also entirely possible that someone from his network (including the Amtsakhara Party) would seek to succeed him with his blessing.[226] Assuming that the early presidential

[219] *Civil Georgia*, March 11, 2013, 18:55.
[220] *Kavkazskii Uzel*, June 14, 2013, 23:53.
[221] *Kavkazskii Uzel*, June 27, 2013, 16:30.
[222] *Kavkazskii Uzel*, June 14, 2013, 23:53.
[223] *Kavkazskii Uzel*, October 29, 2013, 22:28.
[224] Liz Fuller, "Abkhaz Opposition Launches New Challenge to President," Caucasus Report blog, *RFE/RL*, May 1, 2014, http://www.rferl.org/content/abkhazia-opposition-launches-new-challenge-president/25369601.html, accessed June 4, 2014.
[225] See the useful chronology of events compiled by *Kavkazskii Uzel* at http://abkhasia.kavkaz-uzel.ru/articles/243498/, as of June 4, 2014, 11:49.
[226] *Kavkazskii Uzel*, June 4, 2014, 11:45.

elections, now scheduled for August, are won by an opposition force rather than Ankvab or someone from his network, the Abkhaz events of 2014 will go down in regional history as the eleventh patronal presidential network ouster since each polity's initial single-pyramid system was established, and one of only two that clearly fit the irregular as opposed to regular category of regime cycles described in Chapter 4. The logic of regular regime cycles would predict, however, that so long as the constitution remains presidentialist, a tendency toward single-pyramid politics is likely to reemerge in Abkhazia once any new patron is in place.

Armenia after Its Palace Coup: Closure, Crisis, and Closure Again

After its 1998 palace coup, Armenia saw the rise of a new single-pyramid system under Robert Kocharian, who then built up substantial though not overwhelming support and whose network accordingly (if narrowly) survived a significant contestation phase with the 2008 succession to Serzh Sargsyan as president. While Kocharian did not inherit the same degree of disorder that incoming patronal presidents did after revolutions (as in Ukraine or Georgia), the coup had shaken up the relationship among the system's main networks, leading to intensified competition among them and moves by some to establish their own autonomy vis-à-vis Kocharian himself.

Kocharian certainly did not begin his presidency with strong control over the country's most important networks. Instead, this had to be orchestrated over time. He had won his first election shortly after the coup only in a March 1998 runoff against Karen Demirchian, the doyen of Armenia's Soviet era communist network and leader at the time of the People's Party of Armenia.[227] Demirchian then struck an alliance with one of the most important ministers whose defection from Ter-Petrossian had made Kocharian's rise possible, Defense Minister Vazgen Sargsyan. The latter had also become leader of the Republican Party of Armenia (HHK), which represented a large network of veterans from the Karabakh war. This "Unity Coalition" went on to win the relatively competitive 1999 parliamentary elections. Kocharian then felt compelled to appoint Sargsyan prime minister.[228] The Sargsyan-Demirchian alliance thus represented a serious threat to Kocharian's emergent authority, threatening to nip it in the bud. Indeed, both Sargsyan and Demirchian had enormous authority in Armenia itself, whereas Kocharian's own roots were in Nagorno-Karabakh (and this had understandably raised questions about whether he could even be president of Armenia in the first place). Surely confirming some of these worries for Kocharian was that one of Vazgen Sargsyan's first moves as prime minister was to demote Kocharian's close associate Serzh Sargsyan (no relation to Vazgen, and from Karabakh, as Kocharian was) from minister of interior and national security to just minister of national security.[229]

[227] TransCaucasus: A Chronology, v. 7, no. 5, May 1998.
[228] RFE/RL Newsline, June 7, 1999.
[229] Astourian, "Killings in the Armenian Parliament."

The episode that followed and consolidated Kocharian's rule still constitutes one of the most shocking events in post-Soviet politics, one whose origins remain a murky mystery. On October 27, 1999, in full view of television cameras, a group of at least five gunmen strode into the parliament and shot dead parliamentary chairman Demirchian, Prime Minister Sargsyan, two deputy parliamentary chairs, another minister, and four other parliamentarians. The commander of these men let off a stream of rants against what he said were the bloodsuckers he had killed. During a subsequent trial, he insisted he and his fellow gunmen had acted alone, though some of his remarks and those of his associates overheard during the incident indicate he believed he had some kind of help. In addition, it remains puzzling how they were able to enter the parliament with the weapons in the first place.

No evidence has directly linked Kocharian to this event, and plenty of other theories are alive and well in Armenia. Among the theories is that the killings were the work of foreign special services and/or an effort to sabotage a peace deal with Azerbaijan on Nagorno-Karabakh. Whatever the event's origins, its result was that Kocharian's most authoritative potential rivals were removed from the political scene, paving the way for him to build up a single-pyramid system tightly around his own person and his own network.[230] Serzh Sargsyan, Kocharian's close associate from his Karabakh days, who had been demoted by the murdered Vazgen Sargsyan, was soon made head of his presidential administration and then put in charge of Armenian armed forces as defense minister and National Security Council secretary. Vazgen Sargsyan's brother, Aram, briefly filled in as prime minister before Kocharian replaced him in 2000 with Andranik Margaryan, another Karabakh war veteran, who rose to become the dominant leader of the Republican Party.

The next several years followed the familiar pattern by which patronal presidents construct single-pyramid systems. One of the most visible developments was a dramatic tightening of the media space, including the shutdown of the politically independent A1+ television station in 2002[231] and the appearance of heavy bias during elections in favor of the ruling authorities on other channels.[232] The OSCE found an atmosphere of intimidation and fear among Armenian media by 2007,[233] with opposition newspapers at times having their editors jailed on formally unrelated charges[234] or their offices bombed.[235] Opposition forces had their opportunities to campaign significantly restricted, including through stringent formal spending limits.[236] The regime's position in parliament

---

[230] Stephan Astourian, "Killings in the Armenian Parliament: Coup d'Etat, Political Conspiracy, or Destructive Rage?" *Contemporary Caucasus Newsletter*, no. 9, Spring 2000, pp. 1–5, 19.

[231] *RFE/RL Newsline*, April 15, 2005.

[232] *RFE/RL Newsline*, December 12, 2007.

[233] *RFE/RL Newsline*, December 27, 2007.

[234] *RFE/RL Newsline*, January 16, 2007.

[235] *RFE/RL Newsline*, December 14, 2007.

[236] *RFE/RL Newsline*, April 10, 2007.

was anchored by the Republican Party,[237] though Kocharian himself was never its formal leader and ran for election and reelection as an independent, not a party nominee. Instead, his system supplemented the Republican Party with Artur Baghdasarian's Law-Based State Party, which joined the Republicans in coalition after the May 2003 parliamentary elections and by some accounts was formed in collaboration with Kocharian's network, with Serzh Sargsyan its chief patron.[238] Starting in 2003, Republican leader Margaryan served as prime minister and Baghdasarian as parliamentary chair.[239] Also joining the coalition was the Dashnaktsutiun Party, an old organization regarded by some experts as the only party based primarily on values more than on patron-client networks, emphasizing nationalism and socialism and supported strongly by diaspora Armenians. It was thus regarded as a less reliable but sometimes useful partner for the president.[240]

Below the surface, Kocharian oversaw a process whereby networks directly linked to the Karabakh struggle expanded dramatically in business. These networks included those based in the breakaway territory itself as well as many from within Armenia's internationally recognized borders.[241] Rising players included Kocharian's son, Sedrak (cell phone imports); Barsegh Beglarian (gas stations); Mika Badgasarov (oil imports and air travel); and Karen Karapetian (a gas joint venture with Russia).[242] As the latter case of Karapetian illustrates, another new development was the growing presence of Russia in the economy, with many important assets sold to Russian entities to pay off sovereign debt, including in energy, mining, and railroads.[243] Older oligarchic networks described in Chapter 5 including those of Gagik Tsarukian and Khachatur Sukiasian remained in operation, but had to accommodate themselves to the new authorities and enjoyed weaker relationships to them.[244]

These networks and others in the emergent single-pyramid system generally remained loyal to Kocharian while he was not a lame-duck. They helped underpin his reelection in 2003 (again in a runoff, this time against Demirchian's son, Stepan, but with the final result never much in question) and the victory of his "bouquet" of supportive parties in the parliamentary elections that also took place that year, with the Republicans being the leading such party. That

[237] David Petrosyan, political analyst and journalist, author's interview, Yerevan, January 23, 2008.
[238] Astourian, "Killings in the Armenian Parliament," p. 2; *Lenta.ru*, February 29, 2008, 15:07:38.
[239] *RFE/RL Newsline*, June 12, 2003; *RFE/RL Newsline*, June 2, 2003.
[240] Aleksandr Iskandaryan, "Armenia between Autocracy and Polyarchy," *Russian Politics and Law*, v. 50, no. 4, July–August 2012, pp. 23–36, pp. 31–2.
[241] Iskandaryan, "Armenia between Autocracy and Polyarchy," p. 27.
[242] Brian Whitmore, "Armenia: Crisis Spotlights 'Karabakh Clan,'" *Eurasianet*, March 6, 2008.
[243] Armina Bagdasarian and Besik Urigshvili, "Armiane ne smirilis," *The New Times*, March 10, 2008, p. 45.
[244] Iskandaryan, "Armenia between Autocracy and Polyarchy," p. 27.

some fraud was part of his presidential victory was supported by a finding that precincts visited by election observers during the first round registered an average of 6 percent fewer votes for Kocharian than did other precincts despite a near-random distribution of observers.[245]

The expected presidential succession in 2008, however, started to generate considerable intrigue. Kocharian made clear soon after his 2003 reelection that he would not be seeking to alter the constitution so as to obtain a third term.[246] Moreover, it was widely expected in advance that his faithful ally Serzh Sargsyan would be the designated successor.[247] Confirming this expectation, when prime minister and Republican Party chief Margaryan died of long-developing illness in March 2007, it was Sargsyan who succeeded him in the posts of both prime minister and party leader. In this light, a constitutional change that Kocharian pushed through in a 2005 referendum had special short-term significance linked to the succession. While the president still appointed the prime minister (subject to parliamentary approval), the constitutional change removed the president's right to fire him or her. This meant that once Sargsyan was reappointed to this post after the 2007 parliamentary elections, he could not be directly removed, keeping him in the catbird seat for the succession. It also kept alive speculation that Kocharian could become prime minister after leaving the presidency,[248] somewhat mitigating his lame-duck status since he would not be easily removable once made PM and thus might still be in some position to follow through on promises and threats made previously.

The May 12, 2007, parliamentary elections loomed large as a crucial elite primary, widely interpreted as a "dress rehearsal" for the presidential contest.[249] As the balloting approached, two major events sent shock waves through the political establishment. First, major oligarch Gagik Tsarukian announced the creation of the new Prosperous Armenia Party in 2005. Kocharian's chief of staff and prime minister attended its February 2007 congress. Observers in Armenia generally interpreted this party's appearance as having been sanctioned by Kocharian as a way for him to secure a personal power base in the country once Sargsyan became president. It was also widely regarded as an effort to ensure that Sargsyan, who was also Republican Party chief, did not completely dominate parliament.[250] In short, Prosperous Armenia was a kind of political insurance policy by Kocharian lest his colleague's longtime loyalty fade upon rising to the pinnacle of power. Signaling the seriousness

[245] Susan D. Hyde, "The Observer Effect in International Politics: Evidence from a Natural Experiment," *World Politics*, v. 60, no. 1, October 2007, pp. 37–63.

[246] *RFE/RL Newsline*, November 21, 2005.

[247] E.g., *RFE/RL Newsline*, May 26, 2005.

[248] Ilian Cashu, "The Bumpy Transition to Parliamentary Rule In the CIS," End Note, *RFE/RL Newsline*, March 6, 2006.

[249] Emil Danielyan, "West Gives Armenian Leaders a Boost after Disputed Election Win," *Eurasianet*, May 15, 2007.

[250] *RFE/RL Newsline*, February 16, 2007; *RFE/RL Newsline*, March 27, 2007.

of this endeavor, Prosperous Armenia even challenged the Republicans in a mayoral race less than two months before the parliamentary contest.[251] The second major event was the announcement by former president Ter-Petrossian's erstwhile party of power, the Armenian National Movement, that it would return to politics and compete in the 2007 parliamentary elections.[252] Largely discredited by the turmoil and economic collapse of the 1990s, this party nevertheless represented the large extended network of a former patronal president, making it a serious contender even though the former president himself remained quiet.

In the end, with the machine's resources directed primarily in favor of Sargsyan's Republicans,[253] this party received the most votes – just shy of a majority, which could be obtained by aligning with any of the 9 independents who were elected. They nevertheless concluded a coalition with Prosperous Armenia and the Dashnaks.[254] Sargsyan announced that because his party had won at least 25 percent of the vote, he would run for president.[255] With Sargsyan passing this initial viability test, Kocharian nominated him to be prime minister, putting him in pole position for the presidency and thereby signaling his clear intent to back him in the election.[256] Prosperous Armenia itself then endorsed Sargsyan, citing the coalition agreement.[257] A senior Republican official noted that the party's majority also sent a signal to the broader public that it would be best to vote for a president who had a parliamentary majority.[258]

Shaking up Sargsyan's easy election scenario, however, was former president Levon Ter-Petrossian's dramatic announcement in September 2007 that he was reentering politics to free the country from what he said was a corrupt regime. While he had left office highly unpopular and had been politically inactive since his 1998 removal,[259] Ter-Petrossian still had status as the architect of the country's independence, its first president, and informal patron of an extensive network of people who had played major roles in his regime. His network included many businesspeople who owed their holdings at least in part to him through privatization and other actions. Another major asset was his renowned oratorical skill, the same that had helped propel him to the forefront of the national independence movement in the first place in the 1980s. With his flare for the dramatic on full display, Ter-Petrossian announced on

---

[251] *RFE/RL Newsline*, March 27, 2007.

[252] *RFE/RL Newsline*, September 19, 2006.

[253] OSCE ODIHR Election Observation Mission Report, Republic of Armenia Parliamentary Elections 12 May 2007, September 10, 2007.

[254] *RFE/RL Newsline*, June 11, 2007.

[255] *RFE/RL Newsline*, May 17, 2007.

[256] David Petrosyan, political analyst and journalist, author's interview, Yerevan, January 23, 2008.

[257] *RFE/RL Newsline*, December 21, 2007.

[258] Armen Ashotyan, member of parliament of HHK, member of HHK Council, author's interview, Yerevan, January 24, 2008.

[259] *RFE/RL Newsline*, August 20, 2007.

Armenia's Independence Day, September 21, 2007, that he would run again for president, begging forgiveness for allowing the rise of Kocharian and Sargsyan and vowing to stop them for the sake of the nation.[260] His speeches during fall 2007 and early spring 2008 became major events, drawing huge crowds of up to 50,000 (or, to believe organizers, as many as 150,000) to central streets and marches.[261] He not only called the current leadership "robber barons"[262] and "a criminal state,"[263] but blasted the Kocharian-Sargsyan duo for being from Karabakh rather than Armenia itself (essentially robbing Armenia from Armenians).[264] He even accused them of responsibility for the 1999 massacre in parliament, asserting that the officials killed were planning to expose a scheme to swap territory with Azerbaijan and that his victory would be that of the slain.[265] On a more positive note, he called for democratization, the rule of law, better relations with neighbors (including Turkey, Azerbaijan, and Russia), an end to corruption, and the creation of a "meritocratic" society.[266]

His campaign deliberately aimed to induce elite splits and ultimately the collapse of the political machine.[267] Part of this strategy was persistently announcing reports of reputed defections within various administrative structures and predicting the demise of the power *vertikal'*.[268] Another hope was that large protests would undermine the sense of inevitability of Sargsyan's victory. Attempting to spread a sense of momentum, his campaign came up with the novelty of widely distributing DVDs of his speeches, producing several thousand each day by one account. In a January 2008 appearance, he proclaimed the coming of a "DVD revolution."[269] Traveling to Russia, the ex-president even claimed to have secured the Kremlin's backing for his campaign.[270] Ter-Petrossian also reportedly made use of administrative resources at his own disposal, with his associates, for example, giving out food and other basic goods

[260] Armen Bagratuni, "Vremia nestabil'noi stabil'nosti," *Noev Kovcheg*, January 2008, p. 2.

[261] Marianna Grigoryan, "Armenia: Opposition Coalition Fails to Materialize," *Eurasianet*, February 11, 2008; *Polit.Ru*, December 8, 2007, 15:58; *RFE/RL Newsline*, February 19, 2008.

[262] *RFE/RL Newsline*, November 8, 2007.

[263] *Respublika Armenia*, January 23, 2008, p. 2.

[264] Olga Vlasova, Gevorg Davtian, Gevorg Mirzaian, "Desiat' dnei na ploshchadi Svobody," *Ekspert*, No. 10, March 10–16, 2008, pp. 26–8; Whitmore, "Armenia."

[265] *Golos Armenii*, January 24, 2008, p. 2; *Novoe Vremia* (Armenia), January 26, 2008, p. 1; *RFE/RL Newsline*, February 13, 2008.

[266] G. Martirosian, "DVD-revoliutsiia vo imia 'vlast zasluzhennykh,'" *Sobesednik Armenii*, January 25, 2008, p. 2; *Respublika Armenia*, January 23, 2008, p. 2.

[267] Naira Melkumian, "Armenia: Rivals Up the Stakes," Institute of War and Peace Reporting, iwpr.net, February 16, 2008; David Petrosyan, political analyst, author's interview, Yerevan, January 23, 2008.

[268] Gayane Mkrtchian in Gegharkunik, IWPR, "Ter-Petrossian Seeks Rural Vote," in Amnewsservice.org, February 8, 2008; Melkumian, "Armenia."

[269] Martirosian, "DVD-revoliutsiia," p. 2.

[270] *RFE/RL Newsline*, February 19, 2008.

in the Lorii area.[271] And seeking to position himself as the best option for any ambitious or dissatisfied elite regardless of whether they liked him personally, the former chief patron averred from the beginning that if the opposition united around him, he would serve as president for only three years, just enough time to dismantle the Kocharian-Sargsyan regime.[272]

The 2008 succession did catalyze a number of defections to the opposition, though for the most part the single pyramid held and Ter-Petrossian did not manage to rally the most significant figures to his side. The most noteworthy shift was that of parliamentary speaker Baghdasarian. In December 2005, he accused the authorities of "serious ballot-stuffing" in the constitutional referendum earlier that year, and the following May he resigned as speaker, pulling his party out of the ruling coalition. He ran for president himself, however, instead of endorsing Ter-Petrossian.[273] The Dashnaks, while remaining in the propresidential coalition, nevertheless also advanced their own candidate for president. Ter-Petrossian did manage to lure some defectors to his own side, including most notably oligarch Sukiasian,[274] as well as a number of midlevel officials, smaller businesses squeezed by the Karabakh network, one regional television station, and some Karabakh veterans.[275] For the most part, however, any sympathizers he may have had in the ruling system remained publicly silent.

The regime did its best to keep matters that way, seeking to prevent defections and minimize Ter-Petrossian's public support. He was, in the leadership's view, the primary threat in the race. Through biased media and other opportunities to speak out, Sargsyan supporters were happy to remind voters of the economic and political turmoil that had characterized the former president's reign. They accused him of ruining the economy,[276] plotting to betray Nagorno-Karabakh,[277] stealing the 2006 presidential election,[278] and committing many other national sins. To be sure, voters tended to remember the poor state of the economy and other problems that had contributed to his fall from political grace in the late 1990s, and many opponents of Sargsyan indeed regarded Ter-Petrossian as the greater evil.[279] The ex-president responded not

---

[271] Vlasova, Davtian, and Mirzaian, "Desiat' dnei."

[272] *Novoe Vremia* (Armenia), January 22, 2008, p. 2.

[273] Liz Fuller, "Armenian Parties Look Ahead to 2007 Parliamentary Elections," End Note, *RFE/RL Newsline*, January 19, 2006; *RFE/RL Newsline*, May 15, 2006.

[274] Author's interviews with insiders in both the Sargsyan and Ter-Petrossian camps, Yerevan, January 2008.

[275] Gayane Abrahamyan, "Armenia: Governing Party Members, Dashnaks Defect to Ter-Petrossian's Campaign," *Eurasianet*, February 14, 2008; Melkumian, "Armenia"; *RFE/RL Newsline*, December 20, 2007; *RFE/RL Newsline*, February 26, 2008; Whitmore, "Armenia."

[276] *RFE/RL Newsline*, October 30, 2007.

[277] Yu. Barsegov, doctor of law, professor, "Kapituliantskoe Kredo Pretendenta na Post Prezidenta Armenii," *Golos Armenii*, January 22, 2008, p. 5.

[278] *Golos Armenii*, January 24, 2008, p. 1.

[279] *RFE/RL Newsline*, November 21, 2007.

only by blaming such problems of his rule on the transition from communism and the war,[280] but also by openly apologizing for mistakes. No leader was perfect, he pleaded, and 2008 was not about his personal power since he would give up power in three years.[281] But not content to rely on a free and fair debate on the relative merits of the two regimes, the authorities were accused of engaging in a full range of patronal political tactics. These were said to include pressuring opposition with arrest, tax inspection, workplace threats, and vote buying.[282] Sargsyan's team also sought to get out a message based on his record of gradual reform,[283] economic growth,[284] infrastructural development,[285] professional experience,[286] national unity, and the greatest gift a president could give: love.[287] The regime's candidate also prominently met with Russian officials, sending the message that Armenia's most powerful ally in fact supported him rather than Ter-Petrossian.[288]

In the end, the balance of public opinion strongly appears to have worked in favor of Sargsyan. Preelection polls, including those supported by the U.S. Agency for International Development and supervised by the reputable American Gallup agency, showed that he was the favorite to win even a completely honest vote by a large margin, and that Ter-Petrossian had low public appeal.[289] One Armenian pollster reported that Sargsyan drew support in particular because he was seen as having a strong hand, capable of providing order.[290] Some local analysts and opposition figures criticized these survey findings, arguing that the implementing Armenian agency was effectively under the thumb of the authorities and thus covering up what they said was the reality of Kocharian's and Sargsyan's poor standing with the masses.[291] Such objections from opposition figures apparently helped pressure the U.S. Embassy into pulling the plug on a planned exit poll for this election.[292] The embassy, however, defended the quality of the polls,[293] and many independent observers found the overall result quite credible that Sargsyan was more popular than

---

[280] Rita Karapetian, "Former Armenian President Emerges as Contender," Amnewsservice.org, February 8, 2008.

[281] *Novoe Vremia* (Armenia), January 22, 2008, p. 2.

[282] *RFE/RL Newsline*, November 5, 2007; *RFE/RL Newsline*, November 6, 2007; David Shahnazaryan, former minister of national security and leading member of the Armenian National Movement, author's interview, Yerevan, January 23, 2008.

[283] *Novoe Vremia* (Armenia), January 24, 2008, p. 1.

[284] Bagratuni, "Vremia nestabil'noi stabil'nosti."

[285] *Golos Armenii*, January 22, 2008, p. 2.

[286] *Novoe Vremia* (Armenia), January 19, 2008, p. 2.

[287] *Novoe Vremia* (Armenia), January 22, 2008, p. 2.

[288] *Komsomolskaia Pravda*, February 7, 2008.

[289] *RFE/RL Newsline*, January 2, 2007.

[290] Gevork Poghosyan, director, Armenian Sociological Association, author's interview, Yerevan, January 23, 2008.

[291] Petrosyan interview 2008.

[292] *RFE/RL Newsline*, January 22, 2008.

[293] *RFE/RL Newsline*, January 2, 2007.

Ter-Petrossian.[294] According to one analyst, two exit polls by Armenian organizations showed Ter-Petrossian ahead but a third by a British agency (commissioned by Armenian public television) confirmed Sargsyan's win.[295] The OSCE noted a tilted playing field, including media bias in favor of Sargsyan and the use of administrative resources, but ruled that the elections "mostly met OSCE commitments and international standards."[296]

Nevertheless, when the official results reported a Sargsyan victory of 53 percent to 22 percent over Ter-Petrossian, "tens of thousands" of the latter's supporters poured out into the streets for eight days of protest.[297] Sargsyan proposed a coalition government, and others accepted, including Baghdasarian, who became National Security Council secretary.[298] Ter-Petrossian, however, responded that "either Serzhik or the [Armenian] people will leave this country. There can be no other solution."[299] Just days later, around 6:30 in the morning of March 1, the authorities cracked down violently on the crowd, claiming they were provoked. What followed was a major battle in Yerevan that lasted many hours. In one episode around 3:00 pm, opposition forces near the French Embassy "built a barricade out of buses and armed themselves with metal spikes and stones,"[300] smashing and burning a police jeep that drove into the crowd and actually countercharging, sending the police into a panicky retreat. With the authorities now using guns to try to restore order, clashes erupted in different parts of the city, and protesters were reported breaking into and looting stores linked to regime-supporting oligarchs. While the authorities put the death count at eight, others put the toll at forty or more. The protests finally ended early in the morning of March 2, and only when Ter-Petrossian called on his supporters to stop.[301] While his preference to avoid violence can be lauded, some analysts argue that with the outcome of the violence uncertain, he may have lost a chance to lead a revolution. When his official bodyguard unit informed him that he would have to refuse its protection if he stayed at the protest, he opted to keep the service. Georgi Derluguian put it rather bluntly: "If this were Nelson Mandela, he should have refused it. But Ter-Petrossian stayed home."[302]

After Armenia's close call succession, the regime again closed ranks under the new patron, Sargsyan, this time quite quickly. The state of emergency was

[294] Georgi Derluguian, "On ne Mandela," interview in *Ekspert*, No. 10, March 10–16, 2008, pp. 26–8.

[295] David Petrosyan, "Everything as Usual," *The Noyan Tapan Highlights*, no. 7, February 2008, circulated February 23, 2008.

[296] OSCE/ODIHR Election Observation Mission Report, "Republic of Armenia Presidential Election 19 February 2008," May 30, 2008, p. 1.

[297] *RFE/RL Newsline*, February 28, 2008.

[298] *RFE/RL Newsline*, March 3, 2008.

[299] *RFE/RL Newsline*, February 28, 2008.

[300] Institute of War and Peace Reporting, "Armenia's Bloody Saturday," iwpr.net, March 2008.

[301] Ashot Azatian, "Bloody Crackdown Ends Armenian Post-Election Unrest, for Now," *Eurasia Daily Monitor*, March 4, 2008, v. 5, no. 41; Institute of War and Peace Reporting, "Armenia's Bloody Saturday."; Institute of War and Peace Reporting, "Eyewitnesses Tell of Violence, Shootings," iwpr.net, March 2008.

[302] Derluguian, "On ne Mandela."

lifted about three weeks after the violence, though many figures both prominent and minor had been arrested and charged with various crimes.[303] Some
officials who were reputed to have defected to Ter-Petrossian were fired.[304] To
try to calm passions, Sargsyan appointed several figures regarded as "neutral"
to key posts, including those of prime minister and defense minister.[305] He also
amnestied many of the political prisoners from March 2008.[306] Ter-Petrossian
continued to lead large follow-up protests sporadically throughout 2008 and
2009 and even ran atop a party list for the Yerevan city council election in
2009; he lost this effort as well to the ruling Republican Party.[307]

Sargsyan signaled early on that he would run for reelection in the next presidential contest, scheduled for 2013.[308] Clearly no lame-duck, he won early
backing not only from his own core Republican network, but also from allied
networks of Tsarukian (the Prosperous Armenia Party) and Baghdasarian (the
Law-Based State Party).[309] The Republican Party then handily won a majority of seats in the May 2012 parliamentary election, though Ter-Petrossian's
opposition coalition Armenian National Congress eked in too, just 0.08 of
a percentage point above the 7 percent threshold for electoral blocs.[310] This
set the stage for Sargsyan's easy reelection in the February 2013 voting, with
Tsarukian and his Prosperous Armenia once again refraining from running an
alternative candidate, though keeping its distance from Sargsyan as well.[311]
Ter-Petrossian said he was too old to try again, clearing the way for Raffi
Hovannisian to become the only significant opposition candidate, controlling
a small delegation in the parliament.[312] Sargsyan won handily with 59 percent
of the vote. Hovannisian did capture an impressive 37 percent, which inspired
him to lead a series of protests across the country claiming that he had actually
won.[313] These ultimately had little impact on the regime, which largely ignored
them as they faded over the course of 2013.[314] Sargsyan, however, had now
entered his constitutionally final term in office, suggesting that a new fracturing
of the Armenian elite could become likely in the next few years if he could not
sustain substantial public support.

[303] *RFE/RL Newsline*, March 26, 2008; *Polit.Ru*, June 22, 2009, 14:50.

[304] *RFE/RL Newsline*, April 28, 2008.

[305] Richard Giragosian, "New Armenian President Inherits 'Crisis of Confidence'," End Note,
RFE/RL Newsline, April 18, 2008.

[306] *RFE/RL News*, June 1, 2011.

[307] *Polit.Ru*, June 1, 2009, 08:54; Igor Viktorov, "Armeniia na rasput'e," *Polit.Ru*, May 4, 2009,
16:42.

[308] *RFE/RL News*, May 27, 2010.

[309] *RFE/RL News*, June 27, 2011.

[310] *Kavkazskii Uzel*, May 14, 2012, 11:45.

[311] *RFE/RL*, December 25, 2012.

[312] Alexander Jackson, "Assessing Armenia's Presidential Elections," *Caspian Research*, no. 6,
January 22, 2013, 2:33 pm.

[313] Jackson, "Assessing Armenia's Presidential Elections"; *RFE/RL*, February 20, 2013; *RFE/RL*,
February 19, 2013.

[314] Marianna Grigoryan, "Armenia: Opposition Casting About for a New Catalyst," *Eurasianet*,
May 3, 2013, 11:38 am.

Georgia after Shevardnadze and after Saakashvili

Georgia has experienced two patronal presidential ousters since the year 2000, the Rose Revolution and the electoral defeat of President Mikheil Saakashvili's party in the 2012–13 election cycle. Regime dynamics after the Rose Revolution followed the general pattern anticipated in Chapter 4, though with some important twists. Under Mikheil Saakashvili, a core group of modernizing, state-building neoliberals took control after the revolution, one of the rare instances in the post-Soviet history when one can talk about a patronal presidency strongly influenced by something resembling actual ideology. In an effort to push through major market-oriented reforms and insulate themselves from challenges, they strengthened rather than weakened patronal presidentialism and reconstructed a single-pyramid system. One analyst called the result a "hyperpresidency."[315] The most dramatic strengthening of formal presidential powers was rammed through parliament during Saakashvili's very first week in office, reportedly by threatening some deputies still in the parliament with investigation or prosecution.[316] One such change took the right to name some Constitutional Court justices away from the parliament and Supreme Court, rendering this the exclusive prerogative of the presidency.[317] Another gave him a broad right to dissolve parliament, even over budget disputes.[318]

This formal constitutional change helped lead to the marginalization of two figures who had initially, together with Saakashvili, been seen as part of a Rose Revolution triumvirate. Reflecting their standing as revolutionary leaders, Zurab Zhvania and Nino Burjanadze (described in Chapter 7) had become prime minister and parliamentary chair, respectively (Burjanadze keeping her earlier post). But they were sidelined from real decision making in remarkably short order. Burjanadze found herself chairing a parliament that had been greatly weakened. While Zhvania retained a larger role due to his informal clout and ability to work with Saakashvili, he died in his apartment by carbon monoxide poisoning less than two years later, with some blaming Russia (alleging an attempt to destabilize Saakashvili's regime) and others suspecting Saakashvili (alleging an attempt to remove a rival). The official account, made in collaboration with the American FBI, found the tragedy to have been accidental. Informal and formal authority, therefore, became extraordinarily concentrated in a single chief patron just two years after the Rose Revolution.[319]

Accordingly, the country's most potent networks fell quickly into line behind the new patron. One dramatic early sign that elites had reoriented rapidly and

---

[315] Charles H. Fairbanks, Jr., "Georgia's Rose Revolution," *Journal of Democracy*, v. 15, no. 2, April 2004, pp. 110–24.

[316] *Uncertain Democracy: U.S. Foreign Policy and Georgia's Rose Revolution* (Philadelphia: University of Pennsylvania Press, 2009), p. 80.

[317] *RFE/RL Newsline*, January 19, 2005.

[318] Cory Welt, "Georgia's Constitutional Reform," *CACI Analyst*, November 11, 2010.

[319] Mitchell, *Uncertain Democracy*, pp. 82–4.

en masse was the 2004 presidential election, which took place just two months after the Rose Revolution. It produced a stunning 96 percent victory for Saakashvili, a result of which even Turkmenbashi would have been proud. The OSCE observer mission called it an improvement relative to contests recently supervised by Shevardnadze, but also found that old practices of machine politics remained alive and well.[320] The new parliamentary elections that followed produced a huge victory for Saakashvili's National Movement, which soon renamed itself the United National Movement after merging with a smaller party.[321] Networks controlling media moderated their political programming, not eliminating but noticeably scaling back critical coverage of the authorities. NGO leaders became "reluctant to criticize the new government."[322]

If the visible presence of an ideology was one twist on the standard patronal presidential model, a second was the regime's genuine and successful effort to combat certain forms of corruption. In the most dramatic of the reforms, Saakashvili completely dissolved one of the most notoriously corrupt bureaucracies, the traffic police, and reconstituted it with new personnel, high enough wages to live respectably without illicit income, and a strong mandate to stop taking bribes.[323] Amazingly, it worked. Some other state agencies also managed to shed their reputation for rampant bribe taking. Popular trust in the police soared, making Georgia within just a few years a very rare postcommunist country in which the police were a trusted organization. Another remarkable reform was to seize state control over prisons, which had been widely regarded as something like a network of criminal universities for the underworld. Indeed, before Saakashvili, Georgia reportedly could "boast" the largest number of criminal kingpins (*vory v zakone*, or "thieves in law") per capita among the post-Soviet states.[324] One specialist on organized crime who is not particularly enamored of Saakashvili points out how impressive this was: "Nobody before 2004 would have imagined it possible to rein in the vory-v-zakone, but the Saakashvili government managed to do so."[325] All this represented a genuine reduction in the level of patronalism in the polity.

At the same time, it must be kept in mind that this change took place only in a few limited spheres and did not nearly encompass the whole range of patronalistic practices. Indeed, there are ways in which the ending of petty police corruption could actually facilitate a stronger political machine. In a

---

[320] OSCE, ODIHR, *Georgia: Extraordinary Presidential Election, 4 Jan. 2004: OSCE/ODIHR Election Observation Mission Report* (ODIHR, Warsaw, 2004), pp. 1–2.

[321] Mitchell, *Uncertain Democracy*, p. 92; Jonathan Wheatley, *Georgia from National Awakening to Rose Revolution: Delayed Transition in the Former Soviet Union* (Burlington: Ashgate, 2005).

[322] Mitchell, *Uncertain Democracy*, p. 92.

[323] Mitchell, *Uncertain Democracy*, p. 86.

[324] Alexander Kupatadze, "'Transitions after Transitions': Coloured Revolutions and Organized Crime in Georgia, Ukraine, and Kyrgyzstan," PhD Dissertation, University of St. Andrews, 2010, http://hdl.handle.net/10023/1320, pp.126, 180, 183, p. 60.

[325] Kupatadze, *Transitions after Transitions*, p. 130.

society where almost everyone was guilty of something involving a violation of formal law, a more efficient police force that would not look the other way became a potent weapon that the authorities could direct at networks they did not like for one reason or other. In other words, the elimination of street-level bribe taking could make the police an even more effective instrument of selective prosecution directed from the top. Needless to say, businesses wanting to fund opposition politics could be understood for thinking twice about what this might cost them if they therefore found themselves subject to an unwanted investigation into all of their financial histories and relationships.[326]

Accordingly, the new authorities undertook a series of moves to gain control of economic flows that could be used for political purposes. One was to collect funds from people found guilty of corruption. These funds were then put in extrabudgetary "law enforcement development" accounts until the IMF ordered this to stop in late 2005.[327] The government additionally asked for "voluntary contributions" from businesses that would also go into extrabudgetary, though transparently listed, accounts. The IMF also forced these to be liquidated in 2006.[328] One more lasting move was to deprivatize some property, placing it back into state hands through the general prosecutor and Interior Ministry.[329] Even more important for politically influencing business, the regime created a financial police, which became a feared tool of the authorities.[330] For example, after oligarch Badri Patarkatsishvili announced in 2007 that he would challenge Saakashvili in the next presidential election, the financial police seized financial records of one of his major holdings, the company producing the country's famous Borjomi mineral water.[331]

Those who were alarmed by this new concentration of power gathered forces and mobilized a massive protest in 2007. The catalyst was the arrest of Irakli Okruashvili, a former Saakashvili ally during the Rose Revolution who had served as his defense minister. Okruashvili had accused Saakashvili of tolerating large-scale corruption in the government and then resigned.[332] While a regime-friendly interpretation was that Okruashvili had realized he would be

---

[326] Similarly, as we saw in Chapter 7's discussion of Saakashvili's downfall, agents of the state later used the prisons now more fully under its management to terrorize some prisoners, eventually triggering the decisive swing in popular opinion against Saakashvili during the run-up to the 2012 parliamentary election.

[327] Vladimer Papava, "The Political Economy of Georgia's Rose Revolution," *Orbis*, Fall 2006, p. 663.

[328] Vladimer Papava, "Georgia's Hollow Revolution," *Harvard International Review*, February 27, 2008.

[329] Papava, "Georgia's Hollow Revolution."

[330] Transparency International Georgia, report on the results of preelection monitoring, "21 May 2008 Parliamentary Elections," May 15, 2008, as circulated in *Georgia News Digest*, May 19, 2008.

[331] *Polit.Ru*, November 22, 2007, 10:03.

[332] Liz Fuller, "Georgian Authorities Rule Out Concessions to Opposition," End Note in *RFE/RL Newsline*, November 5, 2007.

arrested soon and sought to preempt it by posing as a whistle-blower, to many observers this appeared to be obvious political payback by the regime. Crowds soon reached fifty to seventy-five thousand in the streets of Tbilisi and began calling for the president's resignation. Megaoligarch Patarkatsishvili joined in, a particularly significant act because he was the owner of the popular Imedi television channel.

As tensions escalated, the authorities rallied the full force of a rising patronal president who was not a lame-duck. His forces forcibly broke up the rally, shut down the Imedi television channel, and imposed a state of emergency that included other restrictions on freedom of information and assembly.[333] The president justified such moves as required to battle corruption and to solve other problems facing the country, moves that he said were blocked by an opposition that he variously branded as the beneficiaries of past corruption or as stooges of Russian attempts to destabilize Georgia.[334] With media and the opposition still reeling, Saakashvili called snap elections for less than two months later, in January 2008.[335] Afterward, Imedi was forced out of Patarkatsishvili's hands and wound up under ownership that oversaw a change in coverage to a less critical stance.

While the opposition had mobilized protesters on the same scale as the Rose Revolution had in 2003, and while Saakashvili's popular support had fallen in the run-up to the contest,[336] the crucial difference was that Saakashvili was not a lame-duck in late 2007 as Shevardnadze had been in 2003. Security forces and other key elites in the political machine had little cause to doubt that he was the most likely winner of the standoff, and thus did not defect and instead dutifully carried out his orders. Saakashvili ultimately won the official vote count in the 2008 presidential contest with 52 percent of the ballots, just enough to preclude a runoff. While these elections certainly involved a greater amount of political freedom than the 2007–8 Russian elections, for example, the trend line in Georgia pointed in the direction of political closure, as the logic of patronal presidentialism outlined in Chapter 4 would expect.[337] Oligarch Patarkatsishvili was charged shortly after the election with plotting a coup and planning terrorist acts.[338] He then died of reported heart disease at his mansion in Surrey, England, at age fifty-two in February of that same year.[339] Saakashvili's party also handily won parliamentary elections later that spring.

[333] Mitchell, *Uncertain Democracy*, p. 98; Ghia Nodia, "Georgia," in *Nations in Transit 2008* (New York: Freedom House, 2008), p. 232.

[334] Fuller, "Georgian Authorities."

[335] Mitchell, *Uncertain Democracy*, p. 98; Nodia, "Georgia," p. 232.

[336] Liz Fuller, "Georgian Presidential Ballot a Choice Between Continuity and Radical Change," End Note, *RFE/RL Newsline*, January 4, 2008.

[337] Arch Puddington, "Freedom in Retreat: Is the Tide Turning? Findings of Freedom in the World 2008," Freedom House publication, 2008.

[338] *RFE/RL Newsline*, January 10, 2008.

[339] Nancy MacDonald, "Arkady Shalovich Patarkatsishvili 1955–2008," *McLean's*, February 20, 2008.

Saakashvili's system might be characterized as a "single-pyramid system in a velvet glove." That is, the hard fist of its political machine operated further behind the scenes than in other post-Soviet states and in realms where ordinary citizens were less likely to experience the negative effects directly and routinely (at least, not in ways they could easily link to the regime). Indeed, what Saakashvili did brilliantly was to exert patronal presidential will to remove the aggravating petty corruption that had long been felt by ordinary citizens. His true anticorruption reforms often had an immediate, obvious, and positive impact on ordinary people's quality of life. One example is his reform of the electricity sector. Tbilisi went from being a dark city at night, with only dimly lit streetlights, to one that was demonstratively bright, with lights garishly adorning its most prominent monumental structures in a brash display of the government's new ability to deliver. And so undeniable and popular was the traffic police reform that even opposition politicians would give him credit – including some sworn enemies.[340] As did classic mayoral machines in the United States, Saakashvili paid particular attention to the infrastructure of everyday life, rebuilding roads, repairing schools, enhancing playgrounds.[341]

These visible successes and the regime's communications savvy were particularly effective among Westerners in obscuring the fact that a deeper patronalistic politics remained at the core of Georgian politics throughout Saakashvili's reign. For one thing, his anticorruption reforms were highly visible not only to his own citizens, but especially so to foreign visitors, including diplomats, NGO representatives, and businesspeople. Indeed, Saakashvili's government paid special attention to reducing the red tape and corruption that used to face foreign businesses seeking to operate or invest in Georgia, and he made a major point of communicating all of these advances very systematically to the international community. It helped that Saakashvili himself and many of his young colleagues were not just fluent, but eloquent in English, and what is more, very highly attuned to the ways that influential Westerners tended to talk and think about issues related to democracy and economic reform. Their rhetoric of democracy, pro-Americanism, and aspirations for the EU and NATO resonated strongly in Washington and other Western capitals. All this also helped the Georgian government sustain the notion abroad that it was somehow on a different path. It also helped the country obtain large volumes of aid from Western states, injecting funds into an economy that lacked oil or other highly lucrative sources of rents.

But Saakashvili's system remained a single-pyramid one that did not differ in the fundamentals from those in the other patronal presidentialist countries examined in this volume. Accordingly, it fell victim to a lame-duck syndrome brought on by term limits when the regime suffered a significant drop in popular support, as documented in Chapter 7. Indeed, while there is no denying

---

[340] Author's field observations, Tbilisi, July 2010. Praise for this particular reform was heard among state officials by the author even in the breakaway region of Abkhazia in summer 2010.

[341] Mitchell, *Uncertain Democracy*, p. 86.

that the regime achieved much and improved ordinary people's lives in many ways, substantial problems remained unsolved, the reforms themselves made enemies, and many saw the underlying political machine and reacted negatively. One festering problem was unemployment.[342] His neoliberal reforms dramatically damaged the welfare of much of the intelligentsia that had been patronized by Shevardnadze, and many older workers were "pushed aside" as new and mostly younger people were recruited for state posts. An aggressive effort to enforce laws regulating construction demolished many buildings, with residents being evicted.[343] This meant that opposition criticism could gain traction, as finally took place in 2012, when the prison videotape scandal crystallized a sense of discontent that had already been brewing.[344]

If the Rose Revolution still left Georgia with a presidentialist constitution, producing the trend toward political closure just described, Saakashvili bequeathed his country a divided-executive constitution. As Chapter 7 detailed, he initiated this process more than two years before he would reach his presidential term limit, evidently aiming to ensure that whoever became president could not by himself undo his legacy. Of course, in the end Saakashvili lost control of both the presidency and the parliament to Bidzina Ivanishvili's Georgian Dream coalition. Because this constitution went into full effect only in late 2013, it is far too early to identify its effects on Georgian regime dynamics. The divided-executive constitution by itself should create incentives that would tend to sustain a competing-pyramid system. At the same time, however, the fact that a single coalition won both the parliament and presidency in 2012–13 creates a sense of Ivanishvili's dominance that could, in turn, lead Georgia's networks to orient themselves around him politically. And this could facilitate a new single-pyramid system. Several factors tend to work against such an eventuality, however. For one thing, this coalition is in fact quite diverse, with the crucial parliamentary majority made up of multiple parties (distinct networks) that have rival interests. Should any one of them overreach, therefore, the coalition could collapse. And most in parliament do not have an interest in the new president's emerging as the dominant figure, and so would also likely resist any such efforts on his part. Moreover, Ivanishvili made the very unusual move of actually resigning just after he had reached the pinnacle of formal and informal political power. This is likely to work toward the maintenance of a competing-pyramid system and to complicate any effort to develop a single pyramid of power. The logic of patronal politics from Chapter 4, therefore, would lead us to be cautiously optimistic about democracy in Georgia. But it would also remind us that the most likely

---

[342] Hans Gutbrod, Tbilisi-based expert, author's interview, July 26, 2010.

[343] Salome Asatiani, "Failure to Communicate Dogged Georgian President's First Term," End Note, *RFE/RL Newsline*, December 27, 2007.

[344] George Targamadze, leader of the Christian Democratic Party fraction in parliament, author's interview, Tbilisi, July 31, 2010.

result is *patronal* democracy, in which political corruption and other practices of machine politics remain prominent.

Conclusion

Overall, the post-Soviet experience strongly indicates that so long as either the deeply patronalistic nature of society or the presidentialist character of the constitution is significantly reduced, overthrowing a patronal president is unlikely to lead to lasting democracy. It *is* likely to produce a temporary opening as the expectations of succession that are most likely to give rise to it start to emerge and then as the contestation heats up and produces the ouster. And reestablishing a single-pyramid system under the new patron will take time, meaning that the system will also likely remain competitive for at least some period after the ouster. But without changing the key drivers of single-pyramid politics in focus here, elite networks will have strong incentive to start coordinating again around the new president and the new president will have strong incentive to encourage this process, resulting in a new closing of the regime after its period of competing-pyramid politics. Thus we see that in every case of patronal presidential network ouster in the former USSR where the constitution remained presidentialist, we have witnessed a return to single-pyramid politics, in most cases with levels of closure eventually becoming even greater than they had been before the overthrow after a few years of the time-consuming pyramid-building process. This is essentially the story of Abkhazia after 2005, Armenia after 1998, Georgia after 2003, and Kyrgyzstan after 2005. After presidentialism was restored there in 2010, Ukraine's politics of 2010–13 also fit the pattern.

Ukraine in 2004 and Kyrgyzstan in 2010 confirm this pattern by demonstrating that where presidentialism was eliminated, no significant movement toward a single-pyramid system followed. Instead, the result was a sustained period of much more open competing-pyramid politics. Ukraine's Orange Revolution produced a switch to a formal divided-executive constitution, which, as explained earlier, was a major reason why Ukraine sustained competing-pyramid politics straight through its 2010 presidential election. Kyrgyzstan did the same after its bloody April 2010 revolution, going on to hold two remarkably open elections for both parliament and president although the emergence of the competing-pyramid situation was tragically marred by ethnically charged killings. Georgia may yet provide the first instance of another kind of democratizing exception, where an outgoing patronal president institutes a divided-executive constitution so as to hinder the ability of future presidents to persecute him or reverse his reforms, thereby sowing the longer-run seeds for sustained democratic opening. Ukraine also returned to a divided-executive constitution as of 2014, though it is too early to tell what the effects of this will be.

Of course, Ukraine's experience of 2004–10 also generates some cautionary notes for the prospects of constitutional change to promote long-lasting political opening in highly patronalistic contexts. While a divided-executive constitution does significantly complicate the coordination of elite networks around a single pyramid of patronalistic authority, it does not rule it out entirely. Indeed, decisive electoral victory in a head-to-head competition between networks can create windows of opportunity that skilled and decisive winners can use to undo the opening and even amend the constitution to advance and "lock in" their gains until the next moment of succession. Thus Yanukovych moved quickly after defeating Tymoshenko's network in the 2010 presidential elections to induce critical elite defections that then gained his network control of the prime ministership, uniting both major executive offices under a single network. This, in turn, facilitated the restoration of the 1996 presidentialist constitution and an increased closing of the political system since that time.

Ukraine's experience with a divided-executive constitution also illustrates the danger that divided executives will simply not be able to govern well, too caught up in political infighting to accomplish what people intend their governments to do. This, and the mutual exposure of corruption that can accompany such battles, can threaten to discredit the whole democratic enterprise, generating support for parties and candidates that want to restore presidentialism and "stability." This goes a long way to explaining how Yanukovych was elected president in the first place in 2010.[345] But as Kudelia reminds us, such constant infighting is not an intrinsic feature of divided-executive constitutions and need not be their result.[346] Kyrgyzstan may already be demonstrating as much in the post-Soviet space, though its ethnic and other problems weigh heavily against its counting as a clear-cut success story. Observers should also be watching Georgia closely to see what its new divided-executive constitution yields. And Ukraine's experience after 2010, just as Kyrgyzstan's did after 2005, has taught many that the risks of instability under presidentialism are ultimately even worse. Indeed, one of the central arguments of this book has been that revolution is a fairly normal feature of regime dynamics under patronal presidentialism.

Constitutional choices are not limited to presidentialist and divided-executive constitutions, of course. Parliamentarism is also an option. The following chapter considers the case of Moldova to explore whether parliamentarist constitutions tend to produce substantially distinct regime dynamics in highly patronalistic countries.

[345] Gulnaz Sharafutdinova, *Political Consequences of Crony Capitalism inside Russia* (South Bend, IN: Notre Dame University Press, 2010).
[346] Kudelia, "Institutional Design and Elite Interests."

10

Patronal Parliamentarism

If strong presidencies tend to promote single-pyramid systems and if prime ministers reflecting parliamentary authority in a divided-executive system tend to restrain them, then it might seem logical to go one extra step and conclude, as one article's title puts it, "stronger legislatures, stronger democracy."[1] This does not follow from the logic of patronal politics, however. The "stronger legislatures, stronger democracy" logic assumes constitutions endow an office with powers by stipulating them in a formal constitution. Patronal politics trains our attention instead on how what is written in constitutions shapes what people *expect* from politics in the real world and thus influences both constitution-observing *and constitution-violating* behaviors. And when one looks at what kind of expectations are promoted by parliamentarist constitutions, we see that such constitutions are quite capable of facilitating the emergence of single-pyramid systems much as presidentialist ones are. These effects are somewhat weaker, however, and can be influenced strongly by precisely how formal executive power is arranged by the parliamentarist constitution.[2]

A parliamentarist constitution is one in which the parliament itself formally fills the most important offices of executive power, and this usually means either that there is no directly elected presidency or that any such presidency is allocated only minor or ceremonial formal authority. From the patronal politics perspective, parliamentarist constitutions differ from presidentialist and divided-executive ones in at least two ways that have important implications for regime dynamics. Here we step beyond what was discussed in Chapter 4 and label these ways *executive divisibility* and the *number of formal selectorates*.

[1] M. Steven Fish, "Stronger Legislatures, Stronger Democracy," *Journal of Democracy*, v. 17, no. 1, January 2006, pp. 5–20.

[2] On the importance more generally of not considering parliamentarism and presidentialism as uniform types, see Scott Mainwaring and Matthew S. Shugart, "Juan Linz, Presidentialism, and Democracy: A Critical Appraisal," *Comparative Politics*, v. 29, no. 4, July 1997, pp. 449–71.

Executive divisibility refers to the extent to which formal executive power is concentrated in a single office or divided among multiple offices that are not subordinate to each other. Some parliamentarist constitutions provide for a single leader whose formal powers outweigh those of all the others. In such cases, in the language of Chapter 4, "parliamentarism" can be expected to create essentially the same kind of focal effect and information effect as presidentialism. Ceteris paribus, the fact that a certain network occupies the formally dominant post can both signal that it is the dominant network and make that network a focal point for coordination among elites who want to join a winner but are otherwise uncertain about which network is likely to win. This, in turn, creates expectations of that network's dominance that can make themselves true.[3] One example is the Westminster form of parliamentary rule, in which there is no president and executive power is concentrated in the hands of a government that is selected by the parliament and led by a single person, the prime minister. As the logic of patronal politics would lead us to anticipate, this type of parliamentarist constitution was indeed associated with political closure in highly patronalistic Africa in the 1960s. It had been widely adopted there because of its success in the far less patronalistic context of Great Britain.[4]

But many parliamentarist constitutions feature high executive divisibility. That is, they create multiple offices that are elected by parliament in separate votes, are not subordinated to one another, and have significant authority on paper. This precludes any one executive office from being considered clearly dominant formally. The office of prime minister is almost always one such post. But in some cases, the chair of parliament can also have significant executive powers and, when combined with the parliament's power to elect the prime minister, can be regarded as a post roughly equal to that of the PM. An example is Belarus in the early 1990s, when parliamentary chair Stanislau Shushkevich was considered head of state and roughly the equal of Prime Minister Vyacheslau Kebich. In other cases, such as Moldova in the 2000s, the parliament fills a presidency that has significant executive powers of its own that can rival those of the prime minister or parliamentary chair. In still other cases, the legislature itself can be split, as in India, creating two legislative chamber chairships to fill.

Where parliamentarist constitutions provide for high executive divisibility, one implication is that competition is less likely to be seen as winner-take-all. This is because there is no single post that will signal a network's dominance or

---

[3] This reinforces Steven Roper's observation that an indirectly elected president can be just as powerful as a directly elected one, if not more ("From Semi-Presidentialism to Parliamentarism: Regime Change and Presidential Power in Moldova," *Europe-Asia Studies*, v. 60, no. 1, 2008, pp. 113–26).

[4] Donald L. Horowitz, "Comparing Democratic Systems," *Journal of Democracy*, v. 1, no. 4, Fall 1990, pp. 73–9.

make it the primary focal point for elite coordination in the pursuit of influence and resources. Instead, a power-sharing deal can be struck giving two or more equal networks key formal posts that signal they are both more or less equally powerful players. Such deals can be much more *credible* than typical power-sharing deals made under presidentialism because they are more clearly self-reinforcing. The deal itself effectively gives each network control over informal state-based administrative resources that it can use to defend its position should the other party renege and try to usurp power. Such self-reinforcing deals between rival networks anchored in a constitutional division of executive authority, in turn, tend to promote competing-pyramid politics and complicate attempts to build single-pyramid systems.

Parliamentarist constitutions also stand out by instituting a second formal selectorate for executive leadership. That is, to gain status as chief state executive, a patron must not only officially win a direct popular election (the first selectorate) but *also* win a separate vote among elected legislators (the second selectorate).[5] How challenging this is for the patron can depend on the formal rules for this second vote. Patrons will need greater resources to secure, say, a two-thirds supermajority of legislators than a simple majority. This additional formal step required for attaining a top executive office, then, provides any elite capable of making it into parliament with an additional opportunity to extract concessions from the patron seeking this post. And this creates some additional incentive for opposition. If there is any chance a dominant network will prove unable to secure the necessary majority in parliament on its own, then an opposition network has a chance to wind up with a "golden vote," a vote that could be decisive in enabling the dominant network's patron to claim the formal leadership. Since failure to claim top executive office would likely be interpreted as a sign of weakness, even dominant networks are likely to attach at least some value to holding it. This makes them willing to bargain, thereby encouraging the opposition activity that makes such bargaining necessary. All this distributes more resources to a greater variety of networks, which in turn can open up more space for other networks to operate, making it more difficult for a patron to create a tightly organized power pyramid.

Even where a parliamentary constitution features high executive divisibility and multiple formal selectorates, it still entails a greater risk of single-pyramid politics than a divided-executive constitution for the following reason: An election at a single point in time formally fills all such posts. This creates a greater chance that a single network will be able to gain control of them all, facilitating the emergence of a single-pyramid system to a greater degree than under divided-executive constitutions. Dispersing elections for different top executive

---

[5] The term "selectorate" follows the usage of Bueno de Mesquita et al. and refers to the set of individuals with qualities enabling them potentially to be in a winning coalition, which is the set of individuals whose support is required for the ruler to stay in power. Bruce Bueno de Mesquita, Alastair Smith, Randolph M. Siverson, and James D. Morrow, *The Logic of Political Survival* (Cambridge, MA: MIT Press, 2003).

offices over time reduces the likelihood that one network's momentary surge of public support can enable it to capture the political system as a whole.

This chapter demonstrates these points through the case of Moldova, which wound up the only enduring instance of parliamentarism in the non-Baltic former Soviet space since the 2000s dawned.[6] This case demonstrates that parliamentarism is indeed quite capable of underpinning the construction of a presidential power *vertikal'*, confirming that stronger legislatures do not necessarily mean stronger democracy. Just as presidents should not be too strong, so should parliaments not have too much power. At the same time, analysis of Moldova also shows how parliamentarist constitutions can nevertheless provide incentives that make single-pyramid systems more vulnerable, with Moldova's splintering in 2009 in the face of term limits and an economic crisis. This opened the way for a period of competing-pyramid politics that continues to the day of this writing.

Moldova's 2000 Constitution

Moldova wound up with a parliamentarist constitution in 2000, when in contrast with the rest of the non-Baltic post-Soviet space, its parliament won the initial postindependence struggle for power between parliament and presidency for reasons described in Chapter 6. Parliament eliminated direct presidential elections and claimed the right to choose the president itself, requiring a three-fifths majority vote of parliamentary deputies (that is, at least 61 of 101 legislators). The legislature also stripped the president of some formal powers in the process, including the right to preside over meetings of the government, appoint two Constitutional Court justices, and initiate changes in the constitution.[7] The sitting president at the time of the reform, Petru Lucinschi, blasted the reforms as reducing the presidency to a mere ceremonial post, an interpretation shared by some analysts.[8]

But as one of the reform's chief authors (parliamentary chairman Dumitru Diacov) and others emphasized, the presidency nevertheless retained most of the formal powers it had enjoyed before.[9] Among other things, these included some power to issue decrees having the force of law and the right to nominate the prime minister, initiate legislation and referenda, appoint many important officials, declare war, halt government acts on constitutional grounds pending

---

[6] On post-Soviet Moldovan politics, see also Nicu Popescu, "Moldova's Fragile Pluralism," *Russian Politics and Law*, v. 50, no. 4, July–August 2012, pp. 37–50; and Theodor Tudoriu, "Communism for the Twenty-First Century: The Moldovan Experiment," *Journal of Communist Studies and Transition Politics*, v. 27, no. 2, June 2011, pp. 291–321.

[7] *Infotag*, "Izmeneniia v Konstitutsii: Pliusy i minusy," *Nezavisimaia Moldova*, July 12, 2000, p. 1.

[8] Ilian Cashu, "The Bumpy Transition to Parliamentary Rule in the CIS," End Note in *RFE/RL Newsline*, March 6, 2006.

[9] Dumitru D'iakov, "Novaia konstitutsionnaia real'nost': neskol'ko soobrazhenii," *Nezavisimaia Moldova*, July 13, 2000, p. 1.

a ruling by the Constitutional Court, dissolve parliament under certain limited circumstances, and (vaguely) "take other due measures as to ensure the national security and public order."[10] Moreover, once chosen by parliament, the president could only be removed for violating the constitution and even then only by a two-thirds majority vote in parliament, which also had to gain the agreement of the Constitutional Court.

Two other posts chosen by the parliament also enjoyed significant formal executive powers under the 2000 version of the constitution, much as they had prior to that reform. Most obviously, by virtue of directly managing the day-to-day operations of executive power through the ministries, the prime ministership remained a very significant post. If anything, the reform strengthened this post on paper since, inter alia, the president could no longer chair government meetings.[11] While Diacov claims that the reforms did not strengthen his own post as parliamentary chair, that post retained a good number of important executive functions in addition to its ability to influence parliamentary decision making. These included nominating the prosecutor general, overseeing the national bank, and nominating the chair and members of the Accounts Chamber. Moldova's parliamentarist constitution, therefore, featured relatively high executive divisibility in that multiple executive posts existed that could provide credible formal underpinning for power-sharing deals among different patronal networks in parliament. Credibility is enhanced to the extent that it is more difficult to remove than initially install a figure from any one of these posts. The parliamentary speaker could be replaced only by a two-thirds vote. The prime minister could be removed though a simple vote of no confidence, though this carried risks for parliament because it would open up the possibility of parliamentary dissolution. And removing the president required a two-thirds vote in parliament *and* a Constitutional Court decision.

At the same time, Moldova's constitution contained features typical of parliamentarism that made the rise of single-pyramid politics more likely than under a divided-executive constitution. Most importantly, a single body formed in a single election gained the right to fill all major executive offices. This meant that a single election victory by one network, if it was overwhelming enough, could gain that network control of all executive posts. In addition, the executive posts were not completely independent of each other, and the set of formal interrelationships among these posts was such that one post (in this case, the presidency) was likely to be seen as signaling a slight relative superiority on paper. For one thing, the president was formally head of state. Second, the president retained the right to nominate the prime minister and to dissolve parliament in case the latter proved ineffectual in ways specified in the constitution. And, third, the president was the hardest to remove from office once selected.

---

[10] Geoff Dubrow, "Assessment Report on Moldova Parliament," draft report submitted to the United Nations Development Program, December 24, 2004.
[11] D'iakov, "Novaia konstitutsionnaia real'nost'."

The Rise of Moldova's Communist Machine under Parliamentarism

When adopting the 2000 constitutional reform, Moldova's legislators did not anticipate it would become completely dominated by any single party. Because incumbent President Lucinschi's term was set to expire less than a year after the reform was adopted, parliamentarians expected the sitting parliament, elected in 1998 for a four-year term, to be the one to choose the first president, who would then serve for a full four years. In that parliament, the Party of Communists of the Republic of Moldova (PCRM) had the largest delegation with 40 seats, but this was not nearly enough to elect a parliamentary chair or PM on its own, much less a president. It was also not even enough by itself to block the election of a president despite the high threshold set for filling that office. Instead, Diacov, who as parliamentary chair had guided the reform to passage, expected the new president to be a compromise figure, a technocrat who was not a representative of any party, who had respect across ideological lines, and who could therefore serve as a kind of broker facilitating policy making in a divided parliament.[12] The PCRM perhaps hoped its status as the biggest parliamentary party would enable it to secure the presidency for its leader, Vladimir Voronin, likely as part of a deal letting other forces hold on to the other major executive posts, or perhaps it aimed simply at forcing new elections before the presidency could be filled. Voronin's and Diakov's visions for the first presidency clashed in parliament, as the first two nominees, Voronin and Constitutional Court chair Pavel Barbalat (presented as a respected technocrat), each failed to win over the necessary 61 of parliament's 101 members.

This stalemate put Lucinschi, who had declined to run for reelection under the new system, in position to call early parliamentary elections for 2001. With no single power pyramid dominant and the administrative resources of the state fractured, a highly competitive election led to a landslide victory by a network that did not control any of the state's main executive posts: the Communists. The PCRM had campaigned against the ineffectual authorities and ongoing economic crisis and called for closer relations with Russia.[13] The proportional representation election system and its 6 percent threshold had a major impact on the outcome: The Communists won 50.1 percent of the popular vote, but this translated into a supermajority of 71 of the parliament's 101 seats.[14] This was enough to fill or replace any state executive post unilaterally. The Communists' vote was magnified so strongly because the only other parties/blocs to clear the minimum threshold for winning seats in the party-list competition were the Popular Christian Democratic Party (led by Iurie

---

[12] D'iakov, "Novaia konstitutsionnaia real'nost'."

[13] Igor Botan, executive director of the analytical center ADEPT, author's interview, Chisinau, Moldova, June 30, 2009

[14] This is because the seats were distributed proportionally only among parties that passed the 6 percent threshold, which many parties failed to do. The seats that would have gone to parties winning less than 6 percent were divided up proportionally among the parties that did clear

Rosca and main heir to the country's anti-Soviet nationalist movement) with just 8.2 percent of the vote and a network led by incumbent Prime Minister Dumitru Bragis netting just 13.4 percent. This translated into these parties' winning only 11 and 19 parliamentary seats, respectively. Diacov's own network, running under the label Democratic Party of Moldova, received just 5 percent of the vote, 1 percent shy of the threshold.[15]

Voronin, as Communist leader, thus had his pick of formal posts. Some in the party broached the idea that he might hold both the presidency and prime ministership simultaneously, but in the end he decided the presidency would be more advantageous for securing his position as patron.[16] His choices as to who would fill the other two top formal executive posts appear to have been made at least partly so as to minimize the chance that either post could provide a platform for a subpatron to mobilize a challenge to Voronin's authority. Thus for prime minister, the president nominated Vasile Tarlev, who had been elected to parliament on the Communist list but, significantly, was not a formal party member and lacked a base of his own in the party network. Instead, Tarlev was seen as a technical manager who was in a weak position to build a base of support in the parliament that could hope to challenge Voronin's authority. As Tarlev showed no signs of attempting such a challenge, he was kept on nearly to the end of the Communists' period in power. Voronin's pick for parliamentary chair during his first term was Eugenia Ostapciuc, a core member of his network from the Communist Party leadership, though notably *not* generally regarded as the number two person in the network, having been only number eight on the party's candidate list.[17] She also remained loyal but was replaced in 2005.

Beginning in 2001, then, Moldova increasingly looked much like the post-Soviet patronal presidential countries had looked in the mid-1990s. During that period, one will recall, they had been in the early stages of the time-consuming process of constructing strong centralized political machines out of the rather chaotic competing-pyramid systems that had characterized the initial transition from Soviet rule. One important development was for the Voronin network to establish its economic position in the country. Some business networks associated with the old regime reportedly faced pressure either to work with Voronin's government or to get out. For example, Boris Birshtein, a former Soviet émigré with strong Soviet era Communist Youth League connections who became a major player in Moldova's markets in the 1990s, was denied

the hurdle. In other words, in addition to the 50.1 percent of the parliamentary seats that the Communists won outright, they effectively *also* got 50.1 percent of the seats that other parties would have earned had there been no threshold.

[15] Election results cited in this chapter, unless other sources are given, can be found through the "e-democracy" Web site of the Chisinau-based Association for Participatory Democracy (ADEPT), directed by election expert Igor Botan: http://www.e-democracy.md/en/.

[16] Ilian Cashu, "The Bumpy Transition."

[17] The PCRM's chief subpatron was generally regarded to be Victor Stepaniuc. See, for example, *Tribuna.md*, June 24, 2012, 11:00.

renewal of his 10-year contract with the Information Ministry and ultimately lost control of the NIT television network he had founded. NIT was rumored to have fallen under the influence of the president's son, Oleg Voronin, through a nontransparent ownership structure involving offshore companies. In any case, it soon became known for starkly pro-Communist news coverage.[18]

This was not all. Anatol Stati's massive ASCOM group was reported to have at least initially made its peace with the Voronin system.[19] Voronin's son, Oleg, who had founded a bank in the 1990s, during his father's presidential tenure gained a reputation as one of the country's most important businessmen with holdings in a wide variety of spheres from banking to wine, one of Moldova's most lucrative exports to post-Soviet countries.[20] Initially highly secretive and having what some have described as a murky past, Vladimir Plahotniuc was also reported to have accumulated a fortune at least partly through a close business relationship with Oleg Voronin. His holdings were said to lie in everything from gas stations to mass media, including the country's largest television channel, Prime-TV.[21] By 2005, state-owned media were also found to have displayed a political bias,[22] and for the first time since independence an opposition newspaper, *Kommersant Moldovy*, was shut down.[23] "Unofficial taxes" were also collected from businesses, sources indicated. According to some research, surveys found businesses reporting that they were paying more in bribes, but that these bribes were interfering less with their activities because they had become systematized. By some accounts, part of these funds made their way to election campaigns.[24] During roughly their first year in office, the Communists had also already "replaced 70 percent of the heads of district and appellate courts and managed to increase unilateral legislative authority over selection of Constitutional Court judges."[25]

Voronin also took a page from Ukrainian President Kuchma's playbook and used his network's dominance during his first term to steal opposition thunder by adopting some of their positions and occupying the most promising place on Moldova's political spectrum. This was most pronounced on issues of identity and international orientation, precisely the issues that some have argued tend to be major obstacles for authoritarian consolidation.[26]

[18] Razvan Dumitru, "Politics and Practices in Post-Soviet 'Business': Between Shame and Success," *Revista Martor*, no. 16, 2011, pp. 52–66, p. 63; *Infotag*, April 6, 2012.

[19] Kseniia Il'ina, "La Famiglia," *Kishinevskii Obozrevatel'*, October 21, 2010.

[20] *Kommersant – Vlast'*, no. 36, September 15, 2009.

[21] Graham Stack, "The Talented Mr. Plahotniuc," *BNE Business New Europe*, April 11, 2011.

[22] *RFE/RL Newsline*, May 24, 2005.

[23] Lucan A. Way, "Pluralism by Default in Moldova," *Journal of Democracy*, v. 13, no. 4, October 2002, pp. 127–41, p. 131.

[24] Igor Munteanu, Tatiana Lariushina, and Veaceslav Ionita, *The System of Unofficial Taxation* (Bucharest: Cartier, 2007).

[25] Way, "Pluralism by Default in Moldova," p. 131.

[26] When discussing "pro-Russian" and "pro-Romanian" positions here, we follow Rebecca A. Chamberlain-Creanga ("The Moldovan Parliamentary Election 2010: Towards Stability and Reintegration?" Paper prepared for Kennan Institute Lecture, Woodrow Wilson International

The Communists first rode to power on a platform that was considered "pro-Russian," advocating better relations with Russia, special status for the Russian language, preferential conditions for Russian investment, and working with Russia to secure Moldova's reunification with its breakaway region of Transnistria.[27] This stance had long provoked fierce resistance from nationalist forces oriented more to the European Union and Romania than Russia. Thus when the Communists first grasped the reins of state, Rosca's Christian Democrats unleashed a nearly nonstop series of mass demonstrations designed to thwart Voronin's agenda. In one dramatic episode, the party sustained large street protests for more than 100 days in 2002, ultimately forcing the Communists to back down on their efforts to upgrade the status of the Russian language.[28]

The critical turnaround occurred in November 2003, when Voronin appeared ready to sign a plan negotiated by Putin associate Dmitry Kozak (widely referred to as the Kozak Memorandum) that would have created a Moldovan-Transnistrian federation with a long-term Russian military presence. The Christian Democrats and other opposition forces responded with a furious round of massive street protests. Occurring just after street protests had ousted President Eduard Shevardnadze in Georgia, this must have seemed particularly ominous for Voronin. Various Western leaders also urged him to balk at the deal. Under great pressure, just hours after Russian President Putin announced he would visit Moldova for a signing ceremony, Voronin backtracked and rejected the plan, forcing an irate Putin to cancel his visit.[29] In the wake of this traumatic experience, Voronin repositioned his party's stance, dropping the most inflammatory "pro-Russian" parts of its agenda and instead declaring a strong orientation to Europe, with European Union integration at the center of its political rhetoric along with its traditional emphasis on social issues. While discomfort still remained with Romania in particular, this reorientation gained credibility as Moldova signed an Action Plan with the EU in 2004. With this adroit repositioning, the PCRM successfully claimed the "center" of the identity and foreign policy spectrum. This not only stole the thunder of the main nationalist opposition and insulated him against new challenges from that direction, but also left little room for a revolt for the strongly

Center for Scholars, December 6, 2010, mimeo, p. 5) in treating them not as actual desires to become a republic in a reconstituted USSR or to become a province in Romania, but as broad orientations that reflect different visions of the country's future and are at least partly reflective of social status, generation, and interests.

27 Ilian Cashu, "What Makes an Orange Revolution Unlikely in Moldova?" End Note, *RFE/RL Newsline*, March 4, 2005.

28 Mihai Adauge, secretary of the PPCD, author's interview, December 20, 2008.

29 For a detailed account, see William H. Hill, *Russia, the New Abroad, and the West: Lessons from the Moldova-Transdniestria Conflict* (Baltimore: Johns Hopkins University Press, 2012). Also: Adauge interview 2008; Igor Botan, "Kozak Plan and Implications," *e-democracy*, November 30, 2003, http://www.e-democracy.md/en/monitoring/politics/comments/20031203 1/, accessed June 28, 2012; Aurel Stratan, "Ballooning Westward?" *Transitions Online*, February 21, 2005.

"pro-Russian" end of the political spectrum. The latter political territory thus remained populated only by a handful of minor organizations that were never widely expected to be able to clear the threshold for obtaining parliamentary seats, even with backing from Russia.[30]

As with all of the initial post-Soviet patronal presidents described in Chapter 6, the building of a power pyramid in Moldova did not take place instantly, leaving its politics relatively open during Voronin's first term. Certainly not all oligarchic corporate networks from the 1990s were vanquished or co-opted. The network of Chiril Lucinschi, the former president's son, was one that remained indepedendent. The Communists also did not manage to install their own local political machines everywhere. This was most obvious in the capital city of Chisinau, where the populist mayor Serafim Urechean, first elected in 1994, used his urban machine to anchor anticommunist forces in the run-up to the 2005 parliamentary election. It is also interesting that the Communist Party, despite having had the votes it needed in parliament to change the constitution unilaterally, opted not to alter the way that the president was elected. Indeed, it could have either restored a presidentialist constitution or lowered the three-fifths supermajority requirement to make it easier to retain the presidency without a coalition in the future. The absence of such a change can be explained by the fact that the PCRM's dominance owed largely to this particular variety of parliamentarist system. For one thing, it had only barely won the popular vote in 2001 with 50.1 percent, meaning that its ability to win a direct presidential election was still in question, especially before it had created a strong and proven power *vertikal'*. Moreover, the fact that a two-thirds majority in parliament was needed to elect the presidency meant that the PCRM would be likely to sustain at least the ability to block someone else from taking it even if their parliamentary delegation was cut nearly in half in future elections. Mark Tkaciuk, widely regarded as the Communists' chief strategist, said that such a constitutional change was never even considered during their first term in power.[31]

The Communists mobilized what forces they had managed to put in place for the 2005 parliamentary election, reflecting what might be considered a midpoint in the building of a single-pyramid system. Most major media were found by several studies to have favored the Communists in their news coverage. The state's Moldova 1 television channel – the only TV channel with nationwide coverage – was identified as a particularly egregious offender.[32] Among electronic media, the only exceptions detected by two studies were a radio station and two television channels broadcasting locally in Urechean's

[30] Cashu, "What Makes."

[31] Mark Tkaciuk, author's interview, Chisinau, Moldova, March 20, 2010.

[32] Communist representatives unsurprisingly called some of these findings biased in favor of the opposition. See *RFE/RL Newsline*, February 15, 2005; *RFE/RL Newsline*, March 2, 2005; *RFE/RL Newsline*, March 8, 2005.

Chisinau.[33] Another, however, found no systematic bias one way or the other among a sample of 25 Romanian- and Russian-language print publications.[34] OSCE observers cited "some credible reports of coercion and pressure on public employees to support the incumbents' campaign" and found evidence that police were interfering in certain campaign activities and that employers were pressuring some people not to engage in opposition campaign activities.[35] The government also expelled several Russian political strategists working for opposition parties, saying they lacked required residency or work permits. But many observers interpreted this as aimed against Russian efforts to depose Voronin in retaliation for his 2003 foreign policy reversal.[36]

At the same time, buttressed by the generally positive media coverage, the Communists were generally agreed to have enjoyed considerable popular support in 2005, only slightly down from their electoral high-water mark in 2001. This was widely believed to owe in part to a strong economic recovery that had recently begun, higher social spending, and the start of a program to compensate citizens for savings they had lost during the 1992 hyperinflation in the wake of the USSR's breakup.[37] All this created what Luke March has called a "feel-good factor" in favor of the Communists at the time.[38] The reputable Barometer of Public Opinion series of election surveys conducted by the Institute for Public Policy found that a month before the vote, the Communists had a chance to win as much as 62 percent of the seats.[39]

The official result mobilized by the Communists in the March 6, 2005, parliamentary elections fell short of their 2001 total. They netted just 56 of the parliament's 101 seats on the strength of 46 percent of the popular vote. The only two other parties to clear the election's complicated thresholds for winning parliamentary representation[40] were the Christian Democrats, once again garnering 11 seats with 9 percent of the vote, and a Democratic Moldova Bloc led by Chisinau Mayor Urechean that netted 34 seats on the strength of

[33] *RFE/RL Newsline*, February 8, 2005; OSCE Office for Democratic Institutions and Human Rights, "Republic of Moldova Parliamentary Elections 6 March 2005," OSCE/ODIHR Election Observation Mission Final Report, June 3, 2005, p. 13.

[34] *RFE/RL Newsline*, February 17, 2005.

[35] OSCE Office for Democratic Institutions and Human Rights, "Republic of Moldova Parliamentary Elections 6 March 2005," OSCE/ODIHR Election Observation Mission Final Report, June 3, 2005, pp. 1, 10.

[36] *RFE/RL Newsline*, February 14, 2005.

[37] Cashu, "What Makes"; Stratan, "Ballooning Westward?"

[38] Luke March, "The Consequences of the 2009 Parliamentary Elections for Moldova's Domestic and International Politics: A Narrow Window for Europeanization," paper delivered at the Annual Meeting of the American Association for the Advancement of Slavic Studies, Boston, November 13, 2009.

[39] Institute for Public Policy, "Rezumat de presa: cu privire la barometrul opiniei publice, realizat in ianuarie-februarie 2005," February 20, 2005.

[40] The threshold was 6 percent for officially registered parties, 9 percent for electoral blocs consisting of two parties, and 12 percent for blocs containing three or more parties.

29 percent of the popular vote. Urechean's bloc contained a series of other major anticommunist figures, including former parliamentary chair Diacov, ex-PM Bragis, and Social Liberal Party leader Oleg Serebrian. The OSCE declared the elections to have been generally administered in accordance with the law,[41] though the Communists' vote total wound up being 6 points higher and the Christian Democrats' 5 points lower than predicted by an exit poll funded by a large group of institutions, including the Soros-Moldova Foundation, the OSCE, and the Institute for Public Policy.[42] The Voronin machine had thus gotten off to a relatively strong start in the process of power pyramid building, gradually starting to close the political space and securing a victory in the country's most important elections.[43]

Parliamentarism's Moderate Moderating Effect on the Communist Machine

It is at this point that we start to see one of the key features of the parliamentarist constitution have some moderating effect on single-pyramid formation, its provision for a second formal selectorate. Having won a majority of seats in the parliament, the Communist network now had to obtain a series of votes by the newly elected MPs to place its choices in the top formal executive posts. The posts of speaker and prime minister posed little problem, since the Communists' 56 seats (out of 101) were more than enough to fill these posts. Voronin once again opted to install figures who were not likely to be able or willing to use these posts to provoke splits in the Communist network and challenge Voronin's primacy. For PM, he reappointed the "technical" Tarlev, who had shown no signs of preparing a mutiny. For parliamentary chair, he replaced longtime party member Ostapciuc with nonparty technocrat Marian Lupu, a noncore member of the Voronin network who had been elected to the legislature as only the number 23 person on the Communists' 2005 party list and who had been serving as economy minister.[44] For Voronin to retain the crucial post of president, however, he needed parliamentary allies from beyond his own party list.

After intense bargaining, Voronin managed to piece together a coalition of 75 deputies that included members of both other party lists that won parliamentary seats. This simultaneously secured his own reelection as president and

---

[41] OSCE Office for Democratic Institutions and Human Rights, "Republic of Moldova Parliamentary Elections 6 March 2005," OSCE/ODIHR Election Observation Mission Final Report, June 3, 2005, p. 1.

[42] Adept, "The Exit Poll Results," *e-democracy*, http://www.e-democracy.md/en/elections/parliamentary/2005/exit-poll/, accessed June 28, 2012.

[43] An excellent analysis of these elections is Ryan Kennedy, "Moldova," in Donnacha O Beachain and Abel Polese, eds., *The Colour Revolutions in the Former Soviet Republics* (New York: Routledge, 2010), pp. 62–82.

[44] Lupu later that year became a member of the PCRM.

neutralized his most threatening opposition, facilitating a significant tightening of his political machine during his network's second full term in power. At the same time, the concessions he made appear to have laid the foundation for a later unraveling, when the machine entered a period of expected presidential succession. The following paragraphs examine these particular effects of the formal parliamentarist constitution.

To understand parliamentarism's effects, it is important to consider who precisely defected to the Communists and what they gained in return. Because the Democratic Moldova Bloc led by Urechean was from the beginning a rather loose alliance of patronalistic networks seeking to clear the parliamentary threshold together rather than the formal representation of a single coherent network, few were surprised that Voronin could pick off some of its parliamentarians. One of those was the network of former parliamentary chair Dumitru Diacov in the Democratic Party, who justified his network's joining Voronin at the time as a move to save the country from political crisis at a critical moment.[45] Later, Diacov elaborated that he had thought Voronin could be made into a social democrat and that Voronin had made several promises that in theory were to weaken his ability to dominate Moldovan politics. These promises included depoliticizing the presidency (requiring the president not to be a party member) and lowering the vote threshold required for parties to win parliamentary seats.[46]

Social Liberal Party leader Oleg Serebrian joined Diacov, influenced by Voronin's aforementioned policy shift from the pro-Russian Left to a broadly popular position advocating European integration, a generally pro-Western orientation, and even liberal economic policies, including privatization. These were positions that Voronin promised to maintain and that Serebrian hoped to reinforce through deal making.[47] Serebrian also expected Voronin to keep a promise to allow media freedom. Elaborating on his strategic thinking, the Social Liberal leader explained that he had calculated the Communists had a good chance of obtaining a supermajority had new parliamentary elections been forced by the legislature's failure to elect a president. Had that happened, opposition parties would have lost whatever slim bargaining power they had been enjoying at the time.[48] Neither Diacov nor Serebrian received any of the top three formal executive posts as a result of his deal making. Urechean bitterly branded the defectors "traitors" and conferred his own party's name, the Our Moldova Alliance, on what remained of his bloc, which became the core opposition to Voronin's machine in parliament.[49]

[45] *RFE/RL Newsline*, April 5, 2005.

[46] Dumitru Diacov, author's interview, Chisinau, Moldova, March 27, 2009.

[47] Ilian Cashu, "Politics as Usual in Moldovan Presidential Vote," End Note in *RFE/RL Newsline*, April 7, 2005; *RFE/RL Newsline*, April 5, 2005; *RFE/RL Newsline*, April 5, 2005; Oleg Serebrian, author's interview, Chisinau, Moldova, December 19, 2008.

[48] Serebrian interview 2008.

[49] Ilian Cashu, "Politics as Usual"; *RFE/RL Newsline*, April 5, 2005.

By far the most shocking outcome of the parliamentary bargaining, however, was the decision of Iurie Rosca and his Christian Democrats. The Christian Democrats were seen at the time as "Moldova's most consistent pro-Western party for more than a decade" and the hardest core of the country's anticommunist opposition, with strong roots in the country's independence movement.[50] Indeed, in the wake of the "color revolutions" in Georgia and Ukraine, and with one brewing in Kyrgyzstan at the same time as Moldova's interparty bargaining was occurring, many had thought a revolutionary outcome was possible in Moldova. Not only had the Christian Democrats proven their ability to rock the political establishment with massive protests less than a year and a half before over the Kozak Memorandum; comparing official election results to those of the exit poll mentioned earlier would seem to have given them grounds for claiming that the Communists had stolen a third of their votes and thus put them in strong position to mobilize a serious challenge to the regime. Yet this most likely revolutionary force wound up entering a coalition with its former nemesis, Voronin's Communist Party, without receiving any of the top three executive posts. Rosca came away with only the position of vice-chair of parliament. Some speculate personal material payoffs may have been involved. But since actual public support does matter in highly patronalistic contexts, as discussed extensively earlier, it is hard to see how even the greediest and most cynical of politicians would see a one-off payment alone as being worth such a radical and risky sacrifice of a well-developed reputation that had consistently secured parliamentary representation.[51]

The key to the deal strongly appears to have been the Communists' 2003 foreign orientation volte-face, which had not only stolen some of their pro-Western opponents' thunder, but also put Voronin in position now to co-opt this opposition. In rejecting the Kozak Memorandum and entering into bitter political conflict with Moscow – even to the point of openly aligning with the "Russoskeptic" and Eurocentric regimes of Viktor Yushchenko in Ukraine and Mikheil Saakashvili in Georgia – the Communists now found common cause with the Christian Democrats on the issue most important to the latter's political reputation.[52] Rosca confirms it was the Communists' decision to align with the Christian Democrats in rejecting the Kozak plan in 2003 that gave rise to his surprising "partnership" with Voronin.[53]

[50] Vladimir Socor, "Moldova's Political Sea Change," *Eurasia Daily Monitor*, v. 2, no. 70, April 11, 2005.

[51] Moreover, the present author has not seen any credible reports indicating a sudden, large growth in the personal wealth of Rosca and the large number of associates who went along with him after 2005.

[52] Adauge interview 2008.

[53] Iurie Rosca, author's interview, Chisinau, Moldova, July 7, 2010. Rosca also notes he had found common cause with Voronin before, in particular after he rang the Communist leader up on his cell phone, initially disguising his voice to make sure it was Voronin on the line, to solicit his support for opposing then-President Lucinschi's plans to push through a presidentialist constitution.

Putting pressure on Rosca and his associates were a number of new Western and Western-oriented foreign allies Voronin had won by standing up strongly against Russian influence in the former Soviet space. Saakashvili and Yushchenko both appeared to signal support for Voronin, or at least were understood within the Christian Democratic camp to have done so, as did Romanian President Traian Basescu.[54] Former Lithuanian president and longtime Rosca acquaintance Vytautas Landsbergis, the die-hard anticommunist who had spearheaded his country's fierce drive to leave the USSR under Gorbachev, reportedly advised the Christian Democrats that they should back Voronin to reinforce their country's independence from Russia even if the price had to be slowing democratic reforms.[55] Christian Democrats as well as Social Liberal leader Serebrian also named or alluded to the active role of the conservative former U.S. Congressman John Conlan (R-AZ), who lived in Ukraine and was seen by some as a Yushchenko supporter, in advocating and brokering the deal to build a broad coalition around Voronin to support Moldova's Western orientation, resist Russian influence, and prevent instability.[56] Others reported urging from United States–based nongovernmental organizations, though the American Embassy in Chisinau declared it was not U.S. policy to promote a political alliance around Voronin.[57]

The Communist–Christian Democrat deal was anchored not in giving Rosca or any of his colleagues one of the three most important formal state posts, but by Voronin's promise to carry out ten reforms that Christian Democrats negotiated. Some were in the realm of identity politics, as with a law on the juridical status of Transnistria and a demand that the Russian army leave the territory. Others were aimed, Christian Democrats said, at opening up Moldova's political system, as with the inclusion of "opposition" representatives in organs of power (including election commissions, the Accounts Chamber, and a media monitoring commission), the establishment of parliamentary control over the former KGB, and reduction of the ability of the president to influence judicial appointments.[58]

At the time, Rosca admitted that joining with the Communists was a major risk that could put the party's future in jeopardy, but declared it one worth taking for the sake of Moldova's national unity and future with Europe – essentially opting for an "orange evolution" instead of an Orange Revolution.[59]

---

[54] Adauge interview 2008; Vlad Cubreacov, head of the PPCD parliamentary fraction and party vice president, author's interview, Chisinau, Moldova, March 28, 2009; Socor, "Moldova's Political Sea Change."

[55] Adauge interview 2008.

[56] On his role, see Socor, "Moldova's Political Sea Change." Also multiple interviews by the author with Christian Democrat leaders and Oleg Serebrian.

[57] Oazu Nantoi, author's interview, Chisinau, Moldova, March 28, 2009.

[58] Adauge interview 2008; Cubreacov interview 2009; Rosca interview 2010.

[59] *RFE/RL Newsline*, April 5, 2005; Iurie Rosca, "Moldova's Orange Evolution," *Demokratizatsiya: The Journal of Post-Soviet Democratization*, v. 13, no. 4, pp. 537–43.

While the Christian Democrats would have had a strong vested interest in publicly portraying their fateful move in terms of ideology and national purpose, strategic considerations are also likely to have been in play. With Diacov's network already having agreed to give Voronin the votes he needed in parliament to claim the presidency formally, the Christian Democrats faced the prospect of acceleration in the political closure that had begun in 2005 at the same time that the Communists had essentially stolen their most potent issue. This would have left them highly vulnerable to marginalization as a single-pyramid system emerged. But with Voronin offering them a deal in an effort to co-opt a major political network into his growing machine, the Christian Democrats' choice was largely between accepting and bargaining for what they could in the process, or going to the streets in an effort to overthrow Voronin. But with the Communists clearly enjoying the support of a large plurality of the population, and with so many prominent forces backing the budding machine (including those such as Yushchenko and Saakashvili who otherwise could have lent credibility to a revolutionary uprising), the prospect of successful revolution understandably looked less promising for the party than did cutting a deal. Indeed, this appears to have been at least in part the interpretation of the situation that some Western leaders and lobbyists were pushing on the Western-oriented Christian Democrats and Social Liberals. The latter, in joining the power pyramid, could hope to resist political closure that directly threatened their interests more effectively and to promote policies that were at the core of their reputations.[60] Moldova's parliamentarist constitution, therefore, helped prompt an additional, postelection round of deal making that simultaneously enabled the Communists to broaden their political machine's reach and co-opt a major opposition force but at the cost of making a set of commitments to pursue certain sets of reforms intended by the co-opted parties to weaken Voronin's control over parts of the machine.

Did these Communist promises actually amount to anything? This is a difficult question to answer. It does seem fairly clear that the deals struck by the Democratic Party and Social Liberal Party networks had little pyramid-loosening effect, serving mainly to get Voronin elected president so that he could continue to tighten the screws on his machine. Indeed, before even the end of 2005, both Diacov and Serebrian had accused the Communists of reneging, and Serebrian went on to call for Voronin's impeachment.[61] Asked near the end of Voronin's second term to evaluate the influence other parties could exert on the Communists, Serebrian stated that the president was not even influenced by the Communist Party, much less other parties.[62] To a similar question, Diacov replied that the Communists had initially made some legislative moves

[60] Socor, "Moldova's Political Sea Change."
[61] Cashu, "The Bumpy Transition."
[62] Serebrian interview 2008.

aimed at fulfilling his deal, such as making the presidency a nonparty post and lowering the electoral threshold, but then backed away.[63]

The Christian Democrats have a credible case that they were able to make a moderate difference, securing from Voronin certain formal institutional changes that may have made his machine more vulnerable to toppling under the weight of dynamics related to presidential succession. In interviews shortly before and after the 2009 elections, Christian Democratic leaders claimed that Voronin had actually followed through on most of his 2005 promises to them, including laws giving parties other than the Communists representation in key organs of power including election commissions, consistent calls for the withdrawal of Russian troops from Transnistria, a law on the juridical status of Transnistria, general support for Moldovan independence and integration with Europe rather than Russia, the creation of a parliamentary body to oversee the former KGB, and reduction of the president's power to influence the composition of courts. The primary exception was prosecutorial reform, which they averred was not done by the April 2009 election.[64] Some prominent analysts unconnected with the Communists or Christian Democrats tended to agree that the Christian Democrats had made an impact in getting such legislation passed, with one mentioning the potential of the election commission reform at least somewhat to reduce opportunities for ballot box fraud.[65] The Communists' prime minister for the first three years of the deal, Tarlev, said that the Christian Democrats did not significantly influence government operations during this time but allowed that they did have some impact on legislation.[66]

At the same time, others averred shortly before the April 2009 elections that these concessions were largely in the realm of formal politics, with little visible impact on weakening Voronin's political machine.[67] Christian Democrat leaders admitted that much of their gain wound up being formal in nature and imperfectly implemented, but voiced hope that over time the new norms would have effect.[68] The head of the Christian Democrats' parliamentary faction prior to the April 2009 election, Vlad Cubreacov, was willing to venture that the election commission reform did in fact have a significant impact in the 2007 local elections, in which the Communist Party was surprised by losing a large number of contests at the hands of opposition parties, as will be discussed later.[69]

---

[63] Diacov interview March 2009.

[64] Adauge interview 2008; Cubreacov interview 2009; Rosca interview 2010.

[65] Botan interview 2009; Viorel Cibotaru, director of the European Institute for Political Studies of Moldova, author's interview, Chisinau, Moldova, March 23, 2009.

[66] Vasile Tarlev, author's interview, Chisinau, Moldova, June 25, 2009.

[67] Igor Munteanu, director of the Viitorul Institute for Development and Social Initiatives, author's interview, Chisinau, Moldova, March 24, 2009. Serafim Urechean (author's interview, Chisinau, Moldova, June 25, 2009) was more scathing, saying that the deal did not weaken Voronin and that the election commission reform did not reduce fraud.

[68] Adauge interview 2008; Cubreacov interview 2009.

[69] Cubreacov interview 2009.

Thus while there appears to be some evidence the parliamentarist system helped the Christian Democrats extract some moderate reforms from the Communists that may have slightly complicated attempts to close the political space, it is not surprising that they were unable to leverage the formal laws very strongly into the realm of informal politics. This is because the deal was not anchored in a distribution of the country's top formal executive posts. That could have given the Christian Democrats a credible opportunity to accumulate enough administrative resources of their own to challenge Communist encroachment. But instead, when pressed, Christian Democrat leaders admitted that they had little real ability to hold Voronin to his promises once the latter assumed the presidency. They could rely mainly on the threat of renewed street protests and public shaming through only a limited set of mass media. In effect, they had been counting on their relationship with Voronin personally to seal the deal.[70] Diacov and Serebrian also said that in the end this was all they had to enforce their agreements with Voronin after the latter had taken their votes to become president.[71] In fact, in the bigger picture, the 2005 deal making served the Communists well. Not only were major opposition forces co-opted, but their reputations had been badly damaged in the process. Indeed, the popular support for each of the PCRM's 2005 partners fell precipitously and none made it back into parliament in the April 2009 elections.

Impending Presidential Succession and Cracks in the Communist Pyramid

The greater challenge for the Communists was not the reforms they enacted at the request of the Christian Democrats through the parliamentarism-induced deal of 2005, but the fact that with his reelection, Voronin entered his constitutionally final term as president, raising questions of succession. As the succession approached, however, Voronin was not so vulnerable as highly unpopular patronal leaders like Shevardnadze and Akaev had been, but was entering a moment of economic woes with the onset of the 2008–9 world financial crisis. He thus wielded some real popular support, but also faced significant and growing discontent. Moldova's parliamentarist system, however, meant that networks in Moldova considering the possibility of backing an opposition movement could rationally perceive a greater chance of benefit from doing so than one would have expected had Moldova had a presidentialist constitution. This is because with the parliamentarist system, there could be gains not only from victory, but also from winding up with a "golden ticket" in the form of parliamentary votes that the Communists needed to elect a president. With a golden ticket, they could at least hope to bargain for more meaningful

---

[70] Adauge interview 2008; Cubreacov interview 2009.
[71] Diacov interview March 2009; Serebrian interview 2008.

concessions than Diacov, Serebrian, and Rosca had achieved in 2005. With uncertainty about the future patron and various elites perceiving potential gains from opposition, Moldova began to experience a situation as 2009 approached not unlike that faced by the patronal presidents who had experienced color revolutions earlier in the decade, described in Chapter 7.

During his second term as president, Voronin's authorities undertook a number of actions pushing Moldova even more strongly toward a single-pyramid system, strengthening their own control, and marginalizing opposition networks. Most prominently, prosecutors trained their sights on key figures remaining in the opposition, including Urechean, who had resigned his post as Chisinau mayor in 2005 to accept a seat in parliament. Dramatically, the Communist majority stripped Urechean and other members of his Our Moldova Alliance of their parliamentary immunity from prosecution in October as prosecutors charged them with abuse of office, though they were not convicted.[72] Urechean was later faced with bizarre charges that he was part of an alleged Russian conspiracy to take revenge on its enemies by materially encouraging the Christian Democrats to oust Voronin in a revolution after the 2005 election, after which Rosca would be murdered to open the way to restoring Russian influence.[73] Former Defense Minister Valery Pasat, who had backed Voronin's opposition in 2005, was also accused of playing a key role in this plot after having already been arrested just after the March parliamentary election for supposed contraband arms dealings during his time in office.[74] Social Democratic Party leader Eduard Musuc was arrested for a short period in 2006. After Lucinschi era state privatization director and former businessman Vlad Filat left Diacov's Democratic Party to found his own opposition Liberal Democratic Party, Filat was investigated for supposedly smuggling cigarettes during the 1990s.[75] The only two television networks with nationwide reach by 2009, Moldova 1 and NIT, were, respectively, state-owned or reputedly controlled by circles close to the president's family. They reflected a general tendency for mass media to favor the Communists.[76] Other media increasingly came under pressure. In the run-up to local elections scheduled in 2007, two of the only outlets found not to have displayed a pronounced pro-Communist bias in news coverage in 2005, the Chisinau-based Antena C radio station and Euro TV, were shut down.[77] The incumbent authorities also ended live broadcast of debates in

---

[72] *RFE/RL Newsline*, October 14, 2005.

[73] *Moldova Azi*, January 27, 2009.

[74] *Polit.Ru*, July 16, 2009, 19:26. For more details on Pasat, see "Pasat, Valeriy," *Lenta.ru*, http://lenta.ru/lib/14164073/full.htm, accessed June 30, 2012.

[75] *RFE/RL*, www.rferl.org, November 8, 2008.

[76] Declaration "Ia ne kommunist!" April 7, 2009, 00:39, posted on investigative journalist Natalia Morar's Live Journal blog, http://natmorar.livejournal.com, accessed April 9, 2009; *RFE/RL Newsline*, May 4, 2007.

[77] Ryan Kennedy, "Moldovan Broadcast Privatization: Reform or Censorship?" End Note in *RFE/RL Newsline*, February 22, 2007.

parliament, which had given opposition deputies a chance to reach television audiences.[78]

At the same time, as 2009 approached, the question of succession increasingly created uncertainty regarding the future of Voronin's machine. This uncertainty was magnified by the expectation that opposition forces might be able to force Voronin into concessions even if they could not actually defeat the Communists. During his second term, Voronin did not announce any plans to change the constitution so as to remain in the presidency beyond his second term, and his chief strategist asserted this was never discussed within the top party leadership.[79] Certain actions also sent signals confirming that clinging to the presidency was not his intent, for example, a Communist bill initiated in February 2006 to grant lifelong immunity from prosecution to former presidents for anything they did while in office.[80] The fact that Voronin would be just shy of sixty-eight years old – more than Moldova's average male life expectancy – by the time of the 2009 election and nearly seventy-two by the one scheduled for 2013 also called into question just how long he would be able to hold on even to the party.[81]

The formal presidential succession caused several problems for Voronin. For one thing, he and his advisers recognized that his leaving the presidency could open the way for a split between him and the future president, even if the new president was from his own party.[82] In addition, there was the danger to his authority that such a split within Communist ranks could occur even before the elections should the president announce his preferences too soon, since factions who were not chosen could try to use the parliamentary elections to stage a revolt. Thus Voronin pointedly refused to announce any choice of presidential successor in advance of the parliamentary election.[83] Moreover, seeking to make the formal presidential succession seem to be a minor event, he took pains to emphasize that by leaving the formal post of the presidency, he was not planning to stop being the country's patron in chief. While he did not specify whether he would seek either the formal post of parliamentary chair or prime minister, he did allow: "I will remain chair of the party. And whatever my job title will be after the elections, the party will manage the parliamentary delegation, which will work under my leadership.... If we win and get the necessary number of mandates, the party, in accordance with constitutional norms, will propose candidates for the president and members of the government."[84]

---

[78] Robert Zapadinskii, "'Korolevskie zaitsy', ili net v otechestve svoem poroka, krome oppozitsii," *tribuna redaktora, Kommersant Plus* (Moldova), December 19, 2008, p. 3.

[79] Mark Tkaciuk, author's interview, Chisinau, Moldova, June 25, 2009.

[80] *RFE/RL Newsline*, February 14, 2006.

[81] BBC, "Moldova Country Profile," http://news.bbc.co.uk/2/hi/europe/country_profiles/3038982. stm, accessed June 30, 2012.

[82] Tkaciuk interview 2009.

[83] *Nezavisimaia Moldova*, January 28, 2009.

[84] President Vladimir Voronin, interview with A. Venediktov on Ekho Moskvy Radio, transcript published in *Nezavisimaia Moldova*, February 26, 2009. See also his similar remark on television, reported by *Infotag*, December 11, 2008.

By one account, he compared himself explicitly to Deng Xiaoping, who long ruled without a chief formal state post in China. Voronin asserted, "Whatever I undertake after the elections, I will remain at the heart of everything that happens in the country."[85] The subtext he was trying to communicate was that formal presidential succession would not affect the power of his political machine and thus that elites would be wasting their time breaking ranks to compete for the country's top formal executive posts.

In the context of the upcoming presidential succession, therefore, the nationwide local elections of 2007 came to be seen as an important test of strength for the Voronin machine and different forces considering challenging it or at least staking out distinct bargaining position with it. These were hotly contested, and none more so than the race for Chisinau mayor. This post had become vacant when Urechean resigned to lead his party's new delegation in the parliament in 2005. But four successive elections to replace him had failed as a result of turnout so low that the elections were invalidated. Some of these failures actually reflected opposition success in protesting the way the election was conducted, calling on people not to participate. Indeed, the fact that a hard-core opponent had been mayor for the Communists' entire first term in power meant that the Communists were in a weak position there to push through their own candidate. This helped give public opinion substantial scope to play an important role in that contest.

The fifth attempt took place in 2007, and a Communist candidate was soundly defeated by Dorin Chirtoaca, a twenty-eight-year-old representative of the previously minor Liberal Party led by his uncle, Mihai Ghimpu, a longtime political activist and a leader of the late Soviet era national independence movement.[86] The Liberals, who also won enough votes in the city council election to get Ghimpu elected chairman, attracted supporters of the national independence movement disenchanted with the Christian Democrats after their decision to align with the Communists.[87] The Communists also failed to gain ground in other mayoral and council elections across the country, coming away with control of just 328 mayor's offices out of 898 nationwide, down from 368 elected in 2003. The Communists' main opponents, however, also lost ground as Urechean's Our Moldova Alliance claimed just 155 mayors in its stable, down from 191 in 2003. The gains in the mayoral races were made by other, smaller parties, such as Ghimpu's Liberals and the Democratic Party.[88] The picture was similar for the council races.[89] The Communists were found to

---

[85] Dumitru Ciubasenco, editor in chief of the Russian-language newspaper *Moldavskie Vedomosti*, "Moldova's Communist Leader Seeks to Retain Hold on Power," *RFE/RL*, February 15, 2009.

[86] Ryan Kennedy, "Moldova's Local Elections Reflect National Trends," *RFE/RL Newsline*, June 29, 2007.

[87] Botan interview 2009.

[88] *RFE/RL Newsline*, June 19, 2007.

[89] Kennedy, "Moldova's Local Elections" *RFE/RL Newsline*, June 8, 2007.

have deployed administrative resources at their disposal here, including media bias and voter intimidation.[90] One at least has to entertain the possibility that the election commission reforms obtained from Voronin by the Christian Democrats as part of their power-sharing deal may have played some role in preventing fraud from being used to cover up the Communist losses.

The 2007 local elections had two major implications. First, they gave or confirmed various noncommunist parties' hold over some local administrative resources, especially those connected with mayoral office. Crucially, this included Chisinau, where Chirtoaca was now in charge of sanctioning public protests and doling out various capital city funds. They also gained increasing control over local election commissions, which would make it even harder for the Communists to generate fraudulent results in the 2009 parliamentary elections and, in theory, could give some opposition forces the ability to manipulate results themselves.[91] Second, the 2007 elections confirmed for most that the Communists were not yet invincible. Many concluded from the results that Voronin would not likely be able to secure a sufficient supermajority to control the presidency on his own. This raised the expected gains to networks from challenging the Communists. One could reasonably hope to wind up with a golden ticket – the crucial votes needed to elect a president – or perhaps even a chance either to force the Communists out of power or to compel them to share at least one major executive post with a rival political network.[92]

Consistent with Chapter 4's logic, at this point Voronin began to suffer a series of defections from his single-pyramid system. The first major figure to break with Voronin's system throughout the entire period of his rule was Prime Minister Vasile Tarlev, who after seven years of loyal service stepped down in March 2008.[93] It remains unclear exactly why he resigned, and there is a strong case to be made that he was actually forced to do so by Voronin, who was present at his resignation and actually gave him a state honor.[94] Whether or not resigning was his idea, Tarlev did not remain loyal or even quiet but instead went into opposition and began preparing to challenge the Communists in the April 2009 elections. Asked in late 2008 about the reasons for his resignation, Tarlev volunteered that he began to feel Voronin would not be president for

---

[90] *RFE/RL Newsline*, June 5, 2007; *RFE/RL Newsline*, June 19, 2007.

[91] March, "The Consequences," p. 10.

[92] For example, Oleg Serebrian said in an interview prior to the April 2009 election that the 2007 local election showed that the Communists could not win a supermajority and thus would be unable on their own to win the presidency. He still thought that Voronin could control the country through just the posts of parliamentary chair and prime minister, but expected the Communists to need allies to handle the presidency, a necessity that would weaken Communist control over the country. Serebrian interview 2008.

[93] *RFE/RL Newsline*, March 20, 2008.

[94] Igor Botan, "6th PCRM Congress and Its First Consequences," *e-democracy*, March 31, 2008, http://www.e-democracy.md/en/monitoring/politics/comments/200803311/, accessed October 3, 2013.

much longer, citing his age, and one way or another there would be a change in political generations. Tarlev, only forty-five, said he did not consider himself part of the old generation. He averred that he had a great deal to offer the country with his experience in business and government and alluded to what he perceived as broad support for him as a future leader among both ordinary people and elites. Queried as to why he opted to pursue his goals independently of the Communist network, he replied that there were different groupings within it that were bound to explode at some point, adding that communism was also an idea of the past.[95]

Indeed, the last Barometer public opinion survey taken before Tarlev's resignation found him to be the second-most trusted politician in Moldova with the faith of 40 percent of the population, behind only Voronin with his 44 percent. While the Communists were still revealed to be leading the parliamentary race among parties, a whopping 42 percent of those intending to vote declared that they had not yet decided which party to support, a situation that would surely look encouraging to someone in Tarlev's position. And the survey also confirmed there was vast uncertainty as to who would become the next president, with 66 percent unable to provide a name, and the most mentions given to parliamentary chair Marian Lupu (12 percent) and Tarlev (8 percent).[96]

Certain big business networks were also reported to be backing opposition candidates as April 2009 approached. One sure sign was the appearance of names linked to oligarchs on opposition party lists. Least surprising was Chiril Lucinschi, the businessman son of the former president and Voronin rival who had not succumbed to the Voronin machine. Evidently reflecting a reconciliation between Diacov and the Lucinschi family, Chiril Lucinschi wound up as the fifth candidate on Diacov's Democratic Party list. Lucinschi's network could contribute, among other things, assets in mass media, including ownership of the TV7 television channel, which was generally not biased to the Communists and sometimes broadcast reports friendly to the Democrats.[97] The Liberal Democratic Party of Moldova was founded in 2007 by Vlad Filat, who as director of privatization under President Lucinschi had major connections to big business and by some accounts had accumulated considerable personal wealth during his time in the private sector in the early 2000s. While Filat declared that his own contributions and party dues were enough to sustain the new party project, it quickly attracted some major business figures. Vice president of the ASCOM corporate conglomerate Iurie Leanca appeared as the number ten candidate on Filat's party list, and another major businessman,

[95] Vasile Tarlev, author's interview, Chisinau, Moldova, December 19, 2008.
[96] Institute for Public Policy, "Rezumat de presa: Barometrul de Opinie Publica – Noiembrie 2007," IPP Web site, November 30, 2007, http://www.ipp.md/libview.php?l=ro&idc=156&id=457.
[97] For example, TV7 news broadcasts ("Segodnia v Moldove," 8:30 pm) prior to the April 2009 election observed by the author in Chisinau on March 23, 24, 25, and 26, 2009.

Calin Vieru, the son of a venerated poet, joined in the number seven slot.[98] Another ASCOM vice president, Anatol Salaru, appeared as the number three man on the list of Mihai Ghimpu's Liberal Party, surging in popularity after its impressive win in the Chisinau mayoral race. This strongly suggests that the ASCOM network of Anatol Stati, regarded by many as the richest business-based network operating in Moldova at the time and previously having made peace with the Communist machine, had moved into opposition to Voronin by backing two of the most potent rising opposition party projects.[99] A few figures switched from opposition to the Communists during this period, such as Eduard Musuc, a former anticommunist Chisinau city council member who joined with the PCRM to become city council chair in replacement of the Liberal Party's Ghimpu. But these paled in comparison to the scale of defections by Tarlev and the ASCOM Group.[100]

Despite some key components starting to rattle off, Voronin's machine was put into high gear as the April 5, 2009, parliamentary election neared. One Communist strategy was reportedly to use the opposition's success in the last local elections against them. The central authorities could deny funds and other support to localities controlled by opponents, and then blame them for the consequent failures.[101] As a concrete example, the Justice Ministry froze the accounts of the city of Chisinau, controlled by Liberal Party mayor Chirtoaca, more than once during 2008 and early 2009.[102] This put Voronin in good position to make widely publicized tours of other regions, touting all the progress that had been made there in providing natural gas service, infrastructure, school repairs. Such trips were a central part of his campaign strategy.[103] The Central Election Commission (CEC) ordered two parties to pull television advertisements that criticized the Communists.[104] Prosecutors investigated Urechean and Filat during the final months of the campaign, as described previously.

The just-defected prime minister Tarlev came in for special harassment. State officials initially let him know they would not register a new party before the

---

[98] Party lists of parties in Moldovan national elections can be found on the *e-democracy* Web site of Adept, http://www.e-democracy.md/elections/parliamentary/, accessed February 16, 2014. See also *DECA-press*, January 28, 2009, 16:19, reprinted by *Moldova Azi*, January 28, 2009, 16:19; *Moldavskie Vedomosti*, December 17, 2008, p. 5.

[99] Kseniia Il'ina, "La Famiglia," *Kishinevskii Obozrevatel'*, October 21, 2010.

[100] Elena Moldoveanu and Alexandru Eftode, "The Communists and the Kid," *Transitions Online*, 4 December 4, 2008.

[101] Cibotaru interview 2009. Asked about this practice on Romanian television, Voronin blamed the opposition, saying that the latter sometimes delayed government payments to their own regions so as then to blame the Communists (*Kishinevskie Novosti*, March 27, 2009, p. 1).

[102] *Info-Prim Neo*, January 26, 2009, 18:27.

[103] For example, *Nezavisimaia Moldova*, February 20, 2009; *Nezavisimaia Moldova*, February 26, 2009; NIT channel, "Curier" news broadcast, December 18, 2008, 20:00 Moldova time, observed by author.

[104] *Infotag*, March 11, 2009.

election, and when he responded by becoming formal leader of a preexisting party (the Centrist Union of Moldova), the Ministry of Justice found grounds for refusing to recognize him as its leader. First Deputy Prime Minister Igor Dodon also presided over a meeting with major enterprise representatives that removed Tarlev from his other main formal post, chair of the National Association of Producers.[105] State and other pro-Communist media dragooned Tarlev, citing all kinds of reasons why Voronin had to get rid of him as PM;[106] lambasted other opposition figures;[107] and generally positively reported on the incumbent authorities,[108] including trying to create a sense that a Communist win was inevitable.[109]

Favorite Communist themes included the economic progress the country had made since 2001 and the country's general orientation toward the European Union, though with a dash of Romanophobia thrown in along with calls for better relations with Russia. Russia, it was widely understood by analysts, had now returned to backing Voronin.[110] Electronic media that did not fall in line could be themselves accused of bias (as with Lucinschi's TV7),[111] be warned that their licenses would be revoked and their frequencies put up for bidding later (as with Chisinau's PRO TV), or actually be shut down (as with the Romanian television channel TVR1).[112]

The opposition Liberals, Liberal Democrats, and Our Moldova Alliance campaigned hard against the Communists. With breaking the PCRM's monopoly on power and achieving European integration the centerpieces of their campaigns, these parties jointly pledged they would not vote with Voronin

---

[105] *Moldova Azi,* January 26, 2009; Tarlev interview 2008.

[106] E.g., Sergei Ovcharenko, "Za chto Voronin prognal Tarleva?" *Nezavisimaia Moldova,* February 24, 2009.

[107] For example, a sometimes unattributed video clip to a hard-rock soundtrack was repeatedly played in both Russian and Romanian before and after major news broadcasts on both the NIT and Moldova 1 networks the week of March 23, 2009. It showed Chirtoaca, Filat, and Urechean through editing that made them look violent in street protests. The video concluded with footage of an incident in which a big participant in a Liberal Democratic Party rally in a black jacket with close-cropped hair and a scowl approached pro-Communist journalists and knocked over the camera. Women could be heard crying out in alarm in the background. In at least one instance (just before the "Mesager" news broadcast, March 23, 2009, 21:00), this clip was followed by a Communist ad where a baby-holding woman with milky soft skin said, "I choose stability" to soothing piano music. As an example of negative television news coverage of opposition figures, see the report linking Filat to mafia on NIT, "Curier," Russian-language, March 26, 2009, 20:00.

[108] *Moldova Azi,* February 20, 2009, 18:38; *Moldova Azi,* March 11, 2009, 18:31.

[109] E.g., reporting on polls in the "Curier" news broadcast, NIT channel, December 18, 2008, 20:00.

[110] Cibotaru interview 2009 and, e.g., *Infotag,* February 24, 2009; Moldova1 channel, "Mesager" news program, in Russian, March 24, 2009, 19:00; *Nezavisimaia Moldova,* February 11, 2009; Vladimir Voronin, interview live on NIT TV channel, January 23, 2009, extended quotations in *Nezavisimaia Moldova,* January 27, 2009.

[111] "Segodnia v Moldove" program, TV7 network, March 25, 2009, 20:30.

[112] *Moldavskie Vedomosti,* December 17, 2008, p. 3.

under any circumstance in the new parliament.[113] Filat's Liberal Democrats' central slogan was "Vote without fear."[114] Liberal Party leader Ghimpu stressed anticommunism, declaring that his party could be counted on never to cut a deal with Voronin.[115] Our Moldova Alliance chief Urechean, however, said before the election that he expected a coalition to be the ultimate outcome.[116] All blasted the Communist regime in their ads and interviews. The defecting former PM Tarlev, dogged by state interference in his organization-building plans, ultimately did get on the ballot as Centrist Union leader, campaigning for closer relations with Russia, multinational tolerance (himself being ethnic Bulgarian), and policies friendly to manufacturing.[117] The Christian Democrats circulated negative information about Filat and other rivals competing for the Romania-oriented electorate and attempted to explain to their former voters why they had been right to align with the Communists for the past four years.[118]

Overall, as Voronin's constitutionally final term as president wound to a close, we find significant fissures emerging in his power pyramid. Despite his popular support, Moldova's parliamentary system made it potentially profitable for major political networks to challenge the dominant one – at least, more likely to be profitable than it would be to challenge a popular president in a presidentialist system. This is because even if an opposition coalition could not realistically hope to win complete control over Moldova's parliamentarist system, it could still hope to deny the Communists a three-fifths majority of the seats. In so doing, opposition forces might be able to force the chief patron into a deal that would cede them at least one of the country's chief formal executive posts. And this would give them opportunities to strengthen their own patronal networks. The formal reforms that the Christian Democrats had extracted from the Communists in the previous elections may have reinforced this effect by putting networks other than the Communists' own in formal positions where they could raise the cost of tactics like fraud, as on election commissions.

The result of all this going into the April 5, 2009, parliamentary elections, therefore, was a tough political battle. Voronin's network had significant advantages in popularity and media control despite losing its second-most-popular figure. But opposition networks could still attract enough resources to mount significant resistance, aiming at least to deny the Communists the supermajority they needed to fill all three major executive posts. A preelection Barometer poll accordingly found that the Communists were in range

---

[113] *Moldova Azi*, February 3, 2009, 18:32.
[114] For example, this appeared in a Romanian-language ad aired just before NIT TV network's Russian-language news program "Curier," March 25, 2009, 20:00.
[115] *Infotag*, February 5, 2009, as reprinted in *Moldova Azi*, February 5, 2009.
[116] Serafim Urechean, author's interview, Chisinau, Moldova, December 19, 2008.
[117] *Kommersant Plus* (Chisinau), December 19, 2008, pp. 2–3.
[118] Author's field notes and, e.g., *Moldova Azi*, 26 March 2009, 18:56.

of winning the three-fifths majority they sought, but that a great deal of uncertainty remained.[119]

Moldova's 2009 "Twitter Revolution That Wasn't"

The ultimate result was in fact a "revolution" in the sense the term is used in this book, though it had little to do with the popular online social network that was sometimes cited as a central cause.[120] This revolution also played out according to a parliamentarist logic that differentiates it from the presidential ousters in patronal presidentialist countries documented in Chapter 7.

The drama began on election night, when a Barometer exit poll, cofunded by USAID, indicated that the Communists had won 45 percent of the popular vote and thus 55 of the parliament's 101 seats. This would have been enough to elect a prime minister and parliamentary speaker, but it was short of the 61 needed to elect the president unassisted.[121] As the Central Election Commission processed the results overnight and began announcing preliminary vote totals, however, the Communists' share turned out to be much higher, very close to 50 percent. As more votes were reported, the Communist total crept upward. With 94 percent of the ballots cast considered, the CEC reported on April 6 that Voronin's party had won 49.91 percent and that it was likely to complete the counting by midday. When midday rolled around, the CEC announced that with almost all of the ballots counted (97.93 percent), the Communists were at 49.96 percent of the vote counted. Crucially, this was enough to translate into 61 parliamentary seats – precisely the number Voronin's party needed in order to elect a president unilaterally.[122]

What happened next is the subject of different interpretations. By one prominent journalistic account, groups of outraged youth organized a protest via Twitter and other social media, which attracted more than ten thousand people "seemingly out of nowhere" into Chisinau's streets, with the crowd eventually ransacking the building that houses Moldova's presidency.[123] At best, this

---

[119] Cibotaru interview 2009, based on data summarized in Institute for Public Policy, rezumat de presa, "Barometrul Opiniei Publice – martie 2009," Chisinau, Moldova, copy obtained by the author at the public presentation of the results in Chisinau March 24, 2009.

[120] The term "Twitter Revolution That Wasn't" comes from David J. Kramer and William H. Hill, "Moldova: The Twitter Revolution That Wasn't," *OpenDemocracy*, May 28, 2009. The discussion on the downfall of Voronin's machine in this chapter draws substantially from Henry E. Hale, "Did the Internet Break the Political Machine? Moldova's 2009 'Twitter Revolution That Wasn't,'" *Demokratizatsiya: The Journal of Post-Soviet Democratization*, v. 21, no. 3, Fall 2013, pp. 481–505.

[121] Institute for Public Policy, "Exit Poll aprilie 2009," IPP Web site, http://www.ipp.md/libview. php?l=ro&idc=156&id=453, accessed July 3, 2012.

[122] *Unimedia*, April 6, 2009, 13:09.

[123] For example, reporting out of Moscow and New York, *The New York Times*, April 7, 2009. See also Evgeny Morozov, "Moldova's Twitter Revolution," *Foreign Policy* magazine's "Net.Effect" online portal, April 7, 2009, 2:15 pm, http://neteffect.foreignpolicy.com/posts/2009/04/07/moldovas_twitter_revolution, accessed February 16, 2014; Evgeny Morozov, "Moldova's Twitter

version of events leaves out some crucial pieces of the story. For one thing, rather than having appeared out of nowhere, postelection protests had in fact been planned and even *advertised* by the main opposition parties well before the voting in anticipation of fraud. Moreover, Chisinau city hall – controlled by Liberal Party mayor Chirtoaca – had actually approved it well in advance of election day, officially sanctioning postelection protests for the whole period April 6–20 at the request of the Liberal Democratic Party's Vlad Filat. Many parties had announced their intention to protest then if they found fraud, and by one account protester tents were already being set up in anticipation two days before the voting.[124] And these plans were publicized by using "old-fashioned" television, specifically outlets controlled by patronal networks willing to challenge the Communists. Thus as early as March 26, Chiril Lucinschi's TV7 network had broadcast opposition intentions to protest after the elections.[125] On election night itself, Filat appeared live on Chisinau-based PRO TV to remind citizens that his party had reserved the capital's central square for protesting possible election fraud.[126]

Thus when reports emerged the next day that the Communists were suspiciously likely to win the precise number of seats they needed to control all major state posts despite exit polls saying they got fewer, upset voters already knew where to go to register their feelings, knew they would find supporters among at least three major parties, and knew these actions had the approval of city authorities. Overlapping with these initiatives, two youth groups called for a "Day of National Sorrow" and then a flash mob late in the day on April 6, also in the center of Chisinau and also securing permission from the mayor's office. One of the organizers of the youth protests, journalist Natalia Morar, avers that the youth organizers ceased to play a central role in events after the flash mob at 8:00 pm on April 6. Indeed, Filat appeared before the crowd after the flash mob and reiterated that he had secured permission from the mayor to hold demonstrations for the entire next two weeks, and opposition parties called on protesters to show up the next day (April 7) at 10:00 am for a new round of protests.[127] The announcement of the Communists' likely winning 61 seats, which many considered an outrageous attempt at election manipulation, thus coincided with longtime protest planning and advertising by both political party organizations and youth groups using both traditional

Revolution Is NOT a Myth," *Foreign Policy* magazine's "Net.Effect" online portal, http://neteffect.foreignpolicy.com/posts/2009/04/10/moldovas_twitter_revolution_is_not_a_myth, accessed February 16, 2014.

[124] *Polit.Ru*, April 3, 2009, 11:46.

[125] TV7 network, "Segodnia v Moldove" Russian-language news program, March 26, 2009, 20:30.

[126] *Infotag*, April 6, 2009.

[127] "Zaiavlenie initsiativnoi gruppy po organizatsii flesh-moba 6 aprelia 2009 goda – 'Ia antikommunist'," April 8, 2009, 17:30, posted on Natalia Morar's Live Journal blog, http://natmorar.livejournal.com, accessed April 9, 2009. Morar was a leader of this group as the leader of the association ThinkMoldova.

and nontraditional media. This helped pull thousands into the streets, but most returned home that evening.[128]

On April 7, as opposition party leaders had called for, throngs again gathered in central Chisinau, reportedly in even greater numbers, but this time events took an ugly turn. Protesters clashed with police, throwing stones at, storming, and ransacking the buildings housing the presidency and parliament. They heaved computers and office equipment outside, setting them alight in a bonfire as police tried to disperse the crowd with a water cannon. Curiously culminating the event, the Romanian and European Union flags were hoisted atop the presidential building.[129] Voronin and his allies lambasted their political opponents for causing the "bacchanalia," accusing them of plotting with Romanian[130] special services to destabilize Moldova.[131] The government responded by imposing a visa regime on Romania,[132] expelling Romanian journalists and diplomats,[133] and arresting (among others) masses of protesters, Morar, and Gabriel Stati, son of the director of the ASCOM Group, linked to Filat and Ghimpu in this election.[134] Opposition leaders and sympathizers accused the Communists of using agents provocateurs to infiltrate the peaceful protest and instigate the violence to discredit the opposition, rally opinion against Romania, and create an outcry for stability instead of change. They pointed, for example, to video footage where a particular group can be seen appearing to start violent behavior and a videotaped statement by then-parliamentarian in the Communist delegation Vladimir Turcan (a former interior minister) that he personally arranged for a group of protesters to make their way through the heavily guarded upper floors of the presidential building to raise the EU flag atop it. This, he said, was intended to create a sense the event was over and to get the crowd to disperse. He implied that the protesters violated the agreement by also flying the Romanian flag.[135] This did not end the protests, however. By some reports, accounting department records housed in the presidential building happened to be burned in the process.[136]

---

[128] March ("The Consequences," p. 11) also stresses other conventional media, including text messaging and mobile phones, with only a "small circle of activists" using Twitter, which was emphasized by "Zeitgeist-chasing journalists."

[129] *RFE/RL*, April 7, 2009.

[130] Or Russian, by the Christian Democrats' version of the plot: *Polit.Ru*, April 8, 2009, 22:51.

[131] *RFE/RL*, April 7, 2009; Tudor Sorochanu, "Troianskii kon' Traiana Besescu [*sic*]," *Nezavisimaia Moldova*, April 29, 2009.

[132] *Moldova Azi*, April 29, 2009.

[133] *Infotag*, April 8, 2009.

[134] *Polit.Ru*, April 8, 2009, 15:58; *Polit.Ru*, April 16, 2009, 16:02; *Polit.Ru*, April 24, 2009, 18:27. Simple protesters were soon amnestied (*Polit.Ru*, April 16, 2009, 10:32).

[135] Such videos were shown to the author by Ghimpu in his office on June 25, 2009. Video with Turcan making such statements can be seen on YouTube, uploaded by MoldNews, at http://www.youtube.com/watch?v=ynh8O2y4Fng, accessed July 3, 2012. See also *RFE/RL*, April 7, 2009.

[136] *Infotag*, July 21, 2009.

While the true origins of the violence may never be established beyond doubt, the events did make clear that a revolution is not solely about crowds being able to seize a building that houses the main institutions of power, as some explanations of the color revolutions seemed to assume. Instead, the key is when this causes the political machine itself to disintegrate, a point that effectively means the defection of elite networks in the power pyramid that are necessary to carry out a patron's orders, especially those wielding the means of force. Such disintegration did not happen in Moldova in April 2009, with Voronin still recognized as the most popular and powerful patron in the country. Thus with his power *vertikal'* intact despite the challenge, he was able by April 8 to reclaim the seized government buildings. Voronin announced afterward, "One cannot declare war on one's own children! And thus we made the decision to yield to them for one day everything that was for them so longed for: the offices of the president and of the speaker of parliament, the parliamentary meeting hall, and our telephones and computers. We made the decision to yield to them everything that for them exhausts their whole conception of state authority!"[137]

The Communists did not claim their projected 61-seat supermajority, however. Despite having reported results with 97.93 percent of the ballots counted on April 6 and having promised – prior to the massive protests – that the few remaining ballots would be counted by lunchtime that same day, the Central Election Commission took more than two full days, until the evening of April 8, to present results with 100 percent of the precincts accounted for. In the end, the Communists came away with only 60 seats, one short of the magic number 61.[138] The same day, the CEC chair reportedly checked into the hospital with a heart problem.[139] One interpretation is that under pressure from the protests, the Communists had backtracked on a plan to manufacture a 61-seat majority. Voronin may not have seen this as a very big concession at the time: Shortly before the election, he had reportedly expressed confidence that his party could attract or cajole at least one opposition member of the new parliament to back the Communist candidate for president if necessary.[140] Indeed, the experience of 2005, when Voronin had successfully lured a relative abundance of defectors, might have made this seem quite a reasonable calculation.

The official explanation from the CEC for the counting delay and for the slip in the estimated number of Communist seats was that the remaining votes had been absentee ballots from abroad. These took time to count and wound up going overwhelmingly to Ghimpu's Liberal Party, enough so to drop the overall Communist seat count from 61 to 60.[141] At least one independent

---

[137] *Nezavisimaia Moldova*, April 9, 2009.
[138] *Infotag*, April 9, 2009. This was later confirmed as the final result.
[139] *Polit.Ru*, April 8, 2009, 17:29.
[140] *Polit.Ru*, April 10, 2009, 19:05.
[141] *Infotag*, April 9, 2009.

analyst shortly afterward thought this explanation was credible, calling the slip from 61 to 60 mainly a technical matter of finally having all the ballots in hand and doing the math.[142] Ghimpu, whose Liberal Party picked up the seat in question, averred that the authorities had tried to claim the 61st seat for the Communists, but said they were thwarted not by the protesters but by Liberal Party observers in the foreign precincts, who prevented falsification.[143] While plausible, neither of these explanations would appear particularly compelling. The larger picture of events suggests at least a strong circumstantial case that the opposition-organized protests may have in fact been decisive in persuading incumbent authorities to accept a 60-seat delegation and to use other methods for obtaining the single additional vote in parliament they needed to claim the presidency.

Confident that he would obtain the 61st vote from one of the other parties' delegations, Voronin now had to decide how to allocate the three key executive posts among the many different factions and individuals in the Communist network. He now chose for himself the position of parliamentary chair, which he formally occupied after the new parliament convened. Voronin evidently concluded that his informal power as chief patron would combine effectively with a formal post where he could only be removed by a two-thirds majority in the parliament, making it harder for the next president to remove him even with support from the opposition parties in parliament. The aim of minimizing the chance of a presidential challenge to Voronin was also a chief consideration in his choice for successor as president. After months of speculation, Voronin eventually announced his selection of Zinaida Greceanii, the longtime Finance Ministry official, who had risen through government ranks to become prime minister after Tarlev resigned in 2008. The Communists' chief strategist, Mark Tkaciuk, confirms that the choice of Greceanii was made in large part to preclude the possibility of a future split between Voronin (as parliamentary speaker) and the next president: This could best be achieved if the president were a nonparty technocrat, someone without her own base in parliament that could be used to mount a serious challenge. Greceanii fit this bill perfectly, a respected expert in finance who had never been a PCRM member and was not regarded as a subpatron with her own strong set of personal loyalists or powerful backers other than Voronin's core network.[144] The Communists also hoped that as a technocrat who was not a member of the Communist Party, Greceanii would be seen by the opposition deputies as a compromise candidate worthy of their vote for president.[145]

This choice of Greceanii for president had negative side effects on Voronin's power pyramid, however. Most importantly, it meant that Marian Lupu

[142] Botan interview 2009.
[143] Mihai Ghimpu, author's interview, Chisinau, Moldova, June 25, 2009.
[144] Tkaciuk interview 2009.
[145] Victor Stepaniuc's remarks as reported in *Moldova Azi*, May 20, 2009, 16:55.

was passed over despite being widely considered a leading contender for the presidency. Lupu was a popular parliamentary speaker during 2005–9 who had become a party member in late 2005 and who was seen as building a strong network of his own within the Voronin pyramid. By some accounts, his growing group of supporters had come to include oligarch Vladimir Plahotniuc, who reportedly saw Lupu as a likely presidential successor to Voronin.[146] In opting for Greceanii for president, Voronin reportedly planned for Lupu, seen within the network as having presidential ambitions, to be prime minister instead.[147] For the moment, Lupu accepted his preassigned fate and loyally cast ballots for Greceanii in the parliamentary voting for president on May 20 and June 3.

Perhaps the most remarkable part of Moldova's revolutionary episode – and one that proved decisive – is that the Communists in the end proved unable to gain a single vote from among the 41 deputies elected on the lists of the Liberal Party, Liberal Democratic Party, and Our Moldova Alliance. Each of these parties managed to hold ranks during two successive parliamentary votes for president, on May 20 and June 3. In each case, Communist candidate Greceanii received just 60 votes, 1 shy of the needed 61, thereby forcing new parliamentary elections for July. The Liberals and Liberal Democrats had refused to negotiate at all with the Communists leading up to these votes.[148]

The three main opposition parties' solidarity in this critical moment owes to several factors. For one thing, the son of the ASCOM Group's president had been arrested in the wake of the postelection protests, giving its representatives on the Liberal and Liberal Democratic party lists special cause to keep the party line firm so as to prevent Voronin from claiming all three major state posts for his associates. Ghimpu explained his party's lack of defections by his care in composing the party list so as to ensure loyalty.[149] Urechean, leader of the Our Moldova Alliance, similarly explained his party's solidarity by his caution in selecting candidates for his party's 2009 list, inspired by experiencing the defections from his list in 2005 that allowed Voronin to hold on to the presidency. A key criterion for 2009, he averred, was that he had known all list members personally for a long time and had worked with them – these were core members of his network.[150] Urechean later admitted that he did actually discuss the possibility of a deal with Voronin, but said that the only deal he would have considered would have been one including an opposition president.[151] Communist strategist Tkaciuk asserts that Urechean in fact wanted Voronin to back him (Urechean) for president.[152] But the Communists had

[146] Stack, "The Talented Mr. Plahotniuc."
[147] Tkaciuk interview 2009.
[148] *Infotag*, May 25, 2009.
[149] Ghimpu interview 2009. See also *Infotag*, February 5, 2009, as reprinted in *Moldova Azi*, February 5, 2009.
[150] Serafim Urechean, author's interview, Chisinau, Moldova, June 25, 2009.
[151] *Infotag*, May 25, 2009.
[152] Tkaciuk interview 2009.

from the start ruled out any deal that would have given the opposition the presidency.[153] The Communists reportedly offered many positions other than president and parliamentary chair to Urechean, and Urechean claims that at least one of his deputies was offered 2 million Euros for his vote while others were offered large apartments in Chisinau and even the post of deputy prime minister.[154] But without the presidency, Urechean's personal network in parliament stuck with the Liberals and Liberal Democrats.

Because the voting in parliament was by secret ballot, the three opposition parties opted not to vote against the Communist candidate and they did not simply abstain either. Instead, they actually kept their own deputies physically outside the parliamentary chamber during the voting. This ensured that none could covertly slip a vote for the Communists into the urn in return for a payoff. To ensure each kept the deal to stand firm, Ghimpu, Filat, and Urechean met "constantly" to coordinate, a practice they were to maintain for the early elections that ensued in July.[155]

Badly stung, Voronin regrouped his forces. He secured Greceanii's reelection as prime minister so as to keep her in good position for the next presidential election and retained both the parliamentary speakership and the presidency for himself.[156] Perhaps to demonstrate how generous his party could be to former opposition members who cooperated with him, Voronin made Christian Democrat leader Iurie Rosca deputy prime minister overseeing not only the ministries of defense, interior, and justice, but also potentially lucrative patronage posts.[157] Perhaps also hoping to enhance the chances of these allies of his to make it into parliament, the threshold for winning seats was reduced from 6 percent to 5 percent.[158]

The Communists also unleashed a blistering campaign for the July early elections that Tkaciuk at the time summarized as having one main theme: The Communists are for an independent Moldova while their opponents are enemies of Moldova.[159] Media controlled by the authorities and their allies, as well as Voronin himself and official party ads, appeared almost hysterical in portraying dire threats from Romania, organized crime, and revolutionary disorder. The opposition were said or implied to represent all of these threats. The dangers were symbolized by dramatic video images of the April 7 violence in Chisinau that had culminated in the flying of the *Romanian* flag atop Moldova's presidential building, an apparently clear challenge to Moldova's very sovereignty as a state. The Communists depicted themselves as the saving

[153] *Infotag*, May 25, 2009.
[154] *Moldova Azi*, June 29, 2009, 19:03.
[155] Urechean interview, June 2009.
[156] He was allowed to remain in the presidency until someone else was elected to this office.
[157] *Infotag*, June 18, 2009.
[158] *Infotag*, June 18, 2009; Tudor Sorochanu, "Muzhskoi postupok," *Nezavisimaia Moldova*, June 19, 2009.
[159] Tkaciuk interview 2009.

force of stability and sovereignty.[160] These themes all melded together in a special documentary film called *Attack on Moldova* that was broadcast on the NIT network.[161] At the same time, new Deputy Prime Minister Rosca engaged in a crackdown on campaign finance violations that was widely believed to be directed at the opposition.[162] The ASCOM Group president's son, Gabriel Stati, along with ASCOM's security director, were kept in jail.[163] Even the Liberal Party mayor of Chisinau, Dorin Chirtoaca, was detained by police at one point.[164] Some foreign election observers identified with "color revolutions" were sent home, with a lack of proper accreditation being cited.[165] This time, Voronin boasted, the Communists could get as many as 80 percent of the seats in parliament.[166]

But the opposition's stunning success in denying the Communists a single vote – in a land where many assumed anyone could be bought – arguably dealt the fatal blow to Voronin's power pyramid, setting in motion a chain of events that led to its crumbling and the culmination of Moldova's revolution. Most dramatic was the defection of two major networks in Voronin's system, those of "oligarch" Vladimir Plahotniuc and former parliamentary speaker Marian Lupu. Passed over for the presidency by Voronin in favor of Greceanii, Lupu announced just one week after Greceanii's final defeat that he was leaving the Communist Party.[167]

Lupu explained in an interview shortly afterward that the Communists no longer had anything to offer him were he to stay in the party. He confirmed that Voronin had calculated correctly by choosing Greceanii instead of him as the presidential successor in one sense: Lupu would not have been just a symbolic president of the kind Voronin wanted and thus would have threatened the stability of Voronin's power pyramid.[168] Lupu also emphasized in this interview (as well as publicly) that he and Voronin had developed deep differences in worldview over the years. He claimed that these differences had become too great to bear after the Communists launched what he called "very aggressive" and "nondemocratic" actions following the April 7 events, supplanting

[160] For example, *Infotag*, June 16, 2009; Moldova 1 Channel, "Mesager" news program, Russian-language, June 24, 2009, 19:00; NIT TV (Moldova), "Curier" news program (Russian-language), June 29, 2009, 23:45; and Communist Party TV advertisements shown just before Moldova 1 network, "Mesager" news program, Russian-language, 19:00 Moldova time; before after PRO-TV's news program, June 28, 2009, 19:30; and before NIT TV, "Curier" news program (Russian-language), June 28, 2009, 20:00. On the extent of media bias, see *Moldova Azi*, July 10, 2009.

[161] *Moldova Azi*, June 8, 2009, 19:22.

[162] *Kishinevskii Obozrevatel'*, June 25, 2009, p. 2.

[163] *Moldova Azi*, June 11, 2009, 18:19.

[164] *Infotag*, July 20, 2009.

[165] *Polit.Ru*, July 28, 2009, 17:12.

[166] *Polit.Ru*, June 3, 2009, 17:25.

[167] *Infotag*, June 10, 2009.

[168] Marian Lupu, author's interview, Chisinau, Moldova, June 29, 2009.

the pro-European and democratic agenda that Lupu said he had been pursuing all along within the party.[169] Implicitly recognizing the importance of expectations at this pivotal moment, Lupu added in one public statement:

We should not remain victims of rumors about the omnipotence of the Communist Party – it is strong only so long as we are afraid to stand up against it, and it is weak while certain in imagining itself as the only competent fundamental political force in this country. The April events showed that it is very vulnerable, particularly in moments when the scenario goes out of control. It becomes hysterical, incapable of resolving political conflicts cold-bloodedly and with honor.[170]

Asked in two separate instances why he did not leave the party earlier, Lupu replied he had felt a sense of obligation to the party for having given him his political career. This duty, he said, was paid in full with his complete support of the party in the election campaign that had just ended.[171]

With Lupu's defection came Plahotniuc's. The big businessman had reportedly backed Lupu within Voronin's pyramid to be the president's successor. Thus when Voronin passed Lupu over, Plahotniuc was reported by insiders to have entered into negotiations with political veteran Dumitru Diacov about joining and reinvigorating the latter's Democratic Party together with Lupu. The Democrats had won just 3 percent of the vote in the April election and so were interested in finding a way back to the political big time. Diacov later confirmed that Plahotniuc played a key role in his recruiting Lupu, who shortly after leaving the Communists indeed joined Diacov's Democrats in a move that dramatically shook up the political landscape.[172] Diacov said that pushing Lupu for president was the idea from the start and that this had not been possible for Lupu within the Communist Party.[173]

Explaining his choice for the Democrats, Lupu said that ideally he would have built a new party of his own, but there was no time or money. The Democrats not only offered a developed regional network, but crucially agreed to allow Lupu really to take over the party. This meant not only allowing Lupu to lead the party's candidate list but also installing other people from his personal network in key party posts so that he could actually take it over as party leader.[174]

---

[169] Lupu interview 2009; Marian Lupu, interview in paid-for campaign article in *Moldavskie Vedomosti*, June 26, 2010, p. 3. He also cites disappointment that the party refused to change its name from "Communist."

[170] Marian Lupu, interview in paid-for campaign article in *Moldavskie Vedomosti*, June 26, 2010, p. 3.

[171] Lupu interview 2009; Marian Lupu, interview in paid-for campaign article in *Moldavskie Vedomosti*, June 26, 2010, p. 3.

[172] Stack, "The Talented Mr. Plahotniuc"; *Tribuna.md*, June 15, 2012, 10:18. Lupu earlier had denied reports that Plahotniuc led him out of the Communist Party. See *Infotag*, August 10, 2010.

[173] Dumitru Diacov, author's interview, Chisinau, Moldova, June 25, 2009.

[174] Lupu interview 2009. Diacov (interview June 2009) confirmed this was part of the deal. See also Marian Lupu, interview in paid-for campaign article in *Moldavskie Vedomosti*, June 26, 2010, p. 3. Diacov became honorary chairman of the party.

As for other parties that had courted him, Lupu said, Filat's Liberal Democrats would not cede real control over the party (only backing him as presidential candidate and as top of the candidate list) while others were not consistent with the Left-centrist stance he shared with the Democrats.[175]

While Plahotniuc – who among other things still controlled the large Prime TV network – remained deep behind the scenes at this point, the public fusion of Lupu with the Democrats made the latter a new center of political gravity expected to win a delegation in the next parliamentary elections. This accordingly generated a series of defections of regional elites from other small parties and midlevel technocrats to the Democrats.[176] Relatively few Communist elites joined in, however.[177] There was some notable wavering among mass media after the April election stalemate, with the state-owned Moldova 1 television network broadcasting much more balanced news programming than previously, though in the final weeks of the July election campaign its reporting reverted to form.[178]

The Communists, with their political machine at full throttle as more important pieces were spinning off in a very uncertain political environment, now faced four viable opponents in the party competition. All were mounting fierce attacks on the Communists in their political advertisements, backed by significant administrative support (oligarchic groups, some media, some local administrations).[179] The three party leaders who had held out together in April and May continued their close cooperation, deciding to run separately but as a coordinated team that would once again refuse to compromise with the Communists.[180]

Lupu's reinvigorated Democrats also pledged not to vote for a Communist president.[181] Many observers, including the other anticommunist parties, treated them with some suspicion, wondering whether Lupu's defection was part of an elaborate Communist plot to collect the necessary 61 votes through two parties instead of one. Lupu, according to such a scenario, would rejoin his Communist colleagues in coalition after the voting.[182]

Meanwhile, the economy had begun to deteriorate rapidly in 2009 in the wake of the global financial crisis. A wave of particularly bad economic news

---

[175] Lupu interview 2009.

[176] E.g., *Infotag*, July 3, 2009; *Moldova Azi*, June 30, 2009, 16:44. On his control of Prime TV, see Stack, "The Talented Mr. Plahotniuc."

[177] E.g., *Moldova Azi*, July 1, 2009, 19:01.

[178] *Moldova Azi*, July 10, 2009, 16:28.

[179] *Moldova Azi*, June 29, 2009; Democratic Party ad shown just before Moldova 1 network, "Curier" news program, Russian-language, 19:00 Moldova time; Liberal Party Romanian language ad shown just before Moldova 1 network, "Mesager" news program, Russian-language, 19:00 Moldova time; *Moldova Azi*, July 6, 2009, 19:41.

[180] *Infotag*, June 15, 2009.

[181] Marian Lupu, interview in paid-for campaign article in *Moldavskie Vedomosti*, June 26, 2010, p. 3.

[182] *Infotag*, June 10, 2009; *Infotag*, July 17, 2009.

hit as the midyear point came and went prior to the election.[183] So bad was this news that the Communist-controlled government slashed the budgets of state institutions by 20 percent, including local state administrations. These, in turn, often cut the salaries of their employees, causing embarrassment for Prime Minister Greceanii (the Communists' choice for president) just a week before the crucial election.[184] Surely this must also have reduced incentives for local leaders to carry out any election shenanigans at Communist orders. And this happened despite Voronin's meeting Putin in Moscow and, claiming to have been a victim of an attempted color revolution, securing a $500 million credit to shore up the economy.[185] The Communists nevertheless continued to promise the population economic assistance from the state, including financial aid for agriculture.[186]

When election day rolled around, the Communists claimed about 4 percent more of the vote than had been reflected in an internationally funded Barometer exit poll.[187] Even so, their official share of the ballots had slipped to 45 percent. This proved enough only for 48 parliamentary seats, 3 votes shy even of a simple majority. The other parties to win seats now included not only the Liberals (15 percent), Liberal Democrats (17 percent), and Our Moldova Alliance (7 percent), but also the resurgent Democratic Party (13 percent). Together, these four secured 53 seats.

Rumors soon flew of Voronin's promising large personal payments to Lupu, Diacov, and other Democratic Party deputies in a desperate bid to cling to power. The Democrats were a particularly attractive potential partner for the PCRM because, together, their two delegations would have mustered exactly the 61 votes needed to fill all the country's major executive posts. By some accounts, the Communists were even ready to cede the presidency so long as Voronin could keep the speakership.[188] But Lupu dispelled any suspicions that he might be a "Voronin project" by sticking with the other opposition parties to reject any Communist offer. Instead, he joined the other opposition networks to form a four-party coalition dubbed the "Alliance for European Integration" (AEI). According to the deal, Filat, whose Liberal Democratic Party received the most votes, had his pick of official posts and opted for the prime ministership. Ghimpu was to get the parliamentary speakership, with Urechean accepting a lesser post of first deputy parliamentary speaker because of his party's weak showing. Lupu became the AEI's candidate for

[183] *Infotag*, July 23, 2009.
[184] *Moldova Azi*, July 21, 2009, 17:56.
[185] *Komsomolskaia Pravda v Moldove*, June 25–July 2, 2009, p. 2.
[186] *Moldova Azi*, June 30, 2009, 16:48.
[187] Institute for Public Policy, "Exit Poll 2009: 29 iulie 2009," IPP Web site, http://www.ipp.md/public/files/Barometru/Exit_Poll_29. 07_ora_21_final.pdf, accessed July 5, 2012.
[188] E.g., *The Guardian*, December 2, 2010, 02:00; Dumitru Diacov, author's interview, Chisinau, Moldova, March 17, 2010; Serafim Urechean, author's interview, Chisinau, Moldova, March 19, 2010.

president. Most importantly for the AEI, even before they could elect their own president, Voronin left that office in September, replaced by new parliamentary speaker Ghimpu as acting president pending what the AEI hoped would be Lupu's eventual election.[189]

These events, then, represented the Communists' ouster and the culmination of Moldova's 2009 revolution. This was a revolution that had much more to do with elite network coordination and succession politics than with Twitter or any other social networking platform. Voronin's expected presidential succession had combined with the centrifugal incentives that the parliamentarist constitution gave other networks to undermine his single-pyramid system. But the public at large also played a role through the mass mobilization of April 7 and their patterns of support that influenced how many parliamentary seats each elite group could claim, enabling the opposition to stand down the Communists dramatically. By denying them a single parliamentary vote, they were able to shake widespread expectations of Voronin's future dominance and ultimately shatter them in the July 29 election.

Denouement: The Democratic Upside of Moldova's Parliamentarism

With Voronin no longer expected by elites to dominate Moldovan politics, the country entered into a vibrant period of competing-pyramid politics. The Communist machine had finally been dislodged, but there was no single pre-formed power pyramid to replace it. Instead, it was succeeded by a coalition of rival networks representing distinct business and political interests and views. The relatively high executive divisibility of Moldova's parliamentarist constitution enabled them to strike a power-sharing deal anchored in the country's three chief formal executive posts. This put each network that occupied one of the three posts in position to shore up its own public support and coordinate at least some other networks around its own authority. The resulting combination of relatively even formal power and relatively even public support put each network in position to resist any attempts at power usurpation by any of the other networks. Moreover, Moldova's version of parliamentarism (requiring 61 of 101 parliamentary votes to elect a president) also meant that the opposition coalition could not even finalize its own internal deal without some support from the ousted Communists. And the Communists retained significant media, financial, and regional administrative assets to wield in future battles. This ultimately opened up the political system still further, forcing the AEI itself to compromise with others following what turned out to be nearly two full years of political wrangling.

After the opposition had stood firm against them in the presidential selection process in the spring, in the summer and fall it was the Communists' turn to hold ranks and stymie the new AEI coalition. The AEI had the simple

[189] Ghimpu held both posts until the next election.

majority of votes in parliament it needed to have Filat elected PM and Ghimpu parliamentary chair, and this was quickly achieved. But it would need eight Communist deputies to break with Voronin if it was to get Lupu installed as president.

Lupu initially expressed optimism that there were other Communist deputies waiting to follow his lead in a cascade of defection once they ceased to be afraid.[190] Cracks in the Communist delegation did indeed appear. Two senior figures in the Communist delegation, Victor Stepaniuc (a longtime core party member and reputed rival to Voronin's chief strategist, Tkaciuk, in the network) and Vladimir Turcan (a party nonmember and former first deputy parliamentary chair), called on their colleagues to back Lupu in the second and final attempt to elect the president, on December 7, 2009.

A plenary meeting of the Communist Party leadership, however, decided not only to reject a deal with Lupu but also to boycott the actual voting (which was by secret ballot) so as to prevent any unexpected defections. Stepaniuc and Turcan were warned to heed this boycott, and they ultimately did.[191] As a result, Lupu won only the 53 votes of the AEI deputies. Stepaniuc, Turcan, and two other Communist parliamentarians did wind up abandoning the Communist Party later that month and soon formed a small "United Moldova" party delegation in parliament, but this was too little, too late.[192] This parliament could hold no more presidential elections (two being the limit) and accordingly it was required to dissolve the following year.[193]

Anticipating a new round of political battle with no single overwhelming favorite to win, the country's networks jockeyed for position. Lesser networks increasingly sought to maximize their chances for future political success by identifying and aligning with potential winning patrons and abandoning likely losers. The bigger networks struggled to strengthen their positions as potential winners and thereby attract support from other elites who could help make this a reality.

The AEI took important steps to establish itself as dominant and weaken networks that all the member parties opposed. One important move was to replace the director of the important nationwide Moldova 1 television network, radically changing its coverage from its previous pro-Communist bias to what appeared to be a more balanced editorial policy that did not leave the AEI beyond criticism.[194] While the private NIT network remained quite evidently friendly to the Communists, broadcasting a variety of harshly

[190] *Today's Zaman*, August 1, 2009.
[191] *Moldova Azi*, December 7, 2009, 16:01; *Moldova Azi*, December 7, 2009, 16:02.
[192] *Moldova Azi*, January 13, 2010, 10:55.
[193] The law required parliamentary dissolution after two failures to elect a president, though it also held that the parliament could not be dissolved within a year of the most recent dissolution.
[194] *Moldova Azi*, March 2, 2010, 14:10. An example of more balanced coverage was its broadcast of the news program "Mesager" on March 19, 2010, 19:00.

critical reports about AEI members,[195] it also complained of growing legal harassment from the AEI's prosecutor general's office for its coverage.[196] Prosecutors also filed a case accusing the Communists of illegally obtaining their headquarters building in downtown Chisinau[197] and brought charges against the Communists' former Interior Minister and Chisinau police chief and other Communist era police officials for crimes linked to the April 7 violence, such as the death of a protester.[198] The Ministry of Justice also refused to register a public association linked to Romania on grounds of extremism.[199] While many might regard some or all of these activities as legitimate efforts to restore justice, the point here is that they also served to signal the dominance of the AEI and (in most cases) to weaken their chief opponents, the Communists.

Network realignment proceeded apace during this period, each one seeking to coordinate around a likely winner who would maximize its chances at obtaining the benefits of patronal power in the emergent competing-pyramid system. The Communists continued to experience defections, though these were more of a steady trickle than a cascade. A fifth deputy defected from its parliamentary delegation, leaving it with 43 out of its original 48 as of March 2010, and a few other prominent figures announced they were leaving or resigning leadership posts.[200] Two Chisinau council deputies defected from the Communists to the Liberal Democrats and two Christian Democrats effectively disbanded their own party's official delegation and went over to the Liberals.[201] Voronin's network did manage to tighten its hold on some figures. For example, Igor Dodon, a technocratic economist who had risen to first deputy prime minister in the last Communist government, formally joined the Communist Party.[202] But the overall trend was in the other direction. Regional branches of smaller parties, like the Social-Democratic Party, continued to join with AEI parties. In the case of the Falesti district, the movement was to the Liberal Democrats.[203] The Our Moldova Alliance, which as the weakest member of the AEI could not secure for its leader one of the country's three main executive posts, also suffered hemorrhaging. With polls also showing it unlikely to clear the electoral threshold in the next elections, its parliamentary delegation dropped from

[195] E.g., criticism of the AEI in Konstantin Starysh, anchor and author, "Rezonans" program, NIT network, March 20, 2010, 20:00 and NIT channel, "Curier" Russian-language news program, March 18, 2010, 08:00, author's observations; and favorable coverage of the Communists on NIT TV, "Curier" (Russian-language), March 19, 2010, 20:00.

[196] *Infotag*, March 31, 2010.

[197] *Moldova Azi*, August 6, 2010, 14:13.

[198] *Infotag*, March 4, 2010.

[199] *Moldova Azi*, March 15, 2010, 17:47.

[200] *Imedia English*, March 18, 2010.

[201] *Panorama* (Moldova), March 19, 2010, p. 1.

[202] *Moldova Azi*, March 22, 2010, 17:14.

[203] *Infotag*, July 29, 2010.

7 members to just 4 by July 2010, not enough to remain formally registered in the parliament.[204]

Seeking to avoid what its leaders feared could be a new hung parliament should a new round of legislative elections be held, the AEI attempted to amend the constitution in order to alter the way the president was elected. What followed were seemingly endless public debates in which the AEI parties and the Communists frequently shifted position on related issues, including how the president should be elected, whether any change should be made by a parliamentary two-thirds majority or by referendum, and when such moves should occur. The AEI ultimately opted to reinstitute direct elections for the presidency via a referendum. The Communists declared a boycott of the referendum.[205] In an effort to thwart the boycott, the AEI continued using administrative methods that were now at their disposal, lowering the minimum turnout requirement for a referendum from three-fifths of registered voters to just one-third.[206] Expecting that their effort to restore direct presidential elections would succeed in light of opinion polls showing a vast majority of the population favored it,[207] tension among the AEI's two most popular figures[208] began to break out openly. Filat stated that the Liberal Democrats would run their own candidate instead of backing Lupu, after which he and Lupu engaged in a sharp verbal bout.[209] But the coalition was saved by the Communists, whose boycott contributed to a turnout of just 29 percent in the referendum. This rendered it invalid and thus defeated the attempt to restore direct presidential elections in Moldova.[210] A new parliamentary election, the third in less than two years, was scheduled for November 28, 2010.

With no power vertical in place, this election took place in a highly competitive environment that was judged by observers to be largely free and fair.[211] Campaign themes remained largely unchanged relative to the 2009 elections.[212] One notable development was the political "coming out" of the secretive oligarch Vladimir Plahotniuc, whom the Democratic Party slipped onto its candidate list for the first time just eight days before the election – and in no less than the number two slot, right behind Lupu.[213]

---

[204] *Moldova Azi*, July 16, 2010, 14:28.

[205] *RFE/RL News*, September 6, 2010.

[206] *Moldova Azi*, July 7, 2010, 10:46.

[207] *Infotag*, May 11, 2010.

[208] For poll results, see: *Infotag*, May 11, 2010; *Moldova Azi*, May 26, 2010, 17:08.

[209] *Moldova Azi*, August 4, 2010, 13:09; *Infotag*, August 10, 2010; *Infotag*, August 10, 2010.

[210] *RFE/RL News*, September 6, 2010.

[211] OSCE Office for Democratic Institutions and Human Rights, "Republic of Moldova Early Parliamentary Elections 28 November 2010," OSCE/ODIHR Election Observation Mission Final Report, Warsaw, January 26, 2011.

[212] Chamberlain-Creanga, "The Moldovan Parliamentary Election 2010."

[213] ADEPT, *e-Democracy*, http://www.e-democracy.md/elections/parliamentary/2010/docs/pdm/20101201/, accessed July 6, 2012.

The result was another stalemate. With Urechean's Our Moldova Alliance failing to clear the threshold with only 2 percent of the vote, the AEI was reduced to the three other parties in parliament. These claimed a total of 59 parliamentary seats, with the Liberal Democrats winning the lion's share of 32 (reflecting 29 percent of the vote), the Democrats 15 (13 percent of the vote), and the Liberals 12 (10 percent of the vote). The Communists saw their portion of the ballots decline to 39 percent, yielding 42 seats. This was not enough to block the election of prime minister and parliamentary speaker, but was enough to continue to block the AEI's choice for president. With the Liberal Democrats ascendant, the declining Our Moldova Alliance wound up merging with it.[214] Apparently less optimistic about his chances for becoming president than in 2009, Lupu replaced Ghimpu as parliamentary speaker and acting president while Filat remained prime minister. Ghimpu, whose party had the weakest showing of the three, was forced to wait if he desired one of the country's three top formal executive posts, hoping Lupu could win the presidency and thereby open up for him the parliamentary speaker spot. Still unable to find a presidential candidate able to win the necessary 61 votes, the AEI delayed presidential voting for more than a year after the parliamentary election.

The ice finally began to break in fall 2011. AEI representatives Filat, Lupu, and Plahotniuc agreed to approach the relatively young Communist parliamentarian Igor Dodon about whether he might consider leaving the Communist Party. Dodon had recently lost an extremely close race for Chisinau mayor to the incumbent Liberal Dorin Chirtoaca, and in so doing performed better than had any previous Communist candidate for this office. Feeling that he had demonstrated the value of a reformist approach, Dodon also felt sabotaged by political rivals within the Communist Party and stymied in his efforts to take on a greater leadership role within the party and reform it. Catching him at this moment, Democratic Party and Liberal Democratic Party representatives then made Dodon a conditional promise that the AEI would back Voronin's former prime minister Greceanii (a close Dodon ally still in the Communist parliamentary delegation though not a party member) as a compromise candidate for president. In return, Dodon would have to deliver the parliamentary votes from the Communist fraction that the AEI needed to elect a president.[215] With this promise in hand, Dodon, Greceanii, and a third Communist deputy, Veronica Abramciuc, dramatically announced in November that they were leaving the Communist parliamentary delegation. Moreover, to save the country from crisis, they announced they would vote for an AEI presidential candidate so long as that candidate was nonpartisan.[216] A presidential vote in the parliament was set for December 16, 2011.

[214] Serafim Urechean, interview, *Tribuna.md*, June 9, 2012, 09:00.
[215] Viorel Cibotaru, author's interview, Chisinau, Moldova, May 10, 2012; Igor Dodon, author's interview, Chisinau, Moldova, May 12, 2012; Mihai Ghimpu, author's interview, Chisinau, Moldova, May 10, 2012; *Infotag*, January 24, 2012.
[216] *Infotag*, March 12, 2012.

But as the vote approached, the AEI reneged on the deal and once again nominated Lupu for president, passing over Greceanii.[217] The coalition had apparently hoped that the "Dodon group," now that they had already been lured out of the Communist delegation, would acquiesce and vote for Lupu, who was after all also a former Communist. By some accounts, the reneging occurred after the government of Romania objected in very strong terms to Greceanii, who had been the prime minister to impose a visa regime on Romania and to expel its ambassador during the April 2009 crisis.[218] Dodon, Greceanii, and Abramciuc responded by voting against Lupu, who found himself once again on the losing side of a presidential ballot in parliament.[219] A second vote was scheduled for January 15, 2012. Lupu this time declared he would not run.[220] But as this second voting date approached and no agreement appeared likely, the Constitutional Court declared the first December vote null and void because some deputies had made their votes public when it was supposed to have been a secret ballot.[221] This conveniently meant that the next election could be rescheduled for a later date, buying some time for further negotiations.[222]

The AEI leadership returned to the drawing board, this time determined to find someone who would actually suit the Dodon group, which said that its original offer to back a nonpartisan candidate still stood. According to one insider's account, the Democrats and Liberal Democrats composed an initial list of fourteen names, but each crossed the other's names out except for two, but these two were then vetoed by the Liberal Party. The Liberals then suggested other names, one of which was Nicolae Timofti, a judge and Supreme Magistrate Council chair.[223] A top figure in one of the AEI parties confirmed that none of the negotiating parties wanted "a clearly active person" and that it was evident Timofti could be expected not to interfere in the balance of power within the governing coalition.[224] Ghimpu said that Timofti was also seen as essentially neutral and unlikely to build his own power *vertikal*'.[225] Along with being perceived as unlikely to collaborate with any of the parties, Timofti had the advantage (from the AEI perspective) of having had difficult relations with the Communists. He had been removed as a judge on the Supreme Judicial Chamber (supreme court) by them in 2005 and was installed in his current job reportedly because it was thought he would be less able to cause trouble for the PCRM there.[226] The Dodon group agreed to the choice of Timofti. The

[217] *Infotag*, December 16, 2011.
[218] Cibotaru interview 2012; Ghimpu interview 2012.
[219] *RFE/RL*, December 16, 2011.
[220] *Infotag*, January 9, 2012.
[221] *Infotag*, January 16, 2012.
[222] *RFE/RL*, January 12, 2012.
[223] Ghimpu interview 2012.
[224] Senior figure in one of the AEI parties, author's interview, Chisinau, Moldova, May 2012.
[225] Ghimpu interview 2012.
[226] Arkadie Barbarosie, author's interview, Chisinau, Moldova, May 10, 2012.

Communists called a massive protest to start an hour and a half before the scheduled 3:00 pm vote on March 16, 2012, but the parliamentary leadership moved the vote up to 8:00 am to prevent trouble. Thus early in the morning, in a building surrounded by special troops in bulletproof vests, helmets, and gas masks, Timofti was elected president.[227]

Moldova's three-year political deadlock was finally over, but competition among the country's most influential networks was not – a robust competing-pyramid situation sustained in large part by a parliamentarist constitution with high executive divisibility. With the reputedly neutral Timofti now president, the three-party AEI had only two top executive posts to choose from. As per their earlier agreement, the parties with the most votes would get priority. Thus the Liberal Democrats' Filat retained the prime ministership while the Democrats, giving up the presidency, kept Lupu as parliamentary chair and Plahotniuc as first deputy chair. This left the Liberals out. Ghimpu had accepted this unsatisfactory result as a lesser evil than continued stalemate and feared that the Communists could improve their position should new elections be called.[228] He also calculated, however, that the coalition was sufficiently credibly self-reinforcing to thwart attempts by any of his partners to usurp much power. Filat, who as prime minister and leader of the largest number of AEI deputies was in the strongest position to construct a single-pyramid system of his own, still depended on both the Democrats and Liberals in parliament for his post, constraining his ability to build a power *vertikal'*.[229] And both the Democrats and Liberals, as noted earlier, believed Timofti would also resist such efforts, and indeed the Liberals claimed credit for suggesting him for the presidential post. In one early indication that Timofti was willing to keep AEI coalition members in check, he called for investigation of several raids on Moldovan banks from offshore companies that some linked to the Democrats' Plahotniuc.[230] The Liberal Democrats (among whom the Filat and ASCOM networks were prominent) and the Democrats (with the Plahotniuc and Lucinschi networks centrally placed) were each in strong informal and formal position to resist any encroachment by the other. Indeed, tensions between them frequently bubbled up into media reporting during and after 2012,[231] and each was careful not to let the other gain sole control over state assets that could tip the balance one way or the other.[232]

One point the AEI members could agree on was the threat the Communists posed to their power; thus a number of measures were taken against the PCRM after Timofti's installation that strongly resembled tactics Voronin had once used

---

[227] *Infotag*, March 16, 2012.
[228] Ghimpu interview 2012; *Infotag*, April 5, 2012; *Infotag*, May 5, 2012.
[229] Ghimpu interview 2012.
[230] *Infotag*, June 29, 2012.
[231] *Infotag*, June 18, 2012, 14:00.
[232] E.g., splitting up the Center for Fighting Economic Crimes and Corruption rather than let it fall under either parliament or government: *Tribuna.md*, June 18, 2012, 09:02.

against them. In April 2012, a regulatory agency stripped the nationwide pro-Communist NIT television network (reputedly controlled by former president Voronin's son, Oleg) of its license and forced it off the air, citing biased reporting.[233] The pro-Communist Omega information agency also reported that one of its journalists was badly beaten and suspected political motives since his valuables were not taken.[234] Prime Minister Filat also called for an investigation of railway construction deals involving Oleg Voronin.[235] Perhaps most dramatically, in a move that some considered the price the Liberals had extracted from the coalition in return for agreeing to a junior formal position within it, the AEI voted not only to create a series of museums of "Soviet occupation" and a textbook called *Communist Crimes*, but also to ban communist symbolism in politics outright. Over heated Communist objections, the ban took effect October 1, 2012.[236]

Nevertheless, the Communists stood ready as an ally of convenience in parliament for any AEI member wanting to resist political overstepping on the part of another AEI member, thereby reinforcing the competing-pyramid system. To be sure, the PCRM continued to experience a steady trickle of defections after the AEI finally elected a president. In June 2012, a group of three more parliamentarians led by longtime party heavyweight Vadim Misin declared it was leaving the party in order to create a new one.[237] The PCRM also suffered losses at the regional level, as with the mayor of the Soroca district, who announced he was joining Filat's Liberal Democratic Party so as better to defend the interests of his constituents.[238] Voronin himself admitted the party had lost forty-four hundred members since going into opposition.[239] The Communists still had, however, the single largest party delegation in parliament as well as strong representation in elected organs of local government. It also proved it could rally huge numbers of supporters to the streets, bringing close to one hundred thousand out to protest the parliamentary vote for Timofti, which it argued was illegitimate.[240]

The Communists played their role as "ally of convenience" with strategic gusto. As worries arose that Prime Minister Filat was gaining too much authority, the Plahotniuc-Lupu Democrats teamed up with Communist deputies to oust him from the premiership through a parliamentary vote of non-confidence in March 2013.[241] In evident retaliation, Filat's Liberal Democratic Party joined forces the very next month with the Communists to vote Lupu out as chairman of parliament.[242] By 2014, then, secondary figures from each

[233] *Infotag*, April 6, 2012.
[234] *Panorama* (Moldova), May 9, 2012, p. 3.
[235] *Infotag*, June 25, 2012, 14:00.
[236] *RFE/RL*, October 1, 2012.
[237] *Infotag*, June 7, 2012.
[238] *Tribuna.md*, June 22, 2012, 10:00.
[239] *Tribuna.md*, May 29, 2012, 10:00.
[240] *Reuters*, March 16, 2012, 5:10 pm.
[241] *Infotag*, March 5, 2013.
[242] *Infotag*, April 25, 2013.

of the major governing "pyramids" were occupying the country's top formal posts, Iurie Leanca from the Liberal Democrats as prime minister (also with ties to the ASCOM Group) and Igor Corman from the Democratic Party as parliamentary chair. Plahotniuc resigned his position as MP in late 2013, though he made clear he was remaining active in the larger political network. The Liberal Party did not gain significantly from this infighting between the Democrats and Liberal Democrats. After Liberal leader Ghimpu became increasingly brutal in criticizing Filat, calling him not only corrupt but essentially a Russian stooge, Filat returned fire. Soon, more than half of the Liberals' parliamentary delegation broke with Ghimpu, sending the party into bitter internal feuding. Eventually, the defecting Liberals joined with Filat's Liberal Democrats and the Democrats to form a new coalition, now called the Coalition for Pro-European Governance, leaving Ghimpu and his loyalists in opposition.[243] Moldova as of mid-2014, therefore, featured a robust competing-pyramid system that had sustained itself for five years after the downfall of Voronin's single-pyramid system. It remains possible, however, that this could change, for example, if the Communists are able to take advantage of the resulting political openness to once again win 61 seats in parliamentary elections scheduled for late 2014.

Conclusion

The preceding analysis has illustrated how patronal parliamentarism tends to promote the construction of a single-pyramid system more strongly than divided-executive constitutions do, but that it also involves certain incentives that tend to complicate – relative to patronal presidentialism – any one network's efforts to create such a system. We thus see how, in a single election in 2001, Voronin's Communists were able unilaterally to capture all three major executive posts that Moldova's parliamentarist constitution created. Since he personally could occupy only one of the posts, he avoided the risk that the occupants of the others might start to challenge his authority by carefully choosing people who were in especially weak position to build up the networks in parliament necessary to challenge him. These were typically individuals who had reputations as technocrats rather than network-building politicians and who were usually not actual members of the party. He thereupon began building up a patronal power pyramid much as presidents in post-Soviet presidentialist systems had, starting to squeeze opposition and align other prominent networks (especially business and media) with his power vertical. He was also able to move to the most advantageous position on the political spectrum (a proindependence and pro-EU agenda) and thereby steal some of the thunder from his most potent opposition, the Christian Democratic nationalists. Thus while the Communists failed to win the supermajority that the parliamentarist constitution required for electing all three top executive posts again in the 2005

---

[243] See *Infotag*, April 19, 2013; *Infotag*, May 31, 2013.

elections, they were in good position to co-opt the Christian Democrats and others to reestablish the dominance of Voronin's pyramid for another term.

This co-optation, however, forced the Communists to promise certain concessions. These concessions did more than directly complicate Communist efforts to tighten their pyramid of power (for example, by weakening their grip on election commissions). They also created incentives for other forces to hold out from the Communists so as to gain the power to extract similar, if not bigger, concessions in the future. This combined with a presidential succession crisis induced by Voronin's leaving office in 2009 to enable opposition networks to mount a major challenge. While they did not initially dislodge the Communists from power, through massive protests against apparent fraud and a refusal to accept minor concessions they managed to shake the image of the Communists' inevitable hegemony, especially against the backdrop of brewing economic problems with roots in the global financial crisis. This induced a new round of key elite defections to the opposition, which in turn ultimately led to the Voronin machine's fall from power. What followed was a coalition among three major rival networks that, thanks to the parliamentarist constitution, could be underpinned by the allocation of three significant chief formal executive posts among different networks (or to figures seen as neutral). Thus while the different networks in the resulting Alliance for European Integration (and its successor, the Coalition for Pro-European Governance) did display signs of desiring to amass authority for themselves, they tended to be thwarted by their partners in other key posts at critical junctures. And this, most likely, deterred at least some additional efforts. The result since 2009, therefore, has been a vibrant competing-pyramid system in Moldova underpinned by a parliamentarist constitution with high executive divisibility.

Several important conclusions can be ventured at this point. For one thing, we see that it is a mistake to regard parliamentarist constitutions as inherently working against closure of the political system. Relative to divided-executive constitutions, which generally require a party to win two separate elections through two separate methods of translating votes into seats and often at different points in time, parliamentarist constitutions create an opportunity for a single political network to win control of all major posts in a single battle, a parliamentary election. We saw this not only in Moldova in 2001, but also more recently in Hungary, where the Fidesz Party has been widely criticized after winning a supermajority in parliament for unilaterally changing the constitution to its advantage and moving to close the political system.[244]

---

[244] See Freedom House, "Freedom in the World 2012," available at www.freedomhouse.org, accessed February 17, 2014. Hungary, of course, has lower levels of patronalism than the post-Soviet countries in focus in this volume, making establishment of a power *vertikal'* there more difficult and more likely to meet resistance. We will return to this discussion in Chapter 12.

In addition, we see that revolutions and regime cycles look somewhat different in patronal parliamentarist countries than they do in patronal presidentialist ones. Patronal presidential regime cycles tend to be much more tightly tied to both presidential succession and the degree of public support wielded by the presidential team because the occupancy of a single formal office carries such weight. In patronal parliamentarist countries, depending on which top executive offices exist (executive divisibility) and what the thresholds are for filling them (the share of the second-tier selectorate required for a winning coalition), the expected benefits from distancing one's network from the dominant network are greater. This renders challenges more likely than under patronal presidentialism when a chief patron is not particularly unpopular or in an election that does not involve questions of succession. This accordingly means that any one patron's attempts to steal an election are more likely to provoke a strong reaction from both elites and masses so long as accusations of fraud become both widely known and seen as credible. Thus in Moldova, whether or not there actually was an attempt to steal the April 2009 election, the result appeared highly suspicious and helped generate a mass turnout for protests that opposition elites with the patronal resources they controlled had organized substantially in advance. This may well have prompted the Communists to back away from an attempt to steal the election and resulted in their eventual downfall through new elections.

Third, the Moldovan case provides grounds for questioning the notion that appears in some accounts that identity divides in and of themselves tend to be sources of political openness. Some have written, for example, that Moldova has remained relatively more democratic than most other post-Soviet countries because of inherent social divisiveness, especially that resulting from divisions over whether its identity lies more with the West (including Romania) or the East (including Russia).[245] This identity divide, the account goes, makes it hard for any one force to establish dictatorial control. While there is no denying that Moldova is in fact divided in how elites and citizens perceive their identity, there is little evidence that this has actually thwarted Moldovans' ability to promote authoritarian policies. As we have seen, Voronin found that his political machine enabled him in large part to co-opt his main nationalist opposition in 2005 and craft a moderate pro-European stance that left both pro-Romanian nationalists and pro-Russian nationalists marginalized. Moreover, when the Moldovan polity became intensely polarized on national grounds, this happened largely at the initiative of the Communists themselves. Voronin's forces saw political benefit in attempting to taint their main opposition with the brush of extreme pro-Romanian "unionism," which was supported only by a small minority in Moldova at the time. The strongest pro-Russian forces could likewise be branded as unacceptable extremists.

[245] Dmitrii Furman, "Kommunisty i demokratiia," *Nezavisimaia Moldova*, May 4, 2009; Dmitrii Furman, "Udivitel'naia Moldova," *Rossiia v global'noi politike*, v. 5, no. 5, 2007, pp. 186–96; Way, "Pluralism by Default in Moldova"; Lucan A. Way, "Weak States and Pluralism: The Case of Moldova," *East European Politics and Societies*, v. 17, no. 3, pp. 454–82.

All this was most evident between April and July 2009, when it was the Communists themselves applying the strongest efforts to make national identity issues salient and to polarize the electorate. Thus one cannot say that somehow "identity" bubbled up to block Communist dominance exogenously of the Communists' own strategy of rule. This fits well with patterns in the rest of the former Soviet space, where identity divides have generally not hindered authoritarian developments and have tended instead to be more of a resource in the hands of hybrid regime leaders seeking to manipulate electoral outcomes successfully (a resource that is not always used successfully since it is often employed as a last resort). Key institutional structures, especially formal constitutional arrangements, do a better job of explaining not only patterns but dynamics in regime opening and closure and in the activation and deactivation of identity divides in politics.[246]

Finally, some have argued that hybrid regimes (especially competitive authoritarian regimes) tend to be most stable and most closed when they are based on a dominant political party, which is said to do this work through strong organization and party discipline. This argument has been made to explain Voronin's rise in Moldova with respect to his Communist Party.[247] The problem is that by citing party strength to explain regime strength, one is essentially just pushing back the explanation a small step without really uncovering what makes organizations like parties or states "strong." In Moldova's case, we have seen that while the Communist Party did play an important role, it was not so much party organization, scope, or discipline that mattered, even though these are common stereotypes about the nature of communist parties. If the key was *party* organization and discipline, we would have expected Voronin to put in all the most crucial posts precisely *party* officials, those most subject to the discipline, organization, and loyalty said to be important. But as we have seen, a key to Voronin's success in overcoming the network-fraying incentives of a parliamentarist constitution with high executive divisibility was in fact precisely that he tended to appoint *nonparty* officials to these posts. Most importantly, this included making Tarlev and Greceanii his prime ministers. This is anticipated by the logic of patronal politics, but not by theories focusing on the organization and discipline of parties.

Moreover, the Communist delegation in parliament did experience a major flow of defections from key leaders at precisely the times predicted by the logic of patronal politics. This began when an anticipated presidential succession approached and continued as expectations of the Communists' future

[246] For a fuller version of this argument examining patronal presidential cases, see Hale, "Identity Divides as Authoritarian Resource: Post-Soviet Cases over Twenty Years," paper prepared for presentation at the Association for the Study of Nationalities annual meeting, April 19–21, 2012, Columbia University, New York.

[247] Lucan A. Way, "Authoritarian State-Building and the Sources of Regime Competitiveness in the Fourth Wave: The Cases of Belarus, Moldova, Russia, and Ukraine," *World Politics*, v. 57, January 2005, pp. 231–61.

hegemony were increasingly shaken. Since no major change in Communist organization occurred around this time, such events would seem to weigh against accounts that speculate party organizations are somehow not subject to the same forces that influence the coherence of political organizations more generally, including state organization. More fundamental is the logic of *expectations* that underpins the logic of patronal politics and tells us when organizations are likely to be strong and disciplined in highly patronalistic contexts and when they are likely to break down. The next chapter takes stock of these and other findings in the volume so far, relating them to other factors that are often cited as accounting for at least some part of post-Soviet regime dynamics.

Explaining Post-Soviet Regime Dynamics

Now that the discussion of the details of every highly patronalistic post-Soviet polity is complete, it is appropriate to step back and consider the cumulative findings in light of other factors that have frequently been invoked by observers to explain regime dynamics in Eurasia. This penultimate chapter thus takes on several important tasks. It begins by identifying some of the main lessons learned in this volume's analysis, starting with the need to think differently about formal institutions, less about "regime change," and more in terms of extended patronalistic *networks* and *regime dynamics* that primarily consist of patterns over time in how these networks come to be arranged and rearranged, constituted and reconstituted. Formal institutions like constitutions and elections matter, but in different ways that are not always obvious from a Western perspective. Often they produce *cyclic* patterns of politics that a focus on "transition" or "regime change" can misdiagnose. After summing up these conclusions and the evidence for them, the chapter seeks to identify clearly what this book is *not* about, including explaining important variation in *types* of single-pyramid and competing-pyramid systems as well as in the particular characteristics of the networks that they comprise. Such questions constitute a fecund agenda for future research. The chapter also directly addresses factors that astute readers are sure to notice are deemphasized as explanations of regime dynamics, factors that feature prominently in many other accounts, such as international actors, transnational diffusion processes, leadership characteristics, patterns of private ownership, the spread of social media, and even state strength and weakness. Most of these are shown to represent secondary influences on regime dynamics in the post-Soviet context or to be largely endogenous to the factors emphasized in this volume, though some will prove more important when one shifts from explaining variation within the set of post-Soviet cases to looking at what might make these cases different from those in other parts of the world, the subject of Chapter 12.

A Patronal Politics Perspective on Regime Dynamics

This volume has proceeded from the assumption that much of the world cannot take the rule of law, the lead role of formal institutions, and the primacy of issue- and identity-based politics for granted. Instead, many societies are essentially trapped in a *patronalistic* social equilibrium whereby individuals collectively struggle for economic and political gain (or almost any other kind of gain) primarily through extended networks of actual acquaintance and through personalized rewards and punishments. This contrasts with societies organizing such pursuits around "imagined communities"[1] that unite people who have certain perceived traits in common (such as leftist political views, a common ethnic background, or party membership) but who have not actually met or who are not joined together primarily through chains of common acquaintance and exchange. In more commonly used terms, it is a context where the rule of law and social capital are low and corruption is high, though we must keep in mind that what one society brands as "corrupt" may be legalized in another and thus not formally involve the illegality that the term corruption usually connotes. It is an equilibrium because it represents a kind of self-fulfilling prophecy in which individuals do not generally see themselves as likely to be better off by bucking the patronalistic logic themselves. To refuse to use one's position in the state to help one's relatives and friends, for example, could risk leaving one without crucial favor bank assets that could actually help accomplish the goals of the state in other instances. Such a refusal could also draw the ire of these friends and relatives, who might see such an official as ineffective, selfish, or even arrogant, carrying a holier-than-thou attitude. Similarly, a great deal of research cited earlier has shown that when people believe everyone else is paying bribes to get essential services, they themselves feel justified in doing the same lest they be left the honest "sucker" who stands up for principle but only winds up worse off than everyone else. Given the complexity of society, such expectations can be extremely hard to change. This is especially so when they are embedded in entire elaborate informal or even formal institutions that people simply come to accept as "the way things are." The present author cannot come close to counting the times he has heard local problems written off with a shrugging "What do you expect? This is Russia/Ukraine/Azerbaijan/Moldova/Kazakhstan/Armenia/Kyrgyzstan." Visitors to many other patronalistic parts of the world undoubtedly have heard the same said about other countries by their own residents.

In such a highly patronalistic context, the preceding chapters have attempted to show, it can be helpful to understand politics in terms that are rather different from the way they are understood in less patronalistic contexts. One helpful starting point is to think less in terms of formal institutions such as "political parties" or "state agencies" as the elemental collective actors in society, and

[1] Anderson, *Imagined Communities*.

more in terms of extended patronal networks. These networks are typically led by chief patrons, but do not boil down to these individuals as individuals. They usually have bases in some kind of formal institutions such as a holding company or a state executive office, but the most important of them almost always transcend such entities. Instead, their personalistic reach tends to stretch out to include individuals in a wide variety of other institutions, and their relationships to any given formal institution can change over time without the network itself changing substantially. Business networks, for example, frequently extend into branches of the state, and vice versa, and an oligarch may become a state official without a dramatic change in the composition of his or her network itself. Networks usually do not boil down to actual kinship or ethnic bonds even though the jargon of "clan" and "family" is commonplace and concentrations in certain groups certainly does occur. Major patronal networks in fact are almost always at least somewhat multiethnic and include members through many other kinds of ties that involve significant investment in the interpersonal relationships at hand, including those built among classmates, coworkers, or neighbors. In this sense, the often-exoticized networks of Central Asia are not fundamentally different from patronal networks in Russia or Ukraine.

Politics in highly patronalistic societies is generally best conceived as a dynamic process by which such networks are continually constituted, reconstituted, arranged, rearranged, and dissolved. While the forms of such (re-)constitution and (re-)arrangement are potentially infinite, this volume has focused on one important set of patterns: the dynamic configuration of patronalistic networks between ideal-type single-pyramid and competing-pyramid patterns. Because network survival and well-being depend on having access to power, and because a network's power depends largely on having powerful allies and large numbers of influential members, individuals and networks are likely to gravitate to those networks to which they expect other individuals and networks to gravitate. There is thus an important self-fulfilling prophecy involved in the network politics of highly patronalistic societies: Those networks that are expected to become powerful tend to *become* powerful because this very expectation tends to attract members, who in turn make it more powerful. Put in other words, patronal politics is largely about the efforts of elites and the networks they constitute to *coordinate* their activities such that they do not wind up on a losing side at the same time they have incentive to compete to wind up on top. Elections thus matter less because they are a source of legitimacy or popular mandate and more because they are crucial tests of network strength that facilitate elite coordination around winners and discourage it around losers. In some sense, they are a framework for civil war among networks by peaceful means.

It is in this context that we can also understand how formal constitutions can matter in societies where formal law is frequently disregarded or outright violated. Presidentialist constitutions tend to signal the potential dominance of one single patron and thus generally facilitate the gradual coordination of elite networks around the person of the president, promoting (though not determining) a single-pyramid arrangement. Divided-executive constitutions, on the other hand, tend to complicate such coordination, instead creating incentives for coordination around multiple centers of patronal power and for the formation of a competing-pyramid system.

It is very important not to conflate this analysis with the old debate between parliamentarism and presidentialism, nor with the debate over how powerful parliaments should be. One important reason is that divided-executive constitutions are not parliamentarist constitutions and have crucially different effects in highly patronalistic societies. Parliamentarist constitutions, especially when they provide for a united executive branch, can also promote the coordination of elite networks around a single patron and produce single-pyramid systems that quite closely resemble those that tend to be encouraged by presidentialist constitutions. The extent to which they do so, however, depends on their degrees of executive divisibility and the number of formal selectorates they involve in filling executive posts. That is, the more divided and equally endowed executive posts there are, and the more votes that a network has to win to fill any of these posts with their representative, the greater capacity there is for networks to anchor credible (self-reinforcing) power-sharing deals, weakening the tendency to single-pyramid politics. Even so, however, the fact that a single election win can enable one network to capture every major executive post makes parliamentarism inherently risky in patronal polities: A momentary overwhelming surge in popularity for one party can set in motion a tip toward single-pyramid politics even when the parliamentarist constitution provides for high executive divisibility and multiple formal selectorates. Accordingly, the more that divided-executive constitutions separate the electoral tests of network strength they stipulate through differences in time or election rules, the less likely it is that a single network will capture all chief executive offices.

Stepping back from this discussion of the fundamental differences between parliamentarist, divided-executive, and presidentialist formal constitutions, it is crucial to keep in mind that none of this requires anyone actually to obey the words on the constitution's parchment about which powers the president actually has. Instead, the constitution is simply helping elite networks coordinate both their legal and their constitution-disregarding behavior around either a single patron or multiple patrons. This has several vital implications that we find reflected in the post-Soviet space.

For one thing, because constitutions do not simply "take effect" but instead create incentives for what can be a difficult and contested process of coordination, one would expect time to become an important factor in explaining the degree of openness or closure of a polity at any given moment. The incentives are toward a single-pyramid system with a presidentialist constitution, but to move too fast is for a president to overreach, provoking the very kind of large-scale coordinated defection to the opposition that the president seeks to foreclose. That is, we would expect – and actually find – presidentialist countries to grow increasingly closed over time as the chief patrons are gradually able to coordinate these complicated, extended networks around themselves in a single pyramid of authority. And in the immediate aftermath of a thoroughgoing state collapse, one shaking loose prior conceptions of what constitutes power, one would expect this regular process of single-pyramid formation to become dominant only as leaders gradually learn the new political ropes and as the most incompetent are eliminated through a process akin to natural selection.

Another crucial implication is that this process can be radically disrupted when the expectations of a patron's dominance that underpin it happen to change. When key people constituting a country's main networks start to believe a sitting patron is not likely to be around after a certain point in time to reward loyalty and mete out punishment for behavior undertaken now, they have incentive to start thinking about the future immediately, orienting themselves to whoever they think is most likely to be the next chief patron and is also willing to accept them as allies. They might also consider trying to capture the state for themselves, becoming the dominant network. What had moments before seemed an impregnable single pyramid of patronalistic power can suddenly crumble almost entirely as the coalition of networks that constitute it and carry out its bidding falls apart. In such a situation, each network typically jockeys for position under what its chief patron expects to be a new pyramid of authority, though often without knowing for sure exactly who will wind up being that new pyramid's chief patron and core membership.

The factors that inform networks' expectations as to who is likely to win such struggles thus become particularly potent forces driving regime dynamics in patronalistic societies. The preceding pages have found that these include not only skill in backroom maneuvering and a reputation for wielding the machinery of power effectively, but also genuine public support – at least, when the institution of contested elections is in place. This is because manufacturing an official election result, the recognized measure of relative political power, is easier when one wields genuine popular support relative to rivals and more costly when one lacks it. All other considerations equal, therefore, networks looking to wind up with a future winner are likely to find the most popular potential candidates the most attractive. Competing networks thus also have incentive to cultivate public support, or at least the appearance of it, a goal that can be accomplished in part by organizing or supporting massive street rallies.

When such actions produce an opposition victory in the struggle, they can appear to be "revolutions" even though the underlying political system has not actually changed at all. Revolutions in patronal presidential systems, therefore, should not generally be mistaken for a change in regime.[2] In fact, even if an opposition network captures the presidency in a patronal presidential system after winning support through democratic rhetoric and mobilizing

---

[2] See the definition given in Chapter 1. The question of regime type is discussed further toward the end of this chapter.

prodemocracy masses on the streets, and even if the opposition leaders actually do genuinely intend to democratize, the reappearance of single-pyramid politics is still quite likely for all the reasons documented earlier so long as the patronalistic nature of society and the presidentialist constitution have not changed. This can also be true of patronal parliamentarism under certain widespread circumstances, as Chapter 10 revealed in the case of Moldova. This is the logic of *regime cycles* documented in this volume, cycles whereby periods of gradual regime closure are radically interrupted as expectations of a leader's departure tend to break the emerging single-pyramid arrangement down into a competing pyramid moment, only to drift back to a single-pyramid configuration after the succession struggle is decided. In this sense, then, "revolutions" or other extraconstitutional forms of dominant network ouster can be quite normal features of regime dynamics in patronal presidential polities, indicating the continuity of the existing regime rather than its demise.

Across the former Soviet space nearing on a quarter-century, we have seen these patterns play themselves out in ways that are quite consistent with the specific predictions that Chapter 4 distilled from the logic of patronal politics. For one thing, Chapter 6 showed that after an initial period of irregular regime dynamics, punctuated by the rapid rise and fall of early patronal presidents, regularity eventually emerged with the formation of single-pyramid systems in all but one post-Soviet polity. Remarkably, this pattern holds even in Eurasia's unrecognized quasi-states.

The next three chapters established that regularity in regime cycles continued to dominate irregularity straight through mid-2014 among Eurasia's patronal presidential polities. Six of the ten patronal presidential ousters that occurred after the initial formation of single-pyramid systems strongly fit the pattern of regular "short" regime cycles. This includes not only the three classic color revolutions (Georgia 2003, Ukraine 2004, and Kyrgyzstan 2005), but also the downfall of dominant networks in Abkhazia in 2004, South Ossetia in 2012, and Georgia in 2013. In each of these cases, unpopular presidents fell from power through elections when they were either running up against a term limit or attempting to hand off presidential power to a handpicked successor. Two additional cases (Armenia 1998 and Kyrgyzstan 2010) also fit the anticipated pattern of regular short regime cycles, with patronal presidents meeting their demise when facing a lame-duck syndrome defined by election cycles, though their ousters took place prior to rather in the wake of succession-related elections. One more case, Transnistria, was shown to be defined by "long" regime cycle dynamics, with the president's aging – reaching the symbolic milestone of 70 – a crucial factor in inducing a lame-duck syndrome as the 2011 election approached.[3] Only one patronal presidential network ouster during this period,

---

[3] The ouster of Shevardnadze in the Rose Revolution is also consistent with a long regime cycle pattern. Not only was he in his constitutionally final term in office, but he was also older than age 70. Only four other patronal presidents had reached the age of 70 in office as of the time

the deposing of Viktor Yanukovych in Ukraine's Euromaidan Revolution, is clearly a case of irregularity in regime cycles.[4] Expectations of his demise were generated largely by his own egregious political mistakes against the backdrop of low popular support (even in his native eastern Ukraine) and essentially spontaneous mass protests triggered by Yanukovych's announcement that he would not sign a popular agreement at an approaching European Union summit. Chapter 9 then showed that the larger regime dynamics involved can indeed generally be regarded as cyclic. Each of these presidential ousters was followed by movement back toward single-pyramid politics unless the revolution also resulted in an end to the presidentialist constitution, meaning that the country no longer had a patronal presidentialist system.[5]

Chapter 8 provided additional confirmation of these regularities by examining patterns in patronal presidential polities that have not experienced ousters since their single-pyramid systems were first established. As a rule, presidential networks that survived lame-duck episodes and successfully installed their chosen successors featured incumbent presidents who either were significantly more popular (as with Armenia's Robert Kocharian, Azerbaijan's Heydar Aliyev, Nagorno-Karabakh's Arkady Ghukasian, and Russia's Vladimir Putin) or anointed a political heir who proved capable of winning overwhelming public support of his own in short order (as with the very unpopular Russian President Boris Yeltsin, who chose Putin to succeed him in 1999). Leaders who have not yet experienced any of the regular sources of lame-duck syndromes (old age or succession-related elections) have as a rule been highly resistant to overthrow. As was just mentioned, the toppling of Ukraine's Yanukovych in 2014 is the only clear example of a patronal presidential ouster owing to such irregular regime dynamics as of the time of this writing. The norm is defined by such cases as Azerbaijan's Ilham Aliyev, Belarus's Aliaksandr Lukashenka, Kazakhstan's Nursultan Nazarbaev, and Turkmenistan's Turkmenbashi[6] and Gurbanguly Berdymukhamedov, none of whom became a lame-ducks and all of whom avoided ouster, at least as of mid-2014.

While Chapters 6–9 established these patronal presidential regime dynamics through in-depth process tracing, the pattern also finds quantitative expression. Figure 11.1 tracks Freedom House's index of political rights, a good indicator of levels of political closure, from the point where Figure 6.1 left off (that is, since each country's initial single-pyramid system was created or, in

---

of this writing: Transnistria's Igor Smirnov was ousted via election in late 2011; the time of this writing; Azerbaijan's relatively popular Heydar Aliyev successfully ushered his son into office shortly before dying, while Kazakhstan's Nursultan Nazarbaev and Uzbekistan's Islom Karimov have just recently hit that mark and only Nazarbayev has run for reelection since doing so.

[4] The Abkhaz events of 2014, still developing at the time of this writing, may become counted as the second such case.

[5] It remains too early to judge clearly in the cases of South Ossetia and Transnistria, though events so far are not inconsistent with this pattern.

[6] He died suddenly in office.

a. Parliamentarist:

b. Presidentialist Polities Experiencing No Lame-Duck Syndrome:

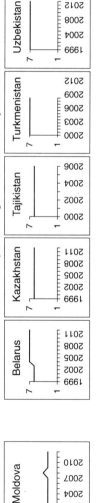

Moldova

Belarus · Kazakhstan · Tajikistan · Turkmenistan · Uzbekistan

c. Polities Experiencing Lame-Duck Syndrome but Substantial Popular Support for President:

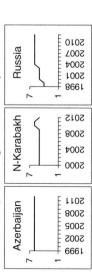

Azerbaijan · N-Karabakh · Russia

d. Polities Experiencing Lame-Duck Syndrome with Low Popular Support for President:

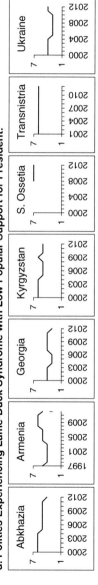

Abkhazia · Armenia · Georgia · Kyrgyzstan · S. Ossetia · Transnistria · Ukraine

FIGURE 11.1. Levels of political closure in post-Soviet polities after the emergence of initial single-pyramid systems to 2012. The starting point here is the year Figure 6.1 ended for each polity. As in Figure 6.1, political closure is measured by Freedom House's Freedom in the World "Political Rights" index (freedomhouse.org), which is represented on the vertical axis. A 7 refers to the least political rights (most political closure), 1 to the most rights (least political closure).

For unrecognized quasi-states, assessments of popular support for presidents do not include populations that were forced to flee or ethnically cleansed, as with the forcibly displaced Georgian residents of Abkhazia. The same is the case for any analogous populations of recognized states.

429

the case of Moldova, a parliamentarist system was adopted).[7] For one thing, it shows how the patronal presidential countries that have not yet faced a lame-duck syndrome have generally experienced steady or gradually tightening political closure.[8] The same is true for polities whose presidents have at some point experienced a lame-duck syndrome but who also have retained substantial support among their current residents.[9] And in the entities that have experienced at least one point when a lame-duck syndrome combined with low presidential popularity, we see evidence of the regime cycles described here. This is most evident in Georgia and Kyrgyzstan, where we see an opening corresponding with each country's color revolution soon followed by a phase of political closure, only to be followed again by an opening after a new presidential ouster. In Armenia, we observe how its 1998 palace coup generated a short-lived political opening that was then followed by a gradual political closure. In Ukraine, the graph reflects a political opening coinciding with the Orange Revolution, and a new, creeping political closure after Yanukovych rose to power and pushed through a reversion to presidentialist basic law. The picture presented by Figure 11.1 is less clear for the unrecognized statelets, as Freedom House did not record a significant increase in political rights after their presidential ousters in 2011 and 2012. We do, however, see the anticipated opening effect after Abkhazia's uncolored revolution, which was followed by another political opening following the incumbent president's death in 2011, which prompted a significant struggle for power among multiple heavyweight networks.

The analysis of post-Soviet cases in Chapters 9 and 10 also bears out Chapter 4's hypotheses as to how the logic of patronal politics should play out under nonpresidentialist constitutions. Because of the length of time it was in effect (2005–10), Ukraine remains the paradigmatic case of a divided-executive constitution in the former Soviet context at the time of this writing. As the theory anticipates, and indeed as was anticipated at the very outset of this period, this formal basic law was shown to have underpinned the most free and competitive politics seen in any post-Soviet country outside the Baltic states.[10] A promising opening relative to its past has so far been sustained in Kyrgyzstan under a new divided-executive constitution adopted in 2010, and Georgia's politics has been increasingly competitive since it started a multiyear shift to

[7] Please refer to the last two footnotes of Chapter 6 for a discussion of the meaning of the Freedom House scores and why Polity IV is unsuitable. For more rigorous analysis of patterns in these data, see other forthcoming work by the author.

[8] The patterns are also consistent with the importance of time discussed earlier, that coordinating networks in a single-pyramid arrangement requires patience and cannot be implemented all at once. Nevertheless, Freedom House political rights scores are a very blunt instrument for this kind of analysis because they can only move up or down in 1-point increments and the scale is limited to the range 1–7 (recall the discussion in Chapter 6).

[9] While Azerbaijan and Russia clearly fit this pattern, Nagorno-Karabakh experienced a slight opening according to Freedom House in 2012.

[10] See Henry E. Hale, "Regime Cycles: Democracy, Autocracy, and Revolution in Post-Soviet Eurasia," *World Politics*, v. 58, no. 1, October 2005, pp. 133–65.

a divided-executive model in 2010, with the new constitution going fully into effect only in late 2013. Researchers will need to watch Ukraine carefully after its reversion to such a constitution in 2014.

This contestation associated with divided-executive constitutions should not be confused with democratization as ordinarily conceived: What happened in Ukraine and what has happened in Kyrgyzstan and Georgia has essentially been a fragmentation of the formerly united political machine, with different branches of the machine openly competing against each other using all methods at their disposal, including highly "corrupt" ones. Ukraine's experience also testifies to the limits of divided-constitutions' potential for true democratization in other ways as well. In its 2010 presidential election, former Prime Minister Viktor Yanukovych's network decisively defeated its chief rivals and quickly capitalized on the expectations of his future dominance this created to induce a series of elite defections and capture not only the presidency but the prime ministership. This enabled him to restore the presidentialist constitution that had existed prior to the Orange Revolution. Divided-executive constitutions do tend to create incentives that promote their own endurance and longer-run political opening, as Ukraine's did in helping defeat multiple prior efforts by Yanukovych or his rivals to build a single-pyramid system prior to 2010. But they are not necessarily permanent and so can themselves be changed at critical junctures. This makes them a significant though vulnerable force for countering tendencies toward single-pyramid configurations of patronalistic countries' main networks. Thus Ukraine's divided-executive constitution coincided with the most sustained period after a political opening before a new round of political closure occurred, as can be seen in Figure 11.1.

Moldova starting in 2001 represents the classic post-Soviet case of patronal parliamentarism, illustrating how it can facilitate single-pyramid politics and regime cycles much like presidentialism but also how it does so with weaker effect, creating more potential for sustained competing pyramid politics under certain conditions. We have seen in Chapter 10's in-depth study how Moldova's parliamentarist constitution helped give rise to a pronounced single-pyramid system under the Communist Party's Vladimir Voronin, a pattern evident in the creeping rise in political closure captured in Figure 11.1 between 2001 and 2008. The detailed case study, however, also revealed that Voronin more times than not needed to strike deals with genuinely autonomous political forces after a parliamentary election in order to keep his network's hold on the position of "president" (which here is a post filled by a parliamentary vote). He easily did this when he was not a lame-duck in 2005, but the deals he cut then did appear to have significant consequences that ultimately made the machine more vulnerable.

The extra vulnerability appears to have mattered when Voronin entered his lame-duck period and also found himself presiding over a period of rapid economic deterioration. His single-pyramid system started to erode as he ran up against his two-term limit in 2009, and a nearly even divide in public support between his own Communist Party and an opposition coalition prevented either side from getting the parliamentary supermajority needed to capture the most important executive post outright. Only in 2012, after three years of stalemate, did a coalition of rival networks emerge in parliament capable of electing someone to this post. Importantly, the person selected was seen as an unassertive compromise figure not clearly attached to any of the main networks, someone capable of playing an arbiter's role while being balanced himself by two other distinct networks occupying the country's two other main executive posts, prime minister and parliamentary chair. This stalemate, now institutionally underpinned in a potentially self-sustaining way, has helped preserve openness in Moldova's polity since 2009, as Figure 11.1 shows. Such a stalemate arguably would not have been possible under most presidentialist constitutions, since direct presidential elections essentially always produce a winner even when levels of support are very close, thereby inducing a tip in network coordination dynamics to the winner. The high divisibility of the executive under Moldova's parliamentarist constitution has also underpinned a self-reinforcing balance of power among networks. This could change, however, should one emerge sufficiently more popular than the others to win control of them all in a future election – a development that could lead to a new round of single-pyramid politics.

Public Opinion and Other Key Subjects Left for Future Research

At this point in the penultimate chapter, it is important to pause for a moment to make clear what this book is and is not about, what it seeks to explain and what it leaves as a future research agenda. The concept of patronal politics is a broad one, and a single volume could hardly do justice to all the major puzzles it helps frame. As the preceding section makes clear, this book has concentrated on documenting and explaining large-scale regime dynamics. In particular, the focus has been on dynamic patterns in how the most important patronalistic networks in a polity arrange and rearrange themselves, with a special emphasis on movement toward or away from ideal-type arrangements that have been dubbed here "single-pyramid systems" and "competing-pyramid systems" – including the possibility of cyclic movement between the two ideal types. This is far, far from everything important about patronal politics. And it is true whether one's perspective is that of the ordinary person, the policy maker, or the social scientist. Each may have many questions that this book helps frame but does not attempt to answer. In this section, some of the biggest such questions are briefly discussed with an eye to where future research might productively go.

What Explains Variation in the Types of Networks Prominent in Different Societies?

The present volume does not seek to explain why different *types* of networks become prominent in different polities at different times. But clearly there are different kinds of patronal networks, as face-to-face personal connections can be based on different sorts of acquaintance. And the preceding pages have called attention to the fact that there is variation across countries and across time in what sorts of networks are most prominent in organizing politics. Different countries feature different degrees to which networks of actual personal acquaintance are forged through ethnicity, region, kinship, friendship, patronage, or service in formal institutions like the Komsomol or the KGB and its successor organizations. While it is common to hear observers declare, for example, that "kinship plays a more important role in Central Asian politics than elsewhere" or that "KGB networks dominate Russia under Putin more than in other countries," such statements are often not backed by rigorous research. And this volume has shown that the larger dynamics of patronal politics (such as the regime cycles characteristic of patronal presidentialism) can be observed regardless of whether a country's major networks have, for example, a major identity or kinship component or not. Nevertheless, it is surely the case that the specific types of networks that a society features – including the relative prominence of former KGB figures in Russia, of figures with ties to Nagorno-Karabakh in Armenia, or of extended kinship networks in Kyrgyzstan – will impact life in these countries in other ways. The precise identification, explanation, and implications of such variation in the context of patronal politics should be a fertile field for future research.

What Are the Different Kinds of Single-Pyramid Systems and Why Do Different Countries Experience Different Kinds?

This book also does not attempt to explain all variation in the particular features of single-pyramid systems. It has, however, called attention to the fact that single-pyramid systems can take a wide variety of forms. One way that single-pyramid systems vary is that they can be composed of – or give the leading roles to – different sorts of networks. Single-pyramid systems composed of different varieties of networks can look quite different to both insiders and outsiders. For example, oligarchic networks with formal bases in the private sector have been much more prominent parts of the single-pyramid systems in Ukraine and Russia than in Belarus or Azerbaijan. Some systems can feature a great diversity in the type of networks they involve, as in Russia, while others seem to reflect a carving up of the political space among highly similar kinds of networks, as with the regionally based political-economic networks of the 1990s and 2000s in Uzbekistan.

There is also the question of how many identifiably distinct major networks the single-pyramid system comprises. Networks themselves can disappear, break up, or otherwise multiply, and the present volume strongly indicates that much of this is endogenous to some of the regime dynamics that are the focus of this book. But there does seem to be meaningful exogenous variation in the number of networks that remain prominent parts of different single-pyramid systems. In the case of Transnistria under Smirnov in the 2000s, for example, one could reasonably conclude that there were only two major networks, Sheriff and the

Smirnov family network. In Kyrgyzstan under Bakiev and Akaev, however, the single-pyramid systems they created integrated a great multiplicity of significant networks.

Single-pyramid systems can also be organized or managed in very different ways. Lukashenka and Nazarbaev, for example, made regular rotation of top leaders distinctive features of their power pyramids in Belarus and Kazakhstan. This feature contrasts rather starkly with single-pyramid systems under the Aliyevs and Putin in Azerbaijan and Russia, both of which have featured a high degree of stability in top cadres. Stylistic differences in single-pyramid management can take on other forms as well. One might contrast Putin's and Aliyev's risk-averse style in Russia and Azerbaijan with the more risk-acceptant behavior of Yeltsin in Russia and Saakashvili in Georgia. Saakashvili also went much further in eliminating petty corruption than did any other, though the result was still a single-pyramid system – just one enveloped in a velvet glove, as it was characterized in Chapter 9. Some single-pyramid systems give prominent roles to a regime party, as in Russia, while others do not, as in Belarus. One might also point to different levels of violence and coercion involved in different single-pyramid systems, with systems like Uzbekistan's being among the most bloody and those like Kazakhstan's much less so.

What this book shows is that despite all of these differences in the form and style of single-pyramid systems, the larger pattern of regime dynamics that the patronal politics logic expects, including regime cycles governed in large part by lame-duck syndromes and levels of popular support, can still be observed. But what it leaves unanswered is what kinds of other effects might result from variation in single-pyramid type when it comes to politics, economics, or society. Identifying and explaining such variation and its impact should be a promising subject of future research.

How Do Competing-Pyramid Situations Vary and Why?

Just as we can find variation in the single-pyramid episodes we observe in the post-Soviet space, so too can we find variation in the periods of competing-pyramid politics that is not directly addressed in the present volume but that warrants documentation and explanation in future work. One of the most obvious questions is why competing-pyramid phases in patronal presidential systems sometimes turn far more deadly than in others. Kyrgyzstan's episodes in 2005 and 2010 each led to bloodshed, with the worst taking place in the latter year, setting in motion events that took the lives of hundreds. Armenia's 2008 contest also involved tragic loss of life. Ukraine's emergent competing-pyramid system is currently embroiled in violence as of mid-2014, though much of this owes to Russia's role. Competing-pyramid phases have been much more peaceful in Moldova, Kazakhstan, and Azerbaijan. Surely it is self-evident why this is deserving of explanation.

Under divided-executive constitutions, we might also expect to find variation in the ferocity of the competition in the associated competing-pyramid systems, with Ukraine 2004–10 registering quite high on this scale. An important agenda for future research, therefore, will be whether Kyrgyzstan and Georgia (which more recently transitioned to such a constitution) will feature the same scale of unbridled political warring or whether these countries' networks prove better able to work together.[11] Naturally, we will also want to observe whether Ukraine's elite, now embarking on a new divided-executive period, has learned from its previous experience and manages to make this sort of constitution work more effectively for governance than in the past.

When patronal presidential ousters occur as presidents become unpopular lame-ducks, there is also variation in precisely how they are ousted. Sometimes this occurs via a presidential election (as with Abkhazia and Ukraine in 2004 as well as Transnistria and South Ossetia in 2011), sometimes through a parliamentary election serving as an "elite primary" (as with Georgia in 2003 and Kyrgyzstan in 2005), and sometimes by means of elite coordination outside the immediate electoral framework (as in Armenia in 1998 and Kyrgyzstan in 2010).

The present book does not directly attempt to explain these and other forms of variation in competing-pyramid phases. Instead, it limits itself to demonstrating that such phases tend to emerge and result in dominant network ouster according to patterns of anticipated possible succession and the level of popular support for the incumbent leadership. Future research will be needed to tell us more precisely whether or (more likely) how the different forms of competing-pyramid politics matter for other outcomes that interest us.

What Explains the Varying Amplitude and Length of Regime Cycles?

While the book has established the importance of regime cycles and the existence of significant regularity in the length of these cycles, it has not sought to make very specific predictions as to precisely how closed the single-pyramid phases will be, how open the competing-pyramid phases will be, and exactly how long either kind of phase will be. To be sure, there are some direct implications for these questions that can be drawn. For example, Chapter 4's theory would lead us to predict that the passage of time without a lame-duck syndrome will tend to lead to higher levels of single-pyramid closure, as would higher levels of support for the patron in chief. And longer term limits and presidents who take office at earlier ages should also tend to make at least the single-pyramid phases longer. Divided-executive constitutions should extend the duration of competing-pyramid systems. But there are many questions beyond these, including some touched on earlier, such as the personal management style of a patronal president and his or her level of risk acceptance. These too should attract the attention of researchers in the future.

---

[11] Suggesting the importance of this possibility in theory is Serhiy Kudelia, "Institutional Design and Elite Interests: The Case of Ukraine," unpublished paper presented at the DC Area Postcommunist Politics Social Science Workshop, George Washington University, January 4, 2012.

What Explains Leadership Popularity?

Perhaps the most important of all of these questions left for future research is the one of leadership popularity. It has been a major theme throughout this volume that public opinion is an immensely important influence on regime dynamics in patronal polities, a key shaper of expectations that impacts patterns of elite coordination. Indeed, it is easy to dismiss elections in these places as corrupt and therefore meaningless, but many reasons have been given as to why this is a major mistake. What this book has not done, however, is attempt to provide a systematic and comprehensive explanation of variation in public opinion. This would simply have been an impossibly large task for a volume that is instead focused on the larger question of regime dynamics. It may have been possible had there existed a well-developed body of research on public opinion in hybrid regimes, one with widely accepted findings that could be reasonably applied as propositions for the present book. But because of a widespread view that public opinion matters little in nondemocratic regimes and because mass surveys can be very expensive, in fact there is precious little such research that is rigorous and of truly high quality.[12] For example, there exists no regularly conducted and widely available survey of public opinion on politics that spans the whole set of post-Soviet polities. While the nondemocratic nature of many of these polities does make such research difficult and the findings hard to interpret, new advances in survey techniques might yet be directed to address these challenges, such as list count experiments that can help measure behaviors people might not want to admit without them having to admit it.[13] And some researchers have managed to have great success in what might initially appear to be remarkably inhospitable Eurasian circumstances.[14] But we are currently left in great want of more such work.

In light of challenges like these, this study's approach has been to show where public opinion has mattered and to use this to argue it is vitally important for us

---

[12] A review of existing research on cases worldwide in this direction is Jennifer Gandhi and Ellen Lust-Okar, "Elections under Authoritarianism," *Annual Review of Political Science*, v. 12, 2009, pp. 403–22. The exceptions on Eurasian countries tend to focus on Russia, as was noted in Chapter 8. See Timothy J. Colton, *Transitional Citizens: Voters and What Influences Them in the New Russia* (Cambridge, MA: Harvard University Press, 2000); Timothy J. Colton and Henry E. Hale, "The Putin Vote: Presidential Electorates in a Hybrid Regime," *Slavic Review*, v. 68, no. 3, Fall 2009, pp. 473–503; William Mishler and John P. Willerton, "The Dynamics of Presidential Popularity in Post-Communist Russia: Cultural Imperative versus Neo-Institutional Choice," *Journal of Politics*, v. 65, no. 1, February 2003, pp. 111–41; Daniel S. Treisman, "Presidential Popularity in a Hybrid Regime: Russia under Yeltsin and Putin," *American Journal of Political Science*, v. 55, no. 3, July 2011, pp. 590–609; Richard Rose, William Mishler, and Neil Munro, *Russia Transformed: Developing Popular Support for a New Regime* (New York: Cambridge University Press, 2006); Stephen White and Ian McAllister, "The Putin Phenomenon," *Journal of Communist Studies and Transition Politics*, v. 24, no. 4, 2008, pp. 604–28; Stephen White, Richard Rose, and Ian McAllister, *How Russia Votes* (Chatham, NJ: Chatham House, 1997).

[13] See Graeme Blair and Kosuke Imai, "Statistical Analysis of List Experiments," *Political Analysis*, v. 20, no. 1, Winter 2012, pp. 47–77.

[14] As just one example, see John O'Loughlin, Vladimir Kolossov, and Gerard Toal, "Inside Abkhazia: Survey of Attitudes in a De Facto State," *Post-Soviet Affairs*, v. 27, no. 1, 2011, pp. 1–36. The same authors also conducted surveys in South Ossetia and Transnistria.

to fund and conduct much more research on these sentiments' origins. That is, for the purposes of this study public opinion has been treated as largely though not entirely exogenous. What the volume has shown is that where leaders lack public support, for whatever reason, they tend to become particularly vulnerable to lame-duck syndromes. For this key argument, there are few grounds for questioning the assumption of popular opinion's exogeneity. It is hard to come up with a mechanism, for example, by which a term limit by itself makes the leader unpopular. Indeed, the volume has presented multiple counterexamples of leaders who have weathered lame-duck phases with strong popular support. These include Russia's Vladimir Putin, Armenia's Robert Kocharian, and Azerbaijan's Heydar Aliyev. And in each case, we have presented evidence of an ousted leader's low popularity (be it from media reports or opinion poll data) from sources prior to the ouster itself, so these are not merely post hoc assessments based on seeing the outcome.

One might still speculate that lame-duck syndromes spur elites to defect who then criticize the regime and make the leader unpopular. But the process tracing provided in Chapter 7 shows that in most cases the problems of regime popularity can be identified prior to significant defections. To be sure, an argument could be made that Kuchma was "sunk" by a covert elite defection in the form of the scandalous leaked Gongadze tape, and Saakashvili was finished off by the prison video released by the defecting Ivanishvili. But Akaev's and Shevardnadze's drops in popularity preceded the defection of the major allies who would become their major challengers. And the same could clearly be said for Ter-Petrossian in Armenia, Ardzinba in Abkhazia, and Bakiev in Kyrgyzstan. And Kuchma's popular support was already not very high in the late 1990s, as was described in Chapter 7. Moreover, Chapter 8 also showed how strong popular support tended to discourage or even reverse initial elite defections during a regime's lame-duck period, as with Putin's rise in 1999–2000 and Heydar Aliyev's dynastic handoff in 2003. Overall, the point is not that there is no endogeneity whatsoever involved in public opinion dynamics. Indeed, lame-duck situations pose at least some risk to even initially popular presidents. Instead, the point is that there is clearly enough about public opinion that is exogenous to the causal factors and outcomes stressed in this volume that it merits treatment as a primary cause – though a cause whose own origins still require more research.

Do the preceding pages suggest any ideas as to where researchers of leadership popularity in patronalistic societies might look? The process-tracing analysis presented in previous chapters suggests public support (or its loss) can result from a wide variety of factors. In our story, we find room for economic performance, media control, highly contingent scandalous events, unpopular leadership decisions, botched management, senses that a leader is past his prime because of old age or infirmity, losses in war, patterns of patronage, personal charisma, perceptions of competence, and senses that there is no alternative – just to mention a few. That the sources of public support for a leader are highly complex should not strike readers in democracies as unusual. Public support is regularly treated as a key determinant of success in elections, and that support is usually found to result from a highly diverse set of influences. Economic factors are singled out for much attention in studies of Western countries, but campaigns and personalities also loom large, as do policy positions, preexisting party and group loyalties, and performance in office on a whole range of issues.[15] While some have made a forceful argument that the economy dominates in Russia,[16] a great deal of other research establishes that this is far from the only factor even there, and probably not even the most important one.[17] Outside Russia, it bears remembering that the Orange Revolution took place during a period of impressive economic growth in Ukraine.[18] And much depends on how today's economic conditions are framed relative to the past or to prior expectations.[19] The economy matters, but it is only one factor. Public support for leadership is highly complex in its origins, not reducing easily to one or two variables that would make it worthwhile to consider public opinion merely a mediating variable in this study. Or at least, we lack sufficient grounds at present for such an analytical move.

The crucial role of public opinion leads us to one particularly important observation regarding the nature of nondemocratic rule under patronal politics. One is that since public support does in fact play an important role in determining which networks are overthrown and which succeed in obtaining power even in patronal presidential systems, then we can in fact talk about a crude but significant *accountability mechanism* built into these systems. When people are the most dissatisfied with their leaders' performance, patronal presidential systems do give them at least some periodic chances to oust them, more so when term limits are on the books and at least some opposition is allowed to compete in elections.[20] Incumbents can manipulate this mechanism by influencing mass media, but the mass dissatisfaction with Soviet and East European Communist Party rule demonstrated that even full control over media cannot eliminate autonomous sources of public opinion.[21]

[15] Classics include Warren E. Miller and J. Merrill Shanks, *The New American Voter* (Cambridge, MA: Harvard University Press, 1996); Samuel L. Popkin, *The Reasoning Voter: Communication and Persuasion in Presidential Campaigns* (Chicago: University of Chicago Press, 1991).

[16] Perhaps most influentially, Treisman, "Presidential Popularity."

[17] Colton, *Transitional Citizens*; Colton and Hale, "The Putin Vote"; Rose, Mishler, and Munro, *Russia Transformed*.

[18] On the variety of other factors leading to social discontent in Ukraine, see Chapter 7 as well as Taras Kuzio, "Democratic Revolutions from a Different Angle: Social Populism and National Identity in Ukraine's 2004 Orange Revolution," *Journal of Contemporary European Studies*, v. 20, no. 1, March 2012, pp. 41–54.

[19] Joshua A. Tucker, *Regional Economic Voting: Russia, Poland, Hungary, Slovakia, and the Czech Republic, 1990–1999* (New York: Cambridge University Press, 2006).

[20] Without term limits or contested elections, the chances for exercising this accountability are reduced but not eliminated, governed by more random sparks for coordinated elite defection and/or the aging of the leader, as noted in Chapter 4.

[21] See Keith Darden and Anna Grzymala-Busse, "The Great Divide: Literacy, Nationalism, and the Communist Collapse," *World Politics*, v. 59, no. 1, October 2006, pp. 83–115; and Jason Wittenberg, *Crucibles of Political Loyalty* (New York: Cambridge University Press, 2006).

Factors That Matter Far Less than Commonly Believed

Some readers might be struck by the small roles this book has assigned to certain factors that are often central to other explanations of "regime change," "levels of democracy," or "revolution" in the postcommunist region. This is not by accident. One of the main arguments presented here is that much of patronal politics is not what it may appear. This means many causes that seem central on the surface are actually of only secondary importance as drivers of regime dynamics. This is not true of all of the factors that do not feature in the chapters so far in this book. Some are unimportant in accounting for variation *among* post-Soviet cases because they are essentially *held constant* in this context. In such instances, a look at broader global patterns might well reveal them to have importance in explaining why the former USSR differs from other parts of the world. This section briefly reviews factors that are not given pride of place here and that are most likely to raise eyebrows among some analysts.

Elite Unity and the Relative Strength of Regime, Opposition, and Civil Society

One set of factors this volume largely dismisses as drivers of regime dynamics consists of "opposition strength," "regime strength," "civil society strength," and "elite unity." In highly patronalistic contexts, it is analytically risky to consider these truly independent variables capable of explaining a given country's "regime type." This is because they can change quite radically and suddenly, depending on what phase of a regime cycle a country happens to be in at a given moment, a cycle that is primarily driven by the key factors emphasized in this book: lame-duck syndromes and public support for the incumbent network.[22] In other words, they are highly endogenous to the logic of patronal politics.[23] Accordingly, at one point in time a particular regime may seem tightly closed, brandishing well-organized mechanisms of repression, only weak civil society resistance, and highly marginalized opposition parties. But politics under such regimes can quite suddenly "awaken" when a chief patron declines in popularity and becomes a lame-duck. Previously loyal elites in such situations start hedging their political bets and even openly defecting, injecting new resources into what had previously seemed to be a feckless opposition and directly helping mobilize

---

[22] Of course, to the extent one defines regime or opposition "strength" as popular support (as opposed to degrees or qualities of organization that are independent of popular support), then this argument is perfectly compatible with the present book's account.

[23] This draws on insights from Graeme B. Robertson, *The Politics of Protest in Hybrid Regimes: Managing Dissent in Post-Communist Russia* (New York: Cambridge University Press, 2011); and Douglass C. North, John Joseph Wallis, Barry R. Weingast, *Violence and Social Orders: A Conceptual Framework for Interpreting Recorded Human History* (New York: Cambridge University Press, 2009); as well as earlier works, notably Michael Bratton and Nicolas van de Walle, *Democratic Experiments in Africa: Regime Transitions in Comparative Perspective* (New York: Cambridge University Press, 1997), which observes that threats to incumbent neopatrimonial regimes often arise from splits within the elite.

civil society activities, including protests against the incumbents.[24] Crucially, this is not a story of Huntington's famous "hard-liners" and "soft-liners" within the regime.[25] It is one of networks with rival political and economic interests that has little to do with democracy itself and much to do with their efforts to coordinate so as to gain, retain, or enlarge their piece of the proverbial pie.

We can thus understand why observers have frequently been surprised at the outbreak of mass protest and revolutions in the postcommunist space and have failed to predict where they will and will not occur. Indeed, *all* of these revolutions were generally surprises, occurring in countries previously considered relatively docile before their "dictators," especially Ukraine and Kyrgyzstan, not to mention Abkhazia or South Ossetia. In retrospect, it is easy to look back and conclude that the original estimates turned out to be wrong and that the state had actually been weak, the elites had actually been divided, and opposition and civil society had actually been strong, just lurking in the shadows in wait of the right moment to spring. Apart from the fact that indices of civil society strength prior to the revolutions do not find that the revolutionary countries stood out clearly or significantly from the nonrevolutionary ones,[26] such retroactive assessments can set the stage for overestimating the country's democratizing potential in the future. Post-Soviet experience shows how elites can strongly reunite after a period of division once a new incumbent patron settles into position and how formerly autonomous civil society and influential opposition parties can be co-opted or marginalized. Few imagined at the height of competing-pyramid politics in Yeltsin-era Russia that anyone could unify that country's fractious oligarchs and governors, or successfully suppress its vibrant opposition. As summed up in the title of one prominent article that appeared at the end of the 1990s, "After Yeltsin Comes ... Yeltsin."[27] But behold.

None of this is to deny that single-pyramid systems can be organized by state leaders in more or less effective ways,[28] that networks can sometimes be permanently opposed to a ruling coalition in the form of opposition parties that

---

[24] Another implication is that regime cycles would also seem capable of significantly influencing the measure of political polarization that Timothy Frye shows tends to hamper market reform, namely, whether parties espousing positions on such reform that differ strongly from the president's position are able to gain sizable parliamentary representation. His case studies seem consistent with this interpretation, with Russian polarization, for example, reportedly declining as Putin tightened his single-pyramid system in the mid-1990s. His other case studies are Uzbekistan, a full autocracy since the mid-1990s, and two East European cases that the next chapter will show can be expected not to experience the same kind of regime cycles as the non-Baltic post-Soviet countries. See Timothy Frye, *Building States and Markets after Communism: The Perils of Polarized Democracy* (New York: Cambridge University Press, 2010).

[25] Samuel P. Huntington, *The Third Wave* (Norman: University of Oklahoma Press, 1991).

[26] Hale, "Regime Cycles."

[27] Daniel S. Treisman, "After Yeltsin Comes ... Yeltsin," *Foreign Policy*, v. 117, Winter 1999–2000, pp. 74–86.

[28] As has been shown by Lucan A. Way, "Authoritarian State-Building and the Sources of Regime Competitiveness in the Fourth Wave: The Cases of Belarus, Moldova, Russia, and Ukraine," *World Politics*, v. 57, January 2005, pp. 231–61.

survive,[29] or that civil society organizations can be more or less capable of sustaining autonomy in the face of regime pressure.[30] But it is to qualify how we should understand the role of these factors: Strong or weak parties/states/organizations are contingent events more than they are permanent "factors." And whether such "events" occur in the first place is likely to be endogenous to the more fundamental factors identified in this volume. Their causal role in patronal regime dynamics is thus best understood as secondary at best, and in many cases essentially epiphenomenal. We thus need to shift the focus of research on such factors to the ways they relate to the patronal politics of expectations and network coordination.

Identity Divides

Countries riven by identity divides do not appear more systematically susceptible to competing- or single-pyramid politics than do others, despite some research suggesting such divides undermine authoritarian rule and other writing suspecting they undermine democracy.[31] To be sure, the revolutions in Ukraine and Kyrgyzstan had strong regional dimensions. But even in these cases reality is much more complex, the divides far from impermeable, and identity politics hardly beyond manipulation by authorities. Chapters 7 and 9 showed, for example, how leading oligarchs from the East and top politicians from the West frequently teamed up when it suited their material and political interests in Ukraine. And while voters regularly cleave along east-west lines in Ukrainian parliamentary elections,[32] Kuchma was able to shift his power base almost entirely from eastern to western Ukraine between the 1994 and 1999 elections. In Kyrgyzstan, the Tulip Revolution may have originated in the South, but it quickly found allies among some of the North's strongest networks (notably Feliks Kulov's), and few experts on this country have argued that these events were related more to identity than material or political interests.[33] In addition, the bulk of patronal presidential ousters needed no strong regional divide to occur, as in Armenia, Georgia, Abkhazia, Transnistria, and South Ossetia.

There are also plenty of instances when the heads of single-pyramid systems who are not lame-ducks have proven able to overpower those who would seek to mobilize identity divides as a way of building up opposition. Kazakhstan provides a case in point, one of the most enduring single-pyramid systems in Eurasia despite inheriting a deep divide between a largely ethnic Russian North and a predominantly ethnic Kazakh South. Moldova's President Voronin supplies

---

[29] Such cases are relatively rare and usually involve networks without major administrative or financial assets, such as Russia's Yabloko Party.

[30] And this is also not to say that civil society organization and training do not do other important things, such as help protests – when they occur – be conducted peacefully.

[31] E.g., Donald L. Horowitz, "Democracy in Divided Societies," *Journal of Democracy*, v. 4, no. 4, October 1993, pp. 18–37; Way, "Authoritarian State-Building."

[32] Timothy J. Colton, "An Aligning Election and the Ukrainian Political Community," *East European Politics & Societies*, v. 25, no. 1, February 2011, pp. 4–27.

[33] Perhaps most authoritatively, Scott Radnitz, *Weapons of the Wealthy: Predatory Regimes and Elite-Led Protests in Central Asia* (Ithaca, NY: Cornell University Press, 2010).

another example. He switched from his earlier pro-Russian position to a pro-EU stance in the run-up to the 2005 election, dramatically co-opting a powerful opposition able to rally tens of thousands in the streets against him.[34]

Two key conclusions would appear in order. One is that identity divides are most likely to work against leaders when they are already unpopular lame-ducks. This can explain why Kuchma could successfully manipulate Ukraine's divide in 1999 but not 2004, and why Voronin rode his country's divide to victory in 2005 but was unable to do so in 2009. It also explains why Kazakhstan's identity bifurcation has never appeared to undermine Nazarbaev, and why Kyrgyzstan's divide was implicated in a revolution after but not before Bakiev's 2009 reelection. The fact that many patronal presidential ousters occurred without identity divides indicates they are far from a necessary cause of authoritarian instability. When a country has them, elites may use them as a convenient way to organize the competition or win support, but when a country does not have them, elites can almost always find other usable battle lines.[35]

A second conclusion is that to the extent identity divides matter, it is likely to be by influencing patterns of support for the president. But as discussed previously, identity is only one factor among many others impacting public opinion, even in countries like Kyrgyzstan and Ukraine. And we must keep in mind that identity divides can also work in favor of a president who is unpopular for other reasons. By stoking identity issues and polarizing the country, such a president can hope to rally a large share of the population to his side against another side despite a dismal record. The balance of evidence, therefore, suggests identity divides have a secondary and overall indeterminate impact on post-Soviet patterns of regime opening and closure.[36]

International Actors
Some readers will be struck by how little impact is ascribed to international actors in driving post-Soviet regime dynamics. The United States, EU, UN, and even Russia appeared in the preceding analysis only occasionally. This is because when one looks closely, deeply, and comparatively at patterns across the post-Soviet space, the largest and most important can be explained quite well without much reference to external actors at all. This is not to say such actors are completely unimportant. Even if they did not have much effect facilitating or inhibiting revolutions or democracy, for example, one might still

---

[34] For a fuller version of the arguments here, see Henry E. Hale, "Identity Divides as Authoritarian Resource: Post-Soviet Cases over Twenty Years," paper prepared for presentation at the Association for the Study of Nationalities annual meeting, April 19–21, 2012, Columbia University, New York. On Moldova, see William H. Hill, *Russia, the New Abroad, and the West: Lessons from the Moldova-Transdniestria Conflict* (Baltimore: Johns Hopkins University Press, 2012).

[35] Supporting this interpretation of identity is Henry E. Hale, *The Foundations of Ethnic Politics: Separatism of States and Nations in Eurasia and the World* (New York: Cambridge University Press, 2008).

[36] This concurs with findings reported in Jan Teorell, *Determinants of Democratization: Explaining Regime Change in the World, 1972–2006* (New York: Cambridge University Press, 2010).

speculate they had a role in determining the extent to which such revolutions involved violence or were able to remain peaceful. This is a task for future research, beyond the scope of this book. But because international factors are prominent in existing literature on regime change and in policy debates, it is worth teasing out a few possible conclusions from the preceding chapters.

Let us turn first to the influence of Western actors on post-Soviet regime dynamics. This volume did find that ousters of dominant networks through elections and protest sometimes did occur where significant Western resources and attention were directed toward this same end, as in Ukraine in 2004. But such ousters were also shown to have taken place where Western interventions were much less pronounced, as in Kyrgyzstan in 2005, or entirely absent, as in Abkhazia in 2004 and South Ossetia in 2011. Ousters were also found to have occurred outside elections and election-related protest, as in Armenia in 1998 and Kyrgyzstan in 2010. While these cannot be accounted for by Western intervention, they were shown in Chapter 7 to fit with the patronal politics framework. And a number of cases were identified in Chapter 8 where oppositions actively attempted to replicate color revolutions in their own countries with the support of Western governments and organizations but failed. Examples include the Belarusan presidential elections of 2001 and 2006 and the Azerbaijan presidential contest of 2003.

EU, American, and more broadly Western actions were at best able to impact propensities to single- or competing-pyramid politics on the margins, when a competing-pyramid situation had arisen for other reasons and the sides were relatively evenly matched. Ukraine in 2004 may be one example where the margins mattered. The Orange Revolution was effectively a stalemate and the ultimate outcome was uncertain as it unfolded. In these conditions, internationally sponsored exit polls, observer missions, statements by prominent American leaders based on this information, and negotiation brokers such as Polish President Aleksander Kwasniewski may well have helped tip expectations in Ukraine toward Yushchenko's ultimate victory, inducing Kuchma to compromise rather than push for outright victory.[37] But this opportunity for international factors to matter was largely served up by domestic factors, especially Kuchma's lame-duck status and low popularity, plus the happenstance that the sides in Ukraine's battle happened to be relatively even.

If we turn our attention to European Union efforts to promote gradual political opening, careful process-tracing analysis of regime dynamics finds little evidence that the European Union was working much democratizing magic in the former Soviet countries, however successful it may have been in the more westerly postcommunist states.[38] Many Eurasian countries at least initially aspired

---

[37] A systematic examination of international influence in the Orange Revolution can be found in Michael McFaul, "Ukraine Imports Democracy: External Influences on the Orange Revolution," *International Security*, v. 32, no. 2, Fall 2007, pp. 45–83.

[38] E.g., Milada A. Vachudova, *Europe Undivided: Democracy, Leverage, and Integration after Communism* (New York: Oxford University Press, 2005).

to joining the EU, but it was clear to elites and masses fairly soon after independence that none of the post-Soviet countries other than the Baltic states had a serious chance of joining in the foreseeable future. That left the EU with very little that could be used to alter elite behavior in ways that could significantly dampen or break the regime cycles this volume has documented. Determined readers can, however, find a few instances in the preceding pages where European forces appear to have influenced regime dynamics. The European Commission's Venice Commission appears to have had at least some role in encouraging Moldova to adopt a proportional-representation election system for parliament in the 1990s, helping put it on the road to parliamentarism rather than presidentialism. It is possible that Georgia's EU aspirations helped convince Saakashvili not to clamp down on political dissent in mass media as tightly as did single-pyramid leaders in Russia and Azerbaijan. And perhaps most dramatically, the prospects for an agreement with the EU provided the trigger for Ukraine's dramatic Euromaidan protests in late 2013, eventually leading to the downfall of Yanukovych's budding single-pyramid system. Chapter 12 will return to this question and consider why the EU has been more successful in influencing regime dynamics in some contexts than others.

Russian intervention, which many argue tends to be a force for regime closure in the post-Soviet region,[39] also appears to have had little decisive influence over post-Soviet regime dynamics outside its borders.[40] If anything, the evidence indicates that Russia has been more effective at helping destabilize incumbents by inducing or accentuating lame-duck syndromes than at determining the outcome of the ensuing succession struggles. In succession struggles themselves, public support appears to play a more important role than Russian preferences. Thus Chapter 7 showed that intense criticism of Bakiev in Russian media, widely accessible in Kyrgyzstan, reinforced other sources of information that were damaging Bakiev's popularity in 2010 after he entered his constitutionally final term in office. Russia's demonstrated displeasure with Transnistria's Igor Smirnov was reported by some sources to have contributed to a sense the aging Smirnov was on his way out and thus a lame-duck. Evidence also indicates Russia was able to help block Jioeva from becoming Kokoity's successor in South Ossetia. But while Russia appears to have had the outcome it wanted in Kyrgyzstan in 2010, its preferred candidate Anatoly Kaminsky lost in Transnistria to Evgeny Shevchuk. Russia also failed to prevent an opposition candidate from ultimately succeeding Kokoity in South Ossetia. And Kremlin efforts to oust other incumbents have dramatically failed and possibly even backfired, helping their objects rally nationalistic support. Examples include Georgia's Saakasvhili in his 2008 reelection and Moldova's Voronin in his 2005 reelection, when neither was a lame-duck. Russia has also been singularly

[39] E.g., David R. Cameron and Mitchell A. Orenstein, "Post-Soviet Authoritarianism: The Influence of Russia in Its 'Near Abroad'," *Post-Soviet Affairs*, v. 28, no. 1, January–March 2012.

[40] This resonates Lucan A. Way, "Explaining the Weakness of International Authoritarian Promotion: The Case of Russia in the 'Near Abroad,'" manuscript, June 2014.

unsuccessful in propping up incumbent networks in lame-duck situations, as in Ukraine in 2004, Abkhazia in 2004, Moldova in 2009, and South Ossetia in 2011–12. Most recently, Russian support failed to save Yanukovych in Ukraine in 2014. There is also little evidence Russia has been able to supply an attractive regime model that others have emulated, especially since others whose systems now appear similar (like Azerbaijan and Kazakhstan) largely preceded Russia in developing this model. Because Russia has had more success in destabilizing incumbent networks than kingmaking – even in territories like South Ossetia that many regard as being actually under Russian occupation – one might even boldly venture that Russia has *net* been an *unintentional* promoter of regime openness. The case of Ukraine in 2014, however, indicates that Russia may now be much more intentionally than before promoting such "openness" (in this case, in the form of domestic conflict) in regimes it does not like.

International Diffusion, Demonstration Effects, and Neighborhood Effects

Dynamics of democratic "diffusion," "contagion," or "demonstration effects" – including those mediated by transnational democracy-promotion networks – have received a great deal of attention in popular and scholarly publications.[41] But they appear not to have been decisive in ousting "dictators," influencing regime-type outcomes, or determining which networks have managed to remain in power in the post-Soviet space. For one thing, any power of example (demonstration effects) would appear to have worked only where leaders were already unpopular lame-ducks. Here a "microcomparison" presented in Chapter 8 is useful to invoke as a telling example. Both Kyrgyzstan and Tajikistan held elections on the very same day in February 2005 that were branded corrupt by international monitors. Both countries were subject to the same power of the example of election-centered protests and revolution in Serbia, Georgia, and Ukraine. Yet only Kyrgyzstan (where the patronal president was an unpopular lame-duck) experienced a new "color revolution" while Tajikistan's patronal president (not an unpopular lame-duck) remained in power. This occurred despite the fact that Tajikistan and Kyrgyzstan were both held up as examples of classic weak states (Tajikistan arguably even the weaker of the two) with minuscule resource endowments, remote locations, regionally oriented identity divides, and impoverished citizens.

Turning to transnational prodemocracy movements and the local youth leaders they helped train to promote democratic breakthroughs via elections and postelection protest, one can surely agree that these have been visible parts of the post-Soviet color revolutions. They also make for a very compelling and hopeful story of how dictators can be brought down by clever, energetic, and impassioned youth through inspiration and training from established

[41] E.g., "Structure and Example in Modular Political Phenomena: The Diffusion of Bulldozer/Rose/Orange/Tulip Revolutions," *Perspectives on Politics*, v. 5, no. 2, June 2007, pp. 259–76; Valerie J. Bunce and Sharon L. Wolchik, *Defeating Authoritarian Leaders in Postcommunist Countries* (New York: Cambridge University Press, 2011).

democracies and successful revolutionaries from other countries. But the pattern of all post-Soviet ousters of patronal presidents since the first appearance of single-pyramid systems in their countries shows that such "dictators" are perfectly capable of falling even without such concerted youth or NGO action. Electoral revolutions involving substantial street mobilization occurred not only in the well-reported and media-savvy movements of Ukraine and Georgia, but also in highly remote places like Abkhazia and South Ossetia. Revolutions in these latter polities in 2004–5 and 2011–12 fit very closely the pattern of regular patronal presidential regime cycles, but featured absolutely nothing in the way of transnational democracy-promotion networks or youth movements attempting to emulate prior "democratic breakthroughs." The electoral revolutions we have seen, therefore, are better understood as regime dynamics typical of single-pyramid systems, with the degree of prodemocracy movement activism primarily adding color to what was already happening for other reasons.

The primacy of patronal politics over various forms of international diffusion also helps us explain why there are so many other instances when transnational prodemocracy networks and local organizations tried hard to emulate the revolutionary tactics of successful ousters in Serbia, Georgia, and Ukraine, but failed. Unsurprisingly, these failures happened primarily when patronal presidents were either not unpopular or not lame-ducks. Examples include Belarus in 2001 and 2006 and Azerbaijan in 2003 and 2005, though one could arguably add most of the national election cycles in Russia under Putin as well as Armenian presidential elections in 2003 and 2008. It is tempting in retrospect to conclude that the failed opposition movements simply did not fully implement the right strategies. Facilitating such a temptation is that failed revolutionaries themselves might believe it and repeat this when interviewed later, blaming themselves or their partners for not doing everything they should have. International actors that were deeply involved in such events might also be expected to claim that their good advice was simply not taken. And they are also likely to take credit for revolutionary successes when they occur regardless of their actual causal role, especially if this helps them obtain continued funding for their activities.

Here it is important to recognize that not just "opposition strength" and "civil society strength" are endogenous to patronal regime dynamics; opposition *strategies* can also be endogenous to them. That is, opposition forces can be more willing and able to unite and conduct innovative, ambitious campaigns when elite jockeying for succession opens up political space for them to do so and elite allies start to hedge their bets (or even defect) in ways that can help them with protection, funding, coordination, and/or organization. Oppositions are also more likely to try harder and display more confidence in their own success[42] when they actually expect they can win, expectations that are strongly driven by the

---

[42] Valerie J. Bunce and Sharon L. Wolchik ("Defeating Dictators: Electoral Change and Stability in Competitive Authoritarian Regimes," *World Politics*, v. 62, no. 1, January 2010, pp. 43–86, p. 67) note the importance of opposition beliefs about the likelihood of success as an important influence on their adopting the strategies they argue are necessary to win.

logic of patronal politics. Simply put, diffusion and demonstration effects have been associated with significant post-Soviet regime dynamics primarily when the workings of patronal politics have made the same outcomes likely for other reasons. And patronal politics has also produced the same outcomes in places that are quite isolated from significant diffusion and demonstration effects.

Twitter and Other Social Media

While many have speculated that various social media might one day open up closed societies and undermine single-pyramid politics, this has not happened yet in Eurasia. In all but one instance (Ukraine 2014) when they have been said to have been important in toppling a single-pyramid patron, that patron was already an unpopular lame-duck. Moreover, social media do not appear to have been necessary or crucial in facilitating mass street mobilization in those cases when leaders were lame-ducks, and media reports tend to exaggerate their role in such instances. For example, while initial newspaper reports by *The New York Times* and other publications led many to brand Moldova's April 2009 events the "Twitter Revolution," a moniker that has unfortunately remained in some circulation, the close analysis of events in Chapter 10 revealed Twitter's role to have been marginal at best. Facebook and Russian-language social media do appear to have influenced the rise of mass protests in Russia in late 2011, though they did not produce Putin's fall from power. And in this particular case, their crucial role was not so much helping opposition forces coordinate their protest actions as showing both fence sitters and Russian authorities in advance that unusually large numbers were going to turn up. This encouraged more fence sitters to appear and prompted Moscow's mayor to sanction the protest officially instead of attempting to thwart it, further contributing to its size and helping avert violence.[43] One might expect, however, that single-pyramid patrons will be likely to find ways to make social media work to their advantage as well, including by providing disinformation and gaining useful advance insight into would-be revolutionary activities.

State Strength, Regime Organization, and Dominant Parties

The dynamics of patronal politics discussed in this volume have been remarkably impervious to how "strong" the state appears to be, how well its repressive and co-optative apparatus is organized, and whether or not the regime features a dominant party – factors that all figure prominently in a growing literature on hybrid regimes and authoritarian institutions.[44] Instead, variables that include

[43] See Chapter 8 and *The New Times*, December 12, 2011, pp. 2–7.

[44] E.g., Jason Brownlee, *Authoritarianism in an Age of Democratization* (New York: Cambridge University Press, 2007); Jennifer Gandhi, *Political Institutions under Dictatorship* (New York: Cambridge University Press, 2008); Barbara Geddes, "What Do We Know about Democratization after Twenty Years?" *Annual Review of Political Science*, v. 2, June 1999, pp. 115–44; Samuel P. Huntington, *Political Order in Changing Societies* (New Haven, CT: Yale University Press, 1968); Milan W. Svolik, *The Politics of Authoritarian Rule* (New York: Cambridge University

state strength, regime structure, and dominant party organization strongly appear endogenous to the logic of patronal politics and the regime cycles it often produces. Indeed, if the most important factor driving Eurasian regime dynamics was the general level of state (or regime party) weakness, we would expect patronal presidential ousters to be distributed essentially randomly over time in the supposedly weak states (or at least randomly over elections, where weakness is often said to be manifested). But this volume has shown that this distribution is not random, instead featuring significant regularity. It has also shown that the theory of regular regime cycles does a much better job of pinpointing not only where but *when* presidential ousters are likeliest to happen – and also what happens next.

At the same time, the logic of patronal politics helps explain what appear to be dramatic changes in the apparent cohesiveness and scope of states, regimes, and dominant parties over time, variation that is often treated as exogenously given by existing theories.[45] For one thing, Chapters 6 and 8 showed that those systems of rule that were widely regarded as the most elaborate, extensive, and well organized have generally only been constructed by patrons who were not unpopular lame-ducks during these periods, such as the machines built by Nazarbaev in Kazakhstan or Putin in Russia. Chapters 6 and 8 also demonstrated that cohesive single-pyramid systems with extensive scope could be created out of environments that at one point featured extreme disorganization and incohesiveness in both state and society. Georgia and Azerbaijan, both widely considered failed states in the 1990s, by the 2000s featured elaborate and cohesive political machines under Aliyev and Saakashvili. Saakashvili was in fact singled out by many Western organizations for praise in state-building accomplishments, and yet he too was ousted when he ran into the twin challenges of a lame-duck syndrome and a major drop in public support. Even Russia, with one of the most tightly organized, extensive, and sophisticated single-pyramid systems in the post-Soviet space, reached this point under Putin after a whole decade of what to many seemed to be insurmountable political "wildness" under Yeltsin (recall "After Yeltsin Comes ... Yeltsin").[46] And Chapter 8 showed that when Putin started to show signs of leaving office as 2008 approached, serious problems emerged within even his regime.

This is not to deny any role to state, regime, and party strength. Instead, it is to argue we need to understand these concepts in the larger context of the logic

---

Press, 2012). Such factors also provide the specific mechanism for how regimes stay in power according to Dan Slater (*Ordering Power: Contentious Politics and Authoritarian Leviathans in Southeast Asia* [New York: Cambridge University Press, 2010], see pp. 18–19), though his chief point is that elite "factions" cooperate to create strong repressive institutions when facing a common domestic redistributive threat.

[45] An exception is Slater (*Ordering Power*), though there is little support in the post-Soviet cases for his argument that domestically driven redistributive movements prompt regime cohesion. There have been few such movements in Eurasia, yet it has seen both the ordering and disordering of regimes in patterns better predicted by the logic of patronal politics.

[46] Treisman, "After Yeltsin Comes ... Yeltsin."

of expectations that is central to patronal politics. When these factors influence large-scale regime dynamics, they do so primarily by shaping the expectations of actors inside and outside the system as to the likely future dominance of the incumbent chief patron(s). A patron who does not arrange his single-pyramid system in a functional way, or who fails to set up procedures by which he can monitor what his subpatrons and clients are doing, risks undermining the expectation that he is likely to stay in power if challenged. Variation in a chief patron's abilities or organizational style, therefore, can impact just how repressive a single-pyramid system feels at any given moment, and open the door to greater or lesser challenges. But the era of completely incompetent patrons largely (though not entirely) passed in the early 1990s, after which point leaders tended to learn how to organize their rule effectively or to be replaced by those who already knew – a process of natural political selection. At the same time, even the strongest organizers with the most extensive state structures could fall victim to a lame-duck syndrome and low popular support. Perhaps the example that makes this point most dramatically from outside the post-Soviet space is the fate of East Germany, as discussed in Chapter 2. The most penetrating and sophisticated repressive apparatus in the world suddenly collapsed when expectations about its future in power shifted as a result of an exogenous cause.[47]

The logic of patronal politics also encourages us to consider something surprising for the literature on nondemocratic regimes: Strong states, regime organization, and dominant parties might have their greatest effects on long-term stability less through their mechanics than *by shaping public opinion*. Strong states and coherent regimes, for example, are useful not only for repression but for actual delivery of social services and visible development projects that populations want. One reason we may see a correlation between regime stability and state-organizational coherence, therefore, may be that such states are better able to deliver over the longer term.

Let us consider dominant parties as a case in point. Dominant parties are often singled out for special attention as regime stabilizers.[48] But how to square this with the preceding chapters' findings? Lukashenka's system has been very successful without a dominant party, and the dominant parties constructed by Shevardnadze and Bakiev did not save them when they became lame-ducks and their popular support fell. This forces those who posit the importance of parties to look for outside explanations as to why some parties are more effective than others in sustaining their leaders' rule. Most have focused on

---

[47] Mancur Olson, "The Logic of Collective Action in Soviet-Type Societies," *Journal of Soviet Nationalities*, v. 1, no. 2, Summer 1990, pp. 8–27.

[48] E.g., Geddes, "What Do We Know"; Henry E. Hale, *Why Not Parties in Russia: Democracy, Federalism, and the State* (New York: Cambridge University Press, 2006); Regina Smyth, Brandon Wilkening, and Anna Urasova [Lowry], "Engineering Victory: Institutional Reform, Informal Institutions, and the Formation of a Hegemonic Party Regime in the Russian Federation," *Post-Soviet Affairs*, v. 23, no. 2, 2007, pp. 118–37; Huntington, *Political Order in Changing Societies*; Svolik, *The Politics of Authoritarian Rule*.

parties as organizations that coordinate elites by virtue of their role as formal institutions.[49] But if we look closely even at those post-Soviet cases where ruling parties are prominent and regarded as regime-stabilizing forces, such as Russia, patronal presidents will very often be found keeping their distance from such parties. Putin, for example, has never been willing to declare himself a formal member of the United Russia Party, and many key figures in his system are also not members. Even in parliamentarist Moldova, where elections have long been by party-list only and where the Communist Party was widely seen as the key organizational tool making Voronin's dominance possible, Chapter 10 demonstrated that he often put key people *who were not party members* in the most important positions other than his own (as with Prime Minister Tarlev) as a way of *strengthening* his own control as chief patron. This strongly indicates that party *organization* itself has not been the chief mechanism underpinning Voronin's and Putin's dominance.

Instead, it may be that regime parties are most effective as vehicles for public support of the regime, as ways that people can form attachments to a coalition of leaders rather than just the leader him- or herself. If a ruling party successfully builds up the scale of attachments that research has found in patterns of American party identification, for example, a single-pyramid system is strengthened in multiple ways. For one thing, the chief patron can rely on it as a kind of crutch when his own popularity falls. And the party's endorsement of a successor can make that candidate the overwhelming favorite once the incumbent enters a lame-duck phase, inducing potential defectors to conclude that they are better off bowing to the inevitable than risking a challenge without the potential to win much public support. We do not see a strong correlation between dominant parties and regime stability because the former USSR does not yet appear to feature dominant parties with such robust support rooted in something other than their main leader's personal popularity, though perhaps some are moving in this direction. Chapter 12 suggests this is another way Eurasia differs from much of Africa and Asia, meaning that parties may matter in global comparative context even while they do not account for much variation within Eurasia yet.

Privatization and Market Economy

A number of works have reasonably argued that those post-Soviet countries that privatized much of their economies thereby also made themselves more vulnerable to elite defection and revolution. Once economic resources are given into the control of private actors, the argument goes, they are more likely to be turned against the regime later.[50] While this makes intuitive sense in

---

[49] Brownlee, *Authoritarianism*; Ora John Reuter and Thomas Remington, "Dominant Party Regimes and the Commitment Problem: The Case of United Russia," *Comparative Political Studies*, v. 42, no. 4, 2009, pp. 501–26; Way, "Authoritarian State-Building."

[50] E.g., Kelly M. McMann, *Economic Autonomy and Democracy: Hybrid Regimes in Russia and Kyrgyzstan* (New York: Cambridge University Press, 2006); Scott Radnitz, "The Color of

environments where formal property rights are taken for granted and informal property rights based on distribution of de facto patronal power are not worth much, it has a harder time explaining the most important regime dynamics in highly patronalistic polities. To be sure, it has been shown that state-owned firms (especially those with less mobile assets) can sometimes be simpler for patronal presidents to use to manufacture votes when they are not lame-ducks.[51] But previous chapters have shown that formally private business can be extremely vulnerable to patronal presidents and placed quite tightly under their political thumbs, as we have seen in extensively privatized Putinite Russia after he had Russia's richest private businessman imprisoned (Mikhail Khodorkovsky). And Putin's Russia has also shown how private firms can be taken (back) into state hands if need be.[52] Moreover, very often state businesses in the post-Soviet space are "privatized" to core members of patronal presidential networks or even to relatives of the president, as Chapter 5 indicated was the case in a number of countries, including Armenia and Kyrgyzstan.[53] That is, while property may be "private sector" on paper, there are many ways that it can be just as much under the control of a patronal president as assets in the state sector.

Conversely, the formal ownership of property by the state does not mean that powerful actors with de facto control over it cannot use it as a power base, even in opposition to patronal presidents when the latter are unpopular lame-ducks. For example, one of the most important defections from Abkhazia's lame-duck President Ardzinba in 2004 was the director of the major state-owned corporation Chernomorenergo, Sergei Bagapsh, who indeed through his defection managed to become president himself in the revolution that followed, as Chapter 7 described. It is not uncommon to see even state officials in noneconomic positions defect in such circumstances. This is because the president's formal ability to hire, fire, and direct loses credibility and thus influence once elites anticipate that he or she will not be in position after a specific near point in the future to carry out threats, fulfill promises, or otherwise enforce orders. In fact, in Armenia in 1998, President Ter-Petrossian's own prime minister and minister of defense were the chief elites who betrayed him after he entered his constitutionally final term in office and his popularity sank in the wake of an unpopular concession in the negotiations over Nagorno-Karabakh. Formal status as private or state property matters much less in governing

---

Money: Privatization, Economic Dispersion, and the Post-Soviet 'Revolutions,'" *Comparative Politics*, v. 42, no. 2, January 2010, pp. 127–46.

[51] Timothy Frye, Ora John Reuter, and David Szakonyi, "Political Machines at Work: Voter Mobilization and Electoral Subversion in the Workplace," *World Politics*, v. 66, no. 2, April 2014, pp. 195–228.

[52] On the politics of nationalization in Russia, see Anna Urasova Lowry, "Between Neopatrimonialism and Developmentalism: Exploring the Causes of Nationalization in Russia," dissertation in political science, Indiana University, 2014.

[53] See also Marlene Laruelle, "Discussing Neopatrimonialism and Patronal Presidentialism in the Central Asian Context," *Demokratizatsiya: The Journal of Post-Soviet Democratization*, v. 20, no. 4, Autumn 2012, pp. 301–24.

regime dynamics in highly patronalistic polities than does the informal relationship to the chief patron.[54]

Resource Rents, Economic Development, and Economic Growth

It is also clear that post-Soviet regime dynamics do not track neatly with economic performance or natural resource endowments such as oil and gas. It is indeed true that so far no presidential ouster has occurred in the truly resource-rich countries of Eurasia (Azerbaijan, Kazakhstan, Russia, and Turkmenistan) since the turmoil of the early 1990s subsided. But Chapter 8 showed that their survival can also be accounted for by the logic of patronal politics, in particular either the absence of lame-duck episodes or popular support for representatives of the incumbent networks (and in Turkmenistan's case, its lack of contested elections altogether for reasons also discussed in Chapter 8). Moreover, post-Soviet experience makes abundantly clear that natural resource wealth is not necessary for a patronal president to build a very tight and long-lived single-pyramid system, with Belarus being a prime example. Indeed, single-pyramid systems have been features of some of the poorest countries in the region, including Tajikistan. General levels of economic development also give us little direct leverage in accounting for post-Soviet regime dynamics. The relatively developed Belarus, Russia, and Kazakhstan have experienced the same broad regime dynamics as have peripheral Tajikistan and Nagorno-Karabakh.

That said, this volume has placed heavy emphasis on the role of popular support for incumbent authorities, and economic growth and changes in personal material welfare have been found by immeasurable volumes of social science research to be a strong influence on how people evaluate the quality of their leadership.[55] The logic of patronal politics would therefore fully expect that economic factors capable of influencing the quality of life of citizens will indeed play an important role in shaping regime dynamics, though primarily by influencing the public's evaluation of how well its chief patrons have performed in office.[56] The 2008–9 global financial crisis, for example, looms large in several of the preceding narratives, contributing to political crises for lame-duck or divided-executive incumbents by damaging their popular standing. But as argued previously, we should not exaggerate the influence of the economy since many other considerations also shape popular support for their political leaders. In addition, the impact of economic growth is complicated by the potential longer-term impact of development, to which the book will turn in Chapter 12.

Public opinion may also help explain why we have not yet witnessed a presidential ouster since the mid-1990s in a major energy exporting state. Existing

---

[54] See also Barbara Junisbai, "Improbable but Potentially Pivotal Oppositions: Privatization, Capitalists, and Political Contestation in the Post-Soviet Autocracies," *Perspectives on Politics*, v. 10, no. 4, December 2012, pp. 891–916.

[55] For an overview of literature on the postcommunist region, see Joshua A. Tucker, "The First Decade of Post-Communist Elections and Voting: What Have We Studied, and How Have We Studied It?" *Annual Review of Political Science*, v. 5, 2002, pp. 271–304.

[56] This is consistent with findings in Teorell, *Determinants of Democratization*.

accounts of the role of oil and gas in political machines have tended to assume these resources strengthen regimes by giving patrons more resources that they can use to pay off clients, keeping them docile and happy, or punish opponents.[57] A few posit that the main effect is to enhance the resolve of elites not to share power since by being richer they have greater reason to fear redistribution if the poor masses actually have their votes counted fairly.[58] This all makes sense, except that we see plenty of very poor countries whose single-pyramid systems have remained strong so long as their leaders have avoided becoming unpopular lame-ducks. The logic of patronal politics would not expect the absolute amount of resources that a chief patron has (whether to hold on to clients or to pay them off) to matter much since it is hard to imagine either patrons or clients ever being content with what they have and not desiring more. Indeed, some leading works on nondemocratic rule posit that greater resources tend to raise the stakes in struggles among networks and therefore lead to fiercer competition for power and a *higher rather than lower risk of ouster*.[59]

Instead, the logic of patronal politics would suggest natural resource wealth matters less by greasing the political machine and more by influencing public opinion. Countries with oil wealth have at least the potential to use these revenues somehow to distribute benefits to the broader public (even if by trickling down through extended patronage networks), to build infrastructure such as roads or gas pipelines to homes, and to invest in improving the economy in other ways. Clearly, a prominent literature on the "resource curse" shows that such resources can also be used poorly, exacerbating economic problems in some parts of society while generating large inequalities that can become the source of resentment. But recent research shows that in fact Eurasia's resource-rich states have not been among these worst offenders. This makes it likely oil wealth has helped contribute to (though not determine) public support for leaderships in at least Azerbaijan, Kazakhstan, and Russia.[60]

Conclusion: Are the Post-Soviet Hybrid Regimes "Regimes"?

One of the central arguments of this book has been that patronal politics frequently features dynamic and often cyclic openings and closures without ever changing the underlying regime, but this does raise the question of what exactly constitutes a "regime" and whether the hybrid regimes we have discussed so far really deserve to be called regimes at all. The political science literature has long featured multiple implied or explicit definitions of "political regime" at the same time it has not subjected this concept to much critical analysis, as Gerardo

---

[57] E.g., Steven Levitsky and Lucan A. Way, *Competitive Authoritarianism: Hybrid Regimes after the Cold War* (New York: Cambridge University Press, 2010).

[58] Thad Dunning, *Crude Democracy: Natural Resource Wealth and Political Regimes* (New York: Cambridge University Press, 2008), p. 11.

[59] Svolik, *The Politics of Authoritarian Rule*, p. 113.

[60] Pauline Jones Luong and Erika Weinthal, *Oil Is Not a Curse: Ownership Structure and Institutions in Soviet Successor States* (New York: Cambridge University Press, 2010).

Munck usefully documents.[61] The field has yet to correct this shortcoming, even in the best works dedicated to what are described as new regime types.[62] Confusing matters is a second usage whereby the term "regime" refers in short-hand to the incumbent leadership of a less-than-democratic country, as in "the Mubarak regime" or "the Chavez regime." What the present treatment under-stands as a "regime" in the sense of "regime type" is a set of procedural and behavioral qualities that Munck distills from the accounts of major theorists. As formulated in Chapter 1, we recall, a *political regime* is a set of rules that are at least strategically accepted and not normatively opposed by major actors and that govern which individuals have access to the most important state positions, how such access is obtained, and how binding state decisions are made.[63]

Crucially, these rules do not need to be formal but can also be informal. What is enduring and more generally regime-constituting about patronalistic hybrid regimes such as those in post-Soviet Eurasia, then, is not any specific set of formal rules, but the deeper, underlying set of understandings (informal rules) governing who has access to state power, how state decisions are made, and how state power is exercised that de facto guide the behavior of the country's most important political actors. Crucial in this regard for patronalistic hybrid regimes would be that power is resolved through contestation among patronal networks that compete in part through formal elections in which at least some networks that are genuinely in the opposition are allowed on the ballot for the most important formal offices. The specific character of this competition can vary dynamically from highly closed single-pyramid systems to relatively open competing-pyramid systems and still leave the basic regime in place. We thus should not discount "hybrid regimes" (those that combine important elements of democracy and autocracy) as "regimes" simply because their formal rules tend to change frequently or because these dynamics make them alternately closer to or more distant from more established regime types like autocracy and democracy.[64] The following chapter relates the post-Soviet cases to other parts of the world.

---

[61] Gerardo L. Munck, "Disaggregating Political Regime: Conceptual Issues in the Study of Democratization," Working Paper no. 228, Helen Kellogg Institute for International Studies, University of Notre Dame, Indiana, August 1996.

[62] E.g., Levitsky and Way, *Competitive Authoritarianism*.

[63] Ibid., pp. 6–8.

[64] It may be useful in some circumstances to think of different kinds of formal constitutions as defining certain patronalistic hybrid regime subtypes, though this risks endowing constitutions in our terminology with an aura of permanence that they do not necessarily deserve and risks treating them as more exogenously given than the logic and empirical practice of patronal politics suggest they in fact are. Thus rather than break down patronalistic hybrid regimes into sub-categories of regime (hybrid regimes with adjectives?), the present study suggests it will be less distracting and more productive to talk instead about different sorts of hybrid regime systems, or the effects of different ways hybrid regimes can be organized. The reference in parentheses is to David Collier and Steven Levitsky, "Democracy with Adjectives: Conceptual Innovation in Comparative Research," *World Politics*, v. 49, no. 3, April 1997, pp. 430–51.

Patronal Politics in Global Comparative Perspective

In considering how the preceding analysis relates to the rest of the world, one can think of the post-Soviet countries as providing something like a pristine context in which to study the fundamental characteristics of patronal politics. It is pristine in the sense that it is unencumbered by certain other factors that can be present in other parts of the world but strongly shape how patronal politics plays out, factors such as a realistic near-term chance of joining the European Union. The preceding chapters have shown that patronal politics does function according to a characteristic logic, one distinct from how politics functions in less patronalistic contexts like those in contemporary Norway or Canada. And since pervasive patronalism is much more common in human history than its absence, including today, the former Soviet world can serve as a useful "baseline" for understanding patterns of real politics that we find in other countries, directing our attention to factors like EU prospects that might shape or alter these baseline patterns in different nations or regions. In this global comparative perspective, at least some of the factors that Chapter 11 concluded were unimportant in accounting for variation within the post-Soviet space now take on more significance as explanations as to how patronal politics might function somewhat differently in other parts of the world.

This final chapter turns to such a global analysis, showing how the logic presented here – factoring in certain contextual variables – can account for regime dynamics in the rest of the postcommunist world. This includes Serbia's democratic breakthrough in 2000, which follows a surprisingly similar "short regime cycle" pattern that has largely been overlooked. It also identifies large-scale factors that have helped tip Latin America's patronal polities toward sustained competing-pyramid politics, but that have produced more mixed results (often quite similar to post-Soviet patterns) in sub-Saharan Africa, Asia, and the Middle East. Indeed, the logic of patronal politics has important implications for how we might understand the series of events now widely known as the Arab Spring. The chapter then identifies a broader comparative research agenda and turns the global analysis back to the post-Soviet states, examining whether these countries might over a much longer period begin to look more like other parts of the world, such as the state failure of Somalia, the open access society of Sweden, the patronal democracy of the Philippines, or the long-term political closure of China. The book then wraps up with implications for policy makers seeking to understand patronal politics and to relate them to policy agendas centered on democracy promotion.

What Distinguishes Eurasia as a Region: High Patronalism, Low Linkage/Leverage

To suggest that the former Soviet space is something like a pristine patronalistic environment is to have in mind that it emerged from a totalitarian system that had destroyed preexisting institutions and ideational commitments to a far greater degree than old regimes typically do. In addition, the totalitarian system itself then disintegrated quite rapidly and extensively, leaving mainly a variety of shards for political entrepreneurs to collect and piece together in new ways, often investing them with new meaning in the process. In this sense, the patterns described in Chapter 11, including what factors are and are not important, can be interpreted as an understanding of what happens under something close to "pure" patronal politics. This analysis can thus provide a useful foundation for thinking about contextual factors that might interact with the patronalistic context to produce different regime dynamics in different parts of the world. This constitutes a major research agenda of its own and so such factors cannot be conclusively identified here. But some suggestions are made in this section to help facilitate future research.

Most obviously, we would expect countries with lower levels of patronalism to feature the regime dynamics described here in a less pronounced way. Because patronalism tends to correlate with weaker rule of law, greater perceived corruption, and scarcer social capital, we can consider at least the following countries to have low levels of patronalism: most West European and North American countries and a few other states such as Australia and Japan that have made the transition to what Douglass North and his colleagues have called an "open access order."[1] We would thus expect such countries to follow a different political logic, one reflecting a nonpatronalistic social equilibrium. As was discussed in Chapter 3, research by Herbert Kitschelt, Zdenka Mansfeldova, Radoslaw Markowski, and Gabor Toka has also established that all of the other postcommunist societies of Europe except Romania, Macedonia, Albania, and Bulgaria feature substantially less patronalism than does the set

---

[1] Douglass C. North, John Joseph Wallis, Barry R. Weingast, *Violence and Social Orders: A Conceptual Framework for Interpreting Recorded Human History* (New York: Cambridge University Press, 2009).

of non-Baltic post-Soviet countries that have been the focus of this book so far.[2] At the same time, they are generally more patronalistic than the classic cases of open access orders. A less patronalistic social equilibrium would be expected to sustain more robust political competition and reduce opportunities for chief patrons to use informal power to produce political closure in the form of single-pyramid systems. This should be the case in these countries even with formal presidentialist constitutions and with parliamentarist constitutions that feature low executive divisibility and few formal selectorates. Patronal networks themselves can be expected to play a lesser role in politics, which increasingly would be expected to revolve increasingly around programmatic issues and causes rather than patronage and selective punishments.

The logic of patronal politics would also suggest, in line with a growing body of research, that the post-Soviet space stands out in important ways because of what Steven Levitsky and Lucan Way call "low linkage and low leverage."[3] That is, Western democracies have relatively little ability to influence regime outcomes there. Levitsky and Way find that two regions, postcommunist Eastern Europe and Latin America, have systematically and historically featured denser ties with Western countries and more structural factors making them vulnerable to Western democratization efforts than countries in the former Soviet Union and Africa. Surely many countries in the Middle East and much of Asia would fall into the latter category as well.[4] Where linkage and leverage are very high, the logic of patronal politics would expect that Western actors may in fact be able to exert enough power to alter the expectations of incumbent and opposition networks as to whether the incumbent leader is likely to remain in power beyond a given point. In high-linkage, high-leverage countries, Western powers are also better able to supply *external* material sustenance and asset protection in *large* enough measure to induce significant networks not to coordinate around a given chief patron's authority. All this serves to weaken or potentially even end the tendency to single-pyramid politics and regime cycles more generally. Thus while levels of Western linkage and leverage *within* the post-Soviet context were nowhere great enough to explain regime dynamics within this set of cases, the logic of patronal politics would not rule out that they could be high enough in other cases to dampen regime cycles by significantly hindering the efforts of patronal presidents to build single-pyramid systems.

---

[2] Herbert Kitschelt, Zdenka Mansfeldova, Radoslaw Markowski, and Gabor Toka, *Post-Communist Party Systems: Competition, Representation, and Inter-Party Cooperation* (New York: Cambridge University Press, 1999), especially p. 39.

[3] Steven Levitsky and Lucan A. Way, *Competitive Authoritarianism: Hybrid Regimes after the Cold War* (New York: Cambridge University Press, 2010), pp. 38–45, p. 40.

[4] Levitsky and Way, *Competitive Authoritarianism*, p. 40. They do not consider the Middle East and most of Asia because they are interested in a specific set of "competitive authoritarian" regimes rather than full autocracies.

The subsequent subsections consider different parts of the world with respect to levels of patronalism and linkage/leverage, showing how variation in these broad "structural" factors can help us account for the degree to which politics there tends to resemble what we see in the "baseline" post-Soviet polities. Special attention is given to non-post-Soviet postcommunist cases because these are frequently considered in the same set as post-Soviet cases in other analyses of regime change, forcing us to show how the present theory relates to them.

Eastern Europe (Also Known as Central, Southern, and Eastern Europe)

Except for Albania, Bulgaria, Macedonia, and Romania, the postcommunist countries of Eastern Europe represent a context that generally features lower levels of patronalism and much higher levels of linkage and leverage than post-Soviet cases. One reason for the latter is the European Union. The highly prosperous EU is widely documented as perhaps the world's most potent source of linkage and leverage capable of undermining single-pyramid politics and perhaps even reducing patronalism itself.[5] In Eastern Europe, the prospect of membership has been both credible and attractive enough that the EU might even be considered a potential "external base" for alternative power pyramids in patronalistic countries that have a chance at membership.

In addition, when considering why East European countries have tended to be more open politically than post-Soviet states, it is worth noting that they have been far less likely to feature presidentialist constitutions. Table 12.1 presents the broad pattern. While one could conceivably argue that lower levels of patronalism might decrease demand for presidentialism, in fact the reason for the prevalence of presidentialism in post-Soviet countries would appear to have more to do with historical contingency linked to precisely how the Soviet "empire" fell apart and what national leaders at the time thought was in their best political interest. As readers will recall from Chapter 5, post-Soviet countries largely owe their legacies of presidentialism to the institutional innovation introduced by Gorbachev in 1990. That year, he imposed the first office of the "presidency" on the USSR's hitherto parliamentarist formal political system and prompted the country's constituent union republics to imitate this move in efforts to gain bargaining power. This put presidential networks in strong position to win the most important power struggles with parliaments during the 1990s, for reasons laid out in Chapter 4. Critically, the postcommunist states of Eastern Europe had for the most part already left the Soviet orbit by the time

---

[5] See in particular Milada A. Vachudova, *Europe Undivided: Democracy, Leverage, and Integration after Communism* (New York: Oxford University Press, 2005).

TABLE 12.1. *Formal Constitutions and Patronalism in Postcommunist Countries since the Mid-1990s*

Degree of Patronalism[b]	Constitution Type[a]		
	Presidentialism	Divided Executive	Parliamentarism
High	Armenia	Ukraine	**Albania**[c]
	Azerbaijan	2006–2010, 2014–	**Moldova 2000–**[c]
	Belarus	Kyrgyzstan 2010–	
	Georgia	**Mongolia**	
	Kazakhstan	**Macedonia**	
	Kyrgyzstan until 2010	**Bulgaria**	
	Moldova until 2000		
	Romania		
	Russia		
	Tajikistan		
	Turkmenistan		
	Ukraine 1991–2006,		
	2010–14		
	Uzbekistan		
Moderate	**Lithuania**		**Estonia**[d]
	Serbia		**Latvia**[c]
	Slovakia 1998–		**Slovakia until 1998**[c]
Low	**Croatia until 2000**	Croatia 2001–	**Czech Republic**[c]
	Poland		**Hungary**[c]
			Slovenia[c]

Note: States effectively under occupation and quasi-states are not included. **Boldfaced** countries are those outside the non-Baltic former Soviet Union.

[a] Author's coding based on definitions in Chapter 4.

[b] Patronalism here is operationalized using the categorization from Kitschelt et al. (*Postcommunist Party Systems*, p. 39) that captures levels of "patrimonialism" in each country's communist legacies, as described in Chapters 2 and 3.

[c] Has a president elected by parliament.

[d] Has a president elected by parliament, but with only symbolic powers.

[e] A directly elected president appoints the PM, but has very weak powers in all other respects and so is coded by local convention as parliamentarist.

of Gorbachev's institutional innovation, so there was no tendency to imitate it. Most of them emerged from Communist rule with nonpresidentialist systems, and many newly elected East European leaders believed their prospects for popular support were increased by avoiding the appearance of imitating Moscow. Now let us look at different sets of East European countries according to constitution type and levels of patronalism to see whether the expected patterns hold.

Nonpresidentialist and Less Patronalistic Countries: Czech
Republic, Estonia, Hungary, Latvia, Slovakia, Slovenia
The logic of patronal politics would suggest that polities with weaker tradi-
tions of patronalism, nonpresidentialist constitutions, and high Western linkage and leverage would give a great deal more mobilizing opportunity to oppositions. We would also expect that incumbent regimes would have substantially
less ability to keep their elites in line when elections provide a focal point for
coordinated action aimed at defeating the regime. The combination of low
patronalism and a nonpresidentialist constitution thus effectively delinks revolution from moments of succession, making regime turnover far more likely to
occur during *any* election in which a country's top offices are at stake. That is,
we would expect "electoral breakthroughs" in such countries to be associated
with low incumbent popularity though *not* systematically with the politics of
succession, as in the post-Soviet space. For these reasons, we would also expect
that incumbent patrons would be far less likely to attempt to steal elections in
the first place, more likely to be challenged when they do, and more likely to
concede quickly when they do and are. And once any such incumbent power
grab is defeated, European Union influence could be expected to be present to
help support the political opening.

This is very much what we find in the parliamentarist and less patronalistic
countries of Eastern Europe. The Czech Republic, Estonia, Hungary, Latvia,
and Slovenia have generally all been free of powerful attempts by incumbent
authorities to monopolize power, and all were successfully integrated into the
European Union.[6] Slovakia in 1998 (a moderately patronalistic country by
the measure of Kitschelt and his fellow researchers) represents the only case in
this same category when a leadership clearly attempted to engineer an election
victory using strong political machine methods against popular opinion. This
was the case of Prime Minister Vladimir Meciar.[7] But he had previously been
ousted from the prime ministership twice since 1991, and in 1998 a well-run
opposition campaign defeated him and he did not even try to resist once the
count was in. Instead, he accepted the results and left office according to constitutionally stipulated procedures.[8] Since that time, no significant reversion
to closed politics has taken place, and the country has joined the European

---

[6] Since a single party won a supermajority in a parliamentarist system in Hungary in 2010 (resulting in its being able to change the constitution unilaterally), many have expressed fears that it
may be reverting to a substantially more closed political system. The logic presented here would
suggest such efforts would be likely to fail in the next election should the party's popular support
drop substantially relative to alternatives.

[7] On the lack of public support for Meciar by 1998, see Valerie J. Bunce and Sharon L. Wolchik,
Defeating Authoritarian Leaders in Postcommunist Countries (New York: Cambridge University
Press, 2011), pp. 59–60.

[8] Valerie J. Bunce and Sharon L. Wolchik, "International Diffusion and Postcommunist Electoral
Revolutions," *Communist and Post-Communist Studies*, v. 39, 2006, pp. 283–304, pp. 290–1.
Slovakia later shifted to a system with a directly elected president who appoints the head of
government.

Union along with all the other parliamentarist East European countries with only moderate or low patronalism. These Slovak events, indeed, would seem to be something quite different from the post-Soviet patronal presidential ousters analyzed in Chapter 7. There were no East European countries with moderate or low patronalism that also had a divided-executive constitution in the 1990s.

Highly Patronalist Countries: Albania, Bulgaria, Macedonia, Romania

As this volume's logic would also expect, the highly patronalistic countries of Eastern Europe have tended to feature more unruly political battles and the greater use of political machine tactics. Albania is the only highly patronalistic East European country with a parliamentarist constitution, and as this book's logic would expect, its politics have been open relative to post-Soviet countries yet slightly more closed than other East European ones.[9] It also remains outside the EU, having failed to meet its criteria for membership. Nevertheless, the EU has been directly involved at key political junctures, among other things helping shape a constitution that intentionally balanced an indirectly elected presidency with a strong prime minister. This balancing (reflecting signficant executive divisibility) has proved important in preventing either side from establishing a single-pyramid system.[10]

Macedonia and Bulgaria feature divided-executive constitutions and have experienced sustained competing-pyramid politics despite periodic political crises and widespread corruption. This reinforces the point made in Chapter 9 that Ukraine's dysfunctional experience with this formal constitutional system need not be typical, and that other countries such as Kyrgyzstan and Georgia that have recently adopted divided-executive constitutions may hope for a better outcome. Of course, Bulgaria and Macedonia have also benefited from very dense and powerful EU linkage and leverage that can act to temper incentives for the most ruthless forms of competition between the separate centers of executive power. In Macedonia, the EU helped discourage ethnic Macedonian networks from running roughshod over ethnic Albanian networks.[11] Thus Bulgaria became a member in 2007 and Macedonia essentially met all criteria but was stymied by Greece because of the latter's claim on the name "Macedonia."[12] Bulgaria's 1996–7 political crisis has been cited by at least one account as an "early precedent" for what it dubs a wave of democratic breakthroughs culminating in the color revolutions. But that study also notes that during this period Bulgaria was

---

[9] For example, compare Gledis Gjipali, "Albania," with the other chapters in *Nations in Transit 2012* (New York: Freedom House, 2013).

[10] Ridvan Peshkopia, *Conditioning Democratization: Institutional Reforms and EU Membership Conditionality in Albania and Macedonia* (New York: Anthem, 2013), especially chapter 3.

[11] Peshkopia, *Conditioning Democratization*.

[12] Vachudova, *Europe Undivided*, chapters 6–7.

already a "poorly functioning but fully democratic state" – exactly what one would expect from a highly patronalistic country with a divided-executive constitution.[13] Indeed, its 1996–7 crisis involved a spirited battle that in part pitted president against prime minister, with the latter initially resigning after a series of "catastrophic" economic failures sparked massive street protests.[14] European linkage and leverage helped pro-European forces defeat the highly unpopular prime minister and his party,[15] who were widely blamed for the economic collapse. They eventually pulled Bulgaria into the EU fold and helped it sustain a robust competing-pyramid system that, much like Ukraine's in 2005–10, featured free and contested elections in a context of substantial continued corruption.[16]

Romania has been Eastern Europe's only patronal presidential state, featuring high levels of patronalism and a presidentialist constitution as defined in Chapter 4. Milada Vachudova reports that European Union incentives and actions constrained its first patronal president, Ion Iliescu, from using the strongest political machine tools that were otherwise available to him. He had indeed begun to employ these tools much as post-Soviet patronal presidents had in the first years after the Soviet bloc's collapse, when the EU itself was just appearing and developing its role.[17] Thus when Iliescu approached the end of his first term in office with low popular support, he and his government strikingly "did not significantly tamper with the 1996 parliamentary or presidential elections" despite having "months of warning" that he was likely to lose.[18] Major warning signs for him had included his unpopular party's losses in the June 1996 local elections (when the opposition captured the Bucharest mayor's office) and the November 3 parliamentary elections, which had triggered a number of defections (including that of his head of secret police) to the opposition before the presidential election two weeks later.[19] Thus even though the opposition campaign and civic activism were "rather low-key,"[20] Iliescu allowed an honest vote count and conceded defeat without a struggle.[21] Thus in a pattern that differs strikingly from the norm in the low linkage and

---

[13] Bunce and Wolchik, *Defeating Authoritarian Leaders*, p. 54.

[14] Venelin I. Ganev, *Preying on the State: The Transformation of Bulgaria after 1989* (Ithaca, NY: Cornell University Press, 2007), p. 139.

[15] Tsveta Petrova, "A Postcommunist Transition in Two Acts: The 1996–97 Antigovernment Struggle in Bulgaria as a Bridge between the 1989–92 and 1996–2007 Democratization Waves in Eastern Europe," in Valerie Bunce, Michael McFaul, and Kathryn Stoner-Weiss, eds., *Democracy and Authoritarianism in the Postcommunist World* (New York: Cambridge University Press, 2010), pp. 107–33.

[16] Georgy Ganev, "Bulgaria," in *Nations in Transit 2012* (New York: Freedom House, 2013).

[17] Vachudova, *Europe Undivided*, chapter 6.

[18] Vachudova, *Europe Undivided*, p. 154.

[19] Vladimir Tismaneanu, "Electoral Revolutions," *Society*, November/December 1997, pp. 61–5, p. 62.

[20] Bunce and Wolchik, *Defeating Authoritarian Leaders*, p. 55.

[21] Tismaneanu, "Electoral Revolutions," p. 62.

low leverage former Soviet space, the presence of high levels of Western linkage and leverage helped Romania successfully nip single-pyramid building in the bud. This set the stage for the European Union to deepen its influence in Romanian domestic politics and eventually pull it into the EU, where it has sustained a robust competing-pyramid system, another example of patronal democracy.

Less Patronalistic Presidentialist Countries: Croatia, Lithuania, Poland, Serbia

The other presidentialist countries of Eastern Europe each featured at least somewhat lower levels of patronalism than Romania according to the Kitschelt-and-company measure. In this set, those with the most credible European Union prospects (Lithuania and Poland) manifested no significant attempts by presidents to monopolize power. Indeed, both joined the EU in the first wave of postcommunist enlargement in 2004.[22] The presidentialist political regimes in Serbia and Croatia, however, emerged out of deadly ethnic wars that made European Union prospects more distant. In the years immediately following the end of fighting, the incumbent presidents there tolerated little opposition, though both presidents and their parties fell from power when succession crises combined with low popular support. And once they fell, with the ethnic conflict further in the past, the EU was there to help seal the political opening.

Croatia. In Croatia, the crucial event was the death of nationalist strongman and separatist war leader Franjo Tudjman in office as president in 1999. This meant that the opposition's well-organized mobilization of discontent met a regime that not only had few patronal resources because of Croatia's low levels of patronalism, but also faced the kind of succession-related uncertainty that would be expected to undermine whatever patronal authority it did have to rely on. After this event, Croatia's democratization was overdetermined. Not only was it a low patronalism country by postcommunist standards, and not only did the EU seriously engage it for membership (ultimately signing a membership treaty with it in 2011),[23] but to help prevent future concentrations of power it transitioned to a divided-executive constitution.[24]

Serbia and the Ouster of Milosevic. The downfall of Slobodan Milosevic in Serbia, strongly presidentialist and more patronalistic than Croatia, even more closely resembles the pattern of leadership ousters found among patronal presidential countries where Western linkage and leverage are low. Most scholarly attention to his ouster in the comparative literature has focused on the highly visible role of clever youth organizations and transnational

---

[22] Vachudova, *Europe Undivided.*

[23] For details, see the European Commission's Web site, http://ec.europa.eu/enlargement/countries/detailed-country-information/croatia/index_en.htm, accessed January 16, 2013.

[24] The author is grateful to Andrew Konitzer for pointing this out. See also the interpretation by Venice Commission experts at http://www.venice.coe.int/docs/2001/CDL(2001)015-bil.pdf, especially pp. 24–5.

democracy-promotion networks that have been quick to claim the credit. Such analyses typically dub these events the "Bulldozer Revolution" and place them either at the start or the pivotal middle in what is depicted as a chain reaction of electoral revolutions.[25] Serbian activists have become widely sought speakers and trainers for those interested in learning how revolutions can be crafted. Yet to the extent Serbian society can be called patronalistic, the logic of patronal politics would call attention to something else that may have been more fundamental: In the period leading up to the 2000 election, Milosevic was an unpopular lame-duck.

When one talked about "President Milosevic" in the first half of the 1990s, he was president of strongly presidentialist *Serbia* rather than of the larger Federal Republic of Yugoslavia, which also contained Montenegro. Unlike Serbia's presidency, the federal presidency was not directly elected and had very weak formal powers, being considered a secondary post.[26] But while the Serbian presidency he held was recognized as the more powerful formal post of the two, Milosevic ran into a big problem: His constitutional limit of two consecutive terms in office was set to expire in 1997. Moreover, this was at the same time his popular support was eroding, with especially strong criticism voiced by those urging even stronger nationalist stances. According to one set of polls, the Serbian president's standing in public eyes had dropped from above 50 percent approval in 1992 to just 12 percent by 1997.[27]

In an effort to make sure he stayed in charge after leaving his post as Serbian president, Milosevic persuaded his party's deputies in the federal parliament to elect him to the federal presidency. But this provoked many of the same problems that many lame-duck patronal presidents faced in post-Soviet countries when they prepared to leave office: key defections and a significant weakening of the political machine. For one thing, at the federal level, the dominant Montenegrin party that had been his ally ruptured, with a major faction opposing his effort to assume formal leadership of the whole federation as a way to prolong his rule. The group that had opposed Milosevic's move then won control of the Montenegrin presidency. Even more dramatically, Milosevic lost control over the Serbian presidency itself. Attempting to usher someone weak enough to control into this formally strong office, Milosevic saw his handpicked heir beaten by a radical nationalist opposition candidate. With Milosevic already in this predicament, his deeply humiliating loss of control over Kosovo in the 1999 war with NATO and the near-collapse

[25] E.g., Mark R. Beissinger, "Structure and Example in Modular Political Phenomena: The Diffusion of Bulldozer/Rose/Orange/Tulip Revolutions," *Perspectives on Politics*, v. 5, no. 2, June 2007, pp. 259–76; Bunce and Wolchik, *Defeating Authoritarian Leaders*.

[26] On these posts and also some of the details that follow in this paragraph, see Sabrina P. Ramet, *Serbia since 1989: Politics and Society under Milosevic and After* (Seattle: University of Washington Press, 2005), pp. 59–60.

[27] Laslo Sekelj, "Parties and Elections: The Federal Republic of Yugoslavia. Change without Transformation," *Europe-Asia Studies*, v. 52, no. 1, January 2000, pp. 57–75, p. 72.

of his economy were absolutely devastating.[28] Lacking strong formal power to rely on, his ability to exercise informal power in the future was under serious question, in turn undermining his ability to shape the expectations of elites and sustain the loyalty of his political machine. Thus one scholarly article published *before* the 2000 presidential election concluded that "the erosion of Milosevic's power is indisputable."[29]

The 2000 election can in fact be seen as Milosevic's last-ditch effort to salvage his position. He pushed through a constitutional amendment that would strengthen the federal presidency by making it for the first time a directly elected post. But when the votes came in showing he had badly lost, confirmed by opposition-sponsored parallel vote counts, the game was up. Milosevic resisted recognition that he had lost in the first round of the September 2000 elections, but opposition forces with EU and other international help successfully mobilized hundreds of thousands of protesters into the streets. At the same time, central figures in his political machine defected.[30] This notably included the military, which thereby "made the endgame almost moot."[31] And once the old regime was decisively ousted, the European Union was there to hold out carrots and sticks for the new authorities, helping consolidate the opening through denser Western linkage and growing leverage.[32] Thus while the bright and creative protesters make for an attractive story line, especially for Westerners who had invested in helping them win, in fact Milosevic faced a large number of factors that all pointed in the direction of his impending downfall and that are likely of more basic importance.

Summing Up Eastern Europe

Overall, Eastern Europe's tendency to feature lower levels of patronalism and higher Western linkage and leverage (especially EU influence) explains why its regime dynamics have tended to differ systematically from those observed in the former Soviet space. These two contextual factors have tended to hinder efforts to build single-pyramid systems regardless of constitutional form, though the fact that Eastern Europe features a greater share of nonpresidentialist constitutions also contributes to its greater political openness. The relatively few serious efforts to usurp power that have occurred have generally been successfully defeated at the next election so long as the public did not back the usurpers. This was the case regardless of whether the opposition was

---

[28] Mark R. Thompson and Philipp Kuntz, "Stolen Elections: The Case of the Serbian October," *Journal of Democracy*, v. 15, no. 4, October 2004, pp. 159–72, p. 165.

[29] Sekelj, "Parties and Elections," p. 72.

[30] Thompson and Kuntz, "Stolen Elections," p. 167.

[31] Paul D'Anieri, "Explaining the Success and Failure of Post-Communist Revolutions," *Communist and Post-Communist Studies*, v. 39, 2006, pp. 331–50, p. 342.

[32] Katya Kalandadze and Mitchell A. Orenstein, "Electoral Protests and Democratization: Beyond the Color Revolutions," *Comparative Political Studies*, v. 42, no. 11, November 2009, pp. 1403–25.

well organized and financed (as in Serbia in 2000) or uncoordinated and low-key (as in Romania in 1996). And the greatest success in subverting democracy occurred in Croatia and Serbia in the 1990s, when their devastating war made European Union prospects most remote. The end of the war sparked a reemergence of these prospects and helped consolidate the democratic openings that occurred once their nondemocratic leaderships toppled after experiencing leadership succession under low popular support.

Africa, Asia, the Middle East (Arab Spring), and Latin America

Turning to the rest of the highly patronalistic world (recall Figure 3.1), we find reason to suspect that regime dynamics there are not fundamentally different from what has been described so far in this book.

Latin America

If we turn first to Latin America, the very high levels of Western linkage and leverage that Levitsky and Way document there can go a long way to explaining why these countries have generally sustained competing-pyramid politics since the end of the Cold War and the fall of many military dictatorships.[33] Much as EU influence helped moderate the propensity of Romania's patronal presidential system to encourage a single-pyramid arrangement of the country's main patronal networks, so have dense and influential American and other Western ties helped do the same in countries such as Argentina, El Salvador, and Mexico despite the regional prevalence of presidentialist constitutions.[34]

Sub-Saharan Africa

African countries would appear to resemble post-Soviet countries in reflecting highly patronalistic societies in places where the West has relatively little linkage or leverage. In the context of the Cold War, single independence movements often won the struggles there for decolonization, with other elites quickly coordinating around their authority. Sometimes this happened with the support of Cold War powers. Political closure was also facilitated by Westminster parliamentarist constitutions, which were initially widespread there but which Chapters 4 and 10 argued tend strongly to promote single-pyramid systems and to be susceptible to regime cycles. These systems tended to break down quickly after independence, much as irregularity in regime cycles occurred in Eurasia in the first years after the USSR's demise and were often replaced by presidentialism or military rule. The result in either case was usually a new single-pyramid system, quite often without any significant political contestation allowed. Without meaningful competition, elections ceased to play a

---

[33] Levitsky and Way, *Competitive Authoritarianism*.
[34] Jose Antonio Cheibub, Zachary Elkins, and Tom Ginsburg, "Latin American Presidentialism in Comparative and Historical Perspective," *Texas Law Review*, v. 89, no. 7, 2011, pp. 1707–39.

significant role coordinating elite maneuvering oriented to presidential ouster or succession, meaning that regime cycles there were more likely to revolve around irregular drivers (such as exogenous shocks) or long-term cyclic drivers like the human life expectancy of leaders.

One very important irregular driver of regime cycles was the demise of Soviet power, which had propped up many African regimes. The USSR's retreat from African politics and eventual collapse helped trigger mass protests, which in turn catalyzed coordinated elite defections in many regimes. This produced Africa's own wave of political opening in the early 1990s and the emergence of its hybrid regimes, supported by the same array of international and domestic considerations that Chapter 4 described as supporting such systems in the post-Soviet space.[35] Also as with the post-Soviet cases, however, the initial openings (with the sudden emergence of competing-pyramid systems) were quickly followed by the reconsolidation of single-pyramid systems in presidentialist countries – evidence again of regime cycling. While further research will be necessary, there is evidence that at least some of these regime cycles are of the regular sort, with phases punctuated by succession-related elections or more vaguely defined by aging leaders. For example, Kenya's dominant network was ousted through an election in 2002 only after its longtime leader Daniel Arap Moi became a lame-duck through term limits.[36] While it may be the case that Africa's independence wars helped forge mass party support in a way that impacts African regime dynamics, this remains an important subject for future research.[37] We will return to the question of ruling parties' popular support later.

The Middle East and the Arab Spring

Regime dynamics in Middle Eastern countries, including the Arab Spring, also appear to follow a broad logic of patronal politics. Most of these countries leading into 2011 were full autocracies, which Chapter 4 argued means three things. First, elections are less likely to structure patterns of coordinated elite network defection related to possible succession. Second, as a result, regime cycles are likely to be of the irregular variety or, in the longer run, regular in being driven by the human life expectancy of leaders and the succession questions that aging raises. Third, because the sources of regular regime cycles tend to organize the impact of other threats to regime control, the chance that any one "irregular" event will become focal for elite defection grows as leaders age (that is, when it becomes clear a succession is in the near-future) and as leaders become more unpopular.

[35] Michael Bratton and Nicolas van de Walle, *Democratic Experiments in Africa: Regime Transitions in Comparative Perspective* (New York: Cambridge University Press, 1997).

[36] Marc Morje Howard and Philip G. Roessler, "Liberalizing Electoral Outcomes in Competitive Authoritarian Regimes," *American Journal of Political Science*, v. 50, no. 2, April 2006, pp. 365–81, p. 377.

[37] Steven R. Levitsky and Lucan A. Way, "Beyond Patronage: Violent Struggle, Ruling Party Cohesion, and Authoritarian Durability," *Perspectives on Politics*, v. 10, no. 4, December 2012, pp. 868–89.

When turning to the 2011 Arab uprisings, one is initially struck by what seems to be a classic case of regime cycle irregularity. For reasons that even the best Middle East experts do not pretend to understand, out of all the events that could possibly have captured Arab hearts and minds, the self-immolation of a frustrated provincial Tunisian fruit vendor sparked a wave of massive protests that rapidly cascaded across the Middle East. It was propagated by regionwide satellite television news networks (the "new Arab public sphere") that framed each successive protest as a chain reaction of popular outrage against corrupt and repressive regimes.[38] Accordingly, the dramatic protests have so far received almost all of the media and scholarly attention on recent regime dynamics in the Arab world.[39]

The patronal politics perspective, however, calls attention to important sources of regime cycle regularity that provide a powerful explanation as to precisely *where these protests actually translated into the ouster of dictators and where they did not.* Perhaps most intriguingly, it highlights the fact that all of the regimes that fell in the wake of this protest wave in 2011 were presidentialist systems with presidents who were not only unpopular but increasingly regarded as lame-ducks as a result of aging and strong expectations of nearing succession. Egypt, Libya, Tunisia, and Yemen each featured elderly leaders who were facing "impending succession crisis" and who were also widely believed to be positioning their own offspring to succeed them, a prospect that "heightened conflict among elites."[40] This expectation of succession "affected every part of the political process" in these countries, often producing splits among those who favored hereditary succession and others whose interests ran against it.[41]

As the logic of patronal politics would lead us to expect, it was in precisely these countries that the suddenly emerging protests were able to provide a focal point for the coordinated defection of elites who were looking to the future and who were dissatisfied with the dynastic option (or doubtful it would succeed). In most cases, the critical elite defections were those of the military itself. These militaries typically represented extensive and elaborate networks of economic interests ranging far beyond the military-industrial complex, classic patronalistic entities. Moreover, the military networks had in at least some cases been

---

[38] Marc Lynch, *The Arab Uprising: The Unfinished Revolutions of the New Middle East* (New York: PublicAffairs, 2012). See also Hamid Dabashi, *The Arab Spring: The End of Postcolonialism* (New York: Zed, 2012); and James L. Gelvin, *The Arab Uprisings: What Everyone Needs to Know* (New York: Oxford University Press, 2012).

[39] Including by some of the same people who focused on the protest element in the color revolutions. For example, see David Patel and Valerie Bunce, "Turning Points and the Cross-National Diffusion of Popular Protest," *APSA CD*, v. 10, no. 1, January 2012, pp. 1, 10–13.

[40] Ellen Lust, "Why Now? Micro Transitions and the Arab Uprisings," *APSA CD*, v. 9, no. 3, October 2011, pp. 1, 3–8, p. 4.

[41] Roger Owen, *The Rise and Fall of Arab Presidents for Life* (Cambridge, MA: Harvard University Press, 2012), p. 139.

in rivalry with the patronal networks of presidential offspring well before the uprisings. Egypt is a stark example of this pattern.[42] Other networks in the old rulers' single-pyramid systems, however, also defected, with tribal networks playing a particularly prominent role abandoning regimes in Yemen and Libya as expectations regarding presidents' ability to hang on to power dimmed.[43]

Moreover, all of the region's monarchies weathered the protest storm. This is unsurprising if succession expectations are decisive: Monarchy provides a mechanism for enhancing elite coordination around a designated successor.[44] It is also interesting that all of the Middle East's more open hybrid regimes[45] (as opposed to full autocracies) survived. This indicates that the political struggles among their most important networks may indeed have been more structured around electoral competition than street protest there, as Chapter 4 anticipates.[46]

The logic of patronal politics also would lead us to expect that where countries emerged from the revolutions with presidentialist constitutions, we would be quite likely to witness a gradual return to single-pyramid politics. But the logic also suggests that an initial period of turmoil is likely before regime cycle regularity comes to dominate; in the short run, leaders are likely to overreach and fall from power early before understandings of power in the new system clarify, and incompetent leaders are selected out through competition or learn to be more effective. As regularity emerges, Chapter 4 indicates that the most likely form of regime would be a hybrid regime. While more time must pass before we can judge, events in the Arab Spring countries as of mid-2014 certainly make this prediction credible.

Asia

Some of the political regimes of Asia are outright dictatorships while others reflect different patterns of patronal politics. Among the dictatorships, the sturdiest have been anchored by homegrown communist parties that at least in some cases (China and Vietnam, if not North Korea) arguably have wielded substantial public support as well, especially in the era of economic growth. On the other end of the regime spectrum, India might be regarded as an example of enduring competing-pyramid politics sustained under a parliamentarist

---

[42] Holger Albrecht and Dina Bishara, "Back on Horseback: The Military and Political Transformation in Egypt," *Middle East Law and Governance*, v. 3, 2011, pp. 13–23; Zoltan Barany, "The Role of the Military," *Journal of Democracy*, v. 22, no. 4, October 2011, pp. 24–35; Eva Bellin, "Reconsidering the Robustness of Authoritarianism in the Middle East: Lessons from the Arab Spring," *Comparative Politics*, v. 44, no. 2, January 2012, pp. 127–51; Gelvin, *The Arab Uprisings*; Owen, *The Rise and Fall*, p. 144.

[43] Jason Brownlee and Joshua Stacher, "Change of Leader, Continuity of System: Nascent Liberalization in Post-Mubarak Egypt," *APSA CD*, v. 9, no. 2, May 2011, pp. 1, 4–9, p. 5; Gelvin, *The Arab Uprisings*; Owen, *The Rise and Fall*.

[44] Jack A. Goldstone, "Weakness and Resilience in Middle Eastern Autocracies," *Foreign Affairs*, v. 90, no. 3, May/June 2011, pp. 8–16; Gordon Tullock, *Autocracy* (New York: Springer, 1987).

[45] Most clearly Iraq and Lebanon.

[46] Apart from armed insurgents in Iraq, of course.

constitution. Under the dominance of the Congress Party, which retained strong political support, India featured something like a relatively liberal single-pyramid system (perhaps akin to that of Georgia under Saakashvili). This system finally fell victim to a decline in public support and ushered in an era of robust competing-pyramid politics at the national level – sometimes branded a "patronage democracy."[47] An interesting topic for research would be whether India's relative liberalism was encouraged more by strong Western linkage and leverage, by institutional features of its parliamentarist constitution, or by leaders committed to making their single-pyramid system more gentle.

Moving farther east, we find a variety of patterns that would seem understandable through the lens of patronal politics. Japan under the Liberal Democratic Party's long postwar dominance could plausibly be put in the same category as Congress Party India. Indeed, Western linkage and leverage were particularly forceful there, beginning with military occupation.[48] Relative openness in Taiwan and South Korea after long periods of Cold War era autocracy can also likely be attributed to very strong Western linkage and leverage after the Cold War. The Philippines, with less dense Western linkage and leverage since the Cold War, has long featured robust patronal politics, though since Ferdinand Marcos fell from power in an early "people power" revolution (when he was aging and had fallen very ill, indicative of long regime cycle dynamics), presidents have been restricted to a single six-year term in office. This effectively renders them lame-ducks from the very start, underpinning lively competing-pyramid politics.[49] Thailand represents an interesting case where an active and popular constitutional monarch representing a vast network of informal economic and political interests (the "network monarchy"), together with the military, may have helped anchor a competing-pyramid system – at least until a May 2014 military coup. The parliament-based government prior to that time represented the other formal executive focal point for elite coordination, and the competition was strongest when the prime minister represented a highly popular alternative patronal network like that of oligarch Thaksin Shinawatra.[50] Whether the 2014

[47] Kanchan Chandra, *Why Ethnic Parties Succeed: Patronage and Ethnic Head Counts in India* (New York: Cambridge University Press, 2004).

[48] Ethan Scheiner, *Democracy without Competition in Japan: Opposition Failure in a One-Party Dominant State* (New York: Cambridge University Press, 2006).

[49] David C. Kang, *Crony Capitalism: Corruption and Development in South Korea and the Philippines* (New York: Cambridge University Press, 2002).

[50] Duncan McCargo, "Network Monarchy and Legitimacy Crises in Thailand," *The Pacific Review*, v. 18, no. 4, December 2005, pp. 499–519. The Thai case leads one to wonder whether it was not in part the monarchy in Great Britain that helped it initially develop its robust competing-pyramid system at the dawn of Western democracy. That is, perhaps the monarchy provided a focal point for patronal network coordination that was an alternative to any prime minister seeking to capitalize on the Westminster parliamentarist system to build a strong single pyramid under his patronage. This could help account for the creation of space for many other patronal networks to flourish relatively independently, though eventually Britain was able to transition to an open access order.

coup will ultimately succeed in restoring a single-pyramid system remains to be seen.

Two other Asian cases deserve special mention because they illustrate the possibility of two somewhat positive futures for the highly patronalistic post-Soviet states: Singapore and Mongolia. Singapore is interesting because it represents one of the few instances where strong single-pyramid leadership in a highly patronalistic country has in fact succeeded in using this power to reduce levels of patronalism dramatically, among other things making Singapore one of the least corrupt countries in the world. Whether this can be replicated in political environments significantly larger than this city-state, however, is open to question. In any case, Singapore is still generally regarded as a hybrid regime. Thus low patronalism does not necessarily mean democracy, though we would expect it to facilitate democracy's proper functioning and hence sustainability whenever a further political opening arrives.[51]

Mongolia represents a second possible outcome, a high-functioning competing-pyramid polity sustained by a divided-executive constitution. After the debacle of patronal democracy in Ukraine after the Orange Revolution, it was not uncommon to hear both observers and insiders cast blame primarily on the divided-executive constitution. According to such arguments, such constitutional forms in highly patronalistic environments are more likely to lead to stalemate and democratic breakdown than to lasting democratic breakthrough. The divided-executive constitutions in the highly patronalistic countries of Eastern Europe (Bulgaria and Macedonia) seem to testify to the contrary, though their relative success could plausibly be attributed instead to EU linkage and leverage. Mongolia's success, however, cannot so easily be chalked up to other factors.

In fact, Mongolia can quite reasonably be considered a "most difficult case" for the argument that divided-executive constitutions are inherently unworkable in patronalistic contexts. It is quite hard to find a country so far removed from Western linkage and leverage as Mongolia. Moreover, it is firmly nested in one of the least hospitable neighborhoods for democracy imaginable, sandwiched between the extremely autocratic China and the more moderate but still nondemocratic Russia. Mongolia is also poor.

Despite these disadvantages, highly patronalistic Mongolia has consistently had "one of the most flourishing democracies in Asia" and been quite effective in policy making, including the conducting of major economic reforms.[52] This is not to say its system is perfectly functional. But surely its experience stands out positively when compared to Ukraine. This suggests policy makers should not be too quick to dismiss divided-executive constitutions, especially

---

[51] This echoes Adam Przeworski and Fernando Limongi, "Modernization: Theories and Facts," *World Politics*, v. 49, no. 2, 1997, pp. 155–83.

[52] Richard Pomfret, "Transition and Democracy in Mongolia," *Europe-Asia Studies*, v. 52, no. 1, January 2000, pp. 149–60.

considering the problems discussed earlier that both presidentialist and parliamentarist formal constitutions can cause for patronal polities.

Are Eurasia's Regime Cycles Ultimately Leading to Sweden, Somalia, or Something Else?

This book has argued that much of post-Soviet politics has been about dynamic continuity once the initial flux of the USSR's demise passed, but this does not mean that the dynamics we see now cannot be laying a foundation for certain kinds of longer-run change. Indeed, some patronal polities in history have experienced long-term regime opening, either as patronal democracies (such as the Philippines) or what North, Wallis, and Weingast have called open access orders (such as Sweden).[53] Others have experienced the long-term stability of a single-pyramid system, as either a hybrid regime (like Tanzania) or full dictatorship (like China). Still others have simply devolved into failed states, the worst possible form of competing-pyramid situation (as in Somalia). Do the first two decades of post-Soviet statehood provide any grounds for thinking that the various polities of Eurasia will eventually escape their tendency to experience regime cycles and wend their way to one of these alternative conditions?

Long-Term Political Closure (Enduring Single-Pyramid Politics)

The logic of patronal politics might lead one to envision several mechanisms by which chief patrons in single-pyramid systems might be able to short-circuit the lame-duck syndrome, avoiding the emergence of competing-pyramid moments and thereby prolonging their regime's rule indefinitely. Here we consider four: dictatorship, popularity, dynasty, and authoritarian institutions (especially parties).

One would be for these regimes simply to move to full dictatorship, effectively banning all opposition from ballots for any major office if not eliminating it entirely. Many enduring regimes worldwide have been full dictatorships, including today's China and Saudi Arabia. Turkmenistan and Uzbekistan have been in this category since the early 1990s, and perhaps other Eurasian polities will follow. It is remarkable, however, that after the very early 1990s, no other post-Soviet state has so far fully gone this route even though few would deny that leaders like Vladimir Putin and Ilham Aliyev could have done so had they wanted to. Instead, the increasing political closure they have displayed appears to be asymptotic, moving ever closer but never quite reaching the line at which all genuine opposition is completely barred from elections to top state posts. And this process tends to fall back whenever these countries experience a lame-duck syndrome with low leadership popularity, and if nothing else leadership aging can eventually bring on such an effect. The countries of Eurasia, therefore, do not appear to be *transitioning* to complete dictatorship.

---

[53] North, Wallis, and Weingast, *Violence and Social Orders.*

It is also conceivable that single-pyramid politics could become habitual if individual patronal presidents sustain popular support and are able repeatedly to confer this support upon handpicked successors, who themselves then prove popular. This kind of regime endurance can then create a sense that the regime's domination is inevitable and that there are no viable alternatives.[54] The problem for this scenario is that popular opinion is extremely difficult to sustain over very long periods, especially when it involves a transfer of power from one leader to another. And while regime longevity can sometimes promote a sense of resigned acceptance, it can also breed patron fatigue and a desire for change – especially as a leadership visibly ages. The supreme patrons of resource-rich states may have an advantage in sustaining popular support because they are in good position to deliver real benefits to their people over a long period. But their support will also be more vulnerable to the vicissitudes of international markets beyond their own control. Russia's experience in 2011 would seem to illustrate this challenge. The Medvedev-Putin Tandem arguably helped sustain the regime's popularity by adding a sense of freshness and new direction, but the announcement of Putin's return helped set in motion a chain of events leading to the largest opposition street protests Moscow had seen since the early 1990s. So far, there is little to suggest that sustained popularity of individual leaders will enable the bulk of Eurasia's states to escape the contestation phases of regime cycles for long.

The Aliyev regime in Azerbaijan suggests dynasty may offer a solution.[55] But more often than not, the grooming of presidential offspring for succession is unpopular because it is easily seen in today's context as illegitimate. Indeed, it has been nearly a century since the creation of the world's last major monarchy, and the overthrow of one dynasty has typically led to its replacement by another form of rule rather than a new dynasty.[56] Dynastic succession also risks alienating other major networks in a single-pyramid system.[57] Public relations disasters involving presidential sons and daughters in Kazakhstan, Kyrgyzstan, and Uzbekistan are clear cases in point, as are the ousters of Arab leaders in 2011. The case of the Aliyevs in Azerbaijan, therefore, would appear to be an exception made possible by the long-term planning of an exceptionally skilled politician (Heydar Aliyev) rather than the harbinger of a new rule to come.

Judging by contemporary world history, a more promising path to sustained single-pyramid politics runs through institutions. The findings of this book suggest that the most effective such institutions, however, are not likely to be those of co-optation and control. This is because even an elaborately organized

---

[54] Some suggest this has already been happening in Russia. See Rose, Mishler, and Munro, *Russia Transformed*.

[55] On how dynasty can facilitate succession, see Tullock, *Autocracy*.

[56] The author is grateful to Georgi Derluguian for pointing this out.

[57] Barbara Junisbai, "Improbable but Potentially Pivotal Oppositions: Privatization, Capitalists, and Political Contestation in the Post-Soviet Autocracies," *Perspectives on Politics*, v. 10, no. 4, December 2012, pp. 891–916.

repressive or co-optative apparatus can rapidly rupture or even dissolve in the face of changed expectations beyond their own control, particularly lame-duck syndromes that can have a wide variety of sources. Instead, the most effective institutions for helping anchor single-pyramid rule are likely to be dominant parties that are not only well organized, but also the bearers of genuine public support *as institutions*, as was discussed in Chapter 11. Such public support, which might resemble enduring party identification in the United States or Great Britain, has the advantage of being conferrable on *whomever the party nominates*. If this support is great enough to make that person the focal point for network coordination in succession elections, then the regime is in strong position not only to weather succession after succession but to survive a bad leader who ruins his own but not his party's reputation. Such parties may well lie behind the endurance of some hybrid regimes in Africa and Asia, helping them survive moments of anticipated succession.

Do we see parties emerging in Eurasia with enough party identification to help regimes weather lame-duck syndromes and thereby endure? American party identification emerged over many decades through cognitive processes among voters that are highly complex and still disputed.[58] Successful African and Asian ruling parties often emerged from long independence struggles against colonial rule or other powerful forces, gaining enduring public support as the vehicles of national salvation.[59] It is unclear whether a similar process is taking place in any of the existing Eurasian single-pyramid systems. Some do not currently have a true dominant party, as in Belarus. Others failed spectacularly, as with the collapses of "parties of power" along with their regimes in Georgia under Eduard Shevardnadze (the Citizens Union of Georgia) and Kyrgyzstan under Kurmanbek Bakiev (the Ak Zhol Party). Uzbekistan's Islom Karimov has hopped from one regime party to another after his initial single-pyramid system was firmly established.

Some dominant parties have been in place in long-enduring regimes. One set of examples includes the Yeni Azerbaijan Party, the People's Democratic Party of Tajikistan, and Kazakhstan's Nur Otan Party. But there is little evidence they are developing support as institutions beyond (respectively) the Aliyev family, Imomali Rahmon, and Nursultan Nazarbaev personally. The ruling party in Armenia (the Republican Party) may be less leader-centric but has not so far managed to win absolute majorities of the party-list vote, though it came very close in 2012. Ukraine's Party of Regions was also less leader-centric, but failed to sustain robust popular support and suffered a dramatic loss of support with the collapse of Yanukovych's regime in 2014. The United Russia Party seemed

---

[58] E.g., Morris Fiorina, *Retrospective Voting in American National Elections* (New Haven, CT: Yale University Press, 1981); Donald Green, Bradley Palmquist, and Eric Schickler, *Partisan Hearts and Minds* (New Haven, CT: Yale University Press, 2002).

[59] On the link between violent independence struggles and strong ruling parties, see Levitsky and Way, "Beyond Patronage."

on track during much of the 2000s to build up a truly stabilizing ruling party with support shown through experimental and other evidence to represent something beyond just support for Putin. Indeed, there is survey evidence that the party has had substantial backing among the masses and that people have been supporting it for reasons far beyond Putin himself.[60] That said, Putin's political evisceration of Dmitry Medvedev in ending the Tandem, the party's subsequent drop in popular support, and Putin's recent flirtation with other movements have called into question whether this initial progress in building up party identification is likely to continue.[61] Patterns of Eurasian party building, therefore, do not currently indicate a clear trend toward the long-term endurance of single-pyramid systems beyond a given leader, though we cannot completely rule this out at present.

State Failure

If the post-Soviet space is unlikely to trend to full autocracy over the next twenty years, might it degenerate into complete and sustained state collapse, a Somalia scenario? To be sure, one can point to some disturbing events that might suggest that at least some countries of Eurasia are heading in this direction. Much of Armenia's top leadership was decimated in the 1999 armed attack on parliament, and it is still in an only partially "frozen" war with Azerbaijan over Nagorno-Karabakh. Kyrgyzstan suffered one violent revolution after another, with the second (in 2010) followed by perhaps the worst ethnic pogrom the post-Soviet world has yet to see. After its peaceful experience with the Orange Revolution, Ukraine surprised many observers in 2014 when its Euromaidan protests descended into violence and unruly opposition forces began seizing control of government buildings in many western regions. When Russia then swiftly annexed Crimea after Viktor Yanukovych was deposed, tensions rose. Deadly fighting began to break out in other regions (especially Donetsk, Luhansk, and Odessa) and pro-Russian separatists managed to take over key buildings and locations in some of these territories by force of arms, with what strongly appeared to be at least tacit Russia support. As of mid-2014, the death toll was mounting as Ukrainian forces worked to retake areas claimed by the separatists. And Russia itself has proven unable to stop a deadly, simmering insurgency in its own North Caucasus despite Putin's otherwise impressive power.

Eurasian regime dynamics, however, do not overall appear to be building up to eventual endemic state failure. For one thing, one of the remarkable qualities of Eurasia's patronal polities appears to be their resilience in the face of what appear to be bouts of state collapse. We saw in the 1990s and early 2000s

---

[60] Evidence is presented in Henry E. Hale and Timothy J. Colton, "Sources of Dominant Party Dominance in Hybrid Regimes: The Surprising Importance of Ideas and the Case of United Russia 1999–2011," unpublished paper, August 21, 2013.

[61] Timothy J. Colton and Henry E. Hale, "Who Defects? Defection Cascades from a Ruling Party and the Case of United Russia 2008–12," unpublished paper; Hale, "The Putin Machine Sputters."

how leaders were eventually able to build single-pyramid systems in virtually all fragments of the former Soviet Union, even those that had been left physically ravaged and emotionally bleeding by civil war, wars for independence, or war with neighbors. The most clearly failed states of the 1990s, Georgia and Azerbaijan, featured strong single-pyramid systems by the 2000s. Time and time again we have seen how apparent state collapses and revolution can be followed by a new round of political machine building. We have even seen remarkably consistent state building in the unrecognized breakaway territories of Abkhazia, Nagorno-Karabakh, South Ossetia, and Transnistria.[62]

One reason this is the case may be that what appears to be an outbreak of "instability" is often a symptom of the regular functioning of patronal presidentialism. This suggests there is somewhat more (informal) institutionalization to these bouts of disorder than often recognized. Kyrgyzstan has suffered multiple revolutions not because it was characterized by endemic state weakness, but because it had a patronal presidentialist constitution and twice happened to have a president who was both a lame-duck and unpopular. Georgia had the same experience, though its second presidential ouster took place in a much more orderly way, perhaps reflecting some learning as Saakashvili realized it was better not to try to claim victory by force. The case of Ukraine is more worrisome, though the chief cause for worry is the strong role the Russian government appears to be playing in working against patronalism's potential for restoring a form of order after a single-pyramid system's rupture.

One may legitimately ask why it is that presidents have more consistently been unpopular in some places, such as Kyrgyzstan and Ukraine, and popular in others, such as Kazakhstan, and one might reasonably speculate that inherent state weakness makes it hard for leaders to win public backing while state strength makes it easier. But both Russia and Belarus show that unpopular leadership is not a fixed trait of a given country, as the highly popular Vladimir Putin and Aliaksandr Lukashenka were both preceded by the equally unpopular Boris Yeltsin and Viacheslau Kebich. Perhaps poverty dooms leaders like those in Kyrgyzstan to be unpopular, but Moldova's Vladimir Voronin wielded substantial public support until the 2008–9 world financial crisis despite ruling one of Europe's poorest countries.

Moreover, the region's leaders appear capable of learning how they might work to prevent major moments of crisis – such as the revolutions characteristic of patronal presidentialism – in the future. After Kyrgyzstan's second revolution, for example, the incoming leadership sought to change the game by instituting a divided-executive constitution, explicitly seeking to restrain any one figure from being able to monopolize enough power to become a dictator and provoke another revolution. Whether this will actually work is another

---

[62] Charles King, "The Benefits of Ethnic War: Understanding Eurasia's Unrecognized States," *World Politics*, v. 53, no. 4, July 2001, pp. 524–52.

question, but at a minimum, there is cause to hope that the post-Soviet space is not trending inexorably to state failure.

Also working in post-Soviet countries' favor is that the most brutal forms of unruly violence have not been a prominent part of its political repertoire since the early 1990s, when violence was mostly associated with separatist conflict. To be sure, there appears to be ample violence in the political competition among Eurasian networks. Recall the 1999 assassinations in Armenia, the suspicious death of opposition party leader Viacheslav Chornovil that same year, the political disappearances in Belarus under Aliaksandr Lukashenka, the Aksy killings in Kyrgyzstan in 2002, the attempted poisoning of Viktor Yushchenko in 2004, the massacre of protesters in Uzbekistan in 2005, the deadly firing on opposition demonstrators in Kyrgyzstan in 2010, the Euromaidan clashes in 2013–14, and innumerable jailings, beatings, or even killings of independent journalists in many of these countries. But in most post-Soviet polities, these remain shocking exceptions, relatively few and far between, rather than a saddening rule as they have been in some countries in the Middle East or Africa. Perhaps most important of all, the region has been almost entirely free of military coups. Indeed, some research has found military intervention to be one of the chief causes of democratic backsliding.[63]

What has restrained naked violence in the post-Soviet context?[64] Merely to cite "state strength" is unsatisfying as an answer. In part, this is because apparent state strength has been shown to vary quite dramatically over time in the same country with the different phases of regime cycles described here. The Eurasian state clearly does not represent the institutional embodiment of the rule of law, and the logic and empirics of regime cycles have found that patrons tend to lose control over state structures (including armed forces) at the very moments when power struggles become most intense.

We need to look beyond states, therefore, to understand why deadly violence is not used more readily as a weapon in competing-pyramid situations. Several answers suggest themselves. Brian Taylor, for one, argues the answer is that the USSR left in place a strong military culture of aversion to direct and autonomous political intervention.[65] One might also point to the fact that the Eurasian countries became independent without having to fight for independence from the USSR in a long military struggle, meaning that they did not emerge with strong victorious armies that might have felt a prerogative to intervene in politics later and had the institutional coherence to do so.

Two other explanations may make the most sense in terms of the logic of patronal politics, however. First, the USSR featured a highly refined and differentiated force structure, with the means of official state violence divided

---

[63] Bratton and van de Walle, *Democratic Experiments in Africa*; Jose Antonio Cheibub, *Presidentialism, Parliamentarism, and Democracy* (New York: Cambridge University Press, 2007).

[64] The author is grateful to Will Reno for posing this question.

[65] Brian D. Taylor, *Politics and the Russian Army: Civil-Military Relations, 1689–2000* (New York: Cambridge University Press, 2003).

up into many separate institutions that had their own troops. These ranged from the different branches of the military to the police to the KGB. In the post-Soviet period, the successors to these different violent networks typically had distinct interests (both professional and business-related) and made separate "deals" with the most important patrons. This meant that they could be divided and conquered more easily. One set of troops could be used to counter (and hence deter) an attempt by another to seize power. Second, the use of violence has almost always proven unpopular when either authorities or oppositions have attempted to employ it in their power struggles. Indeed, one can trace marked declines in presidential popularity in part to such episodes as the murders of journalists Hryhory Gongadze and Georgy Sanaia, the 2002 Aksy killings, the torture of Georgian prisoners under Saakashvili, or the 2014 killings of protesters in the Euromaidan. In fact, each of these events provided fuel for the opposition fire, intensifying people's desire for new leaders and prompting key presidential allies to defect. None of this explains why Eurasian publics might have been less accepting of violence than others, but public opinion does appear to be part of the equation in former Soviet countries.

Overall, while Eurasian events are far from a model of state strength, recent history in this region does not on balance suggest a long-term trend to state failure. To be sure, this statement might seem out of place in mid-2014, as Ukraine teeters on the brink of full-scale civil war and possibly open war with Russia – a development hardly anyone thought could happen so rapidly just nine months ago. So one cannot completely rule out a trend to sustained state failure in Eurasia. But as Georgi Derluguian and Timothy Earle have pointed out with different terminology, patronalism is a highly flexible mechanism for constructing power relationships and establishing some form of order.[66] The networks in single-pyramid systems can come unglued, but they also have a remarkable tendency to recombine anew after even the worst forms of disorder as new expectations regarding future power emerge from the struggles. Civil war by peaceful means can sometimes become actual civil war, but the incentives in Eurasia for organizing the battles in a peaceful way remain substantial.

Long-Term Political Opening

The logic of patronal politics suggests that long-term political opening can take two general forms. One involves a major reduction in a society's level of patronalism along with other institutional reforms that support democratization, the result eventually being something close to an open access order. The second is the stable arrangement of a country's major networks in a competing-pyramid system, something we have called here patronal democracy. The cases

---

[66] Georgi Derluguian and Timothy Earle, "Strong Chieftaincies Out of Weak States, or Elemental Power Unbound," *Comparative Social Research*, v. 27, 2010, pp. 51–76, prepublication draft. They themselves may not share the present author's view regarding the unlikelihood of sustained state failure.

of Eastern Europe indicate that EU membership prospects might be the fastest and most reliable path to either form, but very few post-Soviet states can hold out much hope. Moldova, small and digestible, with a willing "patron" in Romania, may be the only realistic near-term candidate, though Georgia and parts of Ukraine have proven eager even though they are less attractive to the EU itself. One might conceive of at least four other paths to at least one of these types of long-term political opening: leadership self-restraint, institutions, social change, and development, each of which will be discussed briefly. The polities of Eurasia, however, currently do not appear to be firmly on any of them, though constitutional change and development seem to hold out the greatest hope.

Sustained Political Opening through Leadership Self-Restraint. One conceivable path might be just to hope for the right patronal president[67] to come along, someone who will simply abstain from using the patronal power available to her, and then to hope that succeeding leaders follow that precedent. It hardly need be said at this point that this path is unpromising. Leaders typically find it very hard to restrain themselves from using all tools that are at their disposal to achieve their desired ends so long as the costs are not too great. Ironically, the desired ends for which patronal methods are frequently used include even democratization. Perhaps the best evidence is to recall who two of the supposed "authoritarians" who were overthrown in the post-Soviet color revolutions of 2003–5 actually were: Askar Akaev, once regarded as Central Asia's lone democratic leader, and Eduard Shevardnadze, the Soviet foreign minister who ended the Cold War and resigned his post specifically to warn of an impending hard-liner coup in 1991. Others initially regarded as "democrats" also proved quite willing to use the levers of patronalism rather than eschew and eliminate them, ranging from the intellectual Levon Ter-Petrossian to the Columbia-educated Mikheil Saakashvili to the former rebel regional Communist Party boss Boris Yeltsin.

Institutional Sustenance of Competing-Pyramid Politics. It is also possible that formal constitutional developments we have seen recently in Georgia, Kyrgyzstan, and Ukraine constitute the beginning of a trend, the recognition by key players at critical junctures that divided-executive constitutions may ultimately be able to secure their interests better than presidentialist constitutions can. We have seen at least three different paths to such a conclusion in the preceding pages. In Ukraine in 2004, a divided-executive constitution was imposed on a revolutionary network during a stalemate in the streets as the price of its victory, intended by the outgoing patron to protect his interests against the new authorities' gaining too much power. In Kyrgyzstan in 2010, a divided-executive constitution served to anchor a power-sharing deal among revolutionary victors and to help ensure that no one of them would be able to usurp power from the others in the future and set in motion new

[67] Or possibly, in parliamentarist systems, a dominant prime minister.

revolutionary dynamics. The precise motives of Saakashvili in Georgia during 2010–13 remain less clear, as Chapter 9 discussed, but observers generally agree he wanted to weaken future successors either to prevent them from overshadowing him in history or to hinder any effort they might make to prosecute him and his associates. Euromaidan protesters in 2013–14 also made one of their chief goals the restoration of the 2004 divided-executive constitution, and Ukraine's parliament indeed reinstituted it after Yanukovych's downfall. An important question for future research will be why these particular leaders and not others made these moves. Another interesting question is why they opted specifically for divided-executive constitutions instead of parliamentarist ones. Indeed, Moldova remains the only truly parliamentarist post-Soviet polity.[68] At present, however, it would be premature to argue that a broad trend to nonpresidentialist constitutions is sweeping the region. And Ukraine during 2010–14 and Moldova during 2001–9 show that nonpresidentialist constitutions are no guarantee against the rise of a new single-pyramid system. Thus while we cannot rule out that such formal institutional change is starting to lead the region to long-term political opening, the evidence at present is weak.

Breaking Out of the Patronalistic Social Equilibrium. Given that constitutions are not absolutely self-reinforcing in highly patronalistic polities, the most stably open political outcomes would be likely to result from changing the patronalistic nature of society itself. In world historical perspective, however, this would appear quite unlikely in the foreseeable future. For one thing, only a few countries have escaped a patronalistic social equilibrium and achieved something like what North, Wallis, and Weingast have called an open access order, and those few typically did so over the course of a century or two.[69] Only a tiny set stands out for having effected dramatic reductions in the pervasiveness of patronalism within the last half-century, at least as indicated by measures such as corruption and rule of law. Singapore and Chile are perhaps among the best examples, but the former nevertheless remains a hybrid regime while Chilean reforms at times involved brutal repression – far worse than is seen in post-Soviet states with the possible exception of Uzbekistan and Turkmenistan. Another problem is that research is quite divided on precisely how such transitions can come about. Some point to leadership and reforms of the state that can then alter society.[70] But while this path would appear possible, it would not seem to offer much hope given how few leaders have actually had the will, skill, or power actually to pull it off. In the post-Soviet space, Saakashvili has provided the only example of a bold stroke that moved significantly in this direction, but he did not finish the job despite nearly a decade in the presidency. It remains to be seen whether his successors will do so.

---

[68] Parliamentarism has been discussed in some places, as in Ukraine in the late 2000s and early 2010s, but not actually implemented.

[69] North, Wallis, and Weingast, *Violence and Social Orders.*

[70] E.g., Bo Rothstein, "Trust, Social Dilemmas, and Collective Memories," *Journal of Theoretical Politics*, v. 12, no. 4, 2000, pp. 477–501.

Perhaps a competing-pyramid system could, if sustained for a long period, create incentives for a gradual reduction in patronalism. Popular support is likely to matter most directly under competing-pyramid politics, and the masses generally do not like major manifestations of patronalism like official corruption. This gives the sides at least some incentive actually to try to reduce corruption while in power. Of course, working against this incentive is the temptation to continue relying on machine methods in order to weaken one's opponents and manufacture votes for oneself. Corrupt methods may even be in greater short-term demand as each side looks for new ways to gain an advantage in the competition.[71] Some research goes even further, suggesting that politics in competing-pyramid systems tends to be so ugly that it can discredit the whole idea of democracy and foster a longing for a return to single-pyramid politics.[72] But at least competing-pyramid politics creates some real incentive for uprooting patronalism that may kick in over time. The major problem would seem to be the sustainability of the nonpresidentialist constitutions that underpin competing-pyramid systems in the face of early challenges.

The context of patronalism would also be weakened to the extent that politics comes to revolve more around imagined communities, groups of people who act collectively not through chains of actual personal acquaintance but through the conviction that they share common ideas. Such ideas might involve identity, ideology, or more pragmatic policy stands, including preferences for the redistribution of wealth. As was noted in Chapter 4, patronalism is an ideal-type concept. Thus even the most patronalistic environments will experience moments in which people mobilize around imagined communities.[73] Eurasian polities, to be sure, have experienced such episodes. Mobilization in the Armenia-Azerbaijan conflict over Nagorno-Karabakh, for example, is not at root about patronal networks, though networks in each country certainly try to capture the issue and manipulate it to serve their own domestic political purposes. The Euromaidan protests also appear strongly to have been more about imagined community than patronal networks, though so far Ukraine has not generated truly idea-based parties capable of supplanting the patronal networks that dominate the country and that have their own formal party structures.

Political competition almost everywhere in Eurasia remains organized more along patronal lines than imagined communities, and attempts to organize parties primarily in the realm of ideas (even populist efforts aimed at redistribution) have not tended to get as far as those with a strongly patronal core. While different patronal networks associate themselves with different ideas as part of

---

[71] Maria Popova, "Political Competition as an Obstacle to Judicial Independence: Evidence from Russia and Ukraine," *Comparative Political Studies*, v. 43, no. 10, 2010, pp. 1202–29.

[72] Gulnaz Sharafutdinova, *Political Consequences of Crony Capitalism inside Russia* (South Bend, IN: Notre Dame University Press, 2010).

[73] Recall Rogers Brubaker's characterization of nationalism as a "contingent event." Rogers Brubaker, *Nationalism Reframed: Nationhood and the National Question in the New Europe* (New York: Cambridge University Press, 1996), p. 7.

their struggle for popular support, the ideas themselves have generally proven little match for the overwhelming machine power of a single-pyramid patron who is not a lame-duck or who has robust popular support. And while such patrons do generally try to win support through association with certain ideas, they also have an interest in maintaining their political flexibility. Thus the ideas that they tend to emphasize once they obtain power are either abstract goals that unite almost everyone in society, such as patriotism and prosperity, or ideas chosen strategically and contingently to cleave the electorate in a way that helps marginalize an opposition. Putin's promarket anticommunism, for example, has the support of a large majority and helps keep an electorally unviable idea (communism) institutionalized as his main opposition at the national level (the Communist Party network).[74] Perhaps one day such ideas – possibly in the form of party identification – will eventually be taken deeply enough to heart to be able routinely to overpower patronalism's political machinery, replacing it as the primary driver of politics. This must remain a subject for future research, but at the moment there do not appear to be strong grounds for believing this will happen anytime soon.

The most promising way out of the patronalistic social equilibrium over the long haul would seem to be through economic development and associated institutional changes designed to facilitate it, changes one can observe in at least some Eurasian states. High levels of economic development can certainly be achieved in a patronalistic context. At the same time, one would expect that as people become wealthier and develop a broader array of economic relationships, including additional opportunities for earning income, they will become less dependent on particular patrons and more likely to pursue politics based on other issues they care about.[75] Robust economic development also tends to entail dense ties to other developed economies, which today are often open access societies and can provide another set of incentives for opening. In addition, development tends to involve the proliferation of mass media outlets. All this might not translate directly into democracy as certain theories of modernization have suggested. But it may be one reason why some research has found that higher levels of economic development make a political opening more likely to "stick" regardless of how that opening comes about.[76]

The theoretical question, of course, is why patrons would provide for economic development. From the perspective of theories of neopatrimonialism,

---

[74] Timothy J. Colton and Henry E. Hale, "The Putin Vote: Presidential Electorates in a Hybrid Regime," *Slavic Review*, v. 68, no. 3, Fall 2009, pp. 473–503.

[75] Herbert Kitschelt and Steven I. Wilkinson, "Citizen-Politician Linkages: An Introduction," in Herbert Kitschelt and Steven I. Wilkinson, *Patrons, Clients, and Policies: Patterns of Democratic Accountability and Political Competition* (Cambridge: Cambridge University Press, 2007), pp. 1–49.

[76] Adam Przeworski and Fernando Limongi, "Modernization: Theories and Facts," *World Politics*, v. 49, no. 2, 1997, pp. 155–83; Jan Teorell, *Determinants of Democratization: Explaining Regime Change in the World, 1972–2006* (New York: Cambridge University Press, 2010).

this is quite unclear. Such theories tend to assume the merger of property and power leaves no significant room for anything other than short-term material motives. This would seem to leave little reason to expect patronal presidents atop single-pyramid systems actually to pursue any kind of economic "modernization."[77] Instead, they are generally interpreted as kleptocracies.[78]

One important way in which the logic of patronal politics differs from that of neopatrimonialism, however, lies in the strong role that the former posits for public opinion in driving regime dynamics in patronal presidential systems, even where single-pyramid systems appear outwardly robust (though much more so in hybrid regimes rather than full autocracies). The imperative for gaining and sustaining public support – especially if leaders hope to retain power for a long period as they generally do – provides a powerful incentive for patronal presidents to invest in reforms designed to improve economic performance in the long run.[79] Indeed, studies cited earlier found that economic growth was one important source of public support, and there is indication from public rhetoric that leaders understand this connection. Moreover, important research by Anna Lowry finds that the particular patterns of nationalization and privatization in which Russian leaders have engaged over the last two decades cannot be adequately explained by logics of stealing or political control alone, and are instead consistent with a strong developmentalist logic.[80] This certainly resonates with other studies finding that Russia has been pursuing a set of genuine modernization policies at the same time that its politics is also guided by a strongly patronalistic logic, and that in fact something of this sort has been going on for centuries in Russia.[81] One might expect to find similar phenomena in other post-Soviet states to greater or lesser degrees, though clearly there is variation in the level of kleptocracy across the region. Many countries in East Asia, for example, would also fit the model of highly patronalistic polities pursuing rapid development, and these may in the end provide evidence as to how this path to a stable political openness can be realized.

---

[77] This point about the neopatrimonialism literature is made strongly by Anna Urasova Lowry, "Between Neopatrimonialism and Developmentalism: Exploring the Causes of Nationalization in Russia," dissertation in political science, Indiana University, 2014.

[78] This is a particularly common interpretation of Russian politics, reportedly including the U.S. government (*The Guardian*, December 1, 2010). Relatedly, Russia is branded a "predatory" state by Gerald M. Easter, *Capital, Coercion, and Postcommunist States* (Ithaca, NY: Cornell University Press, 2012), e.g., p. 7. U.S. Secretary of State John Kerry on March 3, 2014, called Yanukovych's regime a "kleptocracy" (appearance on NBC's "Meet the Press," author's observation).

[79] I am grateful to Sverker Gustafsson and Georgi Derluguian (private communications) for calling my attention to the development-oriented activity of these states.

[80] Lowry, "Between Neopatrimonialism and Developmentalism."

[81] Derluguian, "Five Centuries of Russia's Modernizations," longer earlier draft (provided by the author) of Derluguian, "The Sovereign Bureaucracy in Russia's Modernizations," Chapter 3 in Piotr Dutkiewicz and Dmitri Trenin, eds., *Russia: The Challenges of Transformation* (New York: NYU Press, 2011), pp. 73–86.

While the phenomenon of the developmentalist patronal presidential state might sound oxymoronic, in fact it captures something of what might be called the art of patronal presidential rule. On one hand, patronal presidents must build and manage the political machinery, coordinating the country's most important networks around their authority through punishments and rewards that keep the dominant network in power. But on the other hand, they also must carefully manage public opinion so that this does not itself create incentives for elite defection to potential rivals. The "art" comes in because these twin imperatives of managing political machinery and sustaining public support can easily contradict each other, as the administrative resources and methods used to stay in power are typically viewed as corruption or worse by the masses. The most successful patronal presidents have mastered the art of finding a balance, though it is rarely a stable one. The good news for the masses is that such dynamics actually can lead not only to greater prosperity, but also to a greater hope for reduced patronalism and ultimately possible movement toward the kind of open access order that North, Wallis, and Weingast describe in their landmark book.[82] This is not a quick fix, however, but a development likely to take more than one generation.

Some Implications for Policy Makers and International Democracy Promotion

On one level, the policy message of this book is to caution against overoptimistic beliefs regarding the power of specific interventions to produce democratization in post-Soviet polities. Not only have the post-Soviet revolutions not tended to produce lasting democratization, instead leading to the reappearance of single-pyramid politics, but the West (including transnational democracy-promotion networks) has had very little ability to influence whether or when they occur.

At the same time, the former USSR countries do provide important "control" cases for establishing that truly dense integration (or at least the real prospect of it) into Western political and economic structures can significantly influence patterns of patronal politics. Cases like Romania, Bulgaria, and Macedonia, especially when compared to cases like Ukraine, Belarus, and Kazakhstan, show that the European Union has been capable of creating incentives that have prevented patronal leaders from successfully building single-pyramid systems even in highly patronalistic polities with presidentialist systems. The most potent influence of the EU appears to be less in facilitating the ouster of particular leaders and more in bringing countries together in all kinds of little ways through robust economic relationships, widespread interpersonal ties, and political engagement. One implication may be that broad economic sanctions on such countries are likely to be less productive in the long run than maintaining and building economic ties.

[82] North, Wallis, and Weingast, *Violence and Social Orders.*

This does not mean that specific actions intended by Western countries to influence regime dynamics cannot matter at the margins, potentially tipping a situation one way or the other when the factors discussed in this book do not point strongly in one direction. For example, providing funding for exit polls where local sources are not forthcoming can help ensure a more credible and democratic vote count, and may provide uniquely credible information that helps one side claim a genuine victory when the outcome is close and contested by convincing some elites that it is indeed the stronger network. The patronal politics logic also has implications for the impact of targeted economic sanctions, those imposed not upon a country as a whole but upon certain individuals or categories of people associated with a given regime. One is that targeted sanctions are unlikely by themselves to provoke the punished networks into opposing or even moderating the behavior of their chief patron. This is because such networks tend to face severe collective action problems in single-pyramid systems, problems that strong patrons can manipulate powerfully. Moreover, in the short run, hurting the position of networks with Western ties and interests is likely to result in the relative strengthening of the position of networks that lack such ties and interests and that therefore are likely to be most hostile to the West. In the longer run, however, such targeted sanctions can create discontent among significant segments of the elite that can facilitate defection at some point in the future once some exogenous factor (such as the approach of a succession-related election) happens to resolve the collective action problem they face in challenging the chief patron. This effect is magnified to the extent that sanctions also have the effect of slowing down the country's economy as a whole, which is likely to make it harder for the patron to sustain popular support over the longer haul.

This study also has a number of other implications for the world of practice. For one thing, it is more likely to be counterproductive than productive to let policy be guided by considerations as to who are the "good guys" and who are the "bad guys" when it comes to democracy – a way of thinking one sometimes hears in Washington as well as other places in the world. As was noted previously, post-Soviet history is replete with examples of good guys turned bad, people in whom Western democratic hopes had been invested but who wound up disappointing. This is not due to any particular personal flaws of those who disillusioned their Western partners, but instead reflects the realities of how patronal power works. No one is saying that we should not be wary of truly bad individuals. Surely it is objectively bad to have a murderous tyrant in place. But policy analysis and practice will be better guided by focusing more intently on the concrete sets of incentives that leaders face than by placing hopes that the right personality has or will finally come along to change the way things are done. Patronalism is a deeply embedded social equilibrium that cannot be undone overnight and that is ignored at a leader's own peril, both politically and physically. Depending on which way the incentives go, bad guys can find themselves acting like democrats and good guys can find themselves behaving like tyrants.

This book also stresses how important it is to think more in terms of regime dynamics than regime change when it comes time to interpret post-Soviet events. All too often, observers treat each new regime movement as indication of a whole new trajectory – or at least a deviation from the old – whereas a deeper look with a broader time frame would tell a different story. What might superficially look like change very often reflects longer-term dynamic continuity, and being aware of this continuity will yield important leverage in anticipating what will come next. This applies not only to apparent "democratic breakthroughs" or "electoral revolutions," which absent dense linkage and leverage have generally been followed by a restoration of single-pyramid politics in patronal presidential countries. It also applies to what may appear to be autocratization. Just as we should not assume a momentary regime opening is permanent, so should we not overestimate the long-run stability of single-pyramid systems like those currently in place in Russia and Kazakhstan, for example. Even moments that look like state failure are sometimes overcome more readily than predicted thanks to the flexible mechanisms of rule that patronal politics provides. Kyrgyzstan, for example, has done much better than anticipated after its 2010 calamity, though of course one still must be wary of setbacks.

Also recommended is a shift away from frames of reference whereby outsiders start with what they think a country needs to do and try to encourage them to do it. More productive are perspectives that begin with the incentives facing patrons and all the major networks in their systems and that then try to figure out what might be productively done (and sustained) from that starting point. Too many hours have been spent, for example, coaching political actors to behave the way actors do in the West without being able to change the fundamental incentives that in fact make it much more productive for these actors to behave very differently. This would mean, among other things, that expert advice is best given not by people who are expert in how things work in Western open access societies. Instead, better expertise is likely to be gained from people with deep understanding of how things work in "the natural state," especially those who have experienced positive actions that can be taken in that context and those who can speak about the experience of those countries that have most recently transitioned from patronalism to an open access order. Expert practitioners in Western societies can still play this role, of course, but they would do well first to receive extensive on-the-ground training (or better still, practical political experience) themselves in the kinds of polities in which they work. Best of all will be advisors who have experience both in highly patronalistic environments and in open access orders, people who understand the implications of patronalism but who also have a vision of how things could operate differently. This is one reason why programs of educational, professional, and intercultural exchange are extremely important: They can give people from the most patronalistic environments a vision of something different but also help people from open access orders start to understand the nature and implications of patronalism.

One such implication concerns recommendations external actors sometimes make regarding which type of constitution is best for a patronalistic society. This book has argued that it is critical not to treat constitutions as documents that will actually be followed, as in most Western legal scholarship. Instead, constitutions in patronalistic societies should be understood as documents that send certain kinds of signals to a country's various patronal networks about who is dominant and who is not, and about when and how challenges to this dominance are likely to take place in the event the incumbent network's popular support drops. This is not the standard debate between presidentialism and parliamentarism, which frequently (though not always) has a formalistic ring to it. Constitutions, crucially, help shape illegal and even constitution-disregarding behavior as well as the actions of law-abiding citizens, and this must be part of the calculus involved in the recommendation. Working with the incentives of patronal leaders also means there are likely to be some circumstances under which even "dictators" can be sold on the idea of certain kinds of constitutional change, such as a shift from presidentialism to parliamentarism or to a divided-executive constitution. These are important opportunities that democratizers should look for.

At the same time, one should also avoid any simplistic conclusions about what particular kind of constitution to recommend. On one hand, divided-executive constitutions do seem to be the most conducive to democratization. On the other hand, Ukraine's experience with such a constitution during 2004–10 was by most ordinary Ukrainians' accounts a debacle, facilitating state paralysis in the face of an enormous economic crisis. If one had a third hand, however, one might point out that Mongolia has done much better with a similar constitution, as have highly patronalistic Bulgaria and Macedonia. Parliamentarist constitutions appear to have rather complex effects, and it is certainly the case that formally stronger parliaments do not necessarily generate more democracy, as Voronin's powerful political machine in Moldova illustrated during 2001–9. For parliamentarism to succeed, much is likely to depend on specific elements of constitutional design itself (notably the degree of executive divisibility and the number of formal selectorates, as Chapter 10 discussed). The larger point is that constitutional design needs to be carefully fit to the structure of society and the trade-offs its people are willing to make between stability and democracy when the two may not go together. Of course, while presidentialism or a single-pyramid-inducing parliamentarist system might provide for more policy coherence, its aura of stability is illusory. It has been patronal presidential systems that have resulted in the most turbulent and deadly collapses, with those in Kyrgyzstan in 2010 and Ukraine in 2014 being the bloodiest examples. The instability just tends to be more concentrated in time at particular points, most notably when presidential succession is perceived to be nearing.

Overall, this book's main recommendation concerns how policy makers and democracy advocates can best understand politics in patronal polities. While there are sometimes opportunities to influence regime dynamics at the margins, and while sometimes the margins matter, international influence is most potent when it is in its most intense form (as in the ability of the EU to exert leverage through the admissions process) or extensive form (as with all the dense inter-personal and economic ties between the West and most of Latin America and other efforts to promote economic development). These remain the most real-istic ways the outside world can assist Eurasian states in making their political battles more like democracy and less like civil war.

References

Daron Acemoglu and James A. Robinson, *Economic Origins of Dictatorship and Democracy* (New York: Cambridge University Press, 2006).

Mikhail N. Afanas'ev, *Klientelizm i rossiiskaia gosudarstvennost'* (Moscow: Moscow Public Science Foundation, 1997).

Askar Akaev, *Trudnaia doroga k demokratii* (Moscow: Mezhdunarodnye otnosheniia, 2002).

Bermet Akaeva, *Tsvety zla: O tak nazyvaemoi "tiul'panovoi revoliutsii" v Kyrgyzstana* (Moscow: Mezhdunarodnye Otnosheniia, 2006).

Shahram Akbarzadeh, "Geopolitics versus Democracy in Tajikistan," *Demokratizatsiya: The Journal of Post-Soviet Democratization*, v. 14, no. 4, Fall 2006, pp. 563–78.

Holger Albrecht and Dina Bishara, "Back on Horseback: The Military and Political Transformation in Egypt," *Middle East Law and Governance*, v. 3, 2011, pp. 13–23.

Gafar Aliev, *Osnovopolozhnik, spasatel' i sozidatel' sovremennogo Azerbaidzhana* (Baku: Shams, 2008).

Leila Alieva, "Azerbaijan's Frustrating Elections," *Journal of Democracy*, v. 17, no. 2, April 2006, pp. 147–60.

Jessica Allina-Pisano, *The Post-Soviet Potemkin Village: Politics and Property Rights in the Black Earth* (New York: Cambridge University Press, 2008).

Gabriel A. Almond, G. Bingham J. Powell, Jr., Russell J. Dalton, and Kaare Strom, *Comparative Politics Today: A World View* (New York: Pearson:, 2008).

James E. Alt and K. Alec Chrystal, *Political Economics* (Berkeley: University of California Press, 1983).

Yu. D. Anchabadze and Yu. G. Argun, *Abkhazy* (Moscow: Nauka, 2007).

Benedict Anderson, *Imagined Communities*, rev. ed. (New York: Verso, 1991).

John Anderson, *Kyrgyzstan: Central Asia's Island of Democracy?* (Amsterdam: Harwood, 1999).

Dominique Arel, "Kuchmagate and the Demise of Kuchma's 'Geopolitical Bluff,'" *East European Constitutional Review*, v. 10, nos. 2–3, Spring/Summer 2001, pp. 54–9.

"Ukraina Vybyraet Zapad, No Ne Bez Vostoka," *Pro et Contra*, v. 9, no. 1, July–August 2005, pp. 39–51.

Irakly Areshidze, *Democracy and Autocracy in Eurasia: Georgia in Transition* (East Lansing: Michigan State University Press, 2007).

Richard Arnold and Andrew Foxall, "Lord of the (Five) Rings: Issues at Sochi, 2014," *Problems of Post-Communism*, January/February 2014, v. 61, no. 1, pp. 3–12.

Stephan Astourian, "Killings in the Armenian Parliament: Coup d'Etat, Political Conspiracy, or Destructive Rage?" *Contemporary Caucasus Newsletter*, no. 9, Spring 2000, pp. 1–5, 19.

Muriel Atkin, "Tajikistan: Reform, Reaction, and Civil War," in Ian Bremmer and Ray Taras, eds., *New States, New Politics* (New York: Cambridge University Press, 1997), pp. 602–33.

"Thwarted Democratization in Tajikistan," in Karen Dawisha and Bruce Parrott, eds., *Conflict, Cleavage, and Change in Central Asia and the Caucasus* (New York: Cambridge University Press, 1997), pp. 277–311.

N. V. Babilunga, S. I. Beril, B. G. Bomeshko, I. N. Galinskii, E. M. Guboglo, V. R. Okushko, and P. M. Shornikov, *Fenomen Pridniestrov'ia*, 2nd ed. (Tiraspol: RIO PGU, 2003).

Elizabeth E. Bacon, *Central Asians under Russian Rule: A Study in Culture Change* (Ithaca, NY: Cornell University Press, 1980).

Sabrina Badger, "Democratisation in an Unrecognized State: Abkhazia, 1994–2007," M.Phil. thesis in Russian and East European Studies, Pembroke College, Oxford, 2008.

Donna Bahry, "The New Federalism and the Paradoxes of Regional Sovereignty in Russia," *Comparative Politics*, v. 37, no. 2, 2005, pp. 127–46.

Margarita M. Balmaceda, "Privatization and Elite Defection in de Facto States: The Case of Transnistria, 1991–2012," *Communist and Post-Communist Studies*, v. 46, no. 4, pp. 445–54.

Zoltan Barany, "The Role of the Military," *Journal of Democracy*, v. 22, no. 4, October 2011, pp. 24–35.

Pranab Bardhan, "Corruption and Development: A Review of Issues," *Journal of Economic Literature*, v. 35, no. 3, September 1997, pp. 1320–46.

Lowell Barrington, *Comparative Politics: Structures and Choices*, 2nd ed. (Boston: Cengage, 2012).

Lowell W. Barrington and Erik S. Herron, "One Ukraine or Many? Regionalism in Ukraine and Its Political Consequences," *Nationalities Papers*, v. 32, March 2004, pp. 53–86.

Robert Bates, "The Impulse to Reform in Africa," in Jennifer Widner, ed., *Economic Change and Political Liberalization in Sub-Saharan Africa* (Baltimore: Johns Hopkins University Press, 1994), pp. 13–28.

Alexander Baturo, *Democracy, Dictatorship, and Term Limits* (Ann Arbor: University of Michigan Press, 2014).

Seymour Becker, *Russia's Protectorates in Central Asia: Bukhara and Khiva, 1865–1924* (New York: RoutledgeCurzon, 2004).

Daniel J. Beers, "Building Democratic Courts from the Inside Out: Judicial Culture and the Rule of Law in Postcommunist Eastern Europe," dissertation in Political Science, Indiana University, 2011.

Mark R. Beissinger, *Nationalist Mobilization and the Collapse of the Soviet State* (New York: Cambridge University Press, 2002).

"The Semblance of Democratic Revolution: Coalitions in Ukraine's Orange Revolution," *American Political Science Review*, v. 107, no. 3, August 2013, pp. 574–92.

"Structure and Example in Modular Political Phenomena: The Diffusion of Bulldozer/Rose/Orange/Tulip Revolutions," *Perspectives on Politics*, v. 5, no. 2, June 2007, pp. 259–76.

Eva Bellin, "Reconsidering the Robustness of Authoritarianism in the Middle East: Lessons from the Arab Spring," *Comparative Politics*, v. 44, no. 2, January 2012, pp. 127–51.

Olga Belova-Gille, "Difficulties of Elite Formation in Belarus after 1991," in Elena Korosteleva, Colin W. Lawson, and Rosalind J. Marsh, eds., *Contemporary Belarus: Between Democracy and Dictatorship* (New York: RoutledgeCurzon, 2003), pp. 53–67.

Graeme Blair and Kosuke Imai, "Statistical Analysis of List Experiments," *Political Analysis*, v. 20, no. 1, Winter 2012, pp. 47–77.

Lisa Blaydes, *Elections and Distributive Politics in Mubarak's Egypt* (New York: Cambridge University Press, 2013)

Stephen Bloom, "Which Minority Is Appeased? Coalition Potential and Redistribution in Latvia and Ukraine," *Europe-Asia Studies*, v. 60, no. 9, November 2008, pp. 1575–600.

Stephen Bloom and Stephen Shulman, "Interest versus Identity: Economic Voting in Ukrainian Presidential Elections," *Post-Soviet Affairs*, v. 27, no. 4, October–December 2011, pp. 410–28.

K. F. Boboev, *Politicheskie partii Tadzhikistana na vyborakh 2005 goda* (Dushanbe: Irfon, 2006).

Carles Boix, *Democracy and Redistribution* (New York: Cambridge University Press, 2003).

Kost' Bondarenko, *Leonid Kuchma: Portret na fone epokhi* (Kharkiv: Folio, 2007).

Anthony Clive Bowyer, "Parliament and Political Parties in Kazakhstan," *Silk Road Paper*, Central Asia-Caucasus Institute and Silk Road Studies Program, Johns Hopkins University SAIS, Washington, DC, May 2008.

Michael Bratton and Nicolas van de Walle, *Democratic Experiments in Africa: Regime Transitions in Comparative Perspective* (New York: Cambridge University Press, 1997).

"Neopatrimonial Regimes and Political Transitions in Africa," *World Politics*, v. 46, July 1994.

Ian Bremmer and Ray Taras, eds., *New States New Politics: Building the Post-Soviet Nations* (New York: Cambridge University Press, 1997).

Ian Bremmer and Cory Welt, "The Trouble with Democracy in Kazakhstan," *Central Asian Survey*, v. 15, no. 2, 1996, pp. 179–99.

Daniel Brower, *Turkestan and the Fate of the Russian Empire* (New York: RoutledgeCurzon, 2003).

Daniel R. Brower and Edward J. Lazzerini, eds., *Russia's Orient: Imperial Borderlands and Peoples, 1700–1917* (Bloomington: Indiana University Press, 1997).

Archie Brown, *The Gorbachev Factor* (New York: Oxford University Press, 1997).

Nathan Brown, *Constitutions in a Nonconstitutional World: Arab Basic Laws and the Prospects for Accountable Government* (Albany, NY: SUNY Press, 2002).

"Dictatorship and Democracy through the Prism of Arab Elections," in Nathan Brown, ed., *Dynamics of Democratization* (Baltimore: Johns Hopkins University Press, 2011), pp. 48–51.

The Rule of Law in the Arab World: Courts in Egypt and the Gulf (New York: Cambridge University Press, 1997).

Jason Brownlee, *Authoritarianism in an Age of Democratization* (New York: Cambridge University Press, 2007).

"Hereditary Succession in Modern Autocracies," *World Politics*, v. 59, no. 4, July 2007, pp. 595–628.

Jason Brownlee and Joshua Stacher, "Change of Leader, Continuity of System: Nascent Liberalization in Post-Mubarak Egypt," *APSA CD*, v. 9, no. 2, May 2011, pp. 1, 4–9, p. 5.

Rogers Brubaker, *Nationalism Reframed: Nationhood and the National Question in the New Europe* (New York: Cambridge University Press, 1996).

Yitzhak Brudny, "Continuity or Change in Russian Electoral Patterns?" in Archie Brown, ed., *Contemporary Russian Politics* (New York: Oxford University Press, 2001), pp. 154–78.

Bruce Bueno de Mesquita, Alastair Smith, Randolph M. Siverson, and James D. Morrow, *The Logic of Political Survival* (Cambridge, MA: MIT Press, 2003).

Valerie J. Bunce, "Rethinking Recent Democratization: Lessons from the Postcommunist Experience," *World Politics*, v. 55, no. 2, January 2003, pp. 167–92.

"Should Transitologists Be Grounded?" *Slavic Review*, v. 54, no. 1, Spring 1995, pp. 111–27.

Valerie J. Bunce and Sharon L. Wolchik, *Defeating Authoritarian Leaders in Postcommunist Countries* (New York: Cambridge University Press, 2011).

"Defeating Dictators: Electoral Change and Stability in Competitive Authoritarian Regimes," *World Politics*, v. 62, no. 1, January 2010, pp. 43–86.

"Favorable Conditions and Electoral Revolutions," *Journal of Democracy*, v. 17, no. 4, October 2006, pp. 5–18.

"International Diffusion and Postcommunist Electoral Revolutions," *Communist and Post-Communist Studies*, v. 39, 2006, pp. 283–304.

Lisa Cameron, Ananish Chaudhuri, Nisvan Erkal, and Lata Gangadharan, "Do Attitudes Towards Corruption Differ across Cultures? Experimental Evidence from Australia, India, Indonesia and Singapore," University of Melbourne Department of Economics Research Paper no. 943, October 2006.

David R. Cameron and Mitchell A. Orenstein, "Post-Soviet Authoritarianism: The Influence of Russia in Its 'Near Abroad,'" *Post-Soviet Affairs*, v. 28, no. 1, January–March 2012.

Donald Carlisle, "Islom Karimov and Uzbekistan: Back to the Future?" in Timothy J. Colton and Robert C. Tucker, eds., *Patterns in Post-Soviet Leadership* (Boulder, CO: Westview Press, 1995), pp. 191–216.

Thomas Carothers, "The End of the Transition Paradigm," *Journal of Democracy*, v. 13, no. 1, January 2002, pp. 5–21.

Christopher D. Carroll, "Macroeconomic Expectations of Households and Professional Forecasters," *Quarterly Journal of Economics*, v. 118, no. 1, February 2003, pp. 269–98.

Julie A. Cassiday and Emily D. Johnson, "A Personality Cult for the Postmodern Age: Reading Vladimir Putin's Public Persona," in Helena Goscilo, ed., *Putin as Celebrity and Cultural Icon* (New York: Routledge, 2013), pp. 37–64.

Center for Political Education, "The Fading Pillars of Power in Belarus: 100 Days of Milinkevich," report, Minsk, February 2006.

Rebecca A. Chamberlain-Creanga, "The Moldovan Parliamentary Election 2010: Towards Stability and Reintegration?" Paper prepared for Kennan Institute Lecture, Woodrow Wilson International Center for Scholars, December 6, 2010, mimeo.

Rebecca Chamberlain-Creanga, "Politics without a 'State': Electoral Reform and Political Party Formation in Secessionist Transnistria – and Its Implications for Conflict Resolution," paper presented at the Annual Meeting of the American Association for the Advancement of Slavic Studies, 2007.

Kanchan Chandra, *Constructivist Theories of Ethnic Politics* (New York: Oxford University Press, 2012).

   Why Ethnic Parties Succeed: Patronage and Ethnic Head Counts in India (New York: Cambridge University Press, 2004).

Mounira M. Charrad and Julia Adams, "Introduction: Patrimonialism, Past and Present," *The Annals of the American Academy of Political and Social Science*, v. 636, July 2011, pp. 6–15.

   eds., special issue of *The Annals of the American Academy of Political and Social Science*, v. 636, July 2011.

H. E. Chehabi and Juan J. Linz, *Sultanistic Regimes* (Baltimore: Johns Hopkins University Press, 1998).

Jose Antonio Cheibub, *Presidentialism, Parliamentarism, and Democracy* (New York: Cambridge University Press, 2007).

Jose Antonio Cheibub, Zachary Elkins, and Tom Ginsburg, "Latin American Presidentialism in Comparative and Historical Perspective," *Texas Law Review*, v. 89, no. 7, 2011, pp. 1707–39.

Liudvig A. Chibirov, *O vremeni, o liudiakh, o sebe (zapiski Pervogo Prezidenta Respubliki Iuzhnaiia Osetiia)* (Vladikavkaz, Russia: Ir, 2004).

Usenaly Chotonov, *Suverennyi Kyrgyzstan: vybor istoricheskogo puti* (Bishkek: Kyrgyzstan, 1995).

Robert K. Christensen, Edward R. Rakhimkulov, and Charles R. Wise, "The Ukrainian Orange Revolution Brought More Than a New President: What Kind of Democracy Will the Institutional Changes Bring?" *Communist and Post-Communist Studies*, v. 38, no. 2, June 2005, pp. 207–30.

M. F. Chudakov, A. E. Vashkevich, S. A. Alfer, M. K. Plisko, and A. O. Dobrovol'skii, *Politicheskie partii: Belarus' i sovremennyi mir*, 2nd ed. (Minsk: Tesei, 2005).

Stephen F. Cohen, *Bukharin and the Bolshevik Revolution: A Political Biography 1888–1938* (New York: Oxford University Press, 1980).

David Collier and Robert Adcock, "Democracy and Dichotomies: A Pragmatic Approach to Choices about Concepts," *Annual Review of Political Science*, v. 2, 1999, pp. 537–65.

David Collier and Steven Levitsky, "Democracy with Adjectives: Conceptual Innovation in Comparative Research," *World Politics*, v. 49, no. 3, April 1997, pp. 430–51.

Ruth Berins Collier and David Collier, *Shaping the Political Arena: Critical Junctures, the Labor Movement and Regime Dynamics in Latin America* (Princeton, NJ: Princeton University Press, 1991).

Kathleen Collins, *Clan Politics and Regime Transition in Central Asia* (New York: Cambridge University Press, 2005).

Timothy J. Colton, "An Aligning Election and the Ukrainian Political Community," *East European Politics & Societies*, v. 25, no. 1, February 2011, pp. 4–27.

Moscow: Governing the Socialist Metropolis (Cambridge, MA: Harvard University Press, 1998).

"Politics," in Colton and Robert Legvold, eds., *After the Soviet Union: From Empire to Nations* (New York: W. W. Norton, 1992), pp. 17–48.

Transitional Citizens: Voters and What Influences Them in the New Russia (Cambridge, MA: Harvard University Press, 2000).

Yeltsin: A Political Life (New York: Basic Books, 2008).

Timothy J. Colton and Henry E. Hale, "The Putin Vote: Presidential Electorates in a Hybrid Regime," *Slavic Review*, v. 68, no. 3, Fall 2009, pp. 473–503.

"Who Defects? Defection Cascades from a Ruling Party and the Case of United Russia 2008–12," unpublished paper.

Timothy J. Colton and Michael McFaul, *Popular Choice and Managed Democracy* (Washington, DC: Brookings Institution Press, 2003).

Timothy Colton and Cindy Skach, "The Predicament of Semi-Presidentialism," in Alfred Stepan, ed., *Democracies in Danger* (Baltimore: Johns Hopkins University Press, 2009).

Alexander Cooley, *Great Games, Local Rules: The New Great Power Contest in Central Asia* (New York: Oxford University Press, 2012).

Michael Coppedge and John Gerring, with David Altman, Michael Bernhard, Steven Fish, Allen Hicken, Matthew Kroenig, Staffan Lindberg, Kelly McMann, Pamela Paxton, Holli A. Semetko, Svend-Erik Skaaning, Jeffrey Staton, and Jan Teorell, "Conceptualizing and Measuring Democracy: A New Approach," *Perspectives on Politics*, v. 9, no. 2, June 2011, pp. 247–67.

Svante Cornell, "Autonomy as a Source of Conflict: Caucasian Conflicts in Theoretical Perspective," *World Politics*, v. 54, no. 2, January 2002, pp. 245–76.

Azerbaijan Since Independence (Armonk, NY: M. E. Sharpe, 2011).

Gary W. Cox, *Making Votes Count: Strategic Coordination in the World's Electoral Systems* (New York: Cambridge University Press, 1997).

James Critchlow, *Nationalism in Uzbekistan: A Soviet Republic's Road to Sovereignty* (Boulder, CO: Westview, 1991).

"Prelude to 'Independence': How the Uzbek Party Apparatus Broke Moscow's Grip on Elite Recruitment," in William Fierman, ed., *Soviet Central Asia: The Failed Transformation* (Boulder, CO: Westview Press, 1991), pp. 131–58.

William Crowther, "Moldova: Caught between Nation and Empire," in Ian Bremmer and Ray Taras, eds., *New States New Politics: Building the Post-Soviet Nations* (New York: Cambridge University Press, 1997), pp. 316–52.

Robert O. Crummey, *Aristocrats and Servitors: The Boyar Elite of Russia, 1613–1689* (Princeton, NJ: Princeton University Press, 1983).

"The Silence of Muscovy," *Russian Review*, v. 46, no. 2, April 1987, pp. 157–64.

Sally N. Cummings, *Kazakhstan: Power and the Elite* (London: I. B. Tauris, 2005).

Hamid Dabashi, *The Arab Spring: The End of Postcolonialism* (New York: Zed, 2012).

John C. K. Daly, "Berdymukhamedov Moves to Eliminate Rivals after Foreign Policy Victories," *Eurasia Daily Monitor*, May 18, 2007.

Robert V. Daniels, *The Rise and Fall of Communism in Russia* (New York: MacMillan 2007).

"Russian Political Culture and the Post-Revolutionary Impasse," *Russian Review*, v. 46, no. 2 April 1987, pp. 165–74.

"Soviet Politics since Khrushchev," in John W. Strong, ed., *The Soviet Union under Brezhnev and Kosygin: The Transition Years* (New York: Van Nostrand Reinhold, 1971).

Paul D'Anieri, "Explaining the Success and Failure of Post-Communist Revolutions," *Communist and Post-Communist Studies*, v. 39, no. 3, September 2006, pp. 331–50.

Understanding Ukrainian Politics: Power, Politics, and Institutional Design (Armonk, NY: M. E. Sharpe, 2007).

Keith Darden, "Blackmail as a Tool of State Domination: Ukraine under Kuchma," *East European Constitutional Review*, v. 10, nos. 2–3, Spring/Summer 2001, pp. 67–71.

"The Integrity of Corrupt States: Graft as an Informal State Institution," *Politics & Society*, v. 36, no. 1, March 2008, pp. 35–60.

Resisting Occupation: Mass Literacy and the Creation of Durable National Loyalties (New York: Cambridge University Press, forthcoming).

Keith Darden and Anna Grzymala-Busse, "The Great Divide: Literacy, Nationalism, and the Communist Collapse," *World Politics*, v. 59, no. 1, October 2006, pp. 83–115.

Partha Dasgupta and Ismail Sarageldin, eds., *Social Capital: A Multifaceted Perspective* (Washington, DC: World Bank, 2000).

Brian L. Davies, *State Power and Community in Early Modern Russia: The Case of Kozlov, 1635–1649* (New York: Palgrave Macmillan, 2004).

Georgi Derluguian, *Bourdieu's Secret Admirer in the Caucasus: A World Systems Biography* (Chicago: University of Chicago Press, 2005).

"Five Centuries of Russia's Modernizations," longer earlier draft (provided by the author) of Derluguian, "The Sovereign Bureaucracy in Russia's Modernizations," Chapter 3 in Piotr Dutkiewicz and Dmitri Trenin, eds., *Russia: The Challenges of Transformation* (New York: NYU Press, 2011), pp. 73–86.

Georgi Derluguian and Timothy Earle, "Strong Chieftaincies Out of Weak States, or Elemental Power Unbound," *Comparative Social Research*, v. 27, 2010, pp. 51–76, prepublication draft.

Jaba Devdariani, "Georgia: Rise and Fall of the Façade Democracy," *Demokratizatsiya: The Journal of Post-Soviet Democratization*, v. 12, no. 1, Winter 2004, pp. 79–115.

Larry Diamond, *Developing Democracy* (Baltimore: Johns Hopkins University Press, 1999).

"Thinking about Hybrid Regimes," *Journal of Democracy*, v. 13, no. 2, April 2002, pp. 21–35.

Larry Diamond and Marc Plattner, eds., *The Global Resurgence of Democracy* (Baltimore: Johns Hopkins University Press, 1996).

Giuseppe Di Palma, *To Craft Democracies: An Essay on Democratic Transition* (Los Angeles: University of California Press, 1990).

Nadia Diuk, "Youth as an Agent for Change: The Next Generation in Ukraine," *Demokratizatsiya: The Journal of Post-Soviet Democratization*, v. 21, no. 2, Spring 2013, pp. 179–96.

Jesse Driscoll, "Commitment Problems or Bidding Wars? Rebel Fragmentation as Peace Building," *Journal of Conflict Resolution*, v. 56, no. 1, February 2012, pp. 118–49.

"Inside Anarchy: Militia Incorporation as State-Building," unpublished paper, February 10, 2009.

Geoff Dubrow, "Assessment Report on Moldova Parliament," draft report submitted to the United Nations Development Program, December 24, 2004.

Raymond M. Duch and Randolph T. Stevenson, "Context and Economic Expectations: When Do Voters Get It Right?" *British Journal of Political Science*, v. 41, no. 1, January 2011, pp. 1–31.

Nora Dudwick, "Political Transformations in Postcommunist Armenia: Images and Realities," in Karen Dawisha and Bruce Parrott, eds., *Conflict, Cleavage, and Change in Central Asia and the Caucasus* (New York: Cambridge University Press, 1997), pp. 69–109.

Razvan Dumitru, "Politics and Practices in Post-Soviet 'Business': Between Shame and Success," *Revista Martor*, no. 16, 2011, pp. 52–66.

Thad Dunning, *Crude Democracy: Natural Resource Wealth and Political Regimes* (New York: Cambridge University Press, 2008).

Maurice Duverger, "A New Political System Model: Semi-Presidential Government," *European Journal of Political Research*, v. 8, no. 2, June 1980, pp. 165–87.

Timothy Earle, *How Chiefs Come to Power: The Political Economy of Prehistory* (Stanford, CA: Stanford University Press, 1997).

Gerald M. Easter, *Capital, Coercion, and Postcommunist States* (Ithaca, NY: Cornell University Press, 2012).

"Preference for Presidentialism: Postcommunist Regime Change in Russia and the NIS," *World Politics*, v. 49, no. 2, January 1997, pp. 184–211.

Restructuring the State: Personal Networks and Elite Identity (New York: Cambridge University Press, 2000).

Adrienne Lynn Edgar, *Tribal Nation: The Making of Soviet Turkestan* (Princeton, NJ: Princeton University Press, 2004).

Robert Elgie, *Semi-Presidentialism: Subtypes and Democratic Performance* (New York: Oxford University Press, 2011).

Zachary Elkins, Tom Ginsburg, and James Melton, *The Endurance of National Constitutions* (New York: Cambridge University Press, 2009).

Gero Erdmann and Ulf Engel, "Neopatrimonialism Reconsidered: Critical Review and Elaboration of an Elusive Concept," *Commonwealth and Comparative Politics*, v. 45, no. 1, February 2007, pp. 95–119.

Ayca Ergun, "The Presidential Election in Azerbaijan, October 2008," *Electoral Studies*, v. 28, no. 4, December 2009, pp. 647–51.

Charles H. Fairbanks, Jr., "Georgia's Rose Revolution," *Journal of Democracy*, v. 15, no. 2, April 2004, pp. 110–24.

James D. Fearon and David D. Laitin, "Explaining Interethnic Cooperation," *American Political Science Review*, v. 90, no. 4, December 1996, pp. 715–35.

Orlando Figes, *A People's Tragedy: The Russian Revolution 1891–1924* (New York: Penguin, 1996).

The Whisperers: Private Life in Stalin's Russia (New York: Metropolitan Books, 2007).

Morris Fiorina, *Retrospective Voting in American National Elections* (New Haven, CT: Yale University Press, 1981).

M. Steven Fish, *Democracy Derailed in Russia: The Failure of Open Politics* (New York: Cambridge University Press, 2005).

Democracy from Scratch (Princeton, NJ: Princeton University Press, 1995).

"The Dynamics of Democratic Erosion," in Richard D. Anderson, Jr., M. Steven Fish, Stephen E. Hanson, and Philip G. Roeder, *Postcommunism and the Theory of Democracy* (Princeton, NJ: Princeton University Press, 2001).

"Stronger Legislatures, Stronger Democracy," *Journal of Democracy*, v. 17, no. 1, January 2006, pp. 5–20.

Aleksandr A. Fisun, *Demokratiia, neopatrimonializm i global'nye transformatsii* (Kharkiv: Konstanta, 2007).

Oleksandr Fisun, "The Dual Spiral of Ukrainian Politics after 2010," PONARS Eurasia Policy Memo no. 165, September 2011.

Oleksandr Fisun and Oleksandr Polishuk, "Ukrainian Neopatrimonial Democracy: Dominant Party-Building and Inter-Elite Settlement in the Semi-Presidential System," paper presented at PONARS Eurasia workshop, Kyiv, November 3–5, 2012.

Sheila Fitzpatrick, *Education and Social Mobility in the Soviet Union 1921–1934* (Cambridge: Cambridge University Press, 1979).

Jonathan Fox, "The Difficult Transition from Clientelism to Citizenship: Lessons from Mexico," *World Politics*, v. 46, no. 2, January 1994, pp. 151–84.

Karl J. Friedrich and Zbigniew K. Brzezinski, *Totalitarian Dictatorship and Autocracy* (Cambridge, MA: Harvard University Press, 1956).

Verena Fritz, *State-Building: A Comparative Study of Ukraine, Lithuania, Belarus, and Russia* (Budapest: Central European University Press, 2007).

Timothy Frye, *Building States and Markets after Communism: The Perils of Polarized Democracy* (New York: Cambridge University Press, 2010).

"A Politics of Institutional Choice – Post-Communist Presidencies," *Comparative Political Studies*, v. 30, October 1997, pp. 523–52.

Timothy Frye, Ora John Reuter, and David Szakonyi, "Political Machines at Work: Voter Mobilization and Electoral Subversion in the Workplace," *World Politics*, v. 66, no. 2, April 2014, pp. 195–228.-

Francis Fukuyama, "The End of History and the Last Man," *The National Interest*, Summer 1989, pp. 3–18.

Dmitry Furman, "Kommunisty i demokratiia," *Nezavisimaia Moldova*, May 4, 2009.

"Udivitel'naia Moldova," *Rossiia v global'noi politike*, v. 5, no. 5, 2007, pp. 186–96.

Jennifer Gandhi, *Political Institutions under Dictatorship* (New York: Cambridge University Press, 2008).

Jennifer Gandhi and Ellen Lust-Okar, "Elections under Authoritarianism," *Annual Review of Political Science*, v. 12, 2009, pp. 403–22.

Jennifer Gandhi and Adam Przeworski, "Authoritarian Institutions and the Survival of Autocrats," *Comparative Political Studies*, v. 40, no. 11, November 2007, pp. 1279–1301.

Georgy Ganev, "Bulgaria," in *Nations in Transit 2012* (New York: Freedom House, 2013).

Venelin I. Ganev, *Preying on the State: The Transformation of Bulgaria after 1989* (Ithaca, NY: Cornell University Press, 2007).

Barbara Geddes, *Politician's Dilemma: Building State Capacity in Latin America* (Berkeley: University of California Press, 1994).

"What Do We Know about Democratization after Twenty Years?" *Annual Review of Political Science*, v. 2, June 1999, pp. 115–44.

Vladimir Gel'man, "The Unrule of Law in the Making: the Politics of Informal Institution Building in Russia," *Europe-Asia Studies*, v. 56, no. 7, November 2004, pp. 1021–40.

"Uroki ukrainskogo," *Polis*, 1 no. 84, February 2005, pp. 36–49.

James L. Gelvin, *The Arab Uprisings: What Everyone Needs to Know* (New York: Oxford University Press, 2012).

Alexander L. George and Andrew Bennett, *Case Studies and Theory Development in the Social Sciences* (Cambridge, MA: MIT Press, 2005).

Alexandra George, *Journey into Kazakhstan: The True Face of the Nazarbayev Regime* (Lanham, MD: University Press of America, 2001).

J. Arch Getty, Practicing Stalinism: *Bolsheviks, Boyars, and the Persistence of Tradition* (New Haven: Yale University Press, 2013)

Tom Ginsburg, James Melton, and Zachary Elkins, "On the Evasion of Executive Term Limits," *William and Mary Law Review*, v. 52, no. 6, 2011, pp. 1807–73.

Tom Ginsburg and Tamir Moustafa, eds., *Rule by Law: The Politics of Courts in Authoritarian Regimes* (New York: Cambridge University Press, 2008).

Gledis Gjipali, "Albania," in *Nations in Transit 2012* (New York: Freedom House, 2013).

Jeannette Goehring, ed., *Nations in Transit 2008: Democratization from Central Europe to Eurasia* (New York: Freedom House, 2008).

Jack A. Goldstone, "Weakness and Resilience in Middle Eastern Autocracies," *Foreign Affairs*, v. 90, no. 3, May/June 2011, pp. 8–16.

Grigorii V. Golosov, "Dmitry Medvedev's Party Reform," *Russian Analytical Digest*, no. 115, June 2012, pp. 8–10.

"The Regional Roots of Electoral Authoritarianism in Russia," *Europe-Asia Studies*, v. 63, no. 4, June 2011, pp. 623–39.

"Russian Political Parties and the 'Bosses': Evidence from the 1994 Provincial Elections in Western Siberia," *Party Politics*, v. 3, no. 1, 1997, pp. 5–21.

"The 2012 Political Reform in Russia: The Interplay of Liberalizing Concessions and Authoritarian Corrections," *Problems of Post-Communism*, v. 59, no. 6, 2012, pp. 3–14.

Thomas Goltz, *Azerbaijan Diary: A Rogue Reporter's Adventures in an Oil-Rich, War-Torn, Post-Soviet Republic* (Armonk, NY: M. E. Sharpe, 1998).

J. Paul Goode, *The Decline of Regionalism in Putin's Russia* (New York: Routledge, 2011).

Mikhail Gorbachev, *Zhizn' i reformy*, book 1 (Moscow: Novosti, 1995).

Thomas Graham, "Novyi rossiiskii rezhim," *Nezavisimaia Gazeta*, November 23, 1995.

Donald Green, Bradley Palmquist, and Eric Schickler, *Partisan Hearts and Minds* (New Haven, CT: Yale University Press, 2002).

Gregory Grossman, "The Second Economy of the USSR," *Problems of Communism*, v. 26, no. 5, September–October 1977, pp. 25–40.

Anna Grzymala-Busse, "The Best Laid Plans: The Impact of Informal Rules on Formal Institutions in Transitional Regimes," *Studies in Comparative International Development*, v. 45, no. 3, September 2010, pp. 311–33.

"Beyond Clientelism: Incumbent State Capture and State Formation," *Comparative Political Studies*, v. 41, nos. 4/5, April/May 2008, pp. 638–73.

Anna Grzymala-Busse and Pauline Jones Luong, "Reconceptualizing the State: Lessons from Post-Communism," *Politics & Society*, v. 30, no. 4, December 2002, pp. 529–54.

Igor' Guzhva and Yuriy Aksenov, "Deti gaza i stali," *Ekspert* (Russia), October 11, 2004.

James Habyarimana, Macartan Humphreys, Daniel N. Posner, and Jeremy M. Weinstein, "Why Does Ethnic Diversity Undermine Public Goods Provision?" *American Political Science Review*, v. 101, no. 4, November 1997, pp. 709–25.

Henry E. Hale, "Cause without a Rebel: Kazakhstan's Unionist Nationalism in the USSR and CIS," *Nationalities Papers*, v. 37, no. 1, January 2009, pp. 1–32.

"Democracy or Autocracy on the March? The Colored Revolutions as Normal Dynamics of Patronal Presidentialism," *Communist and Post-Communist Studies*, v. 39, no. 3, September 2006, pp. 305–29.

"Did the Internet Break the Political Machine? Moldova's 2009 'Twitter Revolution That Wasn't,'" *Demokratizatsiya: The Journal of Post-Soviet Democratization*, v. 21, no. 3, Fall 2013, pp. 481–505.

"Divided We Stand: Institutional Sources of Ethnofederal State Survival and Collapse," *World Politics*, v. 56, no. 2, January 2004, pp. 165–93.

"Explaining Machine Politics in Russia's Regions: Economy, Ethnicity, and Legacy," *Post-Soviet Affairs*, v. 19, no. 3, July–September 2003, pp. 228–63.

"Formal Constitutions in Informal Politics: Institutions and Democratization in Eurasia," *World Politics*, v. 63, no. 4, October 2011, pp. 581–617.

The Foundations of Ethnic Politics: Separatism of States and Nations in Eurasia and the World (New York: Cambridge University Press, 2008).

"Hybrid Regimes: When Democracy and Autocracy Mix," in Nathan Brown, ed., *Dynamics of Democratization* (Baltimore: Johns Hopkins University Press, 2011), pp. 23–45.

"Identity Divides as Authoritarian Resource: Post-Soviet Cases over Twenty Years," paper prepared for presentation at the Association for the Study of Nationalities annual meeting, April 19–21, 2012, Columbia University, New York.

"The Makeup and Breakup of Ethnofederal States: Why Russia Survives Where the USSR Fell," *Perspectives on Politics*, v. 3, no. 1, March 2005, pp. 55–70.

"The Origins of United Russia and the Putin Presidency: The Role of Contingency in Party-System Development," *Demokratizatsiya: The Journal of Post-Soviet Democratization*, v. 12, no. 2, Spring 2004, pp. 169–94.

"The Putin Machine Sputters: First Impressions of Russia's 2011 Duma Election," *Russian Analytical Digest*, no. 106, December 21, 2011, pp. 2–5.

"Regime Cycles: Democracy, Autocracy, and Revolution in Post-Soviet Eurasia," *World Politics*, v. 58, no. 1, October 2005, pp. 133–65.

"Two Decades of Post-Soviet Regime Dynamics," *Demokratizatsiya: The Journal of Post-Soviet Democratization*, v. 20, no. 2, Spring 2012, pp. 71–7.

"The Uses of Divided Power," *Journal of Democracy*, v. 21, no. 3, July 2010, pp. 84–98.

"Why and When Do Patronal Presidents Fall from Power? A Quantitative Study of Eurasian Cases," paper prepared for presentation at the Annual Meeting of the Association for Slavic, East European, and Eurasian Studies (ASEEES), Boston, November 21–4, 2013.

Why Not Parties in Russia: Democracy, Federalism, and the State (New York: Cambridge University Press, 2006).

Henry E. Hale and Timothy J. Colton, "Russians and the Putin-Medvedev 'Tandemocracy': A Survey-Based Portrait of the 2007–08 Election Season," *Problems of Post-Communism*, v. 57, no. 2, March/April 2010, pp. 3–20.

"Sources of Dominant Party Dominance in Hybrid Regimes: The Surprising Importance of Ideas and the Case of United Russia 1999–2011," unpublished paper, August 21, 2013.

"Who Defects? Defection Cascades from a Ruling Party and the Case of United Russia 2008–12," unpublished paper, March 19, 2014.

Henry E. Hale and Robert Orttung, "The Duma Districts: Key to Putin's Power," PONARS Policy Memo, no. 290, September 2003.

Stephen E. Hanson, "Defining Democratic Consolidation," in Richard D. Anderson, Jr., M. Steven Fish, Stephen E. Hanson, and Philip G. Roeder, *Postcommunism and the Theory of Democracy* (Princeton, NJ: Princeton University Press, 2001).

Post-Imperial Democracies: Ideology and Party Formation in Third Republic France, Weimar Germany, and Post-Soviet Russia (New York: Cambridge University Press, 2010).

Time and Revolution: Marxism and the Design of Soviet Institutions (Chapel Hill: University of North Carolina Press, 1997).

Olexiy Haran, "Ukraine: Pluralism by Default, Revolution, Thermidor," *Russian Politics and Law*, v. 50, no. 4, July–August 2012, pp. 51–72.

Vaclav Havel, "The Power of the Powerless," in Paul Wilson, ed., *Open Letters: Selected Writings, 1965–1990* (New York: Vintage Books, 1992).

John Heathershaw, *Post-Conflict Tajikistan: The Politics of Peacebuilding and the Emergence of Legitimate Order* (London: Routledge, 2009).

John Heathershaw and Edmund Herzig, "Introduction: The Sources of Statehood in Tajikistan," *Central Asian Survey*, v. 30, no. 1, March 2011, pp. 5–19.

Michael Hechter, *Principles of Group Solidarity* (Berkeley: University of California Press, 1987).

Stefan Hedlund, *Putin's Energy Agenda: The Contradictions of Russia's Resource Wealth* (Boulder: Lynne Rienner, 2014).

Richard Hellie, "Edward Keenan's Scholarly Ways," *Russian Review*, v. 46, no. 2, April 1987, pp. 177–90.

"Why Did the Muscovite Elite Not Rebel?" *Russian History: Histoire russe*, v. 25, nos. 1–2, 1998, pp. 155–62.

Gretchen Helmke and Steven Levitsky, "Introduction," in Gretchen Helmke and Steven Levitsky, eds., *Informal Institutions and Democracy: Lessons from Latin America* (Baltimore: Johns Hopkins University Press, 2006), pp. 1–30.

Jeffrey Herbst, "Political Liberalization in Africa after Ten Years," *Comparative Politics*, v. 33, no. 3, April 2001, pp. 357–75.

Erik S. Herron, "The Effect of Passive Observation Methods on Azerbaijan's 2008 Presidential Election and 2009 Referendum," *Electoral Studies*, v. 29, no. 3, 2010, pp. 417–24.

Elections and Democracy after Communism? (New York: Palgrave Macmillan, 2009).

"How Viktor Yanukovych Won: Reassessing the Dominant Narratives of Ukraine's 2010 Presidential Election," *East European Politics and Societies*, v. 25, no. 1, February 2011, pp. 47–67.

"Measuring Dissent in Electoral Authoritarian Societies: Lessons from Azerbaijan's 2008 Presidential Election and 2009 Referendum," *Comparative Political Studies*, v. 44, no. 11, November 2011, pp. 1557–83.

Vicki L. Hesli, *Governments and Politics in Russia and the Post-Soviet Region* (Boston: Houghton Mifflin, 2007).

Allen Hicken, "Clientelism," *Annual Review of Political Science*, v. 14, 2011, pp. 289–310.

Brent Hierman, "Sources of Inter-ethnic Trust and Distrust in Central Asia," doctoral dissertation in Political Science, Indiana University, Bloomington, 2011.

John Higley and Michael G. Burton, "The Elite Variable in Democratic Transitions and Breakdowns," *American Sociological Review*, v. 54, no. 1, February 1989, pp. 17–32.

Fiona Hill and Clifford G. Gaddy, *Mr. Putin: Operative in the Kremlin* (Washington, DC: Brookings, 2013).

William H. Hill, *Russia, the New Abroad, and the West: Lessons from the Moldova-Transdniestria Conflict* (Baltimore: Johns Hopkins University Press, 2012).

David Hoffman, *The Oligarchs: Wealth and Power in the New Russia* (New York: PublicAffairs, 2002).

Stephen Holmes, "Back to the Drawing Board: An Argument for Constitutional Postponement in Eastern Europe," *East European Constitutional Review*, v. 2, no. 1, Winter 1993, pp. 21–5.

"Introduction," *East European Constitutional Review*, v. 11, nos. 1–2, Winter/Spring 2002, pp. 90–1.

Slavomir Horak, "Changes in the Political Elite in Post-Soviet Turkmenistan," *China and Eurasia Forum Quarterly*, v. 8, no. 3, 2010, pp. 27–46.

"The Elite in Post-Soviet and Post-Niyazow Turkmenistan: Does Political Culture Form a Leader?" *Demokratizatsiya: The Journal of Post-Soviet Democratization*, v. 20, no. 4, Fall 2012, pp. 371–85.

Donald L. Horowitz, "Comparing Democratic Systems," *Journal of Democracy*, v. 1., no. 4, Fall 1990, pp. 73–9.

"Democracy in Divided Societies," *Journal of Democracy*, v. 4, no. 4, October 1993, pp. 18–37.

Jerry F. Hough, *Democratization and Revolution in the USSR 1985–1991* (Washington, DC: Brookings Institution, 1997).

"Institutional Rules and Party Formation," in Timothy J. Colton and Hough, eds., *Growing Pains: Russian Democracy and the Election of 1993* (Washington, DC: Brookings, 1998), pp. 37–74.

The Logic of Economic Reform in Russia (Washington, DC: Brookings, 2001).

The Soviet Prefects: The Local Party Organs in Industrial Decision-making (Cambridge, MA: Harvard University Press, 1969).

The Soviet Union and Social Science Theory (Cambridge, MA: Harvard University Press, 1977).

Jerry F. Hough and Merle Fainsod, *How the Soviet Union Is Governed* (Cambridge, MA: Harvard University Press, 1979).

Marc Morje Howard and Philip G. Roessler, "Liberalizing Electoral Outcomes in Competitive Authoritarian Regimes," *American Journal of Political Science*, v. 50, no. 2, April 2006, pp. 365–81.

Shireen T. Hunter, "Azerbaijan: Searching for New Neighbors," in Ian Bremmer and Ray Taras, eds., *New States, New Politics* (New York: Cambridge University Press, 1997), pp. 437–72.

Samuel P. Huntington, *Political Order in Changing Societies* (New Haven, CT: Yale University Press, 1968).

The Third Wave (Norman: University of Oklahoma Press, 1991).

Eugene Huskey, "Kyrgyzstan: The Fate of Political Liberalization," in Karen Dawisha and Bruce Parrott, eds., *Conflict, Cleavage, and Change in Central Asia and the Caucasus* (New York: Cambridge University Press, 1997), pp. 242–76.

Eugene Huskey and Gulnara Iskakova, "The Barriers to Intra-Opposition Cooperation in the Post-Communist World: Evidence from Kyrgyzstan," *Post-Soviet Affairs*, v. 26, no. 3, July–September 2010, pp. 228–62.

Susan D. Hyde, "International Dimensions of Elections," in Nathan Brown, ed., *Dynamics of Democratization* (Baltimore: Johns Hopkins University Press, 2011), pp. 266–82.

"The Observer Effect in International Politics: Evidence from a Natural Experiment," *World Politics*, v. 60, no. 1, October 2007, pp. 37–63.

Osmonakun Ibraimov, *Ispytanie istoriei: Razmyshleniia i esse o sud'be Kyrgyzstana* (Moscow: Mezhdunarodnye Otnosheniia, 2008).

Alisher Ilkhamov, "The Limits of Centralization: Regional Challenges in Uzbekistan," in Pauline Jones Luong, ed., *The Transformation of Central Asia* (Ithaca, NY: Cornell University Press, 2004), pp. 159–81.

"Neopatrimonialism, Interest Groups and Patronage Networks: The Impasses of the Governance System in Uzbekistan," *Central Asian Survey*, v. 26, no. 1, March 2007, pp. 65–84.

"Uzbekistan Country Report," in *Bertelsmann Stiftung Transformation Index (BTI) 2012* (Gutersloh: Bertelsman Stiftung, 2012).

Daria Isachenko, "Hyperreality of Statebuilding: The Case of Transdniestrian Region of Moldova," draft paper presented at the International Studies Association Annual Convention, 2008.

Gulnara Iskakova, *Vybory i demokratiia v Kyrgyzstane: Konstitutsionnyi dizain prezidentsko-parlamentskikh otnoshenii* (Bishkek: Biyiktik, 2003).

Aleksandr Iskandaryan, "Armenia between Autocracy and Polyarchy," *Russian Politics and Law*, v. 50, no. 4, July–August 2012, pp. 23–36.

Allen W. Johnson and Timothy Earle, *The Evolution of Human Societies: From Foraging Group to Agrarian State*, 2nd ed. (San Jose, CA: Stanford University Press, 2000).

Juliet Johnson, *A Fistful of Rubles: The Rise and Fall of the Russian Banking System* (Ithaca, NY: Cornell University Press, 2000).

"From Monetary Independence to State Control: Central Banking in the Kyrgyz Republic, 1993–2010," paper presented at a PONARS Eurasia workshop in Bishkek, Kyrgyzstan, June 2011.

Kevin D. Jones, "The Dynamics of Political Protests: A Case Study of the Kyrgyz Republic," Ph.D. dissertation in Public Policy, University of Maryland, August 31, 2007, http://www.lib.umd.edu/drum/handle/1903/7431, last accessed July 17, 2014.

Stephen F. Jones, "Georgia: The Trauma of Statehood," in Ian Bremmer and Ray Taras, eds., *New States, New Politics* (New York: Cambridge University Press, 1997), pp. 505–43.

Barbara Junisbai, "Improbable but Potentially Pivotal Oppositions: Privatization, Capitalists, and Political Contestation in the Post-Soviet Autocracies," *Perspectives on Politics*, v. 10, no. 4, December 2012, pp. 891–916.

"Market Reform Regimes, Elite Defections, and Political Opposition in the Post-Soviet States: Evidence from Belarus, Kazakhstan, and Kyrgyzstan," doctoral dissertation in Political Science, Indiana University, 2009.

"A Tale of Two Kazakhstans: Sources of Political Cleavage and Conflict in the Post-Soviet Period," *Europe-Asia Studies*, v. 62, no. 1, March 2010, pp. 235–69.

Barbara Junisbai and Azamat Junisbai, "Democratic Choice of Kazakhstan: A Case Study in Economic Liberalization, Intraelite Cleavage, and Political Opposition," *Demokratizatsiya: The Journal of Post-Soviet Democratization*, v. 13, Summer 2005, pp. 373–92.

Shairbek Juraev, "Kyrgyz Democracy? The Tulip Revolution and Beyond," *Central Asian Survey*, v. 27, nos. 3–4, September 2008, pp. 337–47.

Katya Kalandadze and Mitchell A. Orenstein, "Electoral Protests and Democratization: Beyond the Color Revolutions," *Comparative Political Studies*, v. 42, no. 11, November 2009, pp. 1403–25.

Stathis Kalyvas, *The Logic of Violence in Civil War* (New York: Cambridge University Press, 2006).

Georgi Kandelaki, "Georgia's Rose Revolution: A Participant's Perspective," *United States Institute of Peace Special Report*, no. 167, July 2006.

David C. Kang, *Crony Capitalism: Corruption and Development in South Korea and the Philippines* (New York: Cambridge University Press, 2002).

Nikolai Karamzin, "A Memoir on Ancient and Modern Russia," in Richard Pipes, ed., *Karamzin's Memoir on Ancient and Modern Russia* (New York: Atheneum, 1986).

Adrian Karatnycky, "Ukraine's Orange Revolution," *Foreign Affairs*, v. 84, no. 2, March–April 2005, pp. 32–52.

Rasma Karklins, *The System Made Me Do It: Corruption in Post-Communist Societies* (Armonk, NY: M. E. Sharpe, 2005).

Terry Lynn Karl, "The Hybrid Regimes of Central America," *Journal of Democracy*, v. 6, no. 3, July 1995, pp. 72–86.

Terry Lynn Karl and Philippe C. Schmitter, "Modes of Transition in Latin America, Southern and Eastern Europe," *International Social Science Journal*, v. 43, June 1991, pp. 269–84.

Heorhii Kas'ianov, *Ukraiina 1991–2007: Narysy novitn'oii istorii* (Kyiv: Nash Chas, 2008).

Daniel Kaufmann, Aart Kraay, and Massimo Mastruzze, "Governance Matters VII: Aggregate and Individual Governance Indicators 1996–2007," report dated June 2008, www-wds.worldbank.org.

Viacheslav Kebich, *Iskushenie vlast'iu: Iz zhizni prem'er-ministra* (Minsk: Paradoks, 2008).

Edward L. Keenan, "Muscovite Political Folkways," *The Russian Review*, v. 45, 1986, pp. 115–81.

"Muscovy and Kazan: Some Introductory Remarks on the Patterns of Steppe Diplomacy," *Slavic Review*, v. 26, no. 4, December 1967, pp. 548–58.

Ryan Kennedy, "Moldova," in Donnacha O Beachain and Abel Polese, eds., *The Colour Revolutions in the Former Soviet Republics* (New York: Routledge, 2010), pp. 62–82.

Mustaq H. Khan, "Markets, States and Democracy: Patron-Client Networks and the Case for Democracy in Developing Countries," *Democratization*, v. 12, no. 5, December 2005, pp. 704–24.

Anatoly Khazanov, *Nomads and the Outside World* (New York: Cambridge University Press, 1984).

Oleg V. Khlevniuk, *Master of the House: Stalin and His Inner Circle* (New Haven, CT: Yale University Press, 2009).

Charles King, "The Benefits of Ethnic War: Understanding Eurasia's Unrecognized States," *World Politics*, v. 53, no. 4, July 2001, pp. 524–52.

The Moldovans: Romania, Russia, and the Politics of Culture (Palo Alto, CA: Hoover Institution Press, 2000).

Herbert Kitschelt, "Clientelistic Linkage Strategies. A Descriptive Exploration," paper prepared for the Workshop on Democratic Accountability Strategies, Duke University, Durham, May 18–19, 2011.

"Linkages between Citizens and Politicians in Democratic Polities," *Comparative Political Studies*, v. 33, nos. 6–7, 2000.

Herbert Kitschelt and Steven I. Wilkinson, "Citizen-Politician Linkages: An Introduction," in Herbert Kitschelt and Steven I. Wilkinson, *Patrons, Clients, and Policies: Patterns of Democratic Accountability and Political Competition* (Cambridge: Cambridge University Press, 2007), pp. 1–49.

eds., *Patrons, Clients, and Policies: Patterns of Democratic Accountability and Political Competition* (Cambridge: Cambridge University Press, 2007).

Herbert Kitschelt, Zdenka Mansfeldova, Radoslaw Markowski, and Gabor Toka, *Post-Communist Party Systems: Competition, Representation, and Inter-Party Cooperation* (New York: Cambridge University Press, 1999).

Valerie Kivelson, *Autocracy in the Provinces: The Muscovite Gentry and Political Culture in the Seventeenth Century* (Stanford, CA: Stanford University Press, 1996).

Georgi Kldiashvili, "The President in Opposition: Georgia's 2012 Parliamentary Elections," *Caucasus Analytical Digest*, no. 43, October 15, 2012, pp. 2–5.

Jack Knight, *Institutions and Social Conflict* (New York: Cambridge University Press, 1992).

Heinz Kohler, *Comparative Economic Systems* (Glenview, IL: Scott, Foresman, 1989).

Nancy Shields Kollmann, "The Façade of Autocracy," in Marker Kaiser, ed., *Reinterpreting Russian History: Readings 860–1860's* (New York: Oxford University Press, 1994).

Kinship and Politics: The Making of the Muscovite Political System (Stanford, CA: Stanford University Press, 1987).

Sergei Kolmakov, "The Role of Financial Industrial Conglomerates in Russian Political Parties," *Russia Watch* (Harvard University), no. 9, January 2003, p. 16.

Pål Kolstø and Helge Blakkisrud, "Living with Non-Recognition: State- and Nation-Building in South Caucasian Quasi-States," *Europe-Asia Studies*, v. 60, no. 3, May 2008, pp. 483–509.

Andrew Konitzer, *Voting for Russia's Governors* (Baltimore: Johns Hopkins University Press, 2005).

Vadim Kononenko and Arkady Moshes, eds., *Russia as a Network State: What Works in Russia When State Institutions Do Not?* (New York: Palgrave Macmillan, 2011).

Vladimir Korobov and Georgii Byanov, "The 'Renewal' of Transnistria," *Journal of Communist Studies and Transition Politics*, v. 22, no. 4, December 2006, pp. 517–28.

Elena Korosteleva, "Questioning Democracy Promotion: Belarus' Response to the 'Colour Revolutions,'" *Democratization*, v. 19, no. 1, February 2012, pp. 37–59.

Stephen Kotkin with a contribution by Jan T. Gross, *Uncivil Society: 1989 and the Implosion of the Communist Establishment* (New York: Random House, 2009).

Lawrence Krader, "Feudalism and the Tatar Polity of the Middle Ages," *Comparative Political Studies in Society and History*, v. 1, no. 1, October 1958, pp. 76–99.

Mark Kramer, "The Collapse of East European Communism and the Repercussions within the Soviet Union," *Journal of Cold War Studies*, v. 5, no. 4, 2003, pp. 178–256.

David J. Kramer and William H. Hill, "Moldova: The Twitter Revolution That Wasn't," *OpenDemocracy*, May 28, 2009.

David J. Kramer, Robert Nurick, Damon Wilson, with Evan Alterman, "Sounding the Alarm: Protecting Democracy in Ukraine," Freedom House Report, April 2011.

Leonid Kravchuk, *Maemo te, shcho maemo: spohady i rozdumy* (Kyiv: Stolittia, 2002).

Robert S. Kravchuk, "The Quest for Balance: Regional Self-Government and Subnational Fiscal Policy in Ukraine," in Taras Kuzio, Robert S. Kravchuk, and Paul D'Anieri, *State and Institution-Building in Ukraine* (New York: St. Martin's, 1999), pp. 155–212.

Serhiy Kudelia, "Betting on Society: Power Perceptions and Elite Games in Ukraine," in Paul D'Anieri, ed., *Orange Revolution and Aftermath: Mobilization, Apathy, and the State in Ukraine* (Washington, DC: Woodrow Wilson Center, 2010), pp. 160–89.

"Clients' Revolt? Explaining the Failure of Government's Patronage in Ukraine's 2010 Presidential Election," paper presented at George Washington University workshop, April 2010.

"Institutional Design and Elite Interests: The Case of Ukraine," unpublished paper presented at the DC Area Postcommunist Politics Social Science Workshop, George Washington University, January 4, 2012.

Emir Kulov, "March 2005: Parliamentary Elections as a Catalyst of Protests," *Central Asian Survey*, v. 27, nos. 3–4, September 2008, pp. 337–47.

Feliks Kulov, *Na perevale* (Moscow: Vremia, 2008).

Alexander Kupatadze, *Organized Crime, Political Transitions, and State Formation in Post-Soviet Eurasia* (New York: Palgrave Macmillan, 2012).

"'Transitions after Transitions': Coloured Revolutions and Organized Crime in Georgia, Ukraine, and Kyrgyzstan," PhD Dissertation, University of St. Andrews, 2010, http://hdl.handle.net/10023/1320, pp.126, 180, 183.

Timur Kuran, "Now Out of Never: The Element of Surprise in the East European Revolution of 1989," *World Politics*, v. 44, no. 1, October 1991, pp. 7–48.

Taras Kuzio, "Ambiguous Anniversary," *Business Ukraine*, November 24–30, 2008, pp. 12–16.

"Democratic Breakthroughs and Revolutions in Five Postcommunist Countries: Comparative Perspectives on the Fourth Wave," *Demokratizatsiya: The Journal of Post-Soviet Democratization*, v. 16, no. 1, Winter 2008, pp. 97–109.

"Democratic Revolutions from a Different Angle: Social Populism and National Identity in Ukraine's 2004 Orange Revolution," *Journal of Contemporary European Studies*, v. 20, no. 1, March 2012, pp. 41–54.

"Strident, Ambiguous and Duplicitous: Ukraine and the 2008 Russia-Georgia War," *Demokratizatsiya: The Journal of Post-Soviet Democratization*, v. 17, no. 4, Fall 2009, pp. 350–72.

Ukraine: A Contemporary History, unpublished draft book manuscript, July 2011.

"Ukraine: Muddling Along," in Sharon L. Wolchik and Jane L. Curry, eds., *Central and East European Politics: From Communism to Democracy* (Lanham, MD: Rowman & Littlefield, 2008), pp. 339–67.

"The 2002 Parliamentary Elections in Ukraine: Democratization or Authoritarianism?" *Journal of Communist Studies and Transition Politics*, v. 19, no. 2, June 2003, pp. 24–54.

David D. Laitin, *Identity in Formation* (Ithaca, NY: Cornell University Press, 1998).

Carl H. Lande, "Networks and Groups in Southeast Asia: Some Observations on the Group Theory of Politics," *American Political Science Review*, v. 67, no. 1, March 1973, pp. 103–27.

Marlene Laruelle, "Discussing Neopatrimonialism and Patronal Presidentialism in the Central Asian Context," *Demokratizatsiya: The Journal of Post-Soviet Democratization*, v. 20, no. 4, Autumn 2012, pp. 301–24.

Alena V. Ledeneva, *How Russia Really Works* (Ithaca, NY: Cornell University Press, 2006).

Russia's Economy of Favours: Blat, Networking, and Informal Exchange (Cambridge: Cambridge University Press, 1998).

John P. LeDonne, "Ruling Families in the Russian Political Order, 1689–1825," *Cahiers du Monde russe et Sovietique*, v. 28, nos. 3–4, July–December 1987, pp. 233–322.

Rene Lemarchand, "Political Clientelism and Ethnicity in Tropical Africa: Competing Solidarities in Nation-Building," *American Political Science Review*, v. 66, no. 1, March 1972, pp. 68–90.

Steven Levitsky and Gretchen Helmke, *Informal Institutions and Democracy: Lessons from Latin America* (Baltimore: Johns Hopkins University Press, 2006).

Steven R. Levitsky and Lucan A. Way, "Beyond Patronage: Violent Struggle, Ruling Party Cohesion, and Authoritarian Durability," *Perspectives on Politics*, v. 10, no. 4, December 2012, pp. 868–89.

Competitive Authoritarianism: Hybrid Regimes after the Cold War (New York: Cambridge University Press, 2010).

"The Rise of Competitive Authoritarianism," *Journal of Democracy*, v. 13, no. 2, April 2002, pp. 51–65.

David Lewis, "The Dynamics of Regime Change: Domestic and International Factors in the 'Tulip Revolution,'" *Central Asian Survey*, v. 27, nos. 3–4, September 2008, pp. 265–77.

Arend Lijphart, "Constitutional Choices for New Democracies," *Journal of Democracy*, v. 2, no. 1, Winter 1991, pp. 72–84.

Staffan I. Lindberg, *Democracy and Elections in Africa* (Baltimore: Johns Hopkins University Press, 2006).

Carl Linden, T. H. Rigby, and Robert Conquest, "Conflict and Authority," discussion in *Problems of Communism*, v. 12, no. 5, September–October 1963, pp. 27–46.

"How Strong Is Khrushchev?" discussion in *Problems of Communism*, v. 12, no. 6, November–December 1963, pp. 56–65.

Juan Linz, "The Perils of Presidentialism," *Journal of Democracy*, v. 1, no. 1, Winter 1990, pp. 51–69.

Juan J. Linz and Alfred Stepan, *Problems of Democratic Transition and Consolidation: Southern Europe, South America, and Post-Communist Europe* (Baltimore: Johns Hopkins University Press, 1996).

Maria Lipman and Nikolay Petrov, eds., *Russia in 2020: Scenarios for the Future* (Washington, DC: Carnegie Endowment, 2011).

Seymour M. Lipset and Stein Rokkan, "Cleavage Structures, Party Systems, and Voter Alignments: An Introduction," in Seymour M. Lipset and Stein Rokkan, eds, *Party Systems and Voter Aligments: Cross-National Perspectives* (New York: Free Press, 1967), pp. 1–64.

Aleksandr Litvinenko, "'Oranzhevaia Revoliutsiia: Prichiny, Kharakter i Rezultaty," in Mikhail Pogrebinsky, ed., *"Oranzhevaia" Revoliutsiia: Versii, Khronika, Dokumenty* (Kyiv: Otima, 2005), pp. 9–18.

Susanne Lohmann, "The Dynamics of Informational Cascades: The Monday Demonstrations in Leipzig, East Germany, 1989–91," *World Politics*, v. 47, no. 1, October 1994, pp. 42–101.

Anna Urasova Lowry, "Between Neopatrimonialism and Developmentalism: Exploring the Causes of Nationalization in Russia," dissertation in political science, Indiana University, 2014.

Petr Luchinskii, *Moldova i Moldavane* (Chisinau: Cartea Moldovei, 2007).

Pauline Jones Luong, *Institutional Change and Political Continuity in Post-Soviet Central Asia* (New York: Cambridge University Press, 2002).

"Politics in the Periphery: Competing Views of Central Asian States and Societies," in Luong, ed., *The Transformation of Central Asia: States and Societies from Soviet Rule to Independence* (Ithaca, NY: Cornell University Press, 2003).

Pauline Jones Luong and Erika Weinthal, *Oil Is Not a Curse: Ownership Structure and Institutions in Soviet Successor States* (New York: Cambridge University Press, 2010).

Samuel Lussac, "The State as a 'Oil' Company? The Political Economy of Azerbaijan," *GARNET Working Paper* No. 74/10, February 2010.

Ellen Lust, "Why Now? Micro Transitions and the Arab Uprisings," *APSA CD*, v. 9, no. 3, October 2011, pp. 1, 3–8.

Ellen Lust-Okar, "Elections under Authoritarianism: Preliminary Lessons from Jordan," *Democratization*, v. 13, no. 3, 2006, pp. 456–71.

Structuring Conflict in the Arab World: Incumbents, Opponents, and Institutions (New York: Cambridge University Press, 2005).

Dov Lynch, "De Facto 'States' around the Black Sea: The Importance of Fear," *Southeast European and Black Sea Studies*, v. 7, no. 3, September 2007, pp. 483–96.

Marc Lynch, *The Arab Uprising: The Unfinished Revolutions of the New Middle East* (New York: PublicAffairs, 2012).

Beatriz Magaloni, *Voting for Autocracy: Hegemonic Party Survival and Its Demise in Mexico* (New York: Cambridge University Press, 2006).

Scott Mainwaring and Matthew S. Shugart, "Juan Linz, Presidentialism, and Democracy: A Critical Appraisal," *Comparative Politics*, v. 29, no. 4, July 1997, pp. 449–71.

Martin Malia, *The Soviet Tragedy: A History of Socialism in Russia, 1917–1991* (New York: Simon & Schuster, 1995).

Erica Marat, "Kyrgyzstan," in *Nations in Transit 2011* (New York: Freedom House, 2011), pp. 297–316.

"Kyrgyzstan," in *Nations in Transit 2012* (New York: Freedom House, 2012), pp.297–316.

"Kyrgyzstan: A Parliamentary System Based on Inter-Elite Consensus," *Demokratizatsiya: The Journal of Post-Soviet Democratization*, v. 20, no. 4, Fall 2012, pp. 325–44.

The Tulip Revolution: Kyrgyzstan One Year After (Washington, DC: Jamestown Foundation, 2006).

Luke March, "The Consequences of the 2009 Parliamentary Elections for Moldova's Domestic and International Politics: A Narrow Window for Europeanization," paper delivered at the Annual Meeting of the American Association for the Advancement of Slavic Studies, Boston, November 13, 2009.

"Managing Opposition in a Hybrid Regime: Just Russia and Parastatal Opposition," *Slavic Review*, v. 68, no. 3, Fall 2009, pp. 504–27.

Sergei Markedonov, "The Unlikely Winners," *Russia Profile.org*, November 15, 2011.

Lawrence P. Markowitz, *State Erosion: Unlootable Resources and Unruly Elites in Central Asia* (Ithaca, NY: Cornell University Press, 2013).

"The Sub-National Roots of Authoritarianism: Neopatrimonialism and Territorial Administration in Uzbekistan," *Demokratizatsiya: The Journal of Post-Soviet Democratization*, v. 20, no. 4, Fall 2012, pp. 387–408.

David Marples, "Outpost of Tyranny? The Failure of Democratization in Belarus," *Democratization*, v. 16, no. 4, August 2009, pp. 756–76.

Monty G. Marshall, *Polity IV Project: Political Regime Characteristics and Transitions 1800–2010* (2011), www.systemicpeace.org.

Monty G. Marshall, Ted Robert Gurr, and Keith Jaggers, "Polity IV Project: Political Regime Characteristics and Transitions, 1800–2009: Dataset Users' Manual," Center for Systemic Peace, www.systemicpeace.org/polity/polity4.htm.

Virginia Martin, *Law and Custom in the Steppe* (Surrey: Curzon, 2001).

Yuri Matsievski, "Change, Transition, or Cycle: The Dynamics of Ukraine's Political Regime in 2004–2010," *Russian Politics and Law*, v. 49, no. 5, September–October 2011, pp. 8–33.

Kimitaka Matsuzato, "All Kuchma's Men: The Reshuffling of Ukrainian Governors and the Presidential Election of 1999," *Post-Soviet Geography and Economics*, v. 42, no. 6, September 2001, pp. 416–39.

"From Belligerent to Multi-Ethnic Democracy: Domestic Politics in Unrecognized States after the Ceasefires," *Eurasian Review*, v. 1, November 2008, pp. 95–119.

"Mezhpravoslavnye otnosheniia i transgranichnye narodnosti vokrug nepriznannykh gosudarstv. Sravnenie Pridniestrov'ia i Abkhazii," in Kimitaka Matsuzato, ed., *Pridniestrov'e v makroregional'nom kontekste chernomorskogo poberezh'ia* (Sapporo: Slavic Research Center, 2008), pp. 192–224.

"Nepriznannye gosudarstva v makroregional'noi politike chernomorskogo poberezh'ia," in Kimitaka Matsuzato, ed., *Pridniestrov'e v makroregional'nom kontekste chernomorskogo poberezh'ia* (Sapporo: Slavic Research Center, 2008), pp. 5–21.

"Patronnoe prezidentstvo i politika v sfere identichnosti v nepreznannoi Abkhazii," *Acta Eurasica*, no. 4, 2006, pp. 132–59.

"A Populist Island in an Ocean of Clan Politics: The Lukashenka Regime as an Exception among CIS Countries," *Europe-Asia Studies*, v. 56, no. 2, March 2004, pp. 235–61.

Eugene Mazo, "Post-Communist Paradox: How the Rise of Parliamentarism Coincided with the Demise of Pluralism in Moldova," *CDDRL Working Papers*, no. 17,

Center on Democracy, Development, and the Rule of Law, Stanford University, August 27, 2004.

Duncan McCargo, "Network Monarchy and Legitimacy Crises in Thailand," *The Pacific Review*, v. 18, no. 4, December 2005, pp. 499–519.

Cynthia McClintock, "Peru's Fujimori: A Caudillo Derails Democracy," *Current History*, v. 92, no. 572, March 1993, pp. 112–20.

"The Prospects for Democratic Consolidation in a 'Least Likely' Case: Peru," *Comparative Politics*, v. 21, no. 2, January 1989, pp. 127–48.

Michael McFaul, "The Fourth Wave of Democracy and Dictatorship: Noncooperative Transitions in the Postcommunist World," *World Politics*, v. 54, no. 2, January 2002, pp. 212–44.

Russia's Unfinished Revolution (Ithaca, NY: Cornell University Press, 2001).

"Transitions from Communism," *Journal of Democracy*, v. 16, no. 4, July 2005, pp. 212–44.

"Ukraine Imports Democracy: External Influences on the Orange Revolution," *International Security*, v. 32, no. 2, Fall 2007, pp. 45–83.

Michael McFaul, Chingiz Mammadov, and Zamira Sydykova, "What's a Corrupt Election among Friends?" *Los Angeles Times*, October 23, 2005.

Eric McGlinchey, *Chaos, Violence, Dynasty: Politics and Islam in Central Asia* (Pittsburgh: Pittsburgh University Press, 2011).

"Exploring Regime Instability and Ethnic Violence in Kyrgyzstan," *Asia Policy*, no. 12, July 2011, pp. 79–98.

Kelly M. McMann, *Economic Autonomy and Democracy: Hybrid Regimes in Russia and Kyrgyzstan* (New York: Cambridge University Press, 2006).

Roy Medvedev, *Aleksandr Lukashenko: Kontury Belorusskoi modeli* (Moscow: BBPG, 2010).

Remiz Mehdiyev, *Azerbaijan – 2003–2008: Thinking about Time* (Baku: Sharq-Qarb, 2010).

Hannes Meissner, "Informal Politics in Azerbaijan: Corruption and Rent-Seeking Patterns," *Caucasus Analytical Digest*, no. 24, February 11, 2011, pp. 6–9.

Ramiz Mekhtiev, *Na puti k demokratii: razmyshliaia o nasledii* (Baku: Sharq-Qarb, 2007).

Ellen Mickiewicz, *Television, Power, and the Public in Russia* (New York: Cambridge University Press, 2008).

Warren E. Miller and J. Merrill Shanks, *The New American Voter* (Cambridge, MA: Harvard University Press, 1996).

William Mishler and John P. Willerton, "The Dynamics of Presidential Popularity in Post-Communist Russia: Cultural Imperative versus Neo-Institutional Choice," *Journal of Politics*, v. 65, no. 1, February 2003, pp. 111–41.

Lincoln Mitchell, *The Color Revolutions* (College Park: University of Pennsylvania Press, 2012).

Uncertain Democracy: U.S. Foreign Policy and Georgia's Rose Revolution (Philadelphia: University of Pennsylvania Press, 2009).

Barrington Moore, Jr., *Soviet Politics: The Dilemma of Power* (Armonk, NY: M. E. Sharpe, 1950).

Christopher Monty, "Stalin, Local Party Secretaries, the Politics of the Lenin Succession, 1922–27," draft paper presented at the Annual Meeting of the Association for Slavic, East European, and Eurasian Studies (ASEEES), Friday, November 22, 2013, Boston.

Robert G. Moser, *Unexpected Outcomes: Electoral Systems, Political Parties, and Representation in Russia* (Pittsburgh: University of Pittsburgh Press, 2001).

Alexander J. Motyl, "The New Political Regime in Ukraine – toward Sultanism Yanukovych-Style?" Cicero Foundation Great Debate Paper, no. 10/06, July 2010.

Gerardo L. Munck, "Disaggregating Political Regime: Conceptual Issues in the Study of Democratization," Working Paper no. 228, Helen Kellogg Institute for International Studies, University of Notre Dame, Indiana, August 1996.

Measuring Democracy: A Bridge between Scholarship and Politics (Baltimore: Johns Hopkins University Press, 2009).

"The Regime Question: Theory Building in Democracy Studies," *World Politics*, v. 54, no. 1, October 2001, pp. 119–44.

Igor Munteanu, Tatiana Lariushina, and Veaceslav Ionita, *The System of Unofficial Taxation* (Bucharest: Cartier, 2007).

Rasim Musabayov and Rakhmil Shulman, *Azerbaijan in 2006–2010: Sociological Monitoring* (Baku: Friedrich Ebert Stiftung and Puls, 2010).

Azerbaijan in 2007: Sociological Monitoring (Baku: Friedrich Ebert Stiftung and Puls, 2008).

Natalia A. Narochnitskaia, *Oranzhevye seti: ot Belgrada do Bishkeka* (St. Petersburg, Russia: Aleteiia, 2008).

Andrew J. Nathan, "A Factionalism Model for CCP Politics," *The China Quarterly*, January–March 1973, pp. 34–66.

Nursultan Nazarbaev, *Bez pravykh i levykh* (Moscow: Molodaia Gvardiia, April 1991).

Viacheslav Nikonov, "'Oranzhevaia' Revoliutsiia v Kontekste Zhanra," in Mikhail Pogrebinsky, ed., *"Oranzhevaia" Revoliutsiia: Versii, Khronika, Dokumenty* (Kyiv: Otima, 2005), pp. 95–105.

David Nissman, "Turkmenistan: Just like Old Times," in Ian Bremmer and Ray Taras, eds., *New States, New Politics* (New York: Cambridge University Press, 1997), pp. 634–53.

Ghia Nodia, "Georgia," in *Nations in Transit 2008* (New York: Freedom House, 2008).

Douglass C. North, *Institutions, Institutional Change and Economic Performance* (New York: Cambridge University Press, 1990).

Douglass C. North and Barry R. Weingast, "Constitutions and Commitment," *Journal of Economic History*, v. 49, no. 4, December 1989, pp. 803–32.

Douglass C. North, John Joseph Wallis, and Barry R. Weingast, *Violence and Social Orders: A Conceptual Framework for Interpreting Recorded Human History* (New York: Cambridge University Press, 2009).

Donnacha O Beachain and Abel Polese, eds., *The Colour Revolutions in the Former Soviet Republics* (New York: Routledge, 2010).

Michael Ochs, "Turkmenistan: The Quest for Stability and Control," in Karen Dawisha and Bruce Parrott, eds., *Conflict, Cleavage, and Change in Central Asia and the Caucasus* (New York: Cambridge University Press, 1997), pp. 312–59.

Guillermo O'Donnell, "Delegative Democracy," *Journal of Democracy*, v. 5, no. 1, January 1994, pp. 55–69.

"On the State, Democratization, and Some Conceptual Problems: A Latin American View with Some Glances at Postcommunist Countries," *World Development*, v. 21, no. 8, August 1993, pp. 1355–69.

Guillermo O'Donnell and Philippe C. Schmitter, *Transitions from Authoritarian Rule: Tentative Conclusions about Uncertain Democracies* (Baltimore: Johns Hopkins University Press, 1986)

Martha Brill Olcott, *Central Asia's Second Chance* (Washington, DC: Carnegie Endowment for International Peace, 2005).

"Democratization and the Growth of Political Participation in Kazakhstan," in Karen Dawisha and Bruce Parrott, eds., *Conflict, Cleavage, and Change in Central Asia and the Caucasus* (New York: Cambridge University Press, 1997), pp. 201–41.

Kazakhstan: Unfulfilled Promise (Washington, DC: Carnegie Endowment, 2002).

Tajikistan's Difficult Development Path (Washington, DC: Carnegie Endowment, 2012).

John O'Loughlin, Vladimir Kolossov, and Gerard Toal, "Inside Abkhazia: Survey of Attitudes in a *De Facto* State," *Post-Soviet Affairs*, v. 27, no. 1, 2011, pp. 1–36.

Mancur Olson, "The Logic of Collective Action in Soviet-Type Societies," *Journal of Soviet Nationalities*, v. 1, no. 2, Summer 1990, pp. 8–27.

Olga Onuch, "Why Did They Join *en Masse*? Understanding 'Ordinary' Ukrainians' Participation in Mass-Mobilization in 2004," *New Ukraine. A Journal of History and Politics*, v. 11, 2011, pp. 89–113.

Robert W. Orttung. "Business and Politics in the Russian Regions," *Problems of Post-Communism*, v. 51, no. 2, March–April 2004, pp. 48–60.

Robert W. Orttung, "Navalny's Campaign to be Moscow Mayor," *Russian Analytical Digest*, no. 136, September 16, 2013, pp. 2–5.

Robert W. Orttung and David Rainbow, "How Do Authoritarian Leaders Stay in Power? Media, Information, and the Opposition in Russia," unpublished manuscript, 2011.

Donald Ostrowski, "The Façade of Legitimacy: Exchange of Power and Authority in Early Modern Russia," *Comparative Studies in Society and History*, v. 44, no. 3, July 2002, pp. 534–63.

Roger Owen, *The Rise and Fall of Arab Presidents for Life* (Cambridge, MA: Harvard University Press, 2012).

Gul Berna Ozcan, *Building States and Markets: Enterprise Development in Central Asia* (Houndmills: Palgrave Macmillan, 2010).

Razmik Panossian, "The Irony of Nagorno-Karabakh: Formal Institutions versus Informal Politics," *Regional & Federal Studies*, v. 11, no. 3, 2001, pp. 143–64.

Vladimer Papava, "Georgia's Hollow Revolution," *Harvard International Review*, February 27, 2008.

"The Political Economy of Georgia's Rose Revolution," *Orbis*, v. 50, no. 4, Fall 2006, pp. 57–67.

Vladimir G. Papava and Teimuraz A. Beridze, *Ocherki politicheskoi ekonomii postkommunisticheskogo kapitalizma* (Moscow: Delo i Servis, 2005).

David Patel and Valerie Bunce, "Turning Points and the Cross-National Diffusion of Popular Protest," *APSA CD*, v. 10, no. 1, January 2012, pp. 1, 10–13.

Anna Persson, Bo Rothstein, and Jan Teorell, "Why Anticorruption Reforms Fail – Systemic Corruption as a Collective Action Problem," *Governance*, v. 26, no. 3, July 2013, pp. 449–71.

Ridvan Peshkopia, *Conditioning Democratization: Institutional Reforms and EU Membership Conditionality in Albania and Macedonia* (New York: Anthem, 2013).

Nikolai Petrov, ed., *Federal'naia Reforma 2000–2004, T. 2. Strategii, Instituty, Problemy* (Moscow, Russia: Moskovskii Obshchestvennyi Nauchnyi Fond, 2005).

Nikolay Petrov, Maria Lipman, and Henry E. Hale, "Three Dilemmas of Hybrid Regime Governance: Russia from Putin to Putin," *Post-Soviet Affairs*, September 2013.

Tsveta Petrova, "A Postcommunist Transition in Two Acts: The 1996–97 Antigovernment Struggle in Bulgaria as a Bridge between the 1989–92 and 1996–2007 Democratization Waves in Eastern Europe," in Valerie Bunce, Michael McFaul, and Kathryn Stoner-Weiss, eds., *Democracy and Authoritarianism in the Postcommunist World* (New York: Cambridge University Press, 2010), pp. 107–33.

Sebastien Peyrouse, "The Kazakh Neopatrimonial Regime and Its Actors: Balancing Uncertainties among the 'Family,' Oligarchs and Technocrats," *Demokratizatsiya: The Journal of Post-Soviet Democratization*, v. 20, no. 4, Fall 2012, pp. 345–70.

"The Rise of Political Islam in Soviet Central Asia," in Hillel Fradkin, Husain Haqqani, and Eric Brown, eds., *Current Trends in Islamist Ideology* (Washington, DC: Hudson Institute, 2007), pp. 40–54.

Turkmenistan: Strategies of Power, Dilemmas of Development (Armonk, NY: M. E. Sharpe, 2011).

Simona Piattoni, "Clientelism in Historical and Comparative Perspective," in Simona Piattoni, ed., *Clientelism, Interests, and Democratic Representation: The European Experience in Historical and Comparative Perspective* (New York: Cambridge University Press, 2001), pp. 1–30.

Richard Pipes, *Russia under the Bolshevik Regime* (New York: Vintage, 1995).

Russia under the Old Regime (New York: Collier, 1974).

The Russian Revolution (New York: Vintage, 1991).

Ann Pitcher, Mary H. Moran, and Michael Johnston, "Rethinking Patrimonialism and Neopatrimonialism in Africa," *African Studies Review*, v. 52, no. 1, April 2009, pp. 125–56.

Marshall T. Poe, *"A People Born to Slavery": Russia in Early Modern European Ethnography, 1476–1748* (Ithaca, NY: Cornell University Press, 2001).

Marshall Poe, "The Truth about Muscovy," *Kritika: Explorations in Russian and Eurasian History*, v. 3, no. 3, Summer 2002, pp. 473–86.

Mikhail Pogrebinsky, "Kak Ukraina Shla k 'Oranzhevoi' Revoliutsii," in Pogrebinsky, ed., *"Oranzhevaia" Revoliutsiia: Versii, Khronika, Dokumenty* (Kyiv: Otima, 2005), pp. 106–18.

Richard Pomfret, "Transition and Democracy in Mongolia," *Europe-Asia Studies*, v. 52, no. 1, January 2000, pp. 149–60.

Grigore Pop-Eleches and Joshua A. Tucker, "Communism's Shadow: Postcommunist Legacies, Values, and Behavior," *Comparative Politics*, v. 43, no. 4, July 2011, pp. 379–408.

Nicu Popescu, "Moldova's Fragile Pluralism," *Russian Politics and Law*, v. 50, no. 4, July–August 2012, pp. 37–50.

Samuel L. Popkin, *The Reasoning Voter: Communication and Persuasion in Presidential Campaigns* (Chicago: University of Chicago Press, 1991).

Maria Popova, "Political Competition as an Obstacle to Judicial Independence: Evidence from Russia and Ukraine," *Comparative Political Studies*, v. 43, no. 10, 2010, pp. 1202–29.

John Duncan Powell, "Peasant Society and Clientelist Politics," *American Political Science Review*, v. 54, no. 2, June 1970, pp. 411–25.

Oleh Protsyk, "Representation and Democracy in Eurasia's Unrecognized States: The Case of Transnistria," *Post-Soviet Affairs*, v. 25, no. 3, 2009, pp. 257–81.

Adam Przeworski, *Democracy and the Market* (New York: Cambridge University Press, 1991).

Adam Przeworski, Michael E. Alvarez, Jose Antonio Cheibub, and Fernando Limongi, *Democracy and Development: Political Institutions and Well-Being in the World, 1950–1990* (New York: Cambridge University Press, 2000).

Adam Przeworski and Fernando Limongi, "Modernization: Theories and Facts," *World Politics*, v. 49, no. 2, 1997, pp. 155–83.

Arch Puddington, "Freedom in Retreat: Is the Tide Turning? Findings of Freedom in the World 2008," Freedom House publication, 2008.

Robert Putnam, *Making Democracy Work* (Princeton, NJ: Princeton University Press, 1993).

Scott Radnitz, "The Color of Money: Privatization, Economic Dispersion, and the Post-Soviet 'Revolutions,'" *Comparative Politics*, v. 42, no. 2, January 2010, pp. 127–46.

"In Georgia, Two Machines Are Better Than One," *ForeignPolicy.com*, September 27, 2012.

"Oil in the Family: Managing Presidential Succession in Azerbaijan," *Democratization*, v. 19, no. 1, February 2012, pp. 60–77.

Weapons of the Wealthy: Predatory Regimes and Elite-Led Protests in Central Asia (Ithaca, NY: Cornell University Press, 2010).

"What Really Happened in Kyrgyzstan?" *Journal of Democracy*, v. 17, no. 2, April 2006, pp. 132–46.

Sabrina P. Ramet, *Serbia Since 1989: Politics and Society under Milosevic and After* (Seattle: University of Washington Press, 2005), pp. 59–60.

David Ransel, "Character and Style of Patron-Client Relations in Russia," in Antoni Maczak, ed., *Klientelsysteme im Europa der Frühen Neuzeit* (Munich: Oldenbourg, 1988), pp. 211–231.

David L. Ransel, *The Politics of Catherinian Russia* (New Haven, CT: Yale University Press, 1975).

John Reed, *Ten Days That Shook the World* (New York: Penguin, 1977).

Thomas F. Remington, *Politics in Russia*, 6th ed. (Boston: Longman, 2010).

David Remnick, *Resurrection: The Struggle for a New Russia* (New York: Random House, 1997).

William Reno, *Warlord Politics and African States* (Boulder, CO: Lynn Rienner, 1998).

Ora John Reuter and Thomas Remington, "Dominant Party Regimes and the Commitment Problem: The Case of United Russia," *Comparative Political Studies*, v. 42, no. 4, 2009, pp. 501–26.

L. H. Rhinelander, "Viceroy Vorontsov's Administration of the Caucasus," in Ronald Grigor Suny, *Transcaucasia: Nationalism and Social Change. Essays in the History of Armenia, Azerbaijan, and Georgia* (Ann Arbor: University of Michigan Press, 1983), pp. 109–40.

Chris Rhomberg, "A Signal Juncture: The Detroit Newspaper Strike and Post-Accord Labor Relations in the United States," *American Journal of Sociology*, v. 115, no. 6, May 2010, pp. 1853–94.

Mykola Riabchuk, *Gleichschaltung: Authoritarian Consolidation in Ukraine 2010–2012* (Kyiv: K.I.S., 2012).

Graeme B. Robertson, "Managing Society: Protest, Civil Society and Regime in Putin's Russia," *Slavic Review*, v. 68, no. 3, Fall 2009, pp. 528–47.

The Politics of Protest in Hybrid Regimes: Managing Dissent in Post-Communist Russia (New York: Cambridge University Press, 2011).

Philip G. Roeder, "Varieties of Post-Soviet Authoritarian Regimes," *Post-Soviet Affairs*, v. 10, no. 1, January 1994, pp. 61–101.

Where Nation-States Come From (Princeton, NJ: Princeton University Press, 2007).

Sandra Elisabeth Roelofs, *The Story of an Idealist* (Tbilisi: LINK, 2010).

Steven D. Roper, "Are All Semipresidential Regimes the Same? A Comparison of Premier-Presidential Regimes," *Comparative Politics*, v. 34, no. 3, April 2002, pp. 253–72.

"From Semi-Presidentialism to Parliamentarism: Regime Change and Presidential Power in Moldova," *Europe-Asia Studies*, v. 60, no. 1, 2008, pp. 113–26.

Iurie Rosca, "Moldova's Orange Evolution," *Demokratizatsiya: The Journal of Post-Soviet Democratization*, v. 13, no. 4, pp. 537–43.

Richard Rose, William Mishler, and Neil Munro, *Russia Transformed: Developing Popular Support for a New Regime* (New York: Cambridge University Press, 2006).

Bo Rothstein, "Trust, Social Dilemmas, and Collective Memories," *Journal of Theoretical Politics*, v. 12, no. 4, 2000, pp. 477–501.

Bo Rothstein and Daniel Eek, "Political Corruption and Social Trust: An Experimental Approach," *Rationality and Society*, v. 21, no. 1, February 2009, pp. 81–112.

Peter L. Roudik, *The History of the Central Asian Republics* (Westport, CT: Greenwood, 2007).

Vladimir Rovdo, "Spetsifika i evoliutsiia politicheskogo rezhima Respubliki Belarus'," *Acta Slavica Iaponica*, v. 21, 2004, pp. 144–80.

Daniel Rowland, "Did Muscovite Literary Ideology Place Any Limits on the Power of the Tsar?" *Russian Review*, v. 49, no. 2, April 1990, pp. 125–55.

Olivier Roy, *The New Central Asia: The Creation of Nations* (New York: NYU Press, 2000).

Dankwart Rustow, "Transitions to Democracy: Towards a Dynamic Model," *Comparative Politics*, v. 2, April 1970, pp. 337–63.

Maxim Ryabakov, "The North-South Cleavage and Political Support in Kyrgyzstan," *Central Asian Survey*, v. 27, nos. 3–4, September 2008, pp. 301–16.

Steven Sabol, *Russian Colonization and the Genesis of Kazak National Consciousness* (New York: Palgrave Macmillan, 2003).

Jeff Sahadeo, *Russian Colonial Society in Tashkent, 1865–1923* (Bloomington: Indiana University Press, 2007).

Richard Sakwa, *The Crisis of Russian Democracy: The Dual State, Factionalism, and the Medvedev Succession* (Cambridge: Cambridge University Press, 2011).

Putin and the Oligarchs: The Khodorkovsky-Yukos Affair (London: I. B. Tauris, 2014).

Russian Politics and Society, 4th ed. (London: Routledge, 2008).

Thomas J. Sargent and Neil Wallace, "Rational Expectations and the Theory of Economic Policy," *Journal of Monetary Economics*, v. 2, no. 2, April 1976, pp. 169–83.

Temir Sariev, *Shakh Kyrgyzskoi demokratii* (Bishkek: Salam, 2008).

Mark Saroyan, *Minorities, Mullahs, and Modernity: Reshaping Community in the Former Soviet Union* (Berkeley: University of California Press, 1997).

Giovanni Sartori, "Concept Misformation in Comparative Politics," *American Political Science Review*, v. 64, no. 4, 1970, pp. 1033–53.

Edward A. D. Schatz, "Framing Strategies and Non-Conflict in Multi-Ethnic Kazakhstan," *Nationalism & Ethnic Politics*, v. 6, no. 2, Summer 2000, pp. 71–94.

Modern Clan Politics: The Power of "Blood" in Kazakhstan and Beyond (Seattle: University of Washington Press, 2004).

"The Soft Authoritarian Tool Kit: Agenda-Setting Power in Kazakhstan and Kyrgyzstan," *Comparative Politics*, January 2009, pp. 203–22.

Andreas Schedler, "The Menu of Manipulation," *Journal of Democracy*, v. 13, April 2002, pp. 36–50.

Ethan Scheiner, *Democracy without Competition in Japan: Opposition Failure in a One-Party Dominant State* (New York: Cambridge University Press, 2006).

Thomas Schelling, *The Strategy of Conflict* (Cambridge, MA: Harvard University Press, 1960).

Sebastian Schiek and Stephan Hensell, "Seeing Like a President: The Dilemma of Inclusion in Kazakhstan," in Susan Stewart, Margaret Klein, Andrea Schmitz, and Hans-Henning Schroder, eds., *Presidents, Oligarchs, and Bureaucrats: Forms of Rule in the Post-Soviet Space* (Burlington: Ashgate, 2012), pp. 203–22.

Steffen W. Schmidt, James C. Scott, Carl Lande, and Laura Guasti, *Friends, Followers, and Factions* (Berkeley: University of California Press, 1977).

John Schoeberlein, "Between Two Worlds," *Harvard International Review*, v. 22, no. 1, Winter 2000, pp. 56–61.

John Schoeberlein-Engel, "Conflict in Tajikistan and Central Asia: The Myth of Ethnic Animosity," *Harvard Middle Eastern and Islamic Review*, v. 1, no. 2, 1994, pp. 1–55.

James C. Scott, "The Analysis of Corruption in Developing Nations," *Comparative Studies in Society and History*, v. 11, no. 3, June 1969, pp. 315–41.

"Corruption, Machine Politics, and Political Change," *American Political Science Review*, v. 63, no. 4, December 1969, pp. 1142–58.

"Patron-Client Politics and Political Change in Southeast Asia," *American Political Science Review*, v. 66, no. 1, March 1972, pp. 91–113.

Laslo Sekelj, "Parties and Elections: The Federal Republic of Yugoslavia: Change without Transformation," *Europe-Asia Studies*, v. 52, no. 1, January 2000, pp. 57–75.

Georgiy Shakhnazarov, *S vozhdiami i bez nikh* (Moscow: Vagrius, 2001).

Gulnaz Sharafutdinova, "Gestalt Switch in Russian Federalism: The Decline in Regional Power under Putin," *Comparative Politics*, v. 45, no. 3, April 2013, pp. 357–76.

Political Consequences of Crony Capitalism inside Russia (South Bend, IN: Notre Dame University Press, 2010).

Eric Shiraev, *Russian Government and Politics* (New York: Palgrave Macmillan, 2010).

Andrei Shleifer and Daniel Treisman, "A Normal Country," *Foreign Affairs*, v. 83, no. 2, March–April 2004, pp. 20–38.

Matthew Soberg Shugart and John M. Carey, *Presidents and Assemblies: Constitutional Design and Electoral Dynamics* (New York: Cambridge University Press, 1992).

Stanislav Shushkevich, *Belovezhskii konsensus i Belarus' (Zametki pervogo)*, unpublished book manuscript, Minsk, 2011, as provided by the author.

Olga Shvetsova, "Resolving the Problem of Pre-Election Coordination: The 1999 Parliamentary Election as Elite Presidential 'Primary,'" in Vicki Hesli and William Reisinger, eds., *Elections, Parties and the Future of Russia* (New York: Cambridge University Press, 2003).

Vitali Silitski, "Beware the People," *Transitions Online*, March 21, 2005.

"Explaining Post-Communist Authoritarianism in Belarus," in Elena Korosteleva, Colin W. Lawson, and Rosalind J. Marsh, eds., *Contemporary Belarus: Between Democracy and Dictatorship* (New York: RoutledgeCurzon, 2003), pp. 36–52.

"Preempting Democracy: The Case of Belarus," *Journal of Democracy*, v. 16, no. 4, October 2005, pp. 83–97.

Alberto Simpser, *Why Governments and Parties Manipulate Elections: Theory, Practice, and Implications* (New York: Cambridge University Press, 2013).

Fredrik M. Sjöberg, "Autocratic Adaptation: The Strategic Use of Transparency and the Persistence of Election Fraud," *Electoral Studies*, v. 33, no. 1, March 2014, pp. 233–45.

"Competitive Elections in Authoritarian States: Weak States, Strong Elites, and Fractional Societies in Central Asia and Beyond," PhD dissertation, Department of Government, Uppsala University, Uppsala, Sweden, 2011.

Cindy Skach, *Borrowing Constitutional Designs: Constitutional Law in Weimar Germany and the French Fifth Republic* (Princeton, NJ: Princeton University Press, 2005).

Alexander Skakov, "Abkhazia at a Crossroads: On the Domestic Political Situation in the Republic of Abkhazia," *Iran & the Caucasus*, v. 9, no. 1, 2005, pp. 159–85.

H. Gordon Skilling and Franklyn Griffiths, eds., *Interest Groups in Soviet Politics* (Princeton, NJ: Princeton University Press, 1970).

Mykhailo Slaboshpyts'kyi, *Peizazh dlia Pomaranchevoii Revoliutsii* (Kyiv: Yaroslaviv Val, 2005).

Dan Slater, *Ordering Power: Contentious Politics and Authoritarian Leviathans in Southeast Asia* (New York: Cambridge University Press, 2010).

Dan Slater and Erica Simmons, "Informative Regress: Critical Antecedents in Comparative Politics," *Comparative Political Studies*, v. 43, no. 7, July 2010, pp. 886–917.

Darrell Slider, "Democratization in Georgia," in Karen Dawisha and Bruce Parrott, eds., *Conflict, Cleavage, and Change in Central Asia and the Caucasus* (New York: Cambridge University Press, 1997), pp. 156–98.

Regina Smyth and Irina Soboleva, "Looking Beyond the Economy: Pussy Riot and the Kremlin's Voting Coalition," *Post-Soviet Affairs*, December 17, 2013.

Regina Smyth, Brandon Wilkening, and Anna Urasova [Lowry], "Engineering Victory: Institutional Reform, Informal Institutions, and the Formation of a Hegemonic Party Regime in the Russian Federation," *Post-Soviet Affairs*, v. 23, no. 2, 2007, pp. 118–37.

Mircea Snegur and Eduard Volkov, *Otkrovennye dialogi* (Chisinau: Draghistea, 2007).

Richard Snyder, "Explaining Transitions from Neopatrimonial Dictatorships," *Comparative Politics*, v. 24, no. 4, July 1992, pp. 379–99.

Michael Sodaro, *Comparative Politics: A Global Introduction* (Columbus, OH: McGraw-Hill, 2007).

Cornelia Soldat, "The Limits of Muscovite Autocracy: The Relations between the Grand Prince and the Boyars in the Light of Iosif Volotskii's Prosvetitel'," *Cahiers du Monde russe*, v. 46, nos. 1–2, January–June 2005, pp. 265–76.

Steven L. Solnick, "Russia's 'Transition,'" *Social Research*, v. 66, Fall 1999, pp. 789–824.

Stealing the State: Control and Collapse in Soviet Institutions (Cambridge, MA: Harvard University Press, 1998).

Svat Soucek, *A History of Inner Asia* (New York: Cambridge University Press, 2000).

Regine Spector, "Securing Property in Post-Soviet Kyrgyzstan," *Post-Soviet Affairs*, v. 24, no. 2, April–June 2008, pp. 149–76.

Alfred Stepan, Juan Linz, and Yogendra Yadav, *Crafting State-Nations: India and Other Multinational Democracies* (Baltimore: Johns Hopkins University Press, 2011).

Susan Stokes, "Perverse Accountability: A Formal Model of Machine Politics with Evidence from Argentina," *American Political Science Review*, v. 99, no. 3, August 2005, pp. 215–25.

Kathryn Stoner-Weiss, "Central Weakness and Provincial Autonomy," *Post-Soviet Affairs*, v. 15, no. 1, January–March 1999, pp. 87–104.

Local Heroes: The Political Economy of Russian Regional Governance (Princeton, NJ: Princeton University Press, 1997).

Maksim Strikha, "Ukrainskie Vybory: Do i Posle," in Mikhail Pogrebinsky, ed., *"Oranzhevaia" Revoliutsiia: Versii, Khronika, Dokumenty* (Kyiv: Otima, 2005), pp. 150–64.

Ronald Grigor Suny, "Elite Transformation in Late-Soviet and Post-Soviet Transcaucasia, or What Happens When the Ruling Class Can't Rule?" in Timothy J. Colton and Robert C. Tucker, eds., *Patterns in Post-Soviet Leadership* (Boulder, CO: Westview, 1995), pp. 141–68.

"On the Road to Independence: Cultural Cohesion and Ethnic Revival in a Multinational Society," in Ronald Grigor Suny, ed., *Transcaucasia, Nationalism, and Social Change* (Ann Arbor: University of Michigan Press, 1996), pp. 377–400.

The Soviet Experiment: Russia, the USSR, and the Successor States (Oxford: Oxford University Press, 1998).

ed., *Transcaucasia: Nationalism and Social Change. Essays in the History of Armenia, Azerbaijan, and Georgia* (Ann Arbor: University of Michigan Press, 1983).

Oleksandr Sushko and Olena Prystayko, "Ukraine," in *Nations in Transit 2009* (New York: Freedom House, 2009).

"Ukraine," *Nations in Transit 2013* (New York: Freedom House, 2013).

Milan W. Svolik, *The Politics of Authoritarian Rule* (New York: Cambridge University Press, 2012).

Sidney Tarrow, "The Strategy of Paired Comparison." *Comparative Political Studies*, v. 43, no. 2, February 2010, pp. 230–59.

Brian D. Taylor, *Politics and the Russian Army: Civil-Military Relations, 1689–2000* (New York: Cambridge University Press, 2003).

State-Building in Putin's Russia: Policing and Coercion after Communism (New York: Cambridge University Press, 2011).

Jan Teorell, *Determinants of Democratization: Explaining Regime Change in the World, 1972–2006* (New York: Cambridge University Press, 2010).

Paul Theroux, "The Golden Man: Saparmurat Niyazov's Reign of Insanity," *The New Yorker*, May 28, 2007, pp. 56–65.

Mark R. Thompson and Philipp Kuntz, "Stolen Elections: The Case of the Serbian October," *Journal of Democracy*, v. 15, no. 4, October 2004, pp. 159–72.

Charles Tilly, *Democracy* (New York: Cambridge University Press, 2007).

European Revolutions, 1492–1992 (Oxford: Blackwell, 1993).

"Parliamentarization of Popular Contention in Great Britain, 1758–1834," *Theory and Society*, v. 26, 1997, pp. 245–73.

Vladimir Tismaneanu, "Electoral Revolutions," *Society*, November/December 1997, pp. 61–5.

Gerard Toal and John O'Loughlan, "Inside South Ossetia: A Survey of Attitudes in a De Facto State," *Post-Soviet Affairs*, v. 29, no. 2, 2013, pp. 136–72.

Ian Traynor, "U.S. Campaign behind the Turmoil in Kiev," *The Guardian*, November 26, 2004.

Daniel S. Treisman, "After Yeltsin Comes ... Yeltsin," *Foreign Policy*, v. 117, Winter 1999–2000, pp. 74–86.

"How Yeltsin Won," *Foreign Affairs*, v. 75, no. 5, September–October 1996, pp. 64–77.

"Presidential Popularity in a Hybrid Regime: Russia under Yeltsin and Putin," *American Journal of Political Science*, v. 55, no. 3, July 2011, pp. 590–609.

The Return: Russia's Journey from Gorbachev to Medvedev (New York: Free Press, 2011).

Alexei Trochev, "A Constitution of Convenience in Ukraine," *Jurist-Forum*, January 18, 2011, http://jurist.org/forum/2011/01/jurist-guest-columnist-alexei-trochev.php, accessed April 24, 2011.

Judging Russia: Constitutional Court in Russian Politics (New York: Cambridge University Press, 2008).

"Meddling with Justice: Competitive Politics, Impunity, and Distrusted Courts in Post-Orange Ukraine," *Demokratizatsiya: The Journal of Post-Soviet Democratization*, v. 18, no. 2, Spring 2010, pp. 122–47, p. 134.

Jessica Trounstine, *Political Monopolies in American Cities: The Rise and Fall of Bosses and Reformers* (Chicago: University of Chicago Press, 2008).

Joshua A. Tucker, "Enough! Electoral Fraud, Collective Action Problems, and the '2nd Wave' of Post-Communist Democratic Revolutions," *Perspectives on Politics*, v. 53, no. 5, 2007, pp. 537–53.

"The First Decade of Post-Communist Elections and Voting: What Have We Studied, and How Have We Studied It?" *Annual Review of Political Science*, v. 5, 2002, pp. 271–304.

Regional Economic Voting: Russia, Poland, Hungary, Slovakia, and the Czech Republic, 1990–1999 (New York: Cambridge University Press, 2006).

Robert C. Tucker, ed., *The Lenin Anthology* (New York: Norton, 1975).

Theodor Tudoriu, "Communism for the Twenty-First Century: The Moldovan Experiment," *Journal of Communist Studies and Transition Politics*, v. 27, no. 2, June 2011, pp. 291–321.

Gordon Tullock, *Autocracy* (New York: Springer, 1987).

Idil Tuncer-Kilavuz, "Political and Social Networks in Tajikistan and Uzbekistan: 'Clan', Region, and Beyond," *Central Asian Survey*, v. 28, no. 3, September 2009, pp. 323–34.

"Understanding Civil War: A Comparison of Tajikistan and Uzbekistan," *Europe-Asia Studies*, v. 63, no. 2, March 2011, pp. 263–90.

Power, Networks and Violent Conflict in Central Asia: A Comparison of Tajikistan and Uzbekistan (New York: Routledge, 2014).

"Understanding Violent Conflict: A Comparative Study of Tajikistan and Uzbekistan," dissertation in Central Eurasian Studies, Indiana University, Bloomington, 2007.

Adam Ulam, *The Bolsheviks: The Intellectual and Political History of the Triumph of Communism in Russia* (New York: Collier, 1965).

Milada A. Vachudova, *Europe Undivided: Democracy, Leverage, and Integration after Communism* (New York: Oxford University Press, 2005).

Nicolas van de Walle, "Meet the New Boss, Same as the Old Boss? The Evolution of Political Clientelism in Africa," in Herbert Kitschelt and Steven I. Wilkinson, eds., *Patrons, Clients, and Policies: Patterns of Democratic Accountability and Political Competition* (Cambridge: Cambridge University Press, 2007).

John M. Veitch, "Repudiations and Confiscations by the Medieval State," *Journal of Economic History*, v. 46, no. 1, March 1986, pp. 31–6.

P. A. Viazemskii, *Zapisnye knizhki (1813–1848)* (Moscow: USSR Academy of Sciences, 1963).

Olga Vlasova, Gevorg Davtian, and Gevorg Mirzaian, "Desiat' dnei na ploshchadi Svobody," *Ekspert*, No. 10, March 10–16, 2008, pp. 26–8.

Vadim Volkov, *Violent Entrepreneurs: The Use of Force in the Making of Russian Capitalism* (Ithaca, NY: Cornell University Press, 2002).

Dmitry Vydrin and Irina Rozhkova, *V ozhidanii geroia: Yezhenedel'nik goda peremen* (Kharkiv: Kankom, 2005).

Christopher Walker, ed., *Nations in Transit 2011: The Authoritarian Dead End in the Former Soviet Union* (New York: Freedom House, 2011).

Christopher Walker and Robert Orttung, "From Revolution to Democracy," *The Wall Street Journal*, March 7, 2011, online version, wsj.com.

Lucan A. Way, "Authoritarian State-Building and the Sources of Regime Competitiveness in the Fourth Wave: The Cases of Belarus, Moldova, Russia, and Ukraine," *World Politics*, v. 57, January 2005, pp. 231–61.

"Deer in Headlights: Incompetence and Weak Authoritarianism after the Cold War," *Slavic Review*, v. 71, no. 3, Fall 2012, pp. 619–46.

"Explaining the Weakness of International Authoritarian Promotion: The Case of Russia in the 'Near Abroad,'" manuscript, June 2014.

"Pluralism by Default in Moldova," *Journal of Democracy*, v. 13, no. 4, October 2002, pp. 127–41.

"The Real Causes of the Color Revolutions," *Journal of Democracy*, v. 19, no. 3, July 2008, pp. 55–69.

"The Sources and Dynamics of Competitive Authoritarianism in Ukraine," *Communist and Post-Communist Studies*, v. 20, no. 1, March 2004, pp. 143–61.

"Weak States and Pluralism: The Case of Moldova," *East European Politics and Societies*, v. 17, no. 3, pp. 454–82.

Max Weber, *Economy and Society*, eds. G. Roth and C. Wittich (Berkeley: University of California Press, 1978), pp. 231–2.

"The Ideal Type," in Max Weber, *The Methodology of the Social Sciences*, translated and edited by Edward A. Shils and Henry A. Finch (Glencoe, Illinois: Free Press, 1949).

Lisa Wedeen, "Conceptualizing Culture: Possibilities for Political Science," *American Political Science Review*, v. 96, no. 4, December 2002, pp. 713–28.

Stephen K. Wegren, ed., *Return to Putin's Russia: Past Imperfect, Future Uncertain* (Lanham, MD: Rowman & Littlefield, 2012).

George Weickhardt, "The Pre-Petrine Law of Property," *Slavic Review*, v. 52, no. 4, 1993, pp. 663–79.

Barry R. Weingast, "The Political Foundations of Democracy and the Rule of Law," *American Political Science Review*, v. 91, no. 2, June 1997, pp. 245–63.

Cory Welt, "Can Georgia Become a Multiparty Democracy?" *Caucasus Analytical Digest*, no. 43, October 15, 2012, pp. 13–15.

"Georgia's Constitutional Reform," *CACI Analyst*, November 11, 2010.

"Georgia's Rose Revolution: From Regime Weakness to Regime Collapse," in Valerie J. Bunce, Michael A. McFaul, and Kathryn Stoner-Weiss, eds., *Democracy and Authoritarianism in the Post-Communist World* (New York: Cambridge University Press, 2010), pp. 155–88.

Jonathan Wheatley, *Georgia from National Awakening to Rose Revolution: Delayed Transition in the Former Soviet Union* (Burlington: Ashgate, 2005).

Stephen White, *Understanding Russian Politics* (Cambridge: Cambridge University Press, 2011).

Stephen White and Elena Korosteleva, "Lukashenko and the Postcommunist Presidency," in Stephen White, Elena Korosteleva, and John Lowehardt, eds. *Postcommunist Belarus* (Lanham, MD: Rowman & Littlefield, 2005), pp. 59–78.

Stephen White and Ian McAllister, "The Putin Phenomenon," *Journal of Communist Studies and Transition Politics*, v. 24, no. 4, 2008, pp. 604–28.

Stephen White, Richard Rose, and Ian McAllister, *How Russia Votes* (Chatham, NJ: Chatham House, 1997).

Stephen White, Richard Sakwa, and Henry E. Hale, eds., *Developments in Russian Politics*, 8th ed.(London: Palgrave Macmillan, 2014).

Sten Widmalm and Sven Oskarsson, eds., *Prometokrati: Mellan Diktatur och Demokrati* (Lund, Sweden: Studentlitteratur, 2010).

John P. Willerton, *Patronage and Politics in the USSR* (Cambridge: Cambridge University Press, 1992).

Andrew Wilson, *Belarus: The Last Dictatorship in Europe* (New Haven, CT: Yale University Press, 2011).

Ukraine's Orange Revolution (New Haven, CT: Yale University Press, 2005).

Virtual Politics: Faking Democracy in the Post-Soviet World (New Haven, CT: Yale University Press, 2005).

Andreas Wimmer, *Ethnic Boundary Making* (New York: Oxford University Press, 2013).

Charles R. Wise and Volodymyr Pigenko, "The Separation of Powers Puzzle in Ukraine: Sorting Out Responsibilities and Relationships between President, Parliament, and the Prime Minister," in Taras Kuzio, Robert S. Kravchuk, and Paul D'Anieri, eds., *State and Institution Building in Ukraine* (New York: St. Martin's, 1999), pp. 25–55.

Jason Wittenberg, *Crucibles of Political Loyalty* (New York: Cambridge University Press, 2006).

Kataryna Wolczuk, *The Moulding of Ukraine: The Constitutional Politics of State Formation* (Budapest: CEU Press, 2001).

David Woodruff, "Khodorkovsky's Gamble: From Business to Politics in the YUKOS Conflict," PONARS Policy Memo no. 308, November 2003.

Money Unmade (Ithaca, NY: Cornell University Press, 1999).

Richard S. Wortman, "'Muscovite Political Folkways' and the Problem of Russian Political Culture," *Russian Review*, v. 46, no. 2, April 1987, pp. 191–7.

Scenarios of Power: Myth and Ceremony in Russian Monarchy From Peter the Great to the Abdication of Nicholas II (Princeton, NJ: Princeton University Press, 2006).

Daniil Yanevsky, *Khronika "Oranzhevoi" Revoliutsii* (Kharkiv: Folio, 2005).

Jan Zaprudnik and Michael Urban, "Belarus: From Statehood to Empire?" in Ian Bremmer and Ray Taras, eds., *New States, New Politics* (New York: Cambridge University Press, 1997), pp. 276–315.

Sergei Zhuk, *Rock and Roll in the Rocket City: The West, Identity, and Ideology in Soviet Dniepropetrovsk, 1960–85* (Washington, DC: Woodrow Wilson Center Press, 2010).

Index

Lightning Source UK Ltd.
Milton Keynes UK
UKOW03f2046260217
295338UK00001B/22/P